A First Course in Scientific Computing

Symbolic, Graphic, and Numeric Modeling Using Maple, Java, Mathematica, and Fortran90

A First Course in Scientific Computing

Symbolic, Graphic, and Numeric Modeling Using Maple, Java, Mathematica, and Fortran90

RUBIN H. LANDAU

Contributors:

Robyn Wangberg (Mathematica),
Kyle Augustson (Fortran90),

M. J. Páez, C. C. Bordeianu,
C. Barnes

PRINCETON UNIVERSITY PRESS

PRINCETON AND OXFORD

Published by Princeton University Press,
41 William Street, Princeton, New Jersey 08540
In the United Kingdom: Princeton University Press,
3 Market Place, Woodstock, Oxfordshire OX20 1SY

Library of Congress Cataloging-in-Publication Data

Landau, Rubin H.

A first course in scientific computing: symbolic, graphic, and numeric modeling using Maple, Java,
Mathematica, and Fortran90 / Rubin H. Landau; contributors, R. Wangberg, K. Augustson
... [et al.].

p. cm.

Includes bibliographical references and index.

ISBN 0-691-12183-4 (cloth : alk. Paper)

1. Science—Data processing. I. Wangberg, R, Augustson K. II. Title

2. Q183.9.L36 2005

3. 502′.85—dc22   2004062443

British Library Cataloging-in-Publication Data is available

The publisher would like to acknowledge the author of this
volume for providing the camera-ready copy from which this book was printed.

Printed on acid-free paper. ∞

pup.princeton.edu

Printed in the United States of America

3 5 7 9 10 8 6 4

ISBN-13: 978-0-691-12183-3 (cloth)

ISBN-10: 0-691-12183-4 (cloth)

*For **Loren Landau***

and your first book

Contents

List of Figures

List of Tables

Preface

This book contains an introduction to scientific computing appropriate for all lower-division college students. Its goal is to make students comfortable using computers to do science and to provide them with tools and knowledge they can utilize throughout their college careers. Its approach is to introduce the requisite mathematics and computer science in the course of solving realistic problems. On that account care is given to indicate how each discipline uses its own language to describe the same concept, how their tools are useful to us, and how computations are often concrete examples of abstract ideas.

This is easier said than done. On the one hand, lower-division students are simultaneously learning elementary mathematics and physics, and so this may be the first place they encounter the science and mathematics used in the problems. On the other hand, in order for the tools and techniques to be useful for more than the assigned problem, we give *more* than an introduction (the original title of this book) to the computational tools. We address the first issue in our teaching by reminding the students that our focus is on having them learn the techniques in the proper context, and that any new science and mathematics they become familiar with will make it easier for them in their other courses. We address the second issue by placing an asterisk * in the title of chapters and sections containing optional materials and by reminding the students of which sections are most appropriate for the problem at hand.

This book covers some of the basics of computation, numerical analysis, and programming from a computational science point of view. We want the reader to acquire some ideas of what is possible with computers, what type of tools there are for it, and how to go about getting all the pieces to work together. After that, it is easy to use on-line help or the references to get more details. As a result, our presentation is more practical and more focused on mathematics and science than an introductory programming or computer science text, with minimal discussion of computer science theory. The book follows our own personal preference for "just enough" computer information in that it avoids going through every option for every command and instead presents realistic examples.

We follow the dictum that science and engineering students learn computing best while sitting down at a computer in a trial-and-error mode. Hence, we adopt a tutorial approach in which readers work along with us in solving a problem, learn by doing, and then work on their own version of the problem (there are also additional exercises at the end of each chapter). We use the command-line mode for the compiled languages that makes the tutorial as universal as possible, and, we believe, is better pedagogically. It then follows that this book is closer to a workbook than a reference book. Yet because one always comes back to find worked examples of commands, it should be valuable for reference as well.

A problem solving environment such as *Maple* or *Mathematica* is probably the easiest way to start scientific computing, is natural to use with trial and error, and is what we do in Part 1. Its graphical interface is friendly, it shows the user a wide spectrum of what can be done with modern computation, such as symbolic manipulations, 2-D, 3-D visualization and linear algebra, and is immediately useful in other courses and for writing technical reports. After the first week with Maple or Mathematica, students with computer fright usually feel better. These environments also demonstrate how computers can give an immediate response in beautiful mathematical notation, or fail at what should be the simplest of tasks.

Part 2 of the text is on Java (or Fortran). We believe that learning to program in a compiled language teaches more of the basics of computation, gets closer to the actual algorithms used, teaches better the importance of logic, and opens up a broader range of technical opportunities (jobs) for the students than the use of a problem solving environment. In addition, compiled languages also tend to be more powerful and flexible for numerically intensive tasks, and students naturally move to them for specialized projects. Likewise, after covering Parts 1 and 2 of the text it may make sense for a student to use environments like *Matlab*, which combine elements of both compiled languages and problem solving environments.

Many students may find that the logic and the precision of language required in programming is more challenging than anything they have ever faced before. Others find programming satisfying and a natural complement to their study of mathematics and foreign languages. We try to decrease the slope of the learning curve by starting the neophytes with sample programs to run and modify, rather than requiring them to write all their own programs from scratch. This process is more exciting, saves a great deal of time otherwise spent in frustrating debugging, and helps students learn by example.

Even though it might not be evident from all the hype about Java and Web computing, Java is actually a good language for beginning science students. It demands proper syntax, produces useful error messages, is consistent and intelligent in handling precision, goes a long way towards being computer-system independent, has Sun Microsystems providing free program-development environments [SunJ], and runs fast enough for nonindustrial purposes (its speed is increasing, as are the number of scientific subroutine libraries being developed in Java).

Part 3 of the text provides a short LATEX survival guide. A number of colleagues have suggested the need for such materials, and since using LATEX is quite similar to compiling a code, it does make a useful extension of the text. Even though we do not try to reveal the full power and complexity of LaTeX, we do give enough of its basic elements for the reader to write beautiful-looking scientific documents.

Depending on how many chapters and modules are used, this book contains enough materials for a one- or two-semester course. Our course has one lecture and two labs every week, with roughly one instructor for every 10 students in lab. Attending lectures and reading the materials before lab are important in acquainting the students with the general concepts behind the exercises and in providing a broad picture of what we are trying to do. The supervised lab is where the real learning occurs.

We believe that a modern student should be acquainted with several approaches to scientific computing. Notwithstanding our avowed claim that there are multiple paths leading to good scientific computing, we have had to make some choices as to what to place in the printed version of this book and what to place on the CD. The basic ideas behind scientific computing are language independent, yet the details are not. For all these reasons we have decided to cover Maple, Java, and LaTeX in the printed version of this book, but to place other languages on the CD that comes with the text.

The CD is platform independent and has been tested on Windows, Macs, and Unix. The Java and Fortran programs are pure text. The Maple and Mathematica files, however, require the respective programs to execute them. The pdf files will require Abode Acrobat, which is free. Any difficulties with the CD should be reported to rubin@physics.orst.edu. Additions and corrections to the CD are found on our Web pages (http://www.physics.orst.edu/~rubin/IntroBook) or through Princeton University Press Web pages (http://pup.princeton.edu/titles/7916.html).

Specifically, the CD contains Java programs, LaTeX files, data files, and various supplementary materials. As indicated, it also contains Maple worksheets with essentially identical materials as in the Maple section of the text but in an interactive format that we recommend over reading the paper version. Furthermore, the CD contains essentially identical materials to the Maple tutorials as Mathematica notebooks. These can be read with Mathematica or printed out as an alternative version of the text. Likewise, the CD also contains the Java materials of the text converted over to Fortran90, as well as the appropriate Fortran programs. Though we do not recommend trying to learn two languages simultaneously, having alternative versions of the text does present some interesting teaching possibilities. Additions and corrections to the CD are found on our Web pages.

Acknowledgements

This book was developed on seven year's worth of students in the introductory scientific computing class at Oregon State University. The course was motivated by the pioneering text by Zachary [Zach 96] and encouraged by [UCES]. The course has been taught by Albert Stetz, David McIntyre, and the author; I am proud to acknowledge their friendship and the inclusion of their materials in the text. I have been blessed with some excellent student assistants without whose efforts the course could not be taught and the materials developed; these include Matt Des Voigne, Robyn Wangberg, Kyle Augustson, Connelly Barnes, and Juan Vanegas. Valuable materials and invaluable friendships have also been contributed by Manuel Páez and Cristian Bordeianu, coauthors of our *Computational Physics* text, and Sally Haerer. They have helped make this book more than the introduction it would have been otherwise. I look forward to their continued collaborations.

Financial support for developing our degree program in computational physics and associated curricular materials comes from the National Science Foundation's Course, Curriculum, and Laboratory Improvement program directed by Duncan McBride, and the Education, Outreach and Training Thrust area of the National Partnership for Computational Infrastructure, under the leadership of Gregory Moses and Ann Redelfs. The courses and materials have benefited from formative and summative assessments by Julie Foertsch of the LEAD Center of the University of Wisconsin. This work has also benefited from formative comments by various reviewers and colleagues, in particular Jan Tobochnik and David Cook. Thanks also goes to my editor, Vickie Kearn at Princeton University Press, who has been particularly insightful, encouraging, and courageous in helping me develop this multidisciplinary text and having it turn out so well, and to Ellen Foos for her caring production of the book. And Jan Landau, always.

RHL

Chapter One

Introduction

1.1 NATURE OF SCIENTIFIC COMPUTING

Computational scientists solve tomorrow's problems with yesterday's computers; computer scientists seem to do it the other way around.

—anonymous

The goal of scientific computing is problem solving. The computer is needed for this, because real-world problems are often too difficult or complex for analytic or human solution, yet workable with the computer. When done right, the use of a computer does not replace our intellect, but rather leverages it by providing a super-calculating machine or a virtual laboratory so that we can do things that were heretofore impossible.

The mathematical modeling and problem-solving orientation of scientific computing places it in the discipline of *computational science*. In contrast, computer science, which studies computers for their own intrinsic interest, provides the underpinning for the development of the hardware and software tools that computational scientists use. As illustrated on the left of Figure 1.1, computational science is a *multidisciplinary* field that combines a traditional discipline, such as physics or finance, with computer science and mathematics, without ignoring the rigor of each. Books such as this, which employs materials from multiple fields, aim to be the central bridge in this figure, connecting and drawing together the three fields.

Studying a multidisciplinary field is challenging. Not only must you learn more than one discipline, you must also work with the separate languages and styles of the different disciplines. To illustrate, a computational scientist may be pleased with a particular solution because it is reliable, self-explanatory, and easy to run on different computers without modification. A computer scientist may view this same solution as lengthy, inelegant, and old-fashioned. Each may be right in the sense that they are making judgments based on the differing values of different disciplines.

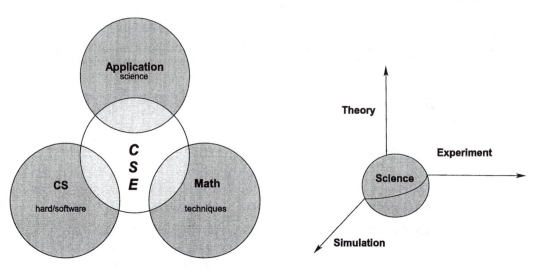

Figure 1.1 *Left:* Computational science is a multidisciplinary field that combines science with computer science and mathematics. *Right:* A new paradigm for science in which simulation plays as essential a role as does experiment and theory.

Another, possibly more fundamental, view of how computation is playing an increasingly important role in science is illustrated on the right of illustrated in Figure 1.1. This symbolizes a paradigm shift in which science's traditional foundation in theory and experiment is extended to include computer simulation. While one may argue that the future will see the CSE on the left of Figure 1.1 get absorbed into the individual disciplines, we think all would agree that the simulation on the right of Figure 1.1 will play an increasing role in science.

1.2 TALKING TO COMPUTERS

As anthropomorphic as your view of computers may be, it is good to keep in mind that a computer always does exactly as told. This means that you should not take the computer's response personally, and also that you must tell the computer exactly what you want it to do. Of course programs can be so complicated that you may not care to figure out what they will do in detail, but it is always possible in principle. Thus it follows that a basic goal of this book is to provide you with enough understanding so that you feel well enough in control, no matter how illusionary, to figure out what the computer is doing.

Before you tell the computer to obey your orders, you need to understand that life is not simple for computers. The instructions they understand are in a *basic machine language*[1] that tells the hardware to do things like move a number stored in one memory location to another location, or to do some simple, binary

---

[1]The "BASIC" (Beginner's All-purpose Symbolic Instruction Code) programming language should not be confused with basic machine language.

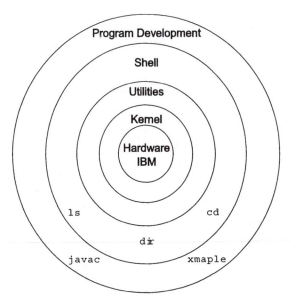

Figure 1.2 A schematic view of a computer's kernel and shells.

arithmetic. Hardly any computational scientist really talks to a computer in a language it can understand. Instead, when writing and running programs, we usually talk to the computer through a *shell* or in a *high-level language*. Eventually these commands or programs all get translated to the basic machine language.

A *shell* is a name for a command-line interpreter, that is, a place where you enter a command for the computer to obey. It is a set of medium-level commands or small programs, run by the computer. As illustrated in Figure 1.2, it is helpful to think of these shells as the outer layers of the computer's *operating system*. While every general-purpose computer has some type of shell, usually each computer has its own set of commands that constitute its shell. It is the job of the shell to run various programs, compilers, and utilities, as well as the programs of the users. There can be different types of shells on a single computer, or multiple copies of the same shell running at the same time for different users. The nucleus of the operating system is called, appropriately, the *kernel*. The user seldom interacts directly with the kernel, but the kernel interacts directly with the hardware.

The *operating system* is a group of instructions used by the computer to communicate with users and devices, to store and read data, and to execute programs. The operating system itself is a group of programs that tells the computer what to do in an elementary way. It views you, other devices, and programs as input data for it to process; in many ways it is the indispensable office manager. While all this may seem unnecessarily complicated, its purpose is to make life easier for you by letting the computer do much of the nitty-gritty work that enables you to think higher-level thoughts and communicate with the computer in something closer to your normal, everyday language. Operating systems have names such as *Unix, OSX, DOS*, and *Windows*.

In Part 1 of this book we will use a high-level *interpreted* language, either Maple or Mathematica. In Part 2 we will use a high-level *compiled* language, either Java or Fortran90. In an interpreted language the computer translates one statement at a time into basic machine instructions. In a compiled language the computer translates an entire program unit all at once. Compiled languages usually lead to faster programs, permit the use of vast libraries of subprograms, and tend to be portable. Interpreted languages appear to be more responsive, interactive, and, consequently, more "user friendly."

When you submit a program to your computer in a compiled language, the computer uses a *compiler* to process it. The compiler is another program that treats your program as a foreign language and uses a built-in dictionary and set of rules to translate it into basic machine language. As you can imagine, the final set of instructions is quite detailed and long, especially after the compiler has made several passes through your program to translate your convoluted logic into fast code. The translated statements ultimately form an *executeable* code that runs when loaded into the computer's memory.

1.3 INSTRUCTIONAL GUIDE

Landau's Rules of Education: Much of the educational philosophy applied in this book is summarized by these three rules:

1. Most of education is learning what the words mean; the concepts are usually quite simple once you understand what you are being told.
2. Confusion is the first step to understanding.
3. Traumatic experiences tend to be the most educational ones.

This book has an attitude, and we hope you will develop one too! We enjoy computing and relish the increased creativity and productivity resulting from powerful computing tools. We believe that computing has so become part of the fabric of science that an introductory scientific computing course should be part of every lower-division university student's education. Hence we deliberately mix the languages of mathematics, science, and computer science. This mix of languages is how modern scientists think about things, and since ideas must be communicated with these same words and ideas, this is how the book is written. However, we are sensitive to the confusion multiple definitions may reap and do provide a section at the end of each chapter indicating some key words and concepts, and a glossary at the end of the book defining many technical terms and jargon.

Because we aim to give an introduction to computational science, we cover some basics of numerical analysis, information about how data are stored, and the concordant limits of computation. However, we present very little discussion of hardware, computer architecture, and operating systems. That is not to say that these are not interesting and important topics, but rather that we want to get the reader busy computing and acquiring familiarity with concrete examples. In our experience, science and engineering students need this practical experience before they can appreciate the more abstract principles of computer science.

We have aimed our presentation at first- and second-year college students. We believe that the chapters and sections not marked optional with an asterisk * provide a good introductory course for them. The inclusion of the optional chapters would raise of the level of the presentation and lead to a longer course. To maintain the logical organization of materials, we have intermixed the optional chapters with the others. However, there should be nothing in the optional chapters that is required in order to understand the chapters that follow.

It is hard to keep up with the rapid changes in computer technology and with the knowledge of how to use them. That is not such a big issue with scientific computing, because it is the basic principles of mathematics, logic, science, and computing that are important, and not the details of hardware and software. Nevertheless, students and faculty often do not enjoy computing because of the frustration and helplessness they feel when computers do not work the way they should. Although we commiserate with those feelings, one of the things we try to teach is that it is not unusual to have new things not work quite right, but that if you relax and follow a trial-and-error approach, then you usually find success working around them.

Be warned, there are some exercises in this book that give the wrong answer, that lead to error messages, or that may "break" the program (but not harm the computer). Learning to cope with the limits of computation gets easier and less traumatic after you have done it a few times. We understand, however, that many instructors may not appreciate a computer's failure that they cannot explain, and so we have assembled an *Instructor's Survival Guide*, available upon request through the Web.

It is important that students become familiar with the material in the text before they come to lab. A lecture helps, but reading and working through the materials is essential. Even though it may not be that hard to work through the problems in lab by having instructors and fellow students prompt you with the appropriate commands to enter, there is little to be gained from that. Our goal is to make this introductory experience very much a "lab" that develops an attitude of experimentation and discovery and that nurtures rewarding feelings when a project finally computes correctly.

Many of the problems we assign require numerical solution and therefore are not covered in elementary texts. These include nonlinear oscillators, the motion of projectiles with drag, and the rotation of cubes about an arbitrary axis. Notwithstanding our prediction that other elementary courses and texts will eventually be more multidisciplinary, some readers may feel that we are requiring them to understand phenomena at a level higher than in their other courses. Our hope is that the readers will recognize that they are pioneers, will be stimulated by their new-found powers, and will help modernize their other courses.

On the technical side, we have developed the materials with Maple 6–9.5, Mathematica 4.2, and the Java Development Kit (JDK or Java 2 Standard Edition, J2SE) [SunJ]. Even though studio and workbench environments are available, we prefer the pedagogical value in using a shell to issue separate commands for compilation and execution, and then having to deal with the source and class files directly. In addition, many students are able to load JDK onto their home computers and work there as well.

We have found that *WinEdt* [WinEdt] and *TextPad* work well to edit and run source code on a Windows platform, and that *Xemacs* [Gnu] with Java tools is excellent for Unix/Linux machines. In addition, *jEdit*, the Open Source programmer's editor [jEdit], is an excellent tool that, because it itself is written in Java, runs on most any platform. Visualization is very important in computational science. It is built into Maple and Mathematica and is excellent. Part of the power of Java is that it has strong graphical capabilities built right into the language, although calling them up is somewhat involved. Consequently, we have adopted the free, open source package *PtPlot* [PtPlot] as our standard approach to plotting with Java. However, *gnuplot* [Gnuplot] and *Grace* [Grace] are also recommended as stand-alone applications. For 3-D graphics, a more specialized application, we give instructions on using *gnuplot* and refer the interested reader to *OpenDx* [DX] and *VisAd* [Visad]. These too are free, powerful, and available for Unix/linux and Windows computers.

1.4 EXERCISES TO COME BACK TO

Consider the following list of problems to which a computational approach could be applied. Indicate with an "M," "J," or "E" whether the best approach would be the use of Maple, Java, or either.

1. calculate the escape velocity from Jupiter
2. write a spreadsheet (accounting) program from scratch
3. solve problems from a calculus textbook
4. prove an algebraic identity
5. determine the time required for a sky diver to reach terminal velocity
6. write a compiler for a programming language

PART 1

MAPLE (OR MATHEMATICA) BY DOING

Chapter Two

Getting Started with Maple

2.1 SETTING UP YOUR WORK SPACE

An important part of scientific computing is being organized. Good organization provides you with more time for the important things like being original and creative in your work, as well as giving you more time to get your work done (or to play). This organizational concept is particularly true for scientific computing, where you may have to deal with many files or many versions of the same file. For students, good organization also keeps you on task.

An important step in organization is knowing where you have stored things. One of the best ways to get organized is to create files in directories and subdirectories (also called folders and subfolders). You need to be able to navigate through your directories, see your files, and tell what is in them by their names. In addition, you need to be able to create, copy, move, and remove files and directories. Finally, you should protect your files from accidental or unintentional intrusions.[1] For whatever operating system you are using, try out and get familiar with the commands to:

- list the names of all files and directories in your working directory or folder
- list the names with details of all files and directories in your working directory or folder
- display the name of the directory in which you are working
- make (create) a directory
- copy file1 to file2 and then delete file1
- copy file1 to a different directory and then delete local file1
- copy file1 to file2, leaving copy of file1

To get started:

- Create a subdirectory Intro in your home directory.
- Create subdirectories Week1, Week2, . . ., Week10 within directory Intro.
- Place a copy of the Maple worksheet version of Appendix B, *Maple Quick*

---

[1]How to do these things under Unix is explained in [L&F 93] or the Web tutorial [UnixWeb].

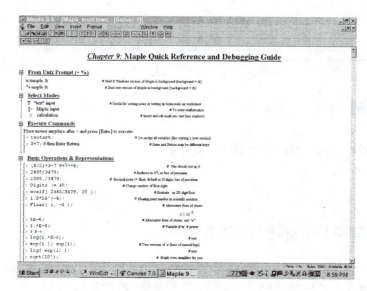

Figure 2.1 An image of Maple's classic desktop environment.

Reference, into the `Intro` directory. One way to do that is to Open the CD file with Maple and then SaveAs into your directory.

* Change to the subdirectory `Week1` and use it for this weeks' work.

2.2 MAPLE'S PROBLEM-SOLVING ENVIRONMENT

Maple is an example of what computer scientists call a *problem-solving environment*. View it as a complete computing system (a really big program) that does nearly everything you need for mathematical calculations and does it within an intuitive, graphical user interface. Maple and its cousins, like Mathematica, extend scientific computations from dealing with numbers to also manipulating algebraic symbols. Even though problem-solving environments are also used for numerical calculations, compiled languages are faster and more flexible. (Matlab, while also called a problem-solving environment by some, is predominantly a friendly interface for doing numerical calculations. It is often used for high-powered design, simulations, and data analysis.)

2.2.1 Look Around, Smell the Roses

Ideally, you are reading this as an electronic Maple worksheet (a file with the suffix `.mws`) within Maple. If not, we recommend that you do so or at least open up a Maple window to experiment with. To do so on a Unix/Linux operating system, type `xmaple &` at a Unix prompt. To do so on other systems, start it as you would any other program. You should get an interface like that in Figure 2.1.

Look around in the window and note how it has dropdown menus and buttons that make it look very much like a word processor or a text editor, with which you may already be familiar. Pull down the menus and take note of the types of functions they perform. Before you get in too deep, note that the File menu has both Close and Exit as options. Close will terminate the Maple window that you are currently working on, while Exit will terminate the entire Maple session.

One of the worst experiences in computing is losing a file containing all of your hard work. Beware, even though you may have assigned a name to a file, its contents do not get permanently stored until you issue the Save or Save As command. Although Maple will usually ask if you want to save a file before discarding it, it is a good idea for you to explicitly save your file in the desired location before exiting or closing. You save a file with the Save command (the Save command under the File pull-down menu). In fact, it is a good idea to save your file on a regular basis while working on it; then even if Maple crashes, you will not lose all your work.

The Save As command under the File pull-down menu lets you change the format of the file as well as the location where it is to be stored. (Make sure you save your files in a directory where you will find them again; the default directory may be in some godforsaken part of the computer.)

Exercise: Now do as you are told!

• Save this worksheet to your home directory or one of your other places.

• Now Close this window and see what happens.

• Now Exit Maple, start it again, and then **Return Here**.   ♠

• Welcome back! Observe that there is a valuable Help menu as the right-most menu. Before you try it out, be warned that the Help window may cover up the window in which you are reading this. You get back to this screen by going to the Window menu, which will show you all the windows that you have open. You select this one to place it on top.

• Try out the Help facility and notice that you can search for commands, search on topics, or go on a tour.

• Try selecting (with your mouse) a word in the preceding text, such as Exit. Then go to the Help menu and note there is automatically a menu item there for help on Exit. Go ahead and read what it says.

• Go to the Help menu again and search for information on Help. Examine the changes in the windowing environment and the arrows on the Help dashboard pointing right and left. They are hyperlinks to other pages for you to try.

• Select (highlight) the above paragraph by dragging your mouse over it (holding down the left mouse button). Now try out the buttons that center the selected text, that right- and left-justify it, and that make it **bold (B),** *italic (I)* or underlined (U). Likewise, you can select some text and change the values in the little white windows to the left of the B button and get all types of formatting options.

While we are talking about what Maple does with text, it is a good idea to experience Maple's active section and subsection notation. Right below this paragraph is a boxed + indicating a collapsed section. Mouse clicking on the + changes it to a − and opens up the material in the section for viewing. Do it now and experience the power of Maple! Clicking on a − reverses the process; do it too to close up the sections.

2.2.2 Try It, You'll Like It!

In a well-designed Maple worksheet, or book for that matter, the section and subsection titles should form an outline of the material covered. This outline assists the learning process, since looking at just the titles of the sections of a document helps map out your journey through the material. Try it with this document:

• Go to the View menu and select Expand All Sections. Then select Collapse All Sections. Imagine how useful collapsing and expanding sections is for writing technical documents; you can first construct an outline by creating the section and subsection titles, and then fill in the material after the logic is clear.

• Whoops! You have now uncovered some of the materials that we have tried to hide in collapsed sections. So, close this document without saving it, and open up the original again.

• **Return Here.** During our ordering you about, you may as well open and close some windows. In fact, it is good to learn how to open and close windows properly before you run the risk of losing some valuable work. Try closing and then opening the window within Maple in which this text appears. With a Windows operating system, a window is closed by depressing the lower most button on the upper right side with the x in it; on a Unix/Linux system, a window is closed by pushing the lower-most button on the upper left side with a − in it, and then selecting the Close option. You will then have to go to the File menu and select Open, or select the name of this file, if Maple was nice enough to write its name there.

• Try minimizing (iconizing) and then maximizing the window within Maple in which this text appears. With a Windows operating system, you minimize and maximize by depressing the lower-most button on the upper right side with an underscore _ in it; on a Unix/Linux system this is done by pushing the lower-most button on the upper right side with a center dot . in it. Then click on the maple-leaf icon to get the full window back.

• Finally, find the button that makes the window in which you are reading this text smaller or larger—but does not close or minimize the window. On a Windows machine that button has a single box, or maybe two overlapping boxes in it; on a Unix machine it is a depressed or raised (shaded) single box.

• Maple is placed in different modes when writing or when doing mathematics. Check that you are still in text [T] mode, go to the Insert menu, and insert a paragraph. This action just makes some space for you to enter the new paragraph, you must still do the writing. To do that, enter text in the space inserted for the new paragraph. Insert a section and enter several lines of nonsense text. Insert two subsections, entering several lines of text after each. Check if your little boxes are working right, and then try deleting your additions when they are in both expanded and collapsed forms.

• Now try playing with the indent buttons (arrows, someplace above the B), as well as the three sizes of magnifying glasses or x's (real cute) that let you progressively enlarge the screen as your eyes get tired (or old). Inspect the explanation of a button's purpose that appears on the information bar at the bottom of your screen when you push that button and hold it down.

• Before you start thinking that Maple is just a program for technical writing, take note of the three adjacent buttons on the task bar (on the top of the window) with Σ, T, and [> on them.

• Press the T button. This action places you in text mode, in which you get these cute windows letting you control the text format, type, and size. Click your mouse into some existing text and start typing something.

• Next push the Σ button and note that it tells you that this is for "inserting inert standard math into a text region." (Inert math looks good but has no symbolic value.) This option is useful for writing reports (like this), since you can insert fancy symbols like $\sum_{i=1}^{\infty} i^{(-2)}$ into your text. Usually inert math is black and active math is red when you enter it. However, some of the colors in this worksheet have been lost as it was transferred down from one generation of Maple to another. We could also have inserted math in executable or active mode as $\sum_{i=1}^{\infty} i^{(-2)}$. If you select either symbol by clicking on it, you can then use the button with the Maple leaf on it to toggle (switch back and forth) between executable and inert modes.

• It sometimes may seem a little hard to get out of the executable math mode. If that happens to you, try pressing the T or the [> button to get back into one of the other modes. Just for fun, use your mouse to select the mathematical summation symbol above (just click on it). You will notice that the Maple command that is used to create this symbol appears in a little window at the top of the screen. Now click on the little x button that appears when the symbol is highlighted, and note how the command gets slipped into the text in place of the symbols. If you highlight the command and click again, the symbol is slipped back into the text. This series of commands acts like another toggle switch.

• Seeing that you have messed up this worksheet over which we have labored so long, you do not want to save it, since that would replace our nice version with your messed-up one. (You may use the Save As option on the File menu to save your messed-up version as a different file.)

2.3 MAPLE'S COMMAND STRUCTURE

At last we will do some mathematics with Maple.

• Pressing the [> button places you in the *execute* mode that permits manipulation of symbols and expressions. The greater-than symbol > is Maple's way of prompting you to enter a command to the right of it (in fact, it is called a "prompt" for just this reason). When you enter commands after the [> prompt, Maple gets to work for you. If you enter commands while Maple is in the text mode, then Maple just copies them onto the worksheet and sits there awaiting your next entry.

• Place Maple into execute mode, tell it to add 3 + 82, and then hit the Enter/Return key. Observe that your command to Maple shows up in red and is in a fixed-width font like a typewriter or a teletype. The teletype font is meant either to evoke the aura of the computing days of the past or to indicate that this is your command to the computer. Check next that Maple speaks back to you in blue and black. If you did as told, Maple has probably responded with a blue streak:

```
Warning, premature end of input
```

This warning is Maple's way of saying that it does not think your command is over yet, even though you appear to think so. To end your command properly you have place a semicolon ; at the end of the line before hitting the Enter key (on some computer systems you may have to hit the Return key).

• So, go back into execute mode [>, insert two prompts into the text, enter 3+82; after the first prompt, and then hit Enter. This command should give 85 as an answer and leave you at the next prompt [>.

• Now use the arrow keys to go back up in this worksheet and fix your previous command by placing the missing ; at its end (after the 82). Then pressing Enter should fix things up. In general, when you make a mistake you can go back to the command you have already entered, correct it, and then hit Enter/Return any place in the command to execute the command again. This correction is a lot better than trying to enter the entire command again, especially when the commands get complicated and you are annoyed with the computer and the slow pace of learning. (It is an often-experienced but not fully tested fact that computers seem to know when you are annoyed with them, and then react by giving you an even harder time.)

• To get the most out of this tutorial you should personally key in the Maple commands rather than cut and paste them to a Maple prompt. In order to force this point, we make some commands inert. A good way to enter commands is to go to the File menu and start a New window within Maple (you may have many windows open simultaneously).

• If you go back to the first [> prompt in the Maple worksheet version of this text and hit Enter, you will note how after executing your command, Maple automatically skips down through the text and output to the next [> prompt and waits there for your next command. In this case, Maple's response means that unless you get into the habit of inserting some extra prompts in your document, you may end up skipping over some valuable material.) So find your way back up to this point in the worksheet and note the action of the Tab key. It jumps you through the worksheet with stops at each prompt or executable expression.

• In the next section you will enter a new calculation on your worksheet directly after the (blue) result of a previous calculation. To do that, place your cursor to the left of the previous result (possibly 85), and press the execute [> button, causing a new execution group to start at that location.

2.3.1 Maple as a Pocket Calculator

Maple does everything a pocket calculator does and much more. It understands the usual arithmetic operators, + and - for addition and subtraction, uses * and / for multiplication and division, and understands either ** or ^ for exponentiation (raising to a power). As an example, $3 \times 45 - 7^6$ would be entered as 3 * 45 - 7 ^ 6, where the spaces do not matter. Go ahead and try it by placing your cursor anywhere after the prompt below and hitting Enter.

> 3 * 45 - 7^6 ;   # This field is a nonexecuted comment

$$-117514$$

Look at how Maple has jumped to the next prompt. If we had not placed an extra [> there, you would have had to look for the cursor and bring it back to here.

2.3.2 Rules of Precedence

When performing calculations like those above, it is important for Maple to know the order in which you want the various operations performed. The order of executions (also followed by most pocket calculators) is

    ^   then   *   or   /   then   +   or   -

There may still be ambiguity, depending upon the way in which you apply this rule. As a case in point, let us say we want to add 4 to 2 and then multiply the sum by 3. Have Maple try this by evaluating the (ambiguous) expression 4 + 2 * 3.

• If you got the answer 10, then you did not do what we wanted. Clearly, this calculation is a case where the order of operations matters. Try (4 + 2) * 3, where the parenthesis makes our intentions clearer.

• Next try $400/10/2$ and explain your result. Because computers tend to do division from left to right (left associative), Maple knows what it is doing, but the result may not be what you want.

• Now see if $400/10/2$ is the same as $(400/10)/2$ or $400/(10/2)$. In the worksheet we give you only one prompt for this as a way of encouraging you to try entering the three commands on a single line with a semicolon ; after each command, but only one Return at the end of the line.

• Remember, if there is a chance that the results may be ambiguous or unclear, use parentheses to force the operations you want and to ensure clarity. For instance, enter 3 ^ 4 ^ 5^ 6.

>   # Enter 3 ^4 ^5 ^6

Maple tells you something is wrong. At times when Maple cannot figure out what you have told it to do, it may respond by just repeating your command back to you (a polite way of suggesting that you get it right next time).

2.4 SUMS AND SUMS

Many problems in science and mathematics require you to evaluate sums. At times the sums are over a finite number of terms, and at other times the number of terms is infinite. With a little cleverness you can write a sum as a single expression. As an instance, here is an infinite sum

$$\sum_{i=0}^{\infty} \frac{(-1)^i \, x^{(2i)}}{(2i)!}$$

The summation index i starts from 0 and runs all the way to infinity. We show two related ways to enter sums into Maple. The first is

```
> Sum((-1)^i * x^(2*i) / (2*i)!, i = 0..infinity);          # Revealing, but inert
```

$$\sum_{i=0}^{\infty} \frac{(-1)^i \, x^{(2i)}}{(2\,i)!}$$

In spite of this output being pretty and being a great way to check that you have entered the sum correctly, it is inert (cannot be used to do the math). The active form for this sum, as well as a number of other functions in Maple, is obtained by writing the function without the capital letter, in this case as `sum(...)`. Try converting the passive sum to an active sum:

```
>                                                           # Paste and edit passive form here
```

If life is fair, you should have obtained $\cos x$ as the value that Maple actually evaluates for the sum. This means that Maple has recognized this infinite sum as the power-series expansion for $\cos x$. Actually, you can have the best of both worlds; use the command `Sum` to have Maple show you what it thinks you want (useful for debugging your typing), and then enter `value(%)` to have Maple perform the calculation:

```
> Sum ( (-1)^i * x^(2*i) / (2*i)!, i = 0..infinity );
```

$$\sum_{i=0}^{\infty} \frac{(-1)^i \, x^{(2i)}}{(2\,i)!}$$

```
> value (%);                                                # Evaluate previous expression
```

$$\cos(x)$$

```
> Sum( (-1)^i*x^(2*i) / (2*i)!, i = 0..infinity ) =         # Use both forms
     sum ( (-1)^i * x^(2*i) / (2*i)!, i = 0..infinity );
```

$$\sum_{i=0}^{\infty} \frac{(-1)^i \, x^{(2i)}}{(2\,i)!} = \cos(x)$$

Take a close look at the `sum()` command we have used here. Like all Maple commands, it has a format that should be followed precisely (although inserting spaces causes no harm). To begin with, note that after the name of the command there is a pair of parentheses. The parentheses contain the *arguments* to the command. In this case, there are two arguments separated by a comma. The first argument or *field* contains the expression to be summed, while the second field contains the range of values to be covered by the summation index.

Descriptions of ranges in Maple are of the form `i = a..b` or `i = a .. b`, where `a` and `b` are the lower and upper limits of the range ($b = \infty$ for our example). If you deviate from this format, Maple may tell you that you did something wrong, or Maple may assume that you know what you are doing (Maple is good at math, not at judging character) and make a reasonable attempt to follow your command. To illustrate, try these:

```
> Sum ( (-1)^i * x^(2*i) / (2*i)!, i =0 .  infinity ) =        # Left off a . in range
        sum ( (-1)^i * x^(2*i) / (2*i)!, i = 0.infinity );
  Error, missing operator or ';'
> Sum ( (-1)^i * x^(2*i) / (2*i)!, i = 0 ..  infty ) =        # Spelled infinity wrong
        sum ((-1)^i * x^(2*i) / (2*i)!, i = 0..infty);
```

$$\sum_{i=0}^{infty} \frac{(-1)^i \, x^{(2\,i)}}{(2\,i)!} = \cos(x) + x^{(2\,infty+2)} + \cdots$$

In the first case you should get an error message, while in the second case Maple evaluated the sum treating infty as if were just another algebraic symbol.

2.4.1 Strings and Quotes

In those cases when there is not an inert form of a command, you can still get Maple to produce output that contains your command and Maple's response on the same line. You accomplish this task with the judicious use of quotes. However, since Maple contains three types of quotes, "double quotes," 'left quotes,' and 'right quotes,' this whole quoting business gets to be rather confusing at times (Landau's second rule):

Maple's quote types.

Example	Name	Function
"a string"	double quotes, quotation marks	creates a string
`John Dull`	left quotes, accents grave, back quotes	delimits names
'x ^ 3'	right quotes, apostrophes	suppresses evaluation

We start with double quotes. Anything placed inside of double quotes becomes a *string*. A string is just a sequence of characters that is treated literally with no inherent meaning or value. As an example, the string "this is now a string" is just letters and spaces to Maple. However, variables can be assigned to strings, as if the strings were their values, and these variables can then be manipulated. (We shall see in our study of Java input and output, that strings are *parsed* to extract their meaning.) Here are some examples:

```
> "3 * 45 - 7 ^ 6" = 3 * 45 - 7 ^ 6;          # String in double quotes, output shows quotes
```

$$"3 * 45 - 7 ^ 6" = -117514$$

```
> `3 * 45 - 7 ^ 6` = 3 * 45 - 7 ^ 6;                    # Left quotes, quotes do not show
```

$$3 * 45 - 7 \, \hat{} \, 6 = -117514$$

> `'3 * 45 - 7 ^ 6' = 3 * 45 - 7 ^ 6;`   # Right quotes, delays execution

$$-117514 = -117514$$

In this case we see that the double quotes showed the command as entered, with the quotes themselves visible in Maple's response. The left (back) quotes produced a similar output, but with the quotes not visible and with a font change. In contrast, the right quotes may have delayed some execution, but not enough for this simple a calculation to stop Maple from returning just a number.

We will often use these left and right quotes to produce nice output and to assist in the learning process. Likewise, you may want to use them to produce nice worksheets. In the next examples we see more clearly that the left quotes just show us what command we have entered, while the right quotes have Maple set the command in proper mathematical notation, but not evaluate the expression:

> `'sum ( (-1)^i * x^(2*i) / (2*i)!, i = 0 .. infinity )'=`   # Delay execution
> `sum ( (-1)^i *x^(2*i) / (2*i)!, i = 0 .. infinity );`

$$\sum_{i=0}^{\infty} \frac{(-1)^i x^{2i}}{2i!} = \cos x$$

> `'sum ( (-1)^i * x^(2*i) / (2*i)!, i = 0 .. infinity )'=`   # Display command
> `sum ( (-1)^i *x^(2*i) / (2*i)!, i = 0 .. infinity );`

$$\text{sum ((-1)^i * x^(2*i) / (2*i)!, i = 0 .. infinity)} = \cos x$$

Now we enter some strings and manipulate them:

> `"a + b " = a + b;`   # Use of string

$$\text{``a+b''} = a+b$$

> `String := "whatever I put here";`   # `String` now a variable

$$String := \text{``whatever I put here''}$$

> `String;`

$$\text{``whatever I put here''}$$

> `"String" = String;`   # LHS = a string

$$\text{``String''} = \text{``whatever I put here''}$$

An important use of the backquote ` is to enclose names containing spaces or special characters that might otherwise give Maple trouble. For example, if the name you give to a variable contains a space, then Maple (and Unix) will assume that it is two names. Yet if you place the two names within back quotes, then the two words will be treated as a single grouping:

```
> My name;                                          # Not acceptable as has blank
  Error, missing operator or ';'
> `My name`;                                        # Now acceptable
```
$$My\ name$$

```
> `My name with colon:`;                            # Colon does not end line
```
$$My\ name\ with\ colon :$$

Scrutinize how the item within left quotes is not the same as a string (which is just a literal recall of the characters); the name in back quotes is the true name of some item in Maple:

```
> `My name` := 10;                                  # Set 'My name' to numeric value.
```
$$My\ name := 10$$

```
> `My name` ;                                       # Print out value of 'My name'
```
$$10$$

```
> `My name` := "Rubin";                             # Set 'My name' to a string
```
$$My\ name := \text{``Rubin''}$$

```
> `My name`;                                        # Print out value of 'My name'
```
$$\text{``Rubin''}$$

See again, in contrast, how right quotes delay the execution of a command:

```
> sin(Pi);                                          # Evaluate the sine of Pi;
```
$$0$$

```
> 'sin(Pi)';                                        # Enter, but do not evaluate the sine of Pi;
```
$$\sin(\pi)$$

```
> eval(%);                                          # Now evaluate the previous expression.
```
$$0$$

In summary, use double quotes " . . . " for strings, left quotes ` . . . ` for a name that contains spaces or special characters, and right quotes ' . . . ' to delay execution of a command.

2.5 EXECUTION GROUPS

In the electronic version of this book, we usually want you to observe the effect of a single, or each group of, commands one at a time. For this reason we often place the symbol [> in our Maple worksheets to stop execution. As a case in point,

```
> 'sin(3.)'  = sin(3.); 'sqrt(10.)'  =  sqrt(10.)
```
$$\sin(3.) = 0.1411200081$$
$$\sqrt{10.} = 3.162277660$$

[>

Monitor how Maple jumps through all these commands in a flash and then stops at the blank prompt. Now remove these lines of output (either by selecting them and hitting the Delete key, or by using the commands in the Edit submenu), place your cursor at the last of the three commands (the one dealing with sqrt(10)), and hit Enter again. What is happening here is easy to understand. The Maple prompt (the symbol that indicates Maple is ready to have a command entered) is the greater-than sign >. The long and short square brackets on the left indicate *execution groups*. The rule is that

> *Maple executes all commands within an execution group and then jumps to the next execution group to resume execution.*

So in our case, we see that Maple stopped at the [> symbol because it is the next execution group, not because it was a blank prompt! To test this rule, select and then delete the blank prompt above this paragraph, and execute the preceding execution group. You should notice that Maple now jumps to the execution group below this paragraph.

An execution group may contain things like text and graphics, in addition to commands, and may get to be quite long. As such, they are a convenient way to organize your worksheets. In this book we will keep our execution groups small in order to encourage you to study the consequence of each command. We suggest that you also keep your execution groups short as a way of reviewing what your worksheet is doing and of checking that it is working properly.

When you insert an execution group, Maple also inserts a command prompt from which you execute commands. To *insert an execution group*:

- Go to the Insert menu.
- Choose Execution Group.
- Choose Before or After Cursor.

To *add more command prompts* to an existing execution group,

- Place the cursor to the left of an existing >.
- Hit the Enter key.
- Check that the new prompt appears above the original >.

On occasion you end up with a bunch of execution groups that would be better off joined together. To *join* two or more *execution groups*:

- Place the cursor in the first of the two execution groups to be joined together.
- From the Edit menu, choose Split or Join, and then Join Execution Groups.
- Press the Enter key.

Alternatively, each computer system has some function keys that let you join and split execution groups rather easily. (They are F3 and F4 on the systems we have tried.) The joining of execution groups works from top to bottom, the splitting from bottom to top. Each time you enter the command, another group gets added or split. To illustrate, the following (whose mathematics we will come to in due course) is a single execution group, with one prompt before and one after the commands:

```
>
> '(x^4 + 7*x - 33)^3' = expand( (x^4 + 7*x - 33)^3 );
> Diff (%, x) = diff(%, x);
>
```

Try splitting this group at the beginning of the `Diff` line to produce two execution groups. Then try joining the split groups into one execution group. Execute the result to make sure both commands are done in a single execution.

2.6 KEY WORDS AND CONCEPTS

active mathematical expression	arithmetic expression	command
execution group	hidden section	inert
mathematical expression	on-line help	prompt
precedence rules	strings	

1. Explain the meaning of these key words.
2. Mathematics is often called the universal language of science. Evaluate this remark in the context of what Maple does.
3. What is the difference between a Maple command and a Maple response?
4. How does Maple differ from a pocket calculator?
5. How does the computer know the difference between a string and the name of a variable?
6. If computers at their heart understand only numbers, how does Maple understand algebraic symbols?

2.7 SUPPLEMENTARY EXERCISES

1. Use the text mode of Maple to write a worksheet containing:
   a. Your name
   b. Your educational level
   c. Your computer experience
   d. What you would like to get out of this course (or book)
   Convert your name into a **bold** font, convert your educational background into *italics*, and underline your experience. It is a good habit to save your worksheet often as you are working on it, and especially before trying to

print it out. Sooner or later it is likely that Maple will freeze up or quit on you and lose track of the active worksheet. That being the case, you will only have to make up the work since your last save.

2. Save your worksheet as a file in the directory Intro and the subdirectory Week1. Do not close the worksheet yet.

3. Print out this first worksheet and hand it in. To do that, you may have to look at the page that comes up when you issue the print command and pick the printer to which you want the output sent.

4. Use the sum command to find a simple expression for the sum of the first n integers, $1 + 2 + \ldots n$. You might want to experiment with the commands simplify(%) and factor(%) to get a compact expression.

5. What is the ratio of $(n+1)!$ to $n!$? How about $(n+50)!$ to $n!$? What happens when you try to calculate the ratio of $(n + m)!$ to $n!$? Use simplify(%) to get a better idea of the result. Do you obtain what you expect to? Explain.

6. Make three different execution groups, with the last two ending in a blank line of execution (that is, as >).

   a. Have each group contain four lines, and have each line raise 2 to a power equal to the sum of the line number plus execution group number.

   b. Now enlarge each execution group so it contains an additional line for input, namely, an extra >.

   c. Add comments on your choice to one of the execution groups.

7. Evaluate

   a. sin(pi), sin(PI), and sin(Pi) and explain,

   b. the natural logarithm of e, the base for natural logarithms,

   c. the natural logarithm of 10,

   d. the logarithm to the base 10 of 10.

8. Explore two ways of accessing Maple's on-line help.

   a. Use Maple to select the word *help* from the above line and then go to the Help menu on the Maple dashboard (in the upper right), and get help on *help*.

   b. Insert an execution group on this worksheet and enter the ?help command.

9. Verify that the following infinite series equals $\pi/4$:

$$1 - \frac{1}{3} + \frac{1}{5} - \frac{1}{7} + \ldots$$

10. (Optional) Although you may not believe it, the following infinite series equals $\pi/4$ for all $0 < x < \pi$:

$$\sin(x) + \frac{\sin(3x)}{3} + \frac{\sin(5x)}{5} + \ldots$$

See if you can manipulate Maple to give this result. Even getting Maple to indicate that the sum is independent of x is a step in the right direction.

11. Use the precedence and arithmetic rules of Maple to predict the values of each of the following expressions:

a. $2 \times 3 + 4/2$

b. $5 - 6 + 7^2$

c. $1 - 2^{3/4}$

12. Use the precedence and arithmetic rules of Maple to predict the values of each of the following expressions:

a. $(4/2)3 - 7^8 + 7**8$

b. $10/14$

c. $10./14$

d. $8/(4/2)$

e. $8/4/2$

f. $6^2 + 5 - 7$

g. $8 + 2^4/2$

13. For the following inputs, what would Maple produce as output:

a. `sum ( (-1)^i / (2*i)!, i = 1 ..  2 )`

b. `Sum ( (-1)^i / (2*i)!, i = 1 ..  2 )`

c. `sum ( (+x)^i / (2*i)!, i = 1 ..  2 )`

Chapter Three

Numbers, Expressions, Functions; Rocket Golf Near Lightspeed

Note to Instructor: This problem, as stated, requires the same level of relativity as covered in elementary physics texts and is thus appropriate for first- or second-year college students. Even if the students do not understand the full implications of the two equations we use, (3.4) and (3.5), it is their application that is the point of this chapter. However, it is conceptually challenging to go further and ask about the golf ball's trajectory as viewed in different frames, as this involves the questions of simultaneity and acceleration in relativity.

3.1 PROBLEM: VIEWING ROCKET GOLF

Michele, a golf fanatic, would like to break the world's record for the fastest golf ball hit. Money being no object, she rents a rocket and hits her golf balls from the moving rocket. The rocket is fast, with a speed of $c/2$, where c is the speed of light (299 792 458 m/s). (This really is fast considering that no object with mass can attain a velocity of c.) As indicated in Figure 3.1, Michele hits her drive with a speed of $U' = 1/\sqrt{3}c$, at an angle $\theta = 30^\circ$, as she measures with respect to

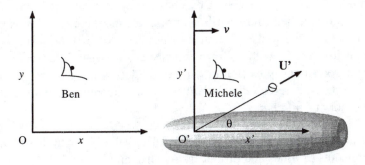

Figure 3.1 Observer Ben on Earth watching Michele on a rocket hitting a golf ball. Ben is at rest in frame O on the left and Michele is moving to the right with velocity v (horizontal arrow) in Frame O'. Michele sees her golf ball hit with velocity U'.

the moving rocket. She observes her drive to remain in the air for a hang time $T' = 2.6 \times 10^7$ seconds (which is almost a year!). Ben, an observer on the earth, sees her rocket moving to the right with a velocity $v = c/2$, and this velocity somehow gets added to that of Michele's golf ball.

Problem a: Since some readers may not be familiar with special relativity, we do not expect you to solve this problem on your own, or even to understand all the equations. Although the theory of special relativity does have it subtleties and fine points, it is accessible to beginning students and we will use only a few simple results. We will lead you through the solution for two cases and then ask you to follow our steps for a third case. This should give you a good working knowledge of some tools (the main focus of this chapter). The third case you work out is the interesting one in which round-off error arising from the use of floating-point numbers ("floats" or "doubles") becomes evident. Usually it takes many computational steps before you see the effect of round-off error, but in this problem it arises fairly simply. Your explicit problem is:

1. How would Ben, watching Michele's drive from the earth, describe the golf ball in terms of its speed, angle ϕ, and hang time T?
2. How would the answer to 1. change if Michele hit her ball to the *left* with the same inclination θ, namely, in a direction opposite to the rocket's velocity?
3. How would the answer to 1. change if Michele hit her ball to the left at an angle $60°$ below the horizon, namely, with $\theta = 240°$?
4. If Michele hit the ball with a speed $U = c$, how would the answers change?

3.2 THEORY: EINSTEIN'S SPECIAL RELATIVITY

Being told that an object is traveling with a velocity near that of the speed of light is a hint that the problem is not a simple mechanics one. Indeed, this means that we need to apply Einstein's special theory of relativity [Smith 65, Ser 00] to it. As indicated in Figure 3.1, we start by considering Ben in a reference frame O with axes (x, y) attached to the earth, and Michele in frame O' with axes (x', y') attached to the moving rocket. Relative to Ben, frame O' (the rocket) is moving along the positive x axis with uniform velocity v. Likewise, Michele feels herself at rest in the rocket and sees Ben moving to the left with velocity $-v$. Both are equally correct and agree on their *relative velocity*; indeed, this is the reason it is called the theory of *relativity*.

Ben and Michele may agree on their relative velocities, but they do not agree on measurements of times and distances. As an example, if Michele says that her golf ball was in the air for a period of time T', then Ben will say that the ball was in the air for a longer time

$$\Delta T = \gamma T' \quad \text{(time dilation)}, \tag{3.1}$$

where γ is a function of relative velocity v that is always greater than 1:

$$\gamma = \frac{1}{\sqrt{1 - v^2/c^2}} > 1. \tag{3.2}$$

In view of the fact that the speed of light c is so much larger than any velocities we normally encounter, γ is usually very close to 1 and only gets large for exceedingly high velocities (normally restricted to elementary particles). The fact that Ben would measure a longer hang time than Michele is called *time dilation* and is often described with the phrase "moving clocks run slow."

The additional result we need from special relativity relates the velocities seen by Michele and Ben. If Michele in the moving rocket O' sees her golf ball having velocity components

$$U' = (U'_x, U'_y), \tag{3.3}$$

then Ben on earth O, will see her golf ball move with velocity components

$$U = (U_x, U_y), \tag{3.4}$$

$$U_x = \frac{U'_x + v}{1 + vU'_x/c^2}, \qquad U_y = \frac{U'_y}{\gamma(1 + vU'_x/c^2)}, \tag{3.5}$$

where γ is the function (3.2) as before. If you study (3.4) a bit, you will notice that the numerator describes the usual addition of relative velocities, while the denominator is the relativistic correction. In turn, the relativistic effects are in the numerator of (3.5).

3.3 MATH: INTEGER, RATIONAL AND IRRATIONAL NUMBERS

There are different types of numbers that are used in mathematics and in computation. For instance, there is a countable infinity of integers, 0, 1, 2, 3, ..., and nearly twice that many if we also include negative integers. Maple stores these integers exactly and tries to retain infinite precision for its pure mathematical operations with them. Yet while a computer program may be smart, the computer is finite and sooner or later it will run out of room if we try to compute with very large numbers that are stored exactly. For this reason computers often store very large (and very small) numbers approximately, using the *floating-point representation*, a variation of scientific notation. We shall discuss that soon.

Even though the number of integers is infinite, there is a yet larger infinity of *rational numbers*, namely, of numbers formed by the ratio of two integers, N/D. Maple stores these rational numbers exactly, by storing the numerator and denominators as integers and then displaying a fraction rather than a bunch of digits. To see what this means in action, enter these operations and interpret the results:

```
1/3;    4/2;    2485/3479;    3(1/3);    3 * (1/3);
```

After the Maple prompts we obtain:[1]

$$1/3 \quad 2 \quad 5/7 \quad 3 \quad 1$$

There are also numbers in our world that cannot be expressed as the ratio of integers, and so would require an infinite number of digits to store. These are called *irrational numbers* and include numbers like π or e (the base of natural logarithms). When Maple encounters irrational numbers, it usually uses the familiar symbol for them rather than approximating them by a fraction or a decimal. By way of example, see what happens when you ask Maple to use some of its built-in functions to determine the angle whose cosine is -1, or raise e to the first power:

```
> arccos(-1);
```
$$\pi$$

```
> 'exp (1)' = exp (1);
```
$$e = e$$

These results are more than pretty symbols. Maple knows the meaning of these and other symbols, as seen from the response to `log(%)`. Here the percent sign % means "the previous expression," and %% means the one before that. Try it:

1. Modify the previous command with `arccos(-1)` and add a `cos(%)` at its end.
2. Likewise, add a `log(%)` to the command `exp(1)`.
3. In both cases explain the effect of execution:

```
> arccos(-1);        cos(%);
```
$$\pi \quad -1$$

```
> 'exp (1)' = exp (1);        log(%);
```
$$e = e, \quad 1$$

Maple understands more than just symbols, it actually knows an incredible amount about a myriad of functions, too. Some common ones are

```
ln(x), log10(x), abs(x), cos(x), sin(x), sqrt(x), arcsin(x), cosh(x).
```

Others are given in an Appendix B or found under Maple's Help menu. Now and then you will need to include π or e, or some other irrational, into one of your commands. Maple normally accepts expressions like `pi`, `Pi`, `PI`, `e`, or `E` as algebraic symbols. You may always define these symbols to be what you want (with techniques that we will get to shortly), but Maple has predefined many such symbols for general use.

---

[1]Instructor's note: Maple interprets 3 (1/3) as a function 3 with argument 1/3 and evaluates it as 3.

So, now we prompt you to run Maple and deduce what it thinks of each. You should have found that `cos(pi)` and `cos(PI)` produce nice output, since Maple recognizes `pi` and `PI` as lower- and uppercase Greek letters. However, they are treated like any other algebraic symbol and do not have values associated with them (unless you have assigned values to them, of course). In contrast, Maple recognizes `Pi` as the ratio of the circumference to the diameter of a circle and evaluates `cos(Pi)` = `-1` just fine. However, we do have to input the rather inelegant `exp(1)` to get the mathematical *e* (this was not true in previous versions of Maple and may well change again).

3.4 CS: FLOATING-POINT NUMBERS

In spite of integers being neat to work with, there are limits to the kind of calculations possible with them. Occasionally you might want to see what the numerical value of an irrational number like π or $\sin(1)$ is, or you may need to deal with a really large number, like the size of the universe. Numbers with decimal points are stored on the computer in a format known as *floating-point notation* or *real*. This notation is similar to scientific or engineering notation of the form

$$\text{mantissa} \times 2^{\text{exponent}}.$$

The term "floating-point" denotes the idea that the decimal (or binary) point moves around or "floats" during calculations in order to keep the number of digits in the mantissa constant.

One easy way to tell Maple that you want to do some work using floating-point numbers ("floats") is to place a decimal point in one of the numbers of your calculation. This automatically makes it a floating-point number, and if one of your numbers is a float, Maple often assumes that you want all the other numbers to be as well. To experience this in action, enter and observe Maple's response to each of the following (we give answers here):

```
1/3,     1/3.,     1./3,     1./3.,     2 + 1./3.
```

$$1/3 \quad 0.3333333333 \quad 0.3333333333 \quad 0.3333333333 \quad 2.333333333$$

The other way to get Maple to do a calculation using floats or reals is to explicitly tell it to evaluate some expression as a floating-point number. This is done with the `evalf` function or command (the `f` means "float"):

```
> eval (1/3) ;        evalf (1/3) ;
```

$$\frac{1}{3}, \quad 0.3333333333$$

```
> evalf (1/3, 40) ;                    # Evaluate as a float with 40 digits
```

$$0.3333333333333333333333333333333333333333$$

If you count the number of 3's in the first case, you will see that Maple has stored 10 decimal places (the word length). This is the default value and is about as good as a pocket calculator. Actually, there is a variable internal to Maple called `Digits` that determines this *number of significant figures*, and it is usually set to 10. You may change the value of `Digits` quite easily if you want more or less precision:

```
> Digits := 4 ;        1/3.;                                    # Sets global number for float digits
```

$$Digits := 4 \qquad 0.3333$$

3.4.1 Powers of 10

We have just seen how Maple stores numbers in floating-point or scientific notation. Unless you are dealing with an exact power of 2, like 256, this floating-point representation of a number is *always* approximate, since only a finite number of digits is used to store the mantissa. In the course of discussing exponents and exponentials, which are related but different, it is useful to see how to enter a number as a power of ten in Maple.[2] Enter each of the following with the spacing exactly as given, and explain Maple's response to each (we give answers here in the printed text):

```
> 3E6;      3 E6;      3E 6;      3.E-6;                         # One good, three bads
```

$$0.3 \, 10^7 \qquad \text{Error, missing operator or ';'} \cdots$$

```
> 3e6;      3*E6;      3.*E6;      3*e6;      3e^1;              # Variations on a theme
```

$$0.3 \, 10^7 \quad 3 \, \text{E6} \quad 3. \, \text{E6} \quad 3 \, \text{e6} \quad 3.$$

```
> ln(1 * e^1);      exp(1);      ln(exp(1));      exp(1.);      ln(exp(1.));
```

$$\ln(e) \quad e \quad 1 \quad 2.718281828 \quad 0.9999999998$$

We deduce from these results that:

- With no spaces, Maple recognizes `3E6` and `3e6` as the floating-point number 3×10^6, with mantissa 3 and (decimal) exponent 6.
- The spaces in `3 E6`, `3E 6`, and `3 e6` lead Maple to believe that `E6`, `3E`, or `e6` are algebraic symbols, in which case it believes you have left out an operand that would connect it to the rest of the expression.
- In contrast, the expressions `3*E6` and `3*e6` are quite acceptable to Maple, and it assumes that you just want to multiply `3` by `E6` and `e6`, respectively. Thus while this representation may look like scientific notation, it is not.

---

[2] Although the computer stores them as powers of 2, it is easier for humans to work with powers of 10.

- Likewise, `e^1` raises the symbol `e` to the first power. Even though this expression looks like the base to the natural logarithm system, evaluating its logarithm shows otherwise.
- The last four cases are illuminating. As we have seen before, Maple has a built-in exponential function `exp()` and it knows that `exp(1)` is the irrational base of the natural logarithm system *e*. Consequently, `ln(exp(1))` = 1 exactly. However, when we repeat these same steps starting with `exp(1.)`, the decimal point places Maple in floating-point mode, in which numbers are stored only approximately, and, consequently, the `ln(exp(1.))` does not exactly equal 1.

3.5 COMPLEX NUMBERS

A complex number is the sum of a real number and an imaginary number. An imaginary number is $\sqrt{-1}$ times a real number.[3] Usually mathematicians and physicists use the symbol i to represent $\sqrt{-1}$, while engineers often use the symbol j; regardless of its name, it is the same number, and it does not really exist in our world. Maple, in turn, marches to its own drummer and uses I to represent $\sqrt{-1}$. To see how this works (we will encounter complex numbers in a number of places again), we give you some examples:

```
> 'sqrt (-1)' = sqrt (-1);                    # What does Maple return?
```
$$\sqrt{-1} = I$$

```
> 1 + (2 + 2*I) / (2 - 2*I);                  # Complex number algebra
```
$$1 + I$$

```
> convert (%, polar);                         # Convert to polar notation (r,θ)
```
$$\mathrm{polar}(\sqrt{2}, \frac{\pi}{4})$$

```
> polar( %% );                                # Alternate way to convert
```
$$\mathrm{polar}(\sqrt{2}, \frac{\pi}{4})$$

```
> sqrt(I);                                    # Square root of i (not obvious answer)
```
$$\frac{\sqrt{2}}{2} + \frac{1}{2} I \sqrt{2}$$

```
> % * %;                                      # Verify result by squaring
```
$$(\frac{\sqrt{2}}{2} + \frac{1}{2} I \sqrt{2})^2$$

```
> simplify (%);                               # Not what expected so simply
```
$$I$$

---

[3]If you need some review of complex numbers, you may want to read the introductory material in Chapter 16 in the Java part of this book.

3.6 EXPRESSIONS

We started our work with Maple by using it as an expensive pocket calculator. You key in commands one at a time and Maple evaluates them one at a time. Maple does much more. One of the truly unique things it does is mathematics, including calculus, with algebraic symbols. Many of the commands in Maple work with either numbers or symbols. We shall see some examples of that.

In a semantic sense, most of the commands that we have so far given to Maple are *expressions* and *statements*. Whereas you may know what these terms mean in common English, they have rather specific meanings in both computer science and mathematics.[4] Expressions are objects that have numerical values (or would have values if the variables contained in them had values). Commands like `1+4;` and `sin(Pi/2)` are expressions with values 5 and 1 respectively. On the other hand, `exp(x) - 1` is also an expression, but it has a numerical value only if `x` has previously been assigned a value. Try it:

```
> exp(x) - 1;
```
Evaluate $e^x - 1$

$$e^x - 1$$

```
> x := 3;        exp(x) - 1;
```
Assign value to x, evaluate $e^x - 1$ again

$$x = 3 \quad e^3 - 1$$

Observe, when Maple just echoes what you entered, it is being diplomatic and telling you that it heard what you have said but cannot do anything about it. If you want more, then you need to tell it more!

3.6.1 restart and unassign

When we refer to a *constant*, we mean an object whose value does not change. As an instance, `PI` = π is such a constant. When we refer to a *variable*, we mean a data item whose value may change. For example, the circumference `C` = `2 * PI * r` will have different values depending upon the radius `r` of the circle. When we refer to a symbol, such as `x`, we view it as one would in algebra; namely, as an abstract object representing something more concrete. Sometimes `x` may have a numerical value, and at other times it may not. In either case we may manipulate it using the rules of algebra and calculus.

When a symbol has been assigned within a worksheet, it normally stays assigned until you change it or until you close that particular worksheet. (It is often useful to have several worksheets open at one time, possibly even different

---

[4]This is an example of *Landau's First Rule of Education*.

versions of the same worksheet.) Every so often you may be happily working away or editing deep within a worksheet that was working just fine for you, and for some reason your statements no longer appear to be working correctly. The problem may be that you have forgotten that some variable has been assigned previously, and you are using it as if it had not been. That being the case, you need to unassign the variables. Also, if you just jump into the middle of a worksheet, you do not know that variables have been assigned or that packages have been called, in which case it would be safest to "start with a clean slate." If Maple really seems to be working improperly, you should save your files, exit Maple, and then start it again.

To start again with all new variables as if it were a whole new session:

```
> restart;                                              # Unassign all variables
```

Unless you have reason not to, it is a good idea to issue the `restart` command at the beginning of each new group of operations.

To unassign a single variable, use single quotes to assign that variable back to a literal or symbolic version of itself, or use the `unassign` command:

```
> x := 10;                                              # The assignment statement
```
$$x := 10$$

```
> x;                                                    # Tell me present value
```
$$10$$

```
> x := 'x';                                             # Assign as symbol. Or use unassign('x');
```
$$x := x$$

```
> x;                                                    # Tell me present value
```
$$x$$

```
> x := 10;     x;     unassign('x');     x;
```
$$x := 10, \quad 10 \quad x := x \quad x$$

3.6.2 Exercise (How Expressions Are Stored)

The factorial operation $n! = n(n-1)(n-2)\cdots(2)(1)$ occurs frequently in mathematics. If n is an integer, then Maple evaluates $n!$ just as you would expect. Run Maple to determine what is the ratio of $(1001)!$ to $1000!$:

```
> 1001!/1000!;                                          # The 1000's should cancel
```
$$1000$$

However, when n is a symbolic variable with no value assigned to it, Maple prefers to store it as $n!$ rather than as the product of many terms. This makes sense because it saves memory and because it makes further manipulations easier:

```
>  (n+1)!/n!;            (n+50)!/n!;                              # Some simple ratios
```

$$\frac{(n+1)!}{n!} \qquad \frac{(n+50)!}{n!}$$

It may appear that Maple is arrogantly repeating to you the command that you have just issued, yet a more understanding view is that Maple does not think like you and so has to be told more explicitly just what you have in mind. In this case, Maple has worked out an answer that apparently looks fine to it, while we might prefer something simpler. So we tell Maple to simplify the answer:

```
>  '(n+1)!/n!'  = simplify((n+1)!/n!);                           # Simplify RHS
```

$$\frac{(n+1)!}{n!} = n+1$$

Exercise: Calculate the ratio of $(n+50)!$ to $n!$, remembering to simplify. Calculate the ratio of $(n+m)!$ to $n!$, where n and m are algebraic. (Maple may output Γ for the gamma function. This is the correct answer. You would have to tell Maple that m and n are integers to get $m!$ as the answer.) ♠

3.7 ASSIGNMENT STATEMENTS

indexStatements

Whereas *expressions* have values, *statements* cause things to happen. In other words, statements have *side effects*, such as assigning values to variables or plotting up some graphs. The most common sort of statement is the assignment statement setting one object equal to another:

```
>  Digits;                                # Expression: current value of Digits
```

$$10$$

```
>  1./3.;                                 # Expression: performs calculation
```

$$0.3333333333$$

```
>  x := 1./3 ;                            # Assignment statement: assigns value to x
```

$$x := 0.3333333333$$

```
>  Digits := 4;     x := 1./3;            # Assignment statements
```

$$Digits := 4 \qquad x := 0.3333$$

We see that the side effects of these statements are that Digits (which determines the precision of floating-point calculations) will subsequently have the value 4, and that x will have the value 0.3333.

Because assignment statements set things equal to each other, they must contain an equal sign. The equal sign := with a colon in front is called an *assignment operator.* It may be thought of as saying "set the variable on my left equal to the value on my right." To a computer this means "go to the location in memory where the value of the variable on my left is stored, and place the value on my right into that memory location." In contrast to conventional programming languages, like C or Java, Maple permits the value on the RHS to be purely symbolic.

In spite of the assignment statements above looking like equations, they do not express the same type of equality as algebraic equations. To illustrate, when we say $x = y$ in algebra, we mean that the objects on both sides of the equal sign are the same. Thus it follows that $y = x$ is also true. Yet when we issued the Maple statement `Digits := 4;`, we are issuing a command to replace whatever was stored in memory as the value of `Digits` with the new value 4. What we most certainly do not want, is $4 = Digits$; namely, to have all values of 4 replaced by the present value of `Digits`, which is usually equal to 10. To make it clear that assignment equality is not the same type of equality as in algebra, the := sign is used instead of the ordinary = equal sign.

On account of computer languages containing two types of equality, you have to exercise some care with your equal signs. To prove the point, if you leave off the colon : Maple does not complain, but the effect is not the same:

```
> restart;   Digits;
```
$$10$$

```
> 1./3;
```
$$0.3333333333$$

```
> Digits = 3;
```
$$10 = 3$$

```
> 1./3;   10;
```
$$0.3333333333 \quad 10$$

Thus we see that when tell Maple `Digits = 3;`, it just tells us that we are stating that $10 = 3$ without resetting the value of `Digits`. As there are no side effects associated with =, no harm is done, but then again, no good is done either. A more proper use of assignment statements is:

```
> y := 3;    y;
```
                                                      # Assign y value 3, then check
$$y := 3, \quad 3$$

```
> x := y;    x;
```
                                                      # Assign x value y
$$x := 3 \quad 3$$

Here we assigned y the value 3 and then assigned x the current value of y. Maple told us that x was assigned the value 3, as expected.

Assignment statements are not limited to numerical values. You are able to assign symbolic values as well:

```
> restart;    x;
```
                                                      # Clear all assigned values, check that $x = x$

$$x$$

```
> x := y;                                                        # Assign y to x
```

$$x := y$$

Now that we have set x equal to y, Maple remembers that y and x are the same, until you assign another value to x.

```
> `x/y` = x/y ;
```

$$x/y = 1$$

3.8 EQUALITY (RHS, LHS)

Maple does have a place for the usual = equal sign. In fact, it uses it in its output, for example, when the solution to an equation is given as $x = y$. Notwithstanding that both sides of an equation are equal to each other, it is often helpful to deal with the left-hand side (LHS) and the right-hand side (RHS) separately:

```
> x := y;                                      # Repeat previous assignment statement
> `x/y` = x/y;                                 # Repeat previous assignment statement
```

$$x := y \qquad x/y = 1$$

```
> rhs(`x/y` = x/y);    lhs(`x/y` = x/y);
```

$$1 \qquad x/y$$

3.9 FUNCTIONS

Mathematicians and scientists make their work easier by employing *functions*. Computer scientists do much the same thing with what they also call *methods* and *subroutines*, although these latter two are able to do more than a simple function might. Consequently, while we will speak of "functions" in Maple and mathematics, when we get to programming we will speak of "methods," which is just another name for the same thing.

As visualized in Figure 3.2, a function $f(x)$ may be thought of as a mathematical meat grinder in which you feed in some variables at one end and get out some values of the function at the other end. As a case in point, $f(x) = 10x^4 \sin(3\,x)$ is such a function. You feed it the variable x, the function multiplies x by 3, evaluates the sine of $3x$, multiplies that by $10x^4$, and then returns the result. In other words, x is the *independent variable* that we choose, and $y = f(x)$ is the *dependent variable*.

We know that this may sound familiar to you, but it is worth repeating that the numbers 3 and 10 occur in our function as *parameters* that are not expected to be changing much. Thus, if we replace these numerical parameters with algebraic symbols $f(x) = A\,x^4 \sin(k\,x)$, then x is still the independent variable,

Figure 3.2 A function as a meat grinder; arguments x and y go in, function $f(x, y)$ comes out.

and A and k are now the parameters, although they are represented by symbols that take on arbitrary values. Apparently, whether a symbol is a variable or a parameter is determined by its use, which we usually figure out from the context. Therefore we also could write our function as a function of three variables, $f(x, k, A) = A\,x^4 \sin(k\,x)$. Functions of more than one variable are called *multivariate functions* and are much like our meat grinder in Figure 3.2, except that we now have a number of ingredients.

When we instruct a computer program such as Maple to create a function for us, we have to decide which symbols are variables and which are parameters. As a rule of thumb, it is probably best to base your decision on convenience: if it is unlikely that the values for the parameters will change, then it is simpler and clearer to build them into the function, for example, 3 and 10 in our function. If it is likely that you will want to change the parameters, for example, to create plots, then it is probably best to treat them as variables.

3.9.1 Built-In Functions (List in Appendix B)

Even though mathematical functions occur in descriptions of our world, computers do not inherently know about them. However, there are often collections of programs called libraries that supplement computer languages and contain many functions and methods. Maple has an extensive library of such functions, and we give a complete list in Appendix B, which you can also get as the Maple's Help menu. Some functions that you may find most useful are:

```
exp(x), ln(x), log10(x), abs(x), sin(x), sqrt(x), arccos(x), cosh(x)
```

Most conventional computer languages handle these common functions as would your calculator; you key in a number, you get back a number. In contrast, symbolic languages also know much about the mathematical properties of these functions so that you can also input symbolic values and have them processed.

In its usual insightful manner, if you give Maple a floating-point number as input, it will evaluate the function numerically. If one argument is symbolic, then Maple will return a symbolic answer. We try this with our example:

```
> x := 10;
```

$$x := 10$$

```
> y := 10 * x^4 * sin(3*x);
```
$$y := 100000 \sin(30)$$

We see that Maple has remembered the value of x from one line to the next (it actually will remember the value of x until we do something to reassign it or until we enter restart). Regardless of the fact that we entered purely numerical values for the argument of the sine function, Maple has still not given us the answer you would get from a calculator! Do not get annoyed. The answer $y = 100000 \sin(30)$ is an exact mathematical expression with no approximations made, and so Maple keeps it that way. If we want a floating-point or decimal number as an answer, then you must force Maple to make the approximation by having it evaluate the answer as a floating-point number:

```
> evalf(%);
```

$$-98803.16241$$

You could also have done this in one step:

```
> y := evalf( 10*x^ 4 * sin(3*x) );
```
$$y := -98803.16241$$

where we have used the := on the LHS to get a nice-looking answer. Alternatively, you could have used a floating-point number in the argument of the function, in which case Maple would automatically convert to floats:

```
> y := 10 * x^4 * sin(3.*x)
```
$$y := -98803.16241$$

Now we try some variations on the preceding commands in which either x is a float, or the factor in front of the sine function is a float:

```
> x := 10.;    y := 10 * x^4 * sin(3*x);                    # x as a float
```
$$x := 10. \quad y := -98803.16241$$

```
> x := 10;        y := 10. *x^4 * sin(3*x);        evalf(%)    # 10 as a float
```
$$x := 10 \quad y := 100000.0 \sin(30) \quad - 98803.16241$$

As we have said before, unless you instruct otherwise, Maple performs all floating-point calculations with 10 significant figures.

3.10 USER-DEFINED FUNCTIONS

In addition to Maple's built-in functions, you can define your own functions and call them anything you want. To name an instance, let us say we want to define the function $10\,x^4\,\sin 3x$ as the function $g(x)$:

```
> restart;                                    # Clear out old assignments
> g := (x) -> 10 * x^4 * sin(3*x);            # Define single-variable function
```

$$g := x \rightarrow 10\,x^4 \sin(3\,x)$$

Survey a few things here. The LHS of := contains the name of the function g being defined. The RHS is immediately followed by the argument x of the function and then an arrow pointing to the function definition. Accordingly, if you think of the function $g(x)$ as "gee of ex," then the g goes to the left of the := and the x goes to the right. Scrutinize how the arrow sign - > is entered as a minus - followed by the greater-than > sign. Maple responds by showing you this so-called *arrow function* or *mapping* in its proper mathematical notation. You then use your function $g(x)$ just like a built-in one. Evaluate $g(10)$ and see if you get the same answer as we did above:

```
>                                             # Enter g(10) or y = g(10)
>                                             # Try a float as the argument to g
```

Defining functions of several variables (multivariates) requires you to add some more variables to the *argument list*. This is a useful way to feed a single-variable function the parameter values it needs. By way of example, to create our old friend $y = A\,x^4 \sin(b\,x)$ as a function of three variables, we replace (x) with (A,b,x):

```
> y := (A, b, x) -> A * x^4 *sin(b*x);        # Define 3-variable function
```

$$y := (A,\, b,\, x) \rightarrow A\,x^4 \sin(b\,x)$$

Use $y(A, b, x)$ to evaluate $10\,x^4$:

```
> y(10, Pi/(2*x), x);                         # 2nd argument always gives sin(Pi/2)
```

$$10x^4$$

3.11 REEXPRESSING ANSWERS

Maple knows that $\sqrt{16}$ is 4 and will evaluate it with no further ado. However, if there is no exact root to some number, then Maple will reduce the number down as far as it is able but may leave some part of the number in root form. Numbers with explicit roots are called *algebraic numbers*. For instance, if we ask Maple to evaluate $(1 + \sqrt{2})^2$:

```
> (1 + sqrt(2))^2;                                          # Should be simple answer
```

$$(1 + \sqrt{2})^2$$

all we get is a pretty form of what we entered. So we will tell Maple that we would like the expanded form of the previous expression:

```
> expand((1 + sqrt(2))^2);                                  # Ah, that is better
```

$$3 + 2\sqrt{2}$$

There are a bunch of Maple commands, such as

```
simplify  factor  allvalues  expand  value  eval  collect  expand  normal
```

that are useful in getting Maple to change the form of its answers to something you might like better. For example, how about some cute cube roots:

```
> (-8)^(1/3);          simplify(%);
```

$$(-8)^{\frac{1}{3}}, \quad 1 + \sqrt{3}\,I$$

where I is the imaginary number.

As we get into more complicated calculations, we shall see that there is little question that Maple does algebra well. However, the results it gives are not always in a form that humans find revealing. Indeed, learning how to use Maple is more than just learning the names and grammar of a whole bunch of commands, it is also acquiring a trademarked trial-and-error state of mind in which you naturally try to manipulate Maple's output until it produces the most mathematically revealing form for you. In this section we look at some manipulations and some "tricks."

Maple is real good at summing finite and infinite series:

```
> sum(i, i = 1 .. n);                                       # Sum the integers from 1 to n
```

$$\frac{(n+1)^2}{2} - \frac{n}{2} - \frac{1}{2}$$

This result is not the outcome $n(n+1)/2$ that we learned in our algebra, so we try to simplify it:

```
> expand(%);           factor(sum(i, i = 1 .. n));          # Try out two
```

$$\frac{1}{2}n^2 + \frac{1}{2}n \qquad \frac{1}{2}n(n+1)$$

Now we produce some other complicated expressions and try to simplify them:

```
> Product(((x^2 + 3*i - 1) / (i+3)), i = 0 .. 10);          # Inert, but revealing
```

$$\prod_{i=0}^{10} \frac{x^2 + 3\,i - 1}{i + 3}$$

> `product((( x^2 + 3*i - 1)/(i+3)), i = 0..10);`   # Active

$$(\frac{y^2}{3}-\frac{1}{3})\,(\frac{y^2}{4}+\frac{1}{2})\,(\frac{y^2}{5}+1)\,(\frac{y^2}{6}+\frac{4}{3})\,(\frac{y^2}{7}+\frac{11}{7})\,(\frac{y^2}{8}+\frac{7}{4})\,(\frac{y^2}{9}+\frac{17}{9})\,(\frac{y^2}{10}+2)\,(\frac{y^2}{11}+\frac{23}{11})\,(\frac{y^2}{12}+\frac{13}{6})\,(\frac{y^2}{13}+\frac{29}{13})$$

> `expand (%);`   # Lots of output to follow

$$\frac{1}{3113510400}\,y^{22}+\frac{1}{20217600}\,y^{20}+\frac{187}{56609280}\,y^{18}+\frac{13}{103680}\,y^{16}+\frac{280831}{94348800}\,y^{14}+\frac{308441}{6739200}\,y^{12}+\frac{8594731}{18869760}\,y^{10}+\cdots$$

> `factor(%);`   # Better

$$\frac{(y-1)\,(y+1)\,(y^2+11)\,(y^2+20)\,(y^2+8)\,(y^2+29)\,(y^2+17)\,(y^2+5)\,(y^2+26)\,(y^2+14)(y^2+2)\,(y^2+23)}{3113510400}$$

You see here that `expand` and `factor` mean the same things as they do in algebra. The command `simplify` uses identities and properties of functions to simplify an expression and has a number of advanced forms (read about them in the Help pages). The `normal` command, on the other hand, is useful for simplifying rational expressions:

> `simplify(cos(x)^2 + sin(x)^2);`   # Simplify using identities

$$1$$

> `normal (product ((( x^2 + 3*i - 1) / (i+3)), i = 0..10));`

$$(x^2-1)\,(x^2+2)\,(x^2+5)\,(x^2+8)\,(x^2+11)\,(x^2+14)\,(x^2+17)\,(x^2+20)(x^2+23)\,(x^2+26)(x^2+29)\,/3113510400$$

3.11.1 Simplifying Examples

> `expand( tan(a + b) );`

$$\frac{\tan(a) + \tan(b)}{1 - \tan(a)\tan(b)}$$

> `combine( % );`   # Fails

$$\frac{-\tan(a) - \tan(b)}{-1 + \tan(a)\tan(b)}$$

> `combine( %, trig );`   # Still fails

$$\frac{-\tan(a) - \tan(b)}{-1 + \tan(a)\tan(b)}$$

> `expand( (1-x)^2 * (x+2) );`

$$-3\,x + 2 + x^3$$

> `combine( % );`   # Fails

$$-3\,x + 2 + x^3$$

```
> simplify( % );                                          # Fails
```
$$-3\,x + 2 + x^3$$

```
> factor( % );                                            # Succeeds
```
$$(x + 2)\,(x - 1)^2$$

```
> expand( exp(a - b) );
```
$$\frac{e^a}{e^b}$$

```
> combine( % );                                           # Succeeds
```
$$e^{(a-b)}$$

```
> simplify( cos(x)^2 - sin(x)^2 );                        # Fails
```
$$\cos(x)^2 - \sin(x)^2$$

```
> combine( cos(x)^2 - sin(x)^2 );                         # Succeeds
```
$$\cos(2y)$$

```
> factor( x^4 - x^2 );
```
$$x^2\,(x - 1)\,(x + 1)$$

```
> 1/(x+1) + 1/(x-1);
```
$$\frac{1}{x + 1} + \frac{1}{x - 1}$$

```
> combine( % );                                           # Fails
```
$$\frac{1}{x + 1} + \frac{1}{x - 1}$$

```
> normal( % );                                            # Sort of succeeds
```
$$\frac{2\,x}{(x - 1)\,(x + 1)}$$

```
> simplify( % );                                          # Really succeeds
```
$$\frac{2\,x}{-1 + x^2}$$

3.11.2 Expressions Behaving Like Functions: eval, evaln

It seems perfectly reasonable to think of a variable like x or y as a symbol that does not vary the way functions do. However, Maple is so smart and has such a good memory that if you set a variable equal to a complicated expression, such as poly-nomial, Maple will treat that variable much as it does the complicated expression and substitute in values for the variables contained in it. Consequently, it should come as no surprise that the manipulations we did on expressions are allowed on variables representing expressions:

```
> restart;    z := (x+2)^15;              # Variable z represents expression
```
$$z := (x + 2)^{15}$$

```
> y := expand (z);
```
$$y := 32768 + x^{15} + 30\,x^{14} + 420\,x^{13} + 3640\,x^{12} + 21840\,x^{11} + \cdots$$

```
> factor (y);
```

$$(x + 2)^{15}$$

Even though we are manipulating z as if it were a function, it is not a true function and does get evaluated differently. To cite an instance, if we enter $z(3)$ as if the expression were a function, we get something interesting but not 5^{15}:

```
> 'z( x = 3 )' = z(3);
```
$$z(x = 3) = (\mathrm{x}(3) + 2)^{15}$$

To evaluate z for $x = 3$, either set $x = 3$ first, or use the `eval` function:

```
> 'z( x = 3 )' = eval (z, x = 3);
```
$$z(x = 3) = 30517578125$$

Seeing that we have brought up the `eval` function, we should also indicate that there is a variant of it called `evaln` that evaluates a variable to a name. Its purpose is essentially the same as the use of quotes to set a variable back to symbolic form after it has been assigned a numerical value, however it is what is needed if you are dealing with subscripted variables:

```
> x := 3;    x;
```
Assign, check value
$$x := 3, \quad 3$$

```
> x := evaln(x);    x;
```
Assign, check value
$$x := x, \quad x$$

3.11.3 Converting Expressions to Functions: unapply

Even though the difference between functions and variables may seem mainly semantic, there are instances where the difference matters. The `unapply` command is used to convert an expression or variable into a true function. The funny name arises from the idea that we normally "apply" a function to a variable to obtain a value, while here we are working backwards and creating a function from a variable. The `unapply` command takes an expression and a variable as its two arguments and returns a function of the second argument:

$$\textit{function} \ = \ \texttt{unapply}\,(\textit{expression, variable})$$

As an instance, here we convert z into the function `zfun(x)` (our name):

```
> z := (x + 2)^15;
```
Define z as polynomial
$$z := (x + 2)^{15}$$

```
> zfun := unapply(z, x);
```
Create function
$$zfun := x \to (x + 2)^{15}$$

```
> expand ( zfun(x) );
```
Check if expand works on `zfun`
$$32768 + x^{15} + 30\,x^{14} + 420\,x^{13} + 3640\,x^{12} + 21840\,x^{11} + \cdots$$

```
> zfun(-1);                                          # Evaluate for x = -1 as check
```

$$1$$

3.12 CS: OVERFLOW, UNDERFLOW, AND ROUND-OFF ERROR

All computers are finite and, alas, Maple is too. This means that if you keep making numbers bigger and bigger, at some point the computer cannot handle them and an *overflow exception* occurs. Likewise, if you keep making numbers smaller and smaller, at some point an *underflow exception* occurs. In addition, since floating-point numbers are stored with a finite number of significant figures, the digit beyond the last one is truncated, and the last digit is rounded off. Similarly, if the truncated digit is greater than 5, then the last stored digit is rounded up, and this leads to *round-off errors*. (For convenience, both truncation and round-off errors are usually called "round-off errors.") In principle, the algorithms used by Maple for calculations have no limit to their precision and should be exact if no floating-point numbers are called. In practice, Maple uses $524,279$ digits, which should not be too hard to live with, but you may ask for more. Serious problems result if you write a program and underflows or overflows occur within it, or if there is a great deal of round-off error.

Enough talk, let us have some fun and see if we are able to *break* Maple using the factorial, $n! = n(n-1)(n-2)\cdots(2)\,(1)$, and powers of 10. Do not worry, you will do no permanent harm and no one will yell at you if you break Maple, although you may lose the active worksheet. In general, you get no warning that Maple is about to break, so drive defensively and *Save Often!* If Maple stops responding for a considerable amount of time, it may be working, or it may be stuck. Before you quit or kill Maple, you may want to try the Stop button in the tool bar and see if Maple responds again. Else you have to quit. Here we challenge Maple and show how it admits failure:

```
> 10^100000 ; 10^1000000 ;              # Increase exponent until integers overflow
> 10.^10000 ; 10.^1000000 ;             # Increase exponent until floats overflow
> 10.^(-100) ; 10.^(-10000) ;           # Decrease exponent until floats underflow
```

'Integer too large for display' $\dfrac{1}{\textit{'Integer too large for display'}}$ $\text{Float}(\infty)$ 0

Because calculations that employ floating-point numbers are are often truncating or rounding off the last digit in the mantissa, and because these errors tend to accumulate in time, their final results may be less precise than the numbers you input. This is called *truncation* and *round-off error*. We use the term "error" here in much the same way one does when speaking about the experimental "error" in a physics laboratory. It is not an error in the sense that you read the meter wrong or had your finger caught in the caliper but is really an uncertainty arising from the finite number of digits used to represent numbers.

To see a living example of round-off error, work through the following commands (we decrease the normal precision to make the effects more evident):

```
> Digits := 4;    x := 1./3;
```
                                                                    # Store only 4 decimal places

$$Digits := 4, \qquad x := 0.3333$$

```
> 2 * x - 2/3;
```
                                                                    # See effect on calculation with floats

$$-0.0001$$

```
> Digits := 10;
```
                                                                    # Repeat with 10 digits

3.13 SOLUTION: VIEWING ROCKET GOLF

Problem a: We will now apply our Maple tools to the relativistic golf-ball problem. Michele on the moving rocket sees her golf ball travel with velocity U' at an angle θ, with a hang time T':

$$U' = \frac{c}{\sqrt{3}}, \quad \theta = 30^\circ, \quad T' = 2.6 \times 10^7,$$

$$U'_x = \frac{c(\theta)}{\sqrt{3}} \cos, \quad U'_y = \frac{c}{\sqrt{3}} \sin(\theta).$$

Ben on the earth observes the rocket moving with a speed $v = c/2$. He sees the golf ball with velocity components U_x and U_y and a hang time of T. The equations of special relativity (that we have not derived and that we do not expect you to fully understand) relate Michele's and Ben's observations

$$U_x = \frac{U'_x + v}{1 + v\,U'_x/c^2}, \quad U_y = \frac{U'_y}{\gamma\,(1 + v\,U'_x/c^2)}$$

$$T = \gamma\,T', \quad \gamma(v) = \frac{1}{\sqrt{1 - v^2/c^2}}.$$

Because the time dilation function $\gamma(v)$ is rather complicated and is used in several places, we start our solution by defining a Maple function for it:

```
> gamma := (v)-> 1/sqrt(1 - v^2/c^2);
  Error, attempting to assign to 'gamma' which is protected
```

Whoops! Although this was the obvious thing to do, it does not work, because Maple apparently has its own function gamma and does not want us to steal its name. On account of this we try defining our function using a capital G:

```
> Gamma := (v)-> 1/sqrt(1 - v^2/c^2);
```

$$\Gamma := v \rightarrow \frac{1}{\sqrt{1 - v^2/c^2}}$$

Ah, that is better. To make life simple for us beginners, let us adopt the convention that we measure all velocities as a fraction of the speed of light c. Thus, rather than saying $v = c/2$, we would just say $v = 1/2$. This will make the equations look simpler and save us some time. This being the case, we redefine Gamma as:

```
> Gamma := (v)-> 1/sqrt(1 - v^2);
```

$$\Gamma := v \rightarrow \frac{1}{\sqrt{1 - v^2}}$$

This function is apparently acceptable to Maple, but we need to test it before we believe it is right. We know by looking at the equation defining $\gamma(v)$ that $\gamma(v = 0) = 1$, and that γ should get progressively larger as v approaches the speed of light c. So we try:

```
> Gamma(0);      Gamma(1/2);      Gamma(1/sqrt(3));      Gamma(99/100);
```

$$1, \quad \frac{2\sqrt{3}}{3}, \quad \frac{\sqrt{6}}{2}, \quad \frac{100\sqrt{199}}{199}$$

These appear to be getting larger, but to be sure let us repeat the calculation using floating-point numbers. We do that by acting on the function with the evalf function or just by placing some decimal points in the arguments. We will be lazy:

```
> Gamma(0);      Gamma(1/2.);      Gamma(1/sqrt(3.));      Gamma(99/100.);
```

$$1, \quad 1.154700538, \quad 1.224744871, \quad 7.088812050$$

Yes, γ does grow as v approaches the speed of light. But what happens if the velocity equals the speed of light?

```
> `Gamma(1)` = Gamma(1);
  Error, (in Gamma) numeric exception:  division by zero
```

Well this does not tell us much, because division by zero is not defined. However in a mathematical sense we really want the limit as v approaches c in infinitesimal steps, and so we will try the limit command:

```
> `Gamma(1)` = limit(Gamma(v), v = 1);
```

$$Gamma(1) = undefined$$

Maple clearly has a problem here, and it is telling us that we did not give it a good enough description of what we want. Well, this is a case where precision in mathematical language is called for. The cause of the problem is that there is an infinity at $v = 1$ (a division by 0), and the limit depends on just how we approach that infinity. As told by the Help reference, we need an option to the limit command to indicate that we are approaching the singularity from the left, namely, from $v < c$:

```
> `Gamma(v=c)` = limit(Gamma(v), v=1,left);
```

$$Gamma(v = c) = \infty$$

This is better. We see that the time dilation factor γ approaches ∞ as the rocket speed approaches the speed of light.

We will discuss plotting in more detail in Chapter 4. Nevertheless, we make here a simple plot of $\gamma(v)$ using Maple's plot command. Because we have set $c = 1$, there are no variables with symbolic values in $\gamma(v)$, and so Maple evaluates it as a number and plots it:

```
> plot(Gamma(v), v=0..1, title='Gamma(v) vs v/c');
```

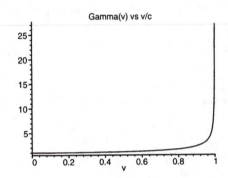

We see that $\gamma(v)$ is essentially 1 until the velocity gets close to the speed of light. Indeed, this is why we do not usually experience relativistic effects in our everyday lives. For the problem at hand, the exact and floating-point values of γ that we will use are:

```
> restart:       Gamma := (v) -> 1/sqrt(1 - v^2):
> 'Gamma(1/sqrt(3))' = Gamma(1/sqrt(3));          evalf(%);
```

$$Gamma(1/sqrt(3)) = \frac{\sqrt{6}}{2} \qquad\qquad 1.224744871$$

The difference in value from 1 indicates that there is a significant relativistic effect for our problem. Specifically, Ben says that the golf ball stayed in the air 22% longer than Michele thought it did:

```
> T := Gamma(1/sqrt(3.))   * 2.6E7;
```

$$T := 0.3184336665\ 10^8$$

Next we calculate the speed U that Ben observes the golf ball to have, knowing that Michele says she hit it with velocity U'. We need then to calculate:

$$U_x = \frac{U'_x + v}{1 + v U'_x}, \qquad\qquad U_y = \frac{U'_y}{\gamma\,(1 + v U'_x)},$$

48

where we have assumed all velocities will be entered as a fraction of c, and so $v = c/sqrt3$. To be flexible, we create functions to calculate these velocity transformations, one of which calls our previously defined Gamma function:

```
> Ux :=(Up, v) -> (Up*cos(theta) + v) / (1 + v*Up*cos(theta));
```

$$Ux := (Up, v) \rightarrow \frac{Up\cos(\theta) + v}{1 + v\,Up\cos(\theta)}$$

```
> Uy := (Up, v) -> Up*sin(theta) / (Gamma(v)*(1 + v*Up*cos(theta)));
```

$$Uy := (Up, v) \rightarrow \frac{Up\sin(\theta)}{\Gamma(v)\,(1 + v\,Up\cos(\theta))}$$

Ben knows Michele's value for θ, and, after converting it to radians, uses it as input:

```
> theta := 30 * Pi/180;                                    # Convert degrees to radians
```

$$\theta := \frac{\pi}{6}$$

```
> convert(theta, degrees);      theta;                     # Check our conversion vs Maple
```

$$30\ degrees \qquad \frac{\pi}{6}$$

```
> UxBen := Ux(1/sqrt(3), 1/2);      evalf(%);              # Ben's $U_x$, as decimal
```

$$UxBen := \frac{4}{5} \qquad 0.8000000000$$

```
> UyBen := Uy(1/sqrt(3), 1/2);      evalf(%);              # Ben's $U_y$, as decimal
```

$$UyBen := \frac{1}{5} \qquad 0.2000000000$$

If nonrelativistic kinematics are applied to this problem, we would see Michele's golf ball moving at the combined speeds of the rocket plus its speed relative to the rocket:

$$U_{\text{nonRel}} = v + U_x = \frac{c}{2} + \frac{c}{\sqrt{3}}\cos(30^o) = c. \tag{3.6}$$

Yet relativity teaches us that this is not possible for anything but light. If we look at the answer we just calculated, we see that the velocity seen by Ben is less than c (1 in our units):

```
> 'UBen' = sqrt(UxBen^2 + UyBen^2);      evalf(%);
```

$$UBen = \frac{\sqrt{17}}{5} \qquad 0.8246211252$$

Now that we have calculated the components U_x and U_y of the velocity in Ben's frame, we calculate the angle ϕ at which Ben sees the golf ball fly off by using the fact that

$$\tan\phi = \frac{U_y}{U_x}, \qquad \text{or} \qquad \phi = \tan^{-1}\frac{U_y}{U_x}. \tag{3.7}$$

Inasmuch as the argument to the arctangent function could be infinite if $U_x = 0$, Maple's arctangent function takes U_y and U_x as separate arguments:

```
> 'phi' = arctan(UyBen, UxBen);        evalf(%);
```

$$\phi = \arctan(\frac{1}{4}) \qquad 0.2449786631$$

```
> convert(%, degrees);                                          # Maple keeps π factor
```

$$\frac{180 \; degrees \; \phi}{\pi} = \frac{44.09615936 \; degrees}{\pi}$$

```
> evalf(%);                                                     # Force Maple to give float
```

$$57.29577950 \; degrees \qquad \phi = 14.03624346 \; degrees$$

Thus we see that while Michele saw her ball fly up at 30 degrees, Ben sees it "pushed forward" to about 14 degrees.

Problem b: In this version of the problem, we have Michele hitting her golf ball backwards, namely, in a direction opposite to the direction of the rocket's flight. If the ball follows the same trajectory as in **Problem a**, only now in the negative x' direction, then it is equivalent to replacing θ by $\pi - \theta$ in the preceding analysis:

```
> theta := (180 - 30)*Pi/180;                                   # Convert degrees to radians
```

$$\theta := \frac{5\pi}{6}$$

```
> convert(theta, degrees);          theta;                      # Check our conversion against Maple's
```

$$150 \; degrees \qquad\qquad \frac{5\pi}{6}$$

```
> UxBen := Ux(1/sqrt(3), 1/2);
```

$$UxBen := 0$$

```
> UyBen := Uy(1/sqrt(3), 1/2);
```

$$UyBen := \frac{1}{3}$$

Assessment: These are interesting results! As expected, if Michele hits her ball in the opposite direction to the rocket's path, the rocket's forward speed cancels out the ball's backwards speed, and Ben sees the ball hit straight up into the air!

This is also an interesting result from the computational point of view, because we got exactly 0 as an answer even though there were a number of steps involved. This is a consequence of our not entering floating-point numbers anywhere in the problem and of Maple being able to do exact arithmetic. However, we could have placed some decimal points in some of the quantities and then ended up with a floating-point computation. We look at what the results would have been if we did the calculation in floating point with six places of precision:

```
> Digits := 6;
```

$$Digits := 6$$

```
> theta := evalf( (180 - 30.5)*Pi/180. );        # Convert degrees to radians
```

$$\theta := 2.60927$$

```
> UxBen := Ux(1./sqrt(3.), 1./2.);
```

$$UxBen := 0.00337563$$

```
> UyBen := Uy(1./sqrt(3.), 1./2.);
```

$$UyBen := 0.337786$$

We see now that with reduced precision, the x component of velocity is no longer exactly zero and that we apparently have only three decimal places of precision. If we ask "what is the relative error in the x component of velocity," the answer would have to be $0.00337563/0 = \infty$. However, we should recognize that the answer $UxBen := 0.003$ is consistent with 0, given the number of decimal places of precision that we have. In view of the fact that it is very hard for floating-point calculations to calculate 0 with high precision, all we may say is that the answer is small and possibly 0. Some further analysis would be needed to see if 0 is really the correct answer.

Problem c: Now repeat this exercise for a golf ball hit at 60° down and backwards, namely, at $\theta = 240^o$. As a consequence of velocities perpendicular to motion not being reversed by a Lorentz transformation, there is no way that this ball will be seen as hit above the horizontal. However, it is possible for the horizontal component of velocity to be reversed by viewing the golf ball in different reference frames, and so it is possible for Ben and Michele to disagree on that.

3.14 EXTENSION: TACHYONS*

One of the principles of relativity is that no particle can be made to go faster than the speed of light. A particle of light, the photon, does travel at the speed of light, yet it has zero mass. To accelerate a particle with mass to $v = c$ would require an infinite amount of energy, since the energy of the particle

$$E = \frac{m_0 \, c^2}{\sqrt{1 - v^2/c^2}} \tag{3.8}$$

is seen to approach infinity as $v \to c$.

The thought has consequently arisen [Fein 76] that if a particle somehow started off its life with $v > c$, then its energy would be finite, albeit imaginary! Such particles are called *tachyons*, from the Greek *tachus* meaning speedy. These would be very strange particles. If you increased their velocities, their energy would decrease, while if you decreased their velocity, their energy would increase, with infinite energy would require to slow them down to c.

Repeat these exercises assuming that Michele's golf ball was a tachyon.

3.15 KEY WORDS AND CONCEPTS

arguments	assignment	complex	equality	exponent
expression	floating-point number	function	imaginary	integer
irrational number	truncation error	overflow	rational number	real
round-off error	side-effect statement	mantissa	underflow	

1. Explain the meaning of these key words.
2. Are irrational numbers irrational only in the decimal system?
3. Do irrational numbers occur in nature?
4. Do floating-point numbers occur in nature?
5. Do floating-point numbers occur in mathematics?
6. What price is paid for Maple's use of infinite precision?
7. Might we be able to eliminate round-off and truncation error if we were more careful in our calculations?
8. What is the difference between a statement of equality and an assignment statement?
9. Explain why it makes sense to think of *functions* as *mappings*.
10. Are integers purer numbers than irrational numbers?
11. Are integers purer numbers than floats?
12. Does the form of a mathematical expression change its meaning?
13. How do you know when to tell Maple to simplify an expression?
14. What is the difference between an expression and a function in Maple?

3.16 SUPPLEMENTARY EXERCISES

1. Make a new worksheet that includes examples of overflow, underflow, and round-off. Save it. *Hint:* 10^(-100) raises 10 to a negative power: 10^{-100}.
2. To see how devious and subtle floating-point arithmetic may be, for `Digits := 2`
   a. Evaluate $2(1./3) - 2./3$.
   b. Evaluate the upward sum $1 - 1/2 - 1/4 - 1/8 - 1/10 - 1/12$.
   c. Evaluate the downward sum $-1/12 - 1/10 - 1/8 - 1/4 - 1/2 + 1$.
   d. Now change the 1's to 1.'s and see what answers you get.
   e. Explain what is happening. (If you happen to know how, do *not* define functions for this problem; Maple is so smart that it may fix up your errors without telling you!)
3. Do you expect the following inputs to give the same results?
   a. `1/3 + 1/3 + 1/3;`
   b. `1./3. + 1./3. + 1./3.;`
   If not, why not?

4. Use Maple to do this complex multiplication and division:
   a. $(10 + 99i)(10 - 99i)$
   b. $(10 + 99i)/(10 - 99i)$
5. Determine a numerical (floating-point) value for
   a. $\log(11)$
   b. $\sin\left(\frac{\pi}{8}\right)$
6. **Type:** Maple has the command `type(expression, datatype)` that tells
   you what kind of data type the expression is. There is a large number of data
   types that Maple recognizes (see help) including:

   ```
   algebraic, Array, array, boolean, complex, constant, cubic,
   _imaginary, equation, even, _numeric, rational, finite, float,
   fraction, function, global, imaginary, infinity, integer,
   laurent, linear, list, listlist, literal, local, logical,
   mathfunc, Matrix, negative, numeric, odd, operator, polynom,
   positive, prime, procedure, quadratic, quartic, radical,
   radnum, rational, scalar, series, set, sqrt, string, symbol,
   table, taylor, undefined, Vector.
   ```

   a. Enter the Maple statement `x := y = 3;` at an execution group.
   b. Test if `x` is a float, a numeric, a boolean, an equation, or a logical.
   c. Test for the type of data that is `y`.
   d. Explain your results.
7. Recall some of the Maple commands we introduced that are used to simplify
   algebraic expressions. Use whatever commands you need to place

   $$\frac{a}{a+b} - \frac{a}{a-b} + \frac{1}{a}$$

   into a simpler form. Add comments to your command lines explaining what
   you are doing.
8. Determine the resistance of three resistors in parallel. Circuit theory tells us
   that the equivalent resistance is

   $$\frac{1}{R} = \frac{1}{R_1} + \frac{1}{R_2} + \frac{1}{R_3}.$$

   Determine the simplest form for R.
9. Write the following numbers in scientific notation so they reflect the given
   number of significant digits:
   a. 25.3 to four significant figures
   b. 0.00005 to two significant figures
   c. 1.351 to two significant figures
   d. 84000 to three significant figures
10. Suppose that the floating-point number system on your computer has two-
    digit mantissas and exponents ranging from -2 to 1. Indicate whether the
    following expressions each would result in overflow, underflow, round-off
    error, or an exact answer:
    a. $20. + 20.$
    b. $50. * 50.$
    c. $20. + 0.01$

    d. $20. * 0.01$

    e. $0.01 + 0.01$

    f. $0.01 * 0.01$

11. (Adapted from [Zach 96]) Indicate with an "R" or "F" which of the following values should be represented with rational numbers and which with floating-point numbers?

    a. the speed of light

    b. the number of protons in an atom

    c. the distance from the Earth to the moon

    d. the acceleration due to gravity on the planet Jupiter

    e. the number of megabytes of memory in a computer

12. You are given the expression $10\,x^4\sin(k\,x)$ to use in Maple.

    a. How would you enter this as a function of the variable x?

    b. How would you enter this as a function of the variables x and k?

    c. How would you enter this as an expression (an object that takes no explicit arguments)?

    d. How would you evaluate the expression for $x = 3$?

    e. How would you evaluate the expression for $x = \sqrt{y}$?

    f. How would you evaluate the function for $x = 3$?

    g. How would you evaluate the function for $x = \sqrt{y}$?

13. What is the effect of the following Maple statements:

    a. `'x/y' := 'z/r';`

    b. `diff(x^3, x);`

    c. `x := 3; x := 'x';`

    d. `evalf(1/3);`

    e. `eval(x^3, x = 1/3);`

    f. `x := (z) -> z^5 - (1/3)*cos(z);`

14. Explain in just a few words what is meant by:

    a. an integer

    b. an irrational number

    c. a floating-point number

    d. truncation error

    e. a statement being different from an expression

    f. `x = y` not being the same as `x := y`.

    g. a complex number

    h. a string

15. Use Maple to simplify (to a form that looks simple to you)

    a. $\dfrac{x+2}{x}$

    b. $\dfrac{(x^2+1)\,\sqrt{x}}{x}$

16. Consider a tachyon with $m_0\,c^2 = 1$. Determine its energy for $\frac{v}{c} = 3, 2$, and 1.

17. Assign the variable y to the expression $\frac{\pi}{6}$, and then evaluate y^3, $y^{\frac{1}{3}}$, and $\tan(y)$ both exactly and numerically.

18. Express $y^8 - 2\,y^4 + 1$ as the product of factors.

19. For $a = 9.2$, $b = 1.5$, and $c = 100$, evaluate $\sqrt{\frac{2a-3b^2}{c^3-20}}$.

20. Much of what we do throughout this book is to examine various data types and the associated methods to handle them. For each data, variable, or expression type on the left, find the best description on the right. Indicate your answer with a letter (some letters may repeat, while others may not be used at all).

string	a	variable with algebraic values
	b	exactly expressible as ratio of two integers
float	c	ordered set of numbers
	d	variable used to store text
class	e	a sequence of numbers
	f	not expressible as ratio of two integers
rational	g	integer appearing within square brackets
	h	data with sign, mantissa, and exponent
floats	i	not expressible as ratio of two floats
	j	constant not changed within program
abstract	k	positive or negative
	l	true or false
final	m	matrix or vector
	n	exactly expressible as ratio of two floats
array	o	a sequence of letters
	p	one symbol, multiple parts
symbolic	q	shared among all methods
	r	float appearing within square brackets
subscript	s	data with mantissa and exponent, but no sign
boolean		
irrational		

Chapter Four

Visualizing Data, Abstract Data Types; Electric Fields of Multipoles

4.1 WHY VISUALIZATION?

One of the most rewarding uses of computers is visualizing the results of calculations. This is done with 2-D and 3-D plots (especially with colored surfaces), with contour maps, and with animations. These types of visualization are sometimes breathtakingly beautiful and often provide deep insight into a problem by letting you see and "handle" the functions with which you are working. Visualization also assists the program debugging process, the development of physical and mathematical intuition, and the all-around enjoyment of your work. Some of the reasons for this may arise from the fact that some large fraction ($\approx 50\%$) of our brain gets involved in visual processing, and if you are able to use this extra brainpower in your scientific work, then you have extended what was otherwise possible with solely logical abilities.

Traditionally, visualization of a scientific problem was the last step in problem solving. After studying tables of numbers for hours and gaining confidence that they are right, a scientist might then go to the trouble of making a bunch of 2-D plots to examine various aspects of the data. Well, in present times computational scientists have demonstrated how much there is to be gained by going beyond 2-D plots. Now it is regular practice to use surface plots, volume rendering (dicing and slicing), and animations (movies). In this chapter we use some of these techniques within the context of visualizing the electric field around charges.

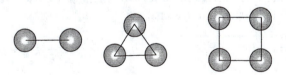

Figure 4.1 Static configurations for two, three, and four electric charges.

4.2 PROBLEM: STABLE POINTS IN ELECTRIC FIELDS

You are given the simple configurations of charges shown in Figure 4.1. The two charges are fixed on a line at coordinates (1,0), (-1,0); the three charges are fixed to the corners of an equilateral triangle at coordinates (0,1), $\sqrt{3}$ (1/2, -1/2), $-\sqrt{3}$ (1/2, -1/2); and the four charges are fixed to the corners of a square at coordinates (1,1), (1,-1), (-1,-1), (-1,1). The origin is at the center of each geometric figure. Your problem is to determine the electric potential at the point (x, y) and see if there might be some points in space at which we a free charge at rest will remain even if perturbed. For the equivalent gravitational problem, these stable points are known as Lagrange points and are the location of asteroids for the Earth-sun system.

4.3 THEORY: STABILITY CRITERIA AND POTENTIAL ENERGY

Coulomb's law tells us that if we have a charge q at the origin, then the electric field $\mathbf{E}$ (the force per unit charge) at a distance r from that charge is

$$\mathbf{E}(r) = \frac{k_e q}{r^2} \hat{\mathbf{r}}. \tag{4.1}$$

where $\hat{\mathbf{r}}$ is a unit vector in the radial (r) direction.[1] Here $k_e = 8.9875\,10^9 Nm^2/C^2$ is Coulomb's constant in SI units, and the electric field $\mathbf{E}$ is directed radially away from the charge. Because $\mathbf{E}$ is a vector, the electric force field about a charge is a vector field with both magnitude and direction at each point. However, no information is lost, and it is much simpler if, instead of the electric force field $\mathbf{E}$, we consider the electric potential field

$$V(r) = \frac{k_e q}{r} \equiv \frac{q}{r}. \tag{4.2}$$

In the second form of this equation, we have left off the electric constant k_e for simplicity; since this affects just the magnitudes of the graphs and not their shapes, it will not change the conclusions we draw. We see that $V(r)$ falls off less rapidly than $\mathbf{E}$ and is a scalar, namely, has no direction associated with it.

Our problem requires us to determine the potentials the for two- and three-charge systems shown in Figure 4.2 and then to look for stable points in these potentials. To determine the potential for two charges, we use Pythagoras's theorem to determine the distance to the charges,

$$r_1 = \sqrt{(x-a)^2 + y^2}, \qquad r_2 = \sqrt{(x+a)^2 + y^2}, \tag{4.3}$$

---

[1]A *vector* is a mathematical object with both magnitude and direction[Ser 00]. They are discussed further in Chapter 7.

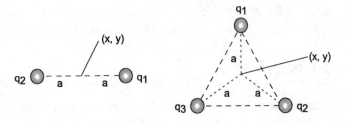

Figure 4.2 Coordinate systems for two- and three-charge configurations.

and then just add up the potentials from the individual charges:

$$V_2(x,\, y) = \frac{q_1}{\sqrt{(x-a)^2 + y^2}} + \frac{q_2}{\sqrt{(x+a)^2 + y^2}}. \tag{4.4}$$

For three charges at the corners of the equilateral triangle, we know the coordinates are $(0, a)$, $(a\cos\theta, -a\sin\theta)$, $(-a\cos\theta, -a\sin\theta)$, where $\theta = 30^o$. Again we use Pythagoras's theorem and add the potentials from the individual charges to obtain

$$V_3(x,\, y) = \frac{q_1}{\sqrt{x^2 + (y-a)^2}} + \frac{q_2}{\sqrt{(x-a\cos\theta)^2 + (y+a\sin\theta)^2}}$$
$$+ \frac{q_3}{\sqrt{(x+a\cos\theta)^2 + (y+a\sin\theta)^2}}. \tag{4.5}$$

These equations for the electric potentials are what we wish to visualize. To make them simpler to visualize, we set $a = 1$ and substitute for θ:

$$V_1(x,\, y) = \frac{q_1}{\sqrt{x^2 + y^2}}, \tag{4.6}$$

$$V_2(x,\, y) = \frac{q_1}{\sqrt{(x-1)^2 + y^2}} + \frac{q_2}{\sqrt{(x+1)^2 + y^2}}, \tag{4.7}$$

$$V_3(x,\, y) = \frac{q_1}{\sqrt{x^2 + (y-1)^2}} + \frac{q_2}{\sqrt{(x - \frac{\sqrt{3}}{2})^2 + (y + \frac{1}{2})^2}}$$
$$+ \frac{q_3}{\sqrt{(x + \frac{\sqrt{3}}{2})^2 + (y + \frac{1}{2})^2}}. \tag{4.8}$$

Owing to its two-dimensional nature, a purely mathematical solution for the equilibrium points in these potentials gets complicated. Instead, we will solve it graphically and rely on our intuitive understanding of how balls roll under the action of gravity. Specifically, we know that a ball released on a surface rolls downhill, and that if the ball is placed in a concave depression, it will remain there. Because the gravitational potential near the Earth's surface is proportional to height, our description of the ball on a surface is equivalent to a description of how a particle behaves in a potential energy field. It therefore follows that charges will "roll down" the electric potential surface and will find a stable position at the concave minimum of the potential. So our problem translates into drawing pictures of the electric potential surfaces and looking for minima at the bottom of hills.

4.4 BASIC 2-D PLOTS: PLOT

Before we get to Maple's plotting commands, let us examine some general principles. First, keep in mind that the point of visualization is to make the science clearer and to better communicate your work to others. So it follows that when you produce a figure, you should look at it and think if there are some better choices of units, ranges of axes, colors, style, et cetera, that might get the message across better and provide better insight. Taking into account that we are dealing with the complexity of human perception and cognition, there may not be one definite way to do things, and some trial and error is necessary to see what looks best.

Our general recommendation for visualization is to make each figure as clear, informative, and self-explanatory as possible. This means labels for various curves and data points, a title, and labels on the axes. We know, you are thinking this is really a lot of work for a lousy assignment or report, and that you do not need all those time-consuming extras to comprehend what is going on. Yet the more often you do it, the quicker and better you get at it, and the more useful will your work be to others (and yourself in the future).

The convention when plotting is to have the independent variable, say x, along the abscissa (horizontal axis) and the dependent variable, say $y = f(x)$, along the ordinate. (Remember that your mouth spreads horizontally across when you say "abscissa" and that it puckers up vertically when you say "ordinate.") If you have trouble deciding which variable is independent, think of an experiment in which you measure the position or velocity of a ball as a function of time. Because you are free to pick the times at which you make the measurement, time is an independent variable. However, once you have chosen the time, nature picks what the position of the ball is at that particular time, so position and velocity are dependent variables.

4.4.1 Loading the plots Package

Maple excels at easily producing graphs of all sorts, and indeed, visualization is one of the most valuable aspects of Maple. Although we will discuss and give examples of a number of possible plots, Maple affords more options than we discuss, and we recommend you look at the commands listed after the `with(plots)` statement and browse the help pages to create just the graph you want. We will first make a simple plot and then embellish it with things like labels and colors.

```
> restart;      with(plots);                          # Loads plotting tools
```

[animate, animate3d, animatecurve, arrow, changecoords, complexplot, complexplot3d, conformal, conformal3d, contourplot, contourplot3d, coordplot, coordplot3d, cylinderplot, densityplot, display, display3d, fieldplot, fieldplot3d, gradplot, gradplot3d, graphplot3d, implicitplot, implicitplot3d, inequal, interactive, listcontplot, listcontplot3d, listdensityplot, listplot, listplot3d, loglogplot, logplot, matrixplot, odeplot, pareto, plotcompare, pointplot, pointplot3d , polarplot, polygonplot, polygonplot3d, polyhedra_supported, polyhedraplot, replot , rootlocus, semilogplot, setoptions, setoptions3d, spacecurve, sparsematrixplot, sphereplot, surfdata, textplot, textplot3d, tubeplot]

We see that in response to the `with(plots)` command, Maple displays all of the plotting commands that are available with this package. (We sometimes use `with(plots):` with a colon rather than a semicolon to avoid the listing.) Now that we have the tools, let us look at the electric potential for a single charge:

```
> V := (r) -> 1/r;
```

$$V := r \to \frac{1}{r}$$

```
> plot( V(r), r = 0 ..  0.2 );                          # Plot function, range
> plot( V(r), r = 1/50 ..  1 );                         # Remove infinity
```

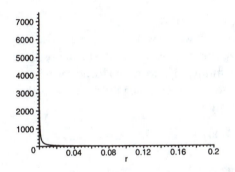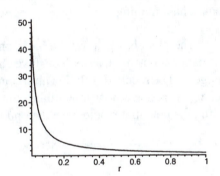

You will observe from the first figure that the second argument to the `plot` command gives the range of values for the abscissa (r in this case). Our interest is really for r between 0 and infinity, but this does not produce such a useful result, since we primarily see the repulsive peak at the origin. In view of that, we get a more revealing plot by not letting r get quite so close to the origin. The second plot eliminates the part of the graph with the infinity at $r = 0$, and so does not fully convey the image that the potential is infinite there. However, we tailor our plot more to our liking by giving some limits to the ordinate (also works if called the generic y):

```
> plot( V(r), r = 0 ..  1, V = 0 ..  10 );              # Limit the y range
> plot( min(V(r), 10), r = 0 ..  1 );                   # Keep ordinate less than 10, another way
```

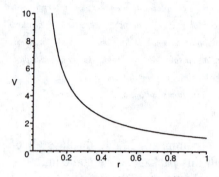
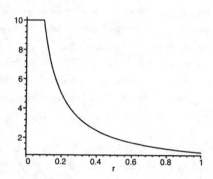

As an alternative, it is possible to tell Maple that you want to see the full dependence of the potential from $r = 0$ to ∞, plot(V(r), r = 0..infinity), but then you lose some details. Try leaving off the range for the abscissa to test Maple's capabilities:

```
> plot( V(r) );
  Plotting error, empty plot
```

You see that because Maple was not given a range of r values to plot, it does not think it has anything to plot (empty plot).

The plot above shows the basic physics. If we view $V(r)$ as an equivalent gravitational potential, a small positive charge (mass) placed near the fixed positive charge will be repelled (roll downhill) out to infinity. There are no locations where a charge remains at rest in equilibrium. If we had fixed a negative charge at the origin, the potential would have the opposite sign:

```
> plot( -V(r), r = 0 .. 1, V = 0 .. -10 );
```

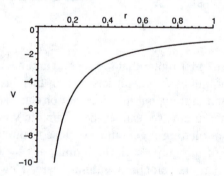

This shows that, regardless of where we place it, our positive test charge will fall into the hole at the origin. As we have just seen by placing a minus sign in front of the first argument to the plot command, it is allowable to have the argument be an expression and not just a function:

```
> plot( -5/r, r = 0 ..  5,V = 0 ..  -20 );                    # Plot explicit expression
```

In summary, the first argument to the `plot` command is the name of the function or expression to be plotted along the ordinate, namely, the dependent variable. The second argument is the range of values for the abscissa, namely, the independent variable. The double period `..` is used to specify the range, so `-10 ..` `10` means from -10 to $+10$. If the upper end of the range is a decimal value, say `.5`, then it is clearer to enter it with a leading zero as `0.5`, so that the range looks like `-10 ..  0.5`, and not the confusing (to the reader and to Maple) `-10...5`.

Before we get on to embellishing the `plot` command, let us have some fun with the pretty graph you just produced:

- Click on the graph to select it. Inspect how a box is formed around it and that there are dark little nodes at the corners and in the middle of the sides.
- Use your mouse to resize the graph by grabbing one of the nodes and dragging it with the mouse button still depressed. Monitor how when a node is selected, a little arrow appears to show you the direction in which the frame can be resized. Resizing is possible diagonally along the corners or horizontally and vertically along the edges.
- Select the graph, copy it (it is placed on the *clipboard*), and then paste it back to the worksheet so that you now have two graphs.
- Make one of your graphs wide and short and the other one tall and thin. Check how the tall one emphasizes the variation in the magnitude of $V(r)$, while the tall one emphasizes the range of r values to which $V(r)$ extends. Both are perfectly legitimate ways to view a function, with one emphasizing the singular nature near the origin and the other the long range.
- Another way to view a function, especially one that has orders of magnitude variation in value, is with a *semilog* or *log-log* plot (although you need to avoid $\log(0)$). In the execution group below, use the `log10( )` function to see how a semilog plot changes the appearance of the same $f(x)$ we have been viewing.
- Next try the explicit semilog plot function `logplot( )`, following the instruction in the comments fields below:

```
> plot( log10(x^2), x = 0 ..  10 );          # Repeat plot with log(V(r))
> logplot( x^2, x = 0 ..  10 );              # Explicit semilog plot; log(1st argument)
```

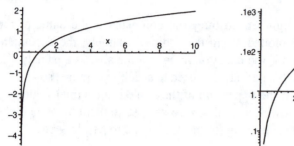 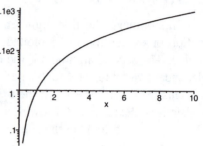

> # Try log-log plot here

4.4.2 Labels and Titles (the Plot Thickens)

Any plot worth looking at is worth explaining. This is done by placing labels along the axes and by placing a title above the curves:

```
> plot( 1/r, r = 1/10 ..  5, labels=['radius r (natural units)','V(r)'],
  title = 'Potential for a positive point charge at the origin' );
```

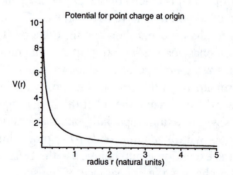

Take stock of how we just added a comma after the range and then added the options, separated by commas, to produce the labels and title. Because there are two axes, the labels field has an entry for the x axis and then the y axis. The labels and title are enclosed in back quotes in order to delimit the expressions:

> # Enter previous `plot` using ordinary accents

Modify the previous command so that the words "abscissa" and "ordinate" appear in the appropriate places and so that the actual expression being plotted appears in the title:

```
>                                                    # Plot with your modified labels and title
```

You may have noticed that we have placed r along the "x-axis" and $V(r)$ along the "y" axis. In fact, there may be cases in which y is the independent variable. Thus you see why it may be better to use the words "ordinate" and "abscissa" than "x" and "y" axes.

4.5 COMPOUND (ABSTRACT) DATA TYPES: [LISTS] AND {SETS}

As we proceed with our exercises in visualization, you will see how to enter arguments to the `plot` commands using different types of parentheses. We recognize that some users may prefer just following the rules without questioning them. Nevertheless, the commands will make more sense, and will be easier to generalize, if you have some understanding of the method behind the madness. And so we now take a little excursion in which we define some terms that are frequently used in mathematics and computer science and employed by Maple commands.

We have already seen a number of ways in which Maple displays data. At times there is just a single symbol, sometimes there is a bunch of symbols separated by commas, sometimes there is a bunch of things in parentheses, and sometimes the symbols are in quotes. To illustrate, in Chapter 5 you will see that when you solve an equation that has several solutions, Maple separates the solutions with commas:

```
> solve( x^4 - 1 = 0, x );
```
$$-1, \ 1, \ I, \ -I$$

```
> solve( x^4 - 1 = 0, x )[1];                        # Solve for only 1 root
```
$$-1$$

Take note of two types of parentheses here and the different forms given for the solutions.

Abstract, compound data types: An *object* in computer science denotes a data type with multiple parts. It may also be called an *abstract* data type, or a *compound* data type. Here the word "abstract" means that there is more to something than meets the eye; namely, the data type may contain multiple parts. Many of the individual symbols or variables used in Maple can be replaced by *objects*. We will discuss objects in more depth when we study Java, which is known as an *object oriented* language.

Data types: In specifying labels for the `plot` command, we placed the x and y labels in square parentheses `[..]`. These are called "brackets." Maple also uses standard parentheses `(..)` and curly parentheses `{..}` called "braces." Brackets and braces are used to construct abstract data types or objects from the more elementary data types we have already seen.

Sequence: A collection of variables (objects or data types) separated by commas is called a *sequence*. As a case in point, the arguments given to the `solve` command above, and indeed to most Maple commands, are variables separated by commas, and, hence, form sequences. While we are speaking of sequences, we may as well indicate that when we give arguments to a Maple command as a comma-separated list, the parenthesis indicate sequence. It is often convenient to let Maple form a sequence for you with the `seq` command:

```
> seq( 2*n-1, n = 1 .. 4 );
```
$$1, \ 3, \ 5, \ 7$$

List: A list is a sequence of numbers, or abstract data types, separated by commas and placed within square brackets. *The order matters for a list*, while it does not for a *set* (to be defined soon). We use a list when we issue the `plot` command:

```
> plot( 1/r, r = 1/10 .. 5, labels=['radius r (natural units)','V(r)'],
  title = 'Potential for point charge at origin' );
```

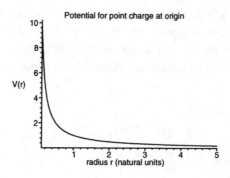

Now we try creating the plot again, this time changing the order of the list:

```
>                                                              # Plot with reordered list
```

Clearly order matters here, as we would not want the labels for the abscissa and ordinates interchanged! You may enter the elements of a list by hand, as in

```
> list1 := [2,4,6,8];
```
$$list1 := [2, \ 4, \ 6, \ 8]$$

Or use Maples `seq` command to help generate the elements of the list:

```
> list2 := [seq(2*n-1, n = 1 .. 4)];
```
$$list2 := [1, \ 3, \ 5, \ 7]$$

The individual elements of a list are referenced via Maple's square bracket notation (a standard way of indicating subscripts):

```
> list2[1]; list1[1]; list2[2]; list1[2];
```

$$1, \qquad 2, \qquad 3, \qquad 4$$

Set: A set is a well-defined collection of related objects or elements with no re-peated element [Fral 76]. In contrast to a list, the order of the elements in a set does *not* matter. Sets are also used as arguments to Maple commands, but only in cases where the order of the elements does matter, for example, a set of equations to be solved. Sets are usually described by enumerating their elements, separated by commas, as a sequence within braces. To prove the point, the sets of equations and solutions used when solving simultaneous equations:

```
> solve({a + 3*b + 4*c = 41, x5*a + 6*b + 7*c = 20}, {a,b});   # Any order for set
> solve({x5*a + 6*b + 7*c = 20, a + 3*b + 4*c = 41}, {b,a});   # Any order for set
```

$$\{a = \frac{c - 62}{-2 + x5}, \qquad b = -\frac{-7c + 4\,x5\,c - 41\,x5 + 20}{3\,(-2 + x5)}\}$$

Maple uses braces to denote sets:

```
> NiceSet := {0, 2, 4, 6};
```

$$NiceSet := \{0, 2, 4, 6\}$$

Seeing that lists and sets both contain comma-separated sequences within them, we emphasize that it is legal for the same element to occur more than once in a list, with the order of the elements in the list part of its definition. As an example, if we define a set with repeated elements in arbitrary order, then Maple will remove the repeats and reorder for us:

```
> MessySet := {6, 4, 0, 4, 2, 0};
```

$$MessySet := \{0, 2, 4, 6\}$$

In contrast, Maple does not change the order or elements of a list:

```
> MessyList := [6, 4, 0, 4, 2, 0];
```

$$MessyList := [6, 4, 0, 4, 2, 0]$$

Arrays: Another data type related to vectors and matrices are arrays. We discuss them in Chapter 7.

4.5.1 Several Curves on One Plot, Sets

We have seen that the first argument to the `plot` command is the function to be plotted. As a case in point, imagine that as part of our charge problem, we want to compare, in a single plot, the r dependence of the potential and the magnitude of the electric field due to both positive and negative charges. Seeing that Maple treats the argument as an object, we substitute the set $\{\frac{1}{r}, \frac{-1}{r}, \frac{1}{r^2}, \frac{-1}{r^2}\}$ as the first argument to the plot command. The fact that we use a set as the object to plot rather than a list $[\frac{1}{r}, \frac{-1}{r}, \frac{1}{r^2}, \frac{-1}{r^2}]$ makes sense since order does not matter and there is no point in plotting identical functions on top of each other:

```
> plot({1/r, -1/r, 1/r^2, -1/r^2}, r = 1/10..5, y = -20..20, labels=['r','V, E']);
```

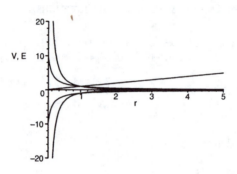

If you are reading the electronic version of this book, you will notice that Maple has chosen a different color for each of the functions. Experiment now with using a list as the first argument and noting how the colors assigned to the curves differ:

```
>                                                        # Use a list [...] for function argument
```

4.5.2 Using the Figure Toolbar

The colors and line formats that Maple picks for graphs may look great on your screen but may not print out or project well (green and yellow are often barely visible). In the next subsection we discuss how to customize the colors to your preference. In this subsection we will explore some of the options using the figure toolbar.

- Select the graph with your mouse (you should notice a box appearing about the graph after it is selected).
- While selected, observe that the second line of the toolbar at the top of your screen now contains icons for graphical options. Explore what each of these icons does. This is both useful and fun.
- Go to the Style pull-down menu and, under Line Width, select Broad. Observe especially the difference it makes for the yellow and green curves. Go to the Legend menu and enable Show Legend.
- Again go to the Legend pull-down, and select Edit Legend. Change the legends so they are $V(r)$, $-V(r)$, $E(r)$, $-E(r)$, and r for the appropriate curves.

- Explore how the different buttons controlling the placement of the axes work.

4.5.3 Customizing Colors and Line Types

Maple automatically chooses different color multifunction plots. You control the
color of your graphs by adding the `color` option to the end of the `plot` command:

```
> plot( [1/r, 1/r^2, r], r = 0 .. 1.5, y = 0..25, color=black );
```

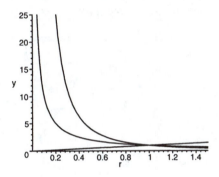

Taking into account that options are objects with multiple parts permitted, you
enter a list (order matters) of colors to specify the colors of each curve:

```
> plot( [1/r, 1/r^2, r], r = 0..1.5, y=0..25, color = [red, blue, maroon] );
```

Likewise, you choose different styles for each curve (like dashed and solid) to help
tell the curves apart, even in basic black. You do that with the `linestyle` option,
which may also be a list for each curve:

linestyle=[1 (solid), **2** (dotted), **3** (dashed), **4** (dot-dashed) **]**

```
>                                        # Plot black with linestyles as list
>                                        # Plot default colors with linestyles as list
```

An especially effective way to distinguish different curves on the same plot without
the use of color, is to draw them with different *thicknesses*. Apply this change with
the `thickness` = n option, where again, a list for the curves is a legal option. The
possible values for `thickness` are: n = 0, 1, 2, and 3, where 0 is the default
thickness.

```
>                                        # Replot with different thickness for each curve
```

4.5.4 Legends, Titles, and Labels

Legends explain to the reader just what is being plotted with each curve. They are invaluable and do wonders for your presentation. When presenting several curves in one plot, it is important that the viewer not only be able to tell them apart by the different color or line style used for each, but also be given information as to what the different curves represent. It is good practice to explain in the caption below a graph what each curve means, as well as in the text (or in your talk) when the graph gets referenced. However, it is also good practice to have a legend in the plot itself explaining what each curve means. Captions and your explanations may get removed, but it is a lot harder to remove a legend.

The legend option specifies a single string or a list of strings in the same order as the curves with a legend for each curve:

```
> plot( [1/r, 1/r^2], r = 0..1.5, y = 0..25, legend = [ `V(r)`, `E(r)` ] );
```

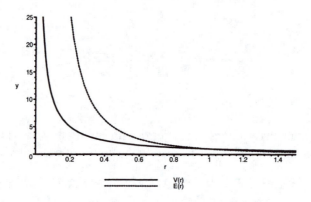

4.5.5 Other Options

As we have said, there are many ways to customize your graph, and Maple's Help pages are a good place to find out about them. Once in a while your graph may not show the features you want, because one function gets very large and Maple automatically adjusts the ordinate range to accommodate that. Here are a number of ways to limit the range of the ordinates:

```
> plot( [sin(x), tan(x),x], x = -Pi..Pi );              # tan(x) overshadows sin(x)
> plot( [sin(x), tan(x), x], x = -Pi..Pi, y = -10..10 );      # Now with y limits
```

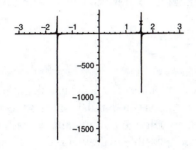

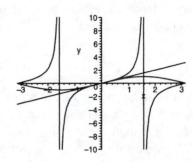

```
> plot( [sin(x), min(10,tan(x) ), x], x = -Pi..Pi );      # Limit +y values to 10
> plot( [sin(x), max(-10,tan(x)), x], x = -Pi..Pi );      # Limit -y values to -10
```

There are occasions when a function falls off slowly, and so you might want to see its behavior for values of its argument from $-\infty$ to $+\infty$. It is clear that Maple is not afraid of big numbers, yet it is nice to see that it makes this type of graph in a finite amount of space:

```
> plot( exp(-x^2), x = -infinity..infinity, title = 'Gaussian' );
> plot( {1/r,1/r^2}, r = 0..infinity, title = 'V and E of Point Charge' );
```

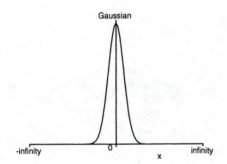

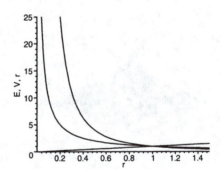

Look at the second plot and its labels along the axes, rather than horizontal. This was accomplished with the commands

```
> plot( [1/r, 1/r^2, r], r = 0..1.5, y = 0..25, labels = ['r', 'E, V, r'] );
> plot( [1/r, 1/r^2, r], r = 0..1.5, y = 0..25, labels = ['r', 'E,V, r'],
        labeldirections = [horizontal, vertical] );      # Rotate coordinate labels
```

4.6 3-D (SURFACE) PLOTS OF ANALYTIC FUNCTIONS

We have examined the potential field $V(r) = 1/r$ surrounding a single charge as a function of r. A 2-D plot is fine for this, since there is only one independent variable r. However, when the same potential is expressed as a function of the Cartesian coordinates x and y,

$$V(x, y) = \frac{1}{\sqrt{x^2 + y^2}},$$

we have two independent variables, x and y, and so need a 3-D visualization. We get that by creating a world in which the z dimension (mountain height) is the value of the potential, and x and y lie on a flat plane below the mountain. Because the surface we are creating is a 3-D object, it is not possible to draw it on a flat screen, and so different techniques are used to give the impression of three dimensions to our brains. We do that by rotating the object, shading it, employing parallax, and so forth.

The command `plot3d` makes a 3-D plot and is just like our old friend `plot`:

```
> restart;      with(plots):                             # Loads tools for you to use
  V := (x,y) -> 1/sqrt( x^2 + y^2 );          # Define function of two variables
> plot3d( V(x,y), x = -4..4, y = -4..4 );                        # Basic form
```

$$V := (x, y) \rightarrow \frac{1}{\sqrt{x^2 + y^2}}$$

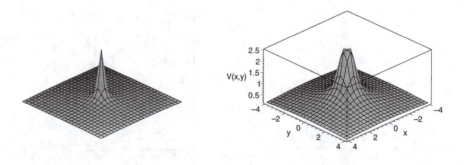

The first plot is a fairly interesting, but it primarily shows the singular nature of the potential near the origin. As seen in the second plot, we get a more useful visualization if we limit the maximum value of V to 2.5 and add labels:

```
> plot3d(min(2.5,V(x,y)), x=-4..4, y=-4..4, axes =BOXED, labels=['x','y','V(x,y)']);
```

We try to make this plot more intuitively informative by making the color red correspond to the highest values of the potential, blue smaller, and green cooler still. Color may be specified as the option `color = red` or with a number. Consequently, we try to be clever and use the actual value of the potential $V(x, y)$ as the color of the graph with `color = V(x,y)` option (yet we minimize the maximum value of the V in order to keep the singularity from confusing the color function).

Seeing as how the potential varies continuously, this means that the color will as well:

```
> plot3d( min(2.5, V(x,y)), x = -4..4, y = -4..4, color = min(2.5, V(x,y)) );
```

Even though there are many options possible as part of the `plot3d` command, it is both easier and more fun to first make a basic plot and then use Maple's graphical user interface (GUI) to modify the plot:

- Select this surface with your mouse (a box with filled little squares on the perimeter should appear).
- Grab the surface by depressing your left (or only) mouse button and holding it down. Now as you move your mouse, the surface will rotate in three dimensions. Make sure to move both right to left, and up and down, in order to get your brain to see the object as three-dimensional.
- With the surface still selected, notice the extra buttons that appear on the control panel. You should experiment and try to make sense of them. Remember that if you hold down a button, a message with the purpose of the button appears at the bottom of the screen. In particular, note:
  a. the different ways to draw axes,
  b. the different ways to render the surface, and
  c. how contour plots compare to the actual surface.

4.6.1 Contours and Equipotential Surfaces

To further help your mind understand that different colors mean different potential values, and that the surface is three-dimensional, we now include the `style = patchcontour` option. This adds contour lines that show different levels of the potential:

```
> V := (x,y) -> 1/sqrt( x^2 + y^2 );
> plot3d( min(2.5,V(x,y)), x = -4..4, y = -4..4, axes = BOXED,
  labels = ['x', 'y', 'V(x,y)'], color = min(2.5,V(x,y)), style = patchcontour );
```

$$V := (x,\ y) \rightarrow \frac{1}{\sqrt{x^2 + y^2}}$$

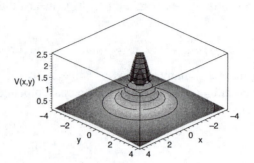

In analogy to gravity, contours lines may be viewed as lines of equal elevation, which means that walking along a contour line does not change your elevation. For our electrical potential, the contours are called equipotential surfaces.

The `contourplot` command also supports the option of making only a 2-D contour plot of the surface (we prefer the 3-D contours to be shown soon). Because the contours are not being projected onto a curved surface or being viewed obliquely, these have the potential of being more precise:

```
> contourplot( V(x,y), x = -4..4, y = -4..4 );
```

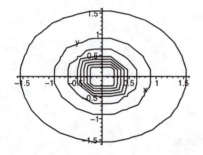
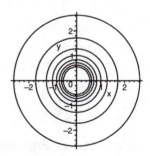

However, we see in the left plot that the equipotential surfaces appear as ellipses, and not the circles to be expected for the symmetric case of a single charge. The reason is that the viewing screen tends to be broader than higher, and so plots are spread out that way. To get a plot with the same scales along the ordinate and abscissa, as done on the right, we add the `scaling = constrained` option:

```
> contourplot( V(x,y), x = -4..4, y = -4..4, scaling = constrained );
```

This produces a more symmetrical figure, but still not round. Apparently, the rapid rise of the potential near the origin is not being handled well by Maple, and so we exclude it by use of the `min` function:

```
> contourplot(min(2,V(x,y)), x = -4..4, y = -4..4, grid=[75,75], scaling=constrained);
```

To produce the circles on the right plot, we actually had to use the `grid = [75,75]` option to increase the default grid Maple uses to evaluate the potential, from the default 25×25 to a finer 75×75.

The contours we have just drawn have all been projected onto the $x - y$ plane. The command `contourplot3d` draws the same contours on a 3-D surface that can be rotated as well for better visualization (looking straight down produces 2-D contours). Actually, `contourplot3d` is faster and more accurate than the 2-D `contourplot` as a consequence of it being written in the compiled language C:

```
> contourplot3d( min(3,V(x,y)), x = -3..3, y = -3..3 );
> contourplot3d( min(3,V(x,y)), x = -3..3, y = -3..3, scaling=constrained );
```

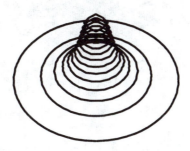

4.7 SOLUTION: DIPOLE AND QUADRUPOLE FIELDS

We have used a number of visualization tools to examine the potential field surrounding a single positive and a single negative charge. The tools only showed us what we probably knew already, namely, that the potential field does not have concave areas in which a charge may remain stably at rest. This was as intended; it is a good idea to learn about new tools by applying them to problems for which you know the right answer. We are now in the position to finally investigate the electric potential due to a dipole and tripole. We start with the dipole configuration shown in Figure 4.2:

$$V_2(x, y) = \frac{q_1}{\sqrt{(x-1)^2 + y^2}} + \frac{q_2}{\sqrt{(x+1)^2 + y^2}}. \qquad (4.9)$$

We start by defining a Maple function:

```
> V2 := (x,y,q1,q2) -> q1/sqrt( (x-1)^2 + y^2) + q2/sqrt( (x+1)^2+y^2 );
```

$$V2 := (x,\ y,\ q1,\ q2) \rightarrow \frac{q1}{\sqrt{(x-1)^2 + y^2}} + \frac{q2}{\sqrt{(x+1)^2 + y^2}}$$

Now we visualize a dipole with one positive and one negative charge:

```
> q1 := 1; q2 := -1;
```
$$q1 := 1, \qquad q2 := -1$$

```
> plot3d( V2(x,y,1,-1), x = -3.5..3.5, y = -3.5..3.5,
    color = min( 3, V2(x,y,1,-1)), labels = ['x','y','V2(x,y)'], axes = boxed);
```

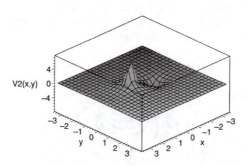

If you grab and rotate this plot you will see that wherever you place a charge, it will either roll downhill away from the positive charge or fall into the hole of the negative charge. There is no stable equilibrium. For that reason enter the commands to look at two charges of the like sign:

```
>                                                    # Make 3-D plot for two positive charges
>                                                    # Make 3-D plot for two negative charges
```

The figure resulting from these commands looks like a saddle. There is a region between the two peaks where it appears that a charge will remain at rest, and where it will roll back towards the midpoint if it is displaced along the positive or negative x axes. However, due to the saddle, if the charge is displaced in the y direction, then it rolls away to infinity. The charge is thus stable for x displacements but unstable for y displacements. This type of equilibrium point is known as a *saddle point*, and occurs for two positive or two negative charges. If the charges have unequal values but the same sign, then the shape gets distorted but still has the same property.

As a check on our analysis, look at the contours for this surface:

```
>                                                    # Create a contourplot3d here
```

You should see the saddle point structure as a single point where two equipotential surfaces cross.

Now we look at the quadrupole potential (we leave the tripole for you). Our intuition tells us that the high degree of symmetry here must lead to a stable position at the center. We define the potential and then we plot it as a 3-D surface and as 3-D contours:

```
> V4 := (x,y) -> 1/sqrt( (x-1)^2 + (y-1)^2 ) + 1/sqrt( (x-1)^2 +
  (y+1)^2) +1/sqrt((x+1)^2 + (y-1)^2 ) + 1/sqrt( (x+1)^2 + (y+1)^2 );
> plot3d(V4(x,y), x = -3.5..3.5, y = -3.5..3.5, color = min(4.5,V4(x,y)),
        labels = ['x', 'y', 'V4(x,y)'], axes = box );
> contourplot3d(min(4.5,V4(x,y)), x = -3..3, y = -3..3, scaling=constrained);
```

$$V_4 := (x, y) \rightarrow \frac{1}{\sqrt{(x-1)^2 + (y-1)^2}} + \frac{1}{\sqrt{(x-1)^2 + (y+1)^2}}$$
$$+ \frac{1}{\sqrt{(x+1)^2 + (y-1)^2}} + \frac{1}{\sqrt{(x+1)^2 + (y+1)^2}}$$

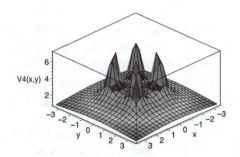 

Indeed, we do see a large central, flat region surrounded by a lip to hold the charge in. We check this out further by looking at some slices through the central region:

```
> plot( V4(x,0), x = -3..3, title = 'V4(x,y=0) vs x');
> plot( min(4,V4(x,x)), x = -3..3, title = 'V4(x=y) vs x' );    # min for details
```

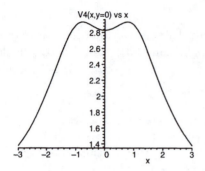
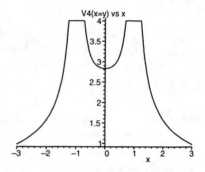

So we see that the central portion of this potential is indeed a flat region with a "lip" all around it. Consequently, a charge placed there will be have no force on it (the flatness) and will be stable for small displacements (the lip).

4.8 EXPLORATION: THE TRIPOLE

Repeat the analysis carried out for the dipole and quadrupole now for the tripole. Be sure to make a 3-D plot with labels and title as well as including contours. Slice your plot through its center to verify that you have found a stable point.

4.9 EXTENSION: YET MORE PLOT TYPES*

4.9.1 2-D Animations

We have just seen that surface-rendering techniques permit us to create images from mathematical functions that give the impression of viewing a true three-dimensional object. This literally gives a new dimension to our visualizations. In addition, if we have plots that show the behavior of some quantity as a function of space, and if this behavior changes gradually with time, then the observation of a sequence of plots of the spatial dependencies, each one for a slightly different time, gives the impression of a continuous evolution of the spatial function in time. The function appears to be alive and, indeed, creating a series of snapshots in time is known as *animation*.

To produce animations, we add the dimension of time to our 2-D plots. To name an instance, let us say we wanted to show the changing temperature distributions along the x direction of a metal bar as it cools with increasing time t. We could plot $T_1(x)$ and then $T_2(x)$ and so forth, where the subscript indicates the time. It is more elegant and concise to envision a single function $T(x, t)$ that contains both the space and time dependencies.

By way of example, if the bar was initially hot in the center, a possible temperature distribution is [Krey 88]

$$T(x,t) = \sin x \, e^{-t} - \frac{\sin 3x \, e^{-9t}}{9}. \tag{4.10}$$

We make a 3-D surface plot of this function from $t = 0$ to 20 and $x = 0$ to π:

```
> plot3d( sin(x) * exp(-0.3*t) - sin(3*x) * exp(-9*0.3*t)/9,
  x = 0..Pi, t = 0..20, axes = BOXED, labels = ['x', 't', 'T(x,t)'] );
```

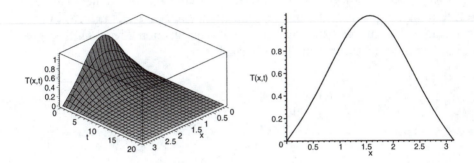

Observe that it is important to label the axes so that you know which variable is time and which is space. Go ahead and grab, enlarge, and rotate the left plot.

The plot on the right uses `animate` to animate this function:

```
> with(plots):      with(plottools):                    # This loads the needed tools
> animate(sin(x) * exp(-0.3*t) - sin(3*x) * exp(-9*0.3*t)/9,
  x = 0..Pi, t = 0..20, labels = ['x', 'T(x,t)'] );
```

Whereas the plot on the right does not look different from a static 2-D plot, if you are reading the electronic version of this book, then you make it come alive by selecting it with your mouse. Then a bunch of buttons appear on the control bar on top that permit you to "play" the animation as you might a CD. Do it now! Investigate the buttons for stop, forward, reverse, fast forward, and fast reverse. However there is also a button that lets the animation loop around and thus play continuously. We recommend that.

An animation works by displaying (flipping through) a sequence of slightly modified images. In movie parlance, these images are called `frames`, and the more you have of them the smoother and slower will be your animation:

```
>                                          # Animate with frames = 100 option
```

4.9.2 3-D Animation

Well, if you have been reading and executing up to this point, it is fairly clear what 3-D animations are about. If you have a function of two space coordinates that also varies in time, then you make a 3-D surface plot to visualize the space dependence at any one time, or an animation to visualize the time dependence of the surface. For example, assume the temperature distribution is now a function of two space coordinates as well as time:

$$T(x, y, t) = \sin x \, e^{-.3t} - \frac{\sin 3x \, e^{-9.9t}}{9} \sin y \, e^{-.3t} - \frac{\sin 3 \, y \, e^{-9.9\,t}}{9}.$$

This is complicated enough that we will define a Maple function rather than try to stuff it into a command. Other than using the name `animate3d`, the format of the command is the same as before. We start with the function $T(x, y, t)$, then give the ranges for each variable, and then the labels:

```
> with(plots):                                          # Load needed tools
```

$$T := (x, \ y, \ t) \rightarrow (\sin(x) \, e^{-0.3\,t} - \frac{1}{9} \sin(3\,x) \, e^{-9.9\,t}) (\sin(y) \, e^{-0.3\,t} - \frac{1}{9} \sin(3\,y) \, e^{-9.9\,t})$$

```
> animate3d( T(x,y,t), x = 0..Pi, y = 0..Pi, t = 0..20, labels=['x','y','T(x,y)'] );
```

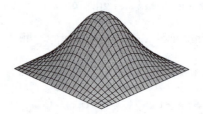

Again, if you are reading the electronic version, then select this plot, play it, and even rotate it while it is vibrating (it looks like a vibrating drum head).

4.9.3 Phase-Space (Parametric) Plots

In science we often encounter several physical quantities that are simultaneous functions of the same variable. For instance, the position $x(t)$, velocity $v(t)$, and acceleration $a(t)$ of a mass undergoing simple harmonic motion are all trigonometric functions of time:

$$x(t) = \sin\omega t, \quad v(t) = -\omega \cos\omega t, \quad a(t) = -\omega^2 \sin\omega t. \qquad (4.11)$$

We easily plot the position and velocity on the same graph; for example,

```
> plot( [sin(wt), -2*cos(wt)], wt = 0..  8*Pi, legend = ['x(wt)','v(wt)'] );
```

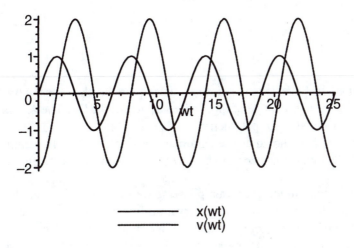

                                   x(wt)
                                   v(wt)

We observe the position and velocity as out of phase, but with the same period.

A more direct way to observe the relation of two dependent variables (x and v in our example) as a function of the same independent variable t is known as a *phase-space* or *parametric plot*. These types of plots have now proven themselves to be highly illuminating and valuable. Phase space is an extension of the usual space of position that also includes velocity as if it were a new dimension, along with position. Explicitly, we plot $x(t)$ along the abscissa as if it were the independent variable and $V(t)$ along the ordinate. In a sense then, a phase-space plot is a plot of $v(x)$.

Recognizing that it might be impossible, or very complicated, to analytically eliminate the time dependencies permitting two functions to be expressed in terms of each other, it is still fairly easy to do this graphically. Explicitly, Maple breaks up the total time interval into a number of steps and then records the pair of values (x, v) for each time step. These values then get plotted as $v(t)$ versus $x(t)$:

```
> plot( [sin(wt), -2*cos(wt), wt = 0..8*Pi], labels = ['Position', 'Velocity'] );
```

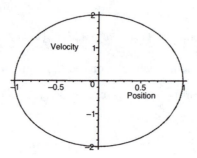

Observe that all we have done here is use a list (square brackets) as the function argument and included the range of time values as part of the list. The general syntax for a two-dimensional (2-D) parametric plot is plot([x(t), y(t), t = a..b], options), where t is known as the parametric variable or simply parameter, and $x(t)$ and $y(t)$ denote the horizontal and vertical functions, respectively.

As far as the output goes, this phase-space plot looks like an ellipse. Yet it has properties that agree with the observations we have made before: when the mass is at its maximum positions, at the extreme right and left edges of the ellipse, the velocity is zero. When the mass has it maximum speed, at the top and bottom of the ellipse, it has zero position, namely, it is passing through its equilibrium position. So while a harmonic oscillator is described via a complicated set of position, velocity, and acceleration functions versus time, in phase space its motion is an elliptical orbit on which the mass passes over and over.

You may be wondering in looking at this graph just how we hit upon the exact range of wt values for which the graph exactly closes on itself. Well, we really did not. In fact, our plot covers two full cycles and plots them on top of each other (which you cannot see). If, on the other hand, your phase-space plot did not form a closed figure, then you would need to run for more values of the time. Try out smaller and smaller ranges for the phase wt in the plot command until you are able to generate 1/2 and 1/4 of an elliptical orbit:

>   # Create some phase-space plots here

As you see from looking at the monitor in front of you, visual displays tend to be broader than they are high. For this reason graphs tend to get stretched horizontally ("scaled") in order to fill the screen. As long as the graph looks good this is not normally a concern, yet it is if you are trying to determine the proper shape of a geometrical figure. For this reason Maple has the scaling = constrained option to avoid undue stretching:

>   # Add scaling = constrained option

4.9.4 Energy Conservation and Implicit Plots

In our discussion of parametric plots, we looked at the position $x(t)$ and velocity $v(t)$ of an oscillator as functions of time. Maple solves numerically for the function $x(v)$ or $v(x)$. There may also be cases where you know some functional relation between two variables, say x and v, and wish to make a plot of x versus v. To cite an instance, let us say that we have a spring with a nonlinear force law so that the potential energy stored in it is

$$V(x) = k\,x^6. \tag{4.12}$$

The kinetic energy of a mass attached to this spring is, as always,

$$K = \frac{1}{2}m\,v^2. \tag{4.13}$$

We know that the sum of kinetic plus potential energy is conserved, which means we have an implicit relation between position and velocity, namely,

$$E = V + K = k\,x^6 + \frac{m\,v^2}{2}. \tag{4.14}$$

This last equation permits us to make a parametric plot even though we do not have explicit solutions for $x(t)$ and $v(t)$. We do it with the `implicitplot` command that plots x versus v given the equation relating the two:

```
> implicitplot( 5*x^6 + (13/2)*v^2 = 1, x = -1..1, v = -1..1 );
```

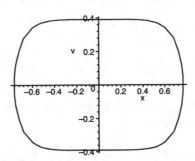

See how this phase-space plot changes if the potential energy varies as x^5.

4.9.4.1 Implicitplot3d

In analogy to the 2-D implicit plots we just made for a nonlinear oscillator, the `implicitplot3d` command plots the 3-D surface defined by some explicit relation between x, y, and z:

```
> implicitplot3d( exp(z^2) = sqrt(x^2 + y^2), x = -3..3, y = -3..3, z = -1..1 );
```

As with other 3-D plots, it is possible to grab and rotate the electronic plot.

4.9.5 Vector Fields: fieldplot and fieldplot3d*

Consider again the electric dipole shown in Figure 4.2. The problem we examined dealt with the electric potential for this type of system. Even though potentials are easier to compute and visualize than fields, it is usually fields that are related to the forces and measured in experiments. As an extension of our charge problem, we now visualize the *electric field* vector $\mathbf{E}(x, y)$ for the dipole,

$$\mathbf{E} = \frac{(\vec{r} - \vec{r_1})}{|\vec{r} - \vec{r_1}|^2} + \frac{(\vec{r} - \vec{r_2})}{|\vec{r} - \vec{r_2}|^2}, \tag{4.15}$$

where the E and r's in this equation are all vector quantities. Mathematically, we determine the electric field as the derivative of the potential using the techniques of vector calculus and then plot the individual components. This is complicated, so let us have Maple do the work.

We start with the x and y components of the electric field E:

```
> Ex := (x, y) -> (x+1) / ((x+1)^2 + y^2) - (x-1) / ((x-1)^2 + y^2);
> Ey := (x, y) -> y / ((x+1)^2 + y^2) - y / ((x-1)^2 + y^2);
```

$$Ex := (x, y) \rightarrow \frac{x+1}{(x+1)^2 + y^2} - \frac{x-1}{(x-1)^2 + y^2}$$

$$Ey := (x, y) \rightarrow \frac{y}{(x+1)^2 + y^2} - \frac{y}{(x-1)^2 + y^2}$$

We visualize the components in two surface plots (we show only one on paper):

```
> plot3d(Ex(x,y), x = -4..4, y = -4..4, labels = ['x','y','E'], axes=boxed);
```

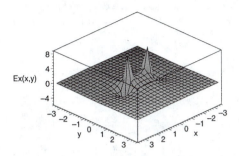

Although this plot shows E_x at each point in space, it is rather hard to get a good feel for the magnitude and direction of the field. For this purpose there is the `fieldplot` command:

```
> fieldplot( [Ex(x,y), Ey(x,y)], x = -4..4, y = -4..4, color = Ex, arrows=THICK );
```

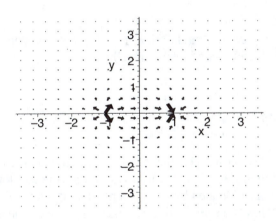

This plot shows the direction of the field as given by direction of arrows, and the magnitude as given by the length of the arrows.

You may not know it from elementary physics classes, but the real world is actually three dimensional. Because of this the electric field actually has a z component as well:

```
> Ez := (x,y,z) -> z / ((x+1)^2 + y^2 + z^2) - z / ((x-1)^2 + y^2 + z^2);
```

$$Ez := (x, \, y, \, z) \rightarrow \frac{z}{(x+1)^2 + y^2 + z^2} - \frac{z}{(x-1)^2 + y^2 + z^2}$$

Here we visualize a 3-D vector field with the `fieldplot3d` command:

```
> fieldplot3d( [Ex(x,y,z), Ey(x,y,z), Ez(x,y,z)],
        x = -4..4, y = -4..4, z = -4..4, arrows = THICK );
```

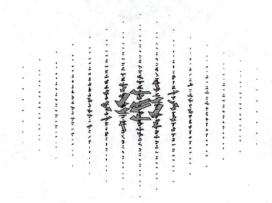

Regardless of how good you might think this plot looks on paper, it truly comes alive when you grab and rotate it electronically.

4.9.6 Polar Plots

Polar coordinates describe a 2-D plane in terms of radius r and orientation θ, rather than the more common Cartesian coordinates x and y. A polar plot is a representation of the function $r(\theta)$ created by placing a point a distance $r(\theta)$ from the origin for each angle θ. They are illuminating because the angle on the plot corresponds to the actual angle of the function's argument, and so the shape of the plot lets you visualize the variation of the function in actual space. If r were independent of θ, then the polar plot would be a circle. Other dependencies are less obvious.

Making polar plots with the `plot` command is similar to making parametric plots, only now we add a `coord = polar` option and use theta instead of time as the parametric variable. Or do it directly with the `polarplot` command:

```
> plot( [r(theta), theta, theta = 0..2*Pi], coords = polar );
> polarplot( [r(theta), theta(theta), theta = 0..2*Pi] );
```

To get a feel for how this works, let us make a polar plot of a function that is independent of θ and has $r = 1$:

```
> plot( [1, theta, theta = 0..2*Pi], coords = polar );
```

```
> polarplot( [ r, theta, theta = 0..2*Pi ] );
```

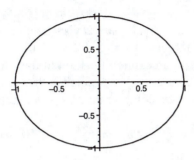

As a more realistic example, consider the expression for the intensity of low-energy X-rays scattered off a reflecting sphere as a function of the scattering angle:

$$\sigma(\theta) = 3 + 2\cos(\theta)^4 + 2\cos(\theta). \tag{4.16}$$

```
> plot( [3+2*cos(theta)^4 + 2*cos(theta), theta, theta = 0..2*Pi], coords = polar );
```

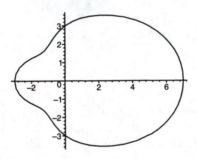

You intuitively feel where the scattering is large and where it is small.

4.9.7 Surface Plots of Complex Functions*

In Chapter 14 we give a review of complex numbers in preparation for representing them as objects in Java. If you are not familiar with complex numbers, then you may want read that review in order to better understand this section.

Maple has the commands `complexplot` and `complexplot3d` for visualizing complex functions. We have found `complexplot3d` the more useful of the two, and will discuss only it. We start with the complex function f of the complex argument $z = x + iy$,

$$f(z) = f(x + iy) = \operatorname{Re} f + i \operatorname{Im} f. \tag{4.17}$$

The command `complexplot3d` makes a 3-D visualization of a complex function or expression. The form of the visualization differs if the input is a implicit function of a complex argument z or an explicit function of the real and imaginary parts x and y. In the latter case `complexplot3d` plots the $\operatorname{Re} f$ while coloring the graphic using the $\operatorname{Im} f$. As an instance, consider the complex function

$$z^2 = (x + iy)^2 = x^2 - y^2 + 2ixy. \tag{4.18}$$

```
> complexplot3d( [x^2 - y^2, 2*x*y], x = -2..2, y = -2..2, axes = framed );
```

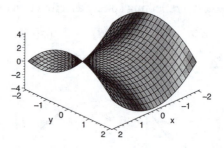

Here the height of the plot is the value $\operatorname{Re} f = x^2 - y^2$, changing sign along the *line $x = y$*, while the color is controlled by $\operatorname{Im} f = 2xy$. We obtain the same plot as before using explicit functions of x and y:

```
> Ref := (x, y) -> x^2 - y^2;
```

$$Ref := (x, y) \rightarrow x^2 - y^2$$

```
> Imf := (x,y) -> 2*x*y;
```

$$Imf := (x, y) \rightarrow 2yx$$

```
> complexplot3d( [Ref, Imf], -2..2, -2..2, axes = framed, labels = [x, y, Ref] );
```

The other approach to visualizing complex functions is to enter complex numbers directly. In this case, `complexplot3d` plots the magnitude of the function and colors the resulting surface with the phase θ, defined as $\tan^{-1}(\operatorname{Re} f / \operatorname{Im} f)$, of the function:

```
> complexplot3d( z^2, z = -2 - 2*I .. 2 + 2*I, axes = framed );
```

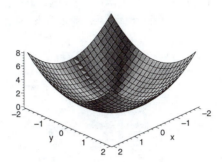

A more realistic example is the complex function

$$f(E) = \frac{1}{E - 2 + i} \tag{4.19}$$

that describes a *resonance* as a function of E that may occur in a circuit containing a resistor, inductor, and capacitor in series (discussed in Chapter 16) or in setting up standing waves in a tube. Regardless of the fact that experiments are done only at pure real values of E, this function has a pole (equals ∞) at a complex energy $E = 2 - i$. To help understand the visualization, we rewrite f in a form with a real denominator (multiply the numerator and denominator by the complex conjugate of the denominator):

$$f(E = x + iy) = \frac{x - 2 - i\,(y + 1)}{(x - 2)^2 + (y + 1)^2}. \tag{4.20}$$

We visualize $f(z)$ using the different forms of `complexplot3d`:

```
> complexplot3d( 1 / (z-2+I), z = 1-3*I..3+2*I, axes = framed );
```

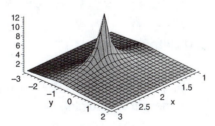

Inasmuch as there are no sign changes here, it must be the modulus of the function that is being plotted. If we look at (4.20) we see that the modulus does have a maximum when $x = 2$ and when $y = -1$, and that the modulus falls off in value as we get away from the pole position. As expected, we see those features on the plot. We visualize the real and imaginary parts of $f(E)$ separately:

```
> Ref := (x,y) -> (x-2) / ((x-2)^2 + (1+y)^2);
> Imf := (x,y) -> -(y +1) / ((x-2)^2 + (1+y)^2);
> complexplot3d( [Ref, Imf], 1..3, -3..2, axes = framed, labels = [ReE,ImE,Ref] );
```

$$Ref := (x,\, y) \rightarrow \frac{x-2}{(x-2)^2 + (1+y)^2}$$

$$Imf := (x,\, y) \rightarrow -\frac{1+y}{(x-2)^2 + (1+y)^2}$$

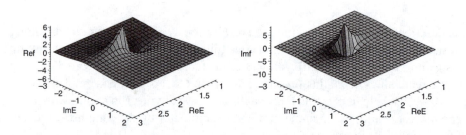

As we see in the plot, there is a sign change at 2 along one of the axes. Consequently, that must be the x axis and the function plotted must be Ref (Imf does not have a sign change). Check next that Ref does not change sign as a function of y, but does have a maximum at $y = -1$ where the denominator gets small. In fact at $(x, y) = (2, -1)$ there is a pole, yet it has residue 0, which we see as a very large oscillation in Ref. To see how the Imf varies as a function of complex energy, we reverse the real and imaginary parts in the argument call:

```
> complexplot3d( [Imf, Ref], 1..3, -3..2, axes = framed, labels = [ReE,ImE,Imf] );
```

4.9.8 Plotting Lists and Sets: pointplot*

If you do measurements in a real lab or run numerical simulations in a virtual lab, you will end up with some numerical data to plot. The data are of the form

$$[\, (x_1,\, y_1),\, (x_2,\, y_2),\, (x_3,\, y_3),\, \cdots (x_N,\, y_N)\,].$$

We will now generate such points, both so that we will have some data to plot, and as a further exercise with sets (not ordered), lists (ordered), and sequences. First we generate a sequence of ordered pairs (each a sublist in square brackets) with the seq command:

```
> sequence = seq( [i, i^2], i = 0..10 );
```
$$sequence = (\,[0,\,0],\,[1,\,1],\,[2,\,4],\,[3,\,9],\,\cdots\,[10,\,100]\,)$$

If we store this sequence in a list, then the order is preserved, yet if we store it as a set, then the order is not:

```
> List := [ seq([i, i^2], i = 0..10) ];          # Generate list, order preserved
> Set  := { seq([i, i^2], i = 0..10) };          # Generate set, order not preserved
```
$$List := [\,[0,\,0],\,[1,\,1],\,[2,\,4],\,\cdots\,[10,\,100]\,]$$
$$Set := \{\,[0,\,0],\,[1,\,1],\,[2,\,4],\,\cdots\,[10,\,100]\,\}$$

The difference becomes evident when we plot the set and list using the `pointplot` command and the `connect = true` option to connects the points. If the points are sequentially ordered, then the list should yield a single-valued function, otherwise the curve will loop back upon itself:

```
> pointplot( List, connect = true );             # Continuous with list
> pointplot( Set,  connect = true );             # Loops back occurs with list
```

4.9.9 Creating Simple Figures: pointplot, pointplot3d*

Here we give some examples of the use of `pointplot` and `pointplot3d` to create simple figures of a barbell (we use the figures in Chapter 7). There are three steps involved. First we plot just the data points using circles for the points. Then we plot lines connecting the data points. Finally we use Maple's `display` command to display both the points and lines on the same graph. In 2-D, the left plot below, we give points as a list of doublets `[x,y]`:

```
> p1 := pointplot( {[-0.7, 0.7],[0.7, -0.7]}, thickness = 2, style = LINE );
> p2 := pointplot({[-0.7, 0.7],[sqrt(2)/2, -0.7]}, symbol = CIRCLE,
  thickness = 2, symbolsize = 45,axes = normal, labels=[x,y]);
> display(p1,p2);
```

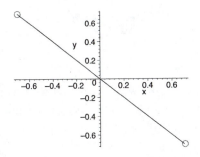 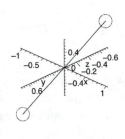

In 3-D, the right plot above, we give the points as a list of triplets [x,y,z]:

```
> p1 := pointplot3d({[-0.7,0,0.7],[0.7, 0, -0.7]}, thickness = 2, style = LINE);
> p2 := pointplot3d({[-0.7,0,0.7],[0.7, 0, -0.7]}, symbol = CIRCLE, thickness = 2,
  symbolsize = 100, axes = normal, labels=[x,y,z]);
> display(p1, p2);
```

4.9.10 Plotting Vectors: arrow*

Maple's `LinearAlgebra` package is discussed in Chapter 7. That package permits us to define vectors, matrices, and arrays of arbitrary sizes and dimensions (although matrices are always 2-D). There you will find some easy-to-use tools for visualizing vectors and matrices. The `arrow` command plots a 3-D vector as an arrow and lets you grab it and rotate it. If the vector is 2-D, then the arrow cannot be rotated. The `display` command lets you place several arrows together. Notwithstanding vectors having more than three components, the `arrow` command works only for 2-D and 3-D vectors.

```
> with(plots):          with(LinearAlgebra):
> Omega := Vector( [1,-3,6] );        L := Vector( [6,0,6] );
> arrow( Omega, color = black, shape = double_arrow);     # Plot Omega as black arrow
> arrow(L);                                                # Not shown
```

$$\Omega := \begin{bmatrix} 1 \\ -3 \\ 6 \end{bmatrix}, \qquad L := \begin{bmatrix} 6 \\ 0 \\ 6 \end{bmatrix}$$

Once we have visualizations of the vectors `L` and `Omega`, we place them on the same graph (the right plot above, which can be grabbed electronically) by assigning objects (named variables) to each arrow, and then displaying the arrows:

```
> w := arrow(Omega, color = black, shape = double_arrow);     # Assign object w
```

```
> L1 := arrow(L):                                          # Assign object L1
> display(w, L1, axes = BOXED, scaling = constrained, labels = [x,y,z],
         title = `Omega (black) and L`);        # Display Omega and L on same graph
> Omega := Vector([1,-3]);
```

We also use the `arrow` command to plot several arrows (or sequences of arrows) at one time. To illustrate, here are the familiar three unit vectors:

```
> arrow({[0,0,1], [0,1,0], [1,0,0]});
```

Study our creation of arrows with the options to control the color and shape of the arrows (see Help `arrow` for other properties). Although there are limited options for the `arrow` command, the `display` command supports the usual ones, such as `labels` and `titles`.

4.10 VISUALIZING NUMERICAL DATA

4.10.1 2-D Plots of Data

Most realistic computations in science produce numerical output, not analytic functions. Possibly in view of the fact that there is more work involved in plotting numerical data than there is for an analytic function, Maple has a number of ways to make 2-D plots of numerical data.[2] In fact, the various packages that are used to extend the basic Maple capabilities, such as those for statistics or linear algebra, often have their own plotting techniques. Here we demonstrate the use of `listplot` from the `plot` package and `scatterplot` from the `statistical` package.

---

[2]David McIntyre assisted with methods for plotting data.

4.10.2 Numerical Plots: listplot

The `listplot` command creates a 2-D plot from a list of numerical data values. If only y values are given, say as the four-element list,

$$Ydata := [1, 8, 27, 100],$$

then `listplot` will assign x values by counting from 1 to 4 to produce

$$\{(1, 1),\ (2, 8),\ (3, 27),\ (4, 400)\}$$

```
> with(plots):       listplot( [1, 8, 27, 100] );       # Plot y with x as order number
```

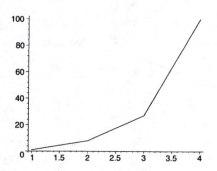

The same plot is obtained if y is entered as a list:

```
> Ydata := [1, 8, 27, 100];                              # Enter y data into list Ydata
> listplot( Ydata );                                     # Plot data object Ydata
```

$$Ydata := [1, 8, 27, 100]$$

If you want to give explicit x values to your data, then you place each (x_i, y_i) value in its own two-element list, and make a big list up of these sublists. This placement and listing produces the left plot below:

$$[\ [x_1,\ y_1], [x_2,\ y_2], [x_3,\ y_3], [x_4,\ y_4]\ ]$$

```
> listplot( [[0, 1], [sqrt(3)/2, 1/2], [-sqrt(3)/2, 1/2] ] );       # Plot list
```

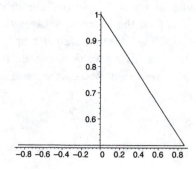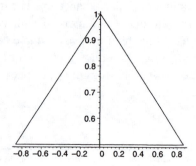

To get the plot to close on itself and thereby form a geometric figure (right plot), we repeat the first point:

```
> listplot( [[0,1], [sqrt(3)/2,1/2], [-sqrt(3)/2,1/2], [0,1]] );  # Repeat 1st pt
```

The above samples are basic commands. There are options for plotting only points, for controlling their size and color, and with `connect = true`, to connect the points in the true order in which they are plotted.

4.10.3 Numerical Plots: scatterplot*

A scatter plot is a plot of points in which the points are not connected. To use the `scatterplot` command, we give as arguments a list of the x values of our data, and a corresponding list of y values:

```
> with(plots):          with(stats[statplots]);            # Load statistics package
> Xdata := [ 0, sqrt(3.)/2, -sqrt(3.)/2 ];                 # [List] of all x values
> Ydata := [ 1, -1/2, -1/2 ];                              # [List] of corresponding y values
```

$$Xdata := [\, 0,\ 0.8660254040,\ -0.8660254040\,]$$

$$Ydata := [\, 1,\ \frac{-1}{2},\ \frac{-1}{2}\,]$$

```
> scatterplot( Xdata, Ydata );                                    # Plot points, basic
> scatterplot( Xdata, Ydata, color = red, symbolsize = 35 );      # Plot + options
```

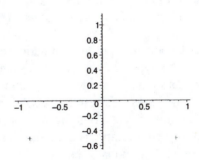

4.10.4 Histograms and Box Plots*

Here we make a histogram and then a box plot of some random data:

```
> data := [-2., -.8, 2., .0, -.5, -.5, 1.6,.8,.5,-.5,-.2, -.2, .2,-.1];
> histogram( data, area = count);
> boxplot( data );
```

$$data := [-2., -0.8, 2., 0., -0.5, -0.5, 1.6, 0.8, 0.5, -0.5, -0.2, -0.2, 0.2, -0.1]$$

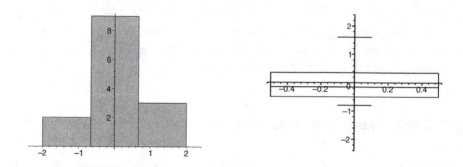

A histogram is used to create bins or bars, with the height of the bar proportional to the number of events that occur within the x values covered by the bar. A box plot is seen to contain a central line showing the median, a lower line showing the first quartile, and an upper line showing the third quartile.

4.10.5 Surface Plots of Data: listplot3d*

We have already seen how to make 3-D or surface plots $z = f(x, y)$ of analytic functions of two variables. Here we describe how to make the same kind of plot from a table of numbers. In Chapter 11 we describe how to use the free, plotting program gnuplot to make surface plots of numerical data (we find gnuplot easier).

Most often, realistic calculations produce numerical data rather than analytic functions as their output. This type of output is a consequence of the real world being less simple than the assumptions made in those models that lead to purely analytic answers. In realistic cases, the resulting equations may still be solved, only they must be solved numerically. Trying to understand if there is meaning in long lists of numbers obtained as output is quite the challenge, yet this point is exactly where visualization tools are most valuable.

While yet to be discussed (we do in Chapter 7), the use of matrices and arrays makes the bookkeeping for multidimensional data rather straightforward. Hence, you may want to review matrices and then return to this subsection.

As with all 3-D visualizations, we want to create a surface in 3-D space that represents our data. Picture data describing the temperature $T(x)$ as a function of distance x along a one-dimensional bar. However, the bar is cooling as a function of time, so there is a temperature distribution for each time that we put together as a function of both time and position $T(t, x)$. Consequently, we will make a graph of

$T(t, x)$ with T as the vertical distance above the plane formed by the time t as one horizontal coordinate and with position x as the other horizontal coordinate. The fact that this 3-D surface does not truly exist in nature is one reason this approach is called "visualization."

The plotting of numerical data is done in two steps. First we read the data into a matrix, with one index for position and other for time. Then we plot the matrix. We have placed some sample $T(t, x)$ data in the file EqHeat_z.dat on the CD, and you should read that file into a convenient location now.

It seems obvious that the data file should contain x and t values with the associated $T(t, x)$ value. Nonetheless, the problem is made simpler by just giving T values, indicated by the subscript _z in the file EqHeat_z.dat. The assumption is that these T values correspond to a rectangular array of uniformly spaced x and t values, and we do not need to know the actual spacing to make the visualization. To see how this works, here are the first three lines in EqHeat_z.dat:

0.	100.	100.	100.	100.	100.	100.	100.	100.	100.	0.
0.	32.5	59.8	78.9	89.5	92.8	89.5	78.9	59.8	32.5	0.
0.	22.7	43.	59.0	69.1	72.5	69.1	59.	43.	22.7	0.

Think of each line of data as a row of a big matrix. Whereas the number of digits used for each number may differ, and so the length of each line may differ, each row has the same number of entries or columns. These data are values of the temperature for increasing x values along the rod. Explicit values of the time are not given, however, subsequent lines (rows of the matrix) contain the temperature distributions for later and later times. In other words, the full matrix is

$$T(x, t) = T(column, row) = z(column, row)$$

where each new row corresponds to the next value of the time. As no explicit values are given for the time or the position, the plotting program will assume uniform spacing and time steps and will assign each integer values, 1, 2, 3 ... for the plot. Think of these as "the first, second, et cetera" times and the "first, second, et cetera" positions.

The data are read into Maple with the readdata command. We view each row of the matrix as a list (order matters)

$$[value\_1, value\_2, \ldots, value\_numcols]$$

and the collection of rows as a list of lists (listlist):

$$[[row1data], [row2data], \ldots [row\ numrows\ data]]$$

Once we know how many rows or columns there are, it is easy to build the matrix with all the elements in their correct rows and columns. We will show you how to make an explicit matrix up out of these data soon, but first we will work with just the z values as a list of lists.

We use the variable `numcols` to tell Maple the number of elements (columns) in each row, and then have Maple count the number of rows:

```
> restart;        with(plots):        with(LinearAlgebra):              # Initialize
> numcols := 11;                                                        # Number columns
```

The data (values of z) are read into the variable (object or abstract data type) that we name data with Maple's `readdata` command. Because files are stored on your individual computer using the local operating system's conventions for files, just how you specify the file name depends somewhat on the computer system you are on and where the file is on that system. For all but the simple Unix version, we have placed a # sign in front of the command so that Maple will treat the command as a comment. Examine the use of left quote or accent grave, ' as opposed to the normal, ' in the command to delineate the name of the data file. To see what works for you, try deleting the comment symbol and seeing if the command completes with no error message:

```
> # data := readdata('EqHeat_z.dat', numcols);          # Unix, file in working directory
> # data := readdata("Mac G3 HD:DMc:EqHeat_z.dat",numcols):     # Apple MacIntosh
> data := readdata("C:\\Documents and Settings\\rubin\\        # Windows extra \
  My Documents\\Rubin\\Books\\Intro\\Maple\\EqHeat_z.dat",numcols);
```
$$data := [\,[0., 100., 100., 100., 100., 100., 100., 100., 100., 100., 0.],$$
$$[0., 32.5, 59.8, 78.9, 89.5, 92.8, 89.5, 78.9, 59.8, 32.5, 0.], \ldots$$

```
> data := readdata("C:/Documents and Settings/rubin/
  Documents/Rubin/Books/Intro/Maple/EqHeat_z.dat", numcols);    # Also for Windows
```
$$data := [[0., 100., 100., 100., 100., 100., 100., 100., 100., 100., 0.], \ldots$$

As you see here from the Maple output, the variable data is a data object composed of a list [...] containing other lists [[...], [...], ...]. Each sublist is the temperature all along the bar at a different time. To look at any individual part of this list, for example, the second row (the second list):

```
> data[2];
```
$$[0., 32.5, 59.8, 78.9, 89.5, 92.8, 89.5, 78.9, 59.8, 32.5, 0.]$$

In case you have trouble reading these files, you may input the data by hand with the list of lists format, `data := [[...], [...], ...]`.

4.10.6 listplot3d

The `listplot3d` command creates a 3-D plot of a list of lists of numeric values. Remaining arguments are interpreted as plot options. See the plot3d help menu for a list of possible options.

```
> listplot3d(data);                                                    # Basic
> listplot3d(data, style=patch, orientation=[-55,30], shading=z);    # Options
```

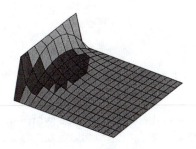

4.11 PLOTTING A MATRIX: MATRIXPLOT*

Another way to make a 3-D plot is with the `matrixplot` command. Though this is an easy command to use, we first need to place the data in a matrix. In Chapter 7 we discuss matrices and give examples of plotting matrices and vectors as well. If you have trouble following the procedure below, you may want to learn some more about matrices in Chapter 7.

We start by reading in the data file. In order to figure out how many rows there are in the matrix without our doing the counting, we use the `nops` (number of operands) command:

```
> restart;   with(plots):      with(linalg):       numcols :=11;
> data := readdata( 'EqHeat_z.dat', numcols );          # Unix, file in working directory
> data := readdata( "Mac G3 HD:DMc:EqHeat_z.dat",numcols ):        # MacIntosh
> data := readdata("C:\\My Documents\\Rubin\\Books\\EqHeat_z.dat", numcols):
                                                                # Windows, note extra \
> data := readdata("C:/Documents and Settings/rubin/
  My Documents/Rubin/Books/Intro/Maple/EqHeat_z.dat", numcols);   # Also Windows
```

$$data := [\,[0., 100., 100., 100., 100., 100., 100., 100., \ldots, 0.\,], \ldots$$

```
> numrows := nops(data);
```
$$numrows := 20$$

We now convert the list named `data` to the matrix named `data_matrix` with the `convert` command:

```
> data_matrix := convert(data,matrix);
```

$$data\_matrix := \begin{bmatrix} 0. & 100. & 100. & 100. & 100. & 100. & 100. & 100. & 100. & 100. & 0. \\ 0. & 32.5 & 59.8 & 78.9 & 89.5 & 92.8 & 89.5 & 78.9 & 59.8 & 32.5 & 0. \\ \vdots & & & & & & & & & & \end{bmatrix}$$

As a check, you should determine the individual element in row 5, column 2. Here we do it for the fifth elements in the second row:

```
> data_matrix[2, 5];                              # Element in row 2, column 5
```
$$89.5$$

4.11.1 Surface Plots with matrixplot*

An entire 2-D matrix is visualized in one step with the `matrixplot` command. This provides a plot that may be grabbed and rotated, which is useful for finding missing elements. The options are much the same as those for `plot3D`:

```
> with(LinearAlgebra):          with(plots):
> Slant := Matrix (<<1,2,3,4> | <5,6,7,8> | <9,10,11,12>>);   # Enter 3 × 4 matrix
> ID := IdentityMatrix(6);                     # The identity matrix of specified dimension
```

$$Slant := \begin{bmatrix} 1 & 5 & 9 \\ 2 & 6 & 10 \\ 3 & 7 & 11 \\ 4 & 8 & 12 \end{bmatrix}, \qquad ID := \begin{bmatrix} 1 & 0 & 0 & 0 & 0 & 0 \\ 0 & 1 & 0 & 0 & 0 & 0 \\ & & \cdots & & & \end{bmatrix}$$

```
> matrixplot( ID, axes = boxed, title = 'Identity Matrix', style = point,
     symbol=CIRCLE, thickness=2, symbolsize = 20 );          # Plot points only
> matrixplot( ID, axes = boxed, title = 'Identity Matrix' );      # Plot surfaces
> matrixplot( Slant, axes = boxed, title = 'Slant Matrix' );      # A new slant
```

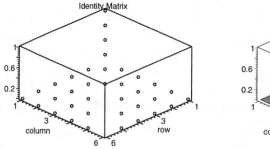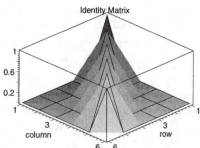

When working with data, the hard part is clearly getting the matrix into Maple. Plotting with the `matrixplot` command is easy. For our data, different rows correspond to different values for the time t, and different columns correspond to different positions x along the bar. The rows will be plotted along the x and y axis in the plot, namely, along the base of the solid figure. The temperature will be plotted as the height of the surface above the base. To help with the visualization, we will also use the color of the surface to convey the temperature (ideally with red being hot and blue cold). We vary the color by using the shading option, with its value set equal to hue; this varies the color through the entire spectrum as a function of the z value:

```
> matrixplot( data_matrix, shading = zhue );                         # Basic
> matrixplot( data_matrix, axes = boxed, labels = [Time, Position, Temp],
title = 'Cooling',orientation = [-20,70], style = patchnogrid, shading = zhue );
```

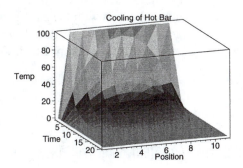

You should see is a colored 3-D surface with many curves drawn on the surface. This is interesting but not necessarily an effective visualization. You are probably the best judge of effectiveness, and to do that you need to try out the options and see what works. So here is another command-line version of matrixplot with many options for things like tick marks at informative places, contours, and better fonts and sizes for the labels:

```
> matrixplot( data_matrix, axes = boxed, labels = [Time, Position, Temp],
  style = patchcontour, labelfont = [HELVETICA,14], axesfont = [HELVETICA,9],
  tickmarks = [4,4,4], title = 'Cooling', titlefont = [HELVETICA,18],
  orientation = [-20,70], shading = zhue );
```

At a Maple prompt, try including and removing some of these options in order to see the effects. Go back to the simplest version of the matrix plot command matrixplot(data) and obtain similar options from within Maple's graphical user interface. In particular, notice how the 3-D effects depend on having made a good choice for the orientation angle.

4.11.2 Non-Uniform x-y Grid with surfdata

The `matrixplot` command assumes the grid spacing is uniform, namely, that the x and y values are uniformly spaced. If they are not, then you need to provide information about how the grid spacing depends on grid location (column and row number). An alternative approach is to read in the set of values (x, y, z) so that you effectively have the function $z(x, y)$. The `surfdata` command is used to plot a surface from a set of (x, y, z) data.

To make a surface plot of data we need data. To start we make a list `data_list` of uniform (x, y) values using the sequence command `seq`. As before, we make each set of (x, y) values into a list and then place all of these sublists into a list of lists. For our temperature example, this placement means we will represent time with the row index, position with the column index, and temperature with the z coordinate. Rather than read in a big file of (x, y, z) values, we will add explicit (x, y) values to our list of data values. We start with the `seq` command that creates a sequence of integers. First we get a sequence of x values from 0 to 100 in steps of 50, and then a sequence of $[x, t]$ with x running from 1 to 1,000 in steps of 100:

```
> numrows;       numcols;
```
$$20, \qquad 11$$

```
> seq( [(j-1) * 10], j = 1..numcols);          # Sequence of x values
```
$$[0], [10], [20], [30], [40], [50], [60], [70], [80], [90], [100]$$

```
> seq( [(i-1) * 50], i = 1..numrows);          # Sequence of t values
```
$$[0], [50], [100], [150], [200], [250], \ldots [950]$$

Now we insert the values of the data matrix to form a list of triplets $[x, y, z]$:

```
> data_list := [seq([ seq( [(i-1) * 50, (j-1)*10,
    data_matrix[i,j]],j = 1..numcols)], i = 1..numrows)];
```

$$\texttt{data\_list} := [[[0, 0, 0.], [0, 10, 100.], [0, 20, 100.], [0, 30, 100.], [0, 40, 100.], \ldots$$

Each point to plot is a set of (x, y, z) values that we are representing in Maple as a sublist. For example, for row 1 and column 2 there is the list

```
> data_list[4,2];
```
$$30$$

We now plot the graph with the `surfdata` command, first in simple form, and then with labels and contours:

```
> surfdata(data_list);                                          # Basic
> surfdata(data_list, labels = [Time, Position, Temperature], axes=boxed,
```

```
style = patchcontour, orientation = [-20,50], shading = zhue); # Options
```

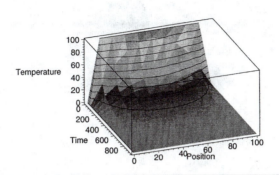

Reading in *(x, y, z)* Data Sets

In a more realistic case our data might be the result of a numerical simulation or a measurement and would reside in an external file. For this purpose we supply the file `EqHeat_xyz.dat` on the CD. We read in these data as before with the `readdata` command, but now with three columns for the values of (x, y, z):

```
> data_list_ex := readdata('EqHeat_xyz.dat', 3);          # Unix read present directory, or:
> data_list_ex := readdata('/home/mcintyre/cpug/heat/EqHeat_xyz.dat',3);
> data_list_ex := readdata("Mac G3 HD:DMc:OSU work:CPUG:EqHeat_xyz.dat", 3):
> data_list_ex:   = readdata("C:/Documents and Settings/rubin/MyDocuments/Rubin/Books/
    Intro/Maple/EqHeat_xyz.dat", 3);                        # Works also on Windows
```

$$data\_list\_ex := [[1., 0., 0.], \cdots$$

```
> data_matrix := convert(data,matrix);                    # Convert data list to matrix
```

$$data\_matrix := \begin{bmatrix} 0. & 100. & 100. & 100. & 100. & 100. & 100. & 100. & 0. \\ \vdots & & & & & & & & \end{bmatrix}$$

```
> type(data, listlist);      type(data, list);           # Is data a list of lists, or a list?
```

$$true, \qquad true$$

```
> type(data_matrix,list);                                 # Is data_matrix a list?
```

$$false$$

where we have tested if `data_matrix` is an array, and if `data` is an array. We then convert from a list of lists to a matrix with the `convert` command:

```
> convert(data, matrix);                                  # Convert variable data to matrix
```

$$\begin{bmatrix} 0. & 100. & 100. & 100. & 100. & 100. & 100. & 100. & 100. & 100. & 0. \\ \vdots & & & & & & & & & & \end{bmatrix}$$

```
> matrixplot( data);                                   # Will work only if data is a matrix
```

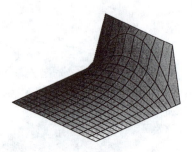

```
> convert(data, listlist);                             # Convert variable data to list of list
> listplot3d(data);                                    # Works only if data is a list; same plot
```

$$[[0., 100., 100., 100., 100., 100., 100., 100., 100., 100., 0.], \ldots$$

4.12 ANIMATIONS OF DATA*

Below we present an animated plot of the wave motion resulting from plucking a string. The string is hanging under its own weight and is affected by friction.[3] This animation comes from a numerical simulation [CP 05] that outputs its results to a file in the gnuplot format used for surface $z(x, y)$ plots. As described in §4.10.5, the data are in the form of a matrix of z values, with the rows of the matrix separated by blank lines. The first row corresponds to time 1, with the place in the row corresponding to different x values. The second row contains all the z values for time 2, and so forth. As we see in the figures, the surface plot shows many ripples corresponding to oscillations of the string, but it is not nearly as effective a visualization as playing the animation below.

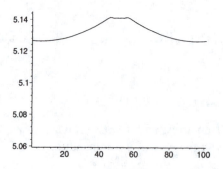

In this section we indicate the steps needed to input numerical data in surface

---

[3]We thank Juan Vanegas for this example.

plot format and convert it into an animation. We start by forming a very long list of data named `data` from the file `function.dat` (Unix reads from the present directory, Windows requires the full path name):

```
> data := readdata( 'function.dat', 1, float ):                    # Unix
> data := readdata( "C:/Documents and Settings/rubin/
      My Documents/Rubin/Books/function.dat", 1, float):       # Windows, note \
> data[1];      data[4];                          # Examine individual elements in a list
```
$$5.126560431, \qquad 5.126343673$$
```
> DATA := array(data):                            # Covert list data to array DATA
> DATA[1];      DATA[4];
```
$$5.126560431, \qquad 5.126343673$$

We next break up the array DATA into a list of sublists. The first sublist `funct[1]` corresponds to row 1 of the original matrix, the second sublist, `funct[2]` corresponds to row 2 of the original matrix, and so forth:

```
> for t from 0 by 1 to 199 do func[t] := [seq(DATA[i],i=101*t+1..101*(t+1))]:
      # For loop repeats for multiple t values
> end do:
```

As a check, we print out the sublist `func[1]`. It is the first row of input and will be the first frame of the movie:

```
> func[1];                                        # Print out individual row
```
$$[5.126560431, 5.126467879, 5.126395193, 5.126342347, 5.126296259, \ldots 5.126560431]$$

Now that we know that the data look good, we plot several of the frames we will put together to form the movie:

```
> listplot( func[0] ); listplot( func[20] );
```

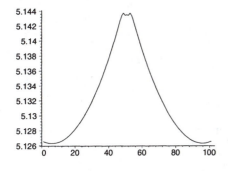 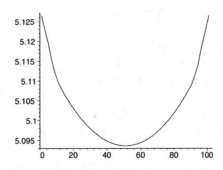

To create the movie, we use the `display` command. Yet, if we try to display several frames together, we just get multiple frames on top of each other. In order not to display all of the frames on top of each other, we use the `seq` command to form a time-ordered sequence of plots. Hence, we have created an animation.

```
> display(seq(listplot( func[t]), t = 1..199), insequence = true) ;# Animation
```

4.13 KEY WORDS AND CONCEPTS

abstract	data type	abscissa	animation
contour plot	dependent variable	implicit plot	independent variable
list	matrix	nonlinear functions	ordinate set
sequence	surface plot	2-D plot	parametric plot
polar plot	potential energy		

1. Is there a direct way of measuring potential energy in nature?
2. Is there a reason electric charges occur always in integer values?
3. How does an abstract data type differ from an algebraic symbol?
4. How do you decide if a variable is *independent* or *dependent*?
5. When might it be a bad idea to use color in your plotting?
6. List three ways in which you may change the interpretation of data by changing the way in which it is presented.
7. What might be a *dishonest* way of presenting your data?
8. Give examples of the type of data that may be appropriate for 1-D, 2-D, 3-D, and 4-D visualizations.
9. When are animations a useful way to display data?
10. How, in a mathematical sense, does a phase-space (parametric) plot differ from an ordinary 2-D plot?
11. What is the difference between a list and a set?
12. How is a table of numerical data similar to, and different from, a mathematical function?
13. Give an example or two of the types of functions that would be visualized best with each of the following plots:
    a. 2-D plot
    b. 3-D plot
    c. multifunction plot
    d. parametric plot
    e. animation
    f. 3-D animation
14. Explain in just a few words what is meant by
    a. an abstract data type
    b. a parametric or phase-space plot
    c. a function of three variables
    d. a set of three variables
    e. a list of three variables

4.14 SUPPLEMENTARY EXERCISES

1. On a single graph, display the functions $x^3 \sin(x)$, $x^3 \cos(x)$, and $x \log(x)$, each in a different color. Use an equal negative and positive x range, and pick that range to obtain the most interesting comparison of the three functions.

2. A graphical approach to solving equations plots the right- and left-hand sides of an equation as two separate functions, and then finds the solution as the value of the abscissa at which the two curves intersect. Use Maple's ability to plot several functions in the same graph to determine the approximate solutions of the following equations:
   a. $\sin(x) = x^2$,
   b. $x^2 + 6x + 1 = 0$,
   c. $H^3 - 9H^2 + 4 = 0$.

3. Do a graphical experiment in which you prove to yourself these very useful mathematical facts:
   a. The exponent e^x grows faster than any power x^n.
   b. The logarithm $\ln(x)$ grows slower than any power x^n. *Hint:* To avoid overflow problems with very large x values, you may want to make semi-log plots.

4. Do a graphical experiment to find the value of n for which these equations are true:
   a. $n \sin(2x) = \sin(x) \cos(x)$,
   b. $n \cos(x)^2 = 1 + \cos(2x)$.

5. If two tones very close in frequency are played together, your ear hears them as a single tone with an oscillating amplitude. Make plots as a function of time of the results of adding the two sine functions

$$\sin(100\,t) + \sin(b\,t).$$

Make a series of plots for b in the range

$$90 < b < 100.$$

Make sure to plot for a long enough range of t values to see at least three cycles of any periodic behavior.

6. Here are nine measurements given in the form (x, y):

   (0, 10.6), (25, 16.0), (50, 45.0), (75, 83.5), (100, 52.8), (125, 19.9), (150, 10.8), (175, 8.25), (200, 4.7)

   Make a plot of these data points.

7. The orbits of planets and comets are known to follow conic sections. Conic sections are the 2-D curves formed when a cone is cut (sectioned) by a plane and are given by the parametric equations in which s is the parameter:
   a. Hyperbola: $(x(s),\ y(s)) = (4\cosh(s),\ 1.4\sinh(s))$
   b. Ellipse: $(x(s),\ y(s)) = (4\cos(s),\ 1.4\sin(s))$
   c. Parabola: $(x(s),\ y(s)) = (s\cos(\theta) - s^2\sin(\theta),\ s^2\cos(\theta) + s\sin(\theta))$, $\theta =$ arbitrary parameter

Make parametric plots of these conic sections. Cover as much range as is needed for the parameter s in order to obtain the full shapes.

8. Planetary orbits are best described by the polar-coordinate form of the conic section:

$$\frac{\alpha}{r} = 1 + \varepsilon \cos(\theta)$$

where ε is the eccentricity and $2\,\alpha$ is the *lataus rectum* of the orbit. An ellipse occurs when $0 < \varepsilon < 1$, a hyperbola for $\varepsilon > 1$, and a parabola for $\varepsilon = 1$. Make polar plots of these three kinds of orbits by using different values of ε. Try also various values for the parameter α (it is inversely proportional to the total energy of the planet).

9. Make a surface plot of the potential:

$$V(x,\,y) = \frac{e^{(-r)}}{r}\cos\left(\frac{x}{r}\right)$$

where $r = \sqrt{x^2 + y^2}$.

10. Make a contour plot of this same potential.

11. A standing wave on a string is described by the equation

$$y(x,\,t) = \sin(10\,x)\cos(12\,t)$$

where x is the distance along the string, y is the height of the disturbance, and t is the time.

a. Create an animation of this function.

b. Create a surface plot of this function, and see if you agree with us that it is not as revealing as the animation.

12. A traveling wave on a string is described by the equation

$$y(x,\,t) = \sin(10\,x - 12\,t)$$

where x is the distance along the string, y is the height of the disturbance, and t is the time.

a. Create an animation of this function.

b. Create a surface plot of this function, and see if you agree with us that it is not as revealing as the animation.

13. Plot the function $f(x) = \sec(x) + 4$ over the interval $[0,\,4\,\pi]$. Seeing that Maple's automatic scaling does not work well here, you will need to specify a range for the ordinates to obtain a useful visualization.

14. Given the points $(1, 0.53)$, $(1.5, 0.65)$, $(2, 0.91)$, $(2.5, 0.95)$, and $(3, 1.10)$, create a plot containing these points as well as the functions $a(x) = \sin\left(\frac{x}{2}\right)$, $b(x) = \frac{x^2}{5}$. Which function fits the data best?

Chapter Five

Solving Equations, Differentiation; Building Towers

5.1 PROBLEM: MAXIMUM HEIGHT OF A TOWER

The Washington monument in the District of Columbia is 555 feet tall and is constructed from 36,000 white granite stones. The weighty marble and granite walls at the base are 15 feet thick, tapering to 18 inches thick at the top of the shaft. [USN&WR]

In our quest to rise above our fellow beings, we wish to build a really tall tower [Zach 96]. We are not that good with big plans, but we are really good at building one-level structures, and so we plan to stack our one-level structures on top of one another until we reach the desired height. Your **problem** is to incorporate into your design the fact that all materials compress when made to bear weight, and thereby to see how this limits the maximum height of the tower.

5.2 MODEL: BLOCK STACKING

We model each level of the tower as a block of thickness t. By working with two blocks in our garage, we have determined that when one block is placed atop another, there is a very small decrease a in the thickness t of the lower block:

$$t \rightarrow t - a. \tag{5.1}$$

After some hard mental processing, we deduce that if we have three blocks stacked atop each other, as in Figure 5.1, then the top block would have thickness t, the middle block thickness $t - a$, and the bottom block $t - 2a$. The double compression

Figure 5.1 A stack of blocks. Observe how the bottom blocks get thinner.

of the bottom block arises because it must support the weight of the two blocks atop it.

5.2.1 Model Problem

Now that we have some idea of the model and tools we are able to apply to our problem, we reformulate it to one we are able to solve. On the other hand, while this is an important part of problem solving, it does means that when we are done solving our problem, we must *verify* that we have a correct mathematical solution and then *validate* that our mathematical solution solves the physical problem:

1. Compute the height of a five-block tower by explicitly entering and summing the thickness of each of the blocks. Observe how the sum is accumulated and use that to deduce an algebraic expression for the height.
2. Suppose you had $10,000$ blocks. You do not want to type in all those terms. Prove that the height H of a tower composed of n levels is:

$$H = nt - \frac{1}{2}n(n-1)a. \qquad (5.2)$$

   Hint: First prove that the sum of the first n integers is $n(n+1)/2$.
3. Check that your expression gives the same answer for the five-story tower as you worked out by hand.
4. Express H as a function $H(n, t, a)$ of three variables.
5. Use your function to determine, for arbitrary t and a, the number of blocks needed to erect a tower of height 200.
6. How many blocks are needed to make a tower of height 200 feet for $t = 15$ feet and $a = 0.001t$?
7. One way of defining maximum height is to imagine adding another level to the tower but not have its height increase (later on we will use a different definition of the maximum height). This is equivalent to finding a solution to the equation

$$H(N_{max}) = H(N_{max} + 1) \qquad (5.3)$$

   Find the algebraic value of N_{max} that satisfies (5.3).
8. Show that the solution to (5.3) corresponds to slipping the additional block onto the bottom of the stack and having it shrink to zero thickness.
9. If $t = 15$ feet and $a = 0.001t$, what is the maximum height of the tower?
10. If we think of N_{max} as a continuous variable and take a mathematical point of view, then the maximum height occurs at the point where an infinitesimal change in n leads to no change at all in the tower's height. Calculus tells us that this occurs when the derivative vanishes, that is, when

$$\frac{dH(n, t, a)}{dn} = 0. \qquad (5.4)$$

Determine this derivative.

11. Determine the value of n that solves (5.4).

12. Explain in your own words why this is not the same as the previous definition we used for maximum.

13. Plot up the results as a check. State in your own words how your graph shows the relation between the two definitions of maximum.

5.3 MATH: EQUATIONS AS CHALLENGES

Consider the equation:

$$a\,x^{20} + b\,x = -c. \tag{5.5}$$

You may think of this equation as a statement of mathematical fact: that the right-hand and left-hand sides of the equation have the same value. You may also view this equation as a challenge: *for given values of the parameters* a, b, *and* c, *find some values of* x *that make both sides equal.* Although equations usually have variables on both sides of the equal sign, nevertheless, it is also legitimate to write them in generic form:

$$f(x) = 0, \tag{5.6}$$
$$a\,x^{20} + bx + c = 0, \tag{5.7}$$

where the second version is for our problem. If $f(x)$ is a symbolic expression, then Maple will automatically search for a symbolic solution of $f(x) = 0$. If $f(x)$ is numeric (contains floats or decimal points), then Maple will conduct a numerical search. We are not using the words "search" and "challenge" just to make mathematics seem exciting. For an arbitrary $f(x)$, there is no guarantee that a solution exists or that Maple will find it even if one does exist.

In many cases, the function $f(x)$ has a form for which no analytic solution exists. To prove the point, even the simple equation

$$x \sin x = 1 \tag{5.8}$$

does not have analytic solutions. However, there may be numeric ones, which leads to the somewhat philosophical question "If it is possible to find a numerical solution, does that mean we should also be able to find an analytic solution if we were smarter?" In some cases the answer is "no," in other cases "yes," and in others "maybe." In any case, it is usually faster for Maple to find a numerical solution than an analytic one. Therefore, if your ultimate interest is in a numerical solution, for example to plot a graph, then it makes good sense to have Maple solve the equation numerically in the first place. If you truly want an analytic solution, you may have to rearrange or simplify the equation so that Maple has a better chance with it, or even try some other program, like Mathematica, that employs different algorithms.

5.4 SOLVING A SINGLE EQUATION: SOLVE, FSOLVE

Maple solves equations with the `solve` command. Let us try it for the general quadratic equation:

```
> solve (a * x^2 + b*x + c = 0, x);          # Find an x that solves the 1st argument
> solve (a * x^2 + b*x = -c, x);                # Alternate way of writing equation
```

$$\frac{-b + \sqrt{b^2 - 4\,a\,c}}{2\,a}, \qquad \frac{-b - \sqrt{b^2 - 4\,a\,c}}{2\,a}$$

We see that there are two roots, and if you look among what might appear to be a garble of symbols, you will see that Maple separates them by a comma (we added some space to make it clearer). Take note that the first argument to `solve` is the equation to be solved, and the second argument is the variable whose value we want as the solution. We suspect that you think it obvious that since $a\,x^2 + b\,x + c = 0$ is a quadratic equation in x, that Maple should know that you want the x values that solve it. Yet from an algebraic point of view, the parameters a, b, and c are also symbols for variables, and you may be interested in the solution of this equation for one of them. So try it and observe the differences:

```
>                                                              # Solve the equation for a, b, and then c
```

As mentioned before, the conventional way to present an equation to be solved is $f(x) = 0$. Yet once one knows the convention, it is no longer necessary to include the $= 0$ part of the equation. For this reason the same `solve` command may be used with just $f(x)$:

```
> solve (a * x^2 + b*x + c, x);                  # Find an x that is a root of 1st argument
```

Sometimes the roots of an expression may be a real number, sometimes a complex number containing the symbol I, sometimes an algebraic expression, and sometimes they cannot be found. As long as the solution is exact, the `solve` command is applicable:

```
>                                                              # Find roots of x^2 - 1, x^2 + 1, x^2 + b
```

Yet sometimes even a simple function does not have exact roots:

```
> solve(x * sin(x) -1);                              # Find the zeros of x sin(x) - 1
```

$$\text{RootOf}(\_Z \sin(\_Z) - 1)$$

Confusion seems appropriate after looking at Maple's response of $\text{RootOf}()$. This is not an answer, but rather an admission of defeat from the internal algorithm used by `solve`. In this case, the transcendental equation $x \sin x - 1 = 0$ does not have an analytic solution, and so it is no surprise that Maple fails. However, because Maple does not know that the analytic solution truly does not exist, but only that it was unable to find it, Maple blames itself and gives you an indication of where it failed. Knowledge of how and where Maple fails may be useful for advanced work, but for beginners it is easier to rearrange the equation and try again. (Soon we will see that the command `fsolve` solves this equation numerically.)

Various formulas give closed-form expressions for the roots of quadratic, cubic, and quartic polynomials. And of course Maple knows them. Maple has tricks for higher-order polynomials, and it will try to use them as much as possible. However, there are some higher-order polynomials whose roots Maple cannot find. We give here a case that works, and invite you to change some powers or add some terms until Maple fails (at least for some of the roots):

```
> solve (x^6 + 2 * x^2 + 3, x);                    # Maple succeeds here
```

$$I, -I, -\frac{\sqrt{2+2I\sqrt{11}}}{2}, \frac{\sqrt{2+2I\sqrt{11}}}{2}, -\frac{\sqrt{2-2I\sqrt{11}}}{2}, \frac{\sqrt{2-2I\sqrt{11}}}{2}$$

```
> solve(x^8 + 2 * x^3 + 5, x) ;
```

$$\mathrm{RootOf}(\%1, index = 1), \ldots$$

```
>                                            # Modify parameters until Maple succeeds
```

5.4.1 Verifying Solutions: eval

It is often convenient to use a variable to represent the equation to be solved and thereby avoid rewriting it many times and having very long commands. Suppose the equation to solve contains the product of factors (which makes it easy for us and Maple to know what the solution should be):

$$(x-a)^2 (x+b)^3 (x-c) = 0. \tag{5.9}$$

We use a symbol like `eqn` to represent the entire equation and then work with it:

```
> eqn := (x-a)^2 * (x+b)^3 *(x-c) = 0;              # Enter equation
```

$$eqn := (x-a)^2 (x+b)^3 (x-c) = 0$$

```
> expand(eqn);                                     # The full form of the equation
```

$$x^6 - x^5 c + 3x^5 b - 3x^4 bc + 3x^4 b^2 - 3x^3 b^2 c + x^3 b^3 - \ldots$$

```
> solve (eqn, x);                          # Solve for roots (obvious from factored form)
```

$$c, \ a, \ a, \ -b, \ -b, \ -b$$

Once we have a solution, we verify it by substituting it back into the equation with the `eval` command:

```
> eval(eqn, x = a);                        # Evaluate equation with substituted solution
```

$$0 = 0$$

5.4.2 Symbolic Solution: roots

The `solve` command is useful for solving equations. Yet sometimes you may have more specialized needs. As an example, you may want to find all the zeros or roots of a polynomial, as well as their multiplicity. The command `roots` is a powerful tool for finding the exact roots of a polynomial (but not the zeros of a transcendental equation). However, it is specialized to mathematical purposes, and we have often found its use less robust and less obvious than `solve`. However, it nicely tells us the multiplicity of the root:

```
> 'roots (x^2 - 1)' = roots (x^2 - 1);
```
$$roots(x^2 - 1) = [\,[1, 1], [-1, 1]\,]$$

Here the notation `[-1,1]` in the output means that -1 is a root with multiplicity 1. However, `roots` is rather limited in that it only works if it is possible to write the roots as algebraic expressions with real integers:

```
> 'roots (x^2 + 1)' = roots (x^2 + 1);           # Fails as they are imaginary
```
$$roots(x^2 + 1) = [\,]$$

In this last case the roots are obviously imaginary, so `roots` just quits. However, adding I as a second argument to `roots` extends the capability of the algorithm to complex numbers:

```
> 'roots( x^2 + 1, I )' = roots ( x^2 + 1, I );        # Find root, complex number OK
> 'roots( x^4 - 4,sqrt(2) )' = roots( x^4-4,sqrt(2) );      # Try and explain
```

$$roots(x^2 + 1, I) = [\,[-I, 1], [I, 1]\,]$$
$$roots(x^4 - 4, \sqrt{2}) = [\,[-\sqrt{2}, 1], [\sqrt{2}, 1]\,]$$

5.4.3 Numerical Solution: fsolve

If `solve` fails to find a solution, or if all you want is a numerical solution, then `fsolve`, which finds solutions numerically, is the tool to use. As a case in point, we have already seen that `solve` cannot solve $x \sin x = 1$, yet Figure 5.2 should convince you that there are an infinite number of x values at which $x \sin x = 1$. The problem is that these values are not exact numbers. This calls for the command `fsolve`, which works just like `solve`, except it uses floating-point numbers and finds numerical solutions:

```
> fsolve (x * sin(x) - 1., x);
```
$$-1.114157141$$

Of course, the above solution is only one solution out of an infinite number, but

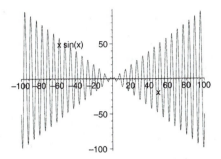

Figure 5.2 A plot showing that $x \sin x$ passes through zero endlessly.

that is because `fsolve` finds only one solution at a time. To find more solutions (one at a time), restrict the range of x by modifying the second argument to provide a range:

```
> fsolve (x * sin(x) - 1, x = 0..2);        # Restrict x to range 0 − 2
> fsolve (x * sin(x) - 1, x = 2..4);        # Restrict x to range 2 − 4
```
$$1.114157141, \qquad 2.772604708$$

5.5 SOLVING SIMULTANEOUS EQUATIONS (SETS)

5.5.1 Algebraic Equations

If you have a few simultaneous equations to solve, then `solve` works just fine. If you have a large number, say five or more, then it is probably more convenient and elegant to set your problem in matrix form and use the techniques of linear algebra. We start with two simultaneous equations in two unknowns x and y:

$$x + 3y + 4 = 41, \qquad (5.10)$$
$$5x + 6y + 7 = 20. \qquad (5.11)$$

First we assign obvious variable names to the equations:

```
> eqn1 := x + 3*y + 4 = 41;
> eqn2 := 5*x + 6*y + 7 = 20;
```
$$eqn1 := x + 3\,y + 4 = 41, \qquad eqn2 := 5\,x + 6\,y + 7 = 20$$

Then we group this set of equations together within braces as {eqn1, eqn2} to form the first argument to `solve`. Recall, a *set* is an unordered sequence of distinct expressions enclosed in braces. As the second argument, we enter the set of variables we want to solve for:

```
> solve({eqn1, eqn2}, {x, y});
```

$$\{y = \frac{172}{9}, \qquad x = \frac{-61}{3}\}$$

Observe how Maple uses braces for its answer *set*. Verify that the same solution is obtained regardless of the order of the equations {eqn1, eqn2} in their set, or of the variables {x,y} in their set:

```
>                                         # Enter interchanged equations and variables
```

This example was fairly obvious, in part, because we used a standard notation for the unknowns and had numerical values for the parameters. Yet consider now the two simultaneous equations:

$$a + 3b + 4c = 41, \tag{5.12}$$
$$5a + 6b + 7c = 20. \tag{5.13}$$

There are clearly two equations and three unknowns a, b, and c. The rules of mathematics being as they are, this means it is possible to solve for any two of the unknowns in terms of the other one, but one unknown will always remain. As before, we first define variable names as labels for the equations:

```
> eqn1 := a + 3*b + 4*c = 41;          eqn2 := 5*a + 6*b + 7*c = 20;
```

$$eqn1 := a + 3b + 4c = 41 \qquad eqn2 := 5a + 6b + 7c = 20$$

We solve simultaneously for {a, b} in terms of the c:

```
> solve( {eqn1, eqn2}, {a, b} );
```

$$\{b = -\frac{13c}{9} + \frac{185}{9}, \qquad a = \frac{c}{3} - \frac{62}{3}\}$$

Modify this solution so that it solves for {b,c} in terms of a.

5.5.2 Numeric Equations

For a change of pace, let us say you want a *numerical* solution of the same two simultaneous equations we previously solved exactly,

$$x + 3y + 4 = 41,$$
$$5x + 6y + 7 = 20.$$

The numerical solution should be faster and more reliable than the exact solution, yet Maple knows that it knows the exact solution, and so returns that from fsolve. However we will get the numerical solution if we use decimal numbers in the equations:

```
>                                          # Enter eqn1, eqn2 with decimals
>                                          # Solve {eqn1,eqn2} with fsolve
```

5.5.3 Nonlinear Equations

Nonlinear equations are exactly what their name implies. They are equations containing functions that are not linear. Whereas quadratic, cubic, and quartic equations are all nonlinear by this definition, Maple knows the closed-form solutions to these types of equations and has no trouble applying them. However, there may not be analytic solutions to other, even simple, nonlinear equations. In those cases the best that Maple does is to find numerical solutions.

Consider the simultaneous, nonlinear equations:

$$\sin(x) + 3\cos(y) = 1, \qquad\qquad (5.14)$$
$$x^2 + y^3 = 12. \qquad\qquad (5.15)$$

Enter these equations as a set and try solving them with `solve`. You should not find much success. So, try solving them with `fsolve`. Use `eval` to check how well the solution satisfies the equations:

```
> eval( eqn1, {x = .  .  , y = .  .} )
> eval( eqn2, {x = .  .  , y = .  .} )
```

5.6 SOLUTION TO TOWER PROBLEM

q: Determine an algebraic expression for the height of a five-block tower. ♠

```
> H := t + (t - a) + (t - 2*a) + (t - 3*a) + (t - 4*a);
```
$$H := 5t - 10a$$

q: Prove that the sum of the first n integers is $n(n+1)/2$. ♠

```
> Sum( i, i = 1..n ) = sum( i, i = 1..n );
> factor( % );
```
$$\sum_{i=1}^{n} i = \frac{(n+1)^2}{2} - \frac{n}{2} - \frac{1}{2}$$
$$\sum_{i=1}^{n} i = \frac{n(n+1)}{2}$$

q: Explain why the height of the tower consisting of n levels is:
$$H = nt - n(n-1)a/2. \quad ♠$$

The total height of n noncompressed blocks is nt. However, with our model, each block other than the top one gets compressed. Consequently, the total height is computed by adding the heights of n successively thinner blocks:

$$H = t + (t - a) + (t - 2a) + \ldots + (n - 1)a$$
$$= nt - a - 2a - \ldots - (n - 1)a = nt - a[1 + 2 + 3 + \ldots + (n - 1)]$$

However, we recognize the series here as the one we have previously summed and so substitute:

```
> H := n*t - a * sum( i, i = 1..n-1 );
> H := n*t - a * factor( sum( i, i = 1..n-1 ) );          # Factor sum
```

$$H := n\,t - a\left(\frac{1}{2}\,n^2 - \frac{1}{2}\,n\right)$$

$$H := n\,t - \frac{a\,n\,(n-1)}{2}$$

q: Check that this is the same answer as before for a five-story tower. ♠

```
> H = eval( H, n=5 );                                     # Evaluate H for n = 5
```

$$n\,t - \frac{a\,n\,(n-1)}{2} = 5\,t - 10\,a$$

This agrees with the explicit five-term calculation, namely, $H = 5\,t - 10\,a$.

q: Express H as a function of three variables, $Hf(n, t, a)$. ♠

```
> Hf := (n, t, a) -> n*t - a*n*(n-1) / 2;
```

$$Hf := (n,\, t,\, a) \to n\,t - \frac{1}{2}\,a\,n\,(n-1)$$

q: Use your function and Maple's `solve` command to determine how many blocks n are needed to make a tower of height 200 for arbitrary t and a. ♠

```
> 'n' = solve( Hf(n, t, a) = 200, n );
```

$$n = \left(\frac{2\,t + a + \sqrt{4\,t^2 + 4\,t\,a + a^2 - 1600\,a}}{2\,a},\; \frac{2\,t + a - \sqrt{4\,t^2 + 4\,t\,a + a^2 - 1600\,a}}{2\,a}\right)$$

We see that there are two solutions for arbitrary t and a, as expected for a quadratic equation. We suspect that only one of them will be physically meaningful.

q: Using your function, solve for the number of blocks of thickness $t = 15$ feet needed to make a tower of height 200 feet if the compression $a = 0.001t$. ♠

```
> 'n' = solve( 200 = Hf(n, 15, 0.001*15 ), n );
```

$$n = (1987.583372,\, 13.41662797)$$

We get two answers, $n = 1987.6$ and $n = 13.4$, neither of them an integer. Because $13 \times 15 = 195$ and $14 \times 15 = 210$, the answer 13.4 is the one we would expect. The 1,988-block tower seems unreasonable and is related to a flaw in our model (as we shall see).

q: Is it possible within our model to add another level to the tower but not have its height increase? Explain how the answer to this question is equivalent to finding a solution to the equation $H(N_{max}) = H(N_{max} + 1)$. ♠

This definition of "maximum" corresponds to adding another block to the tower and not having it get any higher. In some sense this is the maximum height, as adding another block beyond this will actually make the tower shorter in our model. What is happening is that at $n = N_{max}$, the bottom block is being squeezed to zero thickness, and so adding another block gives the bottom block negative thickness. This is clearly a breakdown of our simple model.

q: Find the algebraic value of N_{max} that satisfies this last equation. ♠

```
> restart:     Hf := (n,t,a) -> n*t - a*n*(n-1) / 2;
```

$$Hf := (n, t, a) \to nt - \frac{1}{2}an(n-1)$$

Here we placed both commands on one line and used a colon after `restart` to suppress Maple's response. Now we solve it:

```
> Nmax := solve( Hf(n, t, a) - Hf(n+1, t, a), n );
```

$$Nmax := \frac{t}{a}$$

q: If $t = 15$ feet and $a = 0.001t$, what is the maximum height of the tower? ♠

```
> t := 15;     a := 0.001*t;     Nmax;
```

$$t := 15, \qquad a := 0.015, \qquad 1000.000000$$

We could also do the evaluation more explicitly with `eval`:

```
> Nmax := solve( Hf(n, t, a) - Hf(n+1, t, a), n );
> eval(Nmax, [a = 0.015, t = 15]);
```

$$Nmax := \frac{t}{a}$$

q: Test your function both numerically and symbolically by verifying that adding another level to the maximum number of levels does not increase the height. ♠

```
> Nmax := t/a;
> Hf( Nmax + 1, t, a); Hf(Nmax, t, a);          factor(%);
```

$$\frac{(\frac{t}{a} + 1)t}{2}, \qquad \frac{t^2}{a} - \frac{t(\frac{t}{a} - 1)}{2}, \qquad \frac{t(t+a)}{2a}$$

where we used the `factor` command for simplification.

5.7 DIFFERENTIATION: LIMIT, DIFF, D

Calculus was invented, at least from our point of view, to help solve physics problems. Even today calculus is essential for solving scientific problems, and Maple is good at calculus. When speaking of calculus we usually think of differentiation, integration, and differential equations. We study differentiation in this chapter, integration in Chapter 6, and differential equations in Chapter 15.

Derivatives arose in the study of kinematics, where there was the need to define the velocity of an object at each instant of time. Specifically, instantaneous velocity is defined as the limit of the rate of change of position, for infinitesimally small time intervals:

```
> v(t) = Limit( (x(t + Delta) - x(t) )/Delta, Delta = 0);
```

$$v(t) = \lim_{\Delta \to 0} \frac{x(t + \Delta) - x(t)}{\Delta}$$

Of course you should recognize this limit as the definition of derivative. Indeed, if we use the active form of Maple's `limit` command, we do get the derivative:

```
> Limit( (x(t+Delta)-x(t)) / Delta, Delta = 0 ) =
    limit( (x(t+Delta)-x(t)) / Delta, Delta = 0 );
```

$$\lim_{\Delta \to 0} \frac{x(t + \Delta) - x(t)}{\Delta} = D(x)(t)$$

Here $D(x)$ indicates the derivative of x, and (t) a function of time t.

Maple has the two commands `diff` and `D` for differentiation. The most straightforward is `diff`, although `D` is more powerful and useful. You give `diff` an expression or a function, and it returns the derivative as an expression. However, if you want your derivative to be a function or a mapping, then use `D`. (Alternatively, you may use `unapply` to convert `diff`'s expression into a function.)

5.7.1 Derivative as Expressions: diff

```
> Diff( sin(x), x );                                      # Inert, but pretty diff
```

$$\frac{d}{dx} \sin(x)$$

```
> diff( sin(x), x );                                      # Active form of diff
```

$$\cos(x)$$

Just as we have seen with `sum` and `Sum`, capitalizing the first letter of `diff` produces the inert form `Diff`. In spite of inert forms doing no work, they are valuable as a check that Maple will do the computation you intend:

```
>  Diff( sin(x), x )  = diff( sin(x), x );               # Derivative of expression
> 'diff( sin(x), x )' = diff( sin(x), x );               # Delayed execution on LHS
```

$$\frac{d}{dx} \sin(x) = \cos(x)$$

Here we took the derivative of a built-in function $\sin(x)$. It is also legitimate to use `diff` to take the derivative of a user-defined function:

```
> f := (x) -> ln(x) / (1-x);                             # Define function f(x) = ln(x)/(1 - x)
```

$$f := x \to \frac{\ln(x)}{1 - x}$$

```
> Diff( f(x), x ) = diff( f(x), x );
```

$$\frac{d}{dx}\left(\frac{\ln(x)}{1-x}\right) = \frac{1}{x\,(1-x)} + \frac{\ln(x)}{(1-x)^2}$$

Here we use `diff` to take the derivative of an expression:

```
> Diff( x^7 / (1-x), x ) = diff ( x^7 / (1-x), x);
```

$$\frac{d}{dx}\left(\frac{x^7}{1-x}\right) = \frac{7\,x^6}{1-x} + \frac{x^7}{(1-x)^2}$$

5.7.2 Second Derivatives

To take a second derivative, you differentiate twice in succession, either by repeating the `diff` command or by repeating the x part:

```
> f := (x) -> sin(x);
```

$$f := \sin$$

```
> 'diff( f(x), x )' = diff( f(x), x );                    # Single quotes for delayed execution
```

$$\frac{d}{dx}\,\mathrm{f}(x) = \cos(x)$$

```
> 'diff( %, x )' = diff( %, x );
```

$$\frac{d}{dx}\left(\frac{d}{dx}\,\mathrm{f}(x) = \cos(x)\right) = (-\sin(x) = -\sin(x))$$

```
> Diff( f, x, x ) = diff( f(x), x, x );                   # Curly d's indicate partial derivatives
```

$$\frac{\partial^2}{\partial x^2}\,\sin = -\sin(x)$$

In these commands we started with the function $f(x) = \sin x$ and took the derivative once with respect to x to get df/dx, and then took the derivative of the derivative $d(df/dx)/dx$. Executing the above on $f(x)$, as you see, returns us to $-\sin(x)$. Taking a derivative of some function twice gives you the second derivative $d^2 f/dx^2$.

Another notation for second derivative is to use Maple's *sequence operator* `$`. This operator says to repeat the preceding symbol by the number of times indicated after it. To name an instance, `x$2` is the same as `,x,x`. Thus we express higher derivatives in the succinct forms:

```
> restart; f := (x) -> sin(x);
```

$$f := \sin$$

```
> 'diff( f, x$2 )' = diff( f(x), x$2 );          # Derivative with respect to x²
```

$$\frac{\partial^2}{\partial x^2} f = -\sin(x)$$

```
> 'diff( f, x$3 )' = diff( f(x), x$3 );          # Derivative with respect to x³
```

$$\frac{\partial^3}{\partial x^3} f = -\cos(x)$$

```
> Diff( x^7 / (1-x), x$2 ) = diff ( x^7 / (1-x), x$2 );     # Second derivative
```

$$\frac{d^2}{dx^2} \left(\frac{x^7}{1-x} \right) = \frac{42\,x^5}{1-x} + \frac{14\,x^6}{(1-x)^2} + \frac{2\,x^7}{(1-x)^3}$$

Exercise: Take the first derivative twice of $f(x) = \frac{\ln x}{1-x}$ and see if you get the same answer as taking the second derivative just once. ♠

5.7.3 Partial Derivatives with diff*

If it is legal only only to take a derivative with respect to a variable, then why must we always enter that variable into `diff`? The answer is not trivial. On occasion the expression to differentiate may be one like $f(x) = \sin(x)^b$. To Maple, both x and b are equally good variables for differentiation, and so Maple must be told which one you would like to differentiate with respect to. At the prompts below, take the derivatives and see the differences:

```
>                                          # Derivative of sin(x)ᵇ with respect to x
>                                          # Derivative of sin(x)ᵇ with respect to b
```

When a function contains more than one variable, then the differentiation process is called *partial differentiation*. The resulting derivatives are called *partial derivatives* and in mathematics are denoted with curly d's, for example, $\partial f(x, y)/\partial y$. In addition, since there are several variables, another type of second derivative is formed by differentiating once with respect to each of two different variables. By way of example, we form $\frac{\partial^2}{\partial y\,\partial x} \sin(x)^y$ by first differentiating with respect to x, and then y:

```
> Diff( (sin(x))^y, x, y );          # 2nd partial derivative with respect to x, y
```

$$\frac{\partial^2}{\partial y\,\partial x} \sin(x)^y$$

```
> diff( (sin(x))^y, x, y );                                  # Active form
```

$$\frac{\sin(x)^y \ln(\sin(x))\, y \cos(x)}{\sin(x)} + \frac{\sin(x)^y \cos(x)}{\sin(x)}$$

```
> Diff( (sin(x))^y, y, x )= diff( (sin(x))^y, y, x );    # Another second derivative
```

$$\frac{\partial^2}{\partial x\, \partial y}\sin(x)^y = \frac{\sin(x)^y \ln(\sin(x))\, y\cos(x)}{\sin(x)} + \frac{\sin(x)^y \cos(x)}{\sin(x)}$$

5.7.4 Derivatives of Functions: D

There will be times when you need to have the derivative you calculate be a function or *mapping*. For cases such as these, the D operator is used to take the derivative of a function (not an expression) and to return the result as another function. This type of derivative and functional analysis is more subtle than the derivatives we have been taking with diff, yet sometimes it is needed to get Maple to do what you want. For instance, consider the two expressions for derivatives:

$$\frac{d(\cos t)}{dt}, \qquad \frac{d\cos}{dt}(t).$$

The left expression implies the derivative of $\cos t$ with respect to t, while the right expression indicates a new function, the derivative of $\cos$, that gets evaluated at t. It is the right type of expression that we want to use as a function. You may think that this is just semantics, yet observe that

$$\frac{d}{dt}\cos \pi = \frac{d}{dt}(-1) = 0.$$

Hence, if the t in $d\cos t/dt$ indicates some value, then this is the derivative of a constant, which is clearly 0. Consequently, we must be careful with arguments when we transform one function, such as $\cos$, into another function, such as $d\cos/dt$. The D form of derivative is designed to be used with this type of care. We will look at some examples to see what this means.

Imagine that we are given the position of a mass attached to a nonlinear spring as

$$x(t) = \sin t + 0.3 \sin^2 t.$$

We want to find the velocity $v(t) = dx/dt$ and the acceleration $a(t) = dv/dt$ as functions of time. We first try:

```
> x := (t) -> sin(t) + 0.3*(sin(t))^2;              # Defines function or mapping x(t)
```

$$x := t \rightarrow \sin(t) + 0.3\sin(t)^2$$

```
> v := (t) -> diff( x(t), t );                  # Appears to define v(t) as derivative of x(t)
```

$$v := t \rightarrow \operatorname{diff}(\mathrm{x}(t),\, t)$$

```
> v(1);
 Error, (in v) wrong number (or type) of parameters in function diff
```

The above response shows that `diff(x(t),t)` does not work as a proper function when a number is given as the argument. The reason is that Maple does not accept $v(1)$ as the velocity at `t = 1` although that clearly is what we want. This problem arises from the fact that `diff` does not produce a true function as an answer. One solution, which we find rather awkward, is to use `unapply` to convert the expression into a function:

```
> v := (t) -> diff( x(t), t );                          # Define v(t) as derivative of x(t)
```

$$v := t \to \text{diff}(x(t),\, t)$$

```
> v(t);          v(1);                        # OK for symbol, not OK for numeric argument
```

$$\cos(t) + 0.6\sin(t)\cos(t)$$

```
   Error, (in v) wrong number (or type) of parameters in function diff
> v := unapply ( diff( x(t), t), t );              # Use unapply for proper function
```

$$v := t \to \cos(t) + 0.6\sin(t)\cos(t)$$

```
> 'v(1)' = v(1);
```

$$v(1) = \cos(1) + 0.6\sin(1)\cos(1)$$

In contrast, the command D produces a proper function that is equal to the derivative of the original function. Scrutinize how the arguments of the functions are implicit and do not have to be (and should not be) specified:

```
> x := (t) -> sin(t) + 0.3 * (sin(t))^2;                      # x(t) is arrow function
```

$$x := t \to \sin(t) + 0.3\sin(t)^2$$

```
> D(x);                                          # Form new function = derivative of x
```

$$t \to \cos(t) + 0.6\sin(t)\cos(t)$$

```
> v := D(x);                              # Form v(t) as true arrow function or mapping
```

$$v := t \to \cos(t) + 0.6\sin(t)\cos(t)$$

```
> 'v(1)' = v(1);
```

$$v(1) = \cos(1) + 0.6\sin(1)\cos(1)$$

When the derivative function is used as a regular function, for plotting and so forth, its argument needs to be specified. To cite an instance, here we plot position, velocity, and acceleration:

```
> a := D(v);                                     # Form new function for acceleration
```

$$a := t \to -\sin(t) + 0.6\cos(t)^2 - 0.6\sin(t)^2$$

```
> plot( {x(t), v(t), a(t)}, t = 0..10 );                       # Plot three functions
> plot ( {x(t), D(x)(t), D(D(x))(t)}, t = 0..10 ); # Same plot, using D for derivatives
```

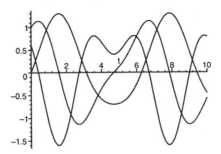

We look now at some more examples of the use of D for creating derivatives of an arrow function:

```
> 'D(g)' = D (g);
```

$$D(g) = D(g)$$

OK, we get back what we entered, which may be correct, but is not exciting. This is related to the fact that Maple does not know anything about g. If we give D a function in which the argument is implicit (not given explicitly), then Maple returns the derivative as an implicit function:

```
> 'D( sin )' = D( sin );                     # Take derivative of sin, an implicit function
```

$$D(\sin) = \cos$$

```
> f := (x) -> ln(x) / (1-x);                 # An explicit, arrow function of x
> 'D (f)' = D (f);                           # Produces arrow function = derivative
```

$$f := x \to \frac{\ln(x)}{1 - x}$$

$$D(f) = (x \to \frac{1}{x\,(1-x)} + \frac{\ln(x)}{(1-x)^2})$$

We see that if $f(x)$ is an explicit function of x, then Maple uses the arrow sign to make it clear to us that we have defined a new function of x.

It is best to think of D(f) as an entirely new function, the derivative, and not as an operator acting on $f(x)$. This point is often confusing in the mathematical notation for mappings and transformations (Landau's second rule). To evaluate this new function obtained by differentiation, we add the argument to D(f), or in this case D(sin):

```
> 'D(sin) (Pi)' = D(sin) (Pi);        'D(sin) (t)' = D(sin) (t);
```

$$D(\sin)(\pi) = -1 \qquad D(\sin)(t) = \cos(t)$$

This makes sense if we think that sin is the argument to the D function and that it creates a new function D(sin). This new function, in turn, is evaluated at an argument x. Naturally, we are allowed to take the function `D(f)` and evaluate it with any argument we want:

```
> 'D(f) (x)' = D(f) (x);          'D(f) (y)' = D(f) (y);
```

$$D(f)(x) = \frac{1}{x\,(1-x)} + \frac{\ln(x)}{(1-x)^2}$$

$$D(f)(y) = \frac{1}{y\,(1-y)} + \frac{\ln(y)}{(1-y)^2}$$

Look at how we do *not* indicate the fact that f is a function of some variable by giving an argument to f within the derivative operation, for example, as `D(f(x))`. Nor do we state with respect to which variable we are taking the derivative.

In that we are not indicating that the derivative is with respect to x, Maple does not view x as a simple argument, but rather as a general variable or function that has yet to be defined. That being the case, if you ask `D` to differentiate $f(x)$, it assumes x is some arbitrary function that may have a derivative of its own:

```
> restart:        f := (x) -> ln(x) / (1-x);        # Clear variables and redefine function
> 'D( f(x) )' = D( f(x) );                                   # Take derivative
```

$$f := x \to \frac{\ln(x)}{1-x}$$

$$D(f(x)) = \frac{D(\ln(x))}{1-x} + \frac{\ln(x)\,D(x)}{(1-x)^2}$$

Likewise, since $f(15)$ is just a number, `D(f(15))` is the derivative of a constant, which of course is zero:

```
> 'D( f(15) )' = D( f(15) );
```

$$D(f(15)) = 0$$

As we have said, if you want to evaluate the derivative function for argument 15, then you should think of `D(f)` as the function:

```
> 'D(f)(15)' = D(f)(15);
```

$$D(f)(15) = -\frac{1}{210} + \frac{1}{196}\ln(15)$$

5.7.5 Second and Partial Derivatives: D

Second derivatives with the `D` operator are formed either by applying `D` twice, or by using the composition operator `@` (which repeats the action of a function, much like `$` repeats the argument):

```
> restart:   f := (x) -> ln(x) / (1-x);
```

```
> 'D( D(f) )' = D( D(f) );                          # Second derivative on arrow function
> '( D@@2 )(f)' = ( D@@2 )(f);                       # Another 2nd derivative on arrow function
```

$$f := x \rightarrow \frac{\ln(x)}{1-x}$$

$$D(D(f)) = (x \rightarrow -\frac{1}{x^2(1-x)} + \frac{2}{x(1-x)^2} + \frac{2\ln(x)}{(1-x)^3})$$

```
> 'D( D(sin) )' = D( D(sin) );                       # Second derivative on built-in function
```

$$D(D(\sin)) = -\sin$$

With functions of several variables (multivariate functions) such as $g(x, y) = \sin x \cos y$, we form different second derivatives by taking the partial derivative with respect to either x or y. You indicate the desired operation to Maple by including a list [in square brackets] of the variable(s) by number that you desire to differentiate with respect to:

```
> g := (x, y) -> sin(x) * cos(y);                    # A function of two variables
> 'D[1](g)' = D[1](g);                               # Derivative with respect to 1st argument
```

$$g := (x, y) \rightarrow \sin(x) \cos(y)$$
$$D_1(g) = ((x, y) \rightarrow \cos(x) \cos(y))$$

```
> 'D[2](g)' = D[2](g);                               # Derivative with respect to 2nd argument
> 'D[1,2](g)' = D[1,2](g);                           # Derivative with respect to 1st & 2nd arguments
```

$$D_2(g) = ((x, y) \rightarrow -\sin(x) \sin(y))$$
$$D_{1,2}(g) = ((x, y) \rightarrow -\cos(x) \sin(y))$$

```
> 'D[2,1](g)' = D[2,1](g);                           # Same answer, order does not matter
> 'D[2,1](g)(Pi/4,Pi/4)' = D[2,1](g)(Pi/4,Pi/4);     # 2nd derivative, explicit
```

$$D_{2,1}(g) = ((x, y) \rightarrow -\cos(x) \sin(y))$$
$$D_{2,1}(g)(\frac{\pi}{4}, \frac{\pi}{4}) = \frac{-1}{2}$$

Check how Maple indicates these second derivatives as arrow functions (mappings). If the function does not have an explicit definition, then the D operator yields an abstract form:

```
> 'D[1,2](n)' = D[1,2](n);                           # 2nd partial undefined function
```

$$D_{1,2}(n) = D_{1,2}(n)$$

Unless the function is very unusual, partial derivatives are generally independent of order:

```
> 'D[1,2](h)' = D [1,2](h); 'D[2,1](h)' = D[2,1](h);    # Independent of order
```

$$D_{1,2}(h) = D_{1,2}(h), \qquad D_{2,1}(h) = D_{1,2}(h)$$

Clearly then, this option gives us another way to determine the second derivative, even for univariate functions:

```
>  'D[1,1](g)' = D[1,1](g);        'D[2,2] (g)' = D[2,2](g);
>  'D[1,1](sin)' = D[1,1](sin);
```

$$D_{1,1}(g) = ((x, y) \rightarrow -\sin(x)\cos(y))$$
$$D_{2,2}(g) = ((x, y) \rightarrow -\sin(x)\cos(y))$$
$$D_{1,1}(\sin) = -\sin$$

5.8 NUMERICAL DERIVATIVES*

Normally you should be happy to have Maple calculate derivatives for you, espe-cially if they are done exactly. If it cannot do it exactly, then let Maple calculate the derivative numerically. We now ask the question, "How does one calculate a derivative numerically?" This query is interesting, as it is useful to understand how Maple does things under cover, as well as being something we will need in Chapter 15, where we undertake a numerical study of projectile motion with fric-tion. Determining a numerical derivative is essentially determining the slope of a function, namely, drawing a tangent to a curve. This is not hard.

Say we want a numerical approximation to the derivative of $f(x) = \sin x$. We know the exact answer,

```
>  f := (x) -> sin(x);        'D(f(x))' = D(f)(x);
```

$$f := \sin \qquad D(f(x)) = \cos(x)$$

The exact derivative is defined as the limit:

$$\frac{df(x)}{dx} \stackrel{\text{def}}{=} \lim_{\Delta x \to 0} \frac{f(x + \Delta x) - f(x)}{\Delta x}. \tag{5.16}$$

Numerical approximations use a similar approach, except that one skips the limit-ing process and simply does the division for a small but finite value of Δ:

$$\frac{df(x)}{dx} \simeq \frac{f(x + \Delta x) - f(x)}{\Delta x}. \tag{5.17}$$

So let us try this out on some typical values. We will start with $x = 1.0$ and $\Delta = 0.1$ (decimal points to ensure that Maple does numerical computations) and compare the approximation to the exact answer:

```
>  'df[exact]/dx' = cos(1.);        'df[approx]/dx' = (sin(1.+0.1) - sin(1.)) / 0.1;
```

$$\frac{df_{exact}}{dx} = 0.5403023059 \qquad \frac{df_{approx}}{dx} = 0.497363753$$

We see that the approximation is at least close. We make the approximation better by using smaller and smaller values for Δ:

```
>  'df[approx]/dx' = (sin(1.+0.01) - sin(1.))  / 0.01;
>  'df[approx]/dx' = (sin(1.+0.001) - sin(1.))  / 0.001;
```

$$\frac{df}{dx}_{approx} = 0.53608598 \qquad 0.5398815$$

The numerical derivative rule we have just outlined is called the *forward-difference approximation* because it moves forward by Δ to sample how the function changes. A more balanced rule that requires no extra computation is known as the *central difference approximation*. It evaluates the function on either side of x and takes that difference:

$$\frac{df}{dx}_{CenDiff} = \frac{f(x + \frac{\Delta}{2}) - f(x - \frac{\Delta}{2})}{\Delta}. \qquad (5.18)$$

We apply it with the same values of Δ as used for the forward difference:

```
>  'df[exact]/dx'= cos(1.);                                      # Exact answer
>  'df[CenDiff]/dx' = ( sin(1.+0.05) - sin(1.-0.05) ) / 0.1;
>  'df[CenDiff]/dx' = ( sin(1.+0.025) - sin(1.-0.025) ) / 0.05;
>  'df[CenDiff]/dx' = ( sin(1.+0.012) - sin(1.-0.012) ) / 0.024;
```

$$\frac{df}{dx}_{exact} = 0.5403023059$$

$$\frac{df}{dx}_{CenDiff} = 0.540077208 \qquad 0.54024603 \qquad 0.54028933$$

We see that even the largest value of Δ yields three places of precision, with the approximation still improving as Δ is made smaller still. Notwithstanding the use of even more precise algorithms in scientific work, our exercise here should convince you that numerical derivatives are generally reliable.

5.9 ALTERNATE SOLUTION: MAXIMUM TOWER HEIGHT

If we think of N_{max} as a continuous variable and take a mathematical point of view, then the maximum height occurs at the point at which an infinitesimal change in n leads to no change at all in the tower's height. We know from calculus that this occurs when the derivative vanishes, that is, when $dH(n, t, a)/dn = 0$:

q: Use Maple's derivative function diff to determine $dH(n, t, a)/dn$. ♠

```
> restart:       Hf := (n, t, a) -> n*t - a*n*(n-1)/2;
> Diff( Hf(n,t,a), n ) = diff( Hf(n,t,a), n );          normal(%);
```

$$Hf := (n, t, a) \rightarrow nt - \frac{1}{2} a n (n - 1)$$

$$\frac{\partial}{\partial n}(nt - \frac{a n (n - 1)}{2}) = t - \frac{a (n - 1)}{2} - \frac{a n}{2}$$

$$\frac{\partial}{\partial n}(nt - \frac{1}{2} a n^2 + \frac{1}{2} a n) = t - a n + \frac{1}{2} a$$

q: Before we defined the "maximum" tower height as one for which $H(N_{max} + 1) = H(N_{max})$, now we want to use calculus. Use Maple's `solve` function to determine the value of n for which $dH/dn = 0$. ♠

```
> 'Nmax' = solve (diff( Hf(n,t,a), n), n );          # Back quotes for string
```

$$Nmax = \frac{2\,t + a}{2\,a}$$

q: Explain in your own words why this is not the same as N_{max}. ♠

Our previous definition of N_{max} was one for which N_{max} and $N_{max}+1$ both gave the same height. That definition gave $N_{max} = t/a$ and $N_{max} + 1 = (t + a)/a$ as producing the same height. The derivative vanishes at $(t + \frac{a}{2})/a$, which is right between our previous two answers. Neither one is really more correct, but they do correspond to different definitions of maximum.

q: Plot up the results as a check. ♠

It is not possible to make plots of symbolic functions, so let us assign values to t and a. We know from our computations that the maximum, in some sense of the word, occurs near $n = 1000$, so we will narrow our plot to that region:

```
> t := 15; a := 0.001*t;
> plot( Hf(n,t,a), n = 0..1200 );          # Broad view shows growth, then curvature
> plot ( Hf(n,t,a), n = 998..1003 );       # Narrow view highlights maximum
```

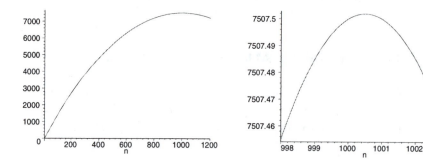

We do indeed see that the maximum height, as determined by the zero of the derivative, occurs at the true maximum of the graph, $n = 1000.5$, but that in terms of integer block numbers, there are maxima at $n = 1000$ and 1001.

5.10 ASSESSMENT AND EXPLORATION

1. How relevant is this model to building actual skyscrapers? Specifically, is it wise to use the same structural design on the top and bottom floors?

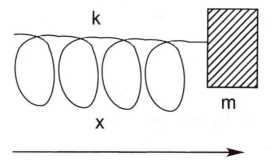

Figure 5.3 A mass m attached to a spring with constant k that is stretched a distance x from its equilibrium position.

2. It is not realistic to have the addition of levels make the tower shorter. Explain in words whether an assumption is at fault, or are we just applying the model beyond its range of applicability.

3. Rather than (5.1), a more realistic model might assume that the blocks get harder to compress at some point and so their thickness never becomes negative. An equation that describes this model may be

$$t = \frac{t_0}{1 + b\,i^2}$$

where t is the thickness of a single block supporting i blocks above it, and $b \simeq 1/100$ is a small number. Obtain an expression from Maple for the total height of a tower of N blocks. *Hint:* while the sum is simple, Maple may not be able to come up with a simple answer. However, numerical evaluation is possible.

4. Use the improved model to derive a Maple function that calculates the height of a tower containing N blocks.

5. Is there a maximum height for the tower now? Plot up the results to be sure.

6. The rate of increase of the tower height with number of blocks is given by the derivative dH/dn. Is there some value of n for which the rate of increase is a maximum? What is the numerical value for the maximum height now (use similar parameter values as before)?

5.11 AUXILIARY PROBLEM: NONLINEAR OSCILLATIONS

A mass $m = 2\,kg$ is attached to a spring as in Figure 5.3. The mass is displaced from its rest position and then released so that it oscillates about the equilibrium position. When the mass is a small distance x from the equilibrium position, the restoring force f tending to bring the mass back to equilibrium is directly proportional to x:

$$f = -k\,x, \tag{5.19}$$

where k is the spring's force constant $k = 25$ Newton/meter. The equation of motion for this system is Newton's second law of motion:

$$f = m\,a, \qquad\qquad -kx = \frac{m\,d^2\,x}{dt^2}. \qquad\qquad (5.20)$$

As shown in the study of *simple harmonic motion*, a solution for the position x as a function of time t is a trigonometric function,

$$\mathrm{x}(t) = \sin(\omega\,t), \qquad\qquad \omega = \sqrt{k/m}. \qquad\qquad (5.21)$$

1. Write a Maple function that returns the position $x(t)$ for any input argument t. (You are given numerical values for m and k, and therefore for ω.)
2. Plot the position for times in the range $0 \le t \le 12$. As always, add labels and a title to your plot.
3. In mechanics we learn that the velocity v is the first derivative of x with respect to time, and that acceleration $a(t)$ is the second derivative:

$$\mathrm{v}(t) = \frac{dx}{dt}, \qquad\qquad a(t) = \frac{dv}{dt} = \frac{d^2\,x}{dt^2}. \qquad\qquad (5.22)$$

   Use Maple's `diff` command to determine analytic expressions for velocity and acceleration as functions of time.
4. Determine whether (5.19) is true for this oscillator, that is, compare $m\,a$ to the force $-k\,x$.
5. Plot $x(t)$, $v(t)$, and $a(t)$ in the same graph for t between 0 and 10, with different colors for each of the three functions.
6. Take your plot and change some lines to dotted and some to bold. Which scheme do you think is clearest?
7. Make a phase-space (parametric) plot of $v(t)$ *versus* $x(t)$ to produce $v(x)$.
8. A more realistic model for an oscillator has the restoring force acting upon the mass depend slightly upon whether the mass is to the right or to the left of the origin (nonlinear terms). For this case the position as a function of time might be described by

$$x(t) = \sin \omega t + b \sin^2 \omega t,$$

   where b (which controls the right-left asymmetry) is a small number compared to 1.
9. Modify your Maple function $x(t)$ to a new one $x(b, t)$ and test that you get the old answer for $b = 0$.
10. For this new oscillator, what are the velocity, acceleration, and force as functions of time? Make several plots for a range of b values between 0 and 1. Add comments to your worksheet indicating for what b values the functions no longer look sinusoidal.
11. Use a 3-D plot with axis and labels to examine x as a function of time for the entire range of b values. Examine the different options for displaying

your surface, as well as different viewing angles. Print out several of the best representations (assume that the printer prints grayscale only). Make sure one of your plots is of only the actual points that are calculated (no connecting lines) and that another one is of contours.

12. Examine the $v(t)$ *versus* $x(t)$ phase-space plot for this anharmonic oscillator for a number of b values.

13. Make a parametric plot of the force $f(t) = ma(t)$ *versus* position $x(t)$ for this anharmonic oscillator. Determining an analytic expression for $f(x)$ would be more difficult.

14. Create two animations of this function, one in which the different frames correspond to different b values, and a second in which the different frames correspond to different times. Look at both and decide which produces the best visualization (animations are usually best to show time dependence).

5.12 KEY WORDS AND CONCEPTS

analytic solution	derivative	derivative operator	limit
mapping	maximum	numerical solution	partial derivative
roots	simultaneous equations	theory *vs.* model	

1. Give three possible meanings of the words *maximum height*.
2. Are mathematical equations always true?
3. Must all equations have analytic solutions?
4. If an equation has a numeric solution, must it also have an analytic solution?
5. Do nonlinear equations occur in nature?
6. How are simultaneous equations different from other types?
7. Are all solutions to an equation equally valid?
8. Are nonlinear equations harder to solve than linear ones? If so, why?
9. Do you have to take a limit to evaluate a derivative?
10. Does it make sense to take the derivative of a function of several variables?
11. What is the difference in Maple between taking the derivative of an expression and a function?
12. Can you take the derivative of a number?

5.13 SUPPLEMENTARY EXERCISES

1. Use both `solve` and `fsolve` to find as many solutions as you are able of
   a. $x^3 + x^2 + x = 1$.
      Beware, this equation may have complex roots that `fsolve` will not show unless you include `complex` in the argument set: (`fsolve(f(x),x,complex)`).
   b. $x^4 + cx^3 + x^2 + x + 1$. *Hint:* you may need to make c numeric.
   c. $\sin(x)^2 = x$. Make a plot to check that your answer is reasonable.
2. Determine the limit
   a. $\lim_{\epsilon \to 0} \frac{\sin(x+\epsilon)-\sin(x)}{\epsilon}$.

b. $\lim_{\epsilon \to 0} \frac{\sin(x+\epsilon/2)-\sin(x-e/2)}{\epsilon}$.

c. $\gamma(v) = \lim_{c \to \infty} \frac{1}{\sqrt{1-v^2/c^2}}$.

d. $\gamma(v) = \lim_{v \to c} \frac{1}{\sqrt{1-v^2/c^2}}$.

3. Determine the first and second derivatives with respect to x of the following expressions:

   a. x^n

   b. $x^{(-n)}$

   c. $\frac{1}{x}$

   d. $\tan x$

   e. $\sin(\sin x)$

   f. $(a x^2 + b x + c)/(d x^2 + e x + f)$

   g. $\sqrt{1 - x^4}$

4. Nonlinear equations are more interesting, but more challenging to solve, than linear equations. They are called nonlinear because the unknown appears to a higher power than the linear first power. Find the solutions of the nonlinear, simultaneous equations:

$$x^2 - 4 y^2 = 1, \qquad\qquad x - 8 y^3 = 3.$$

5. You are given the expression $10 x^4 \sin(k x)$.

   a. Enter this as a Maple expression and determine when it equals 0, and its first and second derivatives.

   b. Enter this as a Maple function and determine when it equals 0, and its first and second derivatives.

6. In mechanics, we often study the position x of an object as a function of time t. If we take the first derivative of the position with respect to time, we get the velocity v as a function of time. In turn, the acceleration a is the second derivative of x with respect to time. In the following exercises, calculate $x(t)$, $v(t)$, and $a(t)$ for each case, and plot all the functions on the same graph as a function of time for $0 \le t \le 10$. Use different colors for each function:

   a. $x(t) = 3 t^2 + 5 t - 13$

   b. $x(t) = \sqrt{t^3}$

   c. $x(t) = (e^t)^t$

7. Here is a real function of the variables x, y, and z:

$$g(x, y, z) = \frac{1}{\sqrt{x^2 + y^2 + z^2}}.$$

Check whether g is a solution of Laplace's differential equation by showing that the sum of these three derivatives equals 0:

$$\frac{d^2 g}{dx^2} + \frac{d^2 g}{dy^2} + \frac{d^2 g}{dz^2} = 0.$$

8. Find the first and second derivatives with respect to x of the functions:

   a. $y = x/(x+1)$
   b. $y = (4\,x^2 + 3\,x)\ln(x)$
   c. $y = \tanh(3\,x)\,e^{\sqrt{5}\,x}$
   d. $y = \sqrt{x^3 + 4\,x^2 + 7\,x + 1}$

9. A rock is hurled upward, and its distance above the ground is given by $y = 210\,t - 34\,t^2$. Use Maple to calculate:
   a. the maximum height from the ground of the rock,
   b. the time at which the rock reaches the maximum height,
   c. the time at which the rock strikes the ground,
   d. the rock's speed when it hits the ground.

10. The resistance R of two resistors in parallel is given by

$$\frac{1}{R} = \frac{1}{R_1} + \frac{1}{R_2}.$$

Solve for R and take the limit as R_2 approaches infinity. Does your answer make sense?

Chapter Six

Integration; Power and Energy Usage (Also 14)

6.1 PROBLEM: RELATING POWER AND ENERGY USAGE

The use of electrical power is characterized by variations of different sorts. There are fluctuations related to the day-night cycle, fluctuations related to the change of seasons (approximately monthly), fluctuations due to weather patterns (daily and long-term), and others [Energy]. As an instance, observe the hourly use of power for Australia during a one-year period shown in Figure 6.1 [D&A 00]. Generally, power consumption peaks in the winter due to heating demands, and peaks again in the summer due to cooling demands. Power usage also shows a year-to-year growth that may be related to population growth and economic development, as well as the seasonal variation that is the most evident, especially when the daily fluctuations are removed by taking averages over weekly periods.

Problem: Determine the total energy used over a three-year period.

6.2 EMPIRICAL MODELS

The data for power usage is just a series of numbers, each for a different time, and therefore not in an appropriate form for analytic integration.[1] We model it approximately with three formulas:

$$P(t) = 4 + [2 + \sin(2\pi t)]\sin(\pi t/91), \tag{6.1}$$

$$P(t) = \left(4 + \frac{t}{365} + \frac{\sin(\pi t/91)}{2}\right)\left(2 + \frac{\sin(2\pi t)^2}{2}\right), \tag{6.2}$$

$$P(t) = \left(4 + \frac{t}{365} + \frac{\sin(\pi t/91)}{2}\right)\left(2 + e^{(-\sin(2\pi t))}\right), \tag{6.3}$$

where the power $P(t)$ is in GW (10^9 watts) and the time t is in days. These formulas try to incorporate the various time dependencies of power usage. Since t is in days, a function of the form $\sin(2\pi t/T)$ is periodic with period T days. There-

---

[1] In Chapter 14 we do this integration numerically with Java. Numeric integration can be used on tables of numbers as well as functions, and is often required for realistic problems.

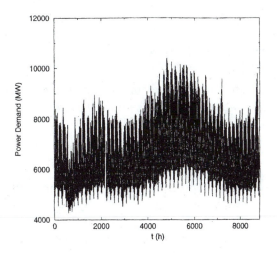 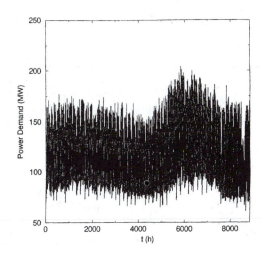

Figure 6.1 Electrical power use for Australia (*left*) and Mad del Plata (*right*) on an hourly basis over a one-year period.

fore $\sin(2\pi t)$ in these models represents a daily variation of power. Likewise, $\sin(\pi t/91)$ has a period of 182 days (half of a year), and so represents a variation that peaks twice during the year. Models 2 and 3 have a term that grows linearly with time to account for year-to-year growth. Finally, model 3 incorporates an exponential time dependence of power use on a daily time scale.

To see if these models look anything like the data, we plot them:

```
> restart;    with(plots):    with(plottools):                    # Model 1
> plot(4 + (2 + sin(2*Pi*t)) * sin(Pi*t/91), t = 0..700, title='Power');
```

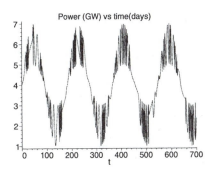

```
>                                              # You plot models 2 and 3 here
```

Indeed, there is a biyearly variation about a nonzero average, a daily variation, and, for models 2 and 3, a long-term growth of the average.

6.3 THEORY: POWER AND ENERGY DEFINITIONS

In common usage, the words "power" and "energy" may differ from their scientific meanings (like paying the "power bill" when you are really buying energy). Power is defined as the rate at which work is done, or energy used:

$$P = \frac{dW}{dt}. \tag{6.4}$$

Consequently, if energy is measured in joules (the System International unit), then power is measured in joules/second or watts (W).

The power company charges you for kilowatt-hours. A kilowatt is 1,000 watts, an hour is 3,600 seconds, and so one kilowatt-hour = 1000 watts $\times$ 3600 sec = 3.6×10^6 joules. Typical costs for a kWh is between 2 and 20 cents, depending on where you live and politics. In any case, you are paying for energy, not power. To set the scale for some realistic numbers, one *horsepower* (hp) equals 746 W. One *energy worker,* the average output power of a human body, is 100 W, significantly less than a horse. A nuclear power plant produces energy at the rate of 1,150 megawatts, significantly more than a horse.

In our problem we are given the power used as a function of time and asked to compute the energy used in three years. Rearranging the definition of power, (6.4) gives the energy used during infinitesimal time dt as

$$dW = P(t)\, dt, \tag{6.5}$$

which gives he total energy used from some time 0 to T as

$$W(T) = \int_0^T P(t)\, dt. \tag{6.6}$$

This means that the solution to our problem is the integration of the three models for power usages, (6.1)–(6.3), which is equivalent to measuring the areas under the $P(t)$ vs. t curves. If an analytic integration is possible, then we will have a function $W(T)$ to use for predicting future energy usage. Otherwise we just have to evaluate the integral numerically and plot the numbers up to see the trends.

6.4 MAPLE: TOOLS FOR INTEGRATION

Integrals were invented to determine quantities such as the potential energy in the interior of a spherical planet:

$$V(R) = \int_0^R 4\,\rho(r)\,\pi\, r\, dr. \tag{6.7}$$

Calculus is still essential for solving scientific problems, and Maple is good at calculus. In the previous chapter we studied the derivative, here we study the *integral*, which is essentially the inverse of the derivative (*antiderivative*). An integral without explicit limits, such as $\int f(x)\,dx$, is an *indefinite integral*. An integral with limits, such as $\int_a^b f(x)\,dx$, is a *definite integral*. The difference is important; an indefinite integral is still a function of x, while a definite integral is just a number. As we are about to see, Maple handles both types of integrals.

6.4.1 Indefinite Integration

The Maple command for integration is int, with inert form Int:

```
> int( y / sqrt(1+x), x );       Int( y / sqrt(1+x), x );        # Evaluate, display
> Int( y / sqrt(1+x), x )  = int( y / sqrt(1+x), x );            # Both together
```

$$2\,y\,\sqrt{1+x} \qquad\qquad \int \frac{y}{\sqrt{1+x}}\,dx$$

$$\int \frac{y}{\sqrt{1+x}}\,dx \;=\; 2\,y\,\sqrt{1+x}$$

Look at the second argument to int. It is the variable with respect to which we want the integration performed. Be careful, it does not have to be x:

```
> Int( y / sqrt(1+x), y ) = int( y / sqrt(1+x), y );        # x ≠ integration variable
```

$$\int \frac{y}{\sqrt{1+x}}\,dy \;=\; \frac{y^2}{2\,\sqrt{1+x}}$$

where, we would have to include the integration constant by hand, if needed. We check the answer via differentiation:

```
> Diff( Int( y / sqrt(1+x), y), y) = diff( Int( y / sqrt(1+x), y ), y);
```

$$\frac{\partial}{\partial y}\left(\int \frac{y}{\sqrt{1+x}}\,dy \right) \;=\; \frac{y}{\sqrt{1+x}}$$

Beware, int does not write out a constant of integration for these indefinite integrals. You will need to include that by hand when appropriate.

6.4.2 Definite Integration

Definite integration includes the integration limits as a second argument in the int command:

```
> Int( x / sqrt(1+x), x = a..b) = int( x/sqrt(1+x), x = a..b );
```

$$\int_a^b \frac{x}{\sqrt{1+x}}\, dx = \frac{2\,(1+b)^{(3/2)}}{3} - 2\,\sqrt{1+b} - \frac{2\,(1+a)^{(3/2)}}{3} + 2\,\sqrt{1+a}$$

In spite of Maple's awesome powers for doing integrals, some functions cannot be integrated analytically:

```
> Int(exp(-x)*sin(x)/sqrt(1+x), x = 0..1) = int(exp(-x)*sin(x)/sqrt(1+x), x = 0..1);
```

$$\int_0^1 \frac{e^{(-x)}\sin(x)}{\sqrt{1+x}}\, dx \;=\; \int_0^1 \frac{e^{(-x)}\sin(x)}{\sqrt{1+x}}\, dx$$

We see that Maple just repeats the integral without evaluating it. This response is Maple's way of saying that it is stumped without losing face. However, even if Maple cannot figure out an exact value for the integral, it should be able to evaluate it numerically. To do that, just tell Maple to evaluate with floats (evalf):

```
> Int( exp(-x)*sin(x) / sqrt(1+x), x = 0..1 ) =
      evalf( int( exp(-x)*sin(x) / sqrt(1+x), x = 0..1 ) );
```

$$\int_0^1 \frac{e^{(-x)}\sin(x)}{\sqrt{1+x}}\, dx = 0.1965185003$$

Now and then you may have to try different approaches to get a workable form for a needed integral, for example,

$$S = \int \sqrt{1+b\,t+c\,t^2}\, dt.$$

Have Maple evaluate this expression for S as an indefinite integral, and then have Maple evaluate this expression for S as the definite integral:

$$\int_0^T \sqrt{1+b\,t+c\,t^2}\, dt.$$

Even the definite integral is terribly complicated. See if substituting some numerical values for the constants helps:

```
>                                                # Assign values to b, c, and T, reevaluate
```

6.4.3 Integrals as Functions

It should be noted that int, like diff, produces an expression, not a function. Use the unapply command to make the indefinite integral $I(x) = \int f(x)\, dx$ into a function of x:

```
> myInt  := unapply( int(y/sqrt( 1+x ), x ), x );          # Form function I(x)
> myInt(z);                                                 # Evaluate function for argument z
```

```
> D(myInt);
```

$$myInt \quad := \quad x \to 2\,y\,\sqrt{x+1}$$

$$x \quad \to \quad \frac{y}{\sqrt{x+1}}$$

In view of the fact that definite integrals are just numbers, the unapply command does not work for them. However, let us imagine an integral as a function of both its upper and lower integration limits:

```
> Int( x/sqrt(1+x), x = y..z ) = int( x/sqrt(1+x), x = y..z );
```

$$\int_y^z \frac{x}{\sqrt{1+x}}\,dx = \frac{2\,(z+1)^{(3/2)}}{3} - 2\,\sqrt{z+1} - \frac{2\,(1+y)^{(3/2)}}{3} + 2\,\sqrt{1+y}$$

The integral clearly depends upon y and z, the endpoints of the interval. Thus we make the integral a function of the endpoints:

```
> myInt := (a, z) -> int( x/sqrt(1+x), x = a..z );
> myInt( a, z );
```

$$myInt := (a,\,z) \to \int_a^z \frac{x}{\sqrt{1+x}}\,dx$$

$$\frac{2\,(z+1)^{(3/2)}}{3} - 2\,\sqrt{z+1} - \frac{2\,(1+a)^{(3/2)}}{3} + 2\,\sqrt{1+a}$$

```
> diff( myInt(a, z), z );    simplify(%);
```

$$\sqrt{z+1} - \frac{1}{\sqrt{z+1}} \qquad \frac{z}{\sqrt{z+1}}$$

6.5 PROBLEM SOLUTION: ENERGY FROM POWER

We now know how to evaluate integrals, so let us do some! We will investigate models 1 and 3 here, and leave model 2 for you. For model 1, let us first define a function for the power, and then look at it to see if it looks OK:

```
> P := (t) -> 4 + ( 2+sin(2*Pi*t) )* sin(Pi*t/91);
> plot( P(t), t = 0..365, title = 'model 1, P(t) vs t, for one year');
```

$$P := t \to 4 + (2 + \sin(2\,\pi\,t))\sin(\frac{1}{91}\,\pi\,t)$$

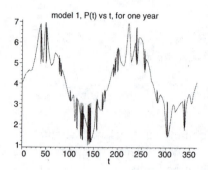

model 1, P(t) vs t, for one year

Now that we know that the integrand looks reasonable, let us integrate it:

```
> Int( P(t), t ) = int( P(t), t );
```

$$\int 4 + (2 + \sin(2\pi t)) \sin(\frac{\pi t}{91}) \, dt =$$

$$4t - \frac{182\cos(\frac{\pi t}{91})}{\pi} + \frac{91}{362} \frac{\sin(\frac{181\pi t}{91})}{\pi} - \frac{91}{366} \frac{\sin(\frac{183\pi t}{91})}{\pi}$$

The expression for the integral is neat and shows that the total energy used has some terms that oscillate as a function of time, as well as a term that increases linearly with time. However, it is missing the integration constant, which is clear since the $t = 0$ value of the integral is $-182/\pi$, when it should be 0. One way of eliminating the need to personally include the integration constant, is to evaluate the integral as a *definite* integral:

```
> Int( P(t), t = 0..T ) = int( P(t), t = 0..T );
```

$$\int_0^T 4 + (2 + \sin(2\pi t)) \sin(\frac{\pi t}{91}) \, dt = \frac{1}{66246} (264984\,\pi\,T - 12056772\cos(\frac{\pi T}{91})$$

$$+ 16653\sin(\frac{181\pi T}{91}) - 16471\sin(\frac{183\pi T}{91}) + 12056772) \,/\pi$$

The above equation is not as neat an expression as the indefinite integral, but it is correct (vanishes at $T = 0$). We define the energy function $E(t)$ as the power integrated up to time T, and evaluate the energy used after one year:

```
> E := (T) -> int( P(t), t = 0..T );
> E(0);                    E(365);
```

$$E := T \to \int_0^T P(t) \, dt$$

$$0, \quad \frac{2}{33123} \frac{-8281\sin(\frac{\pi}{91}) + 24179790\,\pi - 3014193\cos(\frac{\pi}{91}) + 3014193}{\pi}$$

Maple is returning the one-year result as an exact number, which really does not make much sense here, since we want a floating-point number to tell the stockholders. Consequently, we modify the definition of $E(t)$ to float the answer and look at the answers for zero, one, and two years:

```
> E := (T) -> evalf( int(P(t), t = 0..T ) );
> E(0),      E(365),      E(370);
```

$$E := T \rightarrow \text{evalf}(\int_0^T P(t)\,dt)$$

$$0., \qquad\qquad 1460.029026, \qquad\qquad 1481.205658$$

The energy used does appear to be growing year by year, something we here check with a simple plot for 1,000 days:

```
> plot( E(T), T = 0..1000, title = 'Energy (GW) used after T days');
```

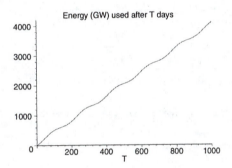

We see a small fluctuation about a linear increase. This does not bode well for the planet!

We now conduct a similar study for model 3. The power function is now:

```
> P := (t) -> ( 4 + 1/365*t + sin(1/91*Pi*t)/2 ) * ( 2 + exp(-sin(2*Pi*t) ) ) );
> plot ( P(t), t = 0..30, title = 'model 3 P(t), for one month' );
> plot ( P(t), t = 0..365, title = 'model 3 P(t), for one year' );
```

$$P := t \rightarrow (4 + \frac{1}{365}t + \frac{1}{2}\sin(\frac{1}{91}\pi t))\,(2 + e^{(-\sin(2\pi t))})$$

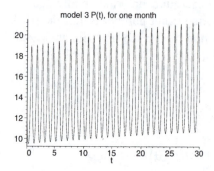

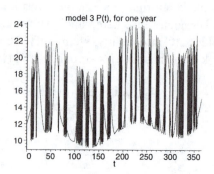

This model looks good and shows an interesting daily and yearly variation. Now that we know that the integrand looks reasonable, let us integrate it:

```
> Int(P(t), t) = int(P(t), t);
```

$$\int (4 + \frac{t}{365} + \frac{1}{2} + \dots$$

Maple appears to give up on us (just repeating the input), so let us try the definite integral form:

```
> Int( P(t), t = 0..T ) = int( P(t), t = 0..T );
```

$$\int_0^T (4 + \frac{t}{365} + \dots$$

Again Maple fails us. Maybe numerical integration works?

```
> Int( P(t), t = 0..365 ) = evalf( int( P(t), t = 0..365 ) );
```

$$\int_0^{365} (4 + \frac{t}{365} + \frac{1}{2} \sin(\frac{\pi t}{91})) (2 + e^{(-\sin(2\pi t))}) \, dt = 5364.722015$$

Yes that works, so let us define an energy function equal to the integral of the power, and plot and evaluate the results:

```
> E := (T) -> evalf( int( P(t), t = 0..T ) );
> E(0), E(365), E(730);
```

$$E := T \rightarrow \text{evalf}(\int_0^T P(t) \, dt)$$

$$0., \qquad\qquad 5364.722015, \qquad\qquad 11921.61441$$

This calculation takes some computer time, since Maple must do a numerical integration, and Maple is slow with numerics. In the present case, we have a highly oscillatory integrand and Maple's adaptive step sizing may have trouble. We are free to try Maple's `plot` command, however, since it uses a minimum of 50 points, this also takes a real long time. Consequently, we use the `resolution` option to set the number of horizontal points to less than the default value of 200:

```
> plot ( E(T), T = 0..1000, resolution = 20, title = 'Energy Used, Model 3 T Days' );
```

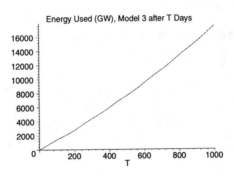

We see, again, a rather linear increase in energy use for the next few years.

6.5.1 Your Solution to Model 2

1. Analyze model 2 in a manner similar to that used for models 1 and 3.
2. These models show a rather linear increase in integrated energy over time. This is a long-range concern, because there is no way for a finite amount of energy to sustain this growth. Regardless of our inability to dictate energy-use policy to the world, modify models 1 and 3 so that the total energy-use growth rate is approximately 10% per year.
3. Devise a model in which the total energy used becomes a constant in time.

6.6 KEY WORDS AND CONCEPTS

definite integral   indefinite integral   integration constant   power vs. energy
integration limits

1. If you buy a truck, do you want it to have lots of power or lots of energy?
2. If an integral represents the area under a curve, how does indefinite integration make sense?
3. How may an integral be thought of as a function?
4. If the definite integral of some expression exists, does that mean that the indefinite integral must also exist?
5. If the indefinite integral of some expression exists, does that mean that the definite integral must also exist?
6. Is it possible to integrate an integral?
7. If the numerical integral of some expression exists, does that mean that the analytic integral must also exist?
8. Is it possible to integrate a function that becomes singular (equal to infinity) within the region of integration?

6.7 SUPPLEMENTARY EXERCISES

Evaluate the following integrals:

1. $\int 3\,x^2 - 5\,x + 8\,dx$
2. $\int \sqrt{x^3 + 5\,x}\,dx$
3. $\int_0^1 e^{\sqrt{x^3+5\,x}}\,dx$
4. $\int \frac{1}{x^2+2\,x+4}\,dx$
5. $\int_{-1}^1 \frac{1}{(x-2)^2}\,dx$
6. $\int_0^\infty e^{(-x^2)}\,dx$
7. $\int \ln(x)\,dx$

Chapter Seven

Matrices and Vectors; Rigid-Body Rotation

7.1 PROBLEM: RIGID-BODY ROTATION

The study of rotations in classical mechanics is an excellent example of the use of vectors and matrices in science. The problem we study is basically an exercise that we work out in full and ask you to repeat for another case. For comparison, we repeat this same problem using Java matrices in Chapter 18. Even if you are not familiar with the physics, we suggest that you work with us through these examples as a review of matrices and as a preview of what is to come; it should also make learning the physics easier in the future.

Problem a (we work this one through for you): Consider Figure 7.1 showing a barbell composed of a mass m_1 attached to mass m_2 by a massless rigid rod of length $2a$. The barbell is fixed at an angle θ with respect to the z axis, and is being rotated with an angular velocity vector ω along the z axis.

a. Use Maple to determine the vector angular momentum $\mathbf{L}$ of this barbell by adding up the angular momenta of the two masses.
b. Use Maple to evaluate the inertia tensor $\{\mathbf{I}\}$ for this barbell.
c. Form the matrix product $\{\mathbf{I}\}\omega$ of the inertia tensor and angular velocity for the barbell. Check that you get the same value for $\mathbf{L}$ as above.
d. Make 3-D plots of $\mathbf{L}$ and ω for three different times, and thereby show that $\mathbf{L}$

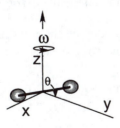

Figure 7.1 A barbell rotating about a fixed axis in the z direction. In Maple you can grab and rotate this `pointplot3d` figure.

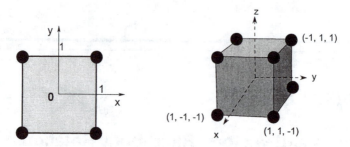

Figure 7.2 *Left:* A 2-D rectangular plate of side 2 with the origin at its center and a mass at each corner. *Right:* A cube of side 2 with the origin at its center and a mass at each corner. In Maple you can grab and rotate these `pointplot3d` figures.

rotates about a fixed ω. A changing **L** implies that there is an external torque being applied to the barbell.

Problem b: Consider the 2-D square plate on the left of Figure 7.2 with a mass m at each corner. It is rotated with these three values for the angular velocity:

$$\omega = \begin{bmatrix} 1 \\ 0 \end{bmatrix}, \qquad \begin{bmatrix} 0 \\ 1 \end{bmatrix}, \qquad \begin{bmatrix} 1 \\ 1 \end{bmatrix}.$$

1. Use Maple to determine the angular momentum vector **L** of the plate by adding up the angular momenta of the individual masses.
2. Use Maple to evaluate the inertia tensor {**I**} for this plate. *Hint:* if this were a solid plate, its inertia tensor would be

$$I = \begin{bmatrix} 1 & 0 \\ 0 & 4 \end{bmatrix}. \qquad (7.1)$$

3. Form the matrix product {**I**}ω of the inertia tensor {**I**} and angular velocity ω for the plate, and check that you get the same value for **L** as before.
4. Make three 3-D plots of **L** and ω for different times, and thereby show that **L** rotates about a fixed ω. From this we deduce that there must be an external torque applied to the plate.
5. Determine the torque acting on the plate. *(optional)*

Problem c: Consider the 3-D cube on the right of Figure 7.2 with a mass m at each corner. It is rotated with these three values for the angular velocity:

$$\omega = \begin{bmatrix} 1 \\ 0 \end{bmatrix}, \qquad \begin{bmatrix} 0 \\ 1 \end{bmatrix}, \qquad \begin{bmatrix} 1 \\ 1 \end{bmatrix}.$$

1. Use Maple to determine the vector angular momentum **L** of the cube by adding up the angular momenta of the individual masses.

2. Use Maple to evaluate the inertia tensor $\{\mathbf{I}\}$ for this cube. *Hint:* if this were a solid cube, its inertia tensor would be

$$I = \begin{bmatrix} +\frac{2}{3} & -\frac{1}{4} & -\frac{1}{4} \\ -\frac{1}{4} & +\frac{2}{3} & -\frac{1}{4} \\ -\frac{1}{4} & -\frac{1}{4} & +\frac{2}{3} \end{bmatrix}.$$

3. Form the matrix product of the inertia tensor and angular velocity $\{\mathbf{I}\}\omega$ for the cube and check that you get the same value for $\mathbf{L}$ as above.
4. Make some 3-D plots of $\mathbf{L}$ and ω for different times. Thereby show that $\mathbf{L}$ rotates about a fixed ω. From this we deduce that there must be an external torque applied to the cube.
5. Determine the torque acting on the cube. *(optional)*

7.2 MATH: VECTORS AND MATRICES

Classical mechanics is an area of physics that studies the motion of particles and objects. Before we describe the motion of a particle, we must first develop a system to specify the location of a particle in space. As illustrated in Figure 7.3, we describe the location $\mathbf{R}$ of a point in space by drawing a set of perpendicular x and y axes, and then drawing a line from the origin O to the point R. An arrow head is usually added to this line segment to show its direction. An arrow in space is the most elementary representation of a *vector*.

We view Figure 7.3 as showing a graphical representation of the displacement vector $\mathbf{R}$. This vector has length or *magnitude* $R = |\mathbf{R}|$, and a direction specified by giving the angle θ that the vector makes with the x axis. A vector is usually denoted by a **bold** symbol, such as $\mathbf{R}$, or sometimes by a symbol with an arrow over it. By convention, the magnitude of a vector is denoted by the same symbol used to denote the vector, only without the bold font or arrows. Even though the direction and magnitude of a vector is a good way to visualize a vector, calculations on vectors are usually easier to perform with the individual *components* of the vector. For our vector $\mathbf{R}$, its components are just its projections along the positive x and y axes:

$$x = R\cos(\theta), \qquad y = R\sin(\theta). \tag{7.2}$$

Thus, if we know R and θ, it is easy to use these equations to calculate x and y, or if we know x and y, R and θ:

$$R = \sqrt{x^2 + y^2}, \qquad \theta = \tan^{-1}\left(\frac{y}{x}\right). \tag{7.3}$$

Usually these components are put together inside some kind of parentheses to indicate that they are the components of a single object. Within the text of a document, they may be written in a horizontal row as (x, y), while in an equation they

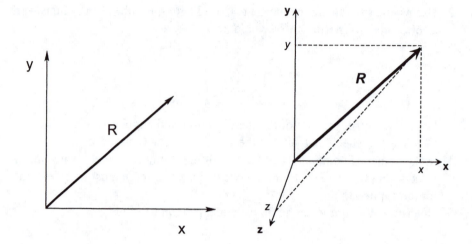

Figure 7.3 *Left:* Representation of a vector as an arrow in 2-D space. *Right:* Representation of a vector as an arrow in 3-D space. The projection of the arrow along each axis equals the components of the vector. In Maple you can rotate the 3-D figure.

may be grouped as a vertical column:

$$R = \begin{bmatrix} x \\ y \end{bmatrix}. \tag{7.4}$$

Whether a vector is viewed as an abstract symbol **R** or as the collection of components, it is the same object being viewed. Multiple representations are a good thing, because sometimes it is easier to perform formal manipulations with abstract symbols rather than individual components, while other times it is easier to perform explicit calculations with the components.

We have drawn the vector **R** as if it were in a plane. If you spent more time away from the computer screen, you might realize that the real world has three dimensions, and we really should be drawing our vectors in a 3-D space with components along the x, y, and z axes. As shown in Figure 7.3, while the trigonometry is more complicated for 3-D vectors than 2-D ones, working with components is much the same, only now **R** has three components:

$$R = \begin{bmatrix} x \\ y \\ z \end{bmatrix}. \tag{7.5}$$

Other vectors in addition to the displacement vector **R** occur regularly in science. Examples include velocity, acceleration, force, and electric and magnetic fields (so you may as well start to understand them now if you do not already). Fortunately, the rules for decomposition into components are the same for all vectors, as are the rules for various algebraic manipulations.

7.2.1 Vector Operations and Matrices

Operating upon vectors that are represented by components is really quite easy, since all you have to do is operate on the individual components using the ordinary rules of algebra. To illustrate, let us say we have vectors A and B represented by their three components,

$$A = \begin{bmatrix} A_x \\ A_y \\ A_y \end{bmatrix}, \qquad B = \begin{bmatrix} B_x \\ B_y \\ B_z \end{bmatrix}. \qquad (7.6)$$

Addition and subtraction are defined as

$$A + B \stackrel{\text{def}}{=} \begin{bmatrix} A_x + B_x \\ A_y + B_y \\ A_z + B_z \end{bmatrix}, \qquad A - B \stackrel{\text{def}}{=} \begin{bmatrix} A_x - B_x \\ A_y - B_y \\ A_z - B_z \end{bmatrix}. \qquad (7.7)$$

Multiplication of vector A by a constant c is defined as

$$c\mathbf{A} \stackrel{\text{def}}{=} \begin{bmatrix} cA_x \\ cA_y \\ cA_z \end{bmatrix}. \qquad (7.8)$$

Two vectors may multiply each other in two ways. The *dot product* is the sum of the product of their corresponding components:

$$\mathbf{A} \cdot \mathbf{B} = \overline{A_x}B_x + \overline{A_y}B_y + \overline{A_z}B_z, \qquad (7.9)$$

where the bar over the components of A indicates complex conjugate. In science, the asterisk * is usually used to indicate complex conjugation, yet is often left off, since the vectors are real. Geometrically, the dot product $\mathbf{A} \cdot \mathbf{B}$ is just the projection of A along the direction of B. In view of the fact that the result is just a *scalar* (a quantity with no direction), the dot product is also known as the *scalar product*.

The second kind of vector multiplication is the *cross product*:

$$\mathbf{A} \times \mathbf{B} = \begin{bmatrix} A_y B_z - A_z B_y \\ A_z B_x - A_x B_z \\ A_x B_y - A_y B_x \end{bmatrix}. \qquad (7.10)$$

Geometrically, the cross product $\mathbf{A} \times \mathbf{B}$ is a new vector perpendicular to the plane formed by A and B, with magnitude $|\mathbf{A}||\mathbf{B}|\sin\theta$, where θ is the angle between the vectors A and B.

7.3 THEORY: ANGULAR MOMENTUM DYNAMICS

A rigid body is one in which the distance between the particles that compose the body do not change [M&T 88]. We imagine such an object rotating about a fixed point O (or about the center of mass of the body). In spite of it being true that each part of a rotating body has a different velocity, all parts have the same angular velocity ω. The velocity of part i is related to ω via:

$$\mathbf{v}_i = \omega \times \mathbf{r}_i, \tag{7.11}$$

where $\mathbf{r}_i$ is a vector from the origin O to part i, and $\times$ represents the vector cross product.

Angular momentum is introduced into mechanics as the rotational analog of linear momentum. It measures the tendency of a rotating object to remain rotating, and has a direction associated with it. For the highly symmetric cases usually studied in elementary physics, the angular momentum and angular velocity vectors are parallel to each other,

$$\mathbf{L} = I\omega, \tag{7.12}$$

with the proportionality constant I called the *moment of inertia*. However, when an object rotates about an axis that is not one of high symmetry, then $\mathbf{L}$ and ω will not be parallel to each other, and a generalization of this equation is needed. The general relation between the angular momentum and the angular velocity follows from expressing the angular momentum of a group of particles as the sum of the angular momentum of each particle:

$$\mathbf{L} = \sum_i \mathbf{r}_i \times \mathbf{p}_i, \tag{7.13}$$

where $\mathbf{p}_i = m_i \mathbf{v}_i$ is the linear momentum of particle i. If we restrict ourselves to the rotation of a rigid body about a fixed point, then the velocity is related simply to the angular velocity, and we have

$$\mathbf{L} = \sum_i m_i \mathbf{r}_i \times (\omega \times \mathbf{r}_i), \tag{7.14}$$

where the right-most vector cross product must be performed first.

We now skip over the details of the derivation and give you the final result. For general problems, such as rotation of the cube in Figure 7.3 about axes along a side of the cube, the angular velocity ω and angular momentum vector $\mathbf{L}$ are related by what Maple calls the dot product of vector ω with the inertia tensor $\{\mathbf{I}\}$:

$$\mathbf{L} = \{\mathbf{I}\}\,\omega. \tag{7.15}$$

Observe how in the above equation we have placed braces around the symbol $\mathbf{I}$. The braces indicate a type of mathematical object, a *tensor*, that transforms one vector into another vector. If the vectors are represented by columns (the usual thing), then we represent the action of a tensor on a vector by the multiplication of that vector by a matrix:

$$\begin{bmatrix} L_x \\ L_y \\ L_z \end{bmatrix} = \begin{bmatrix} I_{xx} & I_{xy} & I_{xz} \\ I_{yx} & I_{yy} & I_{yz} \\ I_{zx} & I_{zy} & I_{zz} \end{bmatrix} \begin{bmatrix} \omega_x \\ \omega_y \\ \omega_z \end{bmatrix}. \tag{7.16}$$

We see by looking at this equation, and by applying the rules of matrix algebra, that this one matrix equation is an elegant way of presenting the three simultaneous linear equations relating the individual angular velocity and angular momentum components to each other:

$$L_x = I_{xx}\omega_x + I_{xy}\omega_y + I_{xz}\omega_z, \tag{7.17}$$

$$L_y = I_{yx}\omega_x + I_{yy}\omega_y + I_{yz}\omega_z, \tag{7.18}$$

$$L_z = I_{zx}\omega_x + I_{zy}\omega_y + I_{zz}\omega_z. \tag{7.19}$$

It is, of course, even easier to write this as one matrix equation $\mathbf{L} = \omega$. In addition, it is much easier to manipulate the matrix equation than the individual equations.

The diagonal elements I_{xx}, I_{yy}, and I_{zz} of the inertia tensor are called the *moments of inertia* about the x, y, and z axes, respectively. They are the same as those used in elementary physics. The off-diagonal elements, such as $I_{xy} = I_{yx}$, are negatives of what are called *products of inertia*, and they are responsible for making ω and $\mathbf{L}$ nonparallel. An explicit expression for the elements of $\mathbf{I}$ is [M&T 88]

$$I_{i,j} = \int \rho(v) \left[\delta_{ij} (\sum_k x_k^2) - x_i x_j \right] dv \tag{7.20}$$

for continuous mass, and

$$I_{i,j} = \sum_a m_a \left[\delta_{ij} (\sum_k x_{a,k}^2) - x_{a,i} x_{a,j} \right] \tag{7.21}$$

for discrete masses. Here the symbol δ_{ij} is the Kronecker delta function,

$$\delta_{i,j} = \begin{cases} 1, & \text{if } i = j \\ 0, & \text{otherwise.} \end{cases} \tag{7.22}$$

7.4 MAPLE: LINEAR ALGEBRA TOOLS

In computing and science, confusion often arises from speaking of *arrays* and *matrices* as much the same thing. An array refers to the bookkeeping device used to store items by placing them in designated rows and columns. A matrix also has its elements stored in rows and columns, but it has well-defined mathematical properties. We shall speak more about this in Chapter 17, where we discuss these objects within the Java framework of programming with a compiled language. Now we shall look at some of the facilities Maple has for handling matrices and their algebraic manipulations. The more elementary tone of the Java chapter on matrices may be more accessible to beginners than this chapter, where Maple's mathematical sophistication requires a higher-level understanding of linear algebra.

In mathematics, the row or column is usually given by a subscript, with the row and column numbers starting from 1. As a case in point, $M_{i,j}$ for an element in row i and column j, with $M_{1,1}$ the first element of the matrix. In computer science, the rows and columns are indicted by indices, for example, `M[i][j]`, with `M[0][0]` the first element. There is essentially no limit to the number of indices an array may have, yet the maximum value that an index may have is limited by the finite amount of computer memory available.[1]

A vector in Maple is represented as a one-dimensional array `v[i]` with index `i` starting from `1`. A matrix in Maple is represented as a two-dimensional array `M[i,j]` with row and column indices `i` and `j` starting from 1.

The branch of mathematics called *linear algebra* deals with matrices. Maple has two packages for linear algebra. The older one, `linalg`, has been superseded by `LinearAlgebra`. The commands are similar, with those in `LinearAlgebra` capitalized, and those in `linalg` in lowercase. In an appendix we give a table showing the equivalent commands in each package. Loading either package shows the commands available:

```
> with(LinearAlgebra);
```

[Add,   Adjoint,   BackwardSubstitute,   BandMatrix,   Basis, BezoutMatrix,   BidiagonalForm,   BilinearForm,   CharacteristicMatrix, CharacteristicPolynomial,   Column,   ColumnDimension,   ColumnOperation, ColumnSpace, CompanionMatrix, ConditionNumber, ConstantMatrix, ConstantVector, CreatePermutation, CrossProduct, DeleteColumn,   DeleteRow, Determinant,   DiagonalMatrix,   Dimension,   Dimensions,   DotProduct, EigenConditionNumbers, Eigenvalues, Eigenvectors, Equal, ForwardSubstitute, FrobeniusForm,   GaussianElimination,   GenerateEquations,   GenerateMatrix, GetResultDataType,   GetResultShape,   GivensRotationMatrix,   GramSchmidt, HankelMatrix,   HermiteForm,   HermitianTranspose,   HessenbergForm, HilbertMatrix,   HouseholderMatrix,   IdentityMatrix,   IntersectionBasis,   IsDefinite, IsOrthogonal, IsSimilar, IsUnitary, JordanBlockMatrix, JordanForm, LA_Main, LUDecomposition, LeastSquares, LinearSolve, Map, Map2, MatrixAdd, MatrixInverse, MatrixMatrixMultiply, MatrixNorm, MatrixScalarMultiply, MatrixVectorMultiply,   MinimalPolynomial,   Minor,   Modular,   Multiply, NoUserValue, Norm, Normalize, NullSpace, OuterProductMatrix, Permanent, Pivot, PopovForm, QRDecomposition, RandomMatrix, RandomVector, Rank, ReducedRowEchelonForm, Row, RowDimension, RowOperation,   RowSpace, ScalarMatrix, ScalarMultiply, ScalarVector, SchurForm,   SingularValues, SmithForm, SubMatrix, SubVector, SumBasis, SylvesterMatrix, ToeplitzMatrix, Trace, Transpose, TridiagonalForm, UnitVector, VandermondeMatrix, VectorAdd, VectorAngle, VectorMatrixMultiply, VectorNorm, VectorScalarMultiply, ZeroMatrix, ZeroVector, Zip]

---

[1]At times the largest value an index assumes is called the *dimension* of the array, while at other times the number of indices is called the dimension of the array. So, be careful! We call the number of indices the dimension.

(The warnings that appear after loading a package do not indicate that anything is wrong. They just indicate that these packages redefine some of the meaning of existing mathematical operations, like norm.) Notwithstanding our preference for the LinearAlgebra package, there are some commands available only in linalg. When you run into that, you may run a linalg command within LinearAlgebra.

7.4.1 Defining Matrices and Vectors

Matrices are input as two-dimensional arrays or with the Matrix command:

```
> with(LinearAlgebra):
> I_plate := Matrix( 2, 2, [ [1,0], [0, 4] ] );        # Define 2 x 2 matrix & elements
```

$$I\_plate := \begin{bmatrix} 1 & 0 \\ 0 & 4 \end{bmatrix}$$

```
> I_sphere := Matrix( 3, 3, [[Ixx,Ixy,Ixz], [Iyx,Iyy,Iyz], [Izx,Izy,Izz] ] );
```

$$I\_sphere := \begin{bmatrix} Ixx & Ixy & Ixz \\ Iyx & Iyy & Iyz \\ Izx & Izy & Izz \end{bmatrix}$$

```
> `I_sphere[2, 3]` = I_sphere[2, 3];                    # Look at individual element
```

$$I\_sphere[2, 3] = Iyz$$

```
> A := Matrix( 3, 3, (i, j) -> i*j^2 );                 # Matrix elements = function (i,j)
```

$$A := \begin{bmatrix} 1 & 4 & 9 \\ 2 & 8 & 18 \\ 3 & 12 & 27 \end{bmatrix}$$

```
> `A[3, 2]` = A[3, 2];                                  # Look at individual element
```

$$A[3, 2] = 12$$

```
> B := Array( 1..3, 1..3, [ [-2,2,-3], [2,1,-6], [-1,-2,0] ] );
```

$$B := \begin{bmatrix} -2 & 2 & -3 \\ 2 & 1 & -6 \\ -1 & -2 & 0 \end{bmatrix}$$

```
> ID := IdentityMatrix(6);                              # The identity matrix of specified dimension
```

$$ID := \begin{bmatrix} 1 & 0 & 0 & 0 & 0 & 0 \\ 0 & 1 & 0 & 0 & 0 & 0 \\ 0 & 0 & 1 & 0 & 0 & 0 \\ 0 & 0 & 0 & 1 & 0 & 0 \\ 0 & 0 & 0 & 0 & 1 & 0 \\ 0 & 0 & 0 & 0 & 0 & 1 \end{bmatrix}$$

You see that the `[i,j]` elements of the matrices are assigned and accessed using the subscript notation `A[i,j]`, just as the elements of a vector are accessed as `v[i]` or `v[j]`. The matrix `I_sphere` is assigned with explicit elements; the matrix `A` is assigned via a functional form for the `[i,j]` element; the matrix `B` is assigned as a list of lists (recall order matters in lists), with each sublist being a row of the matrix, and the major list being a list of rows. The identity matrix `ID` is created just by giving its size.

Now that we have created matrices *row by row* using list of lists, we show how to create them *column by column* using angle brackets `<` and `>` with vertical bars as separators:

```
> A := < <a, d> | <b, e> | <c, f> >;                                  Separated symbols
```

$$A := \begin{bmatrix} a & b & c \\ d & e & f \end{bmatrix}$$

```
> C := Matrix ( < <1, 2, 3, 4> | <5, 6, 7, 8> | <9, 10, 11, 12> > );
```

$$C := \begin{bmatrix} 1 & 5 & 9 \\ 2 & 6 & 10 \\ 3 & 7 & 11 \\ 4 & 8 & 12 \end{bmatrix}$$

Once you have a matrix with numerical elements, it is easy to visualize it via Maple's `matrixplot` command:

```
> with(plots):
> matrixplot(ID, axes = boxed, title =' Identity Matrix');            # Left plot
```

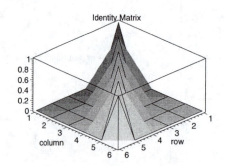
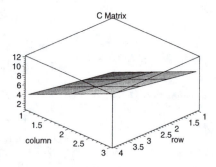

```
> matrixplot( C, axes = boxed, title = 'C Matrix' );                  # Right plot
```

Next we use the `type` function to see if some of the objects we have created are arrays or matrices. We shall see that while an array can be set up to also be a matrix, if the array uses indices that begin with 0, then it cannot be a matrix:

```
> type(M, Matrix);        type(M, Array);                             # Is M a Matrix, Array?
```
$$true \qquad\qquad false$$

7.4.2 Column and Row Vectors

In physics we usually deal with vectors that represent objects having a magnitude and direction in space. We specify the velocity vector by giving its three components:

$$\mathbf{v} = (v_x, v_y, v_z). \tag{7.23}$$

We do this in Maple with the `Vector` command:

```
> restart:  with(LinearAlgebra):
> V := Vector([Vx, Vy, Vz]);                     # Enter column vector; displayed as row
```

$$V := \begin{bmatrix} Vx \\ Vy \\ Vz \end{bmatrix}$$

```
> r := Vector([x,y,z]);                          # Another vector
```

$$r := \begin{bmatrix} x \\ y \\ z \end{bmatrix}$$

```
> V[1];                                          # First element of vector =?
```

$$Vx$$

The `Vector` command manifestly creates a column vector. We may also create a row vector as a matrix with one row. That is, a row vector is the same as a $1 \times N$ matrix. Likewise, a column vector is the same as an $N \times 1$ matrix. Remember, since explicit input of matrix elements are done row by row, a column matrix requires a list of lists, with each sublist containing the one item for that row:

```
> U_col_M := Matrix( [ [10],[20],[30] ] );       # Column vector via list of lists
```

$$U\_col\_M := \begin{bmatrix} 10 \\ 20 \\ 30 \end{bmatrix}$$

```
> U_col_M[2,1];                                  # Look at element in matrix, OK
```

$$20$$

```
> U_col_M := Matrix( <10, 20, 30> );             # Column vector via angle brackets
```

$$U\_col\_M := \begin{bmatrix} 10 \\ 20 \\ 30 \end{bmatrix}$$

```
> `U_col_M[2, 1]` = U_col_M[2, 1];               # Look at element in matrix; it is still OK
```

$$U\_col\_M[2, 1] = 20$$

```
> U_col := <10, 20, 30>;                         # Create column vector, not matrix
```

$$U\_col := \begin{bmatrix} 10 \\ 20 \\ 30 \end{bmatrix}$$

```
> U_col[2, 1];                                        # Look at element in matrix, not OK
.  Error, number of indices exceeds rank
> `U_col[2]` = U_col[2];                              # Look at element in vector, OK as not matrix.
```

$$U\_col[2] = 20$$

```
> U_row_M := Matrix( [a, b, c] );                     # Create row in matrix
```

$$U\_row\_M := \begin{bmatrix} a & b & c \end{bmatrix}$$

```
> `U_row_M[1, 3]` = U_row_M[1, 3];                    # Look at individual elements
```

$$U\_row\_M[1, 3] = c$$

```
> U_row_M[3];                                         # Look at element in vector; not OK for matrix.
  Error, Matrix index out of range
```

7.4.3 Arrays

Arrays in Maple are tables of data or variables with arbitrary numbers of subscripts. Matrices, in contrast, are restricted to just two indices and are mathematical objects. We can define an array in Maple with the `array` command in which we give explicit ranges for each index. However, for intermixing arrays with matrices from the `LinearAlgebra` package, we want Maple to implement the arrays as `rtables`, and so we use the `Array` command:

```
> restart:           with(LinearAlgebra):
> A_1D := Array( 1..4 );                              # Created as rtable (note commas in output)
> Array( 1..2, 1..2, [ [1, 2], [3, 4] ] );           # Create Array and assign elements
> A_3D := Array( 1..4, 1..3, 1..2 );                 # Create 3-D Array, hard to print out
> type(A_1D, Array);        type(a_1D, Array);
> type(A_1D, array);        type(A_3D, Array);
```

$$A_1D := [0, 0, 0, 0]$$

$$\begin{bmatrix} 1 & 2 \\ 3 & 4 \end{bmatrix}$$

$$A_3D := \begin{bmatrix} 1\ldots4 \times 1\ldots3 \times 1\ldots2\ 3 - D\ Array \\ DataType : anything \\ Storage : rectangular \\ Order : Fortran\_order \end{bmatrix}$$

$$\qquad\qquad true \qquad false\ false \qquad\quad true$$

We see that these commands create the 1D array A_1D whose index can vary from 1 to 4, and the 3D array A_3D whose first index varies from 1 to 4, whose second index varies from 1 to 3, and whose third index varies from 1 to 2. These array commands created the two array structures, but have not put any values in them. We assign values explicitly, or with some procedures:

```
> A_1D [1] := A;       A_1D [2] := 55;     A_1D [3] := Pi;
> A_3D [3] := Pi;      A_3D [2] := 55;
> A_1D;
```

$$A\_1D[1] := A \quad A\_1D[2] := 55 \quad A\_1D[3] := Pi \quad A\_3D[3] := Pi \quad A\_3D[2] := 55$$

$$[A,\ 55,\ \pi,\ 0]$$

7.5 MATRIX ARITHMETIC AND OPERATIONS

7.5.1 Multiplication

Matrix multiplication is accomplished with the commands

```
Multiply(A, B)   A.B   MatrixMatrixMultiply(A, B)   evalm(A &* B).
```

The basic mathematical rule showing the dimensions for matrix multiplication is

$$A_{M \times N} = B_{M \times L} C_{L \times N} \tag{7.24}$$

This means that it is legal to multiply the $M \times L$ matrix B by the $L \times N$ matrix C only if the two inner dimensions are the same. The resulting matrix A will have dimension $L \times M$, that is, the two outer dimensions of B and C:

```
> restart:       with(LinearAlgebra):
> A := Matrix( 3, 3, (i,j) -> (i*x)^j );                          # Define matrix A
```

$$A := \begin{bmatrix} x & x^2 & x^3 \\ 2x & 4x^2 & 8x^3 \\ 3x & 9x^2 & 27x^3 \end{bmatrix}$$

```
> B := Matrix(3,3,(i,j) -> i^j);                                  # Define matrix B
```

$$B := \begin{bmatrix} 1 & 1 & 1 \\ 2 & 4 & 8 \\ 3 & 9 & 27 \end{bmatrix}$$

```
> A;        B;                                                    # Check the matrices
```

$$\begin{bmatrix} x & x^2 & x^3 \\ 2x & 4x^2 & 8x^3 \\ 3x & 9x^2 & 27x^3 \end{bmatrix} \qquad \begin{bmatrix} 1 & 1 & 1 \\ 2 & 4 & 8 \\ 3 & 9 & 27 \end{bmatrix}$$

```
> evalm(A &* B);                                     # Matrix multiply of two square matrices
```

$$\begin{bmatrix} x + 2x^2 + 3x^3 & x + 4x^2 + 9x^3 & x + 8x^2 + 27x^3 \\ 2x + 8x^2 + 24x^3 & 2x + 16x^2 + 72x^3 & 2x + 32x^2 + 216x^3 \\ 3x + 18x^2 + 81x^3 & 3x + 36x^2 + 243x^3 & 3x + 72x^2 + 729x^3 \end{bmatrix}$$

```
> A . B;                                                          # Multiply two matrices
```

$$
\begin{bmatrix}
x + 2x^2 + 3x^3 & x + 4x^2 + 9x^3 & x + 8x^2 + 27x^3 \\
2x + 8x^2 + 24x^3 & 2x + 16x^2 + 72x^3 & 2x + 32x^2 + 216x^3 \\
3x + 18x^2 + 81x^3 & 3x + 36x^2 + 243x^3 & 3x + 72x^2 + 729x^3
\end{bmatrix}
$$

> `B . A;`   # Multiply two matrices in reversed order

$$
\begin{bmatrix}
6x & 14x^2 & 36x^3 \\
34x & 90x^2 & 250x^3 \\
102x & 282x^2 & 804x^3
\end{bmatrix}
$$

> `Multiply(A, B);`   # Yet another command for multiply

$$
\begin{bmatrix}
x + 2x^2 + 3x^3 & x + 4x^2 + 9x^3 & x + 8x^2 + 27x^3 \\
2x + 8x^2 + 24x^3 & 2x + 16x^2 + 72x^3 & 2x + 32x^2 + 216x^3 \\
3x + 18x^2 + 81x^3 & 3x + 36x^2 + 243x^3 & 3x + 72x^2 + 729x^3
\end{bmatrix}
$$

> `MatrixMatrixMultiply( A, B );`   `MatrixMatrixMultiply( B, A );`

$$
\begin{bmatrix}
x + 2x^2 + 3x^3 & x + 4x^2 + 9x^3 & x + 8x^2 + 27x^3 \\
2x + 8x^2 + 24x^3 & 2x + 16x^2 + 72x^3 & 2x + 32x^2 + 216x^3 \\
3x + 18x^2 + 81x^3 & 3x + 36x^2 + 243x^3 & 3x + 72x^2 + 729x^3
\end{bmatrix}
$$

$$
\begin{bmatrix}
6x & 14x^2 & 36x^3 \\
34x & 90x^2 & 250x^3 \\
102x & 282x^2 & 804x^3
\end{bmatrix}
$$

The different forms of the command to multiply matrix A by B are seen to all give the same result. Yet the result from $A \times B$ is not the same as $B \times A$ (matrix multiplication is not commutative).

The *identity* or *unit matrix* is always square and must be defined for a specific dimension. It is also worth checking that when multiplying from either side it yields the same answer:

> `ID := IdentityMatrix(3);`   # Create 3×3 identity matrix

$$
ID := \begin{bmatrix}
1 & 0 & 0 \\
0 & 1 & 0 \\
0 & 0 & 1
\end{bmatrix}
$$

> `Multiply( A, ID );`   `ID . A;`   # Check with R and L multiplications

$$
\begin{bmatrix}
x & x^2 & x^3 \\
2x & 4x^2 & 8x^3 \\
3x & 9x^2 & 27x^3
\end{bmatrix}
\qquad
\begin{bmatrix}
x & x^2 & x^3 \\
2x & 4x^2 & 8x^3 \\
3x & 9x^2 & 27x^3
\end{bmatrix}
$$

> `evalm( A &* ID );`   # Multiply by identity matrix

$$
\begin{bmatrix}
x & x^2 & x^3 \\
2x & 4x^2 & 8x^3 \\
3x & 9x^2 & 27x^3
\end{bmatrix}
$$

> `A^2; A . A;`   # Matrix raised to power

$$
\begin{bmatrix}
x^2 + 2\,x^3 + 3\,x^4 & x^3 + 4\,x^4 + 9\,x^5 & x^4 + 8\,x^5 + 27\,x^6 \\
2\,x^2 + 8\,x^3 + 24\,x^4 & 2\,x^3 + 16\,x^4 + 72\,x^5 & 2\,x^4 + 32\,x^5 + 216\,x^6 \\
3\,x^2 + 18\,x^3 + 81\,x^4 & 3\,x^3 + 36\,x^4 + 243\,x^5 & 3\,x^4 + 72\,x^5 + 729\,x^6
\end{bmatrix}
$$

$$
\begin{bmatrix}
x^2 + 2\,x^3 + 3\,x^4 & x^3 + 4\,x^4 + 9\,x^5 & x^4 + 8\,x^5 + 27\,x^6 \\
2\,x^2 + 8\,x^3 + 24\,x^4 & 2\,x^3 + 16\,x^4 + 72\,x^5 & 2\,x^4 + 32\,x^5 + 216\,x^6 \\
3\,x^2 + 18\,x^3 + 81\,x^4 & 3\,x^3 + 36\,x^4 + 243\,x^5 & 3\,x^4 + 72\,x^5 + 729\,x^6
\end{bmatrix}
$$

7.5.1.1 Matrix-Scalar Multiplication

Multiplication of a matrix by a scalar is simple if the scalar is numeric:

```
> 3 * A;
```
                                          # Multiply matrix *A* by number

$$
\begin{bmatrix}
3\,x & 3\,x^2 & 3\,x^3 \\
6\,x & 12\,x^2 & 24\,x^3 \\
9\,x & 27\,x^2 & 81\,x^3
\end{bmatrix}
$$

However, if the scalar is symbolic, the results may not be what you expect:

```
> c * A;
```
                                          # Multiply matrix A by symbol

$$
c \begin{bmatrix}
x & x^2 & x^3 \\
2\,x & 4\,x^2 & 8\,x^3 \\
3\,x & 9\,x^2 & 27\,x^3
\end{bmatrix}
$$

The problem is that Maple does not know what type of an object c is unless you tell it. The most direct way is use the `ScalarMultiply` command:

```
> ScalarMultiply(A, c);
```

$$
\begin{bmatrix}
c\,x & c\,x^2 & c\,x^3 \\
2\,c\,x & 4\,c\,x^2 & 8\,c\,x^3 \\
3\,c\,x & 9\,c\,x^2 & 27\,c\,x^3
\end{bmatrix}
$$

Once in a while, like above, Maple appears to be stubborn in granting our wishes. As is often our approach in these cases, we are patient and request help from the `simplify` command, possibly with `symbolic` or `scalar` as an option:

```
> c * A;        simplify(%);
```
                                                                     # Distribute via simplify

$$
c \begin{bmatrix}
x & x^2 & x^3 \\
2\,x & 4\,x^2 & 8\,x^3 \\
3\,x & 9\,x^2 & 27\,x^3
\end{bmatrix}
\qquad
\begin{bmatrix}
c\,x & c\,x^2 & c\,x^3 \\
2\,c\,x & 4\,c\,x^2 & 8\,c\,x^3 \\
3\,c\,x & 9\,c\,x^2 & 27\,c\,x^3
\end{bmatrix}
$$

```
> c * A;          simplify( %, symbolic);
```

$$
c \begin{bmatrix}
x & x^2 & x^3 \\
2\,x & 4\,x^2 & 8\,x^3 \\
3\,x & 9\,x^2 & 27\,x^3
\end{bmatrix}
\qquad
\begin{bmatrix}
c\,x & c\,x^2 & c\,x^3 \\
2\,c\,x & 4\,c\,x^2 & 8\,c\,x^3 \\
3\,c\,x & 9\,c\,x^2 & 27\,c\,x^3
\end{bmatrix}
$$

```
> c * A;          simplify(%) assuming c::  symbolic;
```

$$c \begin{bmatrix} x & x^2 & x^3 \\ 2x & 4x^2 & 8x^3 \\ 3x & 9x^2 & 27x^3 \end{bmatrix} \qquad \begin{bmatrix} cx & cx^2 & cx^3 \\ 2cx & 4cx^2 & 8cx^3 \\ 3cx & 9cx^2 & 27cx^3 \end{bmatrix}$$

7.5.1.2 Matrix-Vector Multiplication

Now we explore the multiplication of vectors by matrices. Remember the rule showing the dimensions for matrix multiplication:

$$A_{M \times N} = B_{M \times L} C_{L \times N}. \tag{7.25}$$

This means that the number of columns in B must match the number of rows in C. If C is a vector of dimension J, this means that C has J rows and one column (a $J \times 1$ matrix), so $L = J$ and $N = 1$ in the above equation. As a consequence, the matrix B that multiplies a vector of dimension J must be dimension $J \times J$. The result of matrix-vector multiplication is a matrix of $J \times 1$, that is, another a vector:

```
> Vec := Vector([a, b, c]);     ucol := Matrix(3, 1, [[a], [b], [c]]);  # 2 vectors
```

$$Vec := \begin{bmatrix} a \\ b \\ c \end{bmatrix} \qquad ucol := \begin{bmatrix} a \\ b \\ c \end{bmatrix}$$

```
> urow := Matrix(1,3, [d, e, f]);     B := Matrix(3,3, (i,j)-> i^j);  # Row vector
```

$$urow := \begin{bmatrix} d & e & f \end{bmatrix} \qquad B := \begin{bmatrix} 1 & 1 & 1 \\ 2 & 4 & 8 \\ 3 & 9 & 27 \end{bmatrix}$$

```
> Multiply( B, Vec );     Multiply( B, ucol );        # 3 × 3 matrix times 3 × 1 vector
```

$$\begin{bmatrix} a+b+c \\ 2a+4b+8c \\ 3a+9b+27c \end{bmatrix} \qquad \begin{bmatrix} a+b+c \\ 2a+4b+8c \\ 3a+9b+27c \end{bmatrix}$$

```
> 'B * urow' = Multiply(B, urow);                    # 1 × 3 times 3 × 3 not allowed
  Error, first matrix column dimension (3) <> second matrix row dimension (1)
> 'urow * B ' = Multiply( urow, B );                  # Is 1 × 3 times 3 × 3 allowed?
```

$$B\,urow = \begin{bmatrix} d+2e+3f & d+4e+9f & d+8e+27f \end{bmatrix}$$

7.5.2 Matrix Addition and Subtraction

The `LinearAlgebra` package contains a number of ways to perform addition and subtraction of matrices. The `MatrixAdd` and `VectorAdd` methods do the actual work, yet they are called automatically by the more general `Add` command. In addition, there are the shortcuts + and - that work fine (as long as you remember what is a matrix). *Beware:* these commands are real smart and will do the "obvious" thing if you try to add together different combinations of vectors, matrices, and scalars; however, you must ensure that what is obvious to Maple is what you want.

```
> restart:          with(LinearAlgebra):                    # Define matrices A, B
> A := Matrix( 3, 3, (i,j) -> (i*x)^j );        B := Matrix( 3, 3, (i,j) -> i^j );
```

$$A := \begin{bmatrix} x & x^2 & x^3 \\ 2x & 4x^2 & 8x^3 \\ 3x & 9x^2 & 27x^3 \end{bmatrix} \qquad B := \begin{bmatrix} 1 & 1 & 1 \\ 2 & 4 & 8 \\ 3 & 9 & 27 \end{bmatrix}$$

```
> Vec1 := Vector( [a, b, c] );         Vec2 := Vector([1,2,3]);    # Two 3-D vectors
```

$$Vec1 := \begin{bmatrix} a \\ b \\ c \end{bmatrix} \qquad Vec2 := \begin{bmatrix} 1 \\ 2 \\ 3 \end{bmatrix}$$

```
> A + B;        A - B;
```

$$\begin{bmatrix} x+1 & x^2+1 & x^3+1 \\ 2x+2 & 4x^2+4 & 8x^3+8 \\ 3x+3 & 9x^2+9 & 27x^3+27 \end{bmatrix} \qquad \begin{bmatrix} x-1 & x^2-1 & x^3-1 \\ 2x-2 & 4x^2-4 & 8x^3-8 \\ 3x-3 & 9x^2-9 & 27x^3-27 \end{bmatrix}$$

```
> Add( A, B );          MatrixAdd( A, B );                          # Two adds
```

$$\begin{bmatrix} x+1 & x^2+1 & x^3+1 \\ 2x+2 & 4x^2+4 & 8x^3+8 \\ 3x+3 & 9x^2+9 & 27x^3+27 \end{bmatrix} \qquad \begin{bmatrix} x+1 & x^2+1 & x^3+1 \\ 2x+2 & 4x^2+4 & 8x^3+8 \\ 3x+3 & 9x^2+9 & 27x^3+27 \end{bmatrix}$$

```
> Add( Vec1, Vec2 );        Vec1 + Vec2;        A + 2;               # Three adds
```

$$\begin{bmatrix} a+1 \\ b+2 \\ c+3 \end{bmatrix} \qquad \begin{bmatrix} a+1 \\ b+2 \\ c+3 \end{bmatrix} \qquad \begin{bmatrix} x+2 & x^2 & x^3 \\ 2x & 4x^2+2 & 8x^3 \\ 3x & 9x^2 & 27x^3+2 \end{bmatrix}$$

```
> ID := IdentityMatrix(3);
```

$$ID := \begin{bmatrix} 1 & 0 & 0 \\ 0 & 1 & 0 \\ 0 & 0 & 1 \end{bmatrix}$$

```
> A+ 2*ID;        C := Add(A,-lambda);                        # ID implied in 2nd
```

$$\begin{bmatrix} x+2 & x^2 & x^3 \\ 2x & 4x^2+2 & 8x^3 \\ 3x & 9x^2 & 27x^3+2 \end{bmatrix} \qquad C := \begin{bmatrix} x-\lambda & x^2 & x^3 \\ 2x & 4x^2-\lambda & 8x^3 \\ 3x & 9x^2 & 27x^3-\lambda \end{bmatrix}$$

```
> Add(Vec1,1);                                                          # This not permitted
  Error, (in LinearAlgebra:-Add) invalid arguments
> 2*A + 3*B;          Add(Vec1, Vec2, 4, 1);                     # Scalar mult + add, 4 vec1 + vec2
```

$$\begin{bmatrix} 2\,x+3 & 2\,x^2+3 & 2\,x^3+3 \\ 4\,x+6 & 8\,x^2+12 & 16\,x^3+24 \\ 6\,x+9 & 18\,x^2+27 & 54\,x^3+81 \end{bmatrix} \qquad \begin{bmatrix} 4\,a+1 \\ 4\,b+2 \\ 4\,c+3 \end{bmatrix}$$

7.5.3 Other Matrix Operations

Now we define a 3×3 and a 4×4 matrix. The matrix A has three rows, each proportional to the others, and the matrix ID is the 4-D identity matrix:

```
> restart:            with(LinearAlgebra):
> A := Matrix([ [1,2,3], [2,4,6], [3,6,9] ]);          ID := IdentityMatrix(4);
```

$$A := \begin{bmatrix} 1 & 2 & 3 \\ 2 & 4 & 6 \\ 3 & 6 & 9 \end{bmatrix} \qquad ID := \begin{bmatrix} 1 & 0 & 0 & 0 \\ 0 & 1 & 0 & 0 \\ 0 & 0 & 1 & 0 \\ 0 & 0 & 0 & 1 \end{bmatrix}$$

Before we go ahead and evaluate the determinant of each, we observe that the rows in A are not independent, and so its determinant should vanish, while the determinant of a diagonal matrix, such as the identity matrix, is just the product of the diagonal elements:

```
> Determinant(A);          Determinant(ID);          # Determinant vanishes if rows proportional
```

$$0 \qquad 1$$

```
> B := Matrix(3,3, (i,j)-> i^j);          Determinant(B);          # B has independent rows
```

$$B := \begin{bmatrix} 1 & 1 & 1 \\ 2 & 4 & 8 \\ 3 & 9 & 27 \end{bmatrix} \qquad 12$$

```
> Binv := 1/B;                                                  # Inverse exist if nonzero determinant
```

$$Binv := \begin{bmatrix} 3 & \dfrac{-3}{2} & \dfrac{1}{3} \\[2ex] \dfrac{-5}{2} & 2 & \dfrac{-1}{2} \\[2ex] \dfrac{1}{2} & \dfrac{-1}{2} & \dfrac{1}{6} \end{bmatrix}$$

```
> B . Binv;          Binv . B;                                  # B times its inverse, inverse times B
```

$$\begin{bmatrix} 1 & 0 & 0 \\ 0 & 1 & 0 \\ 0 & 0 & 1 \end{bmatrix} \qquad \begin{bmatrix} 1 & 0 & 0 \\ 0 & 1 & 0 \\ 0 & 0 & 1 \end{bmatrix}$$

`> Transpose(A);`   `Trace(A);`   `Trace(ID);`   # Row–column interchange, sum diagonals

$$\begin{bmatrix} 1 & 2 & 3 \\ 2 & 4 & 6 \\ 3 & 6 & 9 \end{bmatrix} \qquad 14 \qquad 4$$

`> A := Matrix([[a,b,c], [a^2,b^2,c^4], [a,b,c^4]]);`   `Ainv := 1/A;`   # Symbolic

$$A := \begin{bmatrix} a & b & c \\ a^2 & b^2 & c^4 \\ a & b & c^4 \end{bmatrix} \qquad Ainv := \begin{bmatrix} -\dfrac{c^3(b-1)}{a} & \dfrac{1}{(a-b)\,a} & -\dfrac{c^3-b}{a} \\ \dfrac{c^3(a-1)}{b} & -\dfrac{1}{(a-b)\,b} & \dfrac{-c^3+a}{b} \\ -\dfrac{1}{(c^3-1)\,c} & 0 & \dfrac{1}{(c^3-1)\,c} \end{bmatrix}$$

`> A.Ainv;`   `Map(simplify, %);`   # A mess, simplified

$$\begin{bmatrix} 1 & 0 & 0 \\ 0 & 1 & 0 \\ 0 & 0 & 1 \end{bmatrix}$$

As we have just seen, the Map command applies a function to each element of its second argument and places the result back into the matrix. If the first argument is a matrix, then each element of the matrix has the function applied to it. If the function takes an argument of its own, that argument may be given as a third argument:

`> restart:  with(LinearAlgebra):`
`> Map(f, x + y*z);`   # Use map on ordinary function

$$f(x) + f(y\,z)$$

`> A := Matrix(3,3, (i,j)-> (i*x)^j);`   # Define matrix A again

$$A := \begin{bmatrix} x & x^2 & x^3 \\ 2\,x & 4\,x^2 & 8\,x^3 \\ 3\,x & 9\,x^2 & 27\,x^3 \end{bmatrix}$$

`> Map(f,A);`   `A;`   # Apply f to each element in A, check

$$\begin{bmatrix} f(x) & f(x^2) & f(x^3) \\ f(2\,x) & f(4\,x^2) & f(8\,x^3) \\ f(3\,x) & f(9\,x^2) & f(27\,x^3) \end{bmatrix} \qquad \begin{bmatrix} f(x) & f(x^2) & f(x^3) \\ f(2\,x) & f(4\,x^2) & f(8\,x^3) \\ f(3\,x) & f(9\,x^2) & f(27\,x^3) \end{bmatrix}$$

`> A:= Matrix(3,3, (i,j) -> (sin(i*x))^j);`   `Map(simplify,A);` # Define, simplify

$$A := \begin{bmatrix} \sin(x) & \sin(x)^2 & \sin(x)^3 \\ \sin(2\,x) & \sin(2\,x)^2 & \sin(2\,x)^3 \\ \sin(3\,x) & \sin(3\,x)^2 & \sin(3\,x)^3 \end{bmatrix} \quad \begin{bmatrix} \sin(x) & 1-\cos(x)^2 & -\sin(x)\,(-1+\cos(x)^2) \\ \sin(2\,x) & 1-\cos(2\,x)^2 & -\sin(2\,x)\,(-1+\cos(2\,x)^2) \\ \sin(3\,x) & 1-\cos(3\,x)^2 & -\sin(3\,x)\,(-1+\cos(3\,x)^2) \end{bmatrix}$$

```
> A:= Matrix(3,3, (i,j) -> (i*x)^j);        Map(diff,A,x);    # Define, take derivative
```

$$A := \begin{bmatrix} x & x^2 & x^3 \\ 2x & 4x^2 & 8x^3 \\ 3x & 9x^2 & 27x^3 \end{bmatrix} \qquad \begin{bmatrix} 1 & 2x & 3x^2 \\ 2 & 8x & 24x^2 \\ 3 & 18x & 81x^2 \end{bmatrix}$$

7.5.4 Vector Operations

Not only does Maple deal with matrices, but it does vector operations, including calculus. We start by setting up a matrix and some vectors with which to experiment. We intermix symbolic and numeric objects:

```
> with(LinearAlgebra):          A := Matrix([ [1,2,3], [2,4,6], [3,6,9] ]);
```

$$A := \begin{bmatrix} 1 & 2 & 3 \\ 2 & 4 & 6 \\ 3 & 6 & 9 \end{bmatrix}$$

```
> ucol := <10, 20, 30>;       urow := [a, b, c];              # Column and row vectors
```

$$ucol := \begin{bmatrix} 10 \\ 20 \\ 30 \end{bmatrix} \qquad urow := [a, b, c]$$

```
> vec := Vector( [x, y*x^2, sin(x)] );                        # A Maple vector
```

$$vec := \begin{bmatrix} x \\ y x^2 \\ \sin(x) \end{bmatrix}$$

As we discussed in §7.2 with the mathematics, there are a number of ways in which one matrix or vector gets multiplied by another. We define some vectors and look at a few ways here:

```
> vec2 := Vector([1,2,3]);      vec3 := <4, 5, 6>;        vec3 := Vector([4, 5, 6]);
```

$$vec2 := \begin{bmatrix} 1 \\ 2 \\ 3 \end{bmatrix} \qquad vec3 := \begin{bmatrix} 4 \\ 5 \\ 6 \end{bmatrix}$$

```
> dot := DotProduct( vec, vec2 );                  # Maple dot product (NB complex conjugation)
```

$$dot := \bar{x} + 2\,\overline{(y x^2)} + 3\sin(\bar{x})$$

As you may recall, the dot product of vectors **A** and **B** equals the length of each vector multiplied by the cosine of the angle between them:

$$\mathbf{A} \cdot \mathbf{B} = |\mathbf{A}||\mathbf{B}|\cos(\theta) = AB\cos(\theta), \qquad (7.26)$$

where $A = |\mathbf{A}|$ is the length (or magnitude or norm, or modulus) of vector $\mathbf{A}$. To check if this relation holds, we will need to determine the length of a vector. Maple has the `VectorNorm` command. However, there are various norms with which mathematicians deal, and what we call the length of a vector is what Maple calls the *2-norm:*

$$\texttt{VectorNorm(V, 2)} = \sqrt{V_x{}^2 + V_y{}^2 + V_z{}^2}. \qquad (7.27)$$

An alternative is to take the dot product of a vector with itself and then take the square root.

First we will determine the magnitude of the two vectors that we dotted into each other, and then check that the deduced value of $\cos(\theta)$ is less than 1 in magnitude. For convenience, we define subscript variables L_2 and L_3 for the lengths:

```
> L[2] := VectorNorm(vec2, 2);        L[2] := sqrt(vec2 . vec2);        # Two ways
```

$$L_2 := \sqrt{14} \qquad L_2 := \sqrt{14}$$

```
> L[3] := VectorNorm(vec3, 2);        L[3] := sqrt(vec3 . vec3);        # Two ways
```

$$L_3 := \sqrt{77} \qquad L_3 := \sqrt{77}$$

```
> cos_theta := DotProduct(vec2, vec3) / L[2] / L[3];        # Cosine angle
```

$$\texttt{cos\_theta} := \frac{16\sqrt{14}\sqrt{77}}{539}$$

```
> evalf(%);                                        # Check that floating-point value < 1
```

$$0.9746318461$$

While we are talking about the magnitude of vectors, it is often useful to deal with vectors that have been normalized to unit length ("unit vectors"). This is done with Maple's `Normalize` command:

```
> NormVec := Normalize( < 1, 2, 3 >, Euclidean);        # Normalize to norm 1
```

$$NormVec := \begin{bmatrix} \frac{\sqrt{14}}{14} \\[2mm] \frac{\sqrt{14}}{7} \\[2mm] \frac{3\sqrt{14}}{14} \end{bmatrix}$$

```
> DotProduct( NormVec, NormVec );                        # Check if normalized (= 1)
```

$$1$$

Now we define two symbolic vectors and take their cross product to check that it agrees with the definition of cross product. After that, we form the cross product of our two numeric vectors, vec2 and vec3, and check that it is perpendicular to both of them (and thus to their plane):

```
> A := Vector([Ax,Ay,Az]);        B := Vector([Bx,By,Bz]);          # 2 vectors
```

$$A := \begin{bmatrix} A_x \\ A_y \\ A_z \end{bmatrix} \qquad B := \begin{bmatrix} B_x \\ B_y \\ B_z \end{bmatrix}$$

```
> CrossProduct( A, B );                          # General form of cross product
```

$$\begin{bmatrix} A_y B_z - A_z B_y \\ A_z B_x - A_x B_z \\ A_x B_y - A_y B_x \end{bmatrix}$$

```
> Vcross := CrossProduct( vec2, vec3 );      # Numeric cross product of vec2 with vec3
```

$$Vcross := \begin{bmatrix} -3 \\ 6 \\ -3 \end{bmatrix}$$

```
> Vcross . vec2;        Vcross . vec3;                # Should get 0 if vectors are orthogonal
```

$$0 \qquad 0$$

We also know that the cross product has a length equal to the product of the lengths of vec2 and vec3 times the sine of the angle between them. So let us compute $\sin(\theta)$ and see if it agrees with the $\cos(\theta)$ we computed from the dot product:

```
> sin_theta := VectorNorm(Vcross, 2)/L[2]/L[3];      evalf(%);      # Exact or useful
```

$$sin\_theta := \frac{3\sqrt{6}\sqrt{14}\sqrt{77}}{1078} \qquad 0.4438141291$$

```
> cos_theta^2 + sin_theta^2;                              # Check via trig identity
```

$$1$$

7.5.5 Vector Calculus*

Vector calculus may appear a little advanced for beginners, but you will have it here when needed. Because the LinearAlgebra package does not have all of the vector calculus commands of the linalg package, we sometimes must intermix the two packages. To illustrate, invoking Curl just returns its name, which means that the LinearAlgebra package does not know what it means. Hence, we use the linalg[curl] from the linalg package (with the derivatives taken with respect to the second argument):

```
> vec := Vector([ x, y * x^2, sin(x)] );
```

$$vec := \begin{bmatrix} x \\ y\,x^2 \\ \sin(x) \end{bmatrix}$$

> Curl(vec, [x,x,x]);   # No exists, use linalg instead

$$\mathrm{Curl}\left(\begin{bmatrix} x \\ y\,x^2 \\ \sin(x) \end{bmatrix}, [x,\,x,\,x] \right)$$

> linalg[curl] (vec, [x,x,x]);   linalg[curl] (vec, [y,y,y]);   Exists

$$[\cos(x) - 2\,y\,x,\ 1 - \cos(x),\ 2\,y\,x - 1] \qquad [-x^2,\,0,\,x^2]$$

> f := vector([x^2, y^3, z^4]):   v := vector([x, y, z]):   # Two vectors
> linalg[diverge] (f, v);   linalg[grad] (x^3, [x,y,x]);   # Operate on them

$$2\,x + 3\,y^2 + 4\,z^3 \qquad [3\,x^2,\,0,\,3\,x^2]$$

7.5.6 Eigenvalues and Eigenvectors*

The command Eigenvectors solves the eigenvalue problem for matrix A:

$$[A]\mathbf{X} = \lambda\mathbf{X}. \tag{7.28}$$

That is, Eigenvectors searches for a set of eigenvectors $[\mathbf{X}]$ and corresponding eigenvalues $[\lambda]$ for which (7.28) holds. The eigenvectors are numbered by the index i, where

$$1 \le i \le D, \tag{7.29}$$

with D the dimension of the space spanned by the eigenvectors. As we shall see, the eigenvectors of A are returned as a matrix with vectors as columns, and so some manipulation is required to extract individual eigenvectors:

> A := Matrix([[-2,2,-3], [2,1,-6], [-1,-2,0]]);   # Enter A's rows

$$A := \begin{bmatrix} -2 & 2 & -3 \\ 2 & 1 & -6 \\ -1 & -2 & 0 \end{bmatrix}$$

> Eigenvectors(A);   # Find eigenvector and eigenvalues of A

$$\begin{bmatrix} -3 \\ -3 \\ 5 \end{bmatrix}, \qquad \begin{bmatrix} -2 & 3 & -1 \\ 1 & 0 & -2 \\ 0 & 1 & 1 \end{bmatrix}$$

> (lambda, VecMatrix) := Eigenvectors(A);   # Place eigenvector in vecs, values in λ

$$\lambda, VecMatrix := \begin{bmatrix} -3 \\ -3 \\ 5 \end{bmatrix}, \quad \begin{bmatrix} 3 & -2 & 1 \\ 0 & 1 & 2 \\ 1 & 0 & -1 \end{bmatrix}$$

```
> lambda[1];      lambda[2];      lambda[3];                # Three eigenvalues
```

$$-3 \qquad -3 \qquad 5$$

```
> Vec1 := Column(VecMatrix, 1);    Vec2 := Column(VecMatrix, 2); # Two eigenvectors
```

$$Vec1 := \begin{bmatrix} 3 \\ 0 \\ 1 \end{bmatrix} \qquad Vec2 := \begin{bmatrix} -2 \\ 1 \\ 0 \end{bmatrix}$$

```
> A.Vec1 = lambda[1].Vec1;                          # Test first eigenvalue with first eigenvector
```

$$\begin{bmatrix} -9 \\ 0 \\ -3 \end{bmatrix} = \begin{bmatrix} -9 \\ 0 \\ -3 \end{bmatrix}$$

```
>                                                    # You test 2nd & 3rd eigenvalues here!
```

This particular eigenvalue problem is a *degenerate* situation in which two of the eigenvalues are equal, and so we do not expect the degenerate eigenvectors to be orthogonal. (Because the matrix A is not Hermitian, we have no guarantee of orthogonality). We will check if they are orthogonal, and then use the Gram-Schmidt orthogonalization procedure to make them orthogonal:

```
> DotProduct(Vec1,Vec2);                             # Equals 0 if orthogonal
```

$$-6$$

```
> NewVecs := GramSchmidt([Vec1, Vec2, Vec3]);    NewVecs[2];    # Extract 2
```

$$NewVecs := \begin{bmatrix} \begin{bmatrix} 3 \\ 0 \\ 1 \end{bmatrix}, \begin{bmatrix} \frac{-1}{5} \\ 1 \\ \frac{3}{5} \end{bmatrix}, \begin{bmatrix} \frac{4}{7} \\ \frac{8}{7} \\ \frac{-12}{7} \end{bmatrix} \end{bmatrix} \qquad \begin{bmatrix} \frac{-1}{5} \\ 1 \\ \frac{3}{5} \end{bmatrix}$$

```
> DotProduct(NewVecs[1], NewVecs[2]);                 # Test if new vectors are orthogonal
```

$$0$$

These same matrix calculations are possible with symbolic matrix elements, although this usually take more time, as the matrices get bigger. As we see below, even with matrices, we sometimes have to coerce Maple into distributing the multiplication and then expanding the products so the answer looks the way we want it to:

```
> restart: with(LinearAlgebra):
> A := Matrix([ [x, -3], [3*x, 4*x] ]);              # Algebraic matrix A
```

$$A := \begin{bmatrix} x & -3 \\ 3x & 4x \end{bmatrix}$$

```
> lambda := Eigenvalues(A);                          # Store eigenvalues in vector
```

$$\lambda := \begin{bmatrix} \frac{5x}{2} + \frac{3\sqrt{x^2-4x}}{2} \\[2mm] \frac{5x}{2} - \frac{3\sqrt{x^2-4x}}{2} \end{bmatrix}$$

```
> (lambda, Xs) := Eigenvectors(A);            # Store both eigenvalues and eigenvectors
```

$$\lambda, Xs := \begin{bmatrix} \frac{5x}{2} + \frac{3\sqrt{x^2-4x}}{2} \\[2mm] \frac{5x}{2} - \frac{3\sqrt{x^2-4x}}{2} \end{bmatrix}, \quad \begin{bmatrix} -\frac{\frac{3x}{2} - \frac{3\sqrt{x^2-4x}}{2}}{3x} & -\frac{\frac{3x}{2} + \frac{3\sqrt{x^2-4x}}{2}}{3x} \\[3mm] 1 & 1 \end{bmatrix}$$

```
> X1 := Column (Xs,1);      X2 := Column (Xs,2);       # Extract two eigenvectors
```

$$X1 := \begin{bmatrix} -\frac{\frac{3x}{2} - \frac{3\sqrt{x^2-4x}}{2}}{3x} \\[3mm] 1 \end{bmatrix} \qquad X2 := \begin{bmatrix} -\frac{\frac{3x}{2} + \frac{3\sqrt{x^2-4x}}{2}}{3x} \\[3mm] 1 \end{bmatrix}$$

```
> A.X1 = lambda[1] . X1;                              # Test first eigenvalue
> A.X1 = Multiply(lambda[1], X1);          # Test first eigenvalue with distributed mult
```

$$\begin{bmatrix} -\frac{x}{2} + \frac{\sqrt{x^2-4x}}{2} - 3 \\[2mm] \frac{5x}{2} + \frac{3\sqrt{x^2-4x}}{2} \end{bmatrix} = \begin{bmatrix} -\frac{(\frac{5x}{2}+\frac{3\sqrt{x^2-4x}}{2})(\frac{3x}{2}-\frac{3\sqrt{x^2-4x}}{2})}{3x} \\[3mm] \frac{5x}{2} + \frac{3\sqrt{x^2-4x}}{2} \end{bmatrix}$$

```
> Map(expand, %);                                    # Expand each element as check
```

$$\begin{bmatrix} -\frac{x}{2} + \frac{\sqrt{x^2-4x}}{2} - 3 \\[2mm] \frac{5x}{2} + \frac{3\sqrt{x^2-4x}}{2} \end{bmatrix} = \begin{bmatrix} -\frac{x}{2} + \frac{\sqrt{x^2-4x}}{2} - 3 \\[2mm] \frac{5x}{2} + \frac{3\sqrt{x^2-4x}}{2} \end{bmatrix}$$

As is true for other Maple calculations, if any one of the numbers in matrix A contains a decimal point, then Maple will interpret this as a request for a floating-point calculation. For matrix calculations, using floats means that the eigenvectors and eigenvalues will be computed numerically and that all elements should be of numeric type. If the calculation is really big, then we recommend a compiled language with a scientific matrix library (we do that in Chapter 17). Here is an example using a numerical form of the previous matrix:

```
> A := Matrix( 10, 10, (i, j)-> (0.1*i )^j);
> Eigenvalues(A);         Eigenvectors(A);
>                                                    # Check precision of solutions via substitution
```

7.5.7 Solution of Linear Equations*

A set of simultaneous linear equations may be written in the matrix form

$$AX = b. \tag{7.30}$$

If we have n equations for n unknowns, then A will be a square matrix of dimension n, **b** a vector of constants with length n, and **X** a vector containing the n unknowns we wish to solve for:

$$X = \begin{bmatrix} x_1 \\ x_2 \\ x_3 \\ x_n \end{bmatrix}. \tag{7.31}$$

The command `LinearSolve(A, b)` finds the vector **X** that solves this equation:

```
> A := Matrix([ [4,-2,1], [3,6,-4], [2,1,8]]);       b := Vector([12, -25,32]);
```

$$A := \begin{bmatrix} 4 & -2 & 1 \\ 3 & 6 & -4 \\ 2 & 1 & 8 \end{bmatrix} \qquad b := \begin{bmatrix} 12 \\ -25 \\ 32 \end{bmatrix}$$

```
> X := LinearSolve (A,b);                         # Solve AX = b for unknown vector X
```

$$X := \begin{bmatrix} 1 \\ -2 \\ 4 \end{bmatrix}$$

```
>                                                 # Check your answer here
```

If you are solving a problem in which you have n equations in m unknowns, then A will have n rows and m columns. For a solution to exist, this situation requires **b** to be a vector of dimension n and **X** a vector of dimension m. If $AX = b$ has no solution, or if Maple cannot find one, then the null sequence NULL is returned. If $AX = b$ has multiple solutions, then Maple will describe the family of solutions parametrically:

```
> A := Matrix([[1,2],[1,3],[1,2]]);       b := <1,-2,1>;   # A = 3 × 2, B = 3 × 1
```

$$A := \begin{bmatrix} 1 & 2 \\ 1 & 3 \\ 1 & 2 \end{bmatrix} \qquad b := \begin{bmatrix} 1 \\ -2 \\ 1 \end{bmatrix}$$

```
> X := LinearSolve(A, b);                                          # Solve
```

$$X := \begin{bmatrix} 7 \\ -3 \end{bmatrix}$$

```
>                                                 # Check your answer here
```

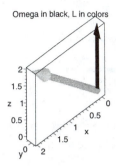

Omega in black, L in colors

Figure 7.4 The angular velocity vector ω in black and the angular momentum vector **L** in gray. In Maple you can grab and rotate this figure.

7.6 SOLUTION: ROTATING RIGID BODIES

We now apply the Maple linear algebra tools to the barbell problem of Figure 7.1. Seeing that the barbell is rotating means that the geometry of this figure is correct only for one instant of time, or for all times in a reference frame rotating with the barbell. We will use that rotating frame and then transform it to a stationary frame later.

We are told that the angular velocity vector of the barbell ω lies along the z axis, as shown in Figure 7.4. This means that the barbell is rotating about the z axis. Clearly, then, this is a 3-D problem, so we define ω as a 3-D vector Ω with only a z component:

```
> restart:with(LinearAlgebra):          Omega := Vector([0,0,omega]);
```

$$\Omega := \begin{bmatrix} 0 \\ 0 \\ \omega \end{bmatrix}$$

We want to use Maple to evaluate the angular momentum via (7.15), which for a barbell with two masses has the simple form:

$$\mathbf{L} = \mathbf{r}_1 \times \mathbf{p}_1 + \mathbf{r}_2 \times \mathbf{p}_2 = m_1 \mathbf{r}_1 \times \omega \times \mathbf{r}_1 + m_2 \mathbf{r}_2 \times \omega \times \mathbf{r}_2. \qquad (7.32)$$

We first enter the vectors using the trigonometry shown in Figure 7.3:

```
> r1 := Vector([-a*sin(theta),0,a*cos(theta)]);   r2 := Vector([a*sin(theta),0,-a*cos(theta)]);
```

$$r1 := \begin{bmatrix} -a\sin(\theta) \\ 0 \\ a\cos(\theta) \end{bmatrix} \qquad r2 := \begin{bmatrix} a\sin(\theta) \\ 0 \\ -a\cos(\theta) \end{bmatrix}$$

This makes sense, since we know that $r_1 = -r_2$ from the figure. Rather than have some very long expressions, we proceed in steps and compute the momentum of each particle next using the cross product:

```
> p1 := m1* CrossProduct(Omega, r1);        p2 := m2* CrossProduct(Omega, r2);
```

$$p1 := m1 \begin{bmatrix} 0 \\ -\omega\, a \sin(\theta) \\ 0 \end{bmatrix} \qquad p2 := m2 \begin{bmatrix} 0 \\ \omega\, a \sin(\theta) \\ 0 \end{bmatrix}$$

As expected, m_1 is moving into the paper (negative y velocity), and m_2 is moving out of the paper. We now compute the angular momentum arising from each mass and add the results:

```
> L1 := CrossProduct(r1, p1);        L2 := CrossProduct(r2, p2);
```

$$L1 := \begin{bmatrix} a^2 \cos(\theta)\, m1\, \omega \sin(\theta) \\ 0 \\ a^2 \sin(\theta)^2\, m1\, \omega \end{bmatrix} \qquad L2 := \begin{bmatrix} a^2 \cos(\theta)\, m2\, \omega \sin(\theta) \\ 0 \\ a^2 \sin(\theta)^2\, m2\, \omega \end{bmatrix}$$

```
> L := L1 + L2;        simplify(%);
```

$$L := \begin{bmatrix} a^2 \cos(\theta)\, m1\, \omega \sin(\theta) + a^2 \cos(\theta)\, m2\, \omega \sin(\theta) \\ 0 \\ a^2 \sin(\theta)^2\, m1\, \omega + a^2 \sin(\theta)^2\, m2\, \omega \end{bmatrix} \quad \begin{bmatrix} a^2 \cos(\theta)\, \omega \sin(\theta)\, (m1 + m2) \\ 0 \\ -a^2\, (-1 + \cos(\theta)^2)\, \omega\, (m1 + m2) \end{bmatrix}$$

We see that even though the angular velocity is always along the z axis, the angular momentum has an x component, in addition to a z component. Furthermore, since we are viewing the system in a rotating frame, an observer in a fixed frame would see the x component of **L** rotate (precess) continuously about a fixed z component.

To visualize this solution, we need to assign numerical values to the masses, lengths, angular velocity, and angles:

```
> m1 := 1;      m2 := 1;      a := 1;      omega := 2;      theta := Pi/4;
```

$$m1 := 1, \qquad m2 := 1, \qquad a := 1, \qquad \omega := 2, \qquad \theta := \frac{\pi}{4}$$

```
> L;        Omega;        map(eval, Omega);
```

$$\begin{bmatrix} 2 \\ 0 \\ 2 \end{bmatrix}, \qquad \begin{bmatrix} 0 \\ 0 \\ \omega \end{bmatrix} \qquad \begin{bmatrix} 0 \\ 0 \\ 2 \end{bmatrix}$$

We now have variables to plot that are numbers and not symbols.

7.6.1 Visualization of Vectors with arrow

Often it is valuable to view a vector as an arrow in space. Maple has the neat command arrow that does just that:

```
> with(plots):          Omega := Vector([0,0,omega]);
```

$$\Omega := \begin{bmatrix} 0 \\ 0 \\ 2 \end{bmatrix}$$

```
> arrow(Omega, color = black, shape = double_arrow);        arrow(L); # Two arrows
```

So we now have visualizations of both **L** and Ω that may be grabbed and rotated. We place them on the same graph by assigning objects to each arrow and then displaying the objects together:

```
> w := arrow(Omega, color = black, shape = double_arrow);   # Assign object to arrow
> L1 := arrow( L ):                                          # Assign object a2 to arrow of L
> display( w, L1, axes = BOXED, scaling = constrained, labels = [x,y,z],
        title = 'Omega in black, L in colors');              # Display both together
```

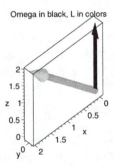

Observe that when we created the arrows we gave some options to the `arrow` command to control the `color` and `shape` of the arrows (use Help `arrow` for other properties of arrows that can be controlled). We have chosen to make Ω black as a way to indicate that it does not move in time (you are free to grab it and move it as you please, however). Notwithstanding the limited number of options available for the `arrow` command, the `display` command permits the usual ones possible for 2-D and 3-D plots (see Chapter 4). For this reason, it is with the `display` command that we placed labels, titles, and constraints on the scaling so that the vertical and horizontal sizes are true.

Now we would like to convey the notion that the angular momentum vector **L** is rotating about the Ω vector (which is fixed along the z axis). We do that by creating vectors with the components that **L** would acquire as it rotates without changing magnitude, and then displaying them all in one plot along with Ω:

```
> L2 := arrow([0,2,2]):  L3 := arrow([-2,0,2]):  L4 := arrow([0,-2,2]):
> display(w, L1, L2, L3, L4, scaling = constrained,        # Three arrows on one graph
   axes = BOXED, labels = [x,y,z], title = `Omega in black, L in colors`);
```

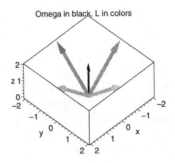

7.6.2 Moment of Inertia for the Barbell

We have just evaluated the angular momentum of the barbell by using the elementary definition of angular momentum for each individual mass, and then adding up the two angular momenta. Even though it is possible to follow this approach for any rigid object, it is easier to get the angular momentum by just multiplying the angular velocity ω by the inertia tensor:

$$\mathbf{L} = \{I\}\omega. \tag{7.33}$$

However, to do that we must first evaluate the inertia tensor for the object under study. We start with the basic definition and apply it to the barbell

$$I_{i,j} = \sum_{a} m_a \left(\delta_{ij} \left(\sum_k x_{a,k}^2\right) - x_{a,i}\, x_{a,j}\right), \tag{7.34}$$

where the sum over a is over the two masses, and i, j, and k take on the values x, y, and z. The x's in this equation describe the location of the two masses in Figure 7.1 in terms of Cartesian coordinates (what we called $\mathbf{r}_1$ and $\mathbf{r}_2$ before):

```
> Omega := Vector([0,0,omega]);                            # Angular velocity vector
```

$$\Omega := \begin{bmatrix} 0 \\ 0 \\ \omega \end{bmatrix}$$

> `x1 := Vector([-a*sin(theta), 0, a*cos(theta)]);`   `x2 := ...;`   # Masses

$$x1 := \begin{bmatrix} -a\sin(\theta) \\ 0 \\ a\cos(\theta) \end{bmatrix} \qquad x2 := \begin{bmatrix} a\sin(\theta) \\ 0 \\ -a\cos(\theta) \end{bmatrix}$$

The angular velocity vector and the positions of the masses are now known. In order to apply the equation for the moment of inertia, we see that x has subscripts indicating both the mass it corresponds to and its component along the x and y axes. Accordingly, we form a matrix x that has two indices:

> `x := Matrix(2,3, [[-a*sin(theta),0, a*cos(theta)], [a*sin(theta),0,-a*cos(theta)]]);`

$$x := \begin{bmatrix} -a\sin(\theta) & 0 & a\cos(\theta) \\ a\sin(\theta) & 0 & -a\cos(\theta) \end{bmatrix}$$

> `x[1,3];`   `x1[3];`   # Check answer, check agree?

$$a\cos(\theta) \qquad\qquad a\cos(\theta)$$

> `m := Vector([m1,m2]);`

$$m := \begin{bmatrix} m1 \\ m2 \end{bmatrix}$$

To keep this treatment simple, we will explicitly write out the a index over particles and have Maple sum over i and j as subscripts. We start by determining the contribution of mass 1 to the moment of inertia:

> `B := Matrix(3,3, (i,j)-> i^j);`   # Test case from before

$$B := \begin{bmatrix} 1 & 1 & 1 \\ 2 & 4 & 8 \\ 3 & 9 & 27 \end{bmatrix}$$

> `delta := IdentityMatrix(3) ;`   `'delta[1,2]' = delta[1,2];`

$$\delta := \begin{bmatrix} 1 & 0 & 0 \\ 0 & 1 & 0 \\ 0 & 0 & 1 \end{bmatrix} \qquad\qquad delta[1,2] = 0$$

> `Inertia := Matrix(3,3, (i,j) -> m1*(delta[i,j]*sum('x1[k]^2', 'k' = 1..3) -x1[i]*x1[j]));`

$$Inertia := \begin{bmatrix} m1\,a^2\cos(\theta)^2 & 0 & m1\,a^2\sin(\theta)\cos(\theta) \\ 0 & m1\,(a^2\sin(\theta)^2 + a^2\cos(\theta)^2) & 0 \\ m1\,a^2\sin(\theta)\cos(\theta) & 0 & m1\,a^2\sin(\theta)^2 \end{bmatrix}$$

> `Inertia := Matrix(3,3,(i,j) -> sum('m[A]*(delta[i,j]*sum('x[A,k]^2', 'k'=1..3)`
      `-x[A,i]*x[A,j])', 'A'=1..2) );`

$$Inertia := \begin{bmatrix} m1\,a^2\cos(\theta)^2 + m2\,a^2\cos(\theta)^2\,,\ 0\,,\ m1\,a^2\sin(\theta)\cos(\theta) + m2\,a^2\sin(\theta)\cos(\theta) \\ 0\,,\ m1\,(a^2\sin(\theta)^2 + a^2\cos(\theta)^2) + m2\,(a^2\sin(\theta)^2 + a^2\cos(\theta)^2)\,,\ 0 \\ m1\,a^2\sin(\theta)\cos(\theta) + m2\,a^2\sin(\theta)\cos(\theta)\,,\ 0\,,\ m1\,a^2\sin(\theta)^2 + m2\,a^2\sin(\theta)^2 \end{bmatrix}$$

To simplify this, we assign the numerical values we had before for the masses, lengths, angular velocity, and angles:

```
> ml := 1;        m2 := 1;        a := 1;        omega := 2;        theta := Pi/4;
```
$$m1 := 1 \qquad m2 := 1 \qquad a := 1 \qquad \omega := 2 \qquad \theta := \frac{\pi}{4}$$

```
> Inertia;
```
$$\begin{bmatrix} 1 & 0 & 1 \\ 0 & 2 & 0 \\ 1 & 0 & 1 \end{bmatrix}$$

```
> with(plots):     matrixplot(Inertia, axes = boxed, title = 'Inertia tensor barbell')
```

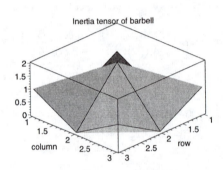

```
> Inertia.Omega;              Inertia;                # Mult, then check if Inertia unchanged
```
$$\begin{bmatrix} 2 \\ 0 \\ 2 \end{bmatrix} \qquad\qquad \begin{bmatrix} 1 & 0 & 1 \\ 0 & 2 & 0 \\ 1 & 0 & 1 \end{bmatrix}$$

7.7 EXPLORATION: PRINCIPAL AXES OF ROTATION*

We have seen that when the inertia tensor contains off-diagonal elements (products of inertia), the angular momentum and angular velocity of a spinning body are not parallel to each other. It would clearly be simpler if we did not have those off-diagonal elements to deal with. In general, what is "simpler" in life depends upon one's view of the world, and the inertia tensor is no different. If we rotate the coordinate system we use to calculate the moment of inertia (still keeping it fixed to the body at the center of mass), then it is usually possible to find an orientation for which the inertia tensor is diagonal. In terms of individual elements, a diagonal matrix is expressed as:

$$I_{i,j} = I_i\,\delta_{i,j}. \tag{7.35}$$

In terms of the matrix representation, this is:

$$\{\mathbf{I}\} = \begin{bmatrix} I_1 & 0 & 0 \\ 0 & I_2 & 0 \\ 0 & 0 & I_3 \end{bmatrix}, \tag{7.36}$$

where we are using $(1, 2, 3)$ to label the (x, y, z) axes in this new system. The set of axes in which the inertia tensor becomes diagonal is called the *principal axes of inertia*.

Finding the principal-axes of inertia is not hard. The whole idea is that the physical angular momentum vector does not change when we choose to view it from different coordinate systems. Therefore when we take the expressions for **L** in the two systems and set them equal, we obtain equations that Maple will solve for us.

We assume that in the principal-axes system, the body is rotating along one of the principal axes, namely, along the 1, 2, or 3 directions. Then the angular momentum **L** and the angular velocity ω will be parallel,

$$\mathbf{L} = I\omega, \tag{7.37}$$

where I is the moment of inertia along the principal axis of rotation (which we cannot yet calculate since we do not know where those axes point). Yet **L** is still the same vector we expressed previously in (7.17)–(7.19) in terms of the products and moments of inertia. By setting the two expressions equal we obtain three simultaneous linear equations for the unknowns I and ω:

$$L_x = I\omega_x = I_{xx}\omega_x + I_{xy}\omega_y + I_{xz}\omega_z, \tag{7.38}$$
$$L_y = I\omega_y = I_{yx}\omega_x + I_{yy}\omega_y + I_{yz}\omega_z, \tag{7.39}$$
$$L_z = I\omega_z = I_{zx}\omega_x + I_{zy}\omega_y + I_{zz}\omega_z. \tag{7.40}$$

We write these three equations in the matrix form:

```
> Matrix([ [I[xx]-I, I[xy], I[xz]], [I[yx], I[yy]-I, I[yz]],
     [I[zx], I[zy], I[zz]-I] ]), Vector([omega[x], omega[y], omega[z]]) = 0;
```

$$\begin{bmatrix} I_{xx} - I & I_{xy} & I_{xz} \\ I_{yx} & I_{yy} - I & I_{yz} \\ I_{zx} & I_{zy} & I_{zz} - I \end{bmatrix}, \begin{bmatrix} \omega_x \\ \omega_y \\ \omega_z \end{bmatrix} = 0$$

The trivial solution is $\omega = 0$. For a nontrivial solution to exist, the matrix on the LHS of this equation must have no inverse. This requires that the determinant of the matrix vanish:

```
> Determinant(Matrix([[I[xx]-I, I[xy], I[xz]], [I[yx],
  Determinant(I[yy]-I, I[yz]], [I[zx], I[zy], I[zz]-I]]));
```

$$I_{xx} I_{yy} I_{zz} + I_{yz} I_{zy} I + I_{zz} I_{xz} I - I_{xx} - I_{xx} I_{yz} I_{zy} - I_{xx} I_{yy} I - I_{yy} - I_{zz} + I$$

$$+I_{yx}\,I_{xy}\,I + I_{yx}\,I_{zy}\,I_{xz} - I_{yx}\,I_{xy}\,I_{zz} - I_{yy}\,I_{zz}\,I + I_{zx}\,I_{xy}\,I_{yz} - I_{zx}\,I_{xz}\,I_{yy} - I_{xx}\,I_{zz}\,I.$$

When the determinant is expanded (something we dare you to try), we are left with a cubic equation in I. The three solutions of this cubic are the three principal moments of inertia, I_x, I_y, and I_z. Once these I's are known, they are substituted back into the matrix equation to determine the angular momenta via:

$$L_x = I_x \omega_x, \tag{7.41}$$
$$L_y = I_y \omega_y, \tag{7.42}$$
$$L_z = I_z \omega_z. \tag{7.43}$$

We enter the inertia tensor for a cube given as part of the **Problem:**

```
> restart:  with(LinearAlgebra):
> Inertia := Matrix([[2/3, -1/4, -1/4], [-1/4, 2/3, -1/4], [-1/4, -1/4, 2/3]]);
```

$$Inertia := \begin{bmatrix} \frac{2}{3} & \frac{-1}{4} & \frac{-1}{4} \\ \frac{-1}{4} & \frac{2}{3} & \frac{-1}{4} \\ \frac{-1}{4} & \frac{-1}{4} & \frac{2}{3} \end{bmatrix}$$

Now we form a diagonal matrix with the value Iprin along the diagonal:

```
> Idiag := Iprin * IdentityMatrix(3);              simplify(%);
```

$$Idiag := Iprin \begin{bmatrix} 1 & 0 & 0 \\ 0 & 1 & 0 \\ 0 & 0 & 1 \end{bmatrix} \qquad Idiag := \begin{bmatrix} Iprin & 0 & 0 \\ 0 & Iprin & 0 \\ 0 & 0 & Iprin \end{bmatrix}$$

Next we form the matrix whose determinant must vanish. We build the matrix up explicitly from its elements:

```
> Inertia - Idiag;
```

$$\begin{bmatrix} \frac{2}{3} - Iprin & \frac{-1}{4} & \frac{-1}{4} \\ \frac{-1}{4} & \frac{2}{3} - Iprin & \frac{-1}{4} \\ \frac{-1}{4} & \frac{-1}{4} & \frac{2}{3} - Iprin \end{bmatrix}.$$

Now we calculate the determinant of this matrix and ask Maple to solve for the value of Iprin for which the determinant vanishes:

```
> Determinant( Inertia - Idiag );
```

$$\frac{121}{864} - \frac{55}{48}\,Iprin + 2\,Iprin^2 - Iprin^3$$

```
> 'I[prin]' = solve( Determinant(Inertia - Idiag), Iprin );
```

$$I[prin] = (\frac{1}{6}, \frac{11}{12}, \frac{11}{12})$$

We should see three principal moments, two of which are equal (a consequence of symmetry). The inertia tensor in the principal-axes frame is thus diagonal:

```
> Idiag := Matrix([ [1/6,0,0], [0,11/12,0], [0,0,11/12] ]);
```

$$Idiag := \begin{bmatrix} \frac{1}{6} & 0 & 0 \\ 0 & \frac{11}{12} & 0 \\ 0 & 0 & \frac{11}{12} \end{bmatrix}$$

Although we cannot derive it all here, the indicial equation that we have deduced above is the same one that arises in the eigenvalue problem. For our problem, the eigenvalues are principal moments of inertia, and the eigenvectors are three values for the angular velocity vector ω. Because each eigenvector is associated with one eigenvalue, the principal moment of inertia, the eigenvectors correspond to values of ω for which $\mathbf{L}$ and ω are parallel. This causes the directions of the eigenvectors to be the same as the directions of the principal axes in space. To verify this for our cube problem:

```
> Inertia := Matrix([[2/3, -1/4, -1/4], [-1/4, 2/3, -1/4], [-1/4, -1/4, 2/3]]);
```

$$Inertia := \begin{bmatrix} \frac{2}{3} & \frac{-1}{4} & \frac{-1}{4} \\ \frac{-1}{4} & \frac{2}{3} & \frac{-1}{4} \\ \frac{-1}{4} & \frac{-1}{4} & \frac{2}{3} \end{bmatrix}$$

```
> Eigenvectors(Inertia);
```

$$\begin{bmatrix} \frac{11}{12} \\ \frac{11}{12} \\ \frac{1}{6} \end{bmatrix}, \begin{bmatrix} 1 & 0 & 1 \\ 0 & 1 & 1 \\ -1 & -1 & 1 \end{bmatrix}$$

We see that Maple first returns a column vector with the same three values of the eigenvalues as we found above. The matrix contains the corresponding three eigenvectors as its columns. Here we separate off the eigenvalues and vectors:

```
> (Is, Omegas) := Eigenvectors( Inertia );        # Store both eigenvalues and eigenvectors
```

$$Is, Omegas := \begin{bmatrix} \frac{1}{6} \\ \frac{11}{12} \\ \frac{11}{12} \end{bmatrix}, \begin{bmatrix} 1 & -1 & -1 \\ 1 & 1 & 0 \\ 1 & 0 & 1 \end{bmatrix}$$

```
> `Is[1]` = Is[1];        omega1 := Column (Omegas,1); ...        # Extract eigenvectors
```

$$Is[1] \;=\; \frac{1}{6} \qquad \omega1 \;:=\; \begin{bmatrix} 1 \\ 1 \\ 1 \end{bmatrix} \qquad Is[2] \;=\; \frac{11}{12} \qquad \omega2 \;:=\; \begin{bmatrix} -1 \\ 1 \\ 0 \end{bmatrix}$$

$$Is[3] \;=\; \frac{11}{12} \qquad \omega3 \;:=\; \begin{bmatrix} -1 \\ 0 \\ 1 \end{bmatrix}$$

We see that the third eigenvalue corresponds to rotations along the diagonal of the cube, while the first two are perpendicular to the diagonal. To actually visualize these eigenvectors, we represent them as arrows with Maple's `arrow` command:

```
> with(plots):          arrow(omega3, axes = BOXED, color=black, labels = [x,y,z]);
```

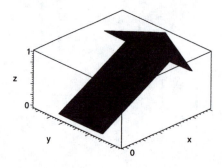

Next, as before, we represent the three omega's as objects and `display` them together:

```
> w3 :=arrow(omega3,axes=BOXED,color=black,labels=[x,y,z]):
> w2 :=arrow(omega2,axes=BOXED):          w1 :=arrow(omega1,axes=BOXED):
> display(w1,w2,w3);
```

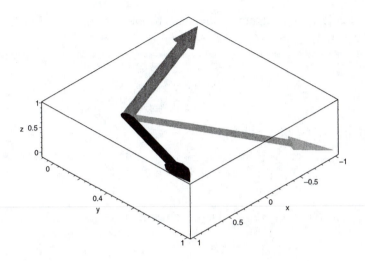

7.8 KEY WORDS AND CONCEPTS

angular momentum	angular velocity	columns & rows	determinant
diagonalization*	dot product	eigenvalues*	eigenvectors*
inertia tensor	linear algebra	linear equations	inverse matrix
matrix arithmetic	moment of inertia	polar coordinates	rigid rotation
vector	scalar multiplication	vector components	vector magnitude
vector direction			

1. Is a vector also a matrix?
2. Is a row vector a matrix?
3. Is a column vector also a matrix?
4. What is the difference between a row and a column vector?
5. Why is the study of matrices and vectors also called linear algebra?
6. How many coordinates are needed to locate a point in space?
7. What meaning is there to a vector having more than three components?
8. Can you add, subtract, and multiply matrices?
9. Can you divide matrices?
10. How are eigenvalues and eigenvectors related?
11. What is the relation between simultaneous equations and matrix equations?

7.9 SUPPLEMENTARY EXERCISES

1. Use Maple's linear algebra commands to find the solution of the simultaneous equations:

$$3x + 2y + z = 11,$$
$$2x + 3y + z = 13,$$
$$x + y + 4z = 12.$$

2. Find the inverse of the matrix:

$$A = \begin{bmatrix} 4 & -2 & 1 \\ 3 & 6 & -4 \\ 2 & 1 & 8 \end{bmatrix}.$$

3. Verify that the inverse A^{-1} found in question 2 works in both directions; that is, that

$$AA^{-1} = A^{-1}A = 1.$$

4. For the same matrix A as in problem 2, find and verify the solution of:

$$AX = B, \qquad B = \begin{bmatrix} 12 \\ -25 \\ 32 \end{bmatrix}.$$

5. In quantum mechanics, the electron's spin is represented by the three Pauli matrices:

$$\sigma_1 = \begin{bmatrix} 0 & 1 \\ 1 & 0 \end{bmatrix}, \quad \sigma_2 = \begin{bmatrix} 0 & -I \\ I & 0 \end{bmatrix}, \quad \sigma_3 = \begin{bmatrix} 1 & 0 \\ 0 & 1 \end{bmatrix}.$$

Many of the properties of angular momenta follow from the properties of these matrices.
a. Enter these three matrices into Maple.
b. Use Maple to show that

$$\sigma_1 \sigma_1 = \sigma_2 \sigma_2 = \sigma_3 \sigma_3 = 1.$$

c. Use Maple to show that

$$\sigma_1 \sigma_2 = I \sigma_3, \qquad \sigma_2 \sigma_3 = I \sigma_1, \qquad \sigma_3 \sigma_1 = I \sigma_2.$$

d. Use Maple to show that for (i, j, k) in cyclic order namely, $[(1, 2, 3), (2, 3, 1), (3, 1, 2)]$,

$$\sigma_i \sigma_j - \sigma_j \sigma_i = 2I \sigma_k.$$

e. Use Maple to show the trace of each of these matrices vanishes,

$$\text{trace } \sigma_i = 0.$$

6. (You do not have to understand the physics here to do this problem.) Consider a hydrogen atom in a magnetic field **B** that points in the y direction. If the electron within the atom is described by the Pauli matrices of problem

5, then the Hamiltonian matrix for this system is a Hermitian matrix of the form:

$$H = \begin{bmatrix} h & -IB \\ IB & h \end{bmatrix},$$

where I is the imaginary number and h is the energy of the atom when there is no magnetic field.

a. The energy of this system is the eigenvalues of this Hamiltonian matrix. Find an analytic expression for the two possible energies for an electron in a magnetic field; namely, find the two eigenvalues of this matrix.

b. Determine the corresponding eigenvectors and show that they are complex yet orthogonal to each other. (Orthogonality is a consequence of the matrix being Hermitian).

7. Determine the relation between the angular momentum and the angular velocities of a uniform plate and cube. Compare that relation to the one we worked out for a plate and cube composed of discrete masses.

8. Consider the matrix:

$$A = \begin{bmatrix} \alpha & \beta \\ -\beta & \alpha \end{bmatrix}.$$

Solve for the complex eigenvalues and eigenvectors of this matrix. *Hint:* your eigenvalues should be $\lambda = \alpha - \beta$, $\lambda = \alpha + I\beta$.

9. In quantum mechanics, a spin 1 particle is described with the three 3×3 matrices:

$$M_1 = \frac{\begin{bmatrix} 0 & 1 & 0 \\ 1 & 0 & 0 \\ 0 & 1 & 0 \end{bmatrix}}{\sqrt{2}}, \qquad M_2 = \frac{\begin{bmatrix} 0 & -I & 0 \\ I & 0 & -I \\ 0 & I & 0 \end{bmatrix}}{\sqrt{2}}, \qquad M_3 = \begin{bmatrix} 1 & 0 & 0 \\ 0 & 0 & 0 \\ 0 & 0 & -1 \end{bmatrix}.$$

a. Show that

$$[M_x, M_y] \overset{\text{def}}{=} M_x M_y - M_y M_x = iM_z,$$

as well as for cyclic permutations of the indices, namely, for index orders yzx and zxy.

b. Show that

$$M_x^2 + M_y^2 + M_z^2 = 2\mathbf{1}$$

where $\mathbf{1}$ is the 3-D identity matrix.

Chapter Eight

Trial-and-Error Searching, Maple Programming; Dipstick Calibration

8.1 PROBLEM: VOLUME OF LIQUID IN SPHERICAL TANKS

A spherical tank of radius $R = 3$ meters is to be used to hold gas. You are given a stick to dip into the tank, and you want to calibrate the scale on it such that it reads the volume of fluid in the tank (see Figure 8.1). Your **problem** is to determine the height of the fluid for a given volume. *Hint:* use an indirect approach by calculating the volume for a series of heights until some height gives you the volume you are looking for.

8.2 MATH: VOLUME INTEGRATION

It seems straightforward to calculate $V(H)$, the volume of the liquid in the tank as a function of height H. Once we have that, the hard problem is to invert the solution, that is determine $H(V)$. Consider Figure 8.1. The volume of a disk of differential thickness dh and radius r is

$$dV = \pi r^2 dh. \tag{8.1}$$

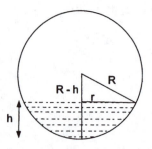

Figure 8.1 A spherical tank of radius R filled with a liquid to height H above its bottom.

Here the height varies over the range $0 \leq h \leq H$, and the radius r is related to the variable height h via Pythagoras's theorem:

$$R^2 = r^2 + (R - h)^2 \qquad \Rightarrow \qquad r^2 = R^2 - (R - h)^2. \qquad (8.2)$$

Indeed, if $h = 2R$, then $r = 0$, as it should. We evaluate the volume by adding up the volumes of all the differential disks:

$$V(H) = \int_0^H \pi r^2 dh = \int_0^H \pi \left[R^2 - (R - h)^2 \right] dh \qquad (8.3)$$

$$= \pi \left[RH^2 - \frac{H^3}{3} \right]. \qquad (8.4)$$

Equation (8.4) gives the volume of fluid as a function of its height. As a check we see that for an empty tank $V(0) = 0$, and that for a full tank $V(2R) = \frac{4}{3}\pi R^3$.

Our problem requires us to deduce the height for a known volume. To do that we rewrite (8.4) as the cubic equation

$$H^3 - 3RH^2 + \frac{3}{\pi}V = 0. \qquad (8.5)$$

For $R = 3$ and a sample volume $V = \frac{4}{3}\pi$, the equation to solve is

$$f(H) = H^3 - 9H^2 + 4 = 0. \qquad (8.6)$$

Here (8.6) is in the standard $f(h) = 0$ form. We know from the geometry of the problem that the solution we want must lie in the range

$$0 \leq H \leq 2R = 6. \qquad (8.7)$$

Because $f(H = 0) = 4$ and $f(H = 2R = 6) = -105$, we know that our function must pass through zero in this range.

Regardless of the existence of closed-form expressions for the solutions of cubic equations, we shall solve it numerically (a procedure you would have to follow anyway if there were higher powers than the third). In spite of the fact that Maple's fsolve command is applicable, we wish to understand what goes on inside that command and to get some programming experience.

8.3 ALGORITHM: BISECTION SEARCHES

A traditional computational technique is "trial and error," in which a program starts with a trial solution, determines how large the error is, and then makes a new guess based on the error. The procedure keeps repeating until the error becomes acceptably small. These trial-and-error programs are interesting to write because they must be intelligent, and interesting to run because you are not sure how long it will take to find a solution, or whether a solution will be found at all.

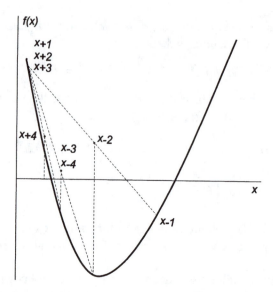

Figure 8.2 A graphical representation of the steps involved in solving for a zero of $f(x)$ using the bisection algorithm. In each step the algorithm takes the midpoint of the interval as its new guess for x, thereby reducing the interval's size by one half. The first interval is (x_1, x_{-1}), the second (x_2, x_{-2}), etc.

The most elementary trial-and-error technique is the *bisection algorithm*. Its basis, shown in Figure 8.2, starts with two values, x_- and x_+, between which we know a zero occurs. We assume that $f(x)$ is negative at x_- and positive at x_+:

$$f(x_-) < 0, \qquad\qquad f(x_+) > 0. \qquad\qquad (8.8)$$

This approach does not limit us in any way, since it just means that if the function changes from positive to negative as x increases, then x_- will be greater than x_+. The algorithm bisects the interval to obtain the midpoint

$$x = \frac{x_+ + x_-}{2}, \qquad\qquad (8.9)$$

and then checks if there is a sign change in the *right* half of the interval. If there is, then it limits the search to the right half-interval only; if not, then it limits the search to the left half-interval. In either case the regions to be searched decrease by one half each time.

In Figure 8.2 the first interval extends from $x_- = x_{+1}$ to $x_+ = x_{-1}$. We bisect that interval at x, and since $f(x) < 0$ at the midpoint, we set $x_- \equiv x_{-2} = x$ and label it x_{-2} to indicate the second step. We then use $x_{+2} \equiv x_{+1}$ and x_{-2} as the next interval and continue the process. We see in the figure that only x_- changes for the first three steps, but that for the fourth step, x_+ finally changes. After that, the changes get too small for us to show.

Table 8.1 Maple's relational operators.

<	less than	<=	less than or equal to	>	greater than
>=	greater than or equal to	=	equals	<>	not equal to

8.4 PROGRAMMING IN MAPLE

We have already done some Maple programming when we defined arrow functions to represent expressions. This is fine as long as the function definition fits on one line. However, sometimes we need to include a number of steps in a calculation, and we cannot do that with an arrow function. In these latter cases we need to write a multiline program, often with logic deciding which path to follow through the program. In the sections to follow we explore some of the features of Maple that are useful for programming. Notwithstanding the usefulness of programming with Maple for honing your programming skills, we recommend that you also experience the more powerful programming possible with compiled languages like Java and Fortran. We do that in Part 2 of this book. Even if you do not intend to be programming in Maple, the programming here will serve well as an introduction to general programming.

8.4.1 Logic

The first step in having the computer make intelligent decisions is having it be able to tell if a statement is true or false. This is accomplished with *Boolean variables*, that is, variables that are either *true* or *false*. Objects that have true and false values may also be constructed from expressions. To construct a Boolean expression, you use relational and logical operators to combine ordinary variables. The relational operators in Maple are as shown in Table 8.1. To prove the point, 1 < 2 is *true*, as is 1 <= 1, while 2 <> 2 is false, as is 2 > 3. To determine what Maple believes to be true, we evaluate an expression as Boolean using the `evalb` command:

```
> evalb(1 > 2);
```
                                                                    # Returns true, false, or fail
$$false$$

```
> T :=1;      Heat :=3;
```
$$T := 1 \qquad Heat := 3$$
                                                                    # Initialize some regular variables

```
> evalb(T <= (Heat -2));    evalb(T <= Heat -2);    evalb(T = Heat);
```
                                                                    # Booleans

$$true \qquad true \qquad false$$

More involved logical expressions are created by combining simple Boolean expressions by use of the three logical, or conditional, operators, and, or, and not. The basic logic behind logical operators is that compound statements constructed

Table 8.2 A truth table showing how Boolean variables combine.

True	**False**	**True**	**False**
true and true	true and false	true or true	false and false
true or false	false or false	not false	not true

from simpler statements obey the truth table, Table 8.2. As an example, here we construct and test some more complex logical expressions:

```
> evalb(4 < 5 and -99 <1);        evalb(1<-99 or -99 <1);   # True and true, False or true
                       true                true
```

8.4.2 Flow Control

The basic logic command used to control program flow is the `if` statement:

*if a statement is true, **then** do something, **else** do something different.*

Maple uses a particular notation for this:

```
if    <logical expression>  then  <statements>
elif  <logical expression>  then  <statements>
elif  <logical expression>  then  <statements>
  .  .  .
else <statements>
end if
```

Here `<logical expression>` is a Boolean expression, `<statements>` is any sequence of Maple statements that you care to include, and `if`, `end if`, `else`, and `elif` are Maple key words (the last is shorthand for `else if`). Take note that every `if` must have a matching `end if`, and that the variables in the logical expressions must have numerical values to avoid complaints from Maple. As we shall see below, it is permissible to use just part of the full construct, if that is all you need. As a case in point, to use just `if` and `then`.

We start with a simple test that may be useful for programming a thermostat. If the temperature T is negative, then we need more `Heat`:

```
> Heat := 2;        T := -3;                            # Set initial value of Heat
```
$$Heat := 2 \qquad T := -3$$

```
> if T <0 then Heat := Heat +1 end if;                  # Increase Heat if cold
```
$$Heat := 3$$

```
> T := 0;        if T <=0 then Heat := Heat +1 end if;                          # More Heat
```

$$T := 0 \qquad Heat := 4$$

We see that Maple discerns whether T is positive or negative and acts appropriately. Maple will then increase the Heat for negative T but not change the Heat for positive T. Try out these same conditions using an if command that tests if T is positive or not negative:

```
>                                                                               # Try it!
```

Up until this point, we have a thermostat that is able to turn up the heat when it is cold but not turn it down when it gets hot. We fix that via two sequential tests:

```
> T := 1;        Heat := 3;
```

$$T := 1 \qquad Heat := 3$$

```
> if T <= 0 then Heat := Heat + 1 end if;
> if T > 0  then Heat := Heat - 1 end if;
```

$$Heat := 2$$

We accomplish the same goal in just one line by invoking the *else if* construct, that Maple calls elif:

```
> T :=1;         Heat :=3;
```

$$T := 1 \qquad Heat := 3$$

```
> if T <= 0 then Heat := Heat + 1 else Heat := Heat - 1 end if;
```

$$Heat := 2$$

In conclusion, it is possible to construct all logical conditions that may exist by combining the simple Boolean operators and expressions. In particular, it is permissible to keep concatenating if statements to be as specific as you like.

8.4.3 for Loop

An essential component of scientific computing involves having the computer repeat a set of commands until some predefined condition is met. This may be until a desired level of precision is achieved, until a matrix or a vector has been spanned, or this may be to step through space or time in discrete steps. We discuss the way to do this in Java in Chapters 12 and 14, where we loop over time steps for projectiles and over space steps for integration. Here we discuss how to do this in Maple.

We have already seen Maple looping in Chapter 5 where we summed up the height of blocks to obtain the height of a tower:

```
> Sum(i, i = 1..100) = sum(i, i = 1..100);
```

$$\sum_{i=1}^{100} i = 5050$$

In this case, Maple has an internal program that loops over the sum. We do the same thing ourselves using Maple's `for` construct:

for <**variable**> from <**expression**> by <**expression**> to <**expression**>,

where not all parts must be used at any one time, although `do` and `end do` are always required. So we write our own `sum`:

```
> mySum := 0;                                                   # Initialize
> for i from 1 to 10 do
> mySum := mySum + i;                        # Prints out intermediate execution
> end do;                                                       # Ends loop
```

$$mySum := 0$$
$$mySum := 1$$
$$\vdots$$
$$mySum := 55$$

Here all the lines between the `do` and `end do` statements get repeated for as long as the condition specified by the `for .. from .. to ..` construct holds true. In the present case, the `for` construct increases `i` from 1 to 10, and the loop increases `mySum` by `i` each time the loop is repeated. For more involved computations there may be many lines between the beginning and end of the `do` loop. As is often the case with loops, some variables must be initialized before the loop begins, as we do here with `mySum := 0;`. Take note, you will avoid the 100 lines of intermediate output by replacing the ";" on the *end do* line with a ":".

For some applications you may wish to change the loop index (counter) by a number other than 1. (Normally you may leave out the `from` and `by` parts of the construct and let them have their default values of 1.) For loops that do not increment by 1, you use the `by` construct and pick what change you would like; for example, here we sum all the even number from 1 to 100:

```
> mySum := 0;                                                   # Initialize
```

$$mySum := 0$$

```
> for i from 0 by 2 to 100 do                          # Increase i by 2
> mySum := mySum + i;                             # No printout as have :
> end do:                                                       # Ends loop
> 'mySum' = mySum;
```

$$mySum = 2550$$

8.4.4 while Loop

You may not always know ahead of time just how often a loop must repeat before the necessary condition is met. In that case you repeat the loop while some condition is true:

> while <**expression**> do <**statements**> end do

To give an instance, let us say we want to keep summing until some sum is greater than 10,000, and then find out what the i value is:

```
> restart:  mySum := 0;      i := 0;                          # Initialize
> while mySum < 10000 do                                      # Repeat while
> mySum := mySum + i;
> i := i + 1;
> end do:                                                     # Ends loop
> 'mySum' = mySum;
> 'i' = i;
```

$$mySum := 0 \qquad i := 0$$
$$mySum = 10011 \qquad i = 142$$

The problem with the while loop is that if the Boolean condition is always true, then the loop is "infinite"; that is, it never end. By way of example, if you change mySum < 10000 to mySum > 0, be prepared to press the stop button!

An addition to the while loop that will keep it from becoming infinite is to *break* the loop, that is, to stop it if some alternative condition is met (say, after 100,000 iterations). For example, here we break the previous while loop when i = 77:

```
> mySum := 0;       i :=0;                                    # Initialize
```

$$mySum := 0 \qquad i := 0$$

```
> while mySum < 10000 do                                      # Do while
> mySum := mySum + i;
> i := i + 1;
> if i = 77 then break end if;                                # Break condition
> end do:                                        # Ends loop; no printout as have :
> 'mySum' = mySum;
> 'i' = i;
```

$$mySum = 2926 \qquad i = 77$$

8.4.5 Procedures (Methods, Multiline Functions)

Though it is satisfying to write worksheets that have intelligence, the use of logic and looping tends to require many lines in order to handle all possible situations that may occur. If all the logic and possible cases are placed together, we may end up with a program that is so long and complicated that it is hard to follow. Consequently, it is useful to do some housekeeping and remove some of the utility commands out from the mainstream of our worksheets. Maple permits this by letting us define our own multiline *procedures* to be called from within a worksheet. Essentially, this is equivalent to defining a function, or what Java calls a *method*.

Here we define a procedure `MySum()` that sums the values of i from `iStart` to `iEnd`, and then uses Maple's `printf` command to print out the results in a general format (the `%g` symbol). The definition of a procedure uses the Maple key word `proc`, takes the arguments `iStart` and `iEnd`, and ends with the key word `end`. Check over the absence of a semicolon or colon on the line containing `proc`, or on the last line before `end`:

```
> restart;
> MySum := proc(iStart, iEnd)                      # Named procedure (argument list)
> local iQuit;                                     # Local variable used only within procedure
> global i, mySum;                                 # Global variable used outside too
> iQuit := 77;
> mySum := 0;                                      # Initialize for each call
> for i from iStart to iEnd do
> mySum := mySum + i;
> if i = iQuit then break end if;
> end do;                                          # Ends loop
> printf("In MySum, at end of do loop, i = %g, mySum = %g", i, mySum)
> end
```

$MySum := \mathbf{proc}(iStart, iEnd)$
$\mathbf{local}\ iQuit;$
$\mathbf{global}\ i, mySum;$
  $iQuit := 77\ ;$
  $mySum := 0\ ;$
  $\mathbf{for}\ i\ \mathbf{from}\ iStart\ \mathbf{to}\ iEnd$
  $\mathbf{do}\ mySum := mySum + i;$
  $\mathbf{if}\ i = iQuit$
   $\mathbf{then\ break}$
   $\mathbf{end\ if}$
   $\mathbf{end\ do};$
    printf(" In MySum, at end of do loop, i = %g, mySum =%g", $i, mySum$)
$\mathbf{end\ proc}$

Observe that Maple returns a statement of what it thinks our procedure is intended to do, with italics used to indicate variable names.

Now we test our procedure by calling `MySum`, as you would any Maple function, with numerical values for the arguments `iStart` and `iEnd`. If the procedure works as intended, Maple should evaluate all the statements within the procedure and then return to the worksheet with values for the global variables:

```
> MySum(0, 10000);
```
$$In\,MySum,\ at\ end\ of\ do\ loop,\ i = 77,\ mySum = 3003$$

```
> 'mySum' = mySum;
```
$$mySum = 3003$$

Here we have called our procedure by name and supplied it with the required two arguments. The values for the internal, or *local*, variables within a procedure are not visible from the outside the procedure:

```
> iQuit;                                        # Local to procedure
```
$$iQuit$$

```
> mySum,        i;                              # Global, visible everywhere
```
$$3003, \qquad 77$$

We see that the internal test causes the loop to break at `i = 77`, and that the value of the variable `mySum` does get returned to the calling program (it should, since we made it *global*). Now let us tell the procedure to end at `iEnd = 70` and not give it a chance to break:

```
> MySum(0, 70);
  In MySum, at end of do loop, i = 71 , mySum = 2485
> 'mySum' = mySum;
> a := mySum;
```
$$mySum = 2485 \qquad a := 2485$$

In summary, the general form of a procedure is:

```
proc   (<arguments>)
local   <list of variables>   global <list of variables>
options <list of options>
<statements>
end;
```

where the first and last lines must always be present.

Exercise: Add the line `> mySum:` as the line before the `> end;` verify that now the value of `mySum` is returned. ♠

8.4.6 Conversion of Procedures to Compiled Code

The code generation package CodeGeneration, and the older codegen, are used
to convert Maple procedures and modules into compiled code. Although we give
no examples, we tell you this for reference purposes.

8.5 SOLUTION: VOLUME FROM DIPSTICK HEIGHT

The solution to our problem requires us to solve for the height h at which

$$f(h) = h^3 - 9h^2 + 12 = 0.$$

We start the solution by defining this function in Maple and then plotting it as a
check that there are solutions in the region of interest:

```
> restart;       f := (h) -> h^3 - 9.*h^2 + 12.;
> plot(f(x), x = 0..9, title = 'Height of Liquid in Sphere');
```
$$f := h \rightarrow h^3 - 9. h^2 + 12.$$

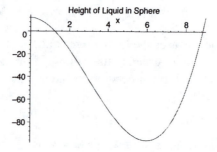

We observe two solutions, namely, two places where $f(h) = 0$. Yet as we discussed when we first set up this problem, the physical solution must lie in the
range $0 < h < 2R = 6$. Consequently only the root near $h = 1.5$ is physical.

As we said, while we have the option of using Maple's fsolve to find the
root, we will find it from scratch by programming up the *bisection algorithm*. We
set the level of desired precision to eps = 0.01, and the range to search in as hhi
= 7,   hlo = 0:

```
> eps := 0.01;       hlo := 0.;       hhi := 7.;                    # Parameters
```
$$eps := 0.01 \qquad hlo := 0. \qquad hhi := 7.$$

We use a *while* loop to narrow down the h range until $eps \leq$
$|(hhi - hlo)/(hhi + hlo)|$ is no longer true:

```
> while abs((hhi-hlo)/(hhi+hlo)) >= eps do
> h := 0.5 * (hlo+hhi):                    # Bisect the interval
> printf(' in loop h = %g', h);               # Print out
> if ( f(hhi) * f(h) <= 0 ) then        # Decide if zero on right or left
> hlo := h;
> else hhi := h;
> end if;
> end do;
```

$$h := 3.5$$

in loop h = 3.5

$$h := 1.75$$

in loop h = 1.75

$$h := 0.875$$

$$\vdots$$

in loop h = 1.244141

This tells us that for a dipstick height $h = 1.244m$ we have a volume $V = 4\pi/3 = 4.19\ m^3$ of fluid in the tank. As a check, we apply Maple's fsolve command

```
> fsolve(f, h, 0..2);
```

$$1.243848483$$

Sure enough, we see that the two answers agree to one place in the fourth decimal place, just the precision we asked our algorithm to produce.

8.6 KEY WORDS AND CONCEPTS

Boolean expressions	Boolean variables	local vs. global	flow control	break
procedure vs. function	volume integration	logical operator	trial and error	loops

1. Why would you ever solve a problem with a *trial-and-error* approach?
2. Can you do arithmetic on Boolean variables?
3. What is meant by *symbolic logic?*
4. How might Boolean variables be related to artificial intelligence (the computer appearing to think)?
5. Can all decision making be reduced to sets of Boolean expressions?
6. Must there always be a relation between the height of a liquid in some vessel and the liquids's volume?
7. If the height of a liquid in some vessel doubles, does that imply that the volume of the liquid must have increased eightfold?
8. Describe what is meant by an *iterative* solution to a problem.
9. Can a program containing correctly programmed Boolean expressions ever give the wrong answer?

10. Can logical conclusions ever be wrong?
11. Is a solution found in 10 steps better than one found in 100 steps?
12. Can a function use another function as part of its definition?

8.7 SUPPLEMENTARY EXERCISES

1. Use the bisection algorithm to calibrate the dipstick. Determine the h's for which the tank is 1/4 full, 1/2 full, 3/4 full, and 99/100 full.
2. Use the `if ... end if` syntax to make a plot of the $\tan\theta$ for $-2\pi \le \theta \le 2\pi$. Limit the ordinate to $|\tan\theta| \le .75$.
3. Write a loop that evaluates the power series for the exponential function $e^{-x} = \sum_{n=0}^{N} \frac{(-x)^n}{n!}$ for $x = 1, 10, 100$. Continue the loop until the next term added to the sum is less than 10^{-6} of the value for the sum.
4. Create a loop that uses the bisection algorithm to find a solution, good to six places, of the equation
$$x = e^{-x}.$$
5. Consider the nonlinear equation for the function $y(x)$:
$$y = \frac{x e^{-y^2}}{1+y^2}.$$
   a. Write a procedure that solves for and returns $y(x)$.
   b. Plot $y(x)$ for $0 < x < 12$.
   c. Write a procedure that computes and returns the derivative dy/dx.
   d. Make a plot of dy/dx for $0 < x < 12$, and check that the derivative does correspond to the slope in the previous graph.
6. (Adapted from [Zach 96]) If a is your age in years, w is your weight in pounds, and h is your height in inches, construct a Boolean expression that will be *true* only when the following statements are true:
   a. you are old enough to obtain a driver's license and you do not weigh 1,000 pounds;
   b. you are not a teenager;
   c. you are either younger than 20 and less than 150 pounds, or older than 40 and greater than 6 feet;
   d. you are neither old enough to vote, tall enough to hit your head on a five-foot door frame, nor the right weight to box as a 132–140 pounder.
7. Let A be your age, Y the number of years you have been in college, and D the number of dollars you have in the bank. Construct a Boolean expressions that will be *true* when the following conditions are met:
   a. you are a millionaire but you are not a senior;
   b. you are either too young to vote or you are not a freshman;
   c. you are either younger than 20 and broke, or older than 90 and have more than $100,000;
   d. you are 16 years old and your number of years in college is greater than the number of dollars you have in the bank.

PART 2

JAVA (OR FORTRAN90) BY DOING

Chapter Nine

Getting Started with Java: Compiling, Interpreting, Executing

9.1 COMPILED LANGUAGES

As we have seen in our work with Maple, a computer is an incredibly powerful and helpful device, when it does what you want. Maple is a fairly easy way to tell the computer what to do and that is why we started with it; you enter a command and Maple responds. If Maple cannot understand your command, or if its response is not what you like, then you just keep changing the command until all is well. In this line-by-line mode with a response after each command line, Maple is acting as an *interpreter*. Having the immediate response of an interpreter is useful, and when it is combined with a friendly graphical user interface (GUI), as in Maple, we have a powerful environment for scientific work.

To provide you with a broader experience in scientific computing than is possible with Maple, we now look at a different approach. Rather than enter commands one at a time, we write a *program* containing all the commands, and then have the computer process (*compile*) them all in one fell swoop.

Just as you probably have found it rather rare to be able to enter many Maple commands without making at least one error, it will also be rather rare that you are able to write a long program perfectly on the first try. However, there are many rewards to be had by trying, and once you get it right it, running it can be a breeze. But not to worry, we will start you with programs to modify rather than making you start from scratch.

To understand the value of a compiled language, imagine telling a story to a bunch of friends at party in which you were restricted to speaking only one sentence at a time, and could not continue your story until someone else responded to each of your sentences. Even though you might be able to get through your story, you could probably weave a better tale if you did not have to stop all the time. Likewise it is with a compiled approach to computing. Though it may take

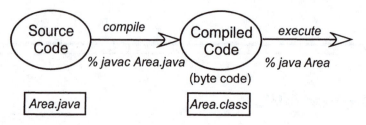

Figure 9.1 Steps in compiling and executing a Java program.

some more skill and time to weave a long program, you should be able to make it do exactly what you want, in exactly the way you want it done. And if the program gets used more than once, for instance to analyze different data sets, you do not have to repeat the process.

Here are some reasons for using Java as your first compiled language:

1. Java is the closest a computer language has ever come to being universal in syntax and execution, secure, and highly flexible.
2. Java is modern in structure, much like C and C++, and essential for computing on the World Wide Web.
3. Java requires the user to be specific about the type of variables declared (strongly *type-cast*) and is very careful about the precision of mathematical functions. This helps a student learn the proper handling of floating-point variables (especially important in scientific computing).
4. Java incorporates the modern, and possibly best, view towards programming known as *object-oriented programming*. C++ is also object-oriented but harder to learn.
5. Java has automatic "garbage collection"; that is, it automatically frees up sections of computer memory once your program stops using them. In C, you must do this yourself (a pain).
6. In our view the error-handling capability of Java, both during compilation and execution, is excellent. It is demanding that its grammar be followed (a good thing) and informative when it is not.
7. Finally, Java is exciting. Much of the excitement has arisen from Java's ability to do Web computing and from the availability of many classes (prepared utility programs to be incorporated into your program).

We have not said that we like Java because it is fast. Compared to Fortran and C, Java is slow, although it has the promise of being much faster. However, since modern computers are so fast, its speed will not affect you until you get into large projects. Likewise, there are fewer scientific libraries of programs for Java than for Fortran and C. However, the availability of libraries is also improving, spurred on, in part, from the developers not having to have a different library for each operating system.

Listing 9.1 Area.java

```
1  //                 Area.java: Area of a circle , sample program
2  public class Area
3  {
4      public static void main( String  args[])
5      {
6      double radius , circum , area , PI = 3.14159265359; // Initialize
7      int modelN = 1;
8      radius = 1.;
9      circum = 2.* PI* radius;
10     area = radius * radius * PI;
11     //                 Screen Output
12     System.out.println("Program number = " + modelN);
13     System.out.println("Radius = " + radius);
14     System.out.println("Circumference = " + circum);
15     System.out.println("Radius = " + radius +", Area = " + area);
16     }
17  }
```

9.2 JAVA PROGRAM PIECES

Whether simple or complex, developing Java programs requires two basic elements. These are indicated in Figure 9.1. One is a *source file* that you have written in Java and has a name ending with .java. The other is the executable file that the computer compiles for only computers to read, and has a name ending with .class. For instance, in Listing 9.1 we give the contents of a source file containing a simple program *Area.java* that calculates the area of a circle. There are a number of actions involved in order for you to convert Area.java into something a computer will understand:

1. You issue a command to *compile* the Java source code from within a *shell* (a command-line interpreter). You know that you are "in" a shell by the command-line prompt, which may contain a > or a %, or something containing the name of the directory/folder in which you are located.

2. The conversion of your program into an executable file is done with the Java compiler at the shell prompt (the second step in Figure 9.1):

> javac Area.java   Run Java compiler on file Area.java

When we illustrate commands like the one above, the first field of characters (>) is the shell's prompt, the second field, in monospaced bold type, is the command that you enter, and the rightmost field is a comment to you that should not be entered.

3. For these commands to work you must issue the `javac` command from within the directory in which the file `Area.java` is stored.[1] If the compilation was successful and you get no error messages, Java will have written another file in the same directory ending with the extension `.class`. In our example, `Area.class`.

4. In Java terminology, the compiled program in the `.class` file contains *byte code*. The term *byte* indicates that the code is compiled to the byte level, and the term *code* is used synonymously with the word "program." Java's universality means that this same `.class` file runs on any operating system, be it Unix, Windows, or Mac. In other compiled languages like Fortran and C, the compiled code contains commands that only one particular computer is able to execute, but it does so immediately. In Java, the compiled code is universal, yet another, internal, step is required before execution.

5. The last processing step in Figure 9.1 is *executing* or *running* your program:[2]

```
> java Area
```
                                                                            Execute byte code `Area.class`

When we issue this execution command `java`, the `.class` extender to `Area` is left off. Java just needs to know that `Area` is the name of the class for it to run the program `Area.class`. If you actually entered `Area.class` or `Area.java` as the program to run, you would get an error message. Go ahead and try `java Area.class`, it does no harm.

9.3 ENTERING AND RUNNING YOUR FIRST PROGRAM

As a general rule, you will not learn to compute just by reading about it. You must do what is necessary to get a program running and giving correct answers before you understand it. Accordingly, before we try to explain what is inside a Java program, let us get some experience with the steps we have outlined so far.

In the code Listing 9.1 is the Java source code for the program `Area.java`. The line numbers on the left are there to help explain the program to you; *do not enter the line numbers in your program*. The lines beginning with a `//`, or between `/*` and `*/`, are comments not read by Java. You do not need to enter these comments into your program, but they do help with understanding and documentation, and you are free to put whatever you want there.

1. Use a *text editor*[3] to enter `Area.java` into a file named `Area.java` in the direc-

---

[1] If you are using a programming environment package such as *Code Warrior*, some of this will be done automatically for you. Nevertheless, it is a good idea to check the location and modification dates of the files you create and use.

[2] In a strict sense this is *interpreting*, because Java executes the `Area.class` file one line at a time. However, most modern Java installations actually recompile the byte code into a completely compiled object code, and then run the recompiled code. In any case, as far as you are concerned Java will follow the commands in your program from top to bottom.

[3] An editor is a program like *Notepad* on a Windows PC, or *nedit* or *Xemacs* on Unix. Word processing

tory for your work. By "enter" we mean key the program in rather than cut and paste it. You may view this as mindless clerical work, but reading and looking at what you are entering helps make this foreign language seem less alien.

2. After you have entered the entire program, Save it into a file named `Area.java` in your personal directory.

3. Open a *shell* in your directory and *compile* `Area.java`:

```
> javac Area.java                          Get help if this will not execute
```

We remind you: the `>` here is the computer's prompt to you; the command you enter is in `bold monospaced font`, and the last field is a comment, not to be entered.

4. If compilation is successful, you will be told nothing (you only get spoken to when you do something wrong). However you can check that a file `Area.class` was created by listing all the files, with creation times, in your working directory:

```
> ls -l                                    From Unix/Linux prompt
> dir A*                                    From Windows command prompt
```

5. If you do have to correct some error (presumably typographical since you are just coping over a running program), open your `Area.java` in an editor and fix it. It is a good idea to keep the editor open in a separate window while you compile in the shell's window. Then Save `Area.java` in the same directory where you are doing the compiling and try compiling again.

6. Get into the habit of saving your files often, and sometimes as backup copies. Saving writes a copy to the hard disk for storage, while closing the file removes it from the grasp of the editor, without necessarily saving it.

7. If you like looking where you should not, use your editor to open and look at the `Area.class` file. Inasmuch as this file is not meant for human comprehension, what you see will not be illuminating. Alternatively, these files are viewable from the shell:

```
> cat Area.class                           Print out on screen for Unix
> type Area.class                          Print out on screen for DOS
```

8. We find ourselves more patient waiting for the computer to do its work if we know what the computer is doing (this also alleviates anxieties that we have done something wrong). On this account *we recommend that you include the* `-verbose` *option in your commands*. We may leave it off in this book to keep things short, but it is fun to include it:

---

programs like *Word* or *Word Perfect* are possible, but you must remember to save the file as *Text* to avoid control characters that will confuse the compiler.

```
> javac -verbose Area.java
```
Tell me what <code>javac</code> is doing

9. Check again that you have created the byte code version of your Java program, namely, that there is a file `Area.class`:

```
> ls -l
> dir
```
List files in Unix/linux
List files in DOS

10. As we see from Figure 9.1, once we have compiled code in `Area.class`, we get the computer to *execute* or *run* it by issuing the `java` command (no `c`) at the prompt with just the class name:

```
> java Area
> java Area.class
```
Execute <code>Area.class</code>
Wrong, cannot have <code>.class</code> extension

You should get output of the form

```
Program number = 1
Radius = 1.0
Circumference = 6.283186
Area = 3.141593
```

11. Now that you have a program that is running, check that it is actually doing as you intended by changing a line in it and seeing how the results change. In particular, try assigning a value to the variable `radius`:

```
6  radius = 1.;
```

12. Use your editor to change this line to `radius = 10.;`, being careful not to leave out the semicolon " `;` " at the end of the line.

13. Save the modified Java source code in the file `Area.java`.

14. Compile the modified file, correcting any errors if necessary.

15. Execute the new `Area.class` file with the command `java Area`, and check that you get $100\,\pi$ as the area.

16. To see how Java responds to not doing things correctly, be adventurous and try below some unconventional variations on the theme:

```
> javac Area
> javac area.java
error: Cannot read: area.java
> java Area.java
> java -verbose Area.java
```
Left off <code>.java</code> after <code>Area</code>
Forget to capitalize
The error message on Unix
Left off <code>c</code> on <code>javac</code>
Really get yelled at for that <code>c</code>!

9.4 LOOKING INSIDE AREA.JAVA

We now look at `Area.java` to get some idea of how a program goes about its business. Though a simple program, it is not trivial in that it contains a number of important parts. Admittedly it is hard to understand at first all that is going on; be patient, after seeing them a few times it begins to make more sense.

// Comments and /* Comments */ At the top of `Area.java` is a `//` and some information about the program. Text following the `//` is a comment unread by Java and placed there as information for the user. The `//` comment may be placed on a line by itself, or after some Java statements. Multiline comments start with a `/*` and end with a `*/`. They too are ignored by Java. We encourage the use of comments and blank lines to make code clearer. Nevertheless, we are frugal in our examples in order to space printed space.

public class Area This line declares the name of the *class* to be `Area`. You may think of the term *class* as the name of our program.[4] Remember that this is exactly the same named used for the file `Area.java` containing the Java source. In fact, if the two do not agree, then Java will complain. The `public` on line 2 indicates that this class may be read by other programs. While speaking of area, notice on line 8 the statement `area = radius * radius * PI`. Here `area` is the name of a variable, and since Java is case sensitive, Java treats it as a completely different name from the class name `Area`.

public static void main(String[] argv) Line 3 contains the important word `main` and means that the *main method* is to follow. A class usually contains a number of *methods*, the term *method* denoting a subprogram that behaves like a mathematical function. It is called a "method" to indicate that it is a method for handling data or variables.

Every Java program that runs directly on a computer, that is, not via a Web browser, must contain a `main` method as the place where execution begins. This simple program contains only one method, the `main` method. The body of the main method is made up of all the lines of code between the first open brace `{` and the last close brace `}`. Usually the `main` method is used as the control unit or administrator for a program; it does not do much in the way of work itself, but instead calls other methods to get the computation done and then collects and organizes their results.

It is probably best for first-time readers to just accept the phrase `public static void main(String[] argv)` as the way to declare a main method, and ignore for now our explanation of what the modifiers and arguments to `main` mean.

---

[4] In a formal sense, a *class* is a collection of data (variables) and methods (functions) that act on those data. In the present case, our class file has only the `main` method.

Nevertheless, we now give some explanation for completeness and for later-time readers.

The modifier `static` before `main` indicates that `main` is a *static* method, and not *dynamic* like an *object*. We talk about objects in Chapters 16 and 18, and suggest you ignore it for now. The modifier `void` before `main` indicates the type of output produced by `main`, in this case nothing. Likewise, the parentheses in `main(String[] argv)` contain the input or arguments supplied to `main`. In this case there is a single argument named `argv` and it is a `String`. The square brackets `[ ]` indicate that `argv` is an array, that is, a subscripted variable.

`double radius, circum, ...; int modelN = 1;` Before you are permitted to use a variable in Java, you must *declare* its name and the type of variable it is. This creates *instances* or records of them so that they may be used later. The first line declares the variables `r`, `area` and `PI` to be `double`, that is, double precision. The next line declares the variable `modelN` to be an `int`, that is, an integer. (We describe the various data types in the next chapter).

Instead of assigning values later, lines 4 and 5 serve double duty by assigning initial values to the variables `PI` and `modelN`. Inspect how in both of these lines there is first a data type (`double` or `int`) and then a series of one or more variables that will be stored with this data type. Any number of variables are permitted on these lines, although it is probably best to add additional declaration lines rather than have one line so long that its end gets hidden beyond the edge of the screen. A semicolon ; is used to end these two statements, as is true for most "action type" statements in Java.

`radius = 1.;` Lines 6, 7, and 8 are *assignment* statements. They compute the numerical value of whatever expression is on the RHS of = and assign that number to the variable named on the LHS of =. Here, "assign" means to store a numerical value in the memory location reserved for that variable. (This is the same as the assignment operator := in Maple, except Java deals only with numerical values.)

Arithmetical operations are denoted by the standard +, -, *, and / symbols. However, the symbol ^, often used for exponentiation, is used for a logical operation *xor* in Java. Instead, use the power function in the Math class, `Math.pow(x,2)`. In this example we squared the variable `radius` by simply using `radius * radius`, but we could also have said `Math.pow(radius,2)`.

system.out.println(...); These lines look worse than they really are and may be used as given until you know better. If you learn to read the `System.out.println` part backwards, you could believe that it says to *print* a *line* out using Java's (the System's) methods to do this. The periods in the command denote the access route. Starting from the top level class, the `System` class, we then access a subclass `out` and one of its methods, the `println(String s)` method. (As an example of another such object-oriented method access, say you make a class `MyClass` with a method `myMethod()`. If you wish to access this method, then call `MyClass.myMethod();`.) Getting back to these output lines, the argument `("Program Number = " + modelN)` means take the string `Program Number = ` and append another string containing the numerical value of the variable `modelN` to the end of it. The appending is done by the `+ modelN` part. Likewise, the output on line 11 starts with a string `Radius = ` and appends the numerical value of `radius` to it. Once these strings are built up (concatenated), they get printed out to your screen, each on a new line. If you do not want Java to place your output on a new line, but instead to continue with the last line, then you would leave off the `ln` part:

```
System.out.print(" Program Number = " + modelN);
```

You are allowed to make the string that gets printed as long as you like by concatenating more and more substrings to it. To cite an instance, on line 13

```
System.out.println("Radius = " + radius +", Area = " + area);
```

after the value of `radius` is added to the string, we add in the string ", Area = " and then add on the value of `area` after that. (When we say "add on the value of," what really is happening is that Java is converting a double to a string, and then adding that string to the end of the previous string).

9.5 KEY WORDS

assignment statement	byte code	class	comments
compile	execution	garbage collection	interpreter
methods	objects	program	shell
source file/code	type-cast	text editor	print
string	main method	running	

9.6 SUPPLEMENTARY EXERCISES

1. Modify `Area.java` into a new program `Volume.java` that calculates the volume of a liquid in a spherical tank of radius R, when the liquid is a height H above the bottom of the tank. We have already studied this problem with Maple in Chapter 8, where we derived that the volume $V = \pi H^2(R - H/3)$. Make sure to test your program for $H = 0$, R, and $2R$, namely, for an empty, a half-full, and a full tank.

2. Explain in just a few words:
   a. what the Java interpreter does;
   b. what the Java compiler does;
   c. how Java differs from an operating system;
   d. what is a shell.

Chapter Ten

Data Types, Limits, Methods; Rocket Golf

10.1 PROBLEM AND THEORY (SAME AS CHAPTER 3)

Michele, our golf fanatic in Figure 3.1 is still in pursuit of the world's record for the fastest golf ball. Recall, she hits her golf balls from a rocket moving to the right with a velocity $v = c/2$ relative to observer Ben on earth, and sees her ball travel with a speed of $U = c/\sqrt{3}$ at an angle $\theta = 30°$ with respect to the moving rocket. She observes her drive to remain in the air for hang time $T' = 2.6 \times 10^7$ seconds.

1. How would Ben, watching Michele's drive from the earth, describe the golf ball in terms of its speed, angle ϕ, and hang time T?
2. How would the answer to 1. change if Michele hit her ball to the left, that is, in a direction opposite to the rocket's velocity?
3. If Michele hit the ball with a speed $U = c$, how would the answers change?

The formulas we need from special relativity relate the description of the same moving object as it appears to observers in different frames. If Michele in O' sees her golf ball having velocity components:

$$U' = (U'_x, U'_y),\tag{10.1}$$

then Ben in O, who sees Michele moving to the right with velocity v, will see her golf ball move with velocity components

$$U = (U_x, U_y),\tag{10.2}$$

$$U_x = \frac{U'_x + v}{1 + vU'_x/c^2}, \qquad U_y = \frac{U'_y}{\gamma(1 + vU'_x/c^2)}\tag{10.3}$$

$$\gamma = \frac{1}{\sqrt{1 - v^2/c^2}}.\tag{10.4}$$

10.2 JAVA'S PRIMITIVE DATA TYPES

Before we begin to calculate with Java, it is in your best interest to explore the limitations of the numerical capabilities of Java. It all arises from the schemes

Table 10.1 Java's basic data types and their sizes in bytes (B).

Name	Type	Bits	Bytes	Range & Precision
boolean	logical	1	-	true or false
char	string	16	2	'\u0000' $\leftrightarrow$ '\uFFFF' (ISO Unicode)
byte	integer	8	1	$-128 \leftrightarrow +127$
short	integer	16	2	$-32,768 \leftrightarrow +32,767$
int	integer	32	4	$-2,147,483,648 \leftrightarrow +2,147,483,648$
long	integer	64	8	$-9,223,372,036,854,775,808 \leftrightarrow$ $9,223,372,036,854,775,807$
float	floating point	32	4	$\pm 1.401298 \times 10^{-45} \leftrightarrow \pm 3.402923 \times 10^{+38}$
double	floating point	64	8	$\pm 4.94065645841246544 \times 10^{-324} \leftrightarrow$ $\pm 1.7976931348623157 \times 10^{+308}$

Table 10.2 The use of three bits a, b, and c, to represent the eight integers from 0 to $2^3 - 1 = 7$.

Binary abc	$= a \times 2^2$	$+ b \times 2^1$	$+ c \times 2^0$	= Decimal
000	0	0	0	0
001	0	0	1	1
010	0	1	0	2
011	0	1	1	3
100	1	0	0	4
101	1	0	1	5
110	1	1	0	6
111	1	1	1	7

computers use to store information. As you have seen in Area.java's statements containing int and double, Java is specific about the types of variable or data with which it deals. Variables are stored as any of Java's primitive data types, or as ones you create yourself. The primitive data types and the amount of memory they occupy are described in Table 10.1. These are rather standard for most modern computer languages. Variables of these types are stored in the computer's memory in small blocks of memory locations called *words*. The amount of memory used to store a variable depends upon what you want to store in the variable, and one of the chores you have in programming is deciding how long you want your variables to be. So, now a word about words.

10.2.1 Integers

The most elementary unit of memory is a little magnet, like a compass needle that points up or down. If we associate "down" with 0 and "up" with number 1, then we have a physical device that stores representations of 0's and 1's. It should then be no surprise to hear that all numbers on the computer are ultimately represented in *binary* form, namely, in terms of the binary digits (abbreviated *bits*) 0 and 1.

Just like the digits in the *decimal* system indicate the number of times that 10^0, 10^1, 10^2, ..., are each contained in a number, so it is with the binary system. As an instance, in Table 10.2 we see the three bits abc representing the eight numbers from 0 to 7. Likewise, N bits are used to represent integers up to 2^N. In practice, since the first bit is used to represent the sign of the integer, we effectively lose one bit, which means that it is possible to represent integers only up to 2^{N-1} with N bits.

Long strings of 0's and 1's are fine for computers but awkward for people. Consequently, binary strings are converted to *octal*, *decimal*, or *hexadecimal* numbers before results are communicated to people. Octal and hexadecimal numbers are fine, but our decimal rules of arithmetic do not work for them, and so they are hard for humans to work with. Converting to decimal numbers makes the numbers easier for us to work with but usually causes some loss in precision.

The point of all this discussion about what goes on in the "guts" of memory is that in one way or another, you must tell Java how many bits you want to have assigned to store the value of each variable. The number of bits is called *word length* and is often expressed in *bytes*, where a byte is a "mouthful of bits":

$$1 \text{ byte} \equiv 1 \text{ B} \overset{\text{def}}{=} 8 \text{ bits}. \tag{10.5}$$

Conventionally, storage size is measured in bytes or kilobytes. For this reason, while one bit is adequate to represent a 0 or 1, two bytes are required to represent a single character, like the letter "a" or "b."

In practice, 8 bits or 1 byte are used to store an integer, in which case the integers lie in the range $1-2^7$ or $1-128$. More usually, 4 B = 32 bits are used for integers, which means that the maximum positive integer is $2^{31} \simeq 2 \times 10^9$. In spite of this seeming to be a large range for numbers, it really is not compared to the range of sizes encountered in the physical world. To illustrate, the ratio of the size of the universe to the size of a proton is 10^{40}. Though Java integers have limited range, they are stored exactly on the computer if they are within this range.

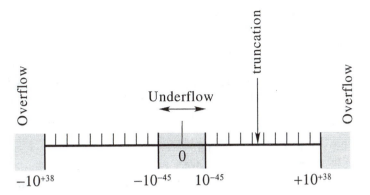

Figure 10.1 An illustration of the limits of single-precision floating point numbers and the consequences of exceeding those limits.

10.2.2 Floating-Point Numbers

Scientific work primarily uses floating-point numbers. In floating-point notation, the number x is stored as a sign, a mantissa, and an exponent:

$$x_{\text{float}} = (-1)^s \times \text{mantissa} \times 2^{\text{exp}}. \qquad (10.6)$$

Here the mantissa contains the *significant figures* of the number, s is the sign bit, and the exponent permits very large, as well as very small, numbers.[1] To prove the point, a single-precision 32-bit word may allocate 8 bits of computer memory for the exponent in (10.6), which leaves 23 bits for the mantissa and 1 for the sign. This 8-bit integer "exponent" has the range $[-127, 128]$. In practical terms this means that single-precision (4-byte) numbers have 6–7 decimal places of precision (1 part in 2^{23}) and magnitudes typically in the range

$$2^{-149} \simeq 10^{-45} \leq \text{single precision} \leq 2^{128} \simeq 10^{38}. \qquad (10.7)$$

These ranges are represented schematically in Figure 10.1. If you write a program requesting *double precision*, then 64-bit (8-byte) words will be used in place of the 32-bit (4-byte) words. With 11 bits used for the exponent and 52 for the mantissa, double-precision numbers have about 16 decimal places of precision and typically have magnitudes in the range

$$10^{-324} \leq \text{double precision} \leq 10^{308}. \qquad (10.8)$$

---

[1] In practice a number called the *bias* is subtracted from the exponent exp so that the stored exponent is always positive.

10.2.3 Naming Convention

We have already seen with the program `Area.java` being stored in the file of the same name, that the name of a class file must match the name of the class. It is also conventional to have the name of the class start with a Capital letter, as we did with `Area.java`.

Regular variables in Java usually are written with lowercase letters. Even though a variable may start with a lowercase letter, it may contain capital letters within, such as `hiMass` and `loMass`. Variable names may contain alphanumeric (letters and numbers) characters and underscore characters (_) but must start with a letter or an underscore. All names are case sensitive, so `IloveYou` and `ILOVEYou` are completely unrelated. We have also seen `PI` spelled with all capital letters. If a piece of variable does not change as the program runs, then it is a *constant* or a `FINAL` and is denoted by all capital letters. Finally, it is illegal to use as names those words that Java has reserved for itself:

Reserved Words

abstract	boolean	break	byte	case	catch	char
class	const	continue	double	default	do	else
extends	final	finally	float	for	goto	if
import	implements	instanceof	int	interface	long	native
new	null	package	private	protected	public	return
short	static	super	switch	synchronized	this	throw
throws	transient	try	void	volatile	while	

Examples of acceptable names are:

```
AlbertEinstein, alEinstein, F_B_I, Herr_Prof_Dr, Geo3rd
```

Examples of unacceptable (space, special character, reserved word, beginning number) names are:

```
Al Einstein, Al*Einstein, final, 3rdGeo
```

10.2.4 Machine Precision

One consequence of computers using the floating-point representation to store numbers is that most numbers are stored with only a limited precision. We see a schematic representation of this in Figure 10.1, where you are to imagine floating-point numbers being stored along the vertical hash marks. If you call for a number that lies between the hash mark, the computer will move you to the closest number. The corresponding loss of precision is called *truncation error*.

The exact precision obtained in a calculation depends on the program. For a single operation, single precision usually yields 6–7 decimal places for a 32-bit word, and double precision 15–16 places. To understand how *machine precision* affects calculations, what would you guess is the result of the simple addition of two single-precision numbers: $7 + 2.0 \times 10^{-8}$?

(a) 7.00000002,   (b) 9×10^{-8},   (c) 7,   (d) 7.02

The correct answer is (c). Because there is no more room left to store the 2.0×10^{-8}, it is lost or truncated from the answer, and the addition gives 7.

This loss of precision is categorized by defining the *machine precision* ϵ_m as the maximum positive number that may be added to the number stored as 1 without changing the number stored as 1 on the computer:

$$1_c + \epsilon_m = 1_c. \tag{10.9}$$

Here the subscript c is a reminder that the variable is the number stored in the computer's memory. Likewise, x_c, the computer's representation of an arbitrary number x, and the actual number x, are related by

$$x_c \simeq x(1 + \epsilon), \qquad |\epsilon| \le \epsilon_m. \tag{10.10}$$

Remember, $\epsilon_m \simeq 10^{-7}$ for single precision and $\epsilon_m \simeq 10^{-16}$ for double precision.

10.2.5 Under- and Overflows

If a single-precision number x is larger than 2^{128}, an *overflow* occurs. If x is smaller than 2^{-149}, an *underflow* occurs. We visualize this in Figure 10.1 by observing that any number that tries to get closer to 0 than 10^{-45} in magnitude falls in the gray region at the center, and leads to underflow. Likewise, any number whose magnitude exceeds 10^{+38} falls in the gray region at the ends of the line, and leads to overflow. The number x_c that the computer stores may end up being NAN (not a number), or a noncomputable infinity, or zero. Because underflow is a loss of information, a scientific programmer should be sensitive to its occurrence. Because the only difference between the representations of positive and negative numbers on the computer is the one sign bit for negative numbers, the same considerations hold for negative numbers.

In our experience, serious scientific calculations almost always require double precision (8B). And if you need double precision in one part of your calculation, you probably need it all over, and that also means double-precision library

Listing 10.1 Limits.java

```
1  /*          Limits.java:        Determine machine precision */
2  public class Limits
3  {    public static void main(String[] args)
4     {   final int N = 60;                              //Declaration
5         int i;                                         //Declaration
6         double eps = 1.0, one_Plus_Eps;                //Declaration
7         for (i = 0; i < N; i = i+1)
8         { eps = eps/2.;
9           one_Plus_Eps = 1.0 + eps;
10          System.out.println("one + eps = " + one_Plus_Eps + ", eps
                = " +eps);   }
11  } }                                                  //End main, end class
12  /* Output:
13  one + eps = 1.5, eps = 0.5
14  one + eps = 1.0000000000000002, eps = 2.220446049250313E−16
15  one + eps = 1.0, eps = 1.1102230246251565E−16 */
```

routines. If you want to be a scientist or an engineer, learn to say "no" to singles and floats.

10.2.6 Experiment: Determine Your Machine's Precision

Listing 10.1 contains the small, but significant, program Limits.java for you to "test-drive" during your "break-in" period with Java. By repeatedly comparing $1 + \epsilon_m$ to 1 as ϵ_m is made smaller, Limits.java determines the machine precision as the value of ϵ_m for which the variable onePlusEps equals 1:

1. Enter Limits.java by hand into a file of the same name, compile it, and run it to determine the machine precision ϵ_m for doubles. If you are going to save the output, or show it to someone else, it is good practice to edit the output file to eliminate the large number of noninformative lines. Once you understand how this program works, you may want to modify it so that it starts closer to the final answer, or so that it runs longer in order to get to the final answer. As is true for many of the programs we give you, they are meant as models for you to modify and extend.

2. Modify Limits.java to determine the machine precision ϵ_m for single-precision numbers (floats). To modify it correctly, you need to change the word double to float in the declaration statements, as well as change numbers like 1.0 to 1.0F throughout the program. The reason for the latter change is that Java automatically assumes that any decimal number is a double, yet by affixing the F you force Java to save the number as a float.

3. **Underflow:** Modify this program to determine the smallest positive single-

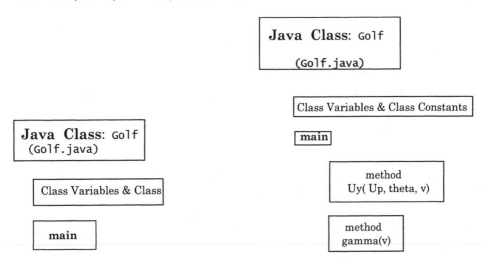

Figure 10.2 *Left:* The structure of a Java class with only a main method. *Right:* The structure of a Java class with two methods.

precision numbers that Java handles. *Hint:* Continuous division of eps by 2 will determine the smallest number within a factor of 2. So, modify the line onePlusEps = 1.0 + eps to a division and increase the value of N so the program repeats for a longer time.

4. **Overflow:** Modify this program to determine the largest positive single-precision numbers that Java handles. *Hint:* Rather than divide by 2, multiply by 2.

5. Determine the underflow and overflow limits (smallest and largest numbers) for double precision.

6. Modify this program to determine the largest and most *negative* integers. *Hint:* Change eps to an integer (int) and keep subtracting 2 to determine the most negative integer; add 2 to determine the most positive integer.

7. Determine Java's value for $3(1/3)$ using double-precision values for 1 and 3, and then integer values for 1 and 3.

10.3 METHODS (FUNCTIONS) AND MODULAR PROGRAMMING

On the left of Figure 10.2 we show a simple Java program. The class's name is Golf and in it is the class definition and the main method. The only conceptual advance beyond the Area.java program of Chapter 9 is that we have included the definition of *class variable* in the box indicating the class definition public class Golf. Class variables are defined just like any other variable, except by doing it at the class level, they may be used by all methods. Variables defined within methods are *local* to that method.

In some ways, having a small program like Area.java do all its computing in the `main` method makes sense. Because execution begins there, you may as well put all the work there so you do not have to look elsewhere to find it. As programs get called on to do more, they tend to get more complicated and harder to follow or modify. Then it makes sense to adopt a modular approach in which a program is divided into several relatively small subprograms, with each subprogram having its own separate function.

In Java, the separate subprograms are separate *methods* and are usually placed within a class of related methods. Often each class has its own main method to begin execution, but that is not necessary. This collection of data (variables) and methods used to manipulate those data is the abstract definition of *class*.

It is a great idea to save time and not repeat yourself, and so it is also possible for methods in one class to call methods from other classes. As an example, the mathematical functions, to be discussed shortly, are in the class named `Math`. We call the method `sin` in that class just by adding a prefix to the method name; for example, `Math.sin`.

On the right of Figure 10.2 we show an example where we have enlarged the class `Golf` to now contain the methods `Uy` and `gamma` as well as `main`. The `main` method may call either of the other methods, and the other methods can call each other as well, but not main. Data is transferred in these calls by means of the argument list and the value of the method (input and output), as well as through the class variables, which may be shared by all methods.

There are many good reasons for writing a program in which there are multiple methods with each method performing a single task (*modular programming*). This lets us build up into complexity with individual modules that are to be written and tested separately, reused in a number of programs, and in which the logic of the program is easy to follow. In good modular programming design, the `main` method is the control unit, or administrator, of the program, and it calls other methods to get the work done without doing any of the work itself. So you get a good idea of what an entire program does just by reading through its `main` method; the details are left to the other methods.

Listing 10.2 Method.java

```
1  //                      Method.java: Example of calling a method
2  public class Method
3  {    public static void main(String[] argv)                 // Main method
4  {    double fVal;
5       int i;
6       for (i=1 ; i <= 100; i=i+1)
7         { fVal = f(i);
8          System.out.println("i= " +i+ " sin(i)+1= " + fVal); }
9  }                                                            // End main
10      public static double f(int y)                           // Method f(y)
```

```
11        { return Math.sin(y) + 1; }
12  }                                                              // End class
```

Enough theory! Now some concrete examples. In Listing10.2 is the program Method.java, containing a main method and a single auxiliary method. The program prints out 100 values of i and the function $f(i) = \sin(i) + 1$ to the computer screen. Observe how the name of the method f is returned as the value of the function. This permits us to use it on line 7 as fVal = f(i).

Also observe that the method f is called with the argument i in main, yet is defined with the argument y in the f method. This is fine. Whereas it is important that the *data types* of the arguments agree in main and in f, the variable names are local to each method and do not have to agree. When the program is executed, actual numbers get passed between main and f (a *value pass*), and not the variable names (a *reference pass*).

Find this program on the disk, copy it to your personal directory, and compile and execute it. Make sure that the name of the file Method.java matches the name of the class. After compilation, there will be another file Method.class containing the compiled byte code. The names of the individual methods do not appear, only the name of the class.

One of the confusing aspects of first learning about methods is that their names seem to be surrounded by so much "junk." Just as you learn to read a newspaper without ever looking at any of the advertisements, so you soon will be able to make sense out of these methods without letting the junk get in your way. The junk arises from the fact that the Java compiler needs to be told in advance what kind of variables will be input and output to a method, and so it requires you to place a whole slew of modifiers in front of and after the method name. As a case in point, when we declared a method on line 10

```
10  public static double f(int y)                        // Declare method f(y)
```

we are just saying that there will be a function $f(y)$ that takes as input the integer y and returns a double for $f(y)$. The public modifier is for access control and means that this method is visible everywhere. The static modifier is related to the *object-oriented* aspects of Java (to be discussed later) and implies that this method is not dynamic so that it may be accessed from the main method.

10.3.1 Main Method

We almost always declare a main method with

```
public static void main(String argv[])                   // Declare main method
```

Table 10.3 Java's mathematical functions.

Math	Java	Math	Java	Math	Java
e $(\ln e = 1)$	`Math.E`	π	`Math.PI`	x^y	`pow(x,y)`
$\sin \theta$	`sin(q)`	$\cos \theta$	`cos(q)`	$\tan \theta$	`tan(q)`
$\sin^{-1} \theta$	`asin(q)`	$\cos^{-1} \theta$	`acos(q)`	$\tan^{-1} \theta$	`atan(q)`
$\tan^{-1}(y/x)$	`atan2(x, y)`	e^x	`exp(x)`	$\ln x$	`log(x)`
random #	`random()`	$\sqrt{x}$	`sqrt(x)`	$|x|$	`abs(x)`
remainder	`IEEEremainder(x,y)`	$\max(x, y)$	`max(x,y)`	$\min(x, y)$	`min(x,y)`
next integer	`ceil(x)`	previous int	`floor(x)`	$\max(x, y)$	`max(x,y)`
nearest integer	`double rint(x)`	nearest int	`round(x)`	$\min(x, y)$	`min(x,y)`

The modifier `static` before `main` indicates that `main` is a *static* method and not *dynamic* like an *object*. We talk about objects in Chapters 16 and 18 and suggest you ignore it for now. The modifier `void` before `main` indicates the type of output produced by `main`, in this case nothing (remember, `main` is an administrator that just watches over the work done by others). Likewise, the parentheses in `main(String[] argv)` contain the input or arguments supplied to `main`. In this case there is a single argument named `argv` and it is a `String`. The square brackets `[ ]` indicate that `argv` is an array, namely, a subscripted variable. Even though the argument to the `main` method may look rather complicated, the good news is that you do not have to supply the argument; `String argv[]` is passed to the main method by the Java interpreter when you run the program.

10.3.2 Mathematical Methods

Java contains a `Math` library or *package* that knows how to compute numerical values for a whole bunch of functions. This collection of methods has the official name `java.lang.Math`. To use a method from this package, for example, `cos` the cos function, you need to tell Java where to find it. It this case you could say `java.lang.Math.cos` or be lazy and use the nickname `Math.cos`. Other examples include `Math.sin(x)` and `Math.sin(Math.PI)`, where `Math.PI` is the numerical value of π. Table 10.3 gives Java's mathematics functions. They all need the `Math.` prefix to work. In most cases, the functions take and return various argument types, such as doubles and floats.

Exercises: Compile and execute the program `TestMath.java` in Listing 10.3 and make sense out of its error message. Replace the `x` assignment statement in the program with each of the following and note the results:

Listing 10.3 TestMath.java

```
1 //                    TestMath.java  test  math  library
2 public class TestMath
3 {    public static final double y= 1.;
4      public static double x;
5      static public void main(String[] args)
6 {    x = sin(y);
7      System.out.println("sin(y)  =  " +x);
8 }}                                                //End main and class
```

```
x = Math.sin(PI);                              // Will not compile
x = Math.sin(Math.PI);                         // Will compile ♠
```

Regardless of the built-in math functions giving accurate answers, they do not know everything about mathematics and will give error messages or nonnumeric answers if pushed too far. Take the previous TestMath program and use it to evaluate:

1. $\sqrt{-1}$
2. $\cos^{-1}(2)$
3. $\log(0)$

10.4 SOLUTION: VIEWING ROCKET GOLF

We will now use Java to solve the same Rocket Golf problem as we did with Maple in Chapter 3. The application of modular programming means that we will now write separate methods, as we did with Maple's user-defined functions, to compute γ, U_x, and U_y, and plot a graph of γ *versus* v using *PtPlot*.[2] Our solution program thus contains a main method, three computational methods, and one plotting method. To determine how round-off error affects the results, we describe and run the program that solves the problem in double precision and ask you to modify it so that it solves the same problem in single precision with floats (we give the results of both, but the source for only double precision).

Listing 10.4 shows the class Golf.java. It takes as input data the angle and velocity of Michele's golf ball and computes the velocities and angles as seen by Ben. If you set the speed of light c equal to a nearly infinite number, the relativistic effects vanish. Observe that we have placed the main method at the top and followed it by the four methods gamma, Ux, Uy, and plotGamma. We like the main method to go first, as it shows from the start how the program works. This is *top-down programming*. Some programmers prefer defining all the methods first before they are called. That is *bottom-up programming*. The Java compiler does

---

[2]We describe the use of *PtPlot* in Chapter 11. We recommend that you read that chapter soon; however, you may work through the present sections just by copying the plotting commands.

not care if you call a method before it is defined; as long as it is defined somewhere within the class file (or in other class files that get included), there will be no error messages.

Listing 10.4 Golf.java

```
1  /*          Golf.java:  Double methods, PtPlots, v in c units */
2  import ptolemy.plot.*;                              // Import PtPlot
3  public class Golf                                   // class begins
4  {    public static void main(String[] args)          // main begins
5  {   double Up, Tp, v, theta, T, ux, uy, UBen, phi;
6      plotGamma();                                    // Call plot method
7      Up= 1.0 / Math.sqrt(3.0);
8      Tp= 2.6e7;
9      v = 0.5;
10     theta = 30.0 * Math.PI / 180.0;
11     System.out.println("Michelle hits the golf ball forward.\n");
12     T = gamma(Up) * Tp;
13     ux = Ux(Up, theta, v);
14     uy = Uy(Up, theta, v);
15     UBen = Math.sqrt(ux * ux + uy * uy);
16     phi =   Math.atan2(uy, ux);
17     System.out.println("According to Ben:");
18     System.out.println("T     = " + T + " s");
19     System.out.println("ux = " + ux);
20     System.out.println("uy = " + uy);
21     System.out.println("UBen  = " + UBen);
22     System.out.println("phi   = " + phi);
23     theta = Math.PI - theta;        // Michelle's angle now backward
24     System.out.println("\nMichelle hits ball backwards\n");
25     T = gamma(Up) * Tp;
26     ux = Ux(Up, theta, v);
27     uy = Uy(Up, theta, v);
28     UBen  = Math.sqrt(ux * ux + uy * uy);
29     phi   = Math.atan2(uy, ux);
30     System.out.println("According to Ben:");
31     System.out.println("T     = " + T + " s");
32     System.out.println("ux = " + ux);
33     System.out.println("uy = " + uy);
34     System.out.println("UBen  = " + UBen);
35     System.out.println("phi   = " + phi);
36  }                     //End of main method, other methods follow
37     public static double gamma(double v)        // gamma(v) function
38  { return 1. / Math.sqrt(1. - v * v);  }
39     public static double Ux(double Up, double theta, double v)
40  { double Upx = Up* Math.cos(theta);
41     return (Upx + v) / (1. + v * Upx);  }
42     public static double Uy(double Up, double theta, double v)
43  { double Upx = Up* Math.cos(theta);
44     double Upy = Up* Math.sin(theta);
45     return Upy /(gamma(v) * (1.0 + v * Upx));  }
46     public static void plotGamma()                 // plot gamma(v)
47  { Plot myPlot = new Plot();                       //Create plot
```

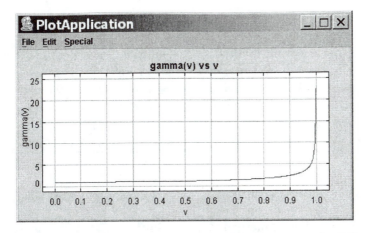

Figure 10.3 A plot of the function $\gamma(v)$ output from the program Golf.java using *PtPlot*. Compare to Maple's plot in Chapter 3.

```
48        myPlot.setTitle("gamma(v) vs v");              //Set title
49        myPlot.setXLabel("v");                         //X axis label
50        myPlot.setYLabel("gamma(v)");                  //Y axis label
51        myPlot.setYRange(0.0, 25.0);                   //Vertical range
52        for (double v = 0.; v < 1.; v += 0.001)
53        { double g = gamma(v);
54          myPlot.addPoint(0, v, g, true); }            //Add data points
55        PlotApplication app = new PlotApplication(myPlot);  //Display
56 }    }                                                //End method, end class
```

Find where the method Uy calls the method gamma. Having one method call another is good modular programming practice. Also note that we have kept the program neat by placing all the plotting commands in the method plotGamma. We thereby keep the technical details from interfering with our ability to see the logical flow of the program, and we permit ourselves to modify the plotting without messing up the rest of the program. The plot obtained is shown in Figure 10.3 and looks much like the Maple plot in Chapter 3.

When comparing the double (ours) and float (your) versions of this program, it is interesting to observe that it is simpler to write Java programs in doubles than floats. The simplicity of doubles is a consequence of Java automatically treating numerical constants as doubles and converting mixed singles plus doubles into doubles, of the math library automatically doing its computations in double precision, and of Java not permitting you to decrease precision (say from double to float) without your acknowledging the fact.

To create a float version of the program, you will have to convert doubles into singles with the *cast* operator (float) and add an F to numerical constants,

Table 10.4 Results of double- and single-precision computations.

Golf.java: double methods	GolfFloat.java: float methods
T = 3.1843366656181317E7 s	T = 3.1843364E7 s
ux = 0.8	ux = 0.8
uy = 0.19999999999999996	uy = 0.2
u = 0.8246211251235323	u = 0.82462114
phi = 0.24497866312686412	phi = 0.24497867

Table 10.5 Results of double- and single-precision computations for the second case.

Golf.java: double methods	GolfFloat.java: float methods
T = 3.1843366656181317E7 s	T = 3.1843364E7 s
ux = -1.4802973661668753E-16	ux = 3.973643E-8
uy = 0.33333333333333326	uy = 0.33333337
u = 0.33333333333333326	u = 0.33333337
phi = 1.5707963267948972	phi = 1.5707963

such as in `1.0F -v * v`, so they are stored as floats:

```
9  v = 0.5F;
10  theta = (float) (30.0 * Math.PI/180.0);
```

The output we obtained for the two cases is compared in Table 10.4. Take stock of how Java prints out only one digit beyond the decimal point, such as in ux = 0.8, as its way of telling you that as far as it knows all other digits beyond the decimal point are zero. This a Java solution to the first part of the problem, where Michele hits the golf ball forward. We see that Java is smart enough to realize that its single-precision calculation with floats has 6–7 places of precision, and so prints out just 8 significant figures (an extra 1 or 2 places so you are able to see the imprecision). In contrast, Java prints out 17 significant figures for doubles, where we expect 15–16 places of precision.

In the second part of the problem, Michele hits the golf ball backward (at $\theta = 150°$). To find a solution to this part of the problem, we will have to modify the program. We changed the line `theta = 30.0 * Math.PI / 180.0;` so that it now reads

```
theta = 150.0 * Math.PI / 180.0;
```

When we ran the modified program we obtained the output in Table 10.5. In these cases we are subtracting two numbers of nearly equal value and so should expect a significant loss of precision. If we look at a number such as u for the backward golf ball (which involves subtractions and is more sensitive), we see

```
u = 0.33333333333333326      u = 0.33333337
```

The above values are clearly the level of precision (size of error) we would expect for a single- and double-precision floating-point calculation: 1 unit in the 16th place for doubles, and 4 units in the 8th place for singles. Even though Maple could do this computation exactly and obtain $1/3$ as the answer, that is not possible with the approximate floating-point representation of numbers used in numeric computations.

When we solve the third part of the problem and look at the x component of velocity that Ben sees for the backward hit, we find that the double- and single-precision calculations give:

```
ux = -1.4802973661668753E-16      ux = 3.973643E-8
```

Within the precision of the calculation, the x velocity is zero. It is not exactly zero, because the numbers used in the calculation are stored with limited precision. We see that it is very hard for floating-point computations to compute exactly zero.

10.4.1 Assessment

One way of interpreting these numbers is to say that the double-precision computation has an error in the 16th decimal place, while the single-precision computation has an error in the 8th place. This is as expected. A more negative way of interpreting these same numbers is to say that the two computations cannot even agree on the sign of the velocity, or to say that the floating-point calculation is wrong by a factor of a million! We personally would say that since the velocity predicted by the program is much smaller than the velocities we used as input, we clearly should suspect the precision of the output. In the present case, we would say that both answers appear consistent with zero, yet we do not believe that we have even one significant figure in the answer.

10.5 YOUR PROBLEM: MODIFY GOLF.JAVA

1. Save and print out a copy of Golf.java from the CD or Web.
2. Draw a box around and label each of the five methods in the program.
3. Label where each method is called.
4. Copy Golf.java into a new file GolfFloat.java. Convert the copy into a single-precision program.
5. Compile and then execute both programs and compare the results for the output (the velocity seen by Ben). We do not expect a large difference for such a simple problem, yet it should be noticeable. The difference might get to be much larger if the calculation were repeated millions of times, as realistic calculations often are.

6. To keep track of your results, make a table of the form:

	U_x^M	U_y^M	U^M	θ^M	U_x^B	U_y^B	U^B	ϕ^B
float								
double								
⋮								

where the superscripts M and B are used for Michele and Ben.

7. Modify both programs so that $\theta = 150°$. This angle corresponds to Michele's ball hit to the left at an angle of $30°$ above the negative x' axis. Enter your results into your table.

8. Compile and execute both programs. Compute the relative error of the double-precision value for ux with respect to the float value for ux:

$$u^{rel} \stackrel{\text{def}}{=} \frac{u^D - u^F}{u^F}. \tag{10.11}$$

Also compute the relative error of the float value for ux with respect to the double value for ux. Compare the two relative errors. Is relative error a useful metric for comparing numbers like these?

9. Modify the double-precision program so that $\theta = 0°$.

10. Compile and execute the program. Record results in your table. According to Ben and equation (10.3), what is the x velocity of Michele's golf ball? What would the x velocity be if nonrelativisitc physics were used? (This corresponds to using these same equations with the speed of light $c = \infty$, so $\gamma = 1$.)

11. Modify the double-precision program so that $\theta = 180°$ and interpret the results.

12. Determine what Ben sees as the x velocity of the golf ball when the golf ball is hit $30°$ below the left horizon, that is, at $\theta = 210°$. Compare this to the result from classical physics.

10.6 COERCION AND OVERLOADING*

We have already told you (and you have probably forgotten) that when you call a method the actual *value* of the argument is *passed* to the methods from the calling program. Remember, main sends only a number to the method, not the name of the argument. On account of this it is quite acceptable to call a method with the variable x as the argument to the method, and then use a different variable like y as the argument within the actual method itself. As a general rule, *methods may change the value of their argument, but may not change the location in memory to which the argument refers.*

The program Change.java in Listing 10.5 is short but with surprising results:

Listing 10.5 Change.java

```
1  //                    Change.java: demo methods use local arguments
2  public class Change
3  {    public static void main(String[] argv)                    // main method
4  {    int x = 0, y = 2;
5       int z;
6       System.out.println("In main, x = "+x+", y = " + y);
7       z = f(x, y);
8       System.out.println("In main, f(x,y) = "  + z);
9       System.out.println("In main, x = "+x+", y = " + y);
10 }                                                    // End main method
11      public static int f(int x, int y)                        // method f
12      { x = y;
13        System.out.println("In f(x,y), x = "+x+", y = " + y);
14        return x*x + y*y; }
15 }                                                    // End class
```

1. Compile and run `Change.java`. You should get the results:

```
In main, x = 0, y = 2
In g(x, y), x = 2, y = 2
In main, f(x, y) = 8
In main, x = 0, y = 2
```

Look at the code and locate the four output statements. Compare them to the printed results. Survey how we start off with $x = 0$ and $y = 2$ in `main`. Then the method `f(x,y)` is called, sets $x = y$, prints out the values $x = 2$, $y = 2$, and returns a value of 8 for `g`. When we get back to `main`, we print out $g(x,y) = 8$, which is the appropriate value for $x = 2$ and $y = 2$, even though in `main`, $x = 0$ and $y = 2$.

What is happening here is simple. The variables in a method are *local* to that particular method and not "seen" by other parts of the program. So, even though they have the same names, the variables x and y in `main` are stored in different memory locations than the variables x and y in the method `f`. Therefore, changing the value of x within the `f(x,y)` method does not change its value in `main`. The changed values within `f(x,y)` do not get returned to `main`. Only the value of the function `f(x,y)` itself is the same in both the calling method and the method called.

In summary, only the single value of the method gets returned by a method, and not the values of the arguments. If multiple values need to be returned, then, as discussed in Chapter 17, an array argument must be used.

2. Copy `Change.java` to `Change2.java`. Modify the function declaration so that the arguments are reversed:

```
16. public static int f(int y, int x)                    // Reversed argument
```

Compile and execute `Change2.java`. This should show you that changing the names of the arguments has no effect as long as the arguments' types still match. This is why these are called "dummy" variables.

3. Notwithstanding the values for variables within a method being local to that particular method, the type of variable given as an argument in the calling program should match the type declared in the method. Exceptions to this rule, known as *method overloading* and *coercion of argument*, we will discuss shortly. So, for example, if a method is declared with the second argument as a `double`, then the call to that method must have the second argument as a `double`. To see what this means, replace the function declaration in line 11 with one that uses `doubles` in place of `ints`:

```
13 public static int g(double x, double y)
```

Recompile `Change.java` and see the results. You should get an error message with a reference to "incompatible types," or "need to cast," or possibly "lowering of precision." These are all signals of inconsistent data types. Some explanation here is worthwhile. Our error is in the assignment statement

```
7      z = f(x, y);
```

In spite of this assignment looking harmless, its offense is that in line 5 we declared the variable z to be an integer, while on line 11 we declared the method f to return a double. As this would lead to a loss of precision, something Java tries to avoid, the Java compiler flags this statement as an error.

Listing 10.6 Change3.java

```
1  //                    Change3.java: Two methods calling each other
2  public class Change3
3  {    public static void main(String[] argv)              //Main method
4  {    double x = Math.PI/4. , y = 2;
5       double z;
6       System.out.println("In main, x = "+x+", y = " + y);
7       z = f(x, y);
8       System.out.println("In main, f(x,y) = "  + z);
9       System.out.println("In main, x = "+x+", y = " + y);
10 }                                                      // End main method
11      public static double f(double x, double y)           //Method f
12        { double w;
13          w = g(x);
14          System.out.println("In f(x,y), x = "+x+", g(x)= " + w);
15          return w*w + y*y; }
16      public static double g(double y)                     //Method g(y)
17        { return Math.pow(Math.tan(y),3); }
18 }
```

4. The *cast* operator is used to tell Java that you really do want to convert data types. Take your latest version of Change.java (the one with the double-precision function), and replace line 7 with one that explicitly *casts* f(x, y) into an integer:

```
7    z = (int) g(x, y);                                    // Cast into integer
11 public static double g(int x, int y)                    // Same as before
```

Recasting the method's return variable explicitly tells the Java compiler that you know you are losing precision with the cast operation, but that it is okay.

5. Up until this point, we have used the main method to call other methods. Actually, there is no restriction that only main may call methods. Thus, in Listing 10.6 we have modified Change.java to Change3.java, which includes a method that calls another method, in this case, one from the Math class. Compile and run change3.java. Compare the output you obtain with the print lines in the code and make sure that you understand why the results are as they are. Check where we have switched to double-precision variables.

Listing 10.7 Overload.java

```
1  //                        Overload.java:     method overloading
2  public class Overload {
3      public static void main(String[] argv) {
4      double x = 2., y = 4., z;
5      int i=3, j=5, k;
6      //        Test choice by argument number
7      z = f(x);
8      z = f(x,y);
9      //        Test choice by argument type or number
10     k = f(i);
11     k = f(i,j);
12     z = f(i,x);
13     }
14     public static double f(double a) {
15     System.out.println("1 double arg, return double");
16         return a*a;   }
17     public static double f(double a, double b) {
18     System.out.println("2 double arg's, return double");
19         return a*a + b*b;  }
20     public static int f(int a) {
21     System.out.println("1 int arg, return int");
22         return a*a*a;  }
23     public static int f(int a, int b) {
24     System.out.println("2 int arg's, return int");
25         return a*b;   }
26     public static int f(int a, double b) {
27     System.out.println("1 int arg + 1 double arg, return int");
28         return (int) a;  }
29 }
```

6. **Method overloading:** Now that we have warned you about how important it is to have the data type of a method's argument be the same in the calling program as it is in the method declaration, we will show you a technique that gets around that restriction. In *method overloading* you define a number of methods all with the same name. For this to work, each method must have either a different selection of argument types or a different number of arguments. You then use the same method name for differing data types, and, incredibly enough, the compiler will choose the proper one based on the unique combination of arguments and return type.

7. Run `Overload.java` in Listing 10.7 to see method overloading in action. This program calls the method `f()` five times, each with a different set of arguments. Java should match the actual method called to the one with the appropriate argument set. Check that you get five lines of output and compare that output to the code to be sure that five different methods were called, all with the same name.

8. Extend `Overload.java` so that it also calls a method `f(double x, double y, double z)` and `f(int i, int j, int k)`.

9. Try to modify and execute `Overload.java` so that there are two versions of `f(double x, int i)`, one that returns a `double`, the other that returns an `int`.

10. **Argument coercion:** Good programming practice dictates that you match argument type in the calling program and the method. Be that as it may, Java may do some automatic conversion for you—as long as it does not lead to a decrease in precision. If you call a method with an argument that does not match the data type declared in the method's definition, Java will convert ("coerce") that argument to match the type in the method's definition. This automatic conversion is called *argument coercion*. Argument coercion is another case in which seeing is believing, and so in Listing 10.8 we present you with our program `Coercion.java`. Compile and execute `Coercion.java`. Check which lines of the code generate the two lines of output and that this truly is an example of argument coercion.

Listing 10.8 Coercion.java

```
1  //                    Coercion.java: Test argument coercion
2  public class Coercion
3  {   public static void main(String[] argv)
4    { int i = 60;                              // Declare instant of int
5      double x = 50.;                          // Declare instant of double
6      //                    Right argument type
7      System.out.println("square of double 50. = "+ square(x));
8      //        Wrong argument type gets coerced
9      System.out.println("square of int 60 = "+ square(i));
10   }                                          // End main
11     public static double square(double x)
12       { return x*x; }
13 }                                            // End class
```

11. Modify `Coercion.java` so that the method uses an integer argument. See now if argument coercion works when a *decrease* in precision would occur.

12. Modify `Coercion.java` so that you test if argument coercion also works with several arguments of the wrong type.

10.7 KEY WORDS

[ ]	array	binary numbers	bits
bytes	class	class variables	argument coercion
local variables	machine precision	memory words	method overload
modular programs	naming convention	overflow	primitive data type
significant figures	double precision	underflow	variable casting
word length			

10.8 SUPPLEMENTARY EXERCISES

1. Explain in just a few words what is meant by:
   a. an integer;
   b. a floating-point number;
   c. a float not being the same as a double;
   d. truncation error;
   e. round-off error;
   f. a string;
   g. machine precision and underflow;
   h. number of significant figures and overflow.
2. Approximately what are the overflow and underflow limits for double-precision computations in Java?
3. Approximately what are the number of significant figures in floats and doubles in Java?
4. **Overloading:** Take all the methods from `Golf` and `GolfFloat` and combine them into one class `GolfBoth`. Copying all the methods means that there will be two versions of each method in this class and that the methods differ only in whether their arguments are floats or doubles. Modify the main program such that all the methods are called with both floats and doubles as arguments. Verify that the appropriate method is being called.
5. Imagine that you have just landed that dream job of yours in the local hamburger joint. Your first assignment is to write a program that figures out what change to make if a person buys one item that costs less than a dollar and pays for it with a dollar bill or coin.
   a. Compute what change in quarters, dimes, and pennies you would give, using the minimum number of coins. *Hint:* Work entirely in integer arithmetic and define the integers: `price`, `change`, `quarters`, `dimes`, and `pennies`. To name an instance, 27 cents would be represented by the

integer 27, and change = 100 - price, quarters = change/25, etc.

    b. Modify the program so that it uses floating-point variables and comment on the different results.

6. Write the following numbers in scientific notation so that they reflect the given number of significant digits:

    a. 25.3 to four significant figures.;

    b. 0.00005 to two significant figures;

    c. 1.351 to two significant figures;

    d. 84000 to three significant figures.

7. Suppose that the floating-point number system on your computer has two-digit mantissas and exponents ranging from -2 to 1. Indicate whether the following expressions each would result in overflow, underflow, round-off error, or an exact answer.

    a. 20. + 20.;

    b. 50. * 50.;

    c. 20. + 0.01;

    d. 20. * 0.01;

    e. 0.01 + 0.01;

    f. 0.01 * 0.01.

8. You have encountered a number of examples in which a program was constructed to contain several methods or functions rather than do all of the computations within the main method. In reflecting on these examples, does dividing a program into methods or functions make it

    a. longer or shorter?

    b. harder or easier to understand?

    c. more or less difficult to debug?

    d. more or less likely to reuse components?

9. Consider a Java program in which the main method uses a method int f(double x, int y) that is defined just once. Indicate whether each of the following is true or false:

    a. the main method must call f with variables having the names of x and y;

    b. the method f may change the values of x and y;

    c. the method f may change the value of $f(x, y)$;

    d. if the main method calls f with two int arguments, f will convert the first one to a double;

    e. the method f returns a double;

    f. the variable type returned by f depends upon the arguments given to it.

10. Indicate the values that Java would produce for the following expressions

    a. 4/2 =

    b. 4/3 =

    c. 3/4 =

    d. 3./4 =

    e. 4/3. =

11. Explain what the values of a and b are at the end of the following bit of code:

```
int i = 3, j = 2;
double a, b, c = 3;
a = 1 + i/j + j/i; b = 1 + c/j + j/c;
```

12. What output is produced by this fragment of code?

```
for (int i = 4; i >= 0; i = i-1) System.out.println("i equals " + i);
```

13. A class consists of a main method with the statement `y = f(x,n)`. The method `f` is defined just once, beginning with the line `double f(double x, int y)`. Indicate whether each of the following is true or false:
   a. the main method must call f with variables named x and y;
   b. the method f may change and return new values for x and n;
   c. the method f returns a value for $f(y, n)$;
   d. the method f returns an int;
   e. the method `f` should have only one argument.

Chapter Eleven

Visualization with Java, Classes, Packages

We have already seen in Maple how helpful visualizations are in understanding results and debugging the computation, and in adding some fun to your work. Fortunately, there is an excellent Java plotting package called *PtPlot* that is both free and easy to use, and in §11.1 we will show you how to use it.[1] In order to use PtPlot, you will need to import a package and work with multiple classes. This is no worse than what we did in Maple. Not only will this use of PtPlot give you some beautiful graphs, it will also give you some experience with objects.

Truly understanding Java's packages, classes, and naming conventions is rather advanced for beginners, and so we will first just give you a sample program to modify, and then tell you about packages and such. We recommend that all users read §11.1, but maybe scan the other sections and treat them as reference materials for the present. In particular, §11.4 on gnuplot will be needed to create 3-D surfaces from data.

11.1 2-D GRAPHS WITHIN JAVA: PTPLOT

One of the exceptional things about Java is that it contains commands that permit you to draw graphs on your computer screen—regardless of your operating system. Yet these commands are rather low level, as we shall see in Chapter 21, and you must attend to a number of details if you want to use them. To avoid all that fuss, we recommend the use of PtPlot [PtPlot] as a basic plotting package for 2-D graphs.[2] PtPlot is free, supported by the University of California, written in Java (and thus runs under Unix, Linux, Mac OS, and MS Windows), is easy to use for 2-D data plotting, and produces attractive graphs.[3] It may be incorporated right into your programs or applets (applets are discussed in Chapter 21), or used as a stand-alone application or applet. We include on the disk the PtPlot Java library; alternatively, you may download the most recent version over the Web.

---

[1] PtPlot is actually part of Ptolemy, an entire computing environment that is powerful, free, and Java-based.
[2] Parts of this chapter were prepared with the help of Connelly Barnes.
[3] For our research publications we use AceGr/Xmgr for 2-D plotting and gnuplot for 3-D surfaces.

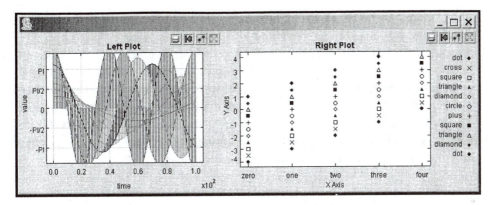

Figure 11.1 Sample output from advanced use of PtPlot in which two plots are placed side by side (see TwoPlotExample.java).

11.1.1 EasyPtPlot.java

Listing 11.1 EasyPtPlot.java

```java
1  //                      EasyPtPlot.java:   simple f(x) plot
2  import ptolemy.plot.*;                      // Plotting package
3  public class EasyPtPlot
4  { public static final double Xmin = -5., Xmax = 5.;   //y automatic
5    public static final int Npoint = 500;
6    public static void main(String[] args)
7    { Plot plotObj = new Plot();             // Create ptPlot object
8      plotObj.setTitle("f(x) vs x");
9      plotObj.setXLabel("x");
10     plotObj.setYLabel("f(x)");
11 //Use: addPoint(int dataSet, double x, double y, boolean connect)
12     double xStep = (Xmax - Xmin) / Npoint;
13     for (double x = Xmin; x <= Xmax; x += xStep)
14     { double y = Math.cos(x);
15       plotObj.addPoint(0, x, y, true); }    //Add point
16     PlotApplication app = new PlotApplication(plotObj);   //Display
17 }}
```

Figure 11.2 is an example of an advanced PtPlot graph. Listing 11.1, containing the program EasyPtPlot.java, is an example of a how to construct a simple graph of $\cos(x)$ *versus* x with PtPlot. Before you try running this program, you need to have PtPlot installed on your computer (see your system administrator or §11.1 to do it yourself). Though we encourage you to use this program as a template, there are several parts of it you will need to understand.

On line 2 we see the statement import ptolemy.plot.*;. This statement copies in or includes the plotting package programs (class files) with your program.[4] In a general sense, PtPlot deals with an *object* that represents your plot.[5] We call this object `myPlot` and create it on line 7. There it is created as a variable type that PtPlot has defined as `Plot`. Here we get some practical experience with them, which will help when we need to understand them. We then add various features, step by step, to `myPlot` to make it just the plot we want. On line 8 we give it a title, and on lines 9 and 10 we label the x and y axes. As is standard with objects in Java, we first give the name of the object and then modify it with "dot modifiers." (These modifiers are like the arguments to Maple's `plot` command, only here the arguments get attached to the objects.)

At this point we could also tell PtPlot what range of x and y values are to be plotted, but we do not! Instead we let PtPlot set the x and y ranges based on the extents of the data it is given. Line 13 begins a `for` loop that repeats itself for a number of increasing x values. (`for` loops are discussed in Chapter 12, "Flow Control via Logic; Projectiles.") During each repetition, line 14 calculates a new value of $y = \cos(x)$ and then line 15 adds a point (x, y) to your plot object. By having `true` as the fourth argument in `myPlot.addPoint(0, x, y, true)`, we are telling PtPlot to connect the previous point to the new one.

You will need to place your own function, or data to be plotted, on line 14 where we call $\cos(x)$. If you have written a method or function whose output you wish to plot, it may be called on line 14. So far, your plot object `myPlot` exists only in the computer's memory. For you to have that plot appear on the computer screen in front of you, you need line 16 to create a `PlotApplication` with your plot as its input.

11.1.2 Running the Sample Program

We have tried to make `EasyPtPlot.java` simple. However, we encourage you to make it fancier by including more options as commands, or by using the pull-down menus in the PtPlot window in which your plot is displayed. We discuss the options below, but before that, we recommend that you run the sample program and see what we are talking about:

1. Compile and execute `EasyPtPlot.java` in the usual way:
   ```
   > javac EasyPtPlot.java                          // Compile EasyPtplot.java
   > java EasyPtPlot                                // Run EasyPtplot.class
   ```

2. You should get a pretty window on your screen just like Figure 11.1. You may move it anywhere on your screen by grabbing the bar on top, and resize it by grabbing a corner and pulling. Try that!

---

[4]More specifically, you are copying a subdirectory `ptolemy`, which, in turn, contains the subdirectory `plot`. The * is a wild-card character, and its use here means to copy all the files (class files) in that subdirectory.
[5]Objects are discussed in Chapters 16 and 18.

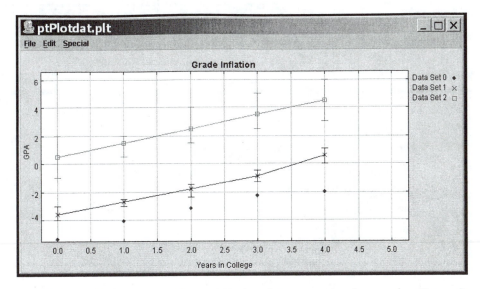

Figure 11.2 Sample output from PtPlot in which three data sets are placed on one plot. Observe the error bars on two sets.

3. By grabbing a corner and pulling, make the window fill about one quarter of your screen.

4. Examine the Edit pull-down menu. Select Edit and pull it down. (Alternatively, the E indicates that this is possible with keystrokes alone. In this case, Alt + E also pulls down the menu.)

5. From the Edit pull-down menu select Format. You should get a window like that in Figure 11.3 that lets you control most of the options in your graph.

6. Experiment with the Format menu. In particular, change the graph so that only points are plotted, with the points being pixels and black, and so that your name is in the title.

7. Select a central portion of your plot and **zoom in** on it by drawing a box (with mouse button depressed) starting from the upper left corner and then moving down before you release the mouse button. You **zoom out** by drawing a box from the lower right corner and moving up. You may also resize your graph by selecting Special/Reset Axes or by resetting the x and y ranges. And of course, you always have the option of starting over by closing the Java window and running the java command again.

8. Scrutinize how you are able to print your graphs under the File menu, as well as write them to file in postscript (.ps format). You may also export plots in various formats.

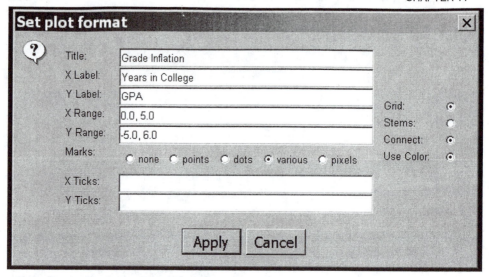

Figure 11.3 The Format submenu located under the Edit menu in a PtPlot application. This submenu
            controls the plot's basic features.

11.1.3 PtPlot Options

Calling PtPlot from Your Program

Plot myPlot = new Plot();	Name and create plot object myPlot
PlotApplication app = new PlotApplication(myPlot);	Display
myPlot.setTitle("f(x) vs x");	Add title to plot
myPlot.setXLabel("x");	Label x axis
myPlot.setYLabel("f(x)");	Label y axis
myPlot.addPoint(0, x, y, true);	Add (x, y) to set 0, connect points
myPlot.addPoint(1, *x*, *y*, false);	Add (x, y) to set 1, no connect points
myPlot.addLegend(0, "Set 0");	Label data set 0 in legend
myPlot.addPointWithErrorBars(0, x, y, yLo, yHi, true);	
	Plot, (x, y - YLo), (x, y + yHi) + error bars
myPlot.clear(0);	Remove all points from data set 0
myPlot.clear(false);	Remove data from all sets
myPlot.clear(true);	Remove all points, default options
myPlot.setSize(500, 400);	Set plot size in pixels (optional)
myPlot.setXRange(-10., 10.);	Set an x range (default fit to data)
myPlot.setYRange(-8., 8.);	Set a y range (default fit to data)
myPlot.setXLog(true);	Use log scale for x axis
myPlot.setYLog(true);	Use log scale for y axis
myPlot.setGrid(false);	Turn off the grid
myPlot.setColor(false);	Color in black and white
myPlot.setButtons(true);	Display zoom-to-fit button on plot
myPlot.fillPlot();	Adjust x, y ranges to fit data
myPlot.setImpulses(true, 0);	Lines from points to x axis, set 0
myPlot.setMarksStyle("none," 0);	Draw none, points, dots, various, pixels
myPlot.setBars(true);	Display data as bar charts
String s = myPlot.getTitle();	Extract title (or other properties)

The program `TwoPlotExample.java` and its data file `data.plt`, taken from the PtPlot Web site, shows how to place two plots side by side, and how to read in a data file containing error bars and various symbols for the points. Here we list some of the options available. More are to be found in the description of the commands (methods) on the PtPlot Web site [PtPlot].

At various times you may have your data in a file, possibly because it came from another application or because you wanted to get it all computed or measured before you started looking at it. If you write your data in a format that PtPlot recognizes, then you will be able to plot it and replot at your pleasure. This may sound like a lot of work, yet most reasonable formats will work. However, you have the option of including some PtPlot formatting commands in the data file.

In the simplest form, a *PtPlot Data Format* is just a text file with a single x, y point per line. For example, Figure 11.2 was produced from a data file with the x and y values separated by spaces, tabs, or commas:

Sample PtPlot Data file `PtPlotdat.plt`

```
1 # This is a comment: Sample data for PtPlot
2 TitleText: Grade Inflation XRange: 0,5 YRange: −5, 6 Grid: on
3 XLabel: Years in College YLabel: GPA Marks: various NumSets:3
4 Color: on
5 DataSet: Data Set 0 Lines:off 0,−5.4 1,−4.1 2,−3.2 3,−2.3 4, −2
6 DataSet: Data Set 1 Lines:on 0,−3.6, −4,−3 1,−2.7, −3, −2.5
7 2,−1.8, −2.4,−1.5 3,−0.9, −1.3, −0.5 4, 0.6, 0,1.1
8 DataSet: Data Set 2 0,0.5, −1,2 1, 1.5, 0.5, 2 2, 2.5, 1.5, 4 3,
9 3.5, 2.5, 5 4, 4.5, 3, 6
```

To plot up your data files, enter

> `java ptolemy.plot.PlotApplication dataFile`   // Plot data in file `dataFile`

This causes the standard PtPlot window to open and display your data. If this does not work, then your CLASSPATH variable may not be defined properly, or PtPlot may not be installed. See "Installing PtPlot" in §C.5.

Reading in your data from the PtPlot window is an alternative. Either use a window that is already open, or issue Java's run command without a file name:

> `java ptolemy.plot.PlotApplication`   // Open PtPlot window

To look at your data from the PtPlot window, choose File → Open → `YourDataFile`. By default, PtPlot will look for files with `.plt` or `.xml` suffixes. However, you may enter any name you want, or pull down the Filter menu and select * to see all of your files. The same holds for the File → SaveAs option. In addition, you may Export your plot as an Encapsulated PostScript (`.eps`) file, a format useful for inserting in documents.

As with any good plot, you should label your axes, add a title, and customize other parts of your plots to make them informative and clear. To do these things, include PtPlot commands with your data, or work with the pull-down menus under Edit and Special in the PtPlot window. The options are essentially the same as ones you would call from your program. Here is a useful list:

TitleText: f(x) vs. x	Add title to plot
XLabel: x	Label x axis
YLabel: y	Label y axis
XRange: 0, 12	Set x range (default: fit to data)
YRange: -3, 62	Set y range (default: fit to data)
Marks: none	(Default) No marks at points, lines connects points
Marks: points	or: dots, various, pixels
Lines: on/off	Do not connect points with lines; default: on
Impulses: on/off	Lines down from points to x axis; default: off
Bars: on/off	Bar graph (turn off lines) default: off
Bars: width (, offset)	Bar graph; bars of width and (optional) offset
DataSet: *string*	Specify data set to plot; *string* appears in legend
x, y	Specify a data point; comma, space, tab separators
move: x, y	Do not connect this point to previous
x, y, yLo, yHi	Plot (x, y - yLo), (x, y + yHi) with error bars

If commands appear before DataSet directives, then the command will apply to all data sets. If commands appear after DataSet directives, then it will apply to that data set only.

11.2 INSTALLING PTPLOT: SEE APPENDIX C*

11.3 CLASSES AND PACKAGES*

Up until this point your programs have contained a single class contained in a file with a .java or .class extension. That class contained a main method and possibly some other methods as well. Just as we encourage you to modify old programs rather than writing all programs from scratch, so we encourage you to include methods you and others have already written and debugged into your new programs. Java contains a large number of *libraries* consisting of collections of methods for various purposes, and you should think of these libraries as *toolboxes* from which you extract individual tools needed for your programs. In fact, the *object-oriented* approach of Java is specifically designed to make reuse of components easier and safer.

Table 11.1 Some of Java's packages and the classes they contain.

Java Package	Classes for
java.lang	Basic elements of Java language
java.util	Utilities; random-number generators, date, time, etc.
java.awt	Abstract Windowing Toolkit; creates graphical interfaces
java.applet	Creates applets and interacts with browsers
java.beans	Creates reusable software components
java.io	Data input and output

11.3.1 Including Packages*

We have already referred to a collection of related methods as a class and, for a broader collection, as a library (like the Math library). In strict Java naming convention, each method would be in a class file, and the libraries would be called *packages*. In general, there are two types of packages: the standard Java packages that constitute the Java language, and user-defined packages that extend standard Java. The PtPlot package is an example of a user-defined package. Some of the standard Java packages are given in Table 11.1.

Because these Java packages contain hundreds or thousands of classes, some organization is necessary to keep track of what each method does. Java does this with a hierarchical directory structure in which there are parent packages containing subpackages, with the subpackages containing more subpackages or various classes. To make the name of each class unique, one precedes it with the names of the package and subpackages that contain this class. As an example, consider the command

```
System.out.println
```

that we have been using to print a line of output on the screen. Here System is the name of the class (classes begin with capital letters) containing many of Java's methods. When we give the combination System.out, we are referring to an object representing the standard *out*put stream. The final println that gets affixed to System.out is the name of the method that prints lines.

To summarize, by convention, the names of classes are capitalized, while the names of packages and methods are lowercase. This is relevant here because the System.out.println command is in the java.lang package, and so the proper full name of the command is actually

```
java.lang.System.out.println
```

which contains the package name as well. Because java.lang is the most basic package, the java compiler automatically looks there to find the methods we invoke. This means we can, fortunately, leave off the `java.lang` prefix. Technically, `java` is the main package and `lang` is a subpackage, but it is easier to just say `java.lang` is the package. We must admit that we sometimes find Java's naming conventions overwhelming. Nevertheless, we will use them when importing packages and in using methods from other classes, so some familiarity is helpful.

You include the classes from a package with the `Import` command. It may be given in one of two forms:

```
import <packageName>.<specific classes>    // Import specific classes from packageName
import <packageName>.*                     // Import all classes from packageName
```

The `import` command tells the Java compiler to look in the package `packageName` for methods that it might not find otherwise. However, for the importation to work the compiler must know *where* the package of classes and their methods are stored on your particular computer. In other words, the compiler needs to know the path to follow through the local disk memory to get to the directory or folder where the classes are stored. For this purpose each computer system, be it Windows, Unix, or Mac OS, has an environmental variable named `CLASSPATH` that contains the explicit path to where the classes are stored on that particular computer. As we show in §C.5 on installing PtPlot, you will need to modify this variable before a package is imported.

Even though what follows is more advanced programming than we do in this book, for completeness we indicate how you could create your own packages. This is done by placing several classes in the same `.java` file and then including a `package` command at the beginning of the file:

```
1   package < mypackage_name >;
2   public class < myclass1_name >
3       {     < normal class structure , multiple methods OK > }
4       public class <myclass2_name>
5       {   < normal class structure , multiple methods OK > }
```

Your package may be a collection of methods *without* any main method, for example, mathematical subroutines that are called from all the programs you write. However, there must be one main method someplace if the program is to run, since execution always begins in a main method. Likewise, the main method must be a public class (other classes are read only the public classes).

11.4 GNUPLOT BASICS

Gnuplot is a versatile 2-D and 3-D graphing package that makes Cartesian, polar, surface, and contour plots. In spite of PtPlot being fine for 2-D plotting with Java,

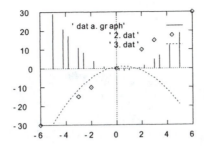

Figure 11.4 A gnuplot graph for three data sets with impulses and lines.

we still have a need for gnuplot's surface plots of numerical data. Gnuplot is open software, available for free on the Web, and produces many output formats.

You begin gnuplot with a file of $(x\ y)$ data points, say, graph.dat. You then issue the **gnuplot** command from a shell or from the Start menu. You then get a new window with the gnuplot prompt gnuplot>.You construct your graph by entering gnuplot commands at the gnuplot prompt or by using the pull-down menus in the gnuplot window:

```
> gnuplot                                          // Start gnuplot program
Terminal type set to 'x11'                         Type of terminal for Unix
gnuplot>                                            The gnuplot prompt
gnuplot>  plot "graph.dat"                          Plot data file graph.dat
```

In Figure 11.4 we plot a number of graphs on the same plot using several data files and the command:

```
gnuplot>  plot 'graph.dat' with impulses, '2.dat', '3.dat' with lines
```

The general form of the 2-D plotting command is:

```
plot {ranges} function {title} {style} {, function ...}
```

with points	Default. Plot symbol at each point
with lines	Plot lines connecting the points
with linespoint	Plot lines and symbols
with impulses	Plot vertical lines from x axis to points
with dots	Plot small dot at each point (scatter plots)

It is necessary to place all file or directory names in single or double quotes and to separate file names with a comma. Explicit values for the x and y ranges are set with the plot options:

```
gnuplot> plot [xmin:xmax] [ymin:ymax] "file"                    Generic
```

Im T(E)

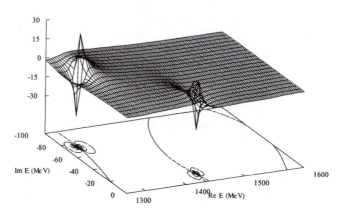

Figure 11.5 Gnuplot's surface plot of a scattering amplitude ImT as a function of complex energy E.

```
gnuplot> plot [-10:10] [-5:30] "graph.dat"                          Explicit
```

11.4.1 Printing Plots

Gnuplot supports a number of printers including PostScript ones. The basic method of printing plots is:

1. Set "terminal type" for your printer.
2. Send the plot output to a file.
3. Replot figure for new output device.
4. Quit gnuplot (or get out of gnuplot window).
5. Print file.

You could also import the file into a word processor to have it appear in a document or into a drawing program to fix it up just right. To see what type of printers and other output devices are supported by gnuplot, enter the set terminal command without any options into a gnu window for a listing of available terminal types. Here is an example of creating a PostScript figure and printing it:

```
gnuplot> set terminal postscript          Choose local printer type
Terminal type set to 'postscript'                 Gnuplot response
gnuplot> set term postscript eps                    Another option
gnuplot> set output "plt.ps"                      Send figure to file
gnuplot> replot                            Plot again so file is sent
gnuplot> quit                               Or get out of gnu window
% lp plt.ps                                     Unix print command
```

11.4.2 Gnuplot Surface (3-D) Plots

The surface (3-D) plot command is `splot`, and it is used in the same manner as `plot`—with the obvious extension from (x, y) to (x, y, z). As discussed in Chapter 4, a surface, such as that in Figure 11.5, is specified by giving just the z values for successive rows, with different rows separated by blank lines:

```
-4.043764                                              Data for 3-D plot
...
-11.000000
```

Because there are no explicit x and y values given, gnuplot labels the x and y axes with the row and column number. At present gnuplot does not have the capability to rotate 3-D plots interactively. Instead, you adjust your plot with the command:

```
gnuplot>  set view rotx, rotz, scale, scalez
```

where $0 \le \texttt{rotx} \le 180°$ and $0 \le \texttt{rotz} \le 360°$ are angles in degrees, and the scale factors control the size. Any changes made to a plot are made when you redraw the plot using the `replot` command.

To see how this all works, here we give a sample gnuplot session that we will use in Chapter 20 to plot a 3-D surface from numerical data. Listing 20.1 contains the actual code used to output data in the form for a gnuplot surface plot.

```
> gnuplot                                       Start gnuplot system from a shell
```

Then, a special gnuplot shell starts up with the prompt `gnuplot>`, and you are ready to give *gnuplot* your subcommands.[6]

```
gnuplot>  set hidden3d                          Hide surface whose view is blocked
gnuplot>  set nohidden3d                        Show surface though hidden from view
gnuplot>  splot 'Laplace.dat' with lines        Surface plot of Laplace.dat with lines
gnuplot>  set view 65,45                         Set x and y rotation viewing angles
gnuplot>  replot                                 See effect of your change
gnuplot>  set contour                            Project contours onto x-y plane
gnuplot>  set cntrparam levels 10                10 contour levels
gnuplot>  set terminal PostScript                Output in PostScript format for printing
gnuplot>  set output "Laplace.ps"                Plot output to be sent to file Laplace.ps
gnuplot>  splot 'Laplace.dat' w l                Plot again, output to file
gnuplot>  set terminal x11                       To see output on screen again
gnuplot>  set title 'Potential V(x,y) vs x,y'   Title graph
gnuplot>  set xlabel 'x Position'                Label x axis
gnuplot>  set ylabel 'y Position'                Label y axis
gnuplot>  set zlabel 'V(x,y)'; replot            Label z axis and replot
```

---

[6]Under Windows, there is a graphical interface that is friendlier than the gnuplot subcommands. The subcommand approach we indicate here is reliable and universal.

gnuplot> `help`	Tell me more
gnuplot> `set nosurface`	Do not draw surface, leave contours
gnuplot> `set view 0, 0, 1`	Look down directly onto base
gnuplot> `replot`	Draw plot again; may want to write to file
gnuplot> `quit`	Get out of gnuplot

For this sample session, the default output for your graph is your terminal screen. To print a paper copy of your graph, we recommend first saving it to a file as a *PostScript* document (suffix `.ps`), and then printing out that file to a PostScript printer. You create the PostScript file by changing the terminal type to `Postscript`, setting the name of the file, and then issuing the subcommand `splot` again. This plots the result out to a file. If you want to see plots on your screen again, you need to set the terminal type to `x11` again (for Unix's *X Windows System*), and then plot it again.

11.5 JAVA ARCHIVES: JAR*

The standard Java Development Kit provides an archive tool `jar` that permits you to compress and decompress files using the *zip* file format. Even if you do not feel the urge at this moment to save disk space by using it, `jar` also lets you create an archive of all your work saved in the directory structure you have already created, and then unpack the archive into a directory with the same structure. This permits you to efficiently and safely save and transfer entire directory structures from one place on the computer to another, or from one computer to another, without worrying about leaving out some important files. What is more, since it is Java, it will work on all computers.

The basics operations with `jar`, made from the command line, are [SunJ]:

> `jar cf archive file1 file2 ...`	Create archive `Archive.jar`
> `jar cvf archive file1 file2 ...`	A verbose creation
> `jar cf archive *`	Archive everything into `Archive.jar`
> `jar tf archive.jar`	View table contents of file `Archive.jar`
> `jar xf archive.jar`	Extract contents of a file `Archive.jar`
> `jar xf archive.jar file1 file2`	Extract `file1, file2`
> `java -jar archive.jar`	Run application in `Archive.jar`
`<applet code = Applet.class archive = "Archive.jar"`	
`width = 350 height = 250> </applet>`	Run applet in `Archive.jar`

Here the options to the `jar` command follow it directly, with several options concatenated (placed end to end). The `c` option indicates that you want to create a `jar` file. The `f` option indicates that you want to use the file that follows the `f` (rather than the standard input or output). The `t` option indicates that you want a table of contents. The `x` option indicates that you want to extract some files. The `v` option may also be included with any of these commands to obtain a verbose version of the action in which `jar` tells you what it is doing as it does it (we recommend that). Check too that we have followed the convention of using a `.jar` extender to `jar` file names, though this is not required.

We have indicated the input files (those to be archived) explicitly as `file1` and `file2`. You are also permitted to use the wild-card symbol `*` to archive *all* the files and subdirectories in the current directory. A particularly valuable feature of `jar` is that if any of the indicated files are directories, then the entire contents of those directories are added to the archive recursively. In turn, when archived directories are extracted, the entire directory and subdirectory structures are extracted.

Here we give an example in which we issue the `jar` command from a directory containing the files `EasyPtPlot.class` and `OOPlanet.java`, and the directory `Plot`, that itself contains a whole bunch of files. We create the archive `All.jar`:

```
> jar cf All.jar *                          Create archive All.jar with everything
```

Whereas there is no indication that this was successful, we check what is in `All.jar` by looking at its table of contents:

```
> jar tf All.jar                            Produce table of contents
EasyPtPlot.class                                         Class file
OOPlanet.java                                           Source File
plot/                                                     Directory
plot/Plot1.class                            File in working directory
plot/Plot2.class
```

If we ask for a verbose form of creation, we would see a list of the file names as they are added to the archive:

```
> jar cvf All.jar                           Verbose archive creation
* added manifest
  adding:  EasyPtPlot.class(in = 807)  (out = 563)(deflated 30%)
  adding:  OOPlanet.java(in = 3141)  (out = 1008)(deflated 67%)
  adding:  plot/(in = 0)  (out= 0)(stored 0%)
  adding:  plot/Plot1.class(in = 687)  (out = 436)(deflated 36%)
  adding:  plot/Plot2.class(in = 782)  (out = 474)(deflated 39%)
```

We see that we also get an indication of how much compression is made for the archived files. The source code is deflated by roughly 2/3, the compiled code by roughly 1/3. Extraction of a single file or of the entire archive is simple:

```
> jar xvf All.jar OOPlanet.java             Extract OOPlanet.java
    extracted:  OOPlanet.java                       jar's response
> jar xvf All.jar *                         Extract everything in All.jar
  extracted:  EasyPtPlot.class
  extracted:  OOPlanet.java
```

```
   created:  plot/                                       Creates directory to place files
 extracted:  plot/Plot1.class
 extracted:  plot/Plot2.class
```

Chapter Twelve

Flow Control via Logic; Projectiles

In this chapter we begin using some of the control structures that make programming so interesting and that make your programs so intelligent. We will have you write your own program to simulate projectile motion, a standard problem of elementary physics. In Chapter 15, "Differential Equations with Java and Maple" we solve this same problem including air resistance. We start with a review of the kinematic equations, which may be scanned by those familiar with it, and then go to describe program design and control structures.

12.1 PROBLEM: FRICTIONLESS PROJECTILE MOTION

Figure 12.1 is the result of a computer simulations showing the trajectory of a projectile fired from a cannon at time $t = 0$, with initial velocity V_0, at an angle θ relative to the horizon. The projectile remains in the air for a total hang time of T and hits the ground a horizontal distance or range $x = R$ away from the origin.

Problem: write a program to simulate the motion of this projectile. Have it:

1. store the initial values V_0, g, and θ as constants;
2. compute the "hang time" T from the equations of kinematics;
3. compute the range R and height H from the equations of kinematics;

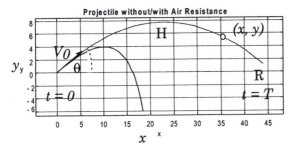
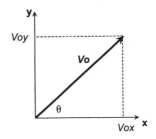

Figure 12.1 *Left:* The trajectory of a projectile fired with initial velocity V_0 in the θ direction. The nonparabolic curve includes air resistance. *Right:* The x and y components of V_0.

4. compute the position (x, y) of the projectile for 100 times starting at $-T/2$ and running in uniform steps to $3T/2$.

12.2 THEORY: KINEMATICS

If we ignore air resistance, a projectile has only the force of gravity acting on it. This force causes the projectile to fall towards the center of the earth with a constant acceleration $g = 9.8m/s^2$. The resulting solutions to the equations of motion are

$$x(t) = V_{0x}t, \quad y(t) = V_{0y}t - \tfrac{1}{2}gt^2. \tag{12.1}$$

Here V_{0x} and V_{0y} are the horizontal and vertical components of the initial velocity, and, as we see from Figure 12.1,

$$V_{0x} = V_0 \cos\theta, \quad V_{0y} = V_0 \sin\theta. \tag{12.2}$$

Likewise, the x and y components of the velocity as functions of time are:

$$v_x(t) = V_{0x}, \quad v_y(t) = V_{0y} - gt \tag{12.3}$$

Although the equations of motion yield x and y as functions of time, they do not tell us the shape of the trajectory. For these simple equations it is easy to derive that the shape is a parabola. We will, instead, determine the shape by plotting up the solution, a simpler approach as the equations become more realistic.

We determine the hang time T by observing that at the time of firing $t = 0$, and landing $t = T$, the projectile has a height $y = 0$. If we set $y = 0$ in (12.1), we obtain an equation for the time at which the height is zero:

$$y(t) = V_{0y}t - \tfrac{1}{2}gt^2 = 0, \quad \Rightarrow \quad V_{0y}t = \tfrac{1}{2}gt^2 \tag{12.4}$$

$$\Rightarrow \quad T = t = \frac{2V_{0y}}{g}, \tag{12.5}$$

where we ignore the $t = 0$ solution. Once we know T we find the range R as the horizontal distance $x(T)$:

$$R = x(T) = V_{0x}\frac{2V_{0y}}{g} = \frac{2V_0^2 \sin\theta \cos\theta}{g}. \tag{12.6}$$

The projectile reaches its maximum height H at the midpoint of the trajectory at time $t = T/2 = V_{0y}/g$:

$$H = y(\frac{T}{2}) = V_{0y}\frac{V_{0y}}{g} - \tfrac{1}{2}g\left(\frac{V_{0y}}{g}\right)^2 \tag{12.7}$$

$$\Rightarrow \quad H = \frac{V_0^2 \sin^2\theta}{2g}. \tag{12.8}$$

12.3 COMPUTER SCIENCE: DESIGNING STRUCTURED PROGRAMS

Now that you are into the program construction business, it is a good idea to understand not only the grammar of the language you are writing in, but also the general
structure that you should be building into your programs. Books have been written
on program design, but then again, it is a good idea not to believe everything you
read! Yet, as seems to be true in much of life, it is helpful to follow the rules until
you know better. Those who have truly mastered a subject may go on and make
new rules. We view programming as a written art that blends elements of science,
mathematics, and computer science into a set of instructions to permit a computer
to accomplish a scientific goal. Good programs should:

- give the correct answers;
- be clear and easy to read, with the action of each part easy to analyze;
- document themselves for the sake of readers and the programmer;
- be easy to use;
- be easy to modify and robust enough to keep giving the right answers;
- be passed on to others to use and develop further.

One way to make your programs clearer is to *structure* them. You may
have already noticed that sometimes we show our coding examples with indentation, skipped lines, and braces placed strategically. This is done to provide visual
clues as to the function of the different program parts (the "structures" in structured programming). In spite of the Java compiler ignoring these visual clues,
human readers are aided in understanding and modifying the program by having it
arranged in a manner that not only looks good, but also makes the different parts
of the program manifest to the eye.

The placement of text on the lines and the skipping of lines to make the
purpose of the programming clearer is known as *structured programming*. We recommend it highly. It is a valuable approach when dealing with control structures,
and particularly so when dealing with one control structure nested within another.
The basic idea is simple: blocks of code performing specified tasks should be indented and physically isolated to set them apart. Even though, in order to conserve
printed space, we do not skip as many lines as we would like to, we recommend
that you do!

12.3.1 Flowcharts and Pseudocode

In Figure 12.2 we present a *flowchart* that illustrates a possible program to compute projectile motion. A flowchart is not meant to be a detailed description of a
program, but rather a graphical aide to help visualize its logical flow. As such, it
is independent of computer language and is useful for developing and understanding the basic structure of a program. We recommend that you draw some type of

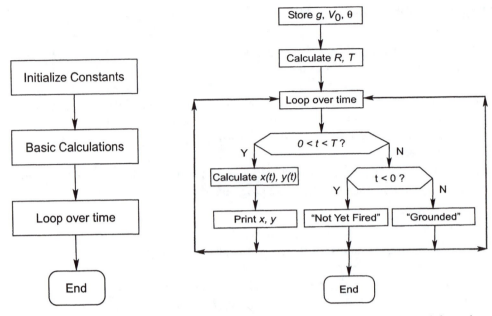

Figure 12.2 A flowchart illustrating a program to compute projectile motion. On the left are the basic components of the program and on the right are details. When writing a program, first map out the basic components, and then design the structure and fill in the details.

flow chart or construct some type of *pseudocode* every time you write a program. Pseudocode is like a text version of a flowchart in that it also leaves out details and instead focuses on the logic:

1. Store g, V_0, and θ.
2. Calculate R and T.
3. Begin repetition loop 100 over times from $-T/2$ to $3T/2$.
    a. Print out "not yet fired" if $t < 0$.
    b. Print out "grounded" if $t > T$.
    c. Calculate and print $x(t)$ and $y(t)$.
    d. Print out error message if $x > R$ or $y > H$.
    e. End loop over time.
4. End program.

   One way of viewing program design is in terms of data flow. Your program starts with some input data, decides what to do with it, does it, and then outputs the results. Usually boxes in flowcharts like Figure 12.3 show actions, while elongated or angled boxes show decisions to be made. The direction of logical flow of the program is shown by the arrows, with flow moving down, except when arrows redirect it.

   For our projectile problem, we need to calculate the position for 100 different times. The easiest way to do this is to have the same block of code repeated

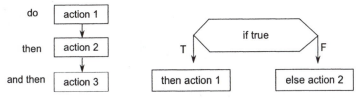

Figure 12.3 *Left:* Sequential or linear programming. *Right:* The if-then-else structure, one of several used in nonlinear programming.

100 times, with only the value of the time t changing. Such a structure is called a *loop*. Like a clock, it will run for a total time

$$T_{\text{total}} = T_f - T_i = \frac{3}{2}T - \frac{-T}{2} = 2T, \qquad (12.9)$$

in steps (ticks) of

$$\Delta t = \frac{2T}{100} = \frac{T}{50}. \qquad (12.10)$$

Whence, the time increases by Δt for each repetition of the loop:

$$t = t + \Delta t, \qquad (12.11)$$

with the program using its intelligence to decide what to compute and print out depending upon the particular value of t.

12.4 FLOW CONTROL VIA LOGIC

One of the most satisfying aspects of programming is getting the computer to do just what you want. Getting it to do what you want is sometimes direct, as when you evaluate functions in a "calculator" mode, and sometimes subtle, as when you try to make the computer act intelligently and "think" logically about what it should do next. Making a program think logically is done by including symbolic logic with *Boolean variables*. A Boolean *variable* is a primitive (built-in) Java data type that is either *true* or *false*. A Boolean *expression* is a combination of variables containing logical operators that evaluate to either *true* or *false*. When Boolean expressions are used with *control structures* in your program, you are able to affect the order in which statements are executed, as well as which statements actually get executed.

12.4.1 Relational and Logical Operators

Conditional operators act between two variables or expressions to form a Boolean expression that is either true or false. There are two types of conditional operators, *relational operators* and *logical operators*. Relational operators start with variables like double x and double y, and create a logical relationship between

Table 12.1 Relational operators of Java.

Operator	Example	Return *true* if
>	$x > y$	x is greater than y
>=	$x >= y$	x is greater than or equal to y
<	$x < y$	x is less than y
<=	$x <= y$	x is less than or equal to y
==	$x == y$	x and y are equal
! =	$x! = y$	x and y are not equal

Table 12.2 Logical operators of Java.

Operator	Example	Name	Return *true* if
&&	x && y	Logical and	x and y both true, conditionally evaluates y
||	x || y	Logical or	either x or y true, conditionally evaluates y
!	!x	Not	x is false
&	x & y	And	x and y both true, always evaluates y
|	x | y	Or	either x or y true, always evaluates y

them, for example, x > y, that is either *true* or *false*. This logical relationship is stored in a Boolean variable that has the value *true* or *false*.

Table 12.1 gives the relational operators, examples of their use, and conditions under which they evaluate to *true* results. In each case, the result is either *true* or *false*. To illustrate, the Boolean variable x > y is *true* if the numerical value of x is greater than the numerical value of y. These relational operators are never used in assignment statements. Indeed, for this reason, we introduce the double equal sign == as a relational operator; x = y is an assignment statement, while x == y is a Boolean variable.

Logical operators combine Boolean variables to create more complex expressions, for example, (x > 3) & (y > 4). Table 12.2 shows Java's logical operators, examples of their use, their logical names, and the conditions under which they evaluate to *true* results.

The basic logic behind logical operators is that if we have a compound statement constructed from two simpler statements, then the truth table, Table 12.3, determines the truth of the compound statement. We see in the truth table that the logical *and* is represented by both & and &&, and that the logical *or* is represented by both | and ||. Either form will work for you. The difference is that the single operator form, such as x | y, always evaluates y even if the result is foretold just

Table 12.3 Truth table.

True	False
true and true	*true and false*
true or true	*false and false*
true or false	*false or false*
!false	*!true*

by evaluating the first variable x. As a case in point, if x is *true*, then x | y is *true* regardless of y. The double operator form evaluates y only if the answer is not foretold by evaluating just x:

```
1 > 4                    false
(1 > 4) | (3 > 2)        true
(1 == 4) & (2 < 1)       false
(1 != 3) & (2 !> 4)      true
```

Believe it or not, what makes the use of logical expressions so powerful is that it is legitimate to combine the different logical expressions to describe the basis for *any* logical decision.

Exercise: If a is your age in years, w your weight in pounds, and h your height in inches, construct Boolean expressions that will be *true* only when the following statements are true:

1. you are old enough to obtain a driver's license but too young to retire, ((a > 16) & (a < 65));
2. you are not a teenager;
3. you are either younger than 20 and less than 150 pounds, or you are older than 40 and more than 6 feet;
4. you are neither old enough to vote, tall enough to hit your head on a five-foot door frame, nor heavy enough to box in the 132–140 pound division. ♠

12.4.2 Control Structures

The combination of Boolean expressions and *control structures* permits you to construct programs that make decisions based on the data at hand. Table 12.4 contains a complete list of the control structures in Java. The type of logic that is possible with these Boolean expressions is shown in the flowcharts of Figures 12.3–12.5. If you look at both the command in the table and the action in the figure together, you should get a good idea of how the command works.

Table 12.4 Logical flow control structures in Java.

Name	Example	Comment
if-then	`if ( (x < 3) && (y == 12) ) z = y*x;`	One-way if.
if-then-else	`if (x <= 0.)  {y = y * y;}` `    else y = 2 * y;`	Two-way if. the catchall

if-then-else-if	`if (score >= 90) {grade='A';}`
	`    else if (score >= 80) {grade='B';}`
	`    else if (score >= 70) {grade= 'C';}`
		Multi-way if
		Any else-if's OK
		Inaccessible if other else true

for	`for (count=0; count<100; count=count+1)` `    {<statements>}`	Initial; for; increment Multi-line code block

do	`do {<statements>} while (<boolean>);`
	`    <labelname>:  x = x*y;  ...`
	`    break <labelname>;`
	`    if (i==99) continue;`
		Goes through at least once
		Control sent to here
		go to labelname
		Jump to loop end

do while	`while (Math.sin(x) < 100.)   {y = y*y;` `    x = x + y;}`	Evaluate as long as true; line to execute
switch	`switch (month) {case 1:  s="Jan"; break;` `    case 12:  s = "Dec"; break;}`	Case 1, break after code block Can have many cases

The left of Figure 12.3 shows *linear* or *sequential* programming, in which the statements are executed in the order in which they are encountered, namely, from top to bottom. Control structures introduce the possibility that the execution of the program may "split" into different paths depending on the values of certain variables, or may repeat certain sections a number of times. If the program does "split," then the programming is no longer sequential.

The *if* and its complete form *if-then-else*, are common control structures. They permit your program to make decisions leading to multiple outcomes, with the decision based on changing situations. To name an instance, *if* it is raining before 10 AM, *then* I will take my umbrella. This structure are enhanced with the *else* option: *if* it is raining before 10 AM, *then* I will take my umbrella, *else* I will take my surfboard.

Consider the flow chart in Figure 12.3 illustrating the *if-then-else* structure, and the example in Table 12.4. First there is a logical expression constructed with the *if* statement. If the logical expression is *true, then* `action 1` is executed, *else* `action 2` is executed. In the Java version of this structure shown in Table 12.4, `action 1` is the block of statements contained within braces that follow the `if` (...) statement (no braces needed if only one statement). If `action 2` is included, it must be preceded with the word *else*. It too may be a single statement or a group of statements. If `action 2` is left off, we end up with an *if-then* statement. The word *then* is assumed in Java but used in other languages.

Figure 12.4 illustrates the *for* loop, probably the most popular control struc-

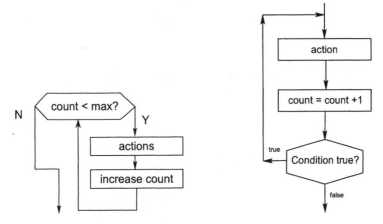

Figure 12.4 *Left:* For-loop iteration (test before action). *Right:* Do-loop iteration (test after action).

ture. The for loop is used to make your program *iterate*; that is, repeat a section of code over and over as long as some condition is true. This is useful for things like summing a series or repeating a calculation until the error gets smaller than some fixed amount. In that a counter is used to keep track of the number of iterations, it is also called a *counting loop*.

In the first line (header) of the *for* structure:

```
for (count = 0; count < 100; count = count + 1)                      // Header
```

there are parentheses containing three fields separated by semicolons. The first one, count = 0, gives the starting value for the counter. The second one, count < 100, gives a Boolean expression. The program will continue to iterate all the statements in braces (*action* in Figure 12.4) following the *for* construct as long as this Boolean expression is true. The third argument in the parentheses, count = count + 1, tells how to change the counter after each iteration of the loop. The iteration ends when the Boolean expression is false, at which point the program jumps to the first executable statement after the braces containing the action.

In general, the braces { and } are needed to indicate the beginning and end of the lines of code controlled by some control structure. They are permitted on lines all by themselves, or combined with lines of code. The structure of the program is probably clearer if the braces are on lines all by themselves and if they are indented to indicate the range of action of the control structure. However, in order to save space on the printed page and keep our codes compact, we may not follow that suggested form in all of our examples. If only a single line of code is being controlled, then it is legal to leave off the braces and place that line of code on the same line as the control structure. This is compact and easy to read.

These few ways to incorporate logic into programs are sufficient for the

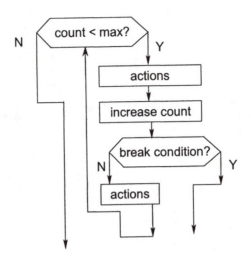

Figure 12.5 A break iteration.

problem at hand. Nevertheless, there are other commands that use a somewhat different approach to control the flow of your program, and we shall now discuss some. Consider again Figure 12.3 illustrating the *if-then-else* structure. We see in Table 12.4 that the *else* part of this control structure may have an *if-then* structure following it to form an *if-then-else-if* structure. What is more, any number of *else-if* statements may be included to handle special cases; for example, we may add more *else-if* statements to assign grades of A+, A-, B+, etc.

Figure 12.4 also illustrates a *do* loop. A *do* loop is very similar to a *for* loop used earlier, except that an *action* code in braces is executed first, and *then* the test is made to determine if the loop is to continue. So it follows that *there will always be at least one iteration of a do loop.*[1]

It is common to have a loop's counter index `count` be an integer, but it is not a requirement. A *for* or *do* loop with noninteger counters is similar to a *while* loop that loops until a general condition becomes *false*. For example, `err > 0.001`. Be that as it may, be warned, round-off error makes it unreliable to demand true equality between two floating-point numbers, or between a float and an integer. By way of example, an ill-advised condition might occur in the *for* loop starting with

```
for ( double x = 0.; x != 100; x = x + 1. )          // May never be satisfied
```

where x may never be *precisely* equal to 100, and so this loop may never end!

---

[1] Hoping not to confuse the reader, we note that the *Do* loop in Fortran executes the action after the test, and is thus equivalent to Java's *for* loop, not the *do* loop.

Table 12.5 Java's increment and decrement operators.

Shorthand	Equivalent Expression	Note
i++	i = i + 1	Evaluate i before increment
i--	i = i - 1	Evaluate i before decrement
++i	i = i + 1	Evaluate i after increment
--i	i = i - 1	Evaluate i after decrement

To make sure that the loop will eventually stop, it is better to use the greater-than and less-than operators. As case in point, we can always satisfy

```
for ( double x = 0.; x <= 100.; x += 1.  )
```

Counting is done so frequently in programming that many programmers prefer to declare the variable used for the loop counter as part of the loop statement itself. For instance, as we did with double x = 0. above, we could have

```
for ( int count = 0; count <= 100; count = count + 1 )
```

Notwithstanding the extra complication of this construction, it has the advantage of declaring locally those variables that are only used locally.

Finally, Table 12.4 and Figure 12.5 show the action of a break statement within a *do* loop. A break statement permits the programming to disrupt the normal order of execution within the *do* loop and send the program out of the loop.

12.4.3 Shorthand Notations

In the for loop in Table 12.4, we incremented the loop counter with the statement count = count + 1;. Regardless of this being perfectly clear, experienced programmers often use shortcuts that are elegant but less clear. Java contains the *increment operator* ++ and the *decrement operator* -- that, respectively, increase or decrease a variable by 1 without the use of an explicit equal sign. As shown in Table 12.5, they are affixed to the front or rear of a variable for slightly different effects. Wherefrom i++ and i-- increment and decrement at the end of the loop, ++i and --i increment and decrement at the beginning of the loop. More specifically, each evaluates to a different value: i++ or i-- *return* the value of i before the increment or decrement, while ++i or --i return the value of i *after* the increment or decrement. Since these operators act on only a single variable, they are called *unary operators*. As an instance, try out this pseudocode:

```
i=5
print i++, ++i
```

Table 12.6 Java's compound assignment operators.

Operator	Example	Equivalent to
+=	x += y	x = x + y
-=	x -= y	x = x - y
*=	x *= y	x = x * y
/=	x /= y	x = x / y
%=	x %= y	x = x % y
&=	x &= y	x = x & y
|=	x |=y	x = x | y
^=	x ^= y	x = x^y

```
i=5
print i--, --i
```

There are occasions when the increment and decrement operators ++ and -- are not flexible enough, like when you want to increase a variable by 2 rather than 1. In these cases the compound assignment operators indicated in Table 12.6 are useful. To cite an instance, x += 1 is equivalent to x = x + 1, which in turn is equivalent to x++. Likewise, x += 2, is equivalent to x = x + 2, and x += y is equivalent to x = x + y. Because these operators act on two variables, they are called *binary operators*.

The switch structure, illustrated in Listing 12.1 gives you a neat way to execute different blocks of code depending upon the value of an integer or Boolean variable. Even though this also is accomplished with a series of if-then statements, as we said, the switch structure is neater. The program Switch.java is used to program our clock radio so that we will wake up to music with our sunlight for different months of the year.

12.5 IMPLEMENTATION: PROJECTILE.JAVA

1. Before you create your own projectile simulation program, write down the equations to be solved and compose a flowchart or pseudocode that shows the logic of your program. Hand these in.
2. As an aide to writing your program, base it on a similar program you already have. That being the case, we suggest that you make of copy of Limits.java and save it as Projectile.java.
3. Add statements to your program, in the part before the *for* loop, that compute and print out T, H, and R. Test it.
4. Modify the *for* loop in Limits.java so that it loops over 100 evenly spaced times from $-T/2$ to $3T/2$.
5. Within the *for* loop, use the *if* statements to decide if the projectile has not yet been fired, if it is in the air, or if it has already hit the ground.

6. Have your program print out explicit values for t, $x(t)$, and $y(t)$. Also have it print out "not yet fired" or "grounded" as appropriate.

7. Have your program make a plot of the particle trajectory, preferably with PtPlot.

Listing 12.1 Switch.java

```
1  //                        Switch.java: demos switch control structure
2  public class Switch
3  {    public static void main(String[] argv)
4  {          int wake;                                    // Declaration
5             for(int month = 12; month > -1; month--)
6  { System.out.println("In for loop month =" +month);
7             switch (month) {                             // Switch structure
8             case 0:
9             System.out.println("last year");
10            break;                                       // Break
11            case 3:
12            wake = 7;
13            System.out.println("February, wake =" +wake );
14            break;
15            case 6:
16            wake = 6;
17            System.out.println("March, wake =" +wake );
18            break;
19            case 12:
20            wake = 9;
21            System.out.println("January, wake =" +wake );
22            break;
23            default: wake = 8;                           // Default
24            break;   }                                   // End switch
25         }}}                                             // End for, main, class
```

12.6 SOLUTION: PROJECTILE TRAJECTORIES

1. Run your program for a variety of initial conditions, namely, for your choice of different values for V_0 and θ. Try some for which you know the expected answer (like $\theta = 0$ and $\theta = \pi/2$).

2. Check that the range R increases as the initial velocity V_0 increases in magnitude, and as the elevation θ increases from 0 to $\pi/4$.

3. Check that the range $R = 0$, but that the hang time $T \neq 0$, for $\theta = 90°$ (this shooting the cannon straight up in the air is not the most clever thing to do).

4. Check that the y values never exceed the maximum height H.

12.7 KEY WORDS

"op" is common computer jargon for "operation," such as in "flops" for "floating-point operations." We use it here to save space as well:

air resistance	Boolean variable	break	conditional op
control structure	counting loop	decrement op	drag
if-then-else	increment op	flow control	flowchart
iteration	linear program	logical operators	operator
pseudocode	relational op	repetition structure	structured program
subroutine libe	switch	unary operator	while loop

12.8 SUPPLEMENTARY EXERCISES

1. Take the program `Limits.java` from Chapter 10 that uses a *for* loop to determine machine precision and make a copy of it.
   a. Compile and run `Limits.java` as a check that it is still running, and to get some output to compare with.
   b. Modify the *for* loop so that the counter is a double-precision variable. You should get all the same results.
   c. Change the *for* loop to a *while* loop that accomplishes the same task. (*Hint:* `while (1.0 + eps != 1.0)` will repeat the loop until there is no difference between the stored values of $1.0 + eps$ and `1.0`.)
   d. Change the *for* loop to a *do* loop that accomplishes the same task.
   e. Include an *if-then* construct in the *for* loop so that the program prints only one line of output, and it is for the first time that `1.0 + eps = 1.0`.
   f. Include an *if-then-else* construct in the *for* loop so that the program prints the message "not there yet" if `1.0 + eps != 1.0`, and then the usual `onePlusEps` and `eps` the first time that `1.0 + eps = 1.0`.

2. If a is your age in years, w is your weight in pounds, and h is your height in inches, construct Boolean expressions that will be *true* only when the following conditions are met:
   a. you are old enough to obtain a driver's license and you do not weigh 1,000 pounds;
   b. you are not a teenager;
   c. you are either younger than 20 and less than 150 pounds, or older than 40 and taller than 6 feet;
   d. you are neither old enough to vote, tall enough to hit your head on a five-foot door frame, nor heavy enough to box in the 132–140-pound division.

3. Let A be your age, Y be the number of years you have been in college, and D be the number of dollars you have in the bank. Construct Boolean expressions that will be *true* when the following conditions are met:
   a. you are a millionaire but you are not a senior;
   b. you are either too young to vote or you are not a freshman;
   c. you are either younger than 20 and broke, or older than 90 and have more than $100,000;
   d. you are 16 years old and your number of years in college is greater than the number of dollars you have in the bank.

Listing 12.2 Iterate.java

```
1                    Iterate.java:  series  expansion  for  1/(1−x)
2  public class Iterate
3  {  public  static  final  int  Nterms=1000;
4     public  static  final  double  Eps=10e−6;
5     static  public  void  main(String[]  args)
6  {    double  sum  =  0.,  x  =  0.5,  term  =  1.;
7        int  i  =0;                        // Repeat  Nterms  times,  or  term < e
8        while  (  (i <= Nterms)  &&  term > Eps)
9  {  sum  =  sum  +  term;
10       term  =   term  *  x;
11       i  =  i+  1;
12       System.out.println("i = "+i+",  sum = "+sum+",  term = "+term
               ); }
13       if  (i  ==  Nterms)  System.out.println("I quit");      // Quit?
14       else  System.out.println("Series = "+sum+",  Exact = "
              +1./(1.−x));
15 }}                                              //End  main,  class
```

4. **Iteration** refers to the repetition of the same lines of code until a condition is satisfied. To illustrate, in Listing 12.2 is a code that computes $1/1 - x$ for $x^2 < 1$ via its infinite series expansion:

$$\frac{1}{1 - x} = 1 + x + x^2 + x^3 + x^4 + \cdots. \qquad (12.12)$$

The summation of terms is repeated 1,000 times or until the new terms have an insignificant effect on the sum ($x^n < 10^{-7}$ sum).

   a. Enter, compile, and execute `Iterate.java`. Check that it runs with no errors.

   b. Try several *positive* values of $x < 1$. Check that convergence is obtained in each case, but with a differing number of terms needed.

   c. See how close you are able to get to $x \simeq 1$ before the algorithm fails, namely, 1,000 summations are made.

   d. The series (12.12) is valid for negative x values, but the code has assumed that $x > 0$. Modify the program so that it will work for negative x, and check your results for $x = -0.5, -0.1$, and -0.9.

Chapter Thirteen

Java Input and Output*

Some of the computing in the chapters to follow is made easier by being able to write output to files, and being able to read from the keyboard or from a file. Even though we will give you the commands needed to do that in those chapters, we will not explain just how they go about doing it. In this optional chapter we do explain some of the theory and details of Java I/O, for those who care to or need to know about them. As we have indicated before, we consider the difficulty of Java's I/O a major weakness of the language for scientific computing, a weakness that is being overcome as this book goes to press. Part of this difficulty arises from the increased security needed to be able to use Java over the Web, and part from Java being designed more for graphical output than text. Already Java 1.5 has added scanner, a version of *scanf*, and we suspect that *printf* will follow shortly [Jgran].

You have seen in Chapter 9, "Getting Started with Java," that we printed out a line of output with the basic Java command:

```
System.out.println("R = " + r + ", A = " +A);
```

Even though this seems rather ungainly for such a simple operation, we advised you to just use it and not worry about its form or meaning. As we get on with more serious computing, it would be nice to have some more control over the input and output (I/O) within our programs. In particular, it is useful to enter input from the keyboard or from a file and to place our output into files that are stored for later use.

In the first part of this chapter we discuss the standard I/O streams of Java and how to use them to read and write files. Rather than give all details of the theory of I/O, we primarily give examples of how these things are done, with little discussion of the various steps that Java must undertake to get them done. In the second part of this chapter we give examples of the use of a freely available package that provides convenient reading and writing of formatted data. That package contains Java versions of the well known C-language *printf* and *scanf* commands.

13.1 BASIC INPUT WITH SCANNER

As this book was going to press, Sun announced their latest version of Java, j2se/1.5.0. It contains the simple scanner command that reads input and converts (parses) it into primitive data types and strings, without the user having to deal with the complication of buffers. While its introduction was too late for us to include in our sample codes, in Listing 13.1 we give ScannerIn.java containing examples of its use with various data types.

Listing 13.1 ScannerIn.java

```
1  //   ScannerIn: Java 1.5+ input via Scanner command
2  import java.io.*;          // Import I/O library
3  import java.util.*;        // Import utilities
4  public class ScannerIn
5  {
6     public static void main(String[] argv)
7     {
8     double r, A;
9     // Connect Scanner to standard input (other also possible)
10    Scanner sc = new Scanner(System.in);
11    System.out.println("Enter your name & r on 1 or more lines");
12    String name = sc.next();         // Read String
13    r = sc.nextDouble();             // Read double
14    System.out.println("Hi "+name);
15    System.out.println("radius = "+r);
16    System.out.println("Key in your age as integer ");
17    int age = sc.nextInt();          //  Read int
18    System.out.println(age+"years old, you don't look it!" );
19    sc.close();                      // Close input
20    A = Math.PI * r * r;
21    System.out.println("Area = "+A);
22 }}
```

13.2 STREAMS: STANDARD OUTPUT, INPUT, AND ERROR

The most basic I/O in Java is that which comes packaged as part of the Java "system." It consists of

System.in	standard input stream (keyboard)
System.out	standard output stream (monitor screen)
System.err	standard error stream (varies)

Here the word *stream* represents a one-way path connecting your program and a device, such as a file. You may issue system-level commands that redirect where the input comes from and where the output goes, but unless you do so, the default input is the keyboard and the default output is the screen. To prove the point, when in Listing 13.2:

Table 13.1 Control characters for formatting output.

Control Character	Effect	Control Character	Effect
\n	new line	\b	backspace
\r	return (no line feed)	\t	tab

Listing 13.2 Area2.java

```
1  public class Area2
2  {   public static void main(String[] args)        //Begin main method
3      {  double r, C, A, PI = Math.PI;        //Declare (instants), assign
4         r = 1.;                                           //Assign r
5         C = 2.* PI* r;                                  //Calculate C
6         A = r * r * PI;                                 //Calculate A
7         System.out.println("R = " + r);                    //Print r
8         System.out.println("C = " + C);                    //Print C
9         System.out.println("\n R = " + r +", A = " + A);
10 } }                                           //End main and class
```

we issue the System.out.println command, we actually are using the println method to send a line of data to be printed on the standard output stream System.out. The method is in the out classes that are part of Java's System.

The original version of Java (1.0) was written so that it transfers data one byte at a time. Java 1.1 and beyond permit I/O using characters as well. Both systems are still part of Java, and commands from each tend to get intermixed. Though you as a programmer are free to go through all the effort of converting your input and output to byte-size chucks, use of the println method does this for you. However, println takes only a single *string* as its argument, which is why we use the + operator to convert doubles and ints to strings that are then concatenated into a single, long string. Here are a few examples:

13.2.1 Screen Output; Area2.java

For beginning work we usually output to the screen. In Listing 13.2 we have Area2.java, a modified version of our old friend Area. It produces the output:

```
R = 1.0
C = 6.283185307179586


R = 1.0, A = 3.141592653589793
```

Survey some new things here. First, how the third println command includes a

Table 13.2 String to primitive type conversion methods.

Conversion Method	Converts to
`Double.parseDouble(String str)`	double
`Double.valueOf(String str).doubleValue()`	double
`Integer.parseInt(String str)`	int
`Integer.valueOf(String str).integerValue()`	int
`Long.parseLong(String str)`	long
`Long.valueOf(String str).longValue()`	long
`Float.parseFloat(String str)`	float
`Float.valueOf(String str).floatValue()`	float
`Boolean.valueOf(String str).booleanValue()`	boolean

\n control character before the symbol R. This causes a "new" or blank line to be inserted in the output, in this case, before the symbol R is printed. (The indentation occurs because there is a blank space after the \n.) Other control characters that you may use to control the format of the output are given in Table 13.1. Another new thing in Area2 is our printing both r and A on the same line:

```
System.out.println("\n R = " + r +", A = " + A);
```

We did this by the concatenation of a string + data conversion + string + data conversion. Some care is needed here in keeping track of where the double quotes begin and end, although you may rest assured that Java will tell you when you do not get it quite right!

13.2.2 Keyboard Input, Screen Output

The keyboard is the standard stream for input, much as the screen is the standard stream for output. We may accomplish all the conversions and transfers needed for output with a single command like `println`, yet an additional step is needed for *input*, because we must *both* transfer a stream of bytes into our program and then convert these bytes into the appropriate data type (such as double, int, or string). Java provides the methods to look after the details, but you must tell Java what it is you want done. In fact, there are a number of different methods to accomplish this task, as you shall see in the examples.

Data read into your program enters as a long string. If you want to assign that long string to a string variable, then no conversion is necessary. If you want to convert that string into double, int, or boolean data types, then you may use the type conversion methods indicated in Table 13.2 [Chap 04, Bron 03, Dav 99]. Observe how the first part of the method name is actually the name of the class to which it belongs, while the second part, after the decimal point, is the method's proper name. So, for example, when we say

```
Double.parseDouble(String str)
```

the method name is parseDouble, and it is contained in the class Double. This agrees with our convention that class names are capitalized, while method names are not. The method's argument is in the parentheses, (String str), with String indicating the data type. In contrast to *primitive* data types, which we declare with lowercase key words like double, Strings are variable-length *objects* that we create, and are therefore declared with the capitalized String.

Before we lose you with all the talk, look at ReadStnd.java in Listing 13.3:

Listing 13.3 ReadStnd.java

```
1  //                    ReadStnd:       standard (keyboard) input stream
2  import java.io.*;                                  // Import I/O library
3  public class ReadStnd {
4  public static final double PI = Math.PI;                    // Constants
5    public static void main(String[] argv) throws IOException   // main
6  { double r, A;                                     // throws exception
7    BufferedReader b = new BufferedReader(new InputStreamReader(
         System.in));
8    System.out.println("Please enter your name");              // Input
9        //    Read & print 1st line; read & convert 2nd line to double
10   String name = b.readLine();
11   System.out.println("Hi "+name+" \n Please enter r");
12   String rS = b.readLine();
13   r = Double.valueOf(rS).doubleValue();
14   A = PI * r * r;                                  // The computation
15   System.out.println("\n Bye "+name+"\t R=  " +r+", A=" +A);
16 } }
```

This code uses the standard input stream (keyboard) and produces the output:

```
Please type in your name
Loren B

Hi Loren B

   Please enter r

10

Bye Loren B R = 10.0, A = 314.1592653589793
```

This example also illustrates a step in the input process known as *buffering*. As a general rule, you do not want your program (software) to interact directly with an I/O device (hardware), as then you may have your fast program waiting for some slow hardware. On these grounds, the data in the input stream gets placed in a *buffer* where it accumulates until there is a full line ready for transmission to your program. So it follows that, like a shock absorber on an automobile smoothing out the ride, a buffer in the I/O streams smooths out the data flow. To include a buffer in the program, on line 7 we have the command

```
BufferedReader b = new BufferedReader(new InputStreamReader(system.in));
```

This means that the standard `java.io` package creates `BufferedReader` objects to buffer the data in the input stream. The method `readLine()` used on line 10 reads the line in the buffer and returns it to the program as a `String`. The reading of the data from the input stream is done by the object `InputStreamReader` (line 7), which is passed to `BufferedReader`. We see (line 10) that we have read in a string `name` with the user's name and stored it as a string. Then (line 12) we read in `String rS`, which we converted to the `double r` with the command `Double.valueOf(rS).doubleValue()`. However, we do not need to convert the string `name` to a string, as it already is one.

Now in Listing 13.4 we give `ReadStnd2.java`, a version of this program that still uses the same `BufferedReader` object but uses the `parse` conversion of the string rather than the `valueOf` form:

Listing 13.4 ReadStnd2.java

```
1  //                             ReadStnd2:  parse input for int, double
2  import java.io.*;                                        //import I/O library
3  public class ReadStnd2
4  {   public static final double PI = Math.PI;
5      public static void main(String[] argv)                          //main
6      throws IOException, FileNotFoundException
7  {   double r, A;                                    //Variables instants
8      BufferedReader b = new BufferedReader(new InputStreamReader(
           System.in));
9      System.out.println("Please enter your age");                   //Input
10     String ageS = b.readLine();                                      //Read
11     int age = Integer.parseInt(ageS);                     //Convert to int
12     System.out.println("Hi at "+age+" yrs,\n Please enter r");
13     String rS = b.readLine();                                       //Read
14     r = Double.parseDouble(rS);                       //Convert to double
15     A = PI * r * r;
16     System.out.println("\n r= " +r+", A= " +A);                   //Screen
17 }}
```

This program produces the output:

```
Please type in your age 101 Hi at 101 years
 Please enter r
1.  Done, R = 1.0, A = 3.141592653589793
```

We see in `ReadStnd2.java` that `Integer.parseInt()` is used to convert a `String` to an `int`, and `Double.parseDouble()` is used to convert a `String` to a `double`.

13.2.3 Keyboard Input via Command Line: CommandLineIn.java

Recall how the main method is always declared with a statement containing `void main(String[] argv)`. The main method gets called by the Java interpreter when you issue the `java` command, and since it is a method, it takes arguments (*parameter list*) and returns values. The word `void` here means that no argument gets returned to the command that calls main, while `String[] argv` means that the argument `argv` is an array (indicated by the `[]`) of the data type `String`. Although we have not done it yet, you are permitted to pass arguments (data) to the main method from the *command line*, that is, from the shell command `java` that you use to run your program. As an example, the program `CommandLineIn.java` in Listing 13.5 accepts and then uses arguments from the command line. Consequently, if you issue the command:

```
> java CommandLineIn Manuel 1.0
```

the string `Manuel` and the double `1.0` will be transferred to the main program for use, and will produce the output:

```
Please enter your name & r as command line arguments
1st argument:  Manuel, 2nd argument:   1.
How's life Manuel?  radius = 1.0
Done Manuel, A = 3.141592653589793
```

Here you are free to use any name and number, or any number of arguments, and the program will have that information transferred to it.

Listing 13.5 CommandLineIn.java

```
1  //                      CommandLineIn:   input via command—line
2  public class CommandLineIn {
3  public static final double PI=Math.PI;                    // Constants
4      public static void main(String[] argv) {
5      double radius, A;
6      System.out.println("Please enter your name and r as command line
              arguments");
7      System.out.println("1st argument: "+ argv[0]+", 2nd argument: "
              +argv[1]);
8      System.out.println("How's life "+ argv[0]+"?");
9      String s = argv[1];                            // String to String
10     radius = Double.valueOf(s).doubleValue();   // strng—Double—double
11     System.out.println("radius = "+radius);
12     A = PI*radius*radius;
13     System.out.println("Done "+argv[0]+ ", A = "+A);
14  }   }
```

Look at `CommandLineIn.java` to see how to create a command-line interpreter in Java. We see first that the main-method declaration on line 4 looks like the usual one (which declares `argv` to be an array of strings). Line 6 reminds the user that she should have entered arguments on the command line, which will be useful the next time the program is run. Line 7 prints out the two strings that are fed to the program through the command line. Seeing that the input is always an array of strings, no conversion is necessary if you want to use elements of the array as a string. This is, in fact, what we do on line 7 with the printouts, and on line 9 with the second argument `s = argv[1]`. However, if you want to use the input string `s` for numerical computation, then you must convert it to the appropriate data type. This is done on line 10, where we first convert the string `s` to a double object with the `Double.valueOf(s)` command, and then convert that object to a static double by appending the `.doubleValue()` method to the object.

13.2.4 File Input and File Output: AFileIO.java, FT.java

Assume you need to store the output of your program in a file or read data from a file. As a case in point, you may want to store data to be plotted by a graphics program, or you may want to read in the results from an experiment so that you may analyze them. The simplest way to do this is by using *command-line redirection* from within the shell in which you are running your program:

```
% java A <infile.dat
```
redirect standard input

will redirect the standard input stream from the keyboard to the file `infile.dat`. Likewise,

```
% java A >outfile.dat
```
redirect standard output

redirects the standard output stream from the screen to the file `outfile.dat`. Or, for complete redirection, you could put both together:

```
% java A <infile.dat >outfile.dat
```
redirect standard I/O

You may also read and write formatted and nonformatted files from within your Java program without any shell commands. Nonformatted files are useful when creating large databases, while formatted files, being simpler to deal with, is all we shall deal with.

Our discussion of the need for buffering when dealing with I/O streams is also true for file I/O. On that account, examine `AFileIO.java` in Listing 13.6. You see that reading a file also uses the `BufferedReader` method. Likewise, we also use the `println` method, but now with a buffer. What is new with file I/O is that we need to create an object that is associated with a physical file on our computer.

Table 13.3 File readers and writers.

Reader	Writer
BufferedReader	PrintWriter
FileReader	FileWriter
	BufferedWriter

Listing 13.6 AFileIO.java

```
1  //                    AFileIO:             Area  with  File  I/O
2  import java.io.*;                          //Import I/O library
3  public class AFileIO {
4  public static final double PI = 3.141593;            // Constants
5     public static void main(String[] argv) throws
6     IOException, FileNotFoundException {       //Main with throw
7     double r, A;                              //declare variables
8     //Ask user to prepare input from file
9     System.out.println("Enter name and r in Name.dat");
10    BufferedReader b = new BufferedReader(new InputStreamReader(new
          FileInputStream("Name.dat")));     //  Open file
11    System.out.println("Hi "+b.readLine());    //Read, print 1st line
12    String s = b.readLine();           //Read 2nd line, convert double
13    r = Double.valueOf(s).doubleValue();       //String to double
14    System.out.println("r = "+r);
15    A = PI * r * r;                            //Do computation
16    System.out.println("Done, look in A.dat");   //Screen print
17    PrintWriter q = new PrintWriter(new FileOutputStream("A.dat"),
          true);
18    q.println("r = " +r);                      //File output
19    q.println("A = "+A);
20  }}
```

Take note of how in AFileIO.java, we open the input file NameAndR.dat and associate it with the object b via the logical but not succinct command:

```
BufferedReader b = new BufferedReader(
    new InputStreamReader( new FileInputStream( "NameAndR.dat" ) ) );
```

We now open output file A.dat and associate it with object q:

```
PrintWriter q = new PrintWriter(
    new FileOutputStream( "A.dat" ), true );
```

Here the words in quotes, "NameAndR.dat" and "A.dat" are the names of physical files on our computer, and unless a more complete path is indicated, they are assumed to reside in the directory from which the java command is issued. The variables FileInputStream and FileOutputStream are objects in which large amounts of data may accumulate. If the data come from an input device, they are accumulated one byte at a time and then passed to the `InputStreamReader` in a large chunk. If the data are to be sent to an output device, it is accumulated in a large chuck from the `FileOutputStream` and then passed to the file, one byte at a time. Java does the same thing in multiple ways. Other options are in Table 13.3.

Once these admittedly awkward commands are issued, reading and writing files is simply accomplished by modifying the objects b and q. For instance, examine the `AFileIO.java` code in Listing 13.6. Check out how the declaration of the main method on lines 5–6 includes the `throws IOException` phrase, as needed when dealing with files. After that, we create an object b (line 11) that represents the input file, and then a second object q (line 19) that represents the output file. After that it is easy to read and write files just by affixing a read or write line method to the object, for example, lines 14 and 20:

```
String s = b.readLine(); q.println("r = " +r);
```

In Listing 13.7 we present the code `FT.java` that uses standard Java to read data from a *file* until it runs out of data (`instring` is `null`), and then places those data into an array for processing. The array is then processed and written to another file. The input file contains data of the form:

```
 0.026643
 0.017807
 0.008962
 0.000107
-0.008756 -0.017628 -0.026508 -0.035396
```

These data are positions $y(t_i)$ of a nonlinear oscillator as a function of time t, measured in discrete steps of h. In other words, the data are $y(0)$, $y(h)$, $y(2h)$, ..., with one y per line, and with each line corresponding to t increasing by h (the actual value of h is not given). The program computes the discrete Fourier transform [CP 05] of these data via:

$$Y_n = \sum_{k=0}^{N-1} \left(\cos(\frac{2\pi n k}{N}) + i \sin(\frac{2\pi n k}{N}) \right) y(t_k), \qquad n = 0, \dots, N-1 \quad (13.1)$$

where N is the number of times at which the input signal was measured. The code is given in Listing 13.7. It produces a file with lines of the form:

```
0   -425.183626    0.0
1   128.80130855519593    964.4441383691654
2   -1.3054384301614006   5.840535198361542
3   31.463783796425304    11.33636196280638
4   12.11948839663997    -0.7004454432124283
5   8.944525602799267    -0.7686320522517022
```

In §13.5 we give another version of this code, which uses formatted output for an improved listing.

Listing 13.7 FT.java

```
1  //              FT.java:     DFT with file IO
2  import java.io.*;
3  public class FT {
4  static final int MAX = 10000;                      // Global Constants
5    public static void main(String[] argv)
6    throws IOException, FileNotFoundException
7  { BufferedReader in = new BufferedReader(new FileReader("Data.in")
       );                        // Create BufferedReader
8    PrintWriter out = new PrintWriter(new FileOutputStream("Data.out
         "), true);               // Create PrintWriter
9    String instring = "";                            // Define variables
10   double imag, real;
11   double input[] = new double[MAX + 1];
12   int i =0, j, k;                                  // Place data into input array
13   while( instring = in.readLine() != null )        // Read till null
14   { Double ins = new Double(instring);             // String to double
15     input[i] = ins.doubleValue();                  // Double to double
16     i = i + 1;
17     for( j = 0; j<i; j++ )                         // Transform, frequency loop
18     { real = imag = 0.0;                           // Initialize
19       for( k = 0; k<i; k++ )                       // Loop over data
20       { real += input[k] * Math.cos( (2*Math.PI*k*j ) / i);
21         imag += input[k] * Math.sin( (2*Math.PI*k*j ) / i); }
22         out.println(" "+j+" "+real+" "+imag);      // File write
23     } }
24   out.close();                                     // close file
25   System.out.println("Output in Data.out");
26 }}
```

13.3 I/O EXCEPTIONS: FILECATCHTHROW.JAVA

You may have noted that the programs containing file I/O have declared their main methods with a statement of the form:

```
main( String[] argv ) throws IOException
```

This is required by the Java compiler when dealing with files. *Exceptions* occur when something goes wrong during the I/O process, such as not finding a file, trying to read past the end of a file, or interrupting the I/O process. In fact, you may get more information of this sort reported back to you by including any of these phrases:

```
FileNotFoundException      EOFException      InterruptedException
```

after the words throws IOException. As an instance, ReadStnd2 in Listing 13.4 contains the statements:

```
public static void main(String[] argv)
      throws IOException, FileNotFoundException
```

where the added comma is to be noted. In this case, we add in the subclass `FileNotFoundException`, which you may have noted in some of the examples.

    Dealing with I/O exceptions is important, since it prevents the computer from locking if a file cannot be read or written. If, for example, a file is not found, then Java will create an `Exception` object and pass it along ("throws exception") to the program that called this main method. This extended declaration creates an object (variable) through which error messages concerning things that can go wrong with your file I/O to be transmitted back to the main method. When you issue the `java` command to run the main method, you will have the error message delivered to you.

Listing 13.8 FileCatchThrow.java

```
1  //                    FileCatchThrow:   throw, catch IO exception
2  import java.io.*;
3  public class FileCatchThrow{
4     public static void main(String[] argv)               //Begin main
5     {double r, circum, A, PI = 3.141593;          //Declare, assign
6        r = 2;
7        circum = 2.* PI* r;                          // Calculate circum
8        A = Math.pow(r,2) * PI;                         // Calculate A
9        try{ PrintWriter q = new PrintWriter(new FileOutputStream("
              FileThrowCatch.out"), true);
10           q.println("r = " + r + ", length, A = " + circum + ", " +
                 A);}      // Print variables
11           catch (IOException ex) { ex.printStackTrace(); } // Catch
12 }}
```

    Just how the program deals with (*catches*) the thrown exception object is beyond the level of this book, although Listing 13.8 does give an example of the `try-catch` construct below. Beware, the file specification on line 11 is for Unix/Linux. For Windows it would be of the form (note double backslash):

```
new FileOutputStream("c:\\jan\\MyDocs\\FileThrowCatch.out"),true);
```

We see here that while the declaration of the main method on line 4 does not contain any statement about an exception being thrown, in its place we have a `try-catch` construct on lines 9–11. The statements within the `try` block are executed, and if they throw an exception, it is caught by the `catch` statement, which prints out a statement to the effect. To illustrate, this program creates a file in the home directory of user `jan`. Well, unless you happen to be user `jan`, an exception should be thrown and you should see the line `Could not write to file` printed out. If you place your user name in place of `jan`, then rather than getting an error message, you should get the file `FileThrowCatch.out` written in your home direc-

Table 13.4 Tag forms for javadoc.

`@author` Loren Rose	before class
`@version` 12.3	before class
`@parameter` sum	before method
`@exception` <exception name>	before method
`@return` weight for trap integration	before method
`@see` <class or method name>	before method

tory. In summary, if you use files, an appropriate `throws IOException` statement is required for successful compilation.

13.4 AUTOMATIC CODE DOCUMENTATION: JAVADOC

In Chapter 14, "Numerical Integration," we present a program `TrapMethods.java` that contained multiline comments of the form:

```
/** TrapMethods.java: with javadoc comments */
public class TrapMethods {
  public static final double A = 0., B = 3.;
  /** main method sums over points
  calls wTrap for trapezoid weight
  calls f(y) for integrand
  @param N number of data points
  @param A first endpoint
  @param B second endpoint  */
```

Here the comments began with a `/**`, rather than the standard `/*`, and ended with the standard `/*`. As usual, Java ignores the text within a comment field but leaves them in the code listing as an aide in understanding the code. What makes these `/**`, or *doc comments* different from the standard ones is that with minimal effort you automatically produce a Web (HTML) page containing these comments, as well as an outline of the formal structure of your entire program.[1] For this to work, the comments must appear before the class or method that they describe and contain key words, such as `@param`.

A sample documentation page, as viewed from a Web browser, is shown in Figure 13.1. This page is named `TrapMethods.html` (it is on the CD) and is produced by operating on your `TrapMethods.java` file with the `javadoc` command:

`% javadoc TrapMethods.java`   Create documentation

Not visible in the figure are the specific definition fields produced by the `@param` tags. Other tags are shown in Table 13.4.

---

[1] Some basics of the World Wide Web are described in Chapter 21, "Web Computing."

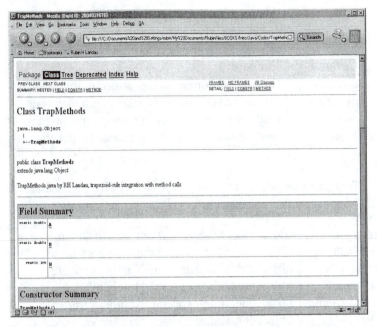

Figure 13.1 A sample of the automatic code documentation produced by running javadoc on the
program TrapMethods.java.

13.5 NONSTANDARD FORMATTED OUTPUT: PRINTF

If you have been trying to make sense of all the ways that Java has to do I/O and
all the commands needed to do it, you may be saying to yourself "there must be
an easier way." Well there are actually numerous *convenience classes* of methods
written to improve upon Java I/O. Unfortunately, none of these convenience classes
are yet part of the Java standard or even universally accepted and maintained by
the Java community.

A particularly attractive and promising package for Java I/O is the *Java
printf package* [Printf]. This package is free for noncommercial use, easy to use,
and provides Java versions of the C-language I/O routines fprintf(), printf(),
and sprintf(), which are the standard for much programming. We recommend
that the interested reader go to its Web site, read over the documentation, browse
the 200 examples, and download the package if interested. The I/O commands are
listed in Table 13.5. These commands are in the package com.braju.format and
in the class Format. Accordingly, to include the needed fprintf methods in your
program, you start your program (before any methods) with the line

```
import com.braju.format.*;
```

Then, just replace System.out.println with Format.printf (since the commands are in the Format class, you affix the class name):

Table 13.5 Nonstandard formatted I/O commands (static methods).

Command	Purpose
fprintf	format and output text to named output stream
printf	format and output text to the standard output
fscanf	read formatted text from named input stream
scanf	read formatted text from standard input stream

Table 13.6 Components of the printf/scanf formatted I/O commands.

Component	Purpose
Parameters p	object used to store input or output stream
NumberVariable	object containing single number from input
IntegerVariable	object containing specific NumberVariable
DoubleVariable	object containing specific NumberVariable
CharacterVariable	object containing specific NumberVariable
StringVariable	object containing specific NumberVariable
intValue()	method to extract integer's value from a NumberVariable
doubleValue()	method to extract double's value from a NumberVariable
charValue()	method to extract characters from a NumberVariable

```
Format.printf("Hello universe!\n");
```

This prints the string Hello universe! and skips a line.

Using the printf/scanf command involves the components shown in Table 13.6. Beware, standard Java contains components, such as

```
Double.valueOf(str).doubleValue(), Integer.valueOf(str).integerValue()
```

that have similar names but are not designed to work with the printf objects. Of course it is the formatting of output that makes the printf package so useful, and it handles many types of output. The basic idea is that to output some data, you have printf convert one of Java's primitive data types into the format you prefer. You denote this by placing the *conversion symbol* % in front of a letter indicating the format you want. As an example, for Al being a String:

Java Statement	Output
`Format.printf( "Hi %s!", p.add(Al) );`	Hi Al!
`Format.printf("%s = %d yrs", p.add(Al).add(9);`	Al =9 yrs

Inspect here how %s outputs a string, while %d outputs an integer.[2] The outputs

---

[2]The use of d for an integer indicates that this is a decimal integer, in contrast to an octal integer. Therefore,

Table 13.7 Sample formatted output for floating-point numbers.

Type	Java Statement	Output
floating	`Format.printf("a=%6.2f, b=%.2f",` `p.add(1.456).add(1.456));`	`a= 1.46, b=1.5`
fixed	`Format.printf("d=%+010f"` `p.add(d));`	`d=-1234.56789`
exponent	`Format.printf("d=%12.1e"` `p.add(d));`	`d= -1.2e+03`
general	`Format.printf("d=%+12.4G"` `p.add(d));`	`d=        -1235`
left general	`Format.printf("d=%-12.4G"` `p.add(d));`	`d= -1235`

are not done directly, but instead get added to a `Parameters` object, which may accumulate other output as well. By way of example, consider the command:

```
Format.printf("%s = %d yrs", p.add(Russ).add(30));
```

The first part of the command says to format for output a `String` (`%s`) and then a decimal integer (`%d`). The second part of the command says to take the converted form of each variable and add each to the object p. The object p, which you may name most anything you want, is a special type of object that holds the parameter list produced by the `printf` command. It is called a `Parameters` object and is created by the default (null) constructor, or with an argument (here a string):

```
Parameters p = new Parameters();          Create empty Parameters object
Parameters p = new Parameters(String Russ);    Create object containing string
```

In our example, the `Parameters` object has the string `Russ` added to it, and then the decimal integer `30` added. More calls to the `get` method will continue to add more output to the `Parameters` object. If you prefer, you may save some space— but this makes commands harder follow and debug—by creating the `Parameters` object within the `printf` command:

```
Format.printf( "M = %15.4e, v = %15.4g", new Parameters(m).add(v) );
```

Now let us look at the commands for fixed-decimal-point floating-point numbers, floating-point numbers in scientific notation, and general floating-point numbers. You use these to control both the total width (number of spaces) used for the output as well as the number of digits that are given to the right of the decimal point. For instance, `%.2f` produces a fixed-decimal-point number with two digits after the decimal point, while `%6.2f` uses a total of six spaces, one for the decimal

---

`%i` also outputs a decimal integer, although this is not true in standard C `printf`. If you want an octal integer, that is converted with `%o`.

point, two after the decimal point, and one before it (including the sign). If the
value for the width is negative, the output is left justified. Some specific examples
are given in Table 13.7.

Listing 13.9 FormatFT.java

```
1  //                    FormatFT.java, file 1, Formatted file O
2  import java.io.*;
3  import com.braju.beta.format.*;                        // Import Format
4  import com.braju.beta.lang.*;
5  public class FormatFT {
6  static final int MAX = 10000;                          // Global constants
7  public static void main(String argv[]) throws IOException,
        FileNotFoundException
8  { Parameters p = new Parameters();
9    Writer out = new FileWriter( "Data.out" );     // Create FileWriter
10   BufferedReader in = new BufferedReader( new FileReader( "Data.in
        " ) ); // Create BufferedReader
11   String s = "";
12   String instring = "";
13   double imag, real;
14   double input[] = new double[MAX + 1];
15   int i =0, j, k;
16   while( instring = in.readLine() != null)    // Place data in array
17     { Double ins = new Double(instring);
18       input[i] = ins.doubleValue();
19       i = i + 1; }
20     for ( j = 0; j<i; j++ )                          // Fourier transform
21     { real = imag = 0.0;                             // Initialize variables
22       for( k = 0; k<i; k++ ) {                        //Loop over data
23         real += input[k] * Math.cos( (2*Math.PI*k*j)/i );
24         imag += input[k] * Math.sin( (2*Math.PI*k*j)/i );  } }
25   s = Format.sprintf("\%d \t \%17.6g \%17.6g \n",p.add(j).add(real
        ).add(imag) );
26   out.write(s);
27   out.close();
28   System.out.println("Output in Data.out");
29 }}
```

In Listing 13.9 we give the complete code `FormatFT.java`. It illustrates
how to use standard Java to read data from a *file* until you run out of data (read
string is null) and then places those data into an array for processing. The array
is then processed and `Format` is used for output. The file is the same series of
positions of an oscillator used in §13.2.4, and the program computes the same
Fourier transform. This produces the formatted output:

```
0              -425.184 0 1
128.801 964.444 2         -1.30544 5.84054 3
31.4638 11.3364 4 12.1195    -0.700445 5              8.94453
-0.768632
```

13.5.1 Formatting Input with Java scanf

Reading in data involves a number of steps. The data are stored on a device in some type of coded format, and so you must first have the computer *parse* or *scan* the data so that there is a copy of it in the computer's RAM. You then must break up the input stream into individual items and then convert those items to numerical values that are then assigned to variables in your program. The `printf` package we have been discussing also includes a `scanf` component that reads in data, much like the analogous command in the C language.

To see how `printf/scanf` works, we give here an annotated example. In trying to make sense of this, it is helpful to remember that the variables representing objects, such as `p` and `num`, just point to a location in memory. To extract the value(s) associated with the object, a method must be applied to it (and that is done with the dot operation that affixes the method to the object):

```
1 import com. braju . format .*;               // Import Format package
2 int n Parameters p = new Parameters ();      // Create p = Parameters
3 NumberVariable num=new IntegerVariable ();          // Create num
4 Format. printf ("Enter an integer: ");          // Formatted output
5 Format. scanf ("\%i", p. add (num));          // Add an integer num to p
6 Format. printf (" \%i and \%i ", p. add (num). add (n));  // Output 2 ints
7 int nValue = p. intValue ();              // Assign value of p to nValue
8 if (nValue == 3) x = x+4;                  // Use nValue in usual way
```

In Listing 13.10 we give the complete code `F2C.java` based on an example taken from the `Format` package. This illustrates how to read from the *standard input stream* both a `double` and a `character`, and then how to process both of them. Some typical output is:

```
Input a T in Fahrenheit: 23.4
23.40 F is -4.78 C Another one? Input a T in Fahrenheit: 96.5
96.50 F is 35.83 C Another one? n
```

Listing 13.10 F2C.java

```
1  import com.braju.beta.format.*;
2  import com.braju.beta.lang.*;
3  class F2C
4  {    public static void main(String args[]) throws Exception {
5       Parameters p = new Parameters();
6       NumberVariable dV = new DoubleVariable();
7       CharacterVariable cV = new CharacterVariable();
8       char ch;
9       do { Format.printf("Input a temperature in Fahrenheit: ");
10           Format.scanf("%e", p.add(dV));
11           double fahrenheit = dV.doubleValue();
12           double celsius = (5.0/9.0)*(fahrenheit -32);
13           Format.printf("%.2f F is %.2f C\n", p.add(fahrenheit).add
                   (celsius));
14           Format.printf("Another one (Y/y)? ");
15           Format.scanf("%c", p.add(cV));
16           ch = cV.charValue();
17       }
18       while( ch == 'y' || ch == 'Y' ); {}
19  }}
```

Chapter Fourteen

Numerical Integration, Nested Loops, Methods;
Power and Energy Usage

In this chapter we explore how computers evaluate integrals numerically. We look at the same energy problem solved with Maple in Chapter 6, where numerical integration also had to be used. This chapter provides a fundamental technique for computational science and a better understanding of calculus. We also gain experience with nested loops, multiple methods, and plotting.

14.1 PROBLEM (SAME AS CHAPTER 6): POWER AND ENERGY

In Chapter 6 we modeled the electrical power use $P(t)$ over time by some simple functions. For example,

$$\text{Model 3:} \quad P_3(t) = \left(4 + \frac{t}{365} + \tfrac{1}{2}\sin\frac{\pi t}{91}\right)\left(2 + e^{-\sin 2\pi t}\right), \quad (14.1)$$

where the power is in GW (10^9 watts) and the time t is in days (the top curve in Figure 14.1). Your **problem** is to determine the total energy used over 1000 days (approximately three years) by evaluating the integral

$$E(100) = \int_0^{100} P_3(t)dt, \quad (14.2)$$

for Model 3, the one that cannot be done analytically.

   The highly oscillatory patterns in Figure 14.1 make (14.2) a challenging integral to evaluate (as demonstrated by the quite different answers obtain by casual application of Maple and Mathematica). Consequently, we want you to compare the results from the two different integration rules (trapezoid and Simpson), and to see if the value for the integral converges as we improve the approximations. There are fancier integration rules, but we leave those to the references [Press 94, CP 05].

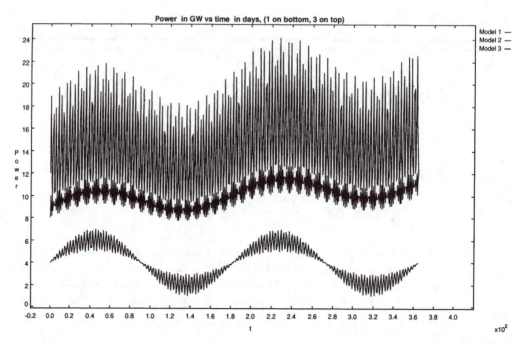

Figure 14.1 Three models of power consumption. The time is in 100 days and the power is in gigawatts.

14.2 ALGORITHMS: TRAPEZOID AND SIMPSON'S RULES

Consider Figure 14.2 showing an arbitrary function $f(x)$ in the interval $a \leq x \leq b$. The definite integral of this function,

$$I = \int_a^b f(x)dx, \tag{14.3}$$

is equal to the area under the curve. A traditional way to measure this area is to plot the integrand on a piece of graph paper and add up the number of little boxes lying below the curve. Seeing that boxes are "quadrilaterals," numerical integration is also called *numerical quadrature*, even when it gets beyond the explicit box-counting stage.

Numerical-integration techniques usually break the total interval up into small columns, as also shown in Figure 14.2, and then use different approximations to determine the area of each column. When the areas of all the columns are added together, we obtain an approximation for the integral as a weighted sum over the integrand $f(x)$ evaluated at points within the integration region:

$$I = \int_a^b f(x)dx \simeq \sum_{i=1}^N f(x_i)w_i. \tag{14.4}$$

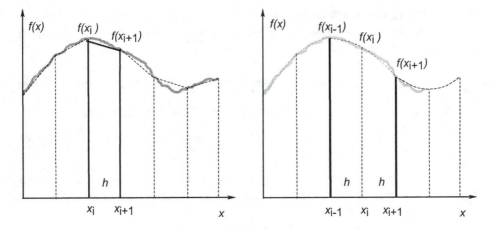

Figure 14.2 *Left:*   Straight-line sections used for the trapezoid rule. An individual trapezoid with
area $\frac{h}{2}[f(x_i) + f(x_{i+1})]$ is highlighted. *Right:*   Parabolas used in Simpson's rule (a
single parabola is fit to each pair of consecutive intervals).

Here the x_is are *integration points* and the w_is are *integration weights*. This is a
handy way to program up an integration algorithm, since we need only change the
specific values for w_i (and maybe x_i) for different rules.

As the number of integration points N is made progressively larger (nar-
rower columns used), the sum in (14.4) should become a progressively better approximation to the integral. However, if too many points are used, then round-off
error tends to accumulate and the approximation stops converging to the exact answer. Consequently, the best integration rules are those which obtain the desired
level of precision with the least number of points.

14.2.1 Trapezoid Rule

The trapezoid rule is the simplest integration algorithm. As shown on the left of
Figure 14.2, we divide the area under $f(x)$ into a series of columns each of width
h, and form trapezoids by approximating the integrand $f(x)$ by a straight line connecting the endpoints of each interval. In this case the integral is approximately
equal to the sum of the areas of the columns.[1] The approximation gets progressively better as the widths of the trapezoids are made progressively smaller, and
the integrand is better approximated by a straight line within the interval.

We first deduce an equation that gives the x value for each integration point.

---

[1]An alternative way of viewing the trapezoid rule is as forming a series of rectangles with horizontal tops, the
height of each rectangle being $(f_i + f_{i+1})/2$. If we use f_i as the height, then we have a version of the trapezoid
rule known as *Euler's rule*.

If we evaluate the function at N points, then we have $N-1$ columns (it takes two points to define one column) covering the range b–a. It follows then that the width of each interval in Figure 14.2 is

$$h = \frac{b-a}{N-1},$$

(14.5)

and the discrete x values. They are thus enumerated with the subscript i:

$$x_i = a + (i-1)h, \quad i = 1, \ N.$$

(14.6)

To calculate the area of each trapezoid in Figure 14.2, we look at the isolated column i. The area of this one trapezoid is its width times its average height:

$$\int_{x_i}^{x_i+h} f(x)dx \simeq \tfrac{1}{2}h[f(x_i) + f(x_{i+1})],$$

(14.7)

which is the same area one gets if each column is considered as a rectangle with the top passing through the midpoint of the slanted top. The total area in the integration region from a to b is the sum of the areas of all the columns:

$$\int_a^b f(x)dx \simeq \frac{h}{2}f(x_1) + hf(x_2) + \ldots hf(x_{N-1}) + \frac{h}{2}f(x_N).$$

(14.8)

Observe that because each internal point gets counted twice, it gets weighted by h, whereas the endpoints get counted just once and so are weighted by only $h/2$. In terms of the notation of our standard integration rule (14.4), the points and weights for the trapezoid rule are:

$$x_i = a + (i-1)h, \quad w_i = \left[\frac{h}{2}, h, \ldots, h, \frac{h}{2}\right], \quad i = 1, \ N.$$

(14.9)

Listing 14.1 Trap.java

```
1  //                    Integ.java:  Trapezoid-rule integration
2  public class Trap
3  {    public static final double A = 0., B =3.;         // Endpoints
4       public static final int N = 100;       // N points (!=intervals)
5       public static void main(String[] args)
6  {    double sum, h, t, w;
7       int i;
8       h = (B - A)/(N - 1);                               // Initialization
9       sum = 0.;
10      for (i=1 ; i <= N; i=i+1)
11      {   t = A + (i-1) * h;
12          if ( i==1 || i==N ) w = h/2.;          // wEnds = h/2, else h
13          else w = h;
14          sum = sum + w * t * t; }
15      System.out.println(sum);
16 }}
17 //                                    OUTPUT 9.000459136822773
```

14.2.1.1 Implementation: Trap/TrapMethods.java

In Listing 14.1 we give you the Java program `Trap.java` that uses the trapezoid rule to evaluate the integral of $\int_0^3 t^2 dt$. This is a simple class with only a `main` method. In Listing 14.2 we give the program `TrapMethods.java` that does the same integration using two methods. If you find this use of methods easy to follow, then use `TrapMethods.java`. Otherwise, start with `Trap.java` and work your way up to `TrapMethods.java`. In both cases the limits of integration A and B and the number of integration points N are declared as constant (`final`) class variables *before* the `main` method. Being `final` means that they cannot be changed by assignment statements, while being class variables means that are available to all methods within the class without having to be passed as arguments. In contrast, the variables that actually vary, `sum`, `h`, `t` and `w`, are declared in `main` and have to be passed to the methods as needed.

Listing 14.2 TrapMethods.java

```
1  //          TrapMethods.java: Trapezoid integration with methods
2  public class TrapMethods
3  {   public static final double A = 0. , B = 3.;          // Endpoints
4      public static final int N = 4;          //N points (!=intervals)
5      public static void main(String[] argv)
6  {   double sum, h, x, w;
7      int i;
8      h = (B - A)/(N - 1);                                 // Step Size
9      sum = 0.;                                            // Initialize
10     for (i=1 ; i <= N; i=i+1) {                          // Sum points
11         x = A + (i-1) * h;                               // x value
12         w = wTrap(i, h);                                 // Call method
13         sum = sum + w * f(x); }
14     System.out.println("Final sum = " + sum);
15  }
16     public static double f(double y)                     // Integrand method
17     { System.out.println("y, f(y) = "+y+", "+y*y);
18         return y*y; }
19     public static double wTrap(int i, double h)          // Weights
20     { double wLocal;
21         if ( i==1 || i==N ) wLocal= h/2.;
22         else wLocal = h;
23         return wLocal; }                                 // Returned value
24  }
```

Good programming is often modular; that is, composed of a number of small subprograms (methods) each of which accomplishes a single, well-defined task. Listing 14.2 gives `TrapMethods.java`, a version of our trapezoid-rule integration program that uses two methods. Observe how on line 13 there is the sum over the weighted integrand calling the method `f(x)`, while on line 16 that method is defined as `f(y)`. As we have said before, this is fine as long as the argument types

are the same. If you look next at line 23 you will notice that the value of the weight
w is the returned value of the function wTrap(i,h), while i and h are passed to the
method as arguments. In contrast, the value of N is used on line 21 but not passed
to the method since it is a global, class variable.

1. Compile and execute Trap.java or TrapMethods.java.
2. Modify it to determine the energy usage $\int_0^{1000} P_3(t)dt$ for Model 3.
3. Incorporate the necessary PtPlot statements in your program to produce a plot
   of Model 3's $P(t)$ for 1000 days, in steps of 0.5 days. §11.1 describes the use
   of PtPlot and gives a sample program whose commands may be incorporated
   in your program.
4. Make a crude graphical estimate (25% accuracy) of the area under your $P_3(t)$
   vs. t curve. Use 10-day column widths, and count the number of boxes in
   each column (count fractionally filled boxes as full if they are more than half
   full), or calculate the area of each trapezoid. Make your boxes big so that
   you do not have too much work to do, and make sure you have the right units
   (energy = GW-days) for your choice of boxes.
5. Compare the answer for the integral from your program using 10-day widths
   with that found from your graph. Do they agree within experimental error?

14.2.1.2 Implementation with Nested Loops

Our approximation to the area under a curve as the sum of columns with straight or
rounded tops should get more accurate as we increase the number of columns N-1.
However, if we make N too large, then round-off error accumulates to the point
where increasing N further leads to a less accurate answer. To get a feel for how
accurate our numerical integration technique is, we want to increase N and see in
what decimal place the answer changes. If the answer changes in, say, the fourth
decimal place, then we would expect the answer to be good to at least three places.

Modify a copy of TrapMethods.java so that it prints out the value of the
integral and the value for eight values in the range $25 \leq N \leq 200$. Rather than
run the program eight times, modify the program so that it loops over eight values
of N:

```
1  for (N = 25; N <= 200; N = N + 25) {          Outer loop increases N
2      ...
3      for (i = 1; i <= N; i++) {       Inner loop sums over columns i
4          ... } }
```

The procedure outlined in this code fragment uses *nested loops*, namely, one *for*
loop contained within another *for* loop. Study how for each value of the total number of points N, everything within the outer loop gets repeated, and this includes the

inner loop's i-summation over the areas of each column. Consequently, it is important to check that the program reinitializes the value of the variables used in the inner loop, in particular, h and sum. If you look at line 8 of the TrapMethods.java, you will notice that the column width h varies with the number of integration points used N. Because of that, we need to begin the *for* loop before line 8. Next notice that the summation over column areas is ended by the right brace on line 15. As a consequence, we need to end the loop over N after line 15.

14.2.2 Improved Method: Simpson's Rule

Simpson's rule for integration will also give us an algorithm of the form (14.4), but with different weights than the trapezoid rule. The integration range is again divided into equal-width columns, with the points given by (14.6). Now, as we show on the right of Figure 14.2, we approximate $f(x)$ at the top of every two columns as a parabola:

$$f(x) = \alpha x^2 + \beta x + \gamma. \qquad (14.10)$$

This is a better than using a straight line. With each parabola containing three unknown parameters, α, β, and γ, we need three values of $f(x)$ to determine them. We do that by having one parabola pass through the tops of two adjacent columns. Whereas the determination of these constants requires some algebra, the idea is simple. What is important is that because parabolas are being fit to successive pairs of columns, *Simpson's rule requires an odd number of integration points N so that there will be an even number of columns.*

14.2.2.1 Simpson's Rule Weights*

After approximating the integrand $f(x)$ by a parabola in (14.10), it is easy to calculate the area of two columns:

$$\int_{x_{i-1}}^{x_{i+1}} (\alpha x^2 + \beta x + \gamma) dx = \frac{\alpha}{3}(x_{i+1}^3 - x_{i-1}^3) + \frac{\beta}{2}(x_{i+1}^2 - x_{i-1}^2) + \gamma(x_{i+1} - x_{i-1}).$$

$$(14.11)$$

However, to make an algorithm out of this we need to express the parameters α, β, and γ in terms of the values of the integrand within the intervals. To do that we evaluate the integrand $f(x)$ at the three integration points $(x_{i-1} = 0, x_i = h, x_{i+1} = 2h)$ and solve for the parameters in terms of them:

$$\alpha = \frac{1}{h^2}\left(\frac{f(x_{i+1}) + f(x_{i-1})}{2} - f(x_i)\right), \qquad (14.12)$$

$$\beta = \frac{1}{h}\left(2f(x_i) - \frac{f(x_{i+1}) + 3f(x_{i-1})}{2}\right), \qquad (14.13)$$

$$\gamma = f(x_{i-1}). \tag{14.14}$$

This leads to the elementary Simpson rule for the area of two columns:

$$\int_{x_{i-1}}^{x_{i+1}} f(x)dx \simeq \frac{hf(x_{i-1})}{3} + \frac{4hf(x_i)}{3} + \frac{hf(x_{i+1})}{3}. \tag{14.15}$$

When we apply Simpson's rule to the entire column, the endpoints of each two-column section get counted twice, since they belong to two different pairs. Yet the first and last endpoints only get counted once:

$$\int_a^b f(x)dx \simeq \frac{h}{3}f(x_1) + \frac{4h}{3}f(x_2) + \frac{2h}{3}f(x_3) + \frac{4h}{3}f(x_4) + \cdots$$
$$+ \frac{4h}{3}f(x_{N-1}) + \frac{h}{3}f(x_N). \tag{14.16}$$

In terms of the notation of our standard integration rule (14.4), Simpson's rule is:

$$x_i = a + (i-1)h, \quad w_i = \left\{ \frac{h}{3}, \frac{4h}{3}, \frac{2h}{3}, \frac{4h}{3}, \cdots \frac{4h}{3}, \frac{h}{3} \right\}, \tag{14.17}$$

where the sequence repeatedly alternates between $4h/3$ and $2h/3$, except for the endpoints. *Remember, N must be odd!*

14.3 ASSESSMENT: WHICH RULE IS BETTER?

1. Modify your trapezoid-rule program so it prints out running values for the sum, the integrand, the weight, and the loop counter i in equation (14.4)'s notation. By "running values" we mean the value of a variable as it actually changes during the calculation. Looking at these values and checking that they change in the way expected is one of the best ways to ensure that your program is working correctly.

2. Modify a copy of your program so it evaluates the integral using Simpson's rule. Make the program smart enough to use only an odd number of points for Simpson's rule. *Hint:* You test if an integer j is even by testing if 2 * (j/2) = j or if j % 2 = 0. The first test takes advantage of the fact that integer arithmetic rounds *down*, while the second test uses a Java method to determine if the remainder is 0 after division by 2.

3. The numerical approximation for integration should improve as the number of points N increases. Make a table or plot showing the level of accuracy obtained for the integral for various numbers of points:

N-1	I (trapezoid)	I (Simpson)
8	-	-
⋮		
512	-	-

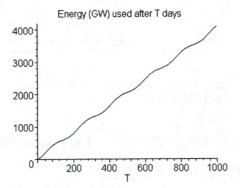

Figure 14.3 Energy consumption as a function of time for model 1 computed with Maple.

4. Make a plot of the energy consumption *versus* time, like that in Figure 14.3, only here for Model 3. How does that compare to the Maple results?

14.4 KEY WORDS AND CONCEPTS

integration	integration points	integration weights	modular programs
nested loops	quadrature	Simpson's rule	trapezoid rule

1. Explain succinctly the difference between the trapezoid and Simpson rules.
2. Is a parabola or a straight line a better approximation for a function?

14.5 SUPPLEMENTARY EXERCISES

1. You are given nonrepeated weights of 1, 2, 4, 8, 16, and 32 kg. Your boss claims that you should be able to use these six weights to weigh any rice sack weighing an integer number of kilograms between 1 and 63. For instance, $63 = 1 + 2 + 4 + 8 + 16 + 32$. Write a program to check if the claim is true. The program should write the sack weight and the weights used.
2. As a more challenging version of the above problem, imagine that you are given a sack of rice of undermined integer weight less than 64 kg. Write a program that determines the sack's weight and the individual weights you used to determine it.
3. The Chinese scholar Sun Tsu in the year 400 BCE found solutions to the problem:

> find an integer such that if divided by 3 the residue is 2, if divided by 5 the residue is 3, and if divided by 7 the residue is 2.

Write a program that finds the numbers less that 500 that satisfy these three conditions.

(These three problems come via courtesy of M. Páez.)

Chapter Fifteen

Differential Equations with Java and Maple;

Projectile Motion with Drag*

In this chapter we solve for projectile motion with drag by solving simultaneous, second-order ordinary differential equations (ODEs) using both Java and Maple. This is a fairly realistic problem that is often missing from undergraduate education, but whose solution looks familiar to students. The ODE solver used in our Java program is simple, useful for other problems as well, and provides some insight into numerical differentiation. The Maple solution, however, gets to be surprisingly involved at times due to the equations being both second-order and coupled, and having a solution that cannot be plotted simply. A comparison of the two approaches is quite educational. We have marked this chapter as optional, in part because there are no new materials that are used elsewhere, and in part because some students may not yet be familiar with differential equations. However the subject matter is important for many fields, and it does provide a good balance to the solution of a partial differential equation studied in Chapter 20.

15.1 PROBLEM: PROJECTILE MOTION WITH DRAG

We want to determine if the inclusion of air resistance in projectile motion leads to trajectories that are much steeper at their ends than their beginnings (golf balls that appear to drop out of the sky). We saw in Chapter 12, "Flow Control via Logic," that frictionless projectile trajectories are parabolas, symmetric about their midpoints, and so do not describe balls dropping out of the sky.

In Figure 12.1 we showed trajectories of a projectile fired from a cannon without friction (solid curve) as well as one with air resistance or drag included (dashed curve). The projectile is fired at time $t = 0$ with velocity V_0 at an angle θ relative to the horizon. It remains in the air for a total or hang time $t = T$ and hits the ground a horizontal distance or range $x = R$ away from the origin, with all these quantities apparently changing if air resistance is included. The problem solution requires us to write a program that predicts or *simulates* these different trajectories for a given set of initial conditions.

15.2 MODEL: VELOCITY-DEPENDENT DRAG

The basic physics behind this problem is Newton's second law of motion, which relates force, mass, and acceleration:

$$\mathbf{F} = m\mathbf{a} = m\frac{d^2\mathbf{x(t)}}{dt^2}, \tag{15.1}$$

where the bold symbols indicate vector quantities. This is a second-order ordinary differential equation. A differential equation because it contains a derivative; an ordinary derivative because there is only one independent variable and so no partial derivatives (no ∂), the time t; and second-order because it is a second derivative. Because the equation of motion involves vectors, there are separate differential equations for the x and y components of each vector:

$$\frac{d^2x}{dt^2} = \frac{1}{m}F_x^f, \qquad \frac{d^2y}{dt^2} = \frac{1}{m}(F_y^f - mg), \tag{15.2}$$

where we have divided through by the mass, switched the derivative to the LHS (a standard form), and substituted components for the frictional force $\mathbf{F}^f$ and the gravitational force.

The force of friction $\mathbf{F}_f$ is not a basic force of nature with a definite form for all situations. Indeed, it is just an approximate description of the physics of viscous flow, with no one expression being accurate for all velocities. We know it always opposes motion, which means it is in a direction opposite to that of the velocity. The simplest model, and the one often studied in texts [M&T 88], assumes that the force of air resistance is proportional to some power n of the projectile's speed:

$$\mathbf{F}^f = -k\,m\,|v|^n\,\frac{\mathbf{v}}{|v_x|}. \tag{15.3}$$

The $\mathbf{v}/|v|$ term ensures that the frictional force changes direction, to keep opposing motion, when the velocity changes sign. If $n = 1$, or any odd power, then we may have the frictional force proportional to $-v^n$ and get the correct sign. However, if n is even, then we have to use these absolute values to ensure the correct sign. Though a frictional force proportional to a power of the velocity is a more accurate description than a constant force, it is still a simplification. Indeed, physical measurements indicate the power n appears to change with velocity, and so the most accurate model would be a numerical one that uses the empirical velocity dependence $n(v)$.

With a simple power-law dependence, the equations of motion take the form:[1]

$$\frac{d^2x}{dt^2} = -k\,v_x^n\,\frac{v_x}{|v_x|}, \qquad\qquad \frac{d^2y}{dt^2} = -g - k\,v_y^n\,\frac{v_y}{|v_y|}. \qquad (15.4)$$

We shall consider three values for n, each of which represents a different model for the air resistance: (1) $n = 1$ for low velocities; (2) $n = \frac{3}{2}$, for medium velocities; and (3) $n = 2$ for high velocities. For comparison, we will compare these solutions with air resistance to the analytic results for the frictionless case:

$$x(t) = v_{0,x}t, \qquad\qquad y(t) = v_{0,y}t - \frac{1}{2}gt^2, \qquad (15.5)$$

$$v_x(t) = v_{x,0}, \qquad\qquad v_y(t) = v_{y,0} - gt. \qquad (15.6)$$

15.3 ALGORITHM: NUMERICAL DIFFERENTIATION

In Chapter 5, "Solving Equations, Differentiation," we used Maple to explore the accuracy of numerical differentiation. We now apply those techniques in the Java solution of differential equations. Most calculus courses start off with the definition of the derivative as:

$$\frac{df(x)}{dx} \stackrel{\text{def}}{=} \lim_{h \to 0} \frac{f(x+h) - f(x)}{h}. \qquad (15.7)$$

It is a challenge to apply this definition on a computer, because its finite word length causes the numerator to fluctuate between 0 and round-off error as the denominator approaches zero. A simple and effective solution is to make h small but not zero:

$$\frac{df(x)}{dx} \simeq \frac{f(x+h) - f(x)}{h}. \qquad (15.8)$$

Equation (15.8), known as the *forward-difference* rule, is not the most accurate approximation [CP 05], but it will suffice.

15.4 MATH: SOLVING DIFFERENTIAL EQUATIONS

When air resistance is present, the force on the projectile depends upon the value of the velocity, which means that the acceleration is not constant. This makes an analytic solution to the differential equation difficult, but it is not a challenge to a numerical solution. The trick is to figure out an approximation that takes the solution at the initial time 0 and advances it a small amount Δt. Because Δt is small, it is not hard to find an approximate solution. One then takes the solution so found and uses it as the new "initial conditions" to provide the solution at time $2\Delta t$. The process is continued until the solution at the desired time is found. With $[x(t = 0),\ y(t = 0)]$ and $[v_x(t = 0),\ v_y(t = 0)]$ as the initial conditions, we have

---

[1]For more realistic models used for friction, these equations may become coupled, e.g., because $(V^2)_x \neq (V_x)^2$. For simplicity, we ignore the coupling of the equations, although the technique for the numerical solution remains unchanged.

all the information we need to start the solution and will keep it going as long as we like.

The simplest algorithm for solving differential equations is a variation of *Euler's rule*. It is based on the fact that for a sufficiently short time interval Δt, we may assume that the acceleration is constant and use the equations for constant acceleration from elementary physics to advance the velocity and position for a short time from t to $t + \Delta t$:

$$x(t + \Delta t) \simeq x(t) + v_x \Delta t + \frac{1}{2} a_x (\Delta t)^2, \quad v_x(t + \Delta t) \simeq v_x(t) + a_x(t) \Delta t. \quad (15.9)$$

Here $a_x(t)$ is the variable acceleration at time t. Likewise, there are similar equations for y and v_y. To make the algorithm simpler, we assume that Δt is so small that the terms quadratic in Δt are negligible with respect to the terms linear in Δt:

$$x(t + \Delta t) \simeq x(t) + v_x \Delta t, \qquad v_x(t + \Delta t) \simeq v_x(t) + a_x(t) \Delta t. \quad (15.10)$$

This means that as long as we keep the time step Δt small, we may ignore the acceleration term in (15.9). The acceleration still affects the solution via (15.10), but it does so by changing the velocity, which, in turn, changes the position. For this simple method to work, we must choose small values of Δt. As a rule of thumb, if the physical system under study has a characteristic time or period of T, then we would start with $\Delta t \simeq T/100$ and then see the effect of decreasing it. A higher-order technique might require fewer steps but use more complicated formulas.

As our example, we take the simple $n = 1$ law for air resistance:

$$\frac{d^2 x}{dt^2} = -k v_x, \qquad \frac{d^2 y}{dt^2} = -g - k v_y. \qquad (15.11)$$

The terms on the right-hand sides of these equations are the accelerations we need for the algorithm. The algorithm starts with the given initial position (the origin) and the velocities $v_{x,0}$, $v_{y,0}$, and then steps through many time steps. We label the time steps with the index $i = 1 \ldots N$. For each time step, the position and velocity will be updated according to the algorithm:

$$x^{i+1} = x^i + v_x^i \, \Delta t, \qquad\qquad y^{i+1} = y^i + v_y^i \, \Delta t, \qquad (15.12)$$

$$v_x^{i+1} = v_x^i - k \, v_x \, \Delta t, \qquad v_y^{i+1} = v_y^i - k \, v_y \, \Delta t - g \, \Delta t. \quad (15.13)$$

The acceleration due to gravity enters only for the y component of velocity, since gravity acts only in the y direction. And as we have said, the forces act by directly changing the velocity, but change the position only indirectly through the changes in velocity.

15.4.1 Implementation: ProjectileAir.java

The implementation of the algorithm is given in the code `ProjectileAir.java` shown in Listing 15.1. The class `ProjectileAir` contains:

1. a `main` method that directs the computation;
2. a `plotNumeric` method that solves the equations of motion numerically and plots the results by calling the `PtPlot` package; and
3. a `plotAnalytic` method that calls the `PtPlot` package to plot the analytic solution for the frictionless case.

Examine how the `PtPlot` package is imported in line 2, before the class `ProjectileAir` is declared. On lines 4 and 5, after the class declaration but before any method declaration, the initial parameters for the problem are set as `final` variables, namely, constants that cannot be modified by any method. Because they are declared as `static class variables`, they will be accessible to all methods within the class, without having to give them as explicit arguments to the methods. However, methods in other classes do not have access to these static class variables.

Observe how on line 10 of `ProjectileAir`, we calculate the hang time T, height H, and range R for a *frictionless* projectile. These are useful to compare with the results from the simulation including air resistance. (If air resistance does not lead to a reduction in all three quantities, then we would suspect our simulation.) A plot object is created and labeled on lines 12–15. After that, data points are added to the plot object using the object-oriented notation `myPlot.addPoint`. The plot is drawn on your screen via the creation of a `PlotApplication` on line 19, and should look like the trajectory in Figure 12.1.

This program makes an indirect use of methods that is worthwhile noting. Normally a method is like a function that takes many arguments but returns only a single value for the function. Here we are repeatedly calling a method that keeps adding data points to an object without ever returning a value to the calling program. As discussed in Chapter 17, the exception to the one-value-returned rule occurs when an object or abstract data type (something with multiple parts) is used as an argument to a method. Because objects have multiple parts they are called *by reference* and not *by value*, which means that a reference to the location in memory where the object resides is passed to the method and not the value of different parts of the object. On account of this, the method may change the values of the different parts of the object (the plot in our case) as it resides in memory, as long as it does not change the location in memory where the object resides.

Observe next how the numerical algorithm used to solve the differential equation is contained in the method `plotNumeric` on line 21. It decides on the value of the time step `dt` by taking the total hang time for frictionless flight and dividing it by the input parameter N. It follows then that *you make the time step* dt *small by making the number of time steps* N *large.* We give some instructions on how to do that in the "Assessment" section. The rest of the method steps through time in small steps, uses Euler's algorithm (15.10) to advance the position and velocity vector, and then adds points to the plot for each time step.

The plotAnalytic method on line 39 is similar to the plotNumeric method, in that it steps through time in small steps and add points to the plot for each time step. However, it computes the position and velocity vectors using the analytic expressions (15.5) for frictionless flight.

15.5 ASSESSMENT: BALLS FALLING OUT OF THE SKY?

1. Compile and run ProjectileAir and check that you get a plot similar to that in Figure 12.1. If your program is not plotting, then you may need to review some of the materials on using PtPlot in Chapter 11, "Visualization with Java."
2. In general, it is not be possible to compare analytic and numerical results to realistic problems, because analytic expressions do not exist. However, we do know the analytic expressions (15.5) for the frictionless case, and we may turn friction off in our numerical algorithm and then compare the two. This is not a guarantee that we have handled friction correctly, yet it is a guarantee that we have something wrong if the comparison fails. Add some lines of code to ProjectileAir.java that calls the plotNumeric method a second time, this time with the friction coefficient $k = 0$.
3. We have deliberately given you a program in which the total number of time steps N is rather *small*, and, inversely, the time step dt is rather *large*. Consequently, the results from the given program will be of low precision. Repeat the calculation with ever-increasing values for N, until you cannot tell the difference on the plot between the numeric and the analytic results for frictionless flight.
4. Once the results look good to you, determine the level of precision of the calculation by comparing the actual numbers for the analytic and the numerical calculations. If necessary, increase N until the relative difference is less than 1%. Use this value of N for future computations.
5. Add lines to the program so that it prints out and plots up the components of the velocity as a function of time.
6. Study your plots of the velocity components *versus* time and draw a line on them that appears to be the terminal velocity for each.
7. Print out several plots showing the effect of air resistance for different initial angles θ. For each, determine the value of R, T, and H, and compare the three with the corresponding values for frictionless flight. All three should decrease.
8. We know that for frictionless flight, the maximum range R occurs for $\theta =$

Listing 15.1 ProjectileAir.java

```
1  //              ProjectileAir.java:    projectile motion with PtPlot
2  import ptolemy.plot.*;
3  public class ProjectileAir {
4  static final double v0 = 22., angle = 34., g = 9.8, kf=0.8;
5  static final int N = 25;                        // Static class variables
6    public static void main(String[] args)
7  { double v0x,v0y, T, H, R;
8    v0x = v0 * Math.cos(angle*Math.PI/180.);
9    v0y = v0 * Math.sin(angle*Math.PI/180.);
10   T = 2*v0y/g;           H = v0y*v0y/(2*g);           R = 2*v0x*v0y/g;
11   System.out.println("Frictionless T, H, R = " +T+", "+H+", " +R);
12   Plot myPlot = new Plot();                      // Create Plot object
13   myPlot.setTitle("Projectile without/with Air Resistance");
14   myPlot.setXLabel("x");
15   myPlot.setYLabel("y");
16   myPlot.setXRange(-R/20, R);
17   plotAnalytic (myPlot, 0);                       // No friction, analytic
18   plotNumeric  (myPlot, 2, kf);                     // Friction, numeric
19   PlotApplication app = new PlotApplication(myPlot);     // Display
20  }                                          //Plot, friction, numeric
21   public static void plotNumeric (Plot myPlot, int set, double k)
22  { double x, y, vx, vy, dt;
23    vx = v0 * Math.cos(angle*Math.PI/180.);
24    vy = v0 * Math.sin(angle*Math.PI/180.);
25    x = 0;      y = 0;
26    dt = 2 * vy / g / N;
27    for (int i = 0; i<N; i=i+1)
28    { vx = vx -k * vx * dt;
29      vy = vy - g * dt - k * vy * dt;
30      x = x + vx * dt;
31      y = y + vy * dt;
32      myPlot.addPoint(set, x, y, true);
33      System.out.println("x = " + x   + " y = " + y); }
34      myPlot.addPoint(set, x, y, true);
35  }                                     // End plotNumeric, start analytic
36   public static void plotAnalytic (Plot myPlot, int set)      //No f
37  { double x, y, v0x, v0y, dt, t;
38    v0x = v0 * Math.cos(angle*Math.PI/180.);
39    v0y = v0 * Math.sin(angle*Math.PI/180.);
40    dt = 2 * v0y / g /N;
41    for (int i = 0; i<N; i=i+1)
42    { t = i * dt;
43      x = v0x * t;
44      y = v0y * t - g * t * t / 2.;
45      myPlot.addPoint(set, x, y, true);
46      System.out.println("Frictionless x = " +x+" y = " + y); }
47  } }                                    //End plotAnalytic, End class
```

$45°$, and that there is the same range for trajectories with θ or $90° - \theta$ (for example, for $30°$ and $60°$). Investigate how both these statements change when drag is included. In other words, if you want to hit your golf ball with a maximum range, should you hit it at an angle that is greater than or less than $45°$?

9. Investigate and describe how the range R varies with initial velocity v_0 for a fixed value of θ. Explain the results you obtain (does it go further, for example?).

10. Up until this point you have looked at results for the model of friction (15.3) with $n = 1$. This corresponds to a low-velocity model. Modify Projectile.java to investigate $n = 2$, (high-velocity model) and $n = 3/2$ (medium-velocity model). To make a realistic comparison, adjust the value of k for the latter two cases such that the initial force of friction, kV_0^n, is the same for all three cases.

15.5.1 Improved Algorithm: Verlet*

In developing the Euler integration algorithm (15.10), we ignored the direct affect of the acceleration on the position, as is present in (15.9). We now want to modify the algorithm so that it includes the acceleration term directly in the solution for $x(t + \Delta t)$. An approach that is nearly as simple as Euler yet appears to work very well is called the *Verlet algorithm*. It uses second-order terms for x_n, but only first-order ones for v_n:

$$x_{n+1} = x_n + v_n \Delta t + \frac{1}{2} a_n (\Delta t)^2, \qquad v_{n+1} = v_n + \frac{1}{2}(a_{n+1} + a_n)\Delta t. \quad (15.14)$$

We see that while the algorithm for the velocity is only first-order in Δt, it makes up for this somewhat by using the average acceleration over the time interval and not just its value at the beginning of the interval. The only problem with this method is that it is not fully self-contained; to determine v_{n+1} you first have to use the Euler method to obtain a_{n+1}.

Exercise: Implement the Verlet algorithm and compare the number of steps needed to obtain the three-place precision with both the Euler and Verlet methods. (The better algorithm should use fewer steps.) ♠

15.6 MAPLE: DIFFERENTIAL-EQUATION TOOLS

Maple is competent at finding solutions to most any differential equation that you give it. It many cases it can find an analytic solution with no help from you, while in other cases you may have to give it some hints based on your understanding of the mathematics of your equation. If all else fails, or if all you want is a plot of the solution, ask Maple to solve the differential equation numerically.

In this section we solve the projectile-with-drag problem in Maple. Because we have already done this with Java, it affords you the opportunity to compare the two approaches to the same problem. You should decide for yourself; we find the Java solution easier and faster.

Warning: Although the commands we have given here appear to work properly on various versions of Maple, we have noted that the *order* in which Maple returns the solution changes with different versions. To cite an instance, $[y(t), x(t)]$ in one case and $[x(t), y(t)]$ in another. Consequently, you may have to reverse the order of some of the arguments in the plotting commands given below.

We start by repeating the differential equations for projectile motion in a uniform gravitational field with no friction, and their solution:

$$\frac{d^2}{dt^2}\, x(t) = 0, \qquad \frac{d^2}{dt^2}\, y(t) = -g, \qquad\qquad (15.15)$$

$$x(t) = v_{o,x}\, t, \qquad y(t) = -g\, t^2 + v_{o,y}\, t. \qquad\qquad (15.16)$$

where we have assumed $x(0) = y(0) = 0$, and used the symbols $v_{o,x}$ and $v_{o,y}$ to denote the x and y components of the initial velocity v_0. We start by solving these equations with Maple and seeing if we get these same solutions. To start simply, first we solve for just the y motion, and then for the simultaneous x and y motions. Then we add in air resistance. This careful approach to a final solution is standard in scientific problem solving.

To keep from repeatedly entering complicated expressions, we give our equations names and enter the names rather than long expressions. We write our differential equations using the `diff` command, and later show how to do it with the D operator (see Chapter 5 for our discussion of derivatives). Yet even if `diff` is used for the equations, D *must* be used for the initial conditions.

There are various ways to enter differential equations, and we demonstrate several of them (all of which give the same answer of course). We use the variables `diff_eq` and `diff_eq2` for two different representations of the equation for the y component of a projectile's motion, and solve each with the `dsolve` command:

```
> restart;      with(DEtools):                                    # Initialize
> Vy := diff(y(t), t);                                # Vy = expression for velocity
```

$$Vy := \frac{d}{dt}\, y(t)$$

```
> diff_eq := diff(Vy, t) = - g;        diff_eq := diff(diff(y(t),t),t) = - g;
> diff_eq := diff(y(t), t, t) = - g;        diff_eq := diff(y(t), t$2) = - g;
> diff_eq := diff(y(t), t$2) + g;                      # Multiple forms, same result
```

$$\textit{diff\_eq} := \frac{d^2}{dt^2}\, y(t) = -g$$

Two simpler ways of entering the same differential equation is with the D operator:

```
> diff_eq2 := (D2)(y)(t) = -g;       diff_eq2 := D(D(y))(t) = -g;       # With D
```

$$diff\_eq2 := (D^{(2)})(y)(t) = -g$$

We solve this equation with the `dsolve`. Even though the command accepts a number of arguments, some of which direct Maple along specified paths for solutions, we leave it all up to Maple:

```
> dsolve(diff_eq);                                                      # Solve ODE with dsolve
```

$$y(t) = -\frac{g\,t^2}{2} + \_C1\,t + \_C2$$

We see that we do indeed get the general solution with integration constants $\_C1$ and $\_C2$ to be determined by the initial conditions (the leading underscores indicate that the computer has chosen these names).

   We incorporate the initial conditions into the solution by setting $\_C1 = Vy0$ and $\_C2 = 0$, or by giving `dsolve` the initial conditions along with the equations and letting it do all the work for us:

```
> init_con := y(0) = 0,       D(y)(0) = Vyo ;                           # Initial conditions
> dsolve( {diff_eq2, init_con}, y(t) );
```

$$init\_con := y(0) = 0, \qquad D(y)(0) = Vyo$$
$$y(t) = -g\,t^2/2 + Vyo\,t$$

This looks great and is the right answer, yet we have had to be careful. First, even if the differential equation is entered with `diff`, the initial conditions *must* be entered with the D. Second, because we have a second-order ODE, there are two initial conditions (displacement and velocity), and we group them as the set `init_con`, with items separated by a comma, but order irrelevant.

   As a check of the solution, we take the derivative of $y(t)$ to obtain an expression for the velocity, and then take the derivative of the velocity to see if we get the acceleration back. To do this, we need to keep in mind that Maple returns an expression in the form of an equation for $y(t)$ as the solution. Even though the expression looks like a function, it is not. Even though it is possible to transform $y(t)$ into a function, the procedure is not straightforward. (One needs to first define a procedure that contains the solution, and then create a function that calls the procedure). We take a simpler approach in which we define the expression `soltn` to contain the solution, and then manipulate `soltn`:

```
> soltn := dsolve( {diff_eq2, init_con}, y(t) );    # Solve ODE with initial conditions
> diff( soltn, t );       diff( soltn, t, t );                          # 1st, 2nd derivatives
```

$$soltn := y(t) = -\frac{1}{2}\,g\,t^2 + Vyo\,t$$

$$\frac{d}{dt}\,\mathrm{y}(t) = -g\,t + Vyo \qquad\qquad \frac{d^2}{dt^2}\,\mathrm{y}(t) = -g$$

15.6.1 Extract Right-Hand Side: rhs

In order to plot the solution, all parameters must be assigned numerical values. In addition, since the expression for the solution is an equation with $y(t)$ on the LHS, we must use Maple's rhs() function to extract the RHS. We extract the velocity and acceleration from the solutions by taking time derivatives:

```
> g := 9.8;        Vyo := 20;
```
$$g := 9.8 \qquad\qquad Vyo := 20$$

```
> plot( rhs(soltn), t = 0..4.2, title = 'y(t) vs t' );         # y(t), left plot
> plot( rhs(diff(soltn, t)), t = 0..5, title = 'v(t) vs t' );  # Vy(t), right plot
> plot( rhs(diff(soltn, t, t) ), t = 0..5, title = 'a(t) vs t' ); # a, right plot
```

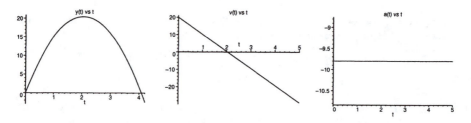

Check over how the velocity starts off positive and then gets more and more negative, and that the acceleration is constant at $g = 9.8$ in the negative y direction.

15.6.2 Second-Order ODE with Plot

Maple has the DEplot command that both solves a differential equation and plots up the solutions. As before, while our solution was analytic and contained initial conditions as parameters, to plot a graph we need to have a completely numeric answer, and so we must assign values to all parameters. The value of the parameter g is assigned first, and the values of the initial conditions are placed within the DEplot command:

```
> restart:     with(DEtools):                              # Initialize, load DEplot
> diff_eq := diff( y(t), t, t ) = - g ;      g := 9.8;              # Enter ODE
```
$$diff\_eq := \frac{d^2}{dt^2}\,\mathrm{y}(t) = -g \qquad g := 9.8$$

```
> DEplot( diff_eq, y(t), t = -0..4.2, [[y(0)=0,D(y)(0)=20 ]] );    # [init conds]
```

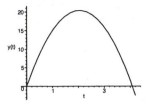

Observe how we include the initial conditions as a *list* for the third argument.

15.6.3 System of ODEs

When the systems in an environment depend on each other, we usually have simultaneous differential equations to solve. As a case in point, in our projectile
problem we have simultaneous equations for the x and y motions (we solved only
for the y motion so far). The same commands and procedures are used for a *set* of
equations as for a single equation. The additional step is to define the variable that
gave the equation to solve to now be a set of equations ("set" because the order
does not matter):

```
> diff_eqs := ( D@@2 ) (y)(t) = -g,    (D@@2) (x)(t) = 0;
```

$$diff\_eqs := (\mathrm{D}^{(2)})(y)(t) = -g, \qquad (\mathrm{D}^{(2)})(x)(t) = 0$$

Here we use D to define the equations, although diff would do. The solution
is obtained by specifying the set of equations {diff_eqs} as the first argument to
dsolve, and the set {y(t), x(t)}, the solution we desire, as the second argument:

```
> dsolve( {diff_eqs}, {y(t), x(t)} );          # Maple will generate integration constants
```

$$\{y(t) = -\frac{g\,t^2}{2} + \_C3\,t + \_C4 \qquad x(t) = \_C1\,t + \_C2\}$$

We see that Maple does find the expected forms of the solution (15.16), with the
constants still to be determined. As before, we include the initial conditions into
the set of equations we give as the first argument to dsolve, this time with four
conditions:

```
> init_cons := y(0)=0,    D(y)(0)=Vyo,    x(0)=0,    D(x)(0)=Vxo ;
```

$$init\_cons := y(0) = 0, \qquad D(y)(0) = Vyo, x(0) = 0, \qquad D(x)(0) = Vxo$$

```
> dsolve( {diff_eqs, init_cons}, {y(t), x(t)} );          # Includes initial condition
```

$$\{y(t) = -\frac{1}{2}g\,t^2 + Vyo\,t, x(t) = Vxo\,t\}$$

Indeed, we get the familiar solutions as a set within braces. If we want numeric values for x and y, we must assign numeric values to the parameters.

15.7 MAPLE SOLUTION: DRAG $\propto$ VELOCITY

We now return to our projectile-with-drag problem, applying some of the Maple tools we have just learned. If the frictional force is proportional to the first power of the velocity, the equations to solve are:

$$\frac{d^2x}{dt^2} = -k\,v_x, \qquad\qquad \frac{d^2y}{dt^2} = -g - k\,v_y. \qquad (15.17)$$

Because the x and y motions are independent, there is no mixing of the x motion into the y equations, and vice versa, and we could actually solve each equation separately. However, simultaneous equations generally are coupled, and we will solve them as if they were. We enter the equations into dsolve as a *set* with elements separated by commas. We use a set because order does not matter, and later we will place brackets around the elements. We define a variable diff_eqs as the set of equations, and then solve the set. Because the equations involve the second derivatives, there will be a diff with respect to t$2 and t:

```
> diff_eqs := diff( x(t), t$2 ) = -k * diff( x(t), t),
     diff( y(t), t$2) = -g -k * diff( y(t), t );
```

$$diff\_eqs := \frac{d^2}{dt^2}\,\mathrm{x}(t) = -k\left(\frac{d}{dt}\mathrm{x}(t)\right), \qquad \frac{d^2}{dt^2}\,\mathrm{y}(t) = -g - k\left(\frac{d}{dt}\mathrm{y}(t)\right)$$

Observe that we must indicate the t dependence of x and y as $x(t)$ and $y(t)$, because otherwise Maple would treat them as constants whose derivatives vanish.

Now we see if Maple is smart enough to find an analytic solution. We enter the set of equations as the first argument to dsolve with braces around diff_eqs to indicate that it is a set:

```
> dsolve({diff_eqs});                              # Solve differential equation
```

$$\{\mathrm{x}(t) = \_C3 + \_C4\,e^{(-k\,t)}, \qquad \mathrm{y}(t) = -\frac{\_C1\,e^{(-k\,t)} + g\,t - \_C2\,k}{k}\}$$

We see that Maple returns a set of solutions with four constants. Good, we are on our way. Rather than solving for the constants in terms of the initial conditions, we define a set of initial conditions, and include them as a second argument to dsolve. We specify initial velocities as the initial values for the first derivatives, and use the D() operator (diff does not work for initial conditions):

```
> InitConds := x(0) = 0,      D(x)(0) = Vox,     y(0) = 0,     D(y)(0) = Voy;
> soltn := dsolve( {diff_eqs,InitConds} );
```

$$InitConds := \mathrm{x}(0) = 0, \qquad \mathrm{D}(x)(0) = Vox, \qquad \mathrm{y}(0) = 0, \qquad \mathrm{D}(y)(0) = Voy$$

$$soltn := \left\{ x(t) = \frac{Vox}{k} - \frac{Vox\, e^{(-kt)}}{k}, \quad y(t) = -\frac{\frac{(g+Voy\,k)\, e^{(-kt)}}{k} + gt - \frac{g+Voy\,k}{k}}{k} \right\}$$

This appears to be the analytic solution we want, and it is worth investigating its properties. Yet before we do that, we need to see if the velocities exhibit reasonable behaviors, that is, if they attain a terminal speed and then stop increasing. We do that by taking the derivative of our solution:

```
> diff(soltn,t);                          # Take derivative of y(t) to get velocity
> diff(y(t),t) = -(-(g+Voy*k)*exp(-k*t)+g)/k};
```

$$\left\{ \frac{d}{dt} x(t) = Vox\, e^{(-kt)}, \qquad \frac{d}{dt} y(t) = -\frac{-(g+Voy\,k)\, e^{(-kt)} + g}{k} \right\}$$

Indeed, we see that the x component of velocity decreases exponentially as a function of time from its initial value and approaches zero for long times. This is a consequence of the frictional force always opposing the velocity in the x direction, but with no other force present to increase the velocity in the x direction. In contrast, the y velocity approaches a terminal value $-g/k$ for long times. This is a consequence of the force of gravity $F = -mg$ exactly balancing the frictional force $F = mkv$ when $v = -g/k$:

```
> Vox := 22*cos(Pi/4);    Voy := 22*sin(Pi/4);    := 9.8;    k := 1.0;
```

$$Vox := 11\sqrt{2} \qquad Voy := 11\sqrt{2} \qquad g := 9.8 \qquad k := 1.0$$

Once the parameters are assigned, we check the solution:

```
> soltn;
```

$$\{x(t) = 11.0000\sqrt{2} - 11.0000\sqrt{2}\, e^{(-1.0t)},$$
$$y(t) = -1.00000\,(9.8 + 11.0\sqrt{2})\, e^{(-1.0t)} - 9.80000\,t + 9.80000 + 11.0000\sqrt{2}\}$$

We see our solution in its numeric form, as a set with a comma separating the equation for $x(t)$ from that of $y(t)$. Though they make the equations hard to read, the zeros after the decimal point indicate the Maple's level of precision for this floating-point calculation (it became floating point when we made g and k floating-point numbers).

15.8 EXTRACT OPERANDS

To plot up the results we need to extract the RHSs of both equations. For a simple expression this was done with the rhs command. Now that soltn is a set of equations, we need to indicate which equation it is in the set that we want the RHS of. For this purpose Maple has the op command to extract *operands* (pieces) from an expression. Consequently, rhs(x) is equivalent to op(2, x). First we test that we know how to extract each equation, and then we take RHSs:

> op(1,soltn);   op(2,soltn);   # Extract operand 1, 2 from soltn

$$x(t) = 11.000 \sqrt{2} - 11.0000 \sqrt{2}\, e^{(-1.0t)}$$
$$y(t) = -1.00000\,(9.8 + 11.0\sqrt{2})\, e^{(-1.0t)} - 9.800000\, t + 9.80000 + 11.0000\sqrt{2}$$

Now that we have a way to separate out each equation, we take the RHSs of each:

> rhs(op(1,soltn));   rhs(op(2,soltn));   # Extract RHSs of x(t), y(t) solution

$$11.00000000 \sqrt{2} - 11.00000000 \sqrt{2}\, e^{(-1.0t)}$$
$$-1.00000\,(9.8 + 11.0\sqrt{2})\, e^{(-1.0t)} - 9.80000\, t + 9.80000 + 11.0000\sqrt{2}$$

At last we have what we need to make our plots. We plot the position and velocity (time derivative) by entering lists (in square brackets) as the first argument to the plot command (a list because order matters for the plot):

> plot([rhs(op(1,soltn)), rhs(op(2,soltn))], t = 0..3, legend = ['x(t)', 'y(t)']);
> plot([diff(rhs(op(1, soltn)), t), diff(rhs(op(2, soltn)), t)],
        t = 0..3, legend = ['Vx(t)', 'Vy(t)']);

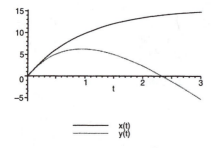

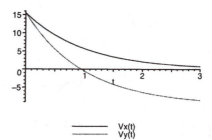

These plots show an initial linear increase of $x(t)$ with time t, as expected for constant velocity. However, as time increases, the action of the frictional force in the x direction is to keep decreasing V_x until, for large time, V_x vanishes (except that the ground gets in the way). Then the x motion ceases and x remains constant. In turn, $y(t)$ shows a parabolic dependence on time initially, as expected for uniform acceleration, but only a linear increase for later times. The linear increase of y with time indicates that v_y has attained its terminal value as the drag force exactly balances that of gravity. As expected from the analytic expressions, and our discussion in the previous paragraph, we see that V_x approaches zero and V_y approaches a constant value for large times (or would if the ground did not get in the way).

The usual plot of a trajectory is a plot of $y(t)$ as the ordinate *versus* $x(t)$ as the abscissa. As you will recall from our discussion of visualization in Chapter 4, this type of plot is known as a *parametric plot*. A parametric plot is constructed by moving the time limits into the list that is used as the first argument (the list contains $\{x(t), y(t)\}$ and the range of t):

```
> plot([rhs(op(1, soltn)), rhs(op(2, soltn)), t = 0..3 ], labels=['x(t)', 'y(t)']);
```

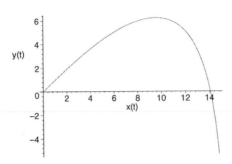

We see a trajectory that is much distorted from the symmetric parabola that occurs for frictionless flight, and looks similar to that computed with Java and shown in Figure 12.1. In fact, this looks very much like the type of trajectory seen for a golf ball or a baseball in which the ball rises at first and then appears to "drop out of the sky" at the end of its trajectory.

15.8.1 Solution for R and T

We now want to determine if we can solve for the range R and hang time T for the general projectile-with-friction problem. We start by again placing our solution in symbolic form:

```
> diff_eqs := diff(x(t), t$) =                          # DE for x, y motion
       -k * diff(x(t), t),      diff(y(t), t$) = -g -k * diff(y(t), t);
```

$$diff\_eqs := \frac{d^2}{dt^2}x(t) = -k\left(\frac{d}{dt}x(t)\right) \qquad \frac{d^2}{dt^2}y(t) = -g - k\left(\frac{d}{dt}y(t)\right)$$

```
> InitConds := x(0) = 0, D(x)(0) = Vox, y(0) = 0, D(y)(0) = Voy;
```

$$InitConds := x(0) = 0, \ D(x)(0) = Vox, \ y(0) = 0, \ D(y)(0) = Voy$$

```
> soltn := dsolve( { diff_eqs, InitConds } );
```

$$soltn := \left\{ x(t) = \frac{Vox}{k} - \frac{Vox\, e^{(-kt)}}{k}, \ y(t) = -\frac{(g+Voy\,k)\,e^{(-kt)}}{k} + gt - \frac{g+Voy\,k}{k} \right\}$$

The range R corresponds to the value of x at which the height $y = 0$ (in addition to the initial firing). We start our solution for the hang time T at which $y(T) = 0$ by extracting $x(t)$ and $y(t)$:

```
> X := rhs(op(1, soltn));        Y := rhs(op(2, soltn));      # Extract RHS x(t), y(t)
```

$$X := \frac{Vox}{k} - \frac{Vox\, e^{(-k\,t)}}{k} \qquad Y := -\frac{\frac{(g + Voy\,k)\, e^{(-k\,t)}}{k} + g\,t - \frac{g + Voy\,k}{k}}{k}$$

Now we use `solve` to find the time T at which $Y(T) = 0$:

```
> solve(Y, t);
```

$$0$$

This just tells us the initial time, which we know, but is not what we want. Instead, let us be more specific and ask for the time at which the height y just becomes negative, namely, when it just hits the ground:

```
> solve(Y < 0, t);
```

We see that Maple returns nothing. It apparently has given up. If we look at the expression for $y(t)$, we see that it contains the time t in both an exponential and a linear term. Apparently, setting $Y = 0$ leads to a transcendental equation that has no analytic solution. The only solution, then, is obtained numerically, and we shall do that with Java (although Maple will also work).

15.9 DRAG $\propto V^2$ (EXERCISE)

Modify the analysis performed for a drag force proportional to the first power of the velocity so that it is appropriate for a force proportional to the square of the velocity. Maple should be able to solve this analytically as well, and you should be able to follow all of the steps we have for Model 1. *Note:* since v^2 does not change sign when v does, you will need to add a $v/|v|$ factor in the frictional force for the y motion (it is not needed for the x motion because the x component of velocity is always positive).

15.10 DRAG $\propto V^{3/2}$

We now want to solve the projectile-with-friction problem for a drag force proportional to the 3/2 power of the velocity. The equations we need to solve are:

$$\frac{d^2 x}{dt^2} = -k\, v_x^{3/2}, \qquad \frac{d^2 y}{dt^2} = -g - k\, v_y^{3/2}\, \frac{v_y}{|v_y|}. \qquad (15.18)$$

The acute reader might notice that there is a problem with this last equation; namely, if v_y is negative, then the square root operation, which is part of raising v_y to the 3/2 power, will return an imaginary number. This is clearly not what we want. We solve that problem by taking the absolute value of v_y before raising it to a power:

$$\frac{d^2y}{dt^2} = -g - k \left|\frac{dy}{dt}\right|^{3/2} \frac{v_y}{|v_y|}. \tag{15.19}$$

This expression is simpler to read and easier to enter into Maple. (An alternative approach would be to use the `sign` function, which extracts the sign of its argument, to keep track of the sign of the velocity and adjust the frictional force appropriately.)

We set about solving this model just as we did the problem with drag proportional to the first power. First we define the set of differential equations and give it the name `diff_eqs`:

```
> restart; with(DEtools):                                    # Clean the slate
> diff_eqs := diff(x(t),t$2) = -k * diff(x(t), t)^(3/2),      # DE
diff(y(t),t$2) = -g - (diff(y(t),t)/abs(diff(y(t),t))) *k*abs(diff(y(t), t))^(3/2);
```

$$diff\_eqs := \frac{d^2}{dt^2} x(t) = -k \left(\frac{d}{dt} x(t)\right)^{(3/2)}, \quad \frac{d^2}{dt^2} y(t) = -g - \left(\frac{d}{dt} y(t)\right) \sqrt{\left|\frac{d}{dt} y(t)\right|} k$$

This looks fine, and so we go on to look for a general solution by first entering the initial conditions:

```
> InitConds := x(0) = 0, D(x)(0) = Vox, y(0) = 0, D(y)(0) = Voy;
```

$$InitConds := x(0) = 0, \qquad D(x)(0) = Vox, \quad y(0) = 0, D(y)(0) = Voy$$

Warning: You may have to stop the following command by hand. We now ask Maple to solve the differential equations labeled `diff_eqs` with the initial conditions labeled `InitConds`:

```
> soltn := dsolve( [diff_eqs, InitConds], [x(t), y(t)] );
```

$$soltn := \cdots \_RootOf \cdots$$

We see from the time it takes Maple to search for a solution, from the volume of output that Maple produces, and from the `_RootOf` command being returned, that Maple is having trouble finding a simple solution to our problem. In any case, an analytic solution with this level of complexity is not illuminating, and probably not even good for computation (the numerous subtractions and evaluations of the multivalued $\tan^{-1}$ and ln functions is error-prone).

Now we try a *numerical* approach. We start it by assigning values to the initial conditions and parameters:

```
> Vox := 22.*cos(Pi/4);    Voy := 22.*sin(Pi/4);    g := 9.8;    k := 1/5.;
```

$$Vox := 15.556349186 \qquad Voy := 15.556349186 \qquad g := 9.8 \qquad k := 0.2000$$

We get a numeric solution using the same procedures as before, only now by including the type=numeric argument to dsolve:

```
> soltn := dsolve( [diff.eqs, InitConds], [x(t), y(t)], type=numeric );
```
$$soltn := \mathbf{proc}(x\_rkf45) \ \ldots \ \mathbf{end \ proc}$$

Regardless of this not appearing to be a clear signal that a solution is in hand, this is Maple's way of telling us that it has written a *procedure* named soltn that will produce a numerical solution to the equations. Recall, a procedure in Maple is like a function that requires more than one line to define. It is like a *method* in Java or a subroutine in Fortran. In the present case the argument to the procedure tells us that the procedure takes an argument and then returns the solution. Since Maple assumes we are solving for $y(x)$, the argument is indicated generically as x. In our case, the second argument to the solve command was the list [x(t), y(t)], and so we are solving for x and y as functions of the time t. Therefore the argument to the procedure is the time t. (The subscript rkf45 to x is meant for aficionados; it indicates that a fourth order Runga-Kutta numerical method is used, and that it uses adaptive step size to obtain fifth-order precision.)

We now have a procedure soltn(t) that numerically solves the differential equations for a single input value of time t and returns [x(t), y(t)] in some form. To see how this works, let us look at the solution returned for time 0 (which should just be the initial conditions we entered):

```
> soltn(0);
```
$$[t = 0., \ x(t) = 0., \ \frac{d}{dt}x(t) = 15.556349186, \ y(t) = 0., \ \frac{d}{dt}y(t) = 15.556349186]$$

OK, the solution appears to be working properly and returning [t,x(t),Vx(t),y(t),Vy(t)]. So we try some nonzero times:

```
> soltn(0.1);        soltn(0.5);
```
$$[t = 0.1, \ x(t) = 1.496606466606704, \ \frac{d}{dt}x(t) = 14.3981782622785151,$$

$$y(t) = 1.44943382860698944, \ \frac{d}{dt}y(t) = 13.47199594152410]$$

$$[t = 0.5, \ x(t) = 6.49693016854386762, \ \frac{d}{dt}x(t) = 10.8534715090049546,$$

$$y(t) = 5.458067069137789, \ \frac{d}{dt}y(t) = 6.980924610035919]$$

We use Maple to pick out the individual pieces of the solution:

```
> Soltn := soltn(0.5);                              # Store list of solutions in Soltn
```
$$Soltn := [t = 0.5, \ x(t) = 6.49693016854386762, \ \frac{d}{dt}x(t) = 10.8534715090049546,$$

$$y(t) = 5.45806706913778950, \ \frac{d}{dt}y(t) = 6.98092461003591946]$$

```
> op(1, Soltn);    op(2, Soltn);  op(3, Soltn);  op(4, Soltn);  op(5, Soltn);
```

$$t = 0.5 \qquad x(t) = 6.49693016854386762 \qquad \frac{d}{dt}x(t) = 10.8534715090049546$$

$$y(t) = 5.45806706913778950 \qquad \frac{d}{dt}y(t) = 6.98092461003591946$$

In order to plot the solutions, we pick off just the RHS of these expressions:

```
> rhs(op(2, Soltn));       rhs(op(4, Soltn));       # Extract RHS of x(t), y(t) in Soltn
```

6.49693016854386762   5.45806706913778950

15.10.1 Defining Functions from Procedures

It seems like we should now be able to plot up the solution. However, Maple's `plot` command accepts expressions and functions as input but not procedures. (We discussed Maple programming and procedures in Chapter 8.) This means we cannot have `plot` call our procedure and plot it. It is not much work to define a function from a procedure and then to plot up the function; essentially, you just define an arrow function as a call to your procedure. Here we do that for the x and y positions and velocities:

```
> X := (t) -> rhs(op(2, soltn(t)));      Y := (t) -> rhs(op(4, soltn(t)));
> Vx := (t) -> rhs(op(3, soltn(t)));     Vy := (t) -> rhs(op(5, soltn(t)));
```

$$X := t \rightarrow \mathrm{rhs}(\mathrm{op}(2, \mathrm{soltn}(t))) \qquad Y := t \rightarrow \mathrm{rhs}(\mathrm{op}(4, \mathrm{soltn}(t)))$$
$$Vx := t \rightarrow \mathrm{rhs}(\mathrm{op}(3, \mathrm{soltn}(t))) \qquad Vy := t \rightarrow \mathrm{rhs}(\mathrm{op}(5, \mathrm{soltn}(t)))$$

```
> plot([X,Y], 0..3, title = "x(t) & y(t), 3/2-power friction");     # Plot 1
> plot([Vx,Vy], 0..3, title = "Vx(t) & Vy(t), 3/2-power friction"); # Plot 2
> plot([X,Y,0..3], title = "y(t) vs x(t) for 3/2-power friction");  # Plot 3
```

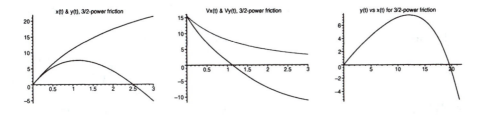

We see similar results to Model 1, only now with an even more drastic "drop out of the sky effect" at the end of the trajectory.

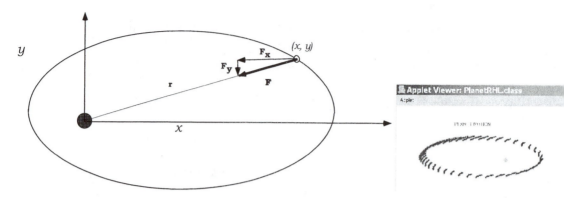

Figure 15.1 *Left:* The gravitational force on a planet a distance r from the sun. The x and y components of the force are indicated. *Right:* Output from the applet PlanetRHL showing the precession of a planet's orbit when the gravitational force $\propto 1/r^4$.

15.11 EXPLORATION: PLANETARY MOTION*

Newton's explanation of the motion of the planets in terms of a universal law of gravitation is one of the great achievements of science. He was able to prove that the planets traveled along elliptical paths with the sun at one vertex, and with periods that agree with observation. All Newton needed to postulate is that the force between a planet of mass m and the sun of mass M is given by

$$F = -\frac{GmM}{r^2},$$
(15.20)

where r is the distance between the planet of mass m and sun of mass M, and G is a universal constant. The minus sign indicates that the force is always attractive and lies along the line connecting the planet and sun, as indicated on the left of Figure 15.1. The hard part for Newton was solving the resulting differential equations, since he had to invent calculus to do it. Whereas the analytic solution is complicated, the numerical solution is not.

Even for planets, the basic equation of motion is

$$\mathbf{F} = m\mathbf{a} = m\frac{d^2\mathbf{x}}{dt^2},$$
(15.21)

with the force now given by (15.20). If we look at Figure 15.1 we see that

$$F_x = F\cos\theta = F\frac{x}{r}, \qquad F_y = F\sin\theta = F\frac{y}{r}, \qquad r = \sqrt{x^2 + y^2},$$
(15.22)

with F given by (15.20). If we write the equation of motion in component form and substitute (15.22) for the force components, we obtain the differential equations we need to solve:

$$\frac{d^2x}{dt^2} = -GM\frac{x}{r^3}, \qquad \frac{d^2y}{dt^2} = -GM\frac{y}{r^3}.$$
(15.23)

15.11.1 Implementation: Planet.java

On the CD you will find the applet `Planet`. We suggest that you run the class file to see how the solution behaves. To keep the calculation simple without changing the physics, assume that the units we use are such that $GM = 1$, and that the initial conditions are [Feyn 63]:

$$x(0) = 0.5, \qquad y(0) = 0, \qquad v_x(0) = 0.0, \qquad v_y(0) = 1.63. \quad (15.24)$$

1. Modify `projectileAir.java` so that it solves (15.23) as functions of time.
2. Make the number of time steps large enough so that the planet's orbit repeats on top of itself.
3. You may need to make the time step small enough so that the orbit closes upon itself (it should) and just repeats. This should be a nice ellipse.
4. Experiment with initial conditions until you obtain the ones that produce a circular orbit (a circle is a special case of an ellipse).
5. Once you have good precision, see the effect of progressively increasing the initial velocity until the orbit opens up and becomes an hyperbola.
6. Use the same initial conditions as produced the ellipse. This time investigate the effect of the power in (15.20) being $1/r^4$ rather than $1/r^2$. You should find that the orbital ellipse now rotates (precesses), as in Figure 15.1.

15.12 KEY WORDS

equations of motion   Euler's method   forward difference
numerical ODE solution   numerical differentiation   ODE

15.13 SUPPLEMENTARY EXERCISES

1. Use Maple, Java, or both to find the solution of the differential equation

$$\frac{dn(t)}{dt} = -\lambda n(t), \quad (15.25)$$

with the initial condition $n(0) = 100$. Plot up the answer for $\lambda = 0.3$.
2. In Chapter 16 you will encounter an RLC electrical circuit and the differential equation describing it. We consider here the same circuit without a capacitor and described by the differential equation

$$V(t) = RI + L\frac{dI}{dt}. \quad (15.26)$$

Solve this equation for the current in the circuit for the same values of R and L as in the problem, and for a constant $V(t)$ (same magnitude as in problem). Plot your solution.

3. Consider exponential growth starting with an initial population $N(0) = 2$.
    a. Solve the equation describing exponential growth

$$\frac{dN(t)}{dt} = \lambda N(t). \qquad (15.27)$$

    Assign the integration constants to correspond to $n(0) = 100$, and $\lambda = 0.3$, and plot up the solution.
    b. Solve for exponential growth with a modulated growth parameter

$$\frac{dy(t)}{dt} = \lambda \left[\frac{10000 - N(t)}{10000} \right] \times N(t). \qquad (15.28)$$

    This is the differential-equation version of the logistics map studied in Chapter 19, "Discrete Math, Arrays as Bins." The term in square brackets is insignificant for small $N(t)$.
4. Solve for and plot up the solution to the differential equation

$$\frac{dy(x)}{dx} = \sin(xy), \qquad (15.29)$$

with initial condition $y(0) = 1$.
    a. Verify that Maple cannot find an analytic solution to this equation.
    b. Have Maple find a numerical solution to this equation.
5. Solve for and plot up the solution to the differential equation

$$\frac{d^2y(x)}{dx^2} = -y(x)^3, \qquad (15.30)$$

subject to the initial conditions $y(0) = 1$, $y'(0) = 0$. *Hint:* If Maple cannot find an analytic solution, you may need to try a numerical one.

Chapter Sixteen

Object-Oriented Programming, Abstract Data;

Complex Currents

Note to the instructor: As an alternative to the full version of this chapter, you may skip the study of the RLC circuit and just focus on the mathematics of complex numbers and their representation in terms of objects. And even with that, you may defer the use of *nonstatic* (object-oriented) methods to a later time.

16.1 PROBLEM: RESONANCE IN RLC CIRCUIT

We are given the circuit shown on the left of Figure 16.1 containing a resistor of resistance R, an inductor of inductance L, and a capacitor of capacitance C. All three elements are connected in series to an alternating voltage source

$$V(t) = V_0 \cos \omega t. \tag{16.1}$$

Problem: Determine the magnitude and time dependence of the current in this RLC circuit as a function of the frequency of the external voltage. We will solve the RLC circuit problem for you within this chapter. *Your problem* is to repeat the calculation for a circuit in which there are two RLC circuits in parallel, as shown on the right of Figure 16.1. You may assume a single value for inductance and capacitance, and three values for resistance:

$$L = 1000 \text{ H}, \qquad C = \frac{1}{1000} \text{ F}, \qquad R = \frac{1000}{1.5}, \ \frac{1000}{2.1}, \ \frac{1000}{5.2} \ \Omega. \tag{16.2}$$

Consider frequencies of applied voltage in the range $0 < \omega < 2/\sqrt{LC} = 2/s$.

16.2 MATH: COMPLEX NUMBERS

Try to remember your first exposure to square roots in elementary school. Though it was straightforward to understand that $5^2 = 25$, it was a challenge to understand that $\sqrt{25} = \pm 5$, and more of a challenge to understand what was the true value of $\sqrt{24}$. For many of us, it was downright impossible to understand the true value of $\sqrt{-1}$. Mathematicians, being a rather clever and proud bunch, have handled this

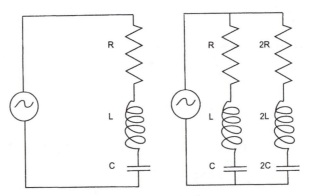

Figure 16.1 *Left:* An RLC circuit connected to an alternating voltage source. *Right:* Two RLC circuits connected in parallel to an alternating voltage. Observe that one of the parallel circuits has double the values of R, L, and C as does the other.

affront to their abilities by inventing the number i as the answer,[1]

$$i \stackrel{\text{def}}{=} \sqrt{-1}, \qquad i^2 = -1, \qquad\qquad (16.3)$$

where the "def" over the equal sign indicates a definition. In this way mathematicians have a way of going ahead with their calculations, even if they do not know what i means. Whereas defining away one's ignorance may appear to be a swindle, mathematicians are an honest bunch at heart and so tell the world that they have really just made up the answer by calling i the *imaginary* number. "Imaginary" is a good name for i, since there is no way to measure this number in the real world, but, then again, there is no law forbidding us from imagining such a number.

In common mathematical usage, i is called *the* imaginary number, while any multiple of i is called *an* imaginary number. So, for example, $2i$, i, and $100i$ are all imaginary numbers. Once we have extended our minds to imagine an imaginary number, it is not much of a stretch to imagine adding a real number to an imaginary number to form something more complex. To name an instance, $1 + i$, $1 + 2i$, and $100 + 76i$. These numbers with both real and imaginary parts are called *complex numbers*.[2] The term "complex" indicates that these numbers have a number of parts, and *not* that they are hard to understand!

Complex numbers are very useful in mathematics and science since they let us double our work output with only the slightest increase in input. This is accomplished by employing the familiar operations of algebra and calculus on complex numbers, and then separating off the real and imaginary parts of the answer at the end. By way of example, even if z is a complex number, z^3/z still equal z^2, without our having to express the individual numbers in terms of their real and imaginary parts.

---

[1] The invention is credited to Girolama Cardana (1501–1576).

[2] The term, as well as much in applied mathematics, is credited to Carl Friedrich Gauss (1777–1855).

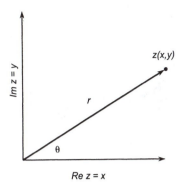

Figure 16.2 Representation of a complex number as a vector in space.

To do algebra with complex numbers, we define the symbol z to represent a number with both real and imaginary parts:

$$z = x + iy. \tag{16.4}$$

In turn, the complex nature of z is indicated by giving its real and imaginary parts:

$$\text{Re } z = x, \qquad\qquad \text{Im } z = y. \tag{16.5}$$

In a strict sense, y is the magnitude of the imaginary part of z, and iy is the imaginary part. Yet y is usually called "the imaginary part."

Because complex numbers have independent real and imaginary parts, a useful way to visualize them is to imagine a coordinate system in which the ordinate points off into imaginary space and the abscissa points off into real space. As seen in Figure 16.2, we then visualize $z = x + iy$ as a point with y projection along the imaginary axis and x projection along the real axis. This is analogous to a *vector* in a 2-D space, except that part of this vector lies in an imaginary space. The analogy between complex numbers and 2-D vectors is taken one step further by applying the *polar coordinate* representation of a vector to complex numbers. On account of this, the point z in Figure 16.2 may be located not only by giving its Cartesian coordinates x and y, but also by specifying it polar coordinates r, the length of the vector from the origin to point z, and θ, the angle that the vector makes with the abscissa. The complex number is the same in either case, and, indeed, the two representations are related via simple trigonometry:

$$
\begin{aligned}
r &= \sqrt{x^2 + y^2}, & \theta &= \tan^{-1}(y/x), \\
x &= r\cos\theta, & y &= r\sin\theta.
\end{aligned}
\tag{16.6}
$$

16.2.1 Complex Arithmetic Review

The essence of the computing aspect of our problem is the programming of the rules of arithmetic for complex numbers. This is an interesting chore because while Java contains all the rules for real numbers, you must educate Java as to the rules for complex numbers. Indeed, since complex numbers are not *primitive data types* like *doubles* and *floats*, we will construct complex numbers as *objects*.[3]

We start with two complex numbers, which we distinguish with subscripts:

$$z_1 = x_1 + i\,y_1, \tag{16.7}$$
$$z_2 = x_2 + i\,y_2. \tag{16.8}$$

The rules of arithmetic follow by applying algebra to the real and imaginary parts:

Addition: $\quad z_1 + z_2 = (x_1 + x_2) + i(y_1 + y_2), \tag{16.9}$

Subtraction: $\quad z_1 - z_2 = (x_1 - x_2) + i(y_1 - y_2), \tag{16.10}$

Multiplication: $\quad z_1 \times z_2 = (x_1 + iy_1) \times (x_2 + iy_2), \tag{16.11}$
$$= (x_1 x_2 - y_1 y_2) + i(x_1 y_2 + x_2 y_1),$$

Division: $\quad \dfrac{z_1}{z_2} = \dfrac{x_1 + iy_1}{x_2 + iy_2} \times \dfrac{x_2 - iy_2}{x_2 - iy_2}, \tag{16.12}$
$$= \frac{(x_1 x_2 + y_1 y_2) + i(y_1 x_2 - x_1 y_2)}{x_2^2 + y_2^2}.$$

In deducing the rule for complex division we employed the fact that a complex number z multiplied by its *complex conjugate*

$$z^* = x - iy, \tag{16.13}$$

always yields a real number:

$$z \times z^* = (x + iy)(x - iy) = x^2 + y^2. \tag{16.14}$$

We observe that this result is the same as the square of the length r defined in (16.6). The length r is commonly referred to as the *modulus* or *magnitude* of the complex number z, and is expressed by using the absolute value symbol: $r = |z|$. The product of the complex number z and its complex conjugate z^* is then

$$zz^* = |z|^2 = r^2. \tag{16.15}$$

Exercise: Consider the complex numbers

$$b = 1 + 2i, \qquad c = 4 + i. \tag{16.16}$$

What are the values of $b + c$, $b - c$, $b \times c$, $|c|$, and b/c?   ♠

---

[3]Because complex numbers are used so often in science and engineering, there is a move afoot to have some future versions of Java incorporate complex numbers as a primitive data type in order to speed up execution and make them easier to use.

We end our little review with an examination of functions of complex numbers. The new idea here is an ingenious theorem, derived by Euler, that if you raise e, the base of the natural logarithm system, to a purely imaginary power, then you get a complex number with a sine and cosine as its real and imaginary parts:

$$e^{i\theta} = \cos\theta + i\sin\theta \qquad \text{(Euler's theorem)}. \qquad (16.17)$$

If the angle θ is real and in radians, then $\cos\theta$ and $\sin\theta$ are identified with the projection of $\exp i\theta$ along the real and imaginary axes, respectively. So if we look at both Figure 16.2 and Eqs. (16.4) and (16.6), we see that it is also possible to express a complex number z in terms of its polar representation:

$$z \equiv x + iy = re^{i\theta} = r\cos\theta + ir\sin\theta. \qquad (16.18)$$

An important application of Euler's theorem is to define what it means to raise a number to a complex power z, for example,

$$e^z = e^{x+iy} = e^x e^{iy} = e^x(\cos y + i\sin y). \qquad (16.19)$$

We shall find (16.19) useful in our exercises.

16.3 THEORY: RESISTANCE BECOMES IMPEDANCE

The basic rules of circuit theory are called Kirchoff's laws [R & M 93], and we now apply one of them to the circuit on the left of Figure 16.1. We work our way around the circuit, setting the external voltage $V(t)$ equal to the sum of the voltage drops across the resistor, the inductor, and the capacitor. If $I(t)$ is the current in the circuit, we end up with the basic differential equation of circuit theory

$$\frac{dV(t)}{dt} = R\frac{dI}{dt} + L\frac{d^2I}{dt^2} + \frac{I}{C}, \qquad (16.20)$$

where we have taken an extra derivative to eliminate an integral. The solution to our problem follows by solving (16.20) when the voltage has the form $V(t) = V_0\cos\omega t$. An elegant way to do that is to recognize that

$$V_0\cos\omega t = \text{Re}\, V_0 e^{-i\omega t} = \text{Re}\,(V_0\cos\omega t - iV_0\sin\omega t). \qquad (16.21)$$

Because (16.20) is a linear equation (only first power of I occurs), the law of linear superposition holds. This means that if we imagine the circuit being driven by a complex voltage source, whose real part is the physical voltage, then the resulting current $I(t)$ will also be complex, with its real part the physical current. Thus we assume that the current has the form

$$I(t) = I_0 e^{-i\omega t}. \qquad (16.22)$$

If we substitute this and the complex $V(t)$ into (16.20), we obtain

$$V_0 e^{-i\omega t} = Z I_0 e^{-i\omega t}. \qquad (16.23)$$

Here Z is called the *impedance* and is the complex expression

$$Z = R + i\left(\frac{1}{\omega C} - \omega L\right). \tag{16.24}$$

Equation (16.23) is the generalization of Ohm's law, $V = IR$, to alternating current circuits.[4] We see that the real part of the impedance is just the resistance R, while the imaginary part (called the *reactance*) is $1/\omega C - \omega L$. As we shall see, the imaginary part of the impedance determines the phase of the current.

16.3.1 Solution for Complex Current

If we now solve (16.23) for the complex current, we obtain

$$I(t) = \frac{1}{Z}V_0 e^{-i\omega t} = \frac{V_0 e^{-i\omega t}}{R + i\left(1/\omega C - \omega L\right)}. \tag{16.25}$$

Eq. (16.25) is more illuminating if the complex impedance is expressed in polar form:

$$Z = |Z|e^{i\theta}, \tag{16.26}$$

$$|Z| = \sqrt{R^2 + (1/\omega C - \omega L)^2}, \quad \theta = \tan^{-1}\left(\frac{1/\omega C - \omega L}{R}\right). \tag{16.27}$$

We see now that the complex current is

$$I(t) = \frac{V_0}{|Z|}e^{-i(\omega t + \theta)}, \tag{16.28}$$

which means that the physical current is its real part:

$$I_{\text{physical}}(t) = \text{Re}I(t) = \frac{V_0}{|Z|}\cos(\omega t + \theta). \tag{16.29}$$

Equation (16.29) states that the amplitude of the current in the circuit is given by the amplitude of the voltage divided by the magnitude of the complex impedance, and that the phase of the current, relative to that of the voltage, is given by θ. If the phase $\theta > 0$, then the current *leads* the voltage in time, that is, the current reaches its maximum before the voltage reaches its maximum. If θ is negative, then the current *lags* the voltage.

Finally, what is to be done if we have two such RLC circuits in parallel, as shown on the right of Figure 16.1. The analysis is the same as that done with ordinary resistors. If two impedances are in series, then they have the same current passing through them. If two impedances are in parallel, then they have the same

---

[4]Some elementary texts may refer to $|Z|$ as the impedance and then use the concept of *phasors* to describe the effect of the impedance on the phase. We view the use of complex impedance as more direct and elegant.

Figure 16.3 An abstract drawing, or what?

voltage across them. If two impedances are connected in series, then the voltages add, and this leads to:

$$Z = Z_1 + Z_2 \qquad \text{(series connection)}. \qquad (16.30)$$

If the impedances are connected in parallel, then the currents add, and this leads to

$$\frac{1}{Z} = \frac{1}{Z_1} + \frac{1}{Z_2} \qquad \text{(parallel connection)}. \qquad (16.31)$$

Hence in the parallel case, the impedances add in inverse, with all the steps of the calculation being performed with complex arithmetic.

16.4 CS: ABSTRACT DATA TYPES, OBJECTS

What do you see when you look at the *abstract* object in Figure 16.3? Some readers may see a face in profile, others may see some parts of human anatomy, and others the total absence of artistic ability. This figure is abstract in the sense that it does not try to present a true or realistic picture of the object, but rather uses a symbol to suggest more than meets the eye.

Abstract or formal concepts pervade mathematics and science because they make it easier to describe nature. For example, we often use the symbol $v(t)$ to denote the velocity of an object as a function of time. Despite velocity being a familiar concept, it is actually abstract in the sense that we cannot see it. What we see is the position of the object as a function of time, and then we infer from that the velocity by determining how rapidly that position is changing.

In computer science we create an abstract object by using a symbol to describe a collection of items. We have already seen that data, or variables in Java and Maple may be integers, floating-point numbers, Booleans, or strings. These types of variables are built into the languages and therefore are called *primitive data types*. In addition, computer languages let the user define *abstract data types* of their own by combining primitive data types into more complicated structures called *objects*. These objects are abstract in the sense that they are named with a single symbol, yet they represent a number of parts.

For instance, one might create an object with parts that contain a student's school record (ID, grades, etc.), as well as other parts that contain methods to calculate the grade point average, etc. Of course, one would need many such objects because there are many students. To distinguish between the general structure of this student-record object and specific record objects for individual students, the general object is called a *class*, while the object for specific cases is called an *instance* of the class, or just an *object*.

In this chapter our objects will be complex numbers, while in other chapters they may be plots, vectors, or matrices. The classes that we form will be combinations of abstract data types and associated methods for modifying those data. The entire class may also be thought of as objects. In a formal sense, computer science requires abstract data types to possess the three properties [Zach 96]:

Typename: procedure to construct the new data type from elementary pieces.

Set values: mechanism for assigning values to the defined data type.

Set operations: rules that permit operations on the new data type (you would not have gone to all the trouble of declaring a new data type unless you were interested in doing something with it).

In terms of these properties, when we declare a variable to be complex we satisfy property (1). When we declare $\text{Re}z = x$ and $\text{Im}z = y$ as *doubles*, we satisfy (2). When we define the rules of arithmetic and trigonometry for complex numbers (as reviewed in § 16.2.1), we satisfy (3).

Before we examine how these properties are applied in our programs, let us review the structure we have been using in our Java programs. When we start off our programs with a declaration statement such as `double x`. This tells the Java compiler the kind of variable x is, so that Java will store it properly in memory and use proper operations on it. The general rule is that *every variable we use in a program must have its data type declared.* For primitive (built-in) data types, we declare them to be `double, float, int, char, long, short,` or `boolean`.

If our program employs some user-defined, abstract data types, then they too must be declared. This declaration must occur even if we do not define the meaning of the data type until later in the program (the compiler checks on that). Consequently, when our program refers to a number z as complex, the compiler must be told at some point that there is *both* a real part x and an imaginary part y that makes up a complex number.

To actually create objects in your Java program, you need class variables and methods that are *nonstatic*. This means we leave off the word `static` in declaring the class and variables. If the class and class variables are no longer static they may be thought of as dynamic. Likewise, methods that deal with objects may be either static or dynamic. The static ones take objects as arguments, much like conventional mathematical functions. In contrast, dynamic methods accomplish the same end by modifying or interacting with the objects. Regardless of our starting our dealings with objects using static methods, you must use dynamic (nonstatic) methods to enjoy the full power of object-oriented programming.

16.4.1 Object Declaration and Construction

Before we start working with objects in a program, it is necessary to understand that even though we may assign a name like x to an object, because objects have multiple components, you do not assign one explicit *value* to the object. It follows then, that when Java deals with objects it does so by *reference*. In plain English this means that the name of the variable *refers to the location in memory* where your object is stored, and not to the explicit values of the object's parts. To see what this means in practise, the class file Complex.java in Listing 16.1 adds and multiplies complex numbers, with the complex numbers represented as objects.

Exercise: 1. Enter the program Complex.java by hand, trying to understand it as best you are able. (Yes, we know that you can just copy it, but then you do not become familiar with the constructs.)

2. Study how the word Complex is a number of things in this program. It is the name of the *class* (line 2), as well as the name of two methods that create the object (lines 7 and 11). Methods, such as these, that create objects are called *constructors*. In spite of neophytes viewing these multiple uses of the name Complex as confusing (Landau's second rule), more experienced users often view it as elegant and efficient. Look closely and take note that this program has nonstatic variables (no static on line 3).

3. Compile and execute this program, and check that the output agrees with the results you obtained in the exercises in §16.2.1.   ♠

The first thing to notice about Complex.java is that the class is declared on line 2 with the statement

```
2 public class Complex
```

The main method is declared on line 23 with the statement

```
23 public static void main(String[] argv)
```

These are the same techniques we have employed before (it is good when some things stay the same in life). However, on line 3 we see that the variables re and im are declared for the entire class with the statement

Listing 16.1 Complex.java

```java
1  //   Complex.java:    Creates "Complex" class with static members
2  public class Complex
3  {    public double re, im;                      //Nonstatic, for entire class
4       public Complex ()                          //Default constructor
5       { re = 0;
6         im = 0; }
7       public Complex(double x, double y)         //Full constructor
8       { re = x;
9         im = y; }
10      //Static method adds 2 complex numbers, returns sum
11      public static Complex add(Complex a, Complex b)
12      { Complex temp = new Complex();             //Create Complex temp
13        temp.re = a.re + b.re;
14        temp.im = a.im + b.im;
15        return temp; }
16      //Static Method multiplies 2 complex numbers, returns product
17      public static Complex mult(Complex a, Complex b)
18      { Complex temp = new Complex();             //Create Complex temp
19        temp.re = a.re * b.re - a.im * b.im;
20        temp.im = a.re * b.im + a.im * b.re;
21        return temp; }
22      //Main method for Complex objects with Static methods
23      public static void main(String[] argv)
24      { Complex a, b;                             //Declare 2 Complex objects
25        a = new Complex();                        // Create the objects
26        b = new Complex(4.7, 3.2);
27        Complex c = new Complex(3.1, 2.4);        //Declare, create in 1
28        System.out.println("a,b = ("+ a.re+","+a.im+"), ("+b.re+","+b
               .im+"),");
29        System.out.println("c = ("+c.re+", "+c.im+")");
30        a = add(b,c);                             //Perform arithmetic
31        System.out.println( "b+c = (" + a.re + ", " + a.im+"), ");
32        a = mult(b,c);
33        System.out.println( "b*c = (" + a.re + ", " + a.im+")");
34 }}
35 // EXPECTED OUTPUT
36 a,b = (0.0,0.0), (4.7,3.2),
37 c = (3.1, 2.4)
38 b+c = (7.800000000000001, 5.6),
39 b*c = (6.890000000000001, 21.200000000000003)
```

```
3  public double re, im;
```

Although this is similar to the declaration we have seen before for class variables, observe that the word `static` is absent. This indicates that these variables are interactive or dynamic, namely, parts of an object. They are dynamic in the sense that they will be different for each object (*instance* of the class) created. That is, if we define `z1` and `z2` to be `Complex` objects, then the variables `re` and `im` will be different for `z1` and `z2`.

We extract the component parts of our complex object by a projection operation. For those readers who know some vector analysis, think of this as similar to extracting the components of a vector in space by taking dot products with the unit vectors to project the vector onto different axes. As with space vectors, the projection operation is denoted by a dot operation:

`z1.re`	real part of object `z1`
`z1.im`	imaginary part of object `z1`
`z2.re`	real part of object `z2`
`z2.im`	imaginary part of object `z1`

This same dot convention is used to access the methods of objects, as we will see below. On line 4 we see a method `Complex` declared with the statement

```
4  public Complex()
```

On line 7 we see a method `Complex` declared, yet again, but with a somewhat different statement:

```
7  public Complex(double x, double y)
```

Some explanation is clearly in order! First notice that both of these methods are nonstatic (no word `static`). In fact, they are the methods that construct our complex number object, which we call `Complex`. Second notice that the name of each of these methods is the same as the name of the class, `Complex`.[5] Indeed, you know that they are special since by convention they are spelled with their first letters capitalized, rather than the lowercase letters usually used for methods, and because these objects have the same name as the class they are in.

The two `Complex` methods are used to *construct* the object, and for this reason are called *constructors*. The first `Complex` constructor on line 4 is seen to be a method that takes no argument and returns no value (yes, this appears rather weird, but be patient). When `Complex` gets called with no argument, as we see on line 25, the real and imaginary parts of the complex number (object) are set to zero. This method is called the *default constructor*, since it does what Java would

---

[5]These two nonstatic methods are special as they permit the parameters characterizing the object that they construct to be passed during a `new` call. However, you probably will not understand this statement until we describe the `new` call.

otherwise do automatically ("by default") when first creating an object, namely, set all of its component parts initially to zero. We have explicitly included it for pedagogical purposes.

Exercise: Remove the default constructor (the one on line 4 that takes no argument) from `Complex.java` and check that you get the same result for the call to `Complex()`. ♠

The `Complex` method on line 7 implements the standard way to construct complex numbers. It is seen to take the two doubles x and y as input arguments, to set the real part of the complex number (object) to x, the imaginary part to y, and then return. This method is an additional constructor for complex numbers but differs from the default constructor by taking arguments. Inasmuch as the nondefault constructor takes arguments while the default constructor does not, Java does not confuse it with the default constructor, even though both methods have the same name.

Okay, let us now take stock of what we have up to this point. On line 3 `Complex.java` has defined the variables `re` and `im` that will be the two separate parts of the created object. As each instance of each object created will have different values for the object's parts, these variables are referred to as *instance variables*. Because the name of the class file and the names of the objects it creates are all the same, it sometimes is useful to use yet another word to distinguish one from the other. Hence the phrase *instance of a class* is used to refer to the created objects (in our example, a, b, and c). This distinguishes them from the definition of the abstract data type.

Now let us look at the `main` method to see how to go about creating objects using the constructor `Complex`. On line 24, in the usual place for declaring variables, we have the statement

```
24  Complex a, b;
```

Because the compiler knows that `Complex` is not one of its primitive (built-in) data types, it assumes that it must be one we have defined. In the present case, the class file contains the nonstatic class named `Complex`, as well as the constructors for `Complex` objects (data types). This means that the compiler does not have to look very far to know what you mean by a *complex* data type. By reason of this, when the statement `Complex a, b;` on line 24 declares the variables a and b to be `Complex` objects, we know that they are manifestly objects since the constructors are *not* static.

Recall that declaring a variable type, such as `double` or `int`, does not assign a value to the variable, but, instead, tells the compiler to add the name of the variable to the list of variables it will encounter. Likewise, the declaration statement

`Complex a, b` lets the compiler know what type of variables these are without assigning values to their parts. To actually *create objects* we have to place numerical values in the memory locations that have been reserved for them. Seeing that an object has multiple parts, we cannot give all its parts initial values with a simple assignment statement like `a = 0;`, so something fancier is called for. This is exactly why the constructor methods are used. Specifically, on line 25 we have the object a created with the statement

```
25  a = new Complex();
```

and on line 26 we have the object b created with the statement

```
26  b = new Complex(4.7, 3.2);
```

Look at how the creation of a new object requires the command `new` to precede the name of the constructor (`Complex` in this case). Also note that line 25 uses the default constructor method to set both the `re` and `im` parts of a to zero, while line 26 uses the second constructor method to set the `re` part of b to `4.7` and the `im` part of b to `3.2`.

Just as we have done with the primitive data types of Java, it is possible to both declare and initialize an object in one statement. Indeed, line 27 does just that for object c with the statement

```
27  Complex c = new Complex(3.1, 2.4);
```

Monitor how the data type `Complex` precedes the variable name c in line 27 because the variable c has not previously been declared; future uses of c should *not* declare or create it again.

16.4.2 Static and Nonstatic Methods

Once our complex-number objects have been declared (added to the variable list) and created (assigned values), it is easy to do arithmetic with them. For those readers seeing objects for the first time, we suggest that you get some experience with object arithmetic using the familiar static methods that we have been using up until now. That is what we do in this section. In the next section §16.4.2.1, which we consider optional for object neophytes, we show how to perform the same object arithmetic using *nonstatic* methods. Undeniably, nonstatic methods are elegant and powerful; however, they do their work in a different way and so may take some getting used to before making sense. We recommend that even the object neophytes read §16.4.2.1 before getting on to the exercises. After that it should be possible to make more sense out of the nonstatic methods and even to repeat the exercises using nonstatic methods (an approach we encourage).

We have now declared and created objects that represent complex numbers.

We know from §16.2.1 all the rules of complex arithmetic and complex trigonometry, so next we will write Java methods to implement these rules. It makes sense to place these methods in the same class file that defines the data type since these associated methods are needed to manipulate objects of that data type. This is an interesting task since it is analogous to the one faced by those people who originally wrote the Java language and had to program up all the methods to do arithmetic with real numbers.

On line 30 in our *main* program we see the statement

```
30  a = add(b, c);
```

This statement says to add the complex number b to the complex number c and then to store the result "as" (in the memory location reserved for) the complex number a. You may recall that we initially set the re and im parts of a to zero in line 25 using the default Complex constructor. This statement will replace the initial zero values with those computed in line 30. Nevertheless, it often helps the debugging process to have zero initial values.

The method add that adds two complex numbers is defined on lines 11–15. It starts with the statement

```
20  public static Complex add(Complex a, Complex b)
```

The method is declared to be *static* and takes as its input arguments the two Complex objects (numbers) a and b. The fact that the word Complex precedes the method's name add signifies that the method will return a Complex number object as its result. We had the option of defining other names like complex_add or plus for this addition method, but we opted to keep things simple instead.

The calculational part of the add method starts on line 12 by declaring and creating a temporary complex number temp that will contain the result of the addition of the complex numbers a and b. As indicated before, the *dot operator* convention with objects means that temp.re will contain the re part of temp and that temp.im will contain the imaginary part. Thus the statements on lines 13 and 14,

```
13  temp.re = a.re + b.re;
14  temp.im = a.im + b.im;
```

add the complex numbers a and b by extracting the real parts of each, adding them together, and then storing the result as the re part of temp. Line 20 determines the imaginary part of the sum in an analogous manner. Finally, the statement

```
21  return temp;
```

returns the object (complex number) temp as the value of add(Complex a, Complex b). Because a complex number has two parts, both parts must be returned to the calling program, and this is what `return temp` does.

16.4.2.1 Nonstatic Methods*

In this section we present a nonstatic approach for dealing with complex objects. If you have just read the section on static methods for dealing with objects and feel somewhat confused by it, we recommend that you jump ahead to the exercises to get some experience with the more elementary aspects of objects before using the nonstatic methods described here. Then come back here to see what nonstatic methods are all about.

The program `ComplexDyn.java` in Listing 16.2 at the end of this section also adds and multiplies complex numbers as objects, but it uses what are called *dynamic, nonstatic*, or *interactive* methods. This is more elegant and powerful, but less like the procedural programming we have been doing up till now. To avoid confusion and to permit you to run both the static and nonstatic versions without them interfering with each other, the nonstatic version is called `ComplexDyn`, in contrast to the `Complex` used for the static method. Inspect how the names of the methods in `ComplexDyn` and `Complex` are the same, although they go about their work differently.

Exercise: 1. Enter the `ComplexDyn.java` class file by hand, trying to understand it in the process. If you have entered `Complex.java` by hand, you may modify that program to save some time (but be careful!).

2. Compile and execute this program, and check that the output agrees with the results you obtained in the exercises in §16.2.1.   ♠

Nonstatic methods go about their work by modifying the properties of the objects to which they are attached (for the present case the objects are complex numbers). In fact, we shall see that nonstatic methods are literally appended to the name of objects much as the endings of verbs are modified when their tenses change. In other words, the method gets appended to the object and in so doing becomes part of the object. To cite an instance, on line 27 we see the operation

```
27  c.add(b);                                        // Nonstatic addition
```

Study the way this statement says to take the complex number object c and modify it using the `add` method that adds b to the object. This results in new values for the parts of object c. Because object c gets modified by this action, line 27 is equivalent to the static operation

```
   c = add(c,b);                                     // Static method equivalent
```

Regardless of the approach, since c now contains the sum c + b, if we want to use c again we must redefine it, as we do on line 30. On line 31 we take object c and multiply it by b with,

```
31  c.mult(b);                                                // Nonstatic multiplication
```

This method changes c to c * b. Thus line 31 has the static-method equivalence

```
    c = mult(c, b);                                           // Static method equivalent
```

We see from these two examples that nonstatic methods are called using the same dot operator that is used to refer to instance variables of an object. On the other hand, static methods take the object as arguments and do not use the dot operator. Thus we called the static methods using add(c,b) and mult(c,b) and called the nonstatic methods using c.add(b) and c.mult(b).

The static methods here do not need a dot operator, since they are called from within the class Complex or ComplexDyn that defined them. However, they would need a dot operator if called from another class. As an instance, you have already seen what we called the method Math.sqrt(x). This is actually the static method sqrt from the class Math. You could call the static add(c,b) method of class Complex by using Complex.add(c,b). This works within Complex as well, but is not required. It is required, however, if add is called from other classes.

Observe now how the object-oriented add method has the distinctive form:

```
public void add(ComplexDyn other)
{this.re = this.re + other.re;
this.im = this.im + other.im;}
```

Line 11 tells us that the method add is nonstatic (the word static is absent), that no value or object is returned (the void), and that there is one argument other of the type ComplexDyn. What is clearly unusual about this nonstatic method is that it is supposed to add two complex numbers together, yet there is only one argument given to the method and no object returned! Indeed, the assumption is that since the method is nonstatic, it will only be used to modify the object that called it. Hence it "goes without saying" that there is an object around for this method to modify, and the this reference is used to refer to "this" calling object. In fact, the reason the argument to the method is conventionally called other, is to distinguish it from the this object that the method will modify. (We are being verbose for clarity's sake: the word "this" may be left out of these statements without changing their actions.) Consequently, when the object addition is done in line 12 with

```
12  this.re = this.re + other.re;                 // Addition of re parts of this and other
```

it is understood that re will refer to the current object being modified (this), while other will refer to the "other" object that is being used to make the modifications.

Listing 16.2 ComplexDyn.java

```
1  //              ComplexDyn.java:    non-static members class
2  public class ComplexDyn
3  { public double re;            // Nonstatic variables: entire class
4    public double im;
5    public ComplexDyn()                          // Default constructor
6      { re = 0;
7        im = 0;  }
8    public ComplexDyn(double x, double y)              // Constructor
9      { re = x;
10       im = y; }
11   public void add(ComplexDyn other)         // Dynamic other + this
12     { this.re = this.re + other.re;
13       this.im = this.im + other.im; }
14   public void mult(ComplexDyn other)         // Dynamic other*this
15   { ComplexDyn ans = new ComplexDyn();            // Intermediate
16     ans.re = this.re * other.re - this.im * other.im;
17     ans.im = this.re * other.im + this.im * other.re;
18     this.re = ans.re;          // Copy value into returned object
19     this.im = ans.im;  }
20   public static void main(String[] argv) // Static Main: object
            indep
21   {   ComplexDyn a, b;                  //Declare 2 Complex objects
22       a = new ComplexDyn();               // Create the objects
23       b = new ComplexDyn(4.7, 3.2);
24       ComplexDyn c = new ComplexDyn(3.1, 2.4);   // Declare, create
25       System.out.println("a,b = ("+ a.re+","+a.im+"),("+b.re+","+b
            .im+"),");
26       System.out.println("c = ("+c.re+", "+c.im+")");
27       c.add(b);                               //Non-static addition
28       a = c;
29       System.out.println("b+c = (" + a.re + ", " + a.im+"),");
30       c = new ComplexDyn(3.1, 2.4);
31       c.mult(b);                       // Non-static multiplication
32       System.out.println("b*c = (" + c.re + ", " + c.im+")");
33  }}
```

16.5 JAVA SOLUTION: COMPLEX CURRENTS

1. Extend the class `Complex.java` or `ComplexDyn.java` by adding new methods to subtract, take the modulus, take the complex conjugate, and determine the phase of complex numbers.

2. Test your methods by checking that the following identities hold for a variety of complex numbers:

$$
\begin{array}{ll}
z + z = 2z, & z + z* = 2\,\mathrm{Re}\,z \\
z - z = 0, & z - z* = 2\,\mathrm{Im}\,z \\
zz* = |z|^2, & zz* = r^2 \quad \text{(which is real)}
\end{array}
\tag{16.32}
$$

Hint: Compare your output to some cases of pure real, pure imaginary, and simple complex numbers that you are able to evaluate by hand.

3. Equations (16.29) and (16.27) are the solution for the current in a single RLC circuit. It tells us that the magnitude of the current is given by

$$|I| = \left|\frac{V_0}{Z}\right|,$$ (16.33)

and that the phase of the current (relative to the $\cos \omega t$ time dependence) is

$$\theta_I = \tan^{-1}\left(\frac{1/\omega C - \omega L}{R}\right).$$ (16.34)

Modify the given complex arithmetic program so that it performs the complex arithmetic required by (16.33). *Hint:* You do not have to solve this from scratch! Instead, use the techniques you have already programmed for determining the magnitude to determine $|I|$.

4. Compute and then make a plot of the magnitude and the phase of the current in the circuit as a function of frequency ω of the external voltage source. For our problem, a good range is $0 \le \omega \le 2$.

5. **Assessment:** You should notice a resonance peak in the magnitude at the same frequency for which the phase vanishes. The smaller the resistance R, the sharper should the circuit pass through resonance. These types of circuits were used in the early days of radio to tune to a specific frequency. The sharper the peak, the better the quality of reception.

6. The second part of the problem, dealing with the two circuits in parallel is very similar to the first part. You need to change only the value of the impedance Z used. To do that, explicitly perform the complex arithmetic implied by (16.31), deduce a new value for the impedance, and then repeat the calculation of the current.

16.6 MAPLE SOLUTION: COMPLEX CURRENTS

Recall from way back in Chapter 3 that Maple knows all about complex numbers and complex arithmetic. Indeed, you have probably already seen an occasional I pop up as the solution to some equations. The point here is that Maple reserves the symbol I as the $\sqrt{-1}$, and this lets us use its I at our pleasure:

```
> restart:              'sqrt (-1)' = sqrt (-1);              # What's returned?
```

$$sqrt\ (-1\ ) = I$$

```
> expand((a + I*b)^2);                                        # See if Maple uses I as √−1
```
$$a^2 + 2\,I\,a\,b - b^2$$

In §16.3 we applied circuit theory and complex analysis to the RLC circuit and found that if the exciting voltage is the real part of

$$V(t) = V_0\,e^{(-I\omega t)},$$ (16.35)

then the current in the circuit is

$$I(t) = \frac{V_0 \cos(\omega t - \theta)}{|Z|}. \tag{16.36}$$

Here Z is the complex impedance,

```
> Z  := R + I * (1/(omega*C) - omega*L);
```

$$Z := R + (\frac{1}{\omega C} - \omega L) I.$$

We will start our Maple investigation by trying to determine magnitude $|Z|$ and phase θ of Z using Maple's capabilities for complex analysis. Whereas needing to know the magnitude and phase of Z is just another way of saying that we need to know Z in polar notation, we have Maple calculate these for us:

```
> Re(Z);                          Im(Z);                                    # ReZ, ImZ
```

$$Re(R + (\frac{1}{\omega C} - \omega L) I) \qquad\qquad Im(R + (\frac{1}{\omega C} - \omega L) I)$$

This is just a fancy way of giving us back the input. The problem is that Maple does not know that ω, R, L, and C are real, and so it cannot do the complex arithmetic. To tell Maple that the constants are real, we tell it what to assume:

```
> assume (R, real); assume(L, real); assume(C, real); assume (omega, real);
> Re(Z);        Im(Z);                                    # Now check again
```

$$R^{\sim} \qquad\qquad \frac{1}{\omega^{\sim} C^{\sim}} - \omega^{\sim} L^{\sim}$$

It has taken some work, but now we are ready for some complex arithmetic. Look at the polar form:

```
> polar(Z);
```

$$polar(\sqrt{R^{\sim 2} + (\frac{1}{\omega^{\sim} C^{\sim}} - \omega^{\sim} L^{\sim})^2}, \quad argument(R^{\sim} + (\frac{1}{\omega^{\sim} C^{\sim}} - \omega^{\sim} L^{\sim}) I))$$

This is giving us the correct magnitude, but Maple appears unable to compute the phase. This seems to be a Maple failure. However, we get it to work by combining the map and evalc commands:

```
> Polar := map( evalc, polar(Z) );                        # Polar is variable name
```

$$Polar := polar(\sqrt{R^{\sim 2} + (\frac{1}{\omega^{\sim} C^{\sim}} - \omega^{\sim} L^{\sim})^2}, \quad arctan(\frac{1}{\omega^{\sim} C^{\sim}} - \omega^{\sim} L^{\sim}, R^{\sim}))$$

Here map applies the procedure evalc to each element of polar(Z) and returns the polar form $(|Z|, \theta)$. This simplifies the elements into the form needed. [It should not be this hard!] We get separate expressions out for the real and imaginary parts by using the command op(numb,expression) to extract the numb-th operand from expression:

```
> op(1,Polar);     op(2,Polar);                              # Extract operands
```

$$\sqrt{R^{\sim2} + (\frac{1}{\omega^{\sim} C^{\sim}} - \omega^{\sim} L^{\sim})^2} \qquad\qquad \arctan(\frac{1}{\omega^{\sim} C^{\sim}} - \omega^{\sim} L^{\sim}, R^{\sim})$$

The expressions we have just derived are the standard ones for the magnitude and the phase of the impedance Z. However, since the current is proportional to $1/|Z|$, we will plot $1/|Z|$. We could compute $1/Z$ and work with that as well.

16.6.1 Maple's Surface Plots of Complex Impedance

We want to examine the current that occurs in the RLC circuit as a function of the driving frequency. We have already discussed in Chapter 4 some of Maple's commands for plotting complex functions. Irrespective of them being illuminating, for the problem given here, we first use plot3d to make the familiar $z(x, y)$ surface plot of the magnitude and phase of the current as functions of *both* the frequency of the external voltage ω and of the resistance R:

```
> restart:           Zinv := 1/(R + I * (1/(omega*C) - omega*L));  # Compute 1/Z
> L := 1000;          C :=1/1000;                            # Assign numerical values
```

$$Zinv := \frac{1}{R + (\frac{1}{\omega C} - \omega L) I} \qquad L := 1000 \qquad C := \frac{1}{1000}$$

```
> assume (R, real);       assume (omega, real);       # Tell Maple the constants are real
> Polar := map( evalc, polar(Zinv) );                 # Convert 1/Z to polar form
> polar(1/((R^2+(1000/omega-1000*omega)^2)^(1/2)),
> arctan(-1000/omega + 1000*omega, R));
```

$$Polar := \mathrm{polar}\left(\frac{1}{\sqrt{R^{\sim2} + (\frac{1000}{\omega^{\sim}} - 1000\,\omega^{\sim})^2}}, \arctan(-\frac{1000}{\omega^{\sim}} + 1000\,\omega^{\sim}, R^{\sim})\right)$$

```
> mag := op(1, Polar);       op(2, Polar);            # Extract magnitude, phase
```

$$mag := \frac{1}{\sqrt{R^{\sim2} + (\frac{1000}{\omega^{\sim}} - 1000\,\omega^{\sim})^2}} \qquad\qquad \arctan(-\frac{1000}{\omega^{\sim}} + 1000\,\omega^{\sim}, R^{\sim})$$

Check out how the magnitude has a maximum when the external frequency $\omega = 1/\sqrt{LC}$. This is the *resonance* frequency. For our choice of constants this corresponds to $\omega = 1$. We now make some plots to see if this is true.

```
> op(1, Polar);        with(plots):
> plot3d(op(1, Polar), omega = 0..2, R = 200..1000, axes = BOXED);  # 1/Z vs ω
```

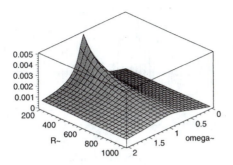

```
> plot3d(op(2,Polar), omega=0..2, R=200..1000, axes = NORMAL);        # θ vs ω
```

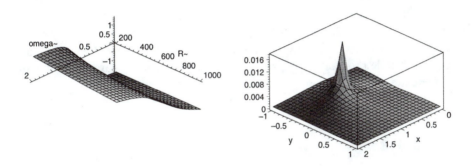

Sure enough, the plot of $1/|Z|$ shows that the magnitude of the current has a maximum at $\omega = 1$. (It helps to grab and rotate these plots to see them better.) We also see that as the resistance R in the circuit is made smaller, the maximum current becomes progressively larger. The second plot of the phase shows that below resonance, $\omega < 1$, the current lags the voltage, while above resonance the current leads the voltage. Another way to visualize complex functions is with the command complexplot3d. It makes a 3-D visualization of a complex function of a complex argument. Here we do it by treating the frequency $\omega = x + iy$ as a complex number:

```
> with(plots):          R := 1000;
> complexplot3d( 1/(R+I*(1/(w*C)-w*L) ), w = 0-I..2+I, axes = BOXED);     # 1/Z
```

We see in the right plot above that there is a sharp peak at $x = \text{Re}(\omega) = 1$, as expected. The color change indicates where $\text{Im}(1/Z)$ changes sign. If we look closely at this graph we will also see that there is a maximum for a negative imaginary value of ω. This is related to how long the resonance stays excited, a statement we do not try to prove here.

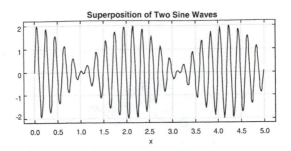

Figure 16.4 Superposition of two waves with similar wave numbers (a PtPlot).

16.7 EXPLORATIONS: OOP WORKED EXAMPLES*

Creating object-oriented programs (OOP) requires a transition from a procedural-programming mindset in which functions take arguments as input and produce answers as output, to one in which objects are created, probed, transferred, and modified. To assist you in the transition, we present here (courtesy of Manuel Páez) two sample procedural programs and their OOP counterparts. In both cases the OOP examples are longer but presumably easier to modify and extend.

16.7.1 OOP Beats

Listing 16.3 Beats.java

```java
1  //                    Beats.java:      plots  beats
2  import ptolemy.plot.*;
3  public class Beats
4  {   public static void main(String[] argv)
5  {
6      double y1, y2, y3, x;
7      int i;
8      x = 0.;                                    // Initial  position
9      Plot myPlot = new Plot();
10     myPlot.setTitle("Superposition of Two Sine Waves");
11     myPlot.setXLabel(" x");
12     for(i = 1;i<501;i++)
13     {   y1 = Math.sin(30*x);                    // Wave 1
14         y2 = Math.sin(33*x);                    // Wave 2
15         y3 = y1+y2;                             // Sum of waves
16         myPlot.addPoint(0,x,y3,true);
17         x = x + 0.01;                           // Small increment in x
18     }
19     PlotApplication app = new  PlotApplication(myPlot);
20 }}
```

First-year physics [Ser 00] usually explains how you obtain beats if you add together two sine functions y_1 and y_2 with nearly identical frequencies,

$$y_3(t) \quad = \quad y_1(t) + y_2(t), \tag{16.37}$$
$$y_1 = A \sin(30\,t), \qquad y_2 = A \sin(33\,t). \tag{16.38}$$

As shown in Figure 16.4, beats look like a single sine wave with a slowly varying amplitude. In Listing 16.3 we give `Beats.java`, a simple program that plot beats.

You see here that all the computation is done in the main program, with no methods called other than those for plotting. On lines 13 and 14 the variables `y1` and `y2` are defined as the appropriate functions of time, and then added together on line 15 to form the beats. Contrast this with the object-oriented program `OOPBeats.java` in Listing 16.4 that produces the same graph.

Listing 16.4 OOPBeats.java

```
1  //                    OOPBeats.java:   OOP Superposition 2 Sine waves
2  import ptolemy.plot.*;
3  public class OOPbeats
4  {     public double A, k1, k2;
5        // Class Constructor, Initializes variables
6        public OOPbeats(double Ampl, double freq1, double freq2) {
7        A = Ampl;                        // Same amplitude for both Sines
8        k1 = freq1;                                    // Freq 1st Sine
9        k2 = freq2;                                  // Freq 2nd Sine }
10       public void sumwaves()                         // Sums 2 waves
11   { int i;
12       double y1, y2, y3, x=0;
13       Plot myPlot = new Plot();
14       myPlot.setTitle("Superposition of two Sines");
15       myPlot.setXLabel(" x");
16       for(i = 1;i<501;i++) {
17           y1 = A*Math.sin(k1*x);                       // 1st Sine
18           y2 = A*Math.sin(k2*x);                       // 2nd Sine
19           y3 = y1 + y2;                              // Superpositon
20           myPlot.addPoint(0, x, y3, true);
21           x = x + 0.01;                            // Increment x  }
22       PlotApplication app = new   PlotApplication(myPlot);
23   }
24       public static void main(String[] argv)        // Class instance
25   {   OOPbeats sumsines = new OOPbeats(1., 30., 33.);      // Instance
26       sumsines.sumwaves();                      // Call sumsins' method
27  }}
```

Here the main program is at the very end, on lines 24–27. It is short because all it does is create an `OOPbeats` object named `sumsines` on line 25 with the appropriate parameters and then, on line 26, sums the two waves by having the method `sumwaves` modify the object. The constructor for an `OOPbeats` object is given on line 6, with the `sumwaves` method given on line 10. The `sumwaves` method takes no

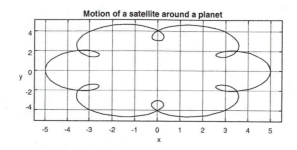

Figure 16.5 The trajectory of a satellite as seen from the sun.

arguments and returns no value; the waves are summed on line 19 and the graph plotted all within the method.

16.7.2 OOP Planet

Listing 16.5 Moon.java

```
1  //                        Moon.java:           moon orbiting a planet
2  import ptolemy.plot.*;
3  public class Moon
4  {    public static void main(String[] argv)
5  {    double Radius, wplanet;          //Planet's orbit r, ang. velocity
6       double radius, wmoon;             //Moon's r, omega wrt planet
7       double time, x, y;                //Position(t) of moon
8       Radius=4.0;                                       //Planet
9       wplanet=2.0;                                //Omega of planet
10      radius=1.0;                                 //Moon's orbit r
11      wmoon=14.0;                             //Oemga moon wrt planet
12      Plot myPlot=new Plot();
13      myPlot.setTitle("Motion of a moon around a planet ");
14      myPlot.setXLabel(" x");
15      myPlot.setYLabel(" y");
16      for(time=0.0;time<3.2;time=time+0.02)
17      {    x=Radius*Math.cos(wplanet*time)+radius*Math.cos(wmoon*time
            );
18           y=Radius*Math.sin(wplanet*time)+radius*Math.sin(wmoon*time
                );
19           myPlot.addPoint(0,x,y,true);    }
20      PlotApplication app=new PlotApplication(myPlot);
21  }}
```

In our second example we add together periodic functions representing positions versus time. One set describes the position of the moon as it revolves around a planet, and the other set describes the position of the planet as it revolves about the sun. Specifically, the planet orbits the sun at a radius $R = 4$ units with an angular frequency $\omega_p = 1$ radian/sec, while the moon orbits the Earth at a radius $r = 1$ unit from the planet and an angular velocity $\omega_s = 14$ radians/sec. In mathematical terms, the position of the planet at time t relative to the sun is described by

$$x_p = R \, \cos(\omega_p \, t),$$
$$y_p = R \, \sin(\omega_p \, t).$$

The position of the satellite, relative to the sun, is given by sums of its position relative to the planet, plus the position of the planet relative to the sun:

$$x_s = x_p + r \, \cos(\omega_s \, t) = R \, \cos(\omega_p \, t) + r \, \cos(\omega_s \, t),$$
$$y_s = y_p + r \, \sin(\omega_s \, t) = R \, \sin(\omega_p \, t) + r \, \sin(\omega_s \, t).$$

So again this looks like beating (if $\omega_s \simeq \omega_p$, and if we plot x or y *versus* t), except now we will make a parametric plot of $x(t)$ *versus* $y(t)$ to obtain a visualization of the orbit.

A procedural program Moon.java to do this summation and to produce the visualization shown in Figure 16.5 is in Listing 16.5.

Exercise: Rewrite the program using OOP.

1. Define a mother class OOPlanet containing:

Radius	planet's orbit radius
wplanet	planet's orbit ω
(xp, yp)	planet coordinates
(getX(double time), getY(double time)	methods for planet coordinates
trajectory()	method for planet's orbit

2. Define a daughter class OOPMoon containing:

radius	radius of moon's orbit
wmoon	frequency of moon in orbit
(xm, ym)	moon coordinates
trajectory()	method for moon's orbit relative to sun

3. The main program must contain one instance of the class planet and another instance of the class Moon, that is, one planet object and one Moon object.
4. Have each instance call its own trajectory method to plot the appropriate orbit. For the planet this should be a circle, while for the moon it should be a circle with retrogrades, as shown in Figure 16.5.   ♠

One solution, which produces the same results as the previous program, is our program OOPlanet.java in Listing 16.6. As with OOPbeats.java, the main program for OOPlanet.java is at the end, on line 56. It is short since all it does is create an OOPMoon object on line 68 with the appropriate parameters, and then have the moon's orbit plotted by applying the trajectory method to the object on line 69.

Listing 16.6 OOPPlanet.java

```java
1  //                    OOPlanet:    Planet  orbiting  Sun
2  import ptolemy.plot.*;
3  public class OOPlanet
4  {   double Radius, wplanet;                          //Orbit r and omega
5      double xp, yp;                                   //Planet coordinates
6      public OOPlanet()                                //default class constructor
7       { Radius = 0.;
8         wplanet = 0.; }
9      //Class constructor, assign variables
10     // @ param Rad the planet radius
11     //@ param pomg planet angular velocity
12     public OOPlanet(double Rad, double pomg) {
13     Radius = Rad;
14     wplanet = pomg;
15     }
16     public double getX( double time )               //get x of planet at t
17      { return   Radius*Math.cos( wplanet*time ); }
18     public double getY( double time )               //get y of planet at t
19      { return   Radius*Math.sin( wplanet*time ); }
20     public void trajectory()                         //trajectory of the planet
21      { double time;
22        Plot myPlot = new Plot();
23        myPlot.setTitle( "Motion of a planet around the Sun" );
24        myPlot.setXLabel(" x");
25        myPlot.setYLabel(" y");
26        for(time = 0.;time <3.2; time = time + 0.02)
27         { xp = getX( time );
28           yp = getY( time );
29           myPlot.addPoint(0, xp, yp, true);  }
30     PlotApplication app = new  PlotApplication( myPlot );
31     }
32 }
33 //planet class ends
34
35 //OOPMoon is daughter class of planet
36 class OOPMoon extends OOPlanet {
37     double radius, wmoon;              //radius, omega of satellite orbit
38     double xm, ym;                     //moon coordinate, wrt to Sun
39     //Default OOPMoon constructor, no arguments
40     public OOPMoon(){
41     radius = 0.;
42     wmoon = 0.;
43     }
44     //Full OOPMoon Constructor
45     public OOPMoon (double Rad, double pomg, double rad, double
          momg) {
46     Radius = Rad;
47     wplanet = pomg;
48     radius = rad;
49     wmoon = momg;
50     }
```

```
51   // trajectory: computes  coordinates  of  moon  relative  to  Sun,
52   // similar  to  one  in  mother  class
53   public void trajectory(){
54   double time;
55   Plot myPlot = new Plot();
56   myPlot.setTitle("Satellite orbit about planet");
57   myPlot.setXLabel(" x");
58   myPlot.setYLabel(" y");
59   for(time = 0.; time <3.2; time = time +0.02){
60       xm = getX(time) + radius*Math.cos(wmoon*time);
61       ym = getY(time) + radius*Math.sin(wmoon*time);
62       myPlot.addPoint(0, xm, ym, true);
63   }
64   PlotApplication app = new  PlotApplication(myPlot);
65   }
66   public static void main(String[] argv){
67   double Rad, pomg, rad, momg;
68   Rad = 4.;                                        // Planet
69   pomg = 2.;                        // angular velocity of planet
70   rad = 1.;                              // satellite orbit radius
71   momg = 14.;                     // ang. vel, satellite around planet
72   // uncomment next 2 lines for planet trajectory and
73       comment other two (Moon) lines
74   // OOPlanet earth = new OOPlanet(Rad, pomg);
75   // earth.trajectory();
76   // next two lines if desire the Moon trajectory
77   // but previous two lines must be commented
78   OOPMoon Selene = new OOPMoon(Rad, pomg, rad, momg);
79   Selene.trajectory();
80   }
81 }
```

What is new about this program is that it contains two classes, OOPlanet beginning on line 3, and OOPMoon beginning on line 39. This means that when you compile the program you should obtain two class files, OOPlanet.class and OOPMoon.class. Yet since execution begins in the main method, and the only main method is in OOPMoon, you need to execute OOPMoon.class to run the program:

```
% java OOPMoon                                    Execute main method
```

Scan the code to see how the class OOPMoon is within the class OOPlanet, and is therefore a *subclass*. Accordingly, OOPMoon is called a *daughter class* and OOPlanet is called a *mother class*. The daughter class inherits the properties of the mother class, as well as having properties of its own. Thus, on lines 51–52 OOPMoon uses the getX(time) and getY(time) methods from the OOPlanet class, without having to say OOPlanet.getX(time) to specify the class name.

16.8 KEY WORDS

abstract data types	reactance	frequency	imaginary number
complex conjugate	constructor	current	default constructor
complex arithmetic	class	impedance	instance of object
instance variable	magnitude	modulus	nonstatic methods
nonstatic variable	object	voltage	polar representation
complex number	reference call	resonance	user-defined data types
object creation			

16.9 JAVA AND MAPLE EXERCISES

1. Complex mathematics is much easier if we have the pure imaginary number $i = \sqrt{-1}$. Define a new complex variable i with a value equal to i. (In Maple, this is just the built-in variable I.)

2. Now that you have a specific variable for i, write some new methods (functions) that compute the following functions of complex numbers (objects):
   a. $\exp(z) = e^{x+iy} = e^x e^{iy} = e^x(\cos y + i \sin y)$
   b. $\sin(z) = (e^{iz} - e^{-iz})/2i$

3. Verify that your methods work by trying some simple cases. (In Maple, compare to the built-in functions that also handle complex numbers.) Examples of simple cases might be the use of complex numbers like $z_1, z_2 = 0, 1, i, 2, 2i, \ldots$, where you can easily figure out the answers.

4. Let $z = 3 + 3\sqrt{(3)}i$.
   a. Determine $|z|$ and check that you get 6.
   b. Determine the phase θ of z and check that you get $\theta = \pi/3$.

5. Find $\mathrm{Re}(2-3i)^2/(2+3i)$, $\mathrm{Im}(1/z^2)$, $|(1+z)/(1-z)|$, and $(2-3i)/(2+3i)$.

6. Consider the complex number $z = x + iy$. Use gnuplot to make a surface plot of $\mathrm{Im}\cos(z)$ and $\mathrm{Re}\cos(z)$.

7. Consider the complex function $f(z) = z^3/(1 + z^4)$.
   a. Make a plot of $f(x)$ *versus* x, that is, assume z is real and vary it along the real axis.
   b. Make surface plots of $\mathrm{Re}z$ and $\mathrm{Im}z$. Restrict the range of x and y values to lie close to where the "action" is.

Chapter Seventeen

Arrays: Vectors, Matrices; Rigid-Body Rotations

Vectors and matrices play key roles in scientific computing. Indeed, much of so-called *high-performance computing* involves computations with very large arrays. These arrays may contain experimental data needing processing, or they may contain the results of a simulation in which the discrete nature of breaking space up into small units leads naturally to the use of arrays. And since real-world problems are often complicated and require high precision (small units), arrays with thousands or millions of elements are not unusual. Even though this means that the matrices used in realistic problems will be big and will require efficient algorithms, often the programs using matrices are simple and direct.

In this chapter we deal with techniques needed to create and manipulate vectors and matrices in Java. We will solve the same problem as we did with Maple in Chapter 7, "Matrices and Vectors; Rigid-Body Rotation." If needed, you should review that chapter for some of the physics and mathematics background (even elementary stuff like what a vector is), and then return here for the Java approach. In an optional section of this chapter we discuss *Jama*, a library of linear algebra methods in Java, that deals with true matrix objects.

It is interesting to observe how the Java and Maple approaches to this problem tend to complement each other. Maple is able to do the calculations symbolically, whereas Java is not. However, Maple is slow in performing numeric calculations involving large matrices, while compiled languages tend to be much faster. In addition, Maple excels in its capacity for interactive 3-D graphics, while this is harder to do in Java or even Mathematica. There are Java packages available that permit interactive 3-D graphics, but they are too complicated or too expensive for us to treat here.

17.1 PROBLEM: RIGID-BODY ROTATIONS

Your problem is similar to the one in Chapter 7. Here we will deal with a plate and a square whose moments of inertia are given, and we will focus on the matrix multiplication that converts the angular velocity ω into the angular momentum $\mathbf{L}$.

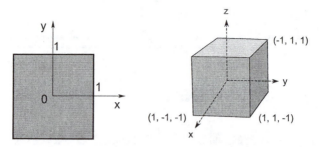

Figure 17.1 *Left:* A plate sitting in the $x - y$ plane with a coordinate system at its center. *Right:* A cube sitting in the center of a three-dimensional coordinate system.

Problem 1: Consider the two-dimensional rectangular metal plate shown on the left of Figure 17.1. It has sides $a = 2$ and $b = 1$, mass $m = 12$, and inertia tensor for axes through the center:

$$\{I\} = \begin{pmatrix} mb^2/12 & 0 \\ 0 & ma^2/12 \end{pmatrix} = \begin{pmatrix} 1 & 0 \\ 0 & 4 \end{pmatrix}. \tag{17.1}$$

The plate is rotated so that its angular velocity vector ω always remains in the $x-y$ plane (which does not mean the plate remains in the $x - y$ plane). Specifically, it is rotated with the three angular velocities:

$$\omega = (1,0), \qquad\qquad \omega = (0,1), \qquad\qquad \omega = (1,1). \tag{17.2}$$

Write a Java program that computes the angular momentum vector **L** via the matrix multiplication $\mathbf{L} = \{I\}\omega$. Plot ω and **L** for each case, and compare the results to those found with Maple.

Problem 2: Consider now the rotation of the cube on the right of Figure 17.1. The cube has side $b = 1$, mass $m = 1$, and, for axes on the corner, an inertia tensor [M&T 88]:

$$\{I\} = mb^2 \begin{pmatrix} +2/3 & -1/4 & -1/4 \\ -1/4 & +2/3 & -1/4 \\ -1/4 & -1/4 & +2/3 \end{pmatrix} = \begin{pmatrix} +2/3 & -1/4 & -1/4 \\ -1/4 & +2/3 & -1/4 \\ -1/4 & -1/4 & +2/3 \end{pmatrix}. \tag{17.3}$$

The cube is rotated along axes passing through two sides and the diagonal, explicitly, with the three angular velocities:

$$\omega = (1,0,0), \qquad\qquad \omega = (0,1,0), \qquad\qquad \omega = (1,1,1). \tag{17.4}$$

Write a Java program that computes the angular momentum vector **L** via the requisite matrix multiplication. Plot ω and **L** for each case, and compare the results to those found with Maple.

17.2 THEORY: ANGULAR-MOMENTUM DYNAMICS

Recall from Chapter 7 that the angular-momentum vector $\mathbf{L}$ is given by the product

$$\mathbf{L} = \{I\}\,\boldsymbol{\omega}. \tag{17.5}$$

Here $\boldsymbol{\omega}$ is the angular-velocity vector and $\{I\}$ is the inertia tensor represented by the matrix $[I_{ij}]$:

$$\{I\} = [I_{ij}] = \begin{pmatrix} I_{xx} & I_{xy} & I_{xz} \\ I_{yx} & I_{yy} & I_{yz} \\ I_{zx} & I_{zy} & I_{zz} \end{pmatrix}. \tag{17.6}$$

Despite the use of x, y, and z to label the three axes being standard in elementary science, the mathematics and the computing gets easier if we label each direction with a number rather than a letter. Consequently, we now change to a notation in which A_0 indicates the component of the vector $\mathbf{A}$ in the x or "0" direction, A_1 indicates the component in the y or "1" direction, and A_2 indicates the component in the z or "2" direction:

$$\begin{pmatrix} A_x \\ A_y \\ A_z \end{pmatrix} \Leftrightarrow \begin{pmatrix} A_0 \\ A_1 \\ A_2 \end{pmatrix}, \quad \begin{pmatrix} I_{xx} & I_{xy} & I_{xz} \\ I_{yx} & I_{yy} & I_{yz} \\ I_{zx} & I_{zy} & I_{zz} \end{pmatrix} \Leftrightarrow \begin{pmatrix} I_{00} & I_{01} & I_{02} \\ I_{10} & I_{11} & I_{12} \\ I_{20} & I_{21} & I_{22} \end{pmatrix}. \tag{17.7}$$

Here we use $0, 1, 2$ for the indices rather than $1, 2, 3$ to be consistent with Java conventions for array elements.

With this new notation, the relation stating that the angular momentum equals the product of the moment of inertia tensor times the angular-velocity vector is represented by the *matrix multiplication*:

$$\begin{pmatrix} L_0 \\ L_1 \\ L_2 \end{pmatrix} = \begin{pmatrix} I_{00} & I_{01} & I_{02} \\ I_{10} & I_{11} & I_{12} \\ I_{20} & I_{21} & I_{22} \end{pmatrix} \begin{pmatrix} \omega_0 \\ \omega_1 \\ \omega_2 \end{pmatrix}. \tag{17.8}$$

In terms of the individual components, (17.8) is an elegant way of representing the three simultaneous equations:

$$L_0 = I_{00}\omega_0 + I_{01}\omega_1 + I_{02}\omega_2, \tag{17.9}$$
$$L_1 = I_{10}\omega_0 + I_{11}\omega_1 + I_{12}\omega_2, \tag{17.10}$$
$$L_2 = I_{20}\omega_0 + I_{21}\omega_1 + I_{22}\omega_2. \tag{17.11}$$

These three equations may also be written in a convenient form for computations:

$$L_k = \sum_{j=0}^{2} I_{kj}\omega_j, \qquad k = 0, 1, 2. \tag{17.12}$$

17.3 CS, MATH: ARRAYS, VECTORS, AND MATRICES

We saw in Chapter 16's dealing with complex-number objects, how the mathematics and the programming become simpler if we deal with a variable's single name, even though it has multiple parts. In computer science we store an entire table of numbers in a single variable when that variable is declared as an *array*. You then deal with the entire array as one symbol, or deal with individual elements in the array via a subscript or index notation. As a case in point, we store the final exam scores of all students in the array `Final[i]`, with the different values of the index `i` referring to different students. In this case, `Final[10] = 99` would be the score of student number `10`, and `Final[100] = 13` would be the (sorrowful) score of student number `100`.

There is no requirement that arrays have only one index. To prove the point, we could use the 2-D array `HW[i][j]` to store all homework scores for all students, with `i` representing the assignment number and `j` representing the student number. It follows then that `HW[2][3] =99` would be second homework score for student number `3`, while `HW[10][500] =12` would be the tenth homework score for student `500`.

You may think of a CS array as an abstraction of the mathematical idea of matrices and vectors. Arrays are collections of values of a certain data types, which themselves may be either abstract or intrinsic types. The values contained in an array are called *elements*, and the shape of an array is referred to its *dimensions*.

Actually, 2-D arrays are stored in Java as a 1-D array, with each element of the 1-D array being another 1-D array representing a row of elements:

$$HW[i][j] = \begin{bmatrix} \boxed{HW[1][1] \quad HW[1][2] \quad HW[1][3]} \\ \boxed{HW[2][1] \quad HW[2][2] \quad HW[2][3]} \\ \boxed{HW[3][1] \quad HW[3][2] \quad HW[3][3]} \end{bmatrix}, \qquad (17.13)$$

where each box is an independent 1-D array. This means, as we shall see, that we may then assign values to each row in a single command, and that we may even make each row independent objects from the other rows.

In mathematics and science we deal with objects called *vectors* and *matrices*. Taking into account that only one index is needed to distinguish the components of a vector, they are stored on a computer in a 1-D *array*. Because matrices have rows and columns, their elements are stored in arrays with two indices. As an example, the matrix I_{xy}, representing the inertia tensor, could have its components stored in the array `I[x][y]`. To repeat, the mathematical objects are vectors and matrices, the computer storage is in single-indexed and double-indexed arrays. (In a later section of this chapter we discuss Jama, an extension of Java that deals with objects that are true matrices.)

As is often the case when science and computer science are combined, confusion results from using different words to describe the same idea. Even worse, we often use the same words to describe different ideas. Of necessity we now must point out that our use of the words "two-dimensional" and "three-dimensional" is from physics, where the number of dimensions of space equals the number of components (indices) that a vector may have, and where the number of values that any one index spans is also equal to the number of dimensions. Yet on a computer, a "three-dimensional array" refers to a data type with three indices, such as A[i][j][k], and there is no limit on the range spanned by any one of the indices i, j, and k. In the latter case, the maximum value of some index is referred to as the "size" or "length" of the array, not its "dimension." To name an example, the two-dimensional physics vectors used to describe motion in a plane are stored in one-dimensional arrays of length 2.

Recall how in Chapter 16, "Object-Oriented Programming," we used a single *object*, or *abstract data type*, to store the real and imaginary parts of a complex number. Java represents arrays as objects, with the size of the object determined by the programmer, and with the individual components of the object referenced by array indices. Explicitly, the elements of an array are referenced by giving each index in a square bracket after the array name, for example, R[1] or I[x][y].

As we saw for complex objects, arrays also must be *declared* and *created*. Declaration tells the compiler the name of the array and the type of data elements to be stored in it. Creation reserves a place in memory for the array elements. The syntax for array *declaration* is similar to that used for primitive data-type declaration, but now with empty square brackets following or preceding the array name:

```
double R[];                                     // Declare R as an array
double[] R;                                     // Alternate declaration
```

After declaring an array to exist, we must also *create* the place in memory for it by using the new operator (as we also did for complex objects):

```
R = new double[3];                              // Create array R
```

As with complex objects, declaration and creation may be combined in one line:

```
double R[] = new double[3];                     // Declare and create array R
```

An important variation on this one-line declaration is the ability to declare, create, and initialize Java arrays in one step with the *initializer* convention. By entering a list of comma-separated values enclosed in curly braces, we accomplish these three tasks in one fell swoop:

```
double R[] = {1.2, 2.4, 4.5};          // Declare, create, and initialize array R
```

where this initializer may be used only in a declaration statement. Observe how
the declaration does not specify the size of the array in these examples. That is
done by the creation step that includes a number within the square brackets, or by
explicit initialization. For the array R this is length 3, which means that it contains
the elements R[0], R[1], and R[2].

   A common error in dealing with arrays is going out of bounds, that is, telling
the computer to go to a location in memory that does not contain any of your
array's elements. This error is easy to make. Even though we declare double
R[length], the last element of the array is R[length-1] since the index count
starts at 0 and not 1. Java is all too happy to tell you (again and again) that you have
made this mistake, and then not compile your program for you; other languages
may let you go beyond the declared size, which is not good because you may end
up someplace where you do not belong.

Listing 17.1 OneDArray.java

```
1  //              OneDarray.java:          using arrays as vectors
2  public class OneDarray
3  { public static void main(String[] argv)                // main method
4    { double A[] = new double [10000];                     // Initialize
5      double B[] = new double [10000];
6      double C[] = new double [10000];
7      int j, k;
8      double startTime , endTime;
9      startTime = System.currentTimeMillis();                 // Present t
10     for (int i=0; i< 10000; i++)
11     {   A[i] = Math.sqrt(i);                    //Assign array elements
12         B[i] = i *i;
13         System.out.println( "i, A[i], B[i] = "
14               + i + ", "+ A[i]+ ", " +B[i] ); }
15     System.out.println(" ");
16     for (int i=0; i< 10000; i++)
17     {   j =  (i + 1);
18         if ( j > 9999 ) j = j - 9999;
19         k =  (i + 2);
20         if ( k > 9999 ) k = k - 9999;
21     C[i] = A[j]*B[k] - A[k]*B[j];
22     System.out.println("i, j, k, C[i] = "
23               + i+ ", " + j+ ", "+ k+ ", " + C[i]);  }
24     endTime = System.currentTimeMillis();
25     System.out.println("time (s) =" + (endTime -startTime)/1000);
26  }}
```

Example and exercise: The program OneDarray.java in Listing 17.1 sets up
two vectors **A** and **B**, each of length 10,000, and then forms the cross product
A × **B**.

1. Compile and execute this program. Examine the way the last line gives you the time it took Java to run your program (execution time). This was obtained by calling the Java utility program, `System.currentTimeMillis()` that reads the clock on the wall in milliseconds.

2. Place the three 1-D vectors A, B, and C into a single 2-D array. You may do this with statements of the form:

```
double Vecs[][] = new double [10] [10000];        // Create A
Vecs[0] [i] = Math.sqrt(i);                        // Set value for a single element
Vecs[1] [i] = i * i;                               // Set value for a single element
```

3. Compile and execute the 2-D version of the program and note how much longer it now takes to run. The extra time arises from the computer having to move through larger blocks of memory.

4. Modify `OneDarray.java` to print out values for A[0], A[999], and A[1000]. Java should not let you access an element that is out of bounds. ♠

17.4 IMPLEMENTATION: INERTIA.JAVA, INERTIA3D.JAVA

For our rotation problem, implemented in `Inertia.java` and `Inertia3D.java`, we will represent the vectors $\mathbf{L}$ and ω with the 1-D arrays L and w, and the inertia tensor $\{I\}$ with the 2-D array I. We have showed you how to declare these arrays in Java and how to reserve memory locations for them, but we have not actually placed any values for them in memory. The most direct way to assign values to an array is by assigning values to each individual element. By way of example, if our angular velocity vector ω were pointing along the x axis with magnitude 10, then we would assign it the three components:

```
w[0] = 10.;      w[1] = 0.;      w[2] = 0.;                // x, y, and z components
```

Declaring values for the moment of inertia tensor I is more interesting since it is a 3×3 array. Again, we explicitly list each individual element, for example,

```
I[0] [0] = 1;      I[0] [1] = 2;      I[0] [2] = 3;
I[1] [0] = 4;      I[1] [1] = 5;      I[1] [2] = 6;
I[2] [0] = 7;      I[2] [1] = 8;      I[2] [2] = 9;
```

In addition to creating multidimensional arrays by using the `new` statement, we may also create them by explicitly listing values for all the elements using the initializer convention. When entering values for an entire array, an entire *row* of values is entered as if it were a single element corresponding to the second index. Wherefrom you may think of a 2-D array in Java as a 1-D array of rows:

```
double I[][] = { {1, 2, 3}, {4, 5, 6}, {7, 8, 9} };      // Declare, initialize 2-D array
```

Indeed, although we will not have any need for it in this chapter, it is also possible to build up an array with each row having a different length, or with the elements of an array being sub-arrays. In this way, arrays are used to build some structured data sets. To repeat, a 2-D array is entered as a 1-D array of 1-D arrays.

The number of elements contained within an array is referred to as its *length*. In Java, an array is an object with length as one of its properties, and we extract that property with a dot operation; for example, A.length is the length of array A:

```
double A[] = new double [10000];                    // Declaration and creation of A
System.out.println("A.length = " + A.length);
Output: A.length = 10000                            // Length of A
```

In ArrayLength.java on the CD, we demonstrate how to determine the length of a 2-D or 3-D array. Recall that a 2-D array is constructed as a 1-D array of rows, with each row stored as independent 1-D arrays. Because each row may have different lengths, we need to specify that row in which we are interested:

```
double B[][] = new double [100] [200];              // 100 rows, each with 200 columns
System.out.println("B.length = " + B.length);
Output: B.length = 100                              // Number rows in B
System.out.println("B[0].length = " + B[0].length);
Output: B[0].length = 200                           // Row 0 length
System.out.println("B[1].length = " + B[1].length);
Output: B[1].length = 200                           // Row 1 length
```

17.4.1 Arrays as Arguments to Methods

Now we break two of the rules we stated in Chapter 10, "Data Types, Limits, Methods." We told you there that a method returns only one number as its value, and that changes made to arguments are not returned to the calling program. The exceptions to these rules occur when an array (or any object) is used as the argument to a method. Inasmuch as an array is an object with multiple parts, when a method is called with an array as an argument, Java passes the location in memory where the object is stored instead of the values of its individual parts. For instance, if we pass the array x[3] as the argument to a method f(x), then method f cannot change the value of the address in memory where storage of the three elements of x begins, but it is free to change the actual values x[0], x[1], and x[2] that are stored there. And since the calling program goes to the same locations in memory, it will find the changed values there. Since the argument to the method is an address that does not get changed, Java does not flag this scheme as an error. For example, the code ArraysEqual.java on the CD shows that if two arrays are set equal to each other, then they share the same locations in memory, and so changing the values of one automatically changes the values of the other.

To see how this works, run the code `ArrayChange.java` in Listing 17.2. Check that all three values of x are changed by the method `f(x)`, but none are returned to `main` as arguments. Nevertheless, the changed values of x are seen by `main` method. In fact, `f` returns nothing to `main`, as indicated in `f`'s declaration statement by `void` as its data type. The `return` statement is needed, but only to get back to `main`.

Listing 17.2 ArrayChange.java

```
1  //                  ArrayChange.java:  modify array in method
2  public class ArrayChange
3  {   public static void main(String[] argv)
4  {   int x[] = {1,2,3};              // Declare x[3], assign 3 values
5      System.out.println("In main, x[0], x[1], x[2] = "+ x[0] +", "
           + x[1] +", "+ x[2]);
6      f(x);                           // Call f(x) to change x
7      System.out.println("In main, x[0], x[1], x[2] = "+ x[0] +", "
           + x[1] +", " +x[2]);
8      public static void f(int x[])            // void as no output
9      {   x[0] = 5;
10         x[1] = 10;
11         x[2] = 15;
12         System.out.println( "In f(x), x[0], x[1], x[2]= "+ x[0] +"
               , " + x[1] +", " + x[2]);
13         return; }                    // Nothing returned
14  }}
```

17.5 JAMA: JAVA MATRIX LIBRARY*

Jama is a basic linear algebra package for Java, developed at the US National Institute of Science [Jama]. We recommend it since it works well, is natural and understandable to non-experts, is free, and helps make scientific codes more universal and portable. Other scientific subroutine libraries in Fortran and C, such as Lapack [LAP 95], have made valuable contributions to science by providing numerical techniques that are more efficient and reliable than those a scientist or engineer might write in the course of solving a problem. Jama provides object-oriented classes that construct true `Matrix` objects, add and multiply matrices, solve matrix equations, and print out entire matrices in aligned row-by-row format. Jama is intended to serve as the standard matrix class for Java.[1]

17.5.1 Jama Examples

The first example deals with 3×1 vectors **b** and **x**, and a 3×3 matrix $[A]$:

---

[1]A sibling matrix package, *Jampack* [Jampack] has also been developed at NIST and the University of Maryland, and it works for complex matrices as well.

```
1  double[][]  array  =  {{1.,2.,3},{4.,5.,6.},{7.,8.,10.}};
2  Matrix  A  =  new  Matrix(array);
3  Matrix  b  =  Matrix.random(3,1);
4  Matrix  x  =  A.solve(b);
5  Matrix  Residual  =  A.times(x).minus(b);
```

The vectors and matrices are declared and created as `Matrix` variables, with **b** given random values. It then solves the 3×3 linear system of equations $\{A\}\mathbf{x} = \mathbf{b}$ with the single command `Matrix x = A.solve(b);`, and computes the residual $\{A\}\mathbf{x} - \mathbf{b}$ with the command `Residual = A.times(x).minus(b);`.

Listing 17.3 JamaEigen.java

```
1  /*      JamaEigen.java:  eigenvalue  problem  with  NIST  JAMA
2  JAMA  must  be  in  same  directory,  or  include  JAMA  in  CLASSPATH
3  uses  Matrix.class,  see  Matrix.java  or  HTML  documentation */
4  import  Jama.*;
5  import  java.io.*;
6  public  class  JamaEigen  {
7    public  static  void  main(String[] argv)  {
8    double[][]  I  =  {  {2./3,-1./4,-1./4},  {-1./4,2./3,-1./4},
         {-1./4,-1./4,2./3}  };
9    Matrix  MatI  =  new  Matrix(I);            // Form  Matrix  from  2D  arrays
10   System.out.print(  "Input  Matrix"  );
11   MatI.print  (10,  5);                        // Jama's  Matrix  print
12   // Jama  eigenvalue  finder
13   EigenvalueDecomposition  E  =  new  EigenvalueDecomposition(MatI);
14   double[]  lambdaRe  =  E.getRealEigenvalues();           // Real  eigens
15   double[]  lambdaIm  =  E.getImagEigenvalues();           // Imag  eigens
16   System.out.println("Eigenvalues:  \t  lambda.Re[] = " + lambdaRe
         [0]+", "+lambdaRe[1]+", "+lambdaRe[2]);
17   Matrix  V  =  E.getV();                     // Get  matrix  of  eigenvectors
18   System.out.print("\n Matrix  with  column  eigenvectors ");
19   V.print  (10,  5);
20   Matrix  Vec  =  new  Matrix(3,1);           // Extract  single  eigenvector
21   Vec.set(  0,  0,  V.get(0,  0)  );
22   Vec.set(  1,  0,  V.get(1,  0)  );
23   Vec.set(  2,  0,  V.get(2,  0)  );
24   System.out.print(  "First  Eigenvector,  Vec"  );
25   Vec.print  (10,5);
26   Matrix  LHS  =  MatI.times(Vec);            // Should  get  Vec  as  answer
27   Matrix  RHS  =  Vec.times(lambdaRe[0]);
28   System.out.print(  "Does  LHS  =  RHS?"  );
29   LHS.print  (18,  12);
30   RHS.print  (18,  12);
31  }}
```

Our second Jama example looks at the same problem examined in §7.7, namely, finding the principle-axes system for a cube. We discussed the idea that there is a coordinate system in which this inertia tensor is diagonal, and that finding such a system entails solving the eigenvalue problem,

$$\{I\}\omega = \lambda\omega, \tag{17.14}$$

where $\{I\}$ is the original inertia matrix, ω is an eigenvector, and λ is an eigenvalue. The program JamaEigen.java in Listing 17.3 solves for the eigenvalues and vectors, and produces output of the form:

```
Input Matrix
     0.66667      -0.25000      -0.25000
    -0.25000       0.66667      -0.25000
    -0.25000      -0.25000       0.66667

Eigenvalues:  lambda.Re[] = 0.1666666666666665,
0.9166666666666666, 0.9166666666666666

Matrix with column eigenvectors               First Eigenvector, Vec
    -0.57735      -0.70711      -0.40825             -0.57735
    -0.57735       0.70711      -0.40825             -0.57735
    -0.57735       0.00000       0.81650             -0.57735

Does LHS = RHS?
    -0.096225044865      -0.096225044865
    -0.096225044865      -0.096225044865
    -0.096225044865      -0.096225044865
```

Look at JamaEigen and notice how on line 8 we first set up the array I with all the elements of the inertia tensor, and then on line 10 we create a matrix MatI with the same elements as the array. On line 13 the eigenvalue problem is solved with the creation of an eigenvalue object E via the Jama command:

```
13  EigenvalueDecomposition E = new EigenvalueDecomposition(MatI);
```

Then on line 14 we extract (get) a vector lambdaRe of length 3 containing the three (real) eigenvalues, lambdaRe[0], lambdaRe[1], lambdaRe[2]:

```
14  double[] lambdaRe = E.getRealEigenvalues();
```

On line 17 we create a 3×3 matrix V containing the eigenvectors in the three columns of the matrix with the Jama command:

```
17  Matrix V = E.getV();
```

which takes the eigenvector object E and gets the vectors from it. Then, on lines 21–23, we form a vector Vec (a 3×1 Matrix) containing a single eigenvector by extracting the elements from V with a get method, and assigning them with a set method:

```
21  Vec.set(0,0,V.get(0,0));
```

Our final Jama example is the program JamaFit.java in Listing 17.4. It demonstrates many of the features of Jama. It makes a least-squares fit [CP 05] of the parabola $y(x) = b_0 + b_1 x + b_2 x^2$ to a set of N_D measured data points:

$$(x_i, y_i \pm \sigma_i), \qquad i = 1, N_D, \tag{17.15}$$

where $\pm\sigma_i$ is the uncertainty in the ith value of y. The fitting is realized by finding a solution to the three simultaneous linear equations:

$$\begin{bmatrix} N_D & S_x & S_{xx} \\ S_x & S_{xx} & S_{xxx} \\ S_{xx} & S_{xxx} & S_{xxxx} \end{bmatrix} \begin{bmatrix} b_0 \\ b_1 \\ b_2 \end{bmatrix} = \begin{bmatrix} S_y \\ S_{xy} \\ S_{xxy} \end{bmatrix}. \qquad (17.16)$$

Here the S's are various sums over the data:

$$S_x = \sum_{i=1}^{N_D} \frac{x_i}{\sigma_i^2}, \quad S_y = \sum_{i=1}^{N_D} \frac{y_i}{\sigma_i^2}, \quad S_{xx} = \sum_{i=1}^{N_D} \frac{x_i^2}{\sigma_i^2}, \quad S_{xy} = \sum_{i=1}^{N_D} \frac{x_i y_i}{\sigma_i^2}. \qquad (17.17)$$

Listing 17.4 JamaFit.java

```java
/*    JamaFit: NIST JAMA matrix libe least-squares parabola fit
 y(x) = b0 + b1 x + b2 xx JAMA libe must be in same directory as
 program, or modify CLASSPATH to include JAMA */
import Jama.*;
import java.io.*;
public class JamaFit
{    public static void main(String[] argv) {
     double []   x = {1., 1.05, 1.15, 1.32, 1.51, 1.68, 1.92};
     double []   y = {0.52, 0.73, 1.08, 1.44, 1.39, 1.46, 1.58};
     double [] sig = {0.1, 0.1, 0.2, 0.3, 0.2, 0.1, 0.1};
     int Nd = 7;                                // Number of data points
     double sig2, s, sx, sxx, sy, sxxx, sxxxx, sxy, sxxy, rhl;
     double [][] Sx = new double[3][3];         // Create 3x3 array
     double [][] Sy = new double[3][1];         // Create 3x1 array
     s= sx = sxx = sy = sxxx = sxxxx = sxy = sxy = sxxy = 0;
     for (int i=0; i <= Nd-1; i++)        // Generate matrix elements
     {    sig2    = sig[i]*sig[i];
          s       += 1./sig2;
          sx      += x[i]/sig2;
          sy      += y[i]/sig2;
          rhl     = x[i]*x[i];
          sxx     += rhl/sig2;
          sxxy    += rhl*y[i]/sig2;
          sxy     += x[i]*y[i]/sig2;
          sxxx    += rhl*x[i]/sig2;
          sxxxx   += rhl*rhl/sig2;
     }                                          // Assign arrays
     Sx[0][0] = s;
     Sx[0][1] = Sx[1][0] = sx;
     Sx[0][2] = Sx[2][0] = Sx[1][1] = sxx;
     Sx[1][2] = Sx[2][1] = sxxx;
     Sx[2][2] = sxxxx;
     Sy[0][0] = sy;
     Sy[1][0] = sxy;
     Sy[2][0] = sxxy;
     Matrix MatSx = new Matrix(Sx);             // Form Jama Matrices
     Matrix MatSy = new Matrix(3, 1);
     MatSy.set(0, 0, sy);
```

```
39    MatSy.set(1, 0, sxy);
40    MatSy.set(2, 0, sxxy);
41    Matrix B = MatSx.inverse().times(MatSy);    // Determine inverse
42    Matrix Itest = MatSx.inverse().times(MatSx);    // Test inverse
43    System.out.print( "B Matrix via inverse" );    // Jama print
44    B.print (16, 14);
45    System.out.print( "MatSx.inverse().times(MatSx) " );
46    Itest.print (16, 14);
47    B = MatSx.solve(MatSy);    // Direct solution too
48    System.out.print( "B Matrix via direct" );
49    B.print (16,14);
50        // Extract using Jama get & Print parabola coefficients
51    System.out.println("FitParabola2 Final Results");
52    System.out.println("\n");
53    System.out.println("y(x) = b0 + b1 x + b2 x^2");
54    System.out.println("\n");
55    System.out.println("b0 = "+B.get(0,0));
56    System.out.println("b1 = "+B.get(1,0));
57    System.out.println("b2 = "+B.get(2,0));
58    System.out.println("\n");
59    for (int i=0; i <= Nd-1; i++) {    // Test fit
60        s=B.get(0,0)+B.get(1,0)*x[i]+B.get(2,0)*x[i]*x[i];
61        System.out.println("i, xi, yi, yfit = "+i+", "+x[i]+", "+y
          [i]+", "+s);}
62  }  }
```

17.6 KEY WORDS

angular momentum	angular velocity	arrays	arrays as arguments
declaration	creation	dimension	eigenvalue problem*
inertia tensor	initializer	linear equations*	matrix library
matrix multiplication	rigid bodies	rotation	

Explain in just a few words what is meant by:

1. a subscript and an array index being different;
2. an abstract data type;
3. a complex number;
4. a Java object;
5. an array;
6. the dimension of an array;
7. the length of an array;
8. a class variable;
9. a local variable;
10. the difference between a class and a method.

17.7 SUPPLEMENTARY EXERCISES

1. Do problems 1 and 2 from the beginning of this chapter!

2. Consider the program `arrayChange.java` given in Listing 17.2. We declared x to be an array of integers, created the array, and assigned it values all on one line with `int x[] = {1,2,3}`. Modify the program so that only the declaration and creation are done in one statement. Do the creation using the `new` command and the assignment in a different statement.

3. We used an integer array as the argument for our method. Modify the program so that `x[]` is now a double of length 5, rather than 3. Test your method by printing out the 5 doubles before and after the method call.

4. There is no reason that the method `f(x[])` cannot also do some calculations and return a value for `f(x[])` as well as changing the values of `x[]`. Modify `ArrayChange.java` so that the method calculates and `main` prints out the norm

$$f(x) = \sqrt{\sum_{i=0} x_i^2}. \qquad (17.18)$$

5. What we have said about methods dealing with single-indexed arrays hold equally true for multi-indexed arrays. Modify the program so that `x[3]` is now the two-indexed array `x[3][2]`, and assign values to `x[i][1]` for `i = 0, 2`.

Chapter Eighteen

Advanced Objects; Baton Projectiles*

In this chapter (coauthored with Connelly Barnes) we look at some additional aspects of object-oriented programming (OOP). These aspects are designed to help make programming more efficient by making the reuse of already-written components easier and more reliable. The ideal is to permit this even for entirely different, future projects, for which you will have no memory or knowledge of the internal workings of the already-written components that you want to reuse. OOP concepts are particularly helpful in complicated projects in which you need to add new features without "breaking" the old ones, and in which you may be modifying code that you did not write.

18.1 PROBLEM: TRAJECTORY OF THROWN BATON

In Chapter 12, "Flow Control via Logic," we examined the motion of a cannonball as it travels through the air, and in Chapter 15 we showed how to include drag. In this chapter we extend our description of frictionless projectile motion to that of a baton that spins as it travels through the air. Figure 18.1 shows the baton as two identical spheres joined by a massless bar. Each sphere has mass m and radius r, with the centers of the spheres separated by a distance L. The baton is thrown with the initial velocity shown on the left of Figure 18.2 (this corresponds to a rotation about the center of the lower sphere).

Problem: Extend the program already developed for projectile motion of a point

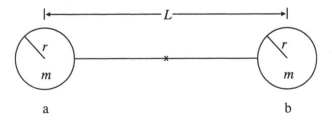

a   b

Figure 18.1 The baton before it is thrown. "x" marks the CM.

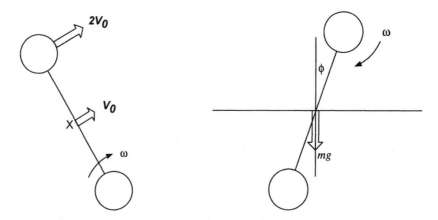

Figure 18.2 *Left:* The initial conditions for the baton as it is thrown. *Right:* The baton spinning in the air under the action of gravity.

particle to an object-oriented program that computes the position and velocity of the baton as a function of time. The program should:

1. plot the position of each end of the baton as a function of time;
2. plot the translational kinetic energy, the rotational kinetic energy, and the potential energy of the baton, all as functions of time;
3. use several classes as building blocks so that you may change one building block without affecting the rest of the program;
4. then be extended to solve for the motion of a baton with an additional lead weight at its center.

18.2 THEORY: COMBINED TRANSLATION AND ROTATION

Classical dynamics describes the motion of the baton as the motion of an imaginary point particle located at the center of mass (CM), plus a rotation about the CM. The CM is located halfway between the spheres and is marked with an X in Figure 18.2. Because the translational and rotational motions are independent, each may be determined separately. This is made easier in the absence of air resistance, since then there are no torques on the baton and the angular velocity w about the CM is constant.

The baton is thrown with an initial velocity as shown on the left of Figure 18.2. The simplest way to view this is as a translation of the entire baton with a velocity $\mathbf{V}_0$, and a rotation of angular velocity w about the CM. To determine w, we note that the tangential velocity due to rotation is

$$v_t = \tfrac{1}{2}wL. \qquad (18.1)$$

For the direction of rotation as indicated in the figure, this tangential velocity gets added to the CM velocity at the top of the baton and gets subtracted from the CM

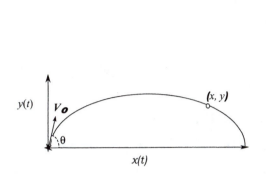
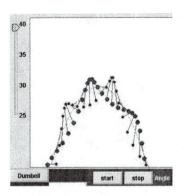

Figure 18.3 *Left:*   The trajectory $(x(t),\ y(t))$ followed by the baton's CM. *Right:*   The applet
JParabola.java showing the entire baton as its CM follows a parabola.

velocity at the bottom. Because the total velocity equals 0 at the bottom, and $2V_0$
at the top, we are able to solve for ω:

$$\tfrac{1}{2}\omega L - V_0 = 0 \qquad \Rightarrow \qquad V_0 = \tfrac{1}{2}\omega L, \quad \Rightarrow \qquad \omega = \frac{2V_0}{L}. \tag{18.2}$$

If we ignore air resistance, the only force acing on the baton is gravity and, as
shown on the right of Figure 18.2, it acts at the CM of the baton. Figure 18.3
shows a plot of the trajectory $(x(t), y(t))$ of the CM. It is the same parabola as followed by the cannonball in Chapter 12, where we found the position and velocity
components of the CM to be:

$$(x_{cm}(t),\ y_{cm}(t)) = \left(V_{0x}t,\ V_{0y}t - \tfrac{1}{2}gt^2 \right) \tag{18.3}$$

$$(v_{x,cm}(t),\ v_{y,cm}(t)) = (V_{0x},\ V_{0y} - gt), \tag{18.4}$$

where the horizontal and vertical components of the initial velocity are:

$$V_{0x} = V_0 \cos\theta, \qquad V_{0y} = V_0 \sin\theta. \tag{18.5}$$

Since the gravitational field does not exert any torques on the baton, and since we
ignore air resistance, the angular velocity $\omega = 2V_0/L$ does not change as the baton
flies through the air. However, since the CM travels along a parabolic trajectory,
the motions of the baton's ends may appear complicated to an observer on the
ground. To describe the motion of the ends, we label one end of the baton a and
the other end b, as shown in Figure 18.1.

For a constant angular velocity ω, the angular orientation ϕ of the baton is

$$\phi(t) = \omega t + \phi_0 = \omega t, \tag{18.6}$$

where we have taken the initial $\phi = \phi_0 = 0$. Relative to the CM, the ends of the
baton are described by the polar coordinates:

$$(r_a, \phi_a) = \left(\tfrac{L}{2},\ \phi(t) \right), \quad (r_b, \phi_b) = \left(\tfrac{L}{2},\ \phi(t) + \pi \right). \tag{18.7}$$

The ends of the baton are also described by the Cartesian coordinates:

$$(x'_a, y'_a) = \left(\tfrac{L}{2}\cos(\omega t),\ \tfrac{L}{2}\sin(\omega t)\right),\quad (x'_b, y'_b) = \left(\tfrac{L}{2}\cos(\omega t + \pi),\ \tfrac{L}{2}\sin(\omega t + \pi)\right).$$
$$(18.8)$$

The baton's ends, as seen by a stationary observer, has the vector sum of the position of the CM plus the position relative to the CM:

$$(x_a,\ y_a) = \left(V_{0x}t + \tfrac{L}{2}\cos(\omega t),\ V_{0y}t - \tfrac{1}{2}gt^2 + \tfrac{L}{2}\sin(\omega t)\right), \qquad (18.9)$$

$$(x_b,\ y_b) = \left(V_{0x}t + \tfrac{L}{2}\cos(\omega t + \pi),\ V_{0y}t - \tfrac{1}{2}gt^2 + \tfrac{L}{2}\sin(\omega t + \pi)\right).$$

If L_a and L_b are the distances of m_a and m_b from CM, the definition of CM tells us that:

$$L_a = \frac{m_b}{m_a + m_b},\quad L_b = \frac{m_a}{m_a + m_b},\quad \Rightarrow \quad m_a L_a = m_b L_b. \qquad (18.10)$$

The moment of inertia of the barbell (ignoring the bar connecting them) is

$$I_{\text{masses}} = m_a L_a^2 + m_b L_b^2. \qquad (18.11)$$

If the bar connecting the masses is uniform with mass m and length L, then it has a moment of inertia about its CM of

$$I_{\text{bar}} = \tfrac{1}{12}mL^2. \qquad (18.12)$$

Because the CM of the bar is at the same location as the CM of the masses, the total moment of inertia for the system is just the sum of the two:

$$I_{\text{tot}} = I_{\text{masses}} + I_{\text{bar}}. \qquad (18.13)$$

The potential energy of the masses is

$$PE_{\text{masses}} = (m_a + m_b)gh = (m_a + m_b)g(V_0\, t\sin(\theta) - \tfrac{1}{2}gt^2), \qquad (18.14)$$

while the potential energy of the bar just has $m_a + m_b$ replaced by m, since both share the same CM location. The rotational kinetic energy of rotation is

$$KE_{\text{Rot}} = \tfrac{1}{2}I\omega^2, \qquad (18.15)$$

with ω the angular velocity and I the moment of inertia for either the masses or the bar (or the sum). The translational kinetic energy of the masses is

$$KE_{\text{Trans}} = \tfrac{1}{2}m\left(\sin(\theta) - g\,t)^2 + (V_0\cos(\theta))^2\right), \qquad (18.16)$$

with $m_a + m_b$ replaced by m for the bar's translational KE.

To get a feel for what the motion of a baton actually looks like, we recommend the reader try out the applet JParabola on the CD (applets are discussed in Chapter 21). A picture of its output is given in Figure 18.2, where we see an interestingly complicated motion. The applet is run from a shell with:

```
% appletviewer jcenterofmass.html
```

18.3 CS: OOP DESIGN CONCEPTS

In accord with Landau's First Rule of Education (§ 1.3), we first describe the words used to describe OOP. Object-oriented programming is programming containing component objects with four characteristics [Smit 91]:

Encapsulation: The data and the *methods* used to produce or access data are encapsulated into entities called *objects*. For our problem, the data are initial positions, velocities, and properties of a baton, and the objects are the baton and the path it follows. As part of the OOP philosophy, data are manipulated only via distinct *methods*.

Abstraction: Operations applied to objects must give what is expected to be standard results according to the nature of the objects. To illustrate, summing two matrices always gives another matrix. By incorporating abstraction into programming, we concentrate more on solving the problem and less on details of the implementation.

Inheritance: Objects inherit characteristics (including code) from their ancestors, yet may be different from their ancestors. A baton inherits the motion of a point particle, which in this case describes the motion of the CM, and extends that by permitting rotations about the CM. In addition, we will form a red baton that inherits the characteristics of a colorless baton, and then has the property of color added to it.

Polymorphism: Methods with the same name may affect different objects in different ways. Child objects may have *member* functions with the same name, but with properties differing from those of their ancestors (analogous to method overload, where the method used depends upon the method's arguments).

We now solve our problem using OOP techniques. Although it is also possible to use the more traditional techniques of procedural programming, this problem contains the successive layers of complexity that are most appropriate for OOP. We will use several source (.java) files for this problem, each yielding a different class file. Each class will correspond to a different physical aspects of the baton, with additional classes added as needed. There will be class Path.java to represent the trajectory of the CM, a class Ball.java to represent the ball on the end of the baton, and a class (Baton.java) to assemble the other classes into an object representing a flying and spinning baton. Ultimately we will combine the classes to solve our problem.

18.3.1 Including Multiple Classes

The codes Ball.java, Path.java, and Baton.java in Listings 18.1–18.3 produce three class files. You may think of each class as an object that may be created, manipulated, or destroyed as needed. (Recall, objects are abstract data types with multiple parts.) In addition, since these classes may be shared with other Java classes, more complicated objects may be constructed by using these classes as building blocks.

To use class files that are not in your working directory, use the import command to tell Java where to find them.[1] For example, in Chapter 11, "Visualization with Java," we used import ptolemy.plot.* to tell Java to retrieve all class files found in the ptolemy/plot directory. A complication arises here in that multiple class files may contain more than one main method. That being the case, Java uses the first main it finds, starting in the directory from which you issued the java command.

In a project where there are many different types of objects (for example, matrices, vectors, batons, and so on), it is a good idea to define each object inside its own .java file (and therefore its own .class file), and to place the main method in a file such as Main.java or ProjectName.java. This separates individual objects from the helper codes that glue the objects together. And since reading a well-written main method should give you a fair idea of what the entire program does, you want to be able to find the main methods easily.

Listing 18.1 Ball.java

```
1  //              Ball.java:  Isolated  Ball  with  Mass  and  Radius
2  //    "Object"  class,  no  main  method,  creates  &  probes  objects
3  public  class  Ball
4  {    public  double  m,  r;  //  Nonstatic  variables  unique  to  ball
5       Ball(double  mass,  double  radius)                    //  Constructor
6    {  m  =  mass;
7        r  =  radius;  }
8       public  double  getM()                                 //  Get  mass
9    {  return  m;  }
10      public  double  getR()                                 //  Get  radius
11   {  return  r;  }
12      public  double  getI()              //  Get  moment  of  inertia
13   {  return  2.0  /  5.0  *  m  *  r  *  r;  }    }
```

---

[1] Actually, the Java compiler looks through all the directories in your classpath and imports the first instance of the needed class that it finds.

18.3.2 Implementation: Ball.java, Path.java Classes

The Ball class in Listing 18.1 creates an object representing a sphere of mass m, radius r, and moment of inertia I. It is our basic building block. Scrutinize the length of the methods in Ball; most are short. Inasmuch as we will be using Ball as a building block, it is a good idea to keep the methods simple and just add more methods to create more complicated objects. Take stock of how similar Ball is to the Complex class in Chapter 16 in its employment of *dynamic (nonstatic)* variables. In the present case, m and r behave like the re and im dynamic variable in the Complex class in that they too act by being attached to the end of an object's name. To prove the point, myBall.m extracts the mass of a ball object.

In case you have forgotten, a *dynamic* variable is one that does not have the word static in front of it (it is also called a *nonstatic* variable). A static variable does not change its value as it is shared among instances (objects) of the class, and so is static. In contrast, a dynamic variable changes according to the object it modifies, and so may assume different values for each object. As an example, myBall.m may be different for each Ball.

In Ball.java we have defined three *dynamic methods*, getM, getR, and getI. When affixed to a particular ball object, these methods extract its mass, radius, and moment of inertia, respectively. Dynamic methods are like dynamic variables in that they behave differently depending on the object they modify. To cite an instance, ball1.getR() and ball2.getR() return different values if ball1 and ball2 have different radii. The getI method computes and returns the moment of inertia $I = \frac{2}{5}mr^2$ of a sphere for an axis passing through its center. The methods getM and getR are *template* methods; namely, they do not compute anything now, but are included to facilitate future extensions. To name an instance, if the Ball class becomes more complex, you may need to sum the masses of its constituent parts in order to return the ball's total mass. With the template in place, you do that without having to reacquaint yourself with the rest of the code first.

Look back now and count all of the methods in the Ball class. You should find four, none of which is a main method. This is fine because these methods are used by other classes, one of which will have a main method.

Exercise: Compile the Ball class. If the Java compiler does not complain, you know Ball.java contains valid code. Next try to run the byte code in Ball.class:

```
> java Ball                                        // Run Ball.class
```

You should get a message that your program has made an error of the type java.lang.NoSuchMethodError, with the word main at the end. This is Java's way of saying you need a main method before executing a class file.   ♠

Exercise: Be adventurous and make a main method for the `Ball` class. Because we have not yet included `Path` and `Baton` objects, you will not be able to do much more than test that you have created the `Ball` object, but that is at least a step in the right direction:

```
1 public static void main(String[] args) {
2       Ball myBall = new Ball(3.2, 0.8);
3       System.out.println("M: " + myBall.getM());
4       System.out.println("R: " + myBall.getR());
5       System.out.println("I: " + myBall.getI());  }
```

This testing code creates a `Ball` object and prints out its properties by affixing `get` methods to the object. Compile and run the modified `Ball.java` and thereby ensure that the `Ball` class still works properly. ♠

Listing 18.2 Path.java

```
1 //                    Path.java:            Parabolic Trajectory Class.
2 public class Path
3 {    public static final double g = 9.8;    // Static, same all Paths
4      public double v0x, v0y;                // Non-static, unique each Path
5      public Path(double v0, double theta)
6      { v0x = v0 * Math.cos(theta * Math.PI / 180.0);
7        v0y = v0 * Math.sin(theta * Math.PI / 180.0); }
8      public double getX(double t) { return v0x * t; }
9      public double getY(double t) { return v0y * t - 0.5*g*t*t; }
10 }
```

The class `Path` in Listing 18.2 creates an object that represents the trajectory $[(x(t), y(t))$ of the center of mass, (18.3). The class `Path` is another building block that we will use to construct the baton's trajectory. It computes the initial velocity components V_{ox} and V_{oy}, and stores them as the dynamic class variables `v0x` and `v0y`. These variables need to be dynamic because each new path will have its own initial velocity. In that the acceleration due to gravity g is a constant, it will be the same for all objects, and thus is declared as a static variable (that does not extract values from objects). Survey how `Path.java` stores g not only as static, but also as a class variable so that its value is available to all methods in the class. The constructor method `Path( )` of the class `Path` takes the polar coordinates (V_0, θ) as arguments and computes the components of the initial velocity, (`v0x`, `v0y`). This too is a building-block class so it does not need a main method.

Exercise: Use the main method below to test the class `Path`. Make a `Path` object and get its properties at several different times. Remember, since this a test code, it does not need to do anything much. Just making an object and checking that it has the expected properties is enough. ♠

```
1  public static void main(String[] args) {
2      Path myPath = new Path(3.0, 45.0);
3      for (double t = 0.0; t <= 4.0; t += 1.0) {
4          double x = myPath.getX(t);
5          double y = myPath.getY(t);
6          System.out.println("t = ", t, " x = ", x, " y = ", y);
       } }
```

18.3.3 Composition, Objects within Objects

A good way to build a complex system is to assemble it from simpler parts. By way of example, automobiles are built from wheels, engines, seats, and so forth, with each of these parts built from simpler parts yet. OOP builds programs in much the same way. We start with the primitive data types of integers, floating-point numbers, and Boolean variables, and combine them into the more complicated data types called objects (what we did combining two doubles into a Complex object). Then we build more complicated objects from simpler objects, and so forth.

The technique of constructing complex objects from simpler ones is called **composition.** As a consequence of the simple objects being contained within the more complex ones, the former are described by *nonstatic class variables.* This means that their properties change depending upon which object they are within. When you use composition to create more complex objects, you are working at a *higher level of abstraction.* Ideally, composition hides the distracting details of the simpler objects from your view so that you focus on the major task to accomplish. This is analogous to first designing the general form of a bridge before worrying about the colors of the cables to be used.

18.3.4 Implementation: Baton.java Class

Now that we have assembled the building-block classes, we combine them to create the baton's trajectory. We call the combined class Baton.java, given in Listing 18.3, and place the methods to compute the positions of ends of the baton relative to the CM in it. Check first that the Baton class and its methods occupies lines 3–24, while the main method is on lines 25–40. Whether main is placed first or last is a matter of taste, Java does not care—but some programmers do very much. Look next at how the Baton class contains the four dynamic class variables, L, w, path, and ball. Being dynamic, their values differ for each baton, and since they are class variables (not within any methods), they may be used by all methods in the class without getting passed as arguments.

Listing 18.3 Baton.java

```
1  //                    Baton.java:    Combines  classes  to  form  Baton
2  import ptolemy.plot.*;
3  public class Baton
4  {    public double L;            // Nonstatic variables unique ea baton
5       public double w;                                        // Omega
6       public Path path;                                  // Path object
7       public Ball ball;                                  // Ball object
8       Baton(Path p, Ball b, double L1, double w1)
9       { path = p;
10        ball = b;
11        L = L1;
12        w = w1; }
13      public double getM()
14          return 2*ball.getM();
15      public double getI()
16          return 2*ball.getI() + 1./2.*ball.getM()*L*L;
17      public double getXa(double t)
18          return path.getX(t) + L/2*Math.cos(w*t);
19      public double getYa(double t)
20          return path.getY(t) + L/2*Math.sin(w*t);
21      public double getXb(double t)
22          return path.getX(t) - L/2* Math.cos(w*t);
23      public double getYb(double t)
24          return path.getY(t) - L/2*Math.sin(w*t);
25      public static void main(String args[])          // Main method
26  {    double x, y;
27      Plot myPlot = new Plot();                        // Create Plot
28      Ball myBall = new Ball(0.5, 0.4);                // Create Ball
29      Path myPath = new Path(15.0, 34.0);              // Create Path
30      Baton myBaton = new Baton(myPath,myBall,2.5,15.0);    // Baton
31      myPlot.setTitle("y vs x");
32      myPlot.setXLabel("x");
33      myPlot.setYLabel("y");
34      for (double t =0.; myPath.getY(t) >= 0.; t +=0.02)
35      {   x = myBaton.getXa(t);
36          y = myBaton.getYa(t);
37          System.out.println("t = " +t+" x = " +x+" y = "+y);
38          myPlot.addPoint(0, x, y, true);    }
39      PlotApplication app = new PlotApplication(myPlot);
40  }}
```

The subobjects used to construct the baton object are created with the statements

```
6    public Path path;                                  // Path subobject
7    public Ball ball;                                  // Ball subobject
```

These statements tell Java that we are creating the variables path and ball to represent objects of the types Path and Ball. To do this, we must place the methods defining Ball and Path in the directory in which we are creating a Baton. The Java compiler is flexible enough for you to declare class variables in any order, or even pass classes as arguments.

The constructor Baton(Path p, Ball b, ...) on line 8 takes the Path and Ball objects as arguments and constructs the Baton object from them. On lines 9 and 10 it assigns these arguments to the appropriate class variables path and ball. We create a Baton from a Ball and a Path such that there is a Ball object at each end, with the CM following the Path object:

```
30 Baton myBaton = new Baton(myPath, myBall, 0.5, 15.);
```

Study how the Baton constructor stores the Ball and Path objects passed to it inside the Baton class, even though Ball and Path belong to different classes.

On lines 13–24 we define the methods to manipulate Baton objects. They all have a get as part of their name. This is the standard way of indicating that a method will retrieve or extract some property from the object to which the method is appended. For instance, Baton.getM returns 2m, that is, the sum of the masses of the two spheres. Likewise, the getI method uses the parallel-axes theorem to determine the moment of inertia of the two spheres about the CM, $I = 2I_m + \frac{1}{2}mL^2$, where m and I_m are the mass and moment of inertia of the object about its center of mass. On lines 17–24 we define the methods getXa, getYa, getXb, and getYb. These take the time t as an argument and return the coordinates of the baton's ends. In each method we first determine the position of the CM by calling path.getX or path.getY, and then add on the relative coordinates of the ends. On line 25 we get to the main method. It starts by creating a Plot object myPlot, a Path object myPath, and a Ball object myBall. In each case we set the initial conditions for the object by passing them as arguments to the constructor (what gets called after the new command).

18.3.5 Composition Exercise

1. Compile and run the latest version of Baton.java. For this to be successful, you must tell Java to look in the current directory for the class files corresponding to Ball.java and Path.java. One way to do that is to issue the javac and java commands with the -classpath option, with the location of the classes following the option. Here the dot . is shorthand for "the current directory":

```
> javac -classpath .  Baton.java          // Include current directory classes
> java  -classpath .  Baton                // Include current directory classes
```

The program should run and plot the trajectory of one end of the baton as it travels through the air, and you should end up with a figure like Figure 18.3.

2. If you want to have the Java compiler automatically include the current directory in the classpath (and to avoid the `-classpath` . option), you need to change your CLASSPATH environment variable to include the present working directory. We explain how to do that in Chapter 11, "Visualization with Java."

3. On line 34 we see that the program executes a `for` loop over values of t for which the baton remains in the air:

```
34  for (double t = 0.0; myPath.getY(t) >= 0.0; t += 0.02)
```

This says to repeat the loop as long as $y(t)$ is positive, namely, as long as the baton is in the air. Of course we could have had the `for` loop remain active for times less than the hang time T, but then we would have had to calculate the hang time! The weakness in our approach is that the loop will be repeat indefinitely if $y(t)$ never becomes negative.

4. Plot the trajectory of end b of the baton on the same graph that contains a's trajectory. You may do this by copying and pasting the `for` loop for a, and then modifying it for b (make sure to change the data-set number in the call to PtPlot so that the two ends are plotted in different colors).

5. Use the Print command within the PtPlot application to print out your graph.

6. Change the mass of the `ball` variable to some large number, for example, 50 kg, in the `Baton` constructor method. Add print statements in the constructor and the main program to show how the `ball` class variable and the `myBall` object were affected by the new mass. You should find that `ball` and `myBall` both reference the same object, since they both refer to the same memory location. In this way changes to one object are reflected in the other object.

In Java, an object is passed between methods and manipulated by *reference*. This means that its address in memory is passed and not the actual values of all the components parts of it. On the other hand, primitive data types like `int` and `double` are manipulated by *value*:

```
1  Ball myBall = new Ball(1.0, 3.0);            Create object
2  Ball p = myBall;                    Now p refers to same object
3  Ball q = myBall;                    Create another reference
```

At times we may actually say that objects "are references." This means that when one object is set equal to another, both objects *point* to the same location in memory (the start location of the first component of the object). Therefore all three variables `myBall`, `p`, and `q` in the above code fragment refer to the same object in memory. When we change the mass of the ball, all three variables will reflect the new mass value. This also works for object arguments: if you pass an object as an argument to a method and the method modifies the object, then the object in the calling program will also be modified.

18.3.6 Extension: Calculating the Baton's Energy

Extend your classes so they plot the energy of the baton as a function of time. Plot the kinetic energy of translation, the kinetic energy of rotation, and the potential energy as functions of time:

1. The translational kinetic energy of the baton is the energy associated with motion of the center of mass. Write a getKEcm method in the Baton class that returns the kinetic energy of translation $KE_{cm}(t) = mv_{cm}(t)^2/2$. In terms of pseudocode, the method is:

```
1 Get present value of Vx.
2 Get present value of Vy.
3 Compute V^2 = Vx^2 + Vy^2.
4 Return mV^2/2.
```

Before you program this method, write getVx and getVy methods that extract the CM velocity from a Baton. Seeing as how the Path class already computes $x_{cm}(t)$ and $y_{cm}(t)$, it is the logical place for the velocity methods. As a guide, we suggest consulting the getX and getY methods.

2. Next we need the method getKEcm in the Baton class to compute $KE_{cm}(t)$. Inasmuch as the method will be in the Baton class, we may call any of the methods in Baton, as well as access the path and ball subobjects there ("subobjects" because they reside inside the Baton object or class). We obtain the velocity components by applying the getV methods to the path subobject within the Baton object:

```
1 public double getKEcm(double t) {
2        double vx = path.getVx(t);
3        double vy = path.getVy(t);
4        double v2 = vx * vx + vy * vy;
5        return getM() * v2 / 2; }
```

Even though the method is in a different class than the object, Java handles this. Study how getM(), being within getKEcm, acts on the same object as does getKEcm without explicitly specifying the object.

3. Compile the modified Baton and Path classes.

4. Modify `Baton.java` to plot the translational kinetic energy of the center of mass as a function of time. Comment out the old `for` loops used for plotting the position of the baton's ends, and add the code:

```
for (double t = 0.0; myPath.getY(t)>= 0.0; t += 0.02) {
    double KEcm = myBaton.getKEcm(t);
    myPlot.addPoint(0, t, KEcm, true);                          }
```

Compile the modified `Baton.java` and check that your plot is physically reasonable. The translational kinetic energy should decrease and then increase as the baton goes up and then comes down.

5. Write a method in the `Baton` class that computes the kinetic energy of rotation about the CM, $KE_r = \frac{1}{2}I\omega^2$. Call `getI` to extract the moment of inertia of the baton, and check that all classes still compile properly.

6. The potential energy of the baton $PE(t) = mgy_{cm}(t)$ is that of a point particle with the total mass of the baton located at the CM. Write a method in the `Baton` class that computes PE. Use `getM` to extract the mass of the baton, and use `path.g` to extract the acceleration due to gravity g. To determine the height as a function of time, write a method `path.getY(t)` that accesses the `path` object. Make sure that the methods `getKEcm`, `getKEr`, and `getPE` are in the `Baton` class.

7. Plot on one graph: the translational kinetic energy, the kinetic energy of rotation, the potential energy, and the total energy. The plots may be obtained with commands such as:

```
for (double t =0.; myPath.getY(t) >= 0.; t += 0.02) {
    double KEcm = myBaton.getKEcm(t);          // KE of CM
    double KEr = myBaton.getKEr(t);            // KE of rotation
    double PE = myBaton.getPE(t);              // Potential
    double total = KEcm + KEr + PE;            // Total Energy
    myPlot.addPoint( 0, t, KEcm, true);        // To data set 0
    myPlot.addPoint( 1, t, KEr, true);         // To data set 1
    myPlot.addPoint( 2, t, PE, true);          // To data set 2
    myPlot.addPoint( 3, t, total, true);  }    // To data set 3
```

Check that all the plotting commands are object-oriented, with `myPlot` being the plot object. Label your data sets with a `myPlot.addLegend` command outside of the `for` loop, and check that your graph is physically reasonable. The total energy and rotational energies should both remain constant in time. However, the gravitational potential energy should fluctuate.

18.3.7 Tutorial: Inheritance and Object Hierarchies

Up until this point we have built up our Java classes via *composition*, namely, by placing objects inside other objects (using objects as arguments). As powerful as composition is, it is not appropriate for all circumstances. For example, you may want to modify the Baton class to create similar, but not identical, objects such as 3-D batons. A direct approach to extending the program would be to copy and paste parts of the original code into a new class, and then modify the new class. However, this is error-prone and leads to long, complicated, and repetitive code. The OOP approach applies the concept of *inheritance* to allow us to create new objects that inherit the properties of old objects but have additional properties as well. This is how we create entire hierarchies of objects.

As an example, let us say we want to place red balls on the end of the baton. We make a new class RedBall that inherits properties from Ball by using the extend command:

```
1  public class RedBall extends Ball {
2          .  .  .
```

As written, this code creates a RedBall class that is identical to the original Ball class. The keyword extends tells Java to copy all of the methods and variables from Ball into RedBall. In OOP terminology, the Ball class is the *parent class* or *superclass*, and the RedBall class is the *child class* or *subclass*. It follows then that a class hierarchy is a sort of family tree for classes, with the parent classes at the top of the tree. As things go, children beget children of their own and trees often grow high.

To make RedBall different from Ball, we add the property of color:

```
1  public class RedBall extends Ball {
2          String getColor ()
3              {return "Red"; }
4          double getR ()
5              {return 1.0;}                    }
```

Now we append the getColor method to a RedBall to find out its color. Consider what it means to have the getR method defined in both the Ball and RedBall classes. We do this because the Java compiler assumes that the getR method in RedBall is more specialized, so it ignores the original method in the Ball class. In computer science language, we would say that the new getR method *overrides* the original method.

18.3.8 Application: Baton with a Lead Weight

As a second example, we employ inheritance to create a class of objects representing a baton with a weight at its center. We call this new class LeadBaton.java and make it a child of the parent class Baton.java. Consequently, the LeadBaton class inherits all of the methods from the parent Baton class, in addition to having new ones of its own:

```
1  // LeadBaton: class inheritance of methods from Baton
2  public class LeadBaton {
3  public double M;                        // Non-static class variables
4  LeadBaton(Path p, Ball b, double L1, double w1, double M1)
5      { super(p, b, L1, w1);              // Baton constructor
6        M = M1; }
7  public double getM()
8    return super.getM() + M;  }           // Call getM in Baton
```

Here the nondefault constructor LeadBaton(...) takes five arguments, while the Baton constructor takes only three. For the LeadBaton constructor to work, it must call the Baton constructor in order to inherit the properties of a Baton. This is accomplished by use of the key word super, which is shorthand for *look in the superclass*, and tells Java to look in the parent, or superclass for the constructor. We may also call methods with the super key word; for example, super.getM() will call the getM method from Baton, in place of the getM method from LeadBaton. Finally, because the LeadBaton class assigns new values to the mass, LeadBaton overrides the getM method of Baton.

Exercise: 1. Run and create plots from the LeadBaton class. Start by removing the main method from Baton.java and placing it in the file Main.java. Instead of creating a Baton, now create a LeadBaton with:

```
LeadBaton myBaton = new LeadBaton(myPath, myBall, 2.5, 15., 10.);
```

Here the 10. argument describes a 10 kg mass at the center of the baton.

2. Compile and run the main method, remembering to use the "-classpath ." option if needed. You should get a plot of the energies of the lead baton *versus* time. Compare its energy to an ordinary baton's and comment on the differences.

3. You should see now how OOP permits us to create many types of batons with only slight modifications of the code. You switch between a Baton and a LeadBaton object with only a single change to main, a modification that would be significantly more difficult with procedural programming. ♠

18.3.9 Encapsulation to Protect Classes

In the previous section we created the classes for Ball, Path, and Baton objects. In all cases the Java source code for each class had the same basic structure: class variables, constructors, and get methods. Yet classes do different things, and it is common to categorize the functions of classes as either:

Interface: how the outside world manipulates an object; all methods that are applied to that object;

Implementation: the actual internal workings of an object; how the methods make their changes.

As applied to our program, the interface for the Ball class includes a constructor Ball, and the getM, getR, and getI methods. The interface for the Path class includes a constructor Path and the getX and getY methods.

Pure OOP strives to keep objects abstract and manipulate them only through methods. This makes it easy to follow and to control where variables get changed, and thereby makes modifying an existing program easier and less error-prone. With this purpose in mind, we separate methods into those that perform calculations and those that cause the object to do things. In addition, to protect your object from being misused by outsiders, we invoke the **private** (in contrast to public) key word when declaring class variables. This ensures that these variables may be accessed and changed only from inside the class. Outside code may still manipulate our objects, but it will have to do so by calling the methods we have tested and know will not damage our objects.

Once we have constructed the methods and made the class variables private, we have objects whose internal codes are entirely hidden to outside users, and thereby protected. As authors, we may rewrite the objects' codes as we want and still have the same working object with a *fixed interface* for the rest of the world. Furthermore, since the object's interface is constant, even though we may change the object, there is no need to modify any code that uses the object. This is a great advance in the ability to reuse code and to use other's people's codes properly.

This two-step process of creating and protecting abstract objects is known as *encapsulation*. An encapsulated object may be manipulated only in a general manner that keeps the irrelevant details of its internal workings safely hidden within. Just what constitutes an "irrelevant detail" is in the eye of the programmer. In general, you should place the private key word before every nonstatic class variable, and then write the appropriate methods for accessing the relevant variables. This OOP process of hiding the object's variables is called *data hiding*.

18.3.10 Encapsulation Exercise

1. Place the `private` key word before all class variables in `Ball.java`. This accomplishes the first step in encapsulating an object. Print out `myBall.m` and `myBall.r` from the main method. The Java compiler should complain, because the variables are now private (visible to `Ball` class member only), and the main method is outside the `Ball` class.

2. Make methods that allow us to manipulate the object in an abstract way; for example, to modify the mass of a `Ball` object and assign it to the private class variable `m`, include the line command `myBall.setM(5.0)`. This is the second step in encapsulation. We already have the methods `getM`, `getR`, and `getI`, and the object constructor `Ball`, but they do not assign a mass to the ball. Insofar as we have used a method to change the private variable `m`, we have kept our code as general as possible and still have our objects encapsulated.

3. When we write `getM()` we are saying that `M` is the *property* to be retrieved from a `Ball` object. Inversely, the method `setM` sets the property `M` of an object equal to the argument that is given. This is part of encapsulation, because with both `get` and `set` methods on hand, you do not need to access the class variables from outside of the class. The use of `get` and `set` methods is standard practice in Java. You do not have to write `get` and `set` methods for every class that you create, but you should create these methods for any class you want encapsulated. If you look back at Chapter 11, "Visualization with Java," you will see that the classes in the PtPlot library have many `get` and `set` methods, for example, `getTitle`, `setTitle`, `getXLabel`, and `setXLabel`.

4. Java's `interface` key word allows us to specify an interface. Here `BallInterface` defines an interface for `Ball`-like objects:

```
1 public interface BallInterface {
2     public double getM();
3     public double getR();
4     public double getI();            }
```

This interface does not do anything by itself, but if you modify `Ball.java` so that `public class Ball` is replaced by `public class Ball implements BallInterface` then the Java compiler will check that the `Ball` class has all of the methods that are specified in the interface. The Java `interface` and `implements` commands are useful for having the compiler check that your classes have all of the required methods.

5. Add an arbitrary new method to the interface and compile `Ball`. If the method is found in `Ball.java`, then the `Ball` class will compile without error.

Listing 18.4 KomplexInterface.java

```
1  //                KomplexInterface:    complex numbers via interface
2  public interface KomplexInterface
3  {    public double getRe();
4       public double getIm();
5       public double setRe();
6       public double setIm();
7       // type = 0: polar representation; other: rectangular
8       public void add(Komplex  other,int type);
9       public void sub(Komplex other,int type);
10      public void mult(Komplex other,int type);
11      public void div(Komplex other,int type);
12      public void conj(int type);              }
```

18.3.11 Extension: Complex Number Objects, Komplex.java

In Listing 18.4 we display our design KomplexInterface.java of an interface for complex numbers. To avoid confusion with the Complex objects of Chapter 16, we call the new objects Komplex. We include methods for addition, subtraction, multiplication, division, negation, and conjugation, as well as get and set methods for the real, imaginary, modulus, and phase. We include all methods in the interface and check that javac compiles the interface without error. Remember, an interface must give the arguments and return type for each method.

We still represent complex numbers in Cartesian or polar coordinates:

$$z = x + iy = re^{i\theta}. \tag{18.17}$$

Insofar as the complex number itself is independent of representation, we should be able to switch between a rectangular or polar representation. This is useful because certain mathematical manipulations are simpler in one representation than the other, for example,

$$\frac{z_1}{z_2} = \frac{a+ib}{c+id} = \frac{ac+bd+i(bc-ad)}{c^2+d^2} = \frac{r_1 e^{i\theta_1}}{r_2 e^{i\theta_2}} = \frac{r_1}{r_2} e^{i(\theta_1-\theta_2)}. \tag{18.18}$$

Listing 18.5 Komplex.java

```
1  //        Komplex: Cartesian/polar complex via interface
2  'type = 0' -> polar representation , else rectangular
3  public class Komplex implements KomplexInterface
4  {    public double mod, theta , re , im;
5       public Komplex ()                              // Default  constructor
6       {    mod = 0;
7            theta = 0;
8            re = 0;
9            im = 0; }
10      public Komplex (double x, double y, int type )       // Constructor
11       { if (type  == 0)
12           {mod = x;  theta = y;}
13           else {re = x; im = y;} }
14      public double getRe () return mod*Math.cos(theta );
15      public double getIm () return mod*Math.sin(theta );
16      public double setRe ()
17      { re = mod*Math.cos(theta );
18        return re;}
19      public double setIm ()
20      { im = mod*Math.sin(theta );
21        return im; }
22      public void add(Komplex other ,int type )
23      { double tempMod=0.;
24       if (type == 0)
25      { tempMod = Math.sqrt(Math.pow(this .mod,2)+Math.pow(other.mod
           ,2)
26           + 2*this .mod*other.mod*Math.cos(this .theta -other.theta ));
27         this .theta = Math.atan2(
28         this .mod*Math.sin(this .theta ) + other.mod*Math.sin(other.
              theta ),
29           this .mod*Math.cos(this .theta ) + other.mod*Math.cos(other
                .theta ));
30        this .mod = tempMod; }
31        else { this .re = this .re + other.re;
32             this .im = this .im + other.im;   } }
33   public void sub(Komplex other ,int type ){
34    if (type == 0)
35    { this .mod = Math.sqrt(Math.pow(this .mod,2)+Math.pow(other.mod
         ,2)-
36     2*this .mod*other.mod*(Math.cos(this .theta )*Math.cos(other.
           theta )+
37    Math.sin(this .theta )*Math.sin(other.theta )));
38     this .theta =
39    Math.atan((this .mod*Math.sin(this .theta )-other.mod*Math.sin(
           other.theta ))/
40    (this .mod*Math.cos(this .theta )-other.mod*Math.cos(other.theta )
           )); }
41     else { this .re = this .re-other.re;
42            this .im = this .im-other.im; }    }
43   public void div(Komplex other ,int type )
44   { if (type == 0) { this .mod = this .mod/ other.mod;
```

```
45              this.theta = this.theta−other.theta; }
46        else{ this.re = (this.re*other.re+this.im*other.im)/
47           (Math.pow(other.re,2)+Math.pow(other.im,2));
48              this.im = (this.im*other.re−this.re*other.im)/
49           (Math.pow(other.re,2)+Math.pow(other.im,2)); } }
50     public void mult(Komplex other,int type){
51        if(type == 0) {
52        this.mod = this.mod*other.mod;
53        this.theta = this.theta+other.theta; }
54        else
55        { Komplex ans = new Komplex();
56           ans.re = this.re*other.re−this.im*other.im;
57           ans.im = this.re*other.im+this.im*other.re;
58           this.re = ans.re;
59           this.im = ans.im;        }}
60     public void conj(int type){
61        if(type == 0){
62        this.mod = this.mod;
63        this.theta = −this.theta; }
64        else{ this.re = this.re;
65              this.im = −this.im;
66     } } }
```

Here is our implementation of an interface that permits us to use either representation when manipulating complex numbers. There are three files, Komplex, KomplexInterface, and KomplexTest, all given in the listings. Because these classes call each other, each must be in a class by itself. However, for the compiler to find all the classes that it needs, all three classes must be compiled with the same javac command:

```
% javac Komplex.java KomplexInterface.java KomplexTest.java
% java KomplexTest                                              // Run test
```

We see that KomplexInterface requires us to have methods for getting and setting the real and imaginary parts of Komplex objects, as well as adding, subtracting, multiplying, dividing, and conjugating complex objects. (In comments we see the suggestion that there should also be methods for getting and setting the modulus and phase.)

The class Komplex contains the constructors for Komplex objects. This differs from our previous implementation Complex by having the additional integer variable type. If type = 0, then the complex number(s) are in polar representation, else they are in the Cartesian representation. So, for example, the methods for arithmetic, such as the add method on line 22, is actually two different methods depending upon the value of type. In contrast, the get and set methods for real and imaginary parts on lines 14–21 are needed only for the polar representation, and so the value of type is not needed.

Listing 18.6 KomplexTest.java

```
1  //              KomplexTest:    test KomplexInterface
2  public class KomplexTest{
3  public static void main(String[] argv){
4  Komplex a, e;
5  e = new Komplex();
6  a = new Komplex(1.0, 1.0,1);
7  Komplex b = new Komplex(1., 2., 1);
8  System.out.println("Cartesian: Re a = "+a.re+", Im a = "+a.im+"");
9  System.out.println("Cartesian: Re b = "+b.re+", Im b = "+b.im+"");
10 b.add(a, 1);
11 e = b;
12 System.out.println("Cartesian: e=b+a="+e.re+" "+e.im+"");
13 // Polar Version, uses get and set methods
14 a = new Komplex(Math.sqrt(2.), Math.PI/4., 0);    // Polar via 0
15 b = new Komplex(Math.sqrt(5.), Math.atan2(2.,1.), 0);
16 System.out.println("Polar: Re a = "+a.getRe()+", Im a = "+a.getIm
       ()+"");
17 System.out.println("Polar: Re b = "+b.getRe()+", Im b = "+b.getIm
       ()+"");
18 b.add(a, 0);
19 e = b;
20 System.out.println("Polar e=b+a = "+e.getRe()+" "+e.getIm()+"");
21 } }
```

18.3.12 Polymorphism, Variable Multityping

Polymorphism allows a variable name that is declared as one type to contain other types as a program runs. The idea may be applied to both the class and the interface. Class polymorphism allows a variable that is declared as one type to contain types it inherits. To illustrate, if we declare `myBaton` of type `Baton`,

```
Baton myBaton;
```

then it is valid to assign an object of type `Baton` to that variable, which is what we have been doing all along. However, it is also permissible to assign a `LeadBaton` object to `myBaton`, and, in fact, it is permissible to assign any other class that inherits from the `Baton` class to that variable:

```
myBaton = Baton(myPath, myBall, 0.5, 15.);          // Usual
myBaton = LeadBaton(myPath, myBall, 0.9, 20., 15.);  // OK too
myBaton = LeadBaton(myPath, myBall, 0.1, 1.5, 80.);  // Also OK
```

Polymorphism applies to the arguments of methods as well. If we declare an argument as type `Baton`, we are saying that the class must be a `Baton`, or else some class that is a child class of `Baton`. This is possible because the child classes will have the same methods as the original `Baton` class (a child class may override a method or leave it alone, but it may not eliminate it).

18.4 KEY WORDS

abstraction	center of mass	child class	composition
data hiding	dynamic methods	dynamic variables	encapsulation
inheritance	interface	multityping	nonstatic variables
object hierarchies	OOP	overriding	parent class
polymorphism	private	programming	reference pass
subclass	subobjects	superclass	templates
translation	rotation		

18.5 SUPPLEMENTARY EXERCISES

Use a Java *interface* to introduce another object corresponding to the polar representation of complex numbers:

$$r = \sqrt{x^2 + y^2}, \qquad \theta = \tan^{-1}(y/x) \qquad (18.19)$$
$$x = r\cos\theta, \qquad y = r\sin\theta.$$

1. Define a constructor `Complex (r, theta, 1)` that constructs the polar representation of a complex number from r and θ. (The 1 is there just to add a third argument and thereby to make the constructor unique.)
2. Define a method (static or nonstatic) that permits conversion from the Cartesian to the polar representation of complex numbers.
3. Define a method (static or nonstatic) that permits conversion from the polar to the Cartesian representation of complex numbers.
4. Define methods (static or nonstatic) for addition, subtraction, multiplication, and division of complex numbers in polar representation. [*Hint:*   multiplication and division are a snap for complex numbers in polar representation, while addition and subtraction are much easier for complex numbers in Cartesian representation.]

Chapter Nineteen

Discrete Math, Arrays as Bins; Nonlinear Bug Dynamics*

This chapter gives an example of how computations are used to model the population dynamics of biological systems. It employs some fairly simple discrete mathematics that leads to some unusual nonlinear behaviors to explore. One-dimensional arrays are used to bin store the results of the simulations, with the arrays then written to a file and visualized with PtPlot. This chapter introduces no new Java tools, but instead reviews a number of previously introduced techniques. So even though there is no advanced material in it, we mark this chapter as optional since it may be skipped without interrupting the logical flow.

19.1 PROBLEM: VARIABILITY OF BUG POPULATIONS

As is true with much in nature, insect populations do not appear to follow any simple patterns. At times they appear stable, at other times they vary periodically, and at still other times they appear chaotic, only to settle down to something simple again.[1]

Problem: Deduce and explore a simple model of the population as a function of time that seems capable of producing complicated behaviors.

19.2 THEORY: SELF-LIMITING GROWTH, DISCRETE MAPS

Imagine a bunch of insects reproducing, generation after generation, in your garden. We start with N_0 of them, in the next generation we have to live with N_1 bugs, and after i generations there are N_n of them to bug us. We want a model for how N_n varies with the discrete generation number n.

We look to the simple model of radioactive decay and growth for guidance.

---

[1] We actually use *chaos* as a technical term meaning complicated behavior in which there does not appear to be any order, but in which there is some simple mathematical description [CP 05].

There we know that an exponential time dependence,

$$N(t) = N(0)e^{\pm\lambda t}, \tag{19.1}$$

follows from the simple discrete law [CP 05]:

$$\Delta N_n = \pm\lambda N_n \Delta t. \tag{19.2}$$

Here λ is a rate constant, N_n is the number of particles present in generation n, and Δt is the time for one generation. The model states that the change in the number of particles in one generation is proportional to the number of particles present and to the length of that generation.

We know that a discrete equation such as (19.2) produces growth or decay for positive or negative values of λ respectively, but not both. If bugs just bred, then an exponential-growth model might make sense; yet bugs cannot live on love alone. As their numbers grow the bugs start running out of food and this leads to their numbers growing only to some maximum value N_*. We modify the simple growth model by introducing a growth rate λ that decreases as the population number reaches some maximum:

$$\lambda = \lambda'(N_* - N_n), \qquad \Rightarrow \qquad \Delta N_n = \lambda' \Delta t (N_* - N_n) N_n. \tag{19.3}$$

We expect that when N_n is small compared to the maximum N_*, the bugs will grow exponentially, but as N_n becomes comparable in magnitude to N_*, the growth rate should decrease and possibly become negative if it exceeds N_*.

To make the mathematics of this model clearer, we change to dimensionless variables

$$x_n = \frac{\lambda' \Delta t}{1 + \lambda' \Delta t N_*} N_n \simeq \frac{N_n}{N_*}, \qquad \mu = 1 + \lambda' \Delta t N_*. \tag{19.4}$$

In terms of these, our model assumes the simple form

$$x_{n+1} = \mu x_n (1 - x_n). \tag{19.5}$$

Here x_n is essentially the fraction of the maximum population attained in generation n, and μ is a constant we call the *survival rate*. The range of variation of these dimensionless parameters are limited to:

$$0 \leq x_n \leq 1, \qquad 0 \leq \mu \leq 4. \tag{19.6}$$

Notwithstanding the simplicity of (19.5) with its one variable x and one parameter μ, it leads to surprisingly complicated behaviors. This is a consequence of its being a *nonlinear equation* in which the variable x occurs to the second power. It is called the *logistics map* [Rash 90], and your **problem** is now reduced to exploring the properties of (19.5).

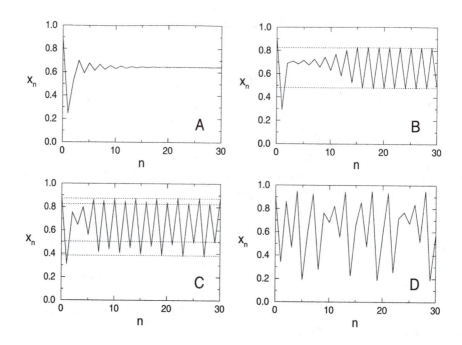

Figure 19.1 The insect population x_n versus generation number n for various survival rates: (A) $\mu = 2.8$, a period-one cycle; (B) $\mu = 3.3$, a period-two cycle; (C) $\mu = 3.5$, a period-four cycle; (D) $\mu = 3.8$, a chaotic regime.

19.3 ASSESSMENT: PROPERTIES OF NONLINEAR MAPS

Rather than do some fancy mathematical analysis [Rash 90] to determine properties of the logistics map (19.5), study it directly on the computer. Write a simple program that uses the logistics map to produce a sequence of population values x_n as a function of the generation number n. Start with a *seed* population $x_0 = 0.75$ and plot up x_n *versus* n for $\mu = (0.4, 2.8, 3.3, 3.5, 3.8)$. The last four simulations should yield results similar to those in Figure 19.1.

Explore other nearby values of μ and identify on printed copies of your graphs the following characteristics:

Transients: Irregular behaviors before reaching a steady state.

Extinction: If the survival rate is too low, the population dies off.

Stable states: Single-population stable states for $\mu < 3$.

Two and three cycles: At two-cycle fixed points, the population jumps back and forth between two semistable x_* values. At three-cycle fixed points the population jumps between three x_* values. These *attractors* occur only for $\mu > 3$.

Intermittency: Try to find solutions for $3.8264 < \mu < 3.8304$ in which the system appears stable for a while but then jumps all around, only to become stable again.

Chaos: The system's behavior in the chaotic region is critically dependent on the exact value of μ and x_0. Systems may start out much the same but end up quite different. Compare the long-term behaviors of starting with the two essentially identical seeds:

$$x_0 = 0.75, \qquad x_0' = 0.75(1 + \epsilon), \qquad (19.7)$$

where $\epsilon \simeq 2 \times 10^{-14}$ for a double-precision calculation. Repeat the experiment with $x_0 = 0.75$, but with what should essentially be two identical survival parameters:

$$\mu = 4.0, \qquad \mu' = 4.0(1 - \epsilon). \qquad (19.8)$$

19.4 EXPLORATION: BIFURCATION DIAGRAM, BUGSORT.JAVA*

Listing 19.1 BugSort.java

```
1  //           BugSort:   Bifurcation diagram for logistic map (sorted)
2  import java.io.*;
3  public class BugSort {
4  static float   m_min = 0.0f ;              // Minimum for m
5  static float   m_max = 4.0f;               // Maximum for m
6  static float   step = 0.1f ;               // Stepsize for m
7     public static void main(String[] argv) throws IOException,
            FileNotFoundException {
8       float   m;
9       float x[] = new float[1000];
10      int i;
11      // Save data in File BugSort.dat
12      PrintWriter w = new PrintWriter( new FileOutputStream( "BugSort.
            dat"), true);
13      for (m = m_min; m <= m_max; m += step)
14      {                                        // Loop for m
15         x[0] = 0.5f;                          // Arbitrary seed
16         //   Skip transients, Record 200 points
17         for (i=1; i <= 200; i++)     x[i] = m*x[i-1] * (1-x[i-1]);
18         for (i=201; i <= 401; i++) x[i] = m*x[i-1] * (1-x[i-1]);
19         for (i=201; i <= 401; i++)            // No dupes
20         {  if ((int) (1000*x[i]) != (int) (1000*x[i-1]) | m <=3.) {
21            x[i] = m*x[i-1] * (1-x[i-1]);
22            w.println( "" + m + " " + x[i]); }
23      } }
24      System.out.println("sorted data in BugsSorted.dat.");
25  } }
```

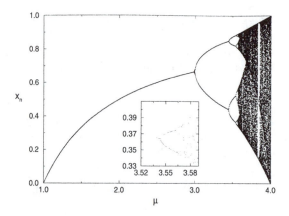

Figure 19.2 The bifurcation plot, attractor populations versus survival rate, for the logistics map.

Listing 19.1 gives our basic program for producing a bifurcation diagram. Computing and watching the population change with each generation gives a good idea of the basic phenomena. However, it is hard to discern the simple and beautiful behavior that lies within these complicated behaviors. One way to gain such understanding is to concentrate on the semistable population values x_* that the system jumps among over time. These are called *attractors* to indicate that the system is somehow attracted to these populations.

A plot of these attractors as a function of the survival parameter μ is an elegant way to summarize the results of extensive computer simulations. One such *bifurcation diagram* is given in Figure 19.2. It shows the output from the program BugSorted.java given here. For each value of μ, hundreds of iterations were made to make sure that all transients died out. The value of x that the system settled down to is recorded as x_*. The doublet of points (μ, x_*) that occur after the transients have died out were then written to a file. To be sure that all attractors have been reached, the calculation is repeated for various values for the initial populations x_0.

19.4.1 Implementation: Bifurcation Diagram

Create your own version of Figure 19.2. To get an idea of how many points may be needed, let us assume that your screen resolution is ∼100 dots per inch and that your laser printer's resolution is ∼300 dots per inch. This means that you are plotting approximately $3000 \times 3000 \simeq 10$ million elements. *Beware:* this will take a long time to print and require more memory than some printers have available.

19.4.2 Binning

1. Break up the range $1 \leq \mu \leq 4$ into 1,000 steps and loop through them. These are the "bins" into which we will place the x_* values.

2. In order not to miss any structures in your bifurcation diagram, loop through a range of initial x_0 values as well.

3. Wait at least 200 generations for the transients to die out, and then print out the next several hundred values of (μ, x_*) to a file.

4. Print out your x_* values to no more than three to four decimal places. You will not be able to resolve more places than this on your plot, and this will keep your output files smaller by permitting you to remove duplicates. It is hard to control the number of decimal places in output with Java's standard print commands. However, you may use the Java version of fprintf to do this and sort the file to remove duplicates.[2] Another approach is to remove two successive x_n values that differ only beyond the third place. We do that in the sample code BugsSorted.java by taking advantage of the fact that x_n is in the range

$$0 \leq x_n \leq 1. \tag{19.9}$$

For this reason, before we write out to a file, we multiply our x_n's by 1,000, cast them as integers, and compare with the previous x_n:

```
if ((int)(1000*x[i]) != (int)(1000*x[i-1]) | m <= 3.)        // Test for dupes
```

If this condition is met, then we know the x_n value differs in the first three decimal places from the previous x_n value.

5. Plot up your file of x_* versus μ. Use small symbols for the points and do not connect them.

6. Enlarge sections of your plot and notice that a similar bifurcation diagram tends to be contained within portions of the original (this is called *self-similarity*).

7. Look over the series of bifurcations occurring at

$$\mu_k \simeq 3, \ 3.449, \ 3.544, \ 3.5644, \ 3.5688, \ 3.569692, \ 3.56989, \ldots \ . \tag{19.10}$$

The end of this series is a region of chaotic behavior.

8. Inspect the way this and other sequences begin and then end in chaos. The changes sometimes occur quickly over a very short range of μ, and so you may have to make plots over a very small range of μ values to see the structures.

---

[2]For example, with the Unix command *sort -u*.

Table 19.1 Maps for generating x_n sequences and bifurcation plots.

Name	$f(x)$
Logistics	$\mu x(1 - x)$
Tent	$\mu(1 - 2\,\lvert x - 1/2 \rvert)$
Ecology	$x e^{\mu(1-x)}$
Quartic	$\mu[1 - (2x - 1)^4]$

9. Close examination of Figure 19.2 shows regions where a very large number of populations suddenly change to very few populations with a slight increase in μ. Whereas these may appear to be artifacts of the video display, this is a real effect and these regions are called *windows*. Check that at $\mu = 3.828427$, chaos turns into a three-cycle population.

19.5 EXPLORATION: OTHER DISCRETE MAPS*

Only nonlinear systems exhibit unusual behavior like chaos. Yet systems are non-linear in any number of ways. Table 19.1 maps that you may use to generate x_n sequences and bifurcation plots.

Chapter Twenty

2-D Arrays: File I/O, PDEs; Realistic Capacitor

The main purpose of this chapter is to get more experience with arrays, and especially with the large 2-D ones used to solve realistic problems. As is often the case with realistic problems, no analytic solution exists and we must employ a variety of techniques to solve our problem. These include breaking space into a discrete lattice and applying a simple algorithm to solve a partial differential equation (PDE), file I/O, and 3-D visualization of numerical data using gnuplot. The simplicity of the solution follows from the use of large arrays that permit us to manipulate thousands or millions of variables with just a few lines of code.

20.1 PROBLEM: FIELD OF REALISTIC CAPACITOR

Figure 20.1, adapted from a first-year physics text, shows an idealized parallel-plate capacitor on the left. The equal spacing and single direction of the electric-field line (arrows) indicate that the field is uniform. On the right is a photograph of the electric field between the plates of a realistic parallel-plate capacitor, visualized by small pieces of thread suspended in oil. Observe how the field fringes out near the ends and extends beyond the ends of the capacitor. Textbooks usually analyze the ideal capacitor because only it can be treated analytically.

Problem: Determine and visualize the electric field within and surrounding a realistic capacitor, and compare to Figure 20.1.

20.2 THEORY AND MODEL: ELECTROSTATICS AND PDES

Capacitors are devices with the *capacity* to store electric charge. They usually consists of two conductors of similar shape separated by a small gap, with equal— but opposite–charge on each conductor. Because the electric field, which would otherwise extend over all of space, is condensed to the region between the plates, capacitors are also called *condensers*.

In spite of real electrical devices being three-dimensional, we model the capacitor, as shown on the left of Figure 20.2, as two wires connected to a battery

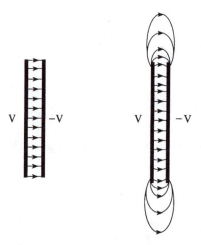

Figure 20.1 *Left*: Electric-field lines betweens the plates of an ideal parallel-plate capacitor. The equal spacing and single direction indicate a uniform field. *Right:* A representation of the field between the plates of a realistic capacitor. The field tends to "fringe" and extend beyond the ends of the plates.

that keeps the top plate at 100 volts and the bottom one at -100 volts. To permit a solution to this capacitor, we need to contain it in a limited space, which we do by placing it inside a charge-free box made from wires that are "grounded" (kept at 0 volts). After we solve this problem, we may make it more realistic still by enlarging the box so that it has no effect on the field near the capacitor. This is little work for us, but much more work for the computer.

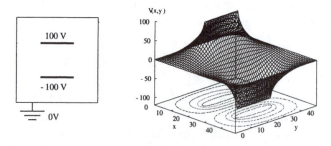

Figure 20.2 *Left:* A parallel-plate capacitor within a grounded box. A realistic capacitor would have the plates closer together in order to condense the field. *Right:* A visualization of the electric potential for this geometry. The contours projected onto the xy plane give the equipotential surfaces.

20.2.1 Laplace's Partial Differential Equation*

Rather than solve for the electric field $\mathbf{E}(x, y)$, we solve for the electric potential $V(x, y)$. This is easier because V is a scalar while $\mathbf{E}$ is a vector, and because the equations for V are simpler. Insofar as the field $\mathbf{E}$ equals the derivative (gradient) of V, the two solutions are equivalent. (Electric-field lines are perpendicular to equipotential surfaces and run from higher to lower potential values.)

Elementary physics texts show how to determine electric-field configurations using Gauss's law. We skip the mathematical manipulations needed to prove it and just state that the solution using Gauss's law is equivalent to finding a solution of the partial differential equation (PDE),

$$\frac{\partial^2 V(x, y)}{\partial x^2} + \frac{\partial^2 V(x, y)}{\partial y^2} = 0. \tag{20.1}$$

This is called Laplace's equation, in honor of the genius who first did those mathematical manipulations. The rounded Ds in (20.1) indicate that the derivatives are partial not *ordinary*. The reason this is a *partial* DE is that the potential function $V(x, y)$ is a function of *both* x and y. We cannot solve the x behavior without simultaneously solving for the y behavior. The real world is full of such equations.

20.3 ALGORITHM: FINITE DIFFERENCES

The simplest method for solving our PDE is illustrated in Figure 20.3 and is known as a *finite-difference technique*. There we see on the left a grid of x and y values, each uniformly spaced by a step size $\Delta x = \Delta y = \Delta$. Rather than trying to find a solution for the continuous range of all possible values of x and y, we try to find the solution only for the finite number of values that lie on the nodes of the grid. Yet even for the small 100×100 grid, this requires solving for 10,000 unknowns. Though not a trivial problem, the use of arrays makes it simple.

Approximating derivatives numerically is quite easy. In fact, in Chapter 15 we show how to do it in order to find a solution of an ordinary differential equation. In the present case, the second partial derivatives are approximated simply as [CP 05]:

$$\frac{\partial^2 V(x, y)}{\partial x^2} \simeq \frac{V(x + \Delta, y) + V(x - \Delta, y) - 2V(x, y)}{\Delta^2}, \tag{20.2}$$

$$\frac{\partial^2 V(x, y)}{\partial y^2} \simeq \frac{V(x, y + \Delta) + V(x, y - \Delta) - 2V(x, y)}{\Delta^2}, \tag{20.3}$$

where Δ is the spacing of the grid in Figure 20.3. After we substitute this expression, and the analogous one for the second y derivative, into Laplace's equation

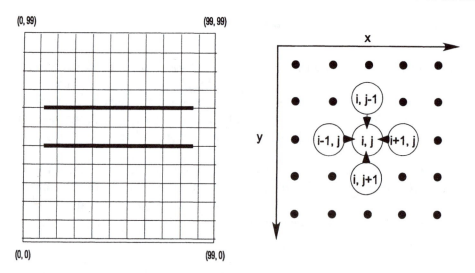

Figure 20.3 *Left:* The capacitor's field is computed only for those (x, y) values on the grid. The voltage of the plates and containing box are kept constant. *Right:* The algorithm for Laplace's equation in which the potential at the point $(x, y) = (i, j)\Delta$ equals the average of the potential values at the four nearest-neighbor points.

(20.1), we obtain a finite-difference approximation to the Laplace equation:

$$V(x, y) \simeq \tfrac{1}{4}[V(x + \Delta, y) + V(x - \Delta, y) + V(x, y + \Delta) + V(x, y - \Delta)],$$

$$\mathtt{V[i][j]} = \tfrac{1}{4}(\mathtt{V[i+1][j]} + \mathtt{V[i-1][j]} + \mathtt{V[i][j+1]} + \mathtt{V[i][j-1]}) . \quad (20.4)$$

Equation (20.4) is the specific implementation of the equation we need to solve in terms of the 2-D Java array elements V[i][j] in which we store the potential values for $x = i\Delta$ and $y = j\Delta$. This equation is visualized on the right of Figure 20.3, which shows that the potential at point (i, j) is the average of the potential values at the four nearest neighbors. If we wrote down this equation for each of the 10,000 points on our grid, we would have 10,000 simultaneous equations for 10,000 simultaneous unknown values of $V_{i,j}$.

Even though it is possible to solve these 10,000 simultaneous equations in a direct fashion, we will follow a simple, indirect approach know as a *relaxation* technique. Equation (20.4) states that a solution for the potential must be the average of the potential values at the four nearest neighbors. With that in mind, we try an iterative approach to finding the solution:

1. Start with an initial guess $V(x, y) = 0$ every place except on the plates.
2. To obtain an improved guess, apply (20.4) to all points in space, except the plates and box.
3. Keep applying (20.4) to obtain an even more approved guess until the improvement becomes smaller than some preset level of tolerance.

There is no guarantee that this relaxation method converges for arbitrary choices of Δ and geometries. Yet if we do come up with a solution that ends up satisfying (20.4), then we have our solution and it's nobody's business how we got it!

20.4 IMPLEMENTATION: LAPLACE.JAVA

The pseudocode for our solution involves an outermost loop for iterations, and inner loops over $Nmax$, x, and y values:

```
1    set potential = 0 on surrounding around box
2    set potential = 100, −100 on upper, plates
3    repeat 1000 times
4        for Nmax x space steps
5        for Nmax y space steps
6            V = average of 4 nearest neighbors
7            keep potential on box & plates fixed
8    print out V
```

This algorithm is well suited to the use of arrays because the indices vary, but not the equations. This means, as we see in Listing 20.1's `Laplace.java`, that it will not take many lines of code to implement. We store the potential $V(x, y)$ in an array `V[i][j]`, with the first index spanning all possible x values and the second index corresponding to all possible y values (measured in steps of Δ). The array is declared as `V[Nmax][Nmax]` on line with 7, and with $Nmax = 100$ steps for the sample program. The voltages of the capacitor plates are kept fixed by lines 13–15, while the boundary conditions for the box are imposed on lines 16–20. The index 25 corresponds to the x value for the left edge of the capacitor, while 75 corresponds to the y value for the lower capacitor and 63 to the y value for the upper capacitor.

Listing 20.1 Laplace.java

```java
1  // Laplace.java:  Solves Laplace equation, finite difference method
2  file output in gnuplot 3−D grid format
3  import java.io.*;
4  public class Laplace {
5  static int  Nmax =  100;                               // Size of box
6    public static void main(String[] argv) throws IOException,
         FileNotFoundException {
7    double V[][] = new double[Nmax][Nmax];
8    int i, j, iter;
9    //                              Save data in file Laplace.dat
10   PrintWriter w = new PrintWriter(new FileOutputStream("Laplace.
         dat"), true);
11   for (i=0; i< Nmax; i++)                         // Initialize array
12     { for (j=0; j< Nmax; j++) { V[i][j] = 0.0; } }
13     for (i = 25; i<= 75; i++)          // Boundary conditions++−*/
14     {   V[i][37] = −100.; /*++−// Plates' potentials
15         V[i][63] = 100.;   }
16     for (i = 0; i< Nmax; i++)                       // Box potential
```

```
17      {    V[0][i]  =  0.0;
18           V[Nmax−1][i]  =  0.;
19           V[i][0]  =  0.;
20           V[i][Nmax−1]  =  0.;      }
21      for (iter=0; iter< 1000; iter++) {            // Iterate 1000 times
22        for (i=1; i<=Nmax−2; i++) {                 // x−direction
23          for(j=1; j<= Nmax−2; j++) {               // y−direction
24
25      V[i][j] = 0.25*(V[i+1][j] + V[i−1][j] + V[i][j+1] + V[i][j−1]);
26
27          if (j ==37 && i >=25 && i <=75) V[i][j] = +100.;    //Plates
28          if (j ==63 && i >=25 && i <=75) V[i][j] = −100.;
29      }}}
30      for (i=0; i<Nmax ; i=i+1) {                   // Write gnuplot 3D format
31        for (j=0; j<Nmax; j=j+1) {
32        w.println(""+V[i][j]+"");}
33        w.println("");      }                       // Blank line between rows
34      System.out.println("data stored in Laplace.dat");
35 }    }                                             // End main, end class
```

The only tricky parts in Laplace.java are ensuring that we do not let the algorithm change the value of the externally applied voltages, and that we do not specify any indices that lie outside of the array. Recall, Nmax-1 is the maximum value possible for an index of the array V[Nmax][Nmax], and so only Nmax-2 is used in the sweeps over space on lines 22–23. Once there are no errors, we just let the program repeat itself 1,000 times and relax into what we hope will be a stable value for the potential.

20.4.1 Laplace.java: Orientation and Visualization

Before trying to modify a complicated or subtle program, it is good to make sure that it runs, and to orient yourself as to how it goes about its business. Likewise, it is good to do some visualizations of the results so that you get a feel for what its output should be. For that purpose, make a copy of Laplace.java to your personal directory and read through it to get a general idea of what it does.

1. Make a paper listing of Laplace.java and draw boxes on it illuminating the following structures in the code:

   a. the loop that initializes the potential to 0;

   b. the loop that keeps the box's potential at 0;

   c. the loops that sets the voltage on the capacitor plates;

   d. the loops that sweep over all x and y values;

e. the loop that implements the algorithm (20.4);

f. the statements that output data;

g. the statement that outputs blank lines.

2. Before you make any modifications, compile and execute Laplace.java. You should get the statement data stored in Laplace.dat printed to your screen.

3. Open the file Laplace.dat with an editor. It should contain the solution $V(x, y)$ in a format that does not bother telling you the x and y values. There are 100 values of V followed by a blank line. These are the values of v[0-99][0]. The second 100 numbers are v[0-99][1], and so forth. The plotting program *gnuplot* automatically uses the row and column indices as the values for x and y it plots, so you do not have to enter them.

4. Use gnuplot (or whatever you have available) to construct 3-D surface plots of the potential *versus* both x and y. Experiment with the options to create the best visualization. We show you how to do this with gnuplot in §11.4, with the explicit command given in §11.4.2. Your plot should look like the RHS of Figure 20.2. The height of the surface represents the value of the potential $V(x, y)$ for the x and y values along the horizontal plane. Take stock of how the potential of the bounding box is always zero, and that of the plates are 100 and -100 volts. On the horizontal plane we have placed contour lines that correspond to curves along which the potential is constant. These contours are also called *equipotential surfaces*. In general, the field is seen to be compressed between the plate and to vary more slowly outside the plates than within.

5. This program uses a Java PrintWriter object to write to a file. The object is created on line 10 and written to on line 30:

```
10  PrintWriter w = new PrintWriter( new FileOutputStream( "Laplace.dat" ), true );
30  w.println(""+V[i][j]+"");
```

While we discuss Java I/O and its complications in Chapter 13, we note a few points here. As you can decipher from line 10, the Printwriter is connected to the file **Lapace.dat** on the computer's hard disk via Java's **FileOutputStream**. The Printwriter object is assigned the variable w to it, so that values of the potential are written to the file by appending the println dot operator to w on line 30.

20.5 EXPLORATION: 2-D CAPACITOR

1. The program Laplace.java assumes that the potential must have relaxed to its final value after 1,000 space iterations. Here is how to decide if this is a good assumption:

a. Modify a copy of `Laplace.java` to output to file `Laplace2.dat`.

b. Rather than try to discern small changes in highly compressed surface plots, use a measure of precision with a numerical value. If you look at the surface plot of the potential in Figure 20.2, you will see that a line along the diagonal samples the whole range of the potential. On this account, define a variable

$$\text{trace} = \sum_i |\text{V[i][i]}| \tag{20.5}$$

and print out the value of `trace` for each iteration. If `trace` changes in the sixth decimal place, you probably have five good places of precision.

c. Next modify the program so that it always obtains at least three places of precision. Define `tol` = `0.001` as the desired relative precision and modify `Laplace.java` so that it stops iterating when the relative change from one iteration to the next is less than `tol`:

$$\left| \frac{\text{trace } - \text{ traceOld}}{\text{traceOld}} \right| < \text{tol.} \tag{20.6}$$

You stop the iteration by issuing the `break` command or by using a `while` loop.

2. Now that you know the code is accurate, make it simulate a more realistic capacitor in which the plate separation is 1/10th of the plate length. You should find the field more condensed between the plates.

3. Compare the results of your simulation to the sketch on the right of Figure 20.1. Whereas we are computing the electric potential, while the sketch is of the electric field, some processing is necessary. We make use of the fact that the electric-field lines point from regions of higher to lower potential, and that the field lines are perpendicular to the equipotential surfaces (the contours in our plots). Though you may try to draw lines perpendicular to the contours projected onto the base of the 3-D plot, it would be easier to look down directly onto the base. Make a 2-D graph, like Figure 20.4, of just the contour lines. The needed gnuplot commands are:

```
gnu> set nosurface
gnu> set view 0,0,1
```


4. Draw in the field lines by hand, starting from the plate at -100 volts, always keeping the field lines perpendicular to the equipotential surfaces and going downhill.

Potential U(x,y) vs x and y

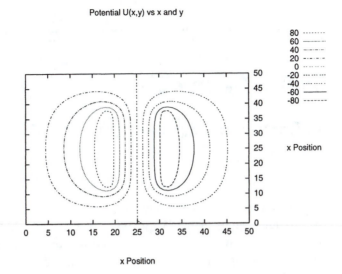

x Position

Figure 20.4 Contour plot of capacitor's equipotential surfaces. The electric-field lines are perpendicular to these contours and point toward lower potential.

20.6 EXPLORATION: 3-D CAPACITOR*

Our solution for the capacitor is general and realistic. However, our model is only two-dimensional (the "plates" are lines not squares). Extend Laplace.java so that the plates have finite dimensions in both the x and y directions. You will now have to solve for $V(x, y, z)$ and make three 3-D surfaces of $V(x, y, z)$ versus $x - y$, $x - z$, and $y - z$.

20.7 KEY WORDS

boundary conditions	equipotential surfaces	electric field	electrostatics
electric potential	equipotential lines	capacitor	gnuplot
hidden lines	finite-difference method	initial conditions	postscript
partial derivatives	reference pass	value pass	contour lines

Chapter Twenty-One

Web Computing, Applets, Primitive Graphics

In this chapter we experience one of Java's unique capabilities, namely, the ability to have its programs run over the World Wide Web (the "Web"). On account of Java's Web prowess being a major force behind its popularity, it is important to learn something about applets, even if it is not enough to become a Web developer. Nevertheless, this chapter may be skipped without serious affect on the chapters to follow.

21.1 WHAT IS WEB COMPUTING?

Up to this point, we have been using Java to write much the same kind of programs you could write with conventional languages like Fortran and C. As indicated in Figure 21.1, we have put our source code in a file such as Applet1.java, and then compiled it with javac into *byte* code that is automatically placed in Applet1.class. We then executed Applet1.class with the java Applet1 command.

A unique aspect of Java is that you may create .class files to be executed via a Web browser on someone else's computer attached to the World Wide Web. Browsers such as *Netscape, Mozilla, Amiya,* and *Internet Explorer* are programs that process files written in the *Hypertext Markup Language* (HTML). Hypertext refers to a document that, in addition to plain text, may also contain multimedia content (figures, data, movies, computer simulations, and sound). HTML is a lan-

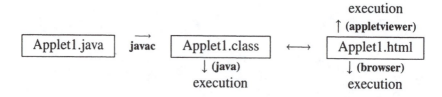

Figure 21.1 When running an applet, a compiled class file is executed from the command line or from a Web browser.

Listing 21.1 CallApplet.html, an HTML file (Web page) that starts off applet `Applet1`.

```
 1 <html>              <!-- Tells browser file type (this is a comment)
        -->
 2 <head>                                    <!-- Begin heading-->
 3 <title> CallApplet.html calls an applet </title>      <!--On top-->
 4 </head>                                    <!--End heading-->
 5 <Body>                                <!--Begin body of page-->
 6 <p>Applet called from this HTML file.</p>        <!--On Browser-->
 7 <applet code="./PlotFourierSeris.class" width=350 height=250>
           <!--Run-->
 8 </applet>                                  <!--End applet-->
 9 </body>                                    <!--End body-->
10 </html>                                    <!--End page-->
```

guage used to create hypertext documents. The "markup" aspect of the language refers to marks, analogous to those used by human typesetters to "mark up" a manuscript in preparation for typesetting, which indicate things like font type and spacings. As we shall see, the marks in HTML are tags like `<em>` enclosed in angle brackets.[1]

All HTML files end with the suffix `.html` (or sometimes `.htm` on *Windows* machines). Browsers read HTML files and both format the text it contains to look like a printed page, and display the referenced multimedia content appropriately. If the browser is modern, it should be equipped with a Java *plug-in* (an addition) that permits it to execute *.class* files. However, browsers cannot compile *.java* files (only developers, like you with SDK, are capable of doing that).

This is actually quite simple with *applets*. The Java programs that we have been writing so far are referred to as *applications*, in recognition of the fact that they *apply* computer science to something useful. Yet if you add two lines and modify one other, you will change an application program into an applet whose `.class` file runs via the Web via a browser. These files are called "applets," since it is envisioned that they will be small applications that will not overload someone else's computer when run over the Web. All applets run on the computer reading the Web page, and not on the server where the page is stored (that is a good thing because educational institutions are terribly underfunded and cannot afford to supply computer time to the whole world.)

An important thing about Java is that the language is written with a high degree of attention to security, which in this case means restricting which areas of memory a program may access. This is a good thing if you are to let someone else's program (applet) run on your computer, and it is one example of how

---

[1] We do not do much with HTML in this chapter. However, in Part 3 of this book we do study another markup language, LATEX.

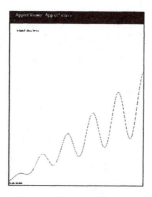

Figure 21.2 A screen dump of the computer screen showing output from Applet1.

Java is designed for Web computing. For this reason, programs that read and write files will not work as applets, since they will not be permitted to write (and possibly damage) files on someone else's computer. Likewise, we have seen that Java methods deal with arrays via *reference calls* in which the address of the array in memory is passed to the method. There are no commands in Java that permit you to manipulate these addresses or go to some other address in memory where you do not belong. This is in contrast to the use of *pointers* in a language like C, where you manipulate memory locations to do some very powerful programming—or do tremendous harm, even if that was not your intention.

The use of applets also protects you, the code provider. On the one hand, you are transmitting only your .class file to the Web computer, and so your source file cannot be damaged, or plagiarized, by the Web user. On the other hand, the .class file is running on *their* computer, not yours, and so regardless of how it fails, it cannot harm you.

21.2 IMPLEMENTATION: GET THIS TO WORK FIRST

If you are on a computer that has been set up to serve documents to the Web (a "Web server"), then the files you place in the directory or folder public_html are viewable by anyone on the Web. It follows that if the *.class* file from your applet program is in public_html, and if this class file is called by some *.html* file, then anyone's browser is used to run your applet on *their* computer, wherever and whatever their computer may be.

To see how this all works (and make more sense of all these words), examine CallApplet.html in Listing 21.1. It is the HTML that calls the applet after being read by a browser, and produces an image on your screen like Figure 21.2. The executeable applet is the compiled version of Applet1.java in Listing 21.2.

1. Save a copy of `CallApplet.html` in your `public_html` directory/folder. If you do not have such a directory, then create one. You can copy `CallApplet.html` from the CD, from the Web, or from Listing 21.1.

Listing 21.2 Applet1.java

```
 1  /*                          Applet1:   applet to plot f(x) */
 2  import java.applet.Applet;                 // Add Applet classes
 3  import java.awt.*;                         // Abstract Windows Toolkit
 4  public class Applet1 extends Applet        // Class definition
 5  { double mx, my, bx, by;          // Class variables for all methods
 6      // paint method. Execution begins here (no main)
 7      g: Graphics context (graph object) passed by browser
 8      public void paint(Graphics g)
 9  { double x, y;                            // World coordinates
10      int gOldX, gOldY, gNewX, gNewY;          // Window coordinates
11      g.drawString("In Applet1.class, f(x) vs x", 40, 40);      // Title
12      System.out.println("In Applet1.class, about to draw graph");
13      world2win(0.0,1.0,1.0,0.0);          // Determine mapping params
14      x = 0.;                                  // First point
15      y = f(x);                             // f(x) = function to plot
16      gOldX = (int)(mx*x+bx);               // Convert to window coords
17      gOldY = (int)(my*y+by);
18      for (x = 0.01; x <= 1.0; x = x+0.01) {       // Step thru points
19        y = f(x);
20        gNewX = (int)(mx*x+bx);             // Convert to window coords
21        gNewY = (int)(my*y+by);
22        System.out.println(" " +x+" , y= "+y+" ");
23        g.drawLine(gOldX, gOldY, gNewX, gNewY);      // Line segment
24        gOldX = gNewX;                      // New point becomes old
25        gOldY = gNewY;   }
26  }
27  public static double f(double x)          // Function to plot
28    { return x/2. + x*0.2*Math.sin(33*x); }
29  void world2win(double xl, double yt, double xr, double yb)
30    { //      mapping (x,y) = world (double) -> window (int)
31    //        x__win = m_x * x + b_x,        y_win = m_y * y + b_y
32    double maxx=350, maxy=250, rm, lm, tm, bm;
33    lm = 0.1 * maxX;                        // Margins, all around
34    rm = 0.9 * maxX;
35    bm = 0.9 * maxY;
36    tm = 0.1 * maxY;
37    mx = (lm-rm)/(xl-xr);                   // Mapping params wrt margins
38    bx = (xl*rm-xr*lm) / (xl-xr);
39    my = (tm-bm) / (yt-yb);
40    by = (yb*tm-yt*bm) / (yb-yt); }
41  }
```

2. Point your browser to the Web page `CallApplet.html`. When opened, this file prints out some lines on the browser's screen and runs the program in the file `Applet1.class`. It knows to run the code *via* the statement on line 8:

```
8 <applet code = "Applet1.class" width = 350 height = 250>          Call applet
```

This command tells the browser to load and run `Applet1.class` and to place the output of the program (a pretty graph) within a window in your browser of size width = 350 pixels × maxY = 250 pixels. A *pixel* stands for "picture element," namely, a single dot on your screen. A typical screen may have an area of 1024 × 768 pixels, so a 350 × 250 graph should appear as a box of about 1/10 the screen size.

3. Normally your browser will run the applet and print out line 6 someplace on your browser's screen (but not if you call the HTML file with the soon-to-be-discussed *appletviewer* command).

4. If you modify an applet that you are developing and want your browser to reload it, you need to depress the shift + reload keys simultaneously. Conversely, if you want to stop the applet from running, then pushing the back arrow on the browser seems safest. (Closing the browser window may still leave the applet running.)

5. `appletviewer`:   The SDK developer's kit provides a shell command that activates an applet without a browser:

```
> appletviewer CallApplet1.html                          Execute applet from within shell
```

The applet does not look quite the same within appletviewer as it does with a browser, but this is a convenient and fast way to develop applets.

6. Examine the graph drawn by your applet. Not bad for something we have done from scratch? One of the amazing things about Java is that this class file produces an identical graph on every Java-enabled computer system.

a. Use the View/Page Source button on your browser to see the source HTML file that the browser is *rendering* on the screen for you. Look at line 8 calling the Java program `Applet1.class`.

b. Instruct your browser to save this Web page in the appropriate directory for this chapter (File/Save As ... button on your browser). The file should have the name `CallApplet.html`. It should be similar to the file in Listing 21.1.

7. Point your browser to `Applet1.java` and open it (the file is on the CD). Study `Applet1.java`. This is the Java source code, given in Listing 21.2, for an applet to draw a graph. Your browser will be able to read this file as text, list it on your screen, but not compile or execute it. Examine how the variable `g` represents a `Graphics` object that ultimately becomes the graph on your screen. The `paint` method draws the graph, and the `world2win` method determines the parameters needed to scale the graph so that it fits in the window on your computer screen.

You will modify the `paint` method as part of your exercise.

8. Tell your browser to save `Applet1.java` in the appropriate directory for this week's work. (Doing that with the File>Save As commands is safer than cut and paste.)

9. `Applet1.class:`   This is a compiled byte code to be called by your browser as it reads `CallApplet.html`. Feel free to look at it, but it will not tell you much, as it is not meant to be read by humans.

10.   Create your own personal copy of `Applet1.class` by compiling `Applet1.java`.

11. Open your copy of `CallApplet.html` with your browser (File > Open Page > Browse). If you did all the copying and compiling correctly, this should plot the graph again.

12. Try out the alternate method for executing applets, issuing `appletviewer` from a shell:

`>  appletviewer CallApplet.html`   View applet from a shell

13. Try using the command `java Applet1` to execute `Applet1.class`.

21.2.1 Understanding Applet1.java

Look inside `Applet1.java` to see what makes it go. On lines 2 and 3 we find:

```
2  import java.applet.Applet;                              // Add Applet classes
3  import java.awt.*;                                     // Add Abstract Windows Toolkit
```

These *import* commands tells the Java compiler to include packages of class files that extend Java beyond the basic classes. The `java.applet` package contains the class `Applet` that is needed to create applets. Consequently, when on line 4 we have the statement:

```
4  public class Applet1 extends Applet                        // Class definition
```

the word "extends" means that `Applet1` inherits all the general properties of an `Applet`, as defined in `java.applet`. These include an applet's ability to be displayed in a window, its ability to respond to events like the click of a mouse, and its being killed when no longer needed. Line 4 is how we declare our `Applet1` to be an Applet. The compiler understands what an `Applet` is after the importation of line 2.

What is new in this program, aside from it being an applet, is that it draws graphical objects on your computer screen. Regardless of our graphics not being as fancy as what is possible with Java, the mere fact that we are able to write graphic commands that will run on most every computer is a major advance towards system-independent computing. The Abstract Windows Toolkit `java.awt` contains the classes for creating graphical objects such as lines, strings, rectangles, and ovals.[2]

Other than lines 2–4, the rest of the program has the same structure as the applications you have been writing up until now. However, they start their lives differently. As a consequence of applets beginning their execution from a Web browser, which is inherently a graphical interface, the applet must be "painted" onto a browser's Web page. Thus, an applet's execution begins in a method named `paint`, in contrast to the `main` method where execution begins for an application. If we had written an application, line 8 might declare our *main* method. Instead, execution of the applet begins with the call to the `paint` method:

```
8  public void paint(Graphics g)                          // Execution begins here
```

You are free to put whatever you want in the `paint` method, but you must call it `paint` and it must have a graphical object as its argument. It is through this graphics context, g in our case, that the browser and applet communicate.

21.2.1.1 Transformation of Coordinates

We want to plot

$$f(x) = \frac{x}{2} + 0.2x \, \sin(33\,x), \qquad \text{for} \qquad 0.0 \le x \le 1.0. \qquad (21.1)$$

Because $f(0) = 0$ and $f(1) \simeq 0.7$, we need to plot ordinates in the range $0 \le y \le 1$. These ranges for x and y are called actual or *world values* or coordinates. The plotting in our applet is done with basic Java graphics that deal with the display screen's *pixels*. A typical screen, indicated on the left of Figure 21.3, may be 1,024 pixels wide and 768 pixels high. To draw our graph we need to convert the x and y values from (21.1) into pixel counts or *window coordinates* that fit on the screen. We assume a linear mapping between the two,

$$x_{win} = m_x \, x + b_x, \qquad y_{win} = m_y \, y + b_y, \qquad (21.2)$$

where the m's and b's are constants that we need to determine. The method `world2sc` solves for these constants and in the process as converts the values of x and y in `doubles` into `ints` needed for pixel values. To be safe, we leave a 10% margin around the graph.

---

[2]A useful reference on this subject is the free textbook by D. Eck [Eck 02]. Other books often examine older versions of Java, even if they call them Java2, Java3, or Java4. Eck uses JFC (Java Foundation Class) and swing.

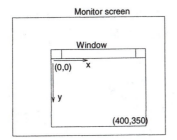
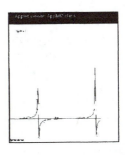

Figure 21.3 *Left:* The coordinate system used to define the window (pixel) coordinates. The upper left corner corresponds to the point (0,0), the width of the window is 400 pixels, and the height is 350 pixels. The y_{win} coordinate increases downwards. *Right:* An image of the computer screen showing Applet2.

Rather than try to draw a smooth curve through 100 points (possible using *splines* [CP 05]), we draw 100 little straight lines connecting old points, (gOldX, gOldY) to new points (gNewX, gNewY) and hope that your eyes are not good enough to notice the steps. The for loop that generates the 100 line segments starts on line 18, and the actual drawing is done on line 23. Seeing that pixel coordinates are all integers, on lines 16–17 and 20–21 we use the *cast* operator (int) to convert or "cast" a double into an integer (recall, we must do this explicitly since Java will not let us reduce precision unless we insist).

21.3 EXPLORATION: MODIFY APPLET1.JAVA

1. Copy the files CallApplet.html and Applet1.java into new files Applet2.html and Applet2.java respectively.

2. Modify both these files so they will work as the applet Applet2.java. You will need to make the names of the Java source and class file consistent. This also means that you will have to compile Applet2.java to produce Applet2.class, since a direct renaming of Applet1.class will not work.

3. Check that opening Applet2.html in your browser draws the graph again.

4. Modify the program Applet2.java so that it also draws an x axis and a y axis with the graph. It should look like the right drawing in Figure 21.3.

   a. *Hint 1:* Draw a long line using the g.drawLine command on line 31, only now draw it from the origin to the edge of the box.

   b. *Hint 2:* It is easy to draw an axis outside of the piece of real estate you have reserved on the screen, and then not see the line at all (what a bummer). Accordingly, it is a good idea to make your program change progressively so that at first you draw the axes well within the reserved box and then see how close you can get the axes to the edges of the boxes before they disappear.

5. Modify the source code to plot the function $f(x) = \tan(5x)$. To keep your curve within the boundary, like Figure 21.3, you may have to divide $f(x)$ by 100.

6. Make the straight-line nature of the drawing more evident by experimenting with the number of steps used in the program and observing the results. For example, try using 1/10 the number of steps, and 10 times the number of steps. Is there a limit to how smooth a graph you are able to create?

21.4 EXTENSION: PTPLOT AS APPLET*

Listing 21.3 PlotFourierSeries.java defines a class `PlotFourierSeries` derived from `PlotApplet` that configures and constructs a PtPlot.

```
1  // PlotFourierSeries.java   by   Edward A. Lee
2  package ptolemy.plot.demo;
3  import ptolemy.plot.Plot; import ptolemy.plot.PlotApplet;
4  public class PlotFourierSeries extends PlotApplet
5  {
6      public String getAppletInfo() {return "PlotFourierSeries\n";}
7      public void init()            // Initialize the applet
8      {   super.init();
9          Plot plot = (Plot)plot();
10         plot.setTitle("Fourier Series for Square Wave");
11         plot.setXRange(0, 400);
12         plot.setMarksStyle("none");
13         plot.addLegend(0, "ideal");
14         plot.addLegend(1, "1 sinusoid");
15         for (int j = 2; j <= 10; j++)
16             {plot.addLegend(j, j + " sinusoids");}
17         boolean first = true;
18         plot.addPoint(0, 0.0, 0.0, false);
19         for (int i = 0; i <= 400; i++)
20     {   double approximation = 0.0;
21             for (int j = 1; j <= 10; j++)
22             {   double sig = 4*Math.sin(i*2*Math.PI*(2*j-1)/400.)/(
                   Math.PI*(2*j-1));
23                 approximation += sig;
24                 plot.addPoint(j,(double)i,approximation,!first); }
25     first = false;
26     if (i <= 200) {plot.addPoint(0, (double)i, 1.0, true); }
27     if (i >= 200) {plot.addPoint(0, (double)i, -1.0, true); }
28     }
29         plot.addPoint(0, 400.0, 0.0, true);
30     } }
```

21.5 EXTENSION: APPLET WITH BUTTON INPUT*

Listing 21.4 AppletWindow.java by Manuel Páez.

```
1   // AppletWindow.java:      plots f(x)
2
3   import java.applet.Applet;           // add Applet classes
4   import java.awt.*;                    //  Abstract Windows Toolkit
5   import java.awt.event.ActionListener;    //  Button Listeners
6   import java.awt.event.ActionEvent;
7
8   public class AppletWindow extends Applet implements ActionListener
9   {   TextField text1, text2, text3, text4;     // class variables
10      String b1s="Start"; Button b1=new Button(b1s);
11      double mx, my, bx, by, xl, xr, yt, yb;
12
13               // paint method. Execution begins here (no main)
14               // g: Graphics context (the graph object) passed by
                    browser
15
16      public void paint(Graphics g) {
17        double x, y;                        // world coordinates
18        int gOldX, gOldY, gNewX, gNewY;       // window coordinates
19        String st1=text1.getText();          // string to double
20        xl = Double.valueOf(st1).doubleValue();
21        String st2 = text2.getText();
22        xr = Double.valueOf(st2).doubleValue();
23        String st3 = text3.getText();
24        yb = Double.valueOf(st3).doubleValue();
25        String st4 = text4.getText();
26        yt = Double.valueOf(st4).doubleValue();
27        System.out.println("In Applet1.class, about to draw graph");
28        world2win(xl, yt, xr, yb);      // determine mapping params m,
                    b
29        // Step through the points
30        x = 0.;                          // first point
31        y = f(x);                        // f(x) = function to plot
32        gOldX = (int)(mx*x+bx);          // convert to window coordinates
33        gOldY = (int)(my*y+by);
34        for (x = 0.01; x <= 1.0; x = x+0.01)
35        {   y = f(x);
36          gNewX = (int)(mx*x + bx);   // convert to window
                    coordinates
37          gNewY = (int)(my*y + by);
38          System.out.println(" " +x+" , y= "+y+" ");
39          g.drawLine(gOldX, gOldY, gNewX, gNewY);         // draw
                    segment
40          gOldX = gNewX;               // new point becomes old
41          gOldY = gNewY;
42      } }
43
44      public static double f(double x)        // function to plot
45      { return x/2. + x*0.2*Math.sin(33*x); }
```

```
46        // method world2win computes mapping parameters
47
48     public void world2win(double xl,double yt,double xr,double yb)
49     {                              // (x,y) = world (double) -> window (
         int)
50       double maxX=450, maxY=350, rm, lm, tm, bm;          // bigger
         window
51       lm = 0.1 * maxX;                                    // margins, all
         around
52       rm = 0.9 * maxX;
53       bm = 0.9 * maxY;
54       tm = 0.1 * maxY;
55       mx = (lm-rm)/(xl-xr);                               // mapping params wrt
         margins
56       bx = (xl*rm-xr*lm) / (xl-xr);
57       my = (tm-bm) / (yt-yb);
58       by = (yb*tm-yt*bm) / (yb-yt);          }
59
60     public void init() {                    // labels, text fields for
         buttons
61       add(b1);
62       b1.addActionListener(this);
63       add(new Label("x_min:", Label.RIGHT));
64       text1=new TextField(7);
65       add(text1);
66       text1.setText("0.0");
67       add(new Label("x_max:",Label.RIGHT));
68       text2=new TextField(7);
69       add(text2);
70       text2.setText("1.0");
71       add(new Label("y_min:", Label.RIGHT));
72       text3=new TextField(7);
73       add(text3);
74       text3.setText("0.0");
75       add(new Label("y_max:", Label.RIGHT));
76       text4=new TextField(7);
77       add(text4);
78       text4.setText("1.0");
79     }
80
81     public void actionPerformed(ActionEvent e) { //   Buttons
82     String tst;
83     tst=e.getActionCommand();
84     if (b1s.equals(tst)) {    // Find the Range
85         repaint();
86 }      } }
```

Now that we have learned how to do some elementary things with applets, it is time to examine to do some fancy things with them. Examine `AppletWindow.java` in Listing 21.4. It is a modification of our basic graph-plotting applet that takes user input for the minimum and maximum values of x and y to be plotted. Compile this source file and create `AppletWindow.class`.

The plotting part of this applet is the same as our previous one, yet it has some new features. On lines 6–7 we import some `awt` classes to handle events entered by depressing buttons. Next note on line 10 that we now have a *button* object defined for the Start button, and a string containing the word "start" to place on top of this button. Scrutinize next on line 11 how we declare two graphical *TextField* objects to contain the minimum and maximum values of x and y as read from the screen. On lines 21–28 we convert these graphical objects into strings, and then convert the strings into doubles. Other new operations are present in the `init` method on lines 72–92, and the `actionPerformed` method on lines 93–97. The `init` method adds the new buttons to the screen and sets up the links to transfer data into the program, while the `actionPerformed` method responds to the depression of the Start button and repaints the screen.

21.6 EXTENSION: AWT, JFC, AND SWING*

Sun Microsystems, the inventor and keeper of Java, has announced that the Abstract Windows Toolkit (`awt`) is being replaced by the *Java Foundation Classes (JFC)*. JFC also contains the *Swing* classes `javax.swing.*` to replace the AWT scrollbars, buttons, textfields, and other graphics user interface components that are sensitive to bugs. As things go, AWT is still functional, the applet we have written should work for still some time. However, it is not recommended to mix Swing and AWT components, and to satisfy forward-looking readers, we now rewrite our AWT applet, `Applet1.java` as the swing-class applet `Japplet1.java`. Note the new components:

1. The Swing component set contains *containers*, that is, windows that contain groups of controls or other containers. In the Swing hierarchy, the top-level containers provide places for containers of lesser hierarchy. Some of the top-level containers are **JApplet, JPanel**, and **JDialog**.
2. Components are added to containers of lower hierarchy. One such level of hierarchy is **contentPane**, an internal component of each top-level container into which all visible components are placed.
3. The JPanel class directs the distribution of *atomic* components in the drawing area. JPanel, as well as the other top-level containers, has a content pane into which the Swing components are added.
4. A Swing application usually contains two top-level containers, such as *frame (JFrame)* or *applet (JApplet)*, and *panel*, as well as *atomic* components like buttons, combo boxes, sliders, and text fields. A JApplet is a class that allows applets to use Swing features.
5. An individual Swing component may contain one JFrame and several JPanes. The JFrame provides the window for the application.

21.6.1 Building a JApplet*

Listing 21.5 gives JApplet1, which has the same functionality as our previous graphing applet, only now with the Swing set. (An additional example is provided in Chapter 18, "Advanced Objects; Baton Projectiles.") We recommend that the interested reader look at listing 21.5 for further JApplet experience.

Listing 21.5 JApplet1.java by Manuel Páez.

```java
import java.awt.*;
import javax.swing.*;

public class  JApplet1 extends JApplet{
   GraphPanel graphPan;        // Tell class AJp1 another class

    public void init(){
    graphPan = new GraphPanel();
    getContentPane().add(graphPan, BorderLayout.CENTER);
  }
  public class GraphPanel extends JPanel{
  double mx,my,bx,by;

    GraphPanel()        //constructor for white background
    {setBackground(Color.white); }

    public double f(double x)
    {return x/2. + x*0.2 * Math.sin(33*x);}

    void world2sc(double xl,double yt,double xr,double yb)
    {
    double maxx,maxy,rm,lm,tm,bm;
    maxx = 350;     //screen max width
    maxy = 250;     //screen max height
    lm = 0.1*maxx;  //left margin 1/10 of maximum
    rm = 0.9*maxx;    //right screen margin to plot figure
    bm = 0.9*maxy;    //bottom margin
    tm = 0.1*maxy;    //upper margin
    mx = (lm-rm)/(xl-xr); //this and next 3 are global varibles
    bx = (xl*rm-xr*lm)/(xl-xr);
    my = (tm-bm)/(yt-yb);
    by = (yb*tm-yt*bm)/(yb-yt);
  }
   public void paintComponent(Graphics g)
 {
   super.paintComponent(g);     //calls paintComponent
   double x,y;              //world coordinates
   int goX,goY,gnX,gnY;          //window coordinates
   g.drawString("In Ap1.class, f(x) vs x", 40, 40);  // Add title
   System.out.println("In Applet.class, about to draw graph");
   world2sc(0.0,1.0,1.0,0.0);   //to produce constants mx,my,bx,
         by
```

```
42      //called with left, top, right and bottom world extremes
43      // Step through the points
44      x = 0.00;          //first point
45      y = f(x);
46      goX = (int)(mx*x+bx);     //convert to window coordinates
47      goY = (int)(my*y+by);     //with linear transformations
48      for (x = 0.01;x<=1.0; x = x+0.01)
49        { y = f(x);
50           gnX = (int)(mx*x+bx);     //new point converted to
51           gnY = (int)(my*y+by);     //window coordinates
52           g.drawLine(goX, goY, gnX, gnY);     //plot line segment
53           goX = gnX;  //for next iteration old point is now the
54           goY = gnY;  //just calculated
55        }
56      }
57    }//JPanel
58  }//JApplet
```

Given the preceding theory for JApplets, we now try to design one. We know we must have a class inherited from the JApplet, and another class inherited from the JPanel class. In addition, we shall draw our objects in the content pane of the object of JPanel. On line 4 we import awt in order to use the graphics() class, and on line 5 we import the Swing package to build a JApplet and a JPanel. Execution of the applet begins in the paintComponent(Graphics g) method on line 11, where the browser transmit the Graphics object g. This object is called the *graphics context* because it provides the context and methods for painting. To cite an instance, it contains information on the window size, the clipping region, the color, and the font, as well as the methods to draw a line, a rectangle, an oval, and so forth. Initialization is done in the init() method on line 45, which is called automatically.

The definition of the class Apj1 as derived from JApplet occurs on line 39. We see that Apj1 inherits all the properties and methods of JApplets. The statement on line 40 declares an instance of a new class derived from JPanel. The init() method on line 45 initializes the applet by declaring an instance of the class GraphPanel, which is defined as a class of the type JPanel with the JApplet class. This gets added to the content Pane of the JApplet. Finally, on line 56 the constructor of the GraphPanel class is defined, with the color white declared for the panel background. The remainder of the JApplet contains much the same code as Applet1.java.

21.7 EXAMPLE: BATON APPLET, JPARABOLA.JAVA*

In Figure 18.3 we show the output of the applet Jparabola.java written by Manuel Pàez (and found on the disk). This applet implements the OOP and physics

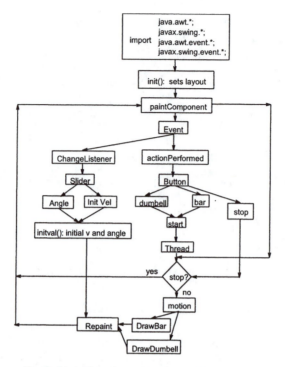

Figure 21.4 Flowchart of the applet JParabola.

ideas we have been discussing, and is available on the CD. We encourage all readers to try out the applet, even if they do not look inside to see what makes it work. In this section we describe what makes it work.

As indicated by the flowchart in Figure 21.4, Jparabola starts by importing the necessary classes. It then sets the layout for the applet and then calls the method paintComponent to analyze the events needed to start the applet's thread (pressing the buttons dumbell/bar followed by start). Events changing the initial velocity are originated by the slider bars. If the stop button is pressed, the thread stops and the program waits for further events.

When the applet is loaded by a browser, the browser (or appletviewer) transfers to it a graphics context in which to plot elements. The applet is initialized with the init() method and continues with the paintComponent method that sets watchers to the action of the buttons, sliders, and system actions. If the start button is pressed, a thread to start the motion is begun, and the motion continues until it is stopped or the projectile hits the ground.

Because the Applet uses the swing technology, it needs instances of JApplet andJPanel. From these it constructs three classes:

1. `JParabola`: inherits properties of `JApplet` and contains other two classes.
2. `ParabolaPanel`: inherits properties of `JPanel` and implements `Runnable`. Because a `Thread` is defined, the object `ActionListener` is implemented in order to listen for the buttons that generate actions.
3. `ListenToSlider`: controls the action of the sliders and creates instance of `ChangeLister`.

As was needed for our most elementary applet, `JParabola` contains class variables used in transforming from world (x, y) to window (X, Y) coordinates. In addition, `JParabola` contains class variables used in transforming time and energy to window (T, E). The `init()` method establishes the layout for the applet. It contains a main JPanel, `ParabolaPanel`, which uses a BorderLayout:

1. **North:** a JSlider to select the initial angle of the projectile.
2. **West:** another JSlider to select the initial velocity of the projectile.
3. **Center:** on the left, the location of the graphs for the parabolic motion, on the right, the energy graphs.
4. **South:** another JPanel `formsPan` using a BorderLayout with a button and JTextFields to set the dumbell's masses and length. Also buttons to start or stop the motion, with similar button on the right for a solid bar.

ParabolaPanel: The class `ParabolaPanel` inherits properties of a JPanel, and contains methods:

1. `ParabolaPanel():`   class constructor and variable initializer.
2. `world2sc():`   transforms world to global coordinates.
3. `energycoor():`   transforms world to global coordinates for E and t.
4. `xyaxis():`   plots the x-y axis of right graph.
5. `initval():` uses JSliders to determine initial velocity of projectile.
6. `DrawDumbell()`, `DrawBar():`   draws trajectory and plots energy.
7. `motion():` computes and plots (x, y), and calls method to add rotation.
8. `run():`   in action until stop button pressed or motion ends. Freezes motion for several milliseconds so that user sees the positions of the dumbell and steps through the time used in `motion` method.
9. `setInitAngle`, `setInitVel:`   converts JSlider readings to doubles, draws initial velocity vector.
10. `beginMov():`   called when "start" depressed, starts thread, sets time to 0.
11. `paintComponent():`   the main program, the internal thread that continuously watches these programs.
12. `actionPerformed():`   listens for events caused from buttons and reads JTextFieldsds.

The class `class ListenToSlider` implements ChangeListener and continuously detects the JSliders to see if they have moved. Its call to method `beginMov` starts the motion thread.

21.7.1 Exercises for JParabola

1. Observe the motion of the dumbell for different masses and lengths, and how the heavier mass remains closer to the parabolic COM trajectory.
2. Does the time in the air depend upon the mass?
3. What properties of the baton's motion change when the mass increases?
4. Is the baton at rest at the highest point in its trajectory?
5. Is the sum of the translational KE + PE constant?
6. Is total energy constant?
7. Is rotational energy constant?

21.8 KEY WORDS

applet	appletviewer	application	browser
byte code	HTML	hypertext	just-in-time compiler
markup language	pixels	WWW	

21.9 SUPPLEMENTARY EXERCISES

1. You are writing a Java program or applet designed to run over the World Wide Web. Explain in just a few words the purpose or content of each of the following:
   a. Program.java
   b. javac
   c. java
   d. Program.html
   e. Program.class
   f. appletviewer
2. Explain in just a few words:
   a. what makes the *main* method different from all other methods;
   b. what is a Web browser;
   c. what is special about the *paint* method in an applet;
   d. on what computer does an applet run;
   e. on what computer is an applet compiled;
   f. how you get an applet to write out to a file.

PART 3

LaTeX SURVIVAL GUIDE

Chapter Twenty-Two

LaTeX for Text: Scientific Document Processing, Markup Language

22.1 WHY LaTeX?

In the 1980's Donald Knuth created a revolutionary computer program called TeX ("tech") for producing book-quality technical documents [Knuth 86] that rivaled the documents produced by a professional human typesetter. In 1985 Leslie Lamport combined a number of TeX commands into a set of higher-level macros known as LaTeX [Lap 85] that has fewer details to worry about than TeX. At present LaTeX is widely used for scientific journals, books, and reports, and for good reason. LaTeX automatically generates tables of contents, lists of figures, cross-references, equations, section and figure numbers, indexes, and bibliographies. Nevertheless, it is the mathematics that LaTeX does better than any other electronic system. This chapter describes enough of the basic elements of LaTeX for you to produce your own beautiful-looking scientific documents [Wilk 95].

To produce a LaTeXdocument, all you have to do is prepare a source file with some LaTeX commands embedded at the correct places, and then compile the source. Because the source file is an ASCII file, it is possible to write and read it on any computer system with no special programs. Of course one needs a copy of the LaTeX program to typeset this ASCII file, but the program is free and readily available.

The basic steps for using LaTeX are shown in Figure 22.1. It is seen to be quite similar to compiling and running a code, and so makes a useful last part for this book. By convention, the LaTeX source file has a `.tex` extender and the compiled version of the source has a `.dvi` extender. We have called our source file `Paper.tex` and the compiler has produced the *device-independent* file `Paper.dvi` from it. A `.dvi` file is independent of any specific computer system or hardware, and is viewed on a computer screen with a program known as a *viewer*, or converted to a PostScript (`.ps`) or Portable Document Format (`.pdf`) file to be sent to a printer or posted on the Web.

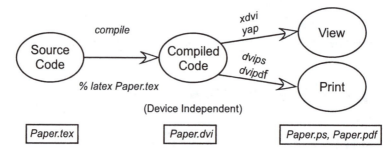

Figure 22.1 The steps followed and utilities used in preparing a document with LaTeX. The source file is Paper.tex, the device-independent file is Paper.dvi, and the file ready for printing/posting is Paper.ps or Paper.pdf.

The theory behind LaTeX is that authors should worry about the contents of a document and leave the format up to the computer. In practice there are a number of steps to follow before authors see their documents typeset. This is in contrast to WYSIWYG (what you see is what you get), in which the formulas appear on the computer screen as you enter them. We personally prefer a markup-language approach for complicated documents, especially if that document is to be placed in a digital library. We find that not having to concentrate on how things look until after the writing is over lets us get the hard part of creation done first. However, there are a number of LaTeX commands to learn, and debugging complicated equations can be challenging. Nevertheless, a thing of beauty is a joy forever.

22.2 STRUCTURE OF A LaTeX DOCUMENT

LaTeX is a member of a class of languages known as *markup languages*.[1] The term "markup" comes from the printing trade, where an editor would "markup" a document by inserting symbols to indicate properties such as font size and spacing. This same purpose is served by the LaTeX commands, only in this case they are not for a human typesetter to follow, but for a computer. Inasmuch as LaTeX is a compiled, in contrast to an interpreted, language, when you are done with the writing, the compiler will read your entire document, place the tables, figures, and so forth, in the best places throughout your document, and then cross-reference the whole thing. Like other compilers, you may have to remove all errors before the compiler produces anything, and the compiler may need to make several passes through the document to get it all right.

22.3 SAMPLE INPUT FILE (SAMPLE.TEX)

A LaTeX source file has two basic parts:

---

[1] Others include HTML, XML, GML, and MATHML.

```
1    \documentclass[options]{classname}
2       ...
3            Part I: preamble
4       ...
5       \begin{document}
6       ...
7            Part II: actual document
8       ...
9       %%\end{document}
```

The first part is the preamble, and it starts with a statement of the type of document your document is to be. The choices, `classname = article, report, book, slides`, or `letter`, seem to cover most everything. Older versions of LATEX started with a `\documenttype` command, but the newer LATEX 2e uses the `\documentclass` command. The `[options]` argument might include the font sizes (in points)— 10 pt (default), 11 pt, or 12 pt—as well as `onecolumn` (default), or `twocolumn`, `oneside` or `twoside`, or `landscape`. With `\documentclass{article}` you obtain a document in 10 pt font. The preamble might also include macros (commands) that you have defined for your own use, and commands for including special packages, for example, for dealing with graphics.

To give you a real example, here, and on the CD is `Sample.tex`, an edited version of a problem set with a comment following the `%`:

```
\documentclass{article}
\begin{document}

\section{Sample \LaTeX\ Output}\index{Comments!Latex@\LaTeX}

\noindent This document consists of bits and pieces of a final
examination given at \textbf{\large Oregon State University}. The
material is from the text \emph{Computational Physics} \cite{CP},
which does not cost much \$\$.

We have left off anything fancy, like title page, from the
preamble and used an enumerated list environment
(\tell{enumerate}), with mathematics environment inserted as
needed. An \emph{Environment} usually begins with
\verb+\begin{name}+ and ends with \verb+\end{name}+.

% This is a one-line comment beginning with %; it does not get printed.

\begin{enumerate}

\item Given $N=6$ random numbers distributed between 0 and 10,
\[ 3, 7, 3, 1, 8, 2 \]

\begin{enumerate}
    \item Use this sequence to simulate a random walk and determine
          if the distance from the origin $R = \sqrt{N}$.
    \item Use this sequence to determine an approximate value for the
          double integral
```

```
    \begin{equation}
    \int_0^1 \int_0^1 {dx\,dy\over  x^2+y^2}
    \end{equation}

\end{enumerate}

\item Given the Schr\"{o}dinger equation for two coupled wave functions
$\psi_1$ and $\psi_2$,
    \begin{eqnarray}
  {-\hbar^2 \over 2m_1} {d^2 \psi_1 (x)\over dx^2} + V(x)\psi_1(x) +
               U(x)\psi_2(x)   &=& E \psi_1(x) \label{eq.1} \\
  {-\hbar^2 \over 2m_2} {d^2 \psi_2 (x)\over dx^2} + V(x)\psi_2(x) +
               U(x)\psi_1(x)&=& E \psi_2(x) \label{eq.2}
    \end{eqnarray}
Express equations (\ref{eq.1}) and (\ref{eq.2}) in the dynamical
form appropriate for numerical integration:
\[
{d \textbf{y}(t)\over dt} = \textbf{f(y},t)
\]
\end{enumerate}
%\end{document}
```

When we apply LaTeX to these paragraphs we produce the text:

22.4 SAMPLE LaTeX OUTPUT

This document consists of bits and pieces of a final examination given at **Oregon State University**. The material is from the text *Computational Physics* [CP 05], which does not cost much $$.

We have left off anything fancy, like title page, from the preamble and used an enumerated list environment (enumerate), with mathematics environment inserted as needed. An *Environment* usually begins with \begin{name} and ends with \end{name}.

i) Given $N = 6$ random numbers distributed between 0 and 10,

$$3, 7, 3, 1, 8, 2$$

(a) Use this sequence to simulate a random walk and determine if the distance from the origin $R = \sqrt{N}$.

(b) Use this sequence to determine an approximate value for the double integral

$$\int_0^1 \int_0^1 \frac{dx\,dy}{x^2 + y^2} \tag{22.1}$$

ii) Given the Schrödinger equation for two coupled wave functions ψ_1 and ψ_2,

$$\frac{-\hbar^2}{2m_1} \frac{d^2\psi_1(x)}{dx^2} + V(x)\psi_1(x) + U(x)\psi_2(x) = E\psi_1(x) \tag{22.2}$$

$$\frac{-\hbar^2}{2m_2} \frac{d^2\psi_2(x)}{dx^2} + V(x)\psi_2(x) + U(x)\psi_1(x) = E\psi_2(x) \tag{22.3}$$

Express equations (22.2) and (22.3) in the dynamical form appropriate for numerical integration:

$$\frac{dy(t)}{dt} = \mathbf{f(y}, t)$$

22.4.1 Brief Look at Input File

Most of the characters in our input file `Sample.tex` are the same as in the output. However, mathematical symbols, Greek, and some special characters are entered with commands: the math symbols and Greek, because they do not appear on the keyboard, the special characters because LATEX uses them within its own commands.

Look at the commands in `Sample.tex`. You will notice that LATEX commands usually consist of a backslash \ followed by a word. As an instance, we use \item, \begin{equation}, and \emph{Computation Physics} respectively. The Greek letter ψ was produced with \psi, and the mathematical symbol $\sqrt{N}$ with \sqrtN. As we also see in these examples, the special characters { and } are used to enclose the argument to a LATEX command. To illustrate, the $\sqrt{}$ is applied to N via \sqrtN, and both the words *Computational* and *Physics* are emphasized by \emph{Computational Physics}. Of special importance in this file is the dollar sign $. When used as part of the text to indicate a dollar sign, it is entered as \$. When used as part of LATEX command to switch between text and math modes, it is entered as $, for example:

```
coupled wave functions $\psi_1$ and $\psi_2$
```
coupled wave functions ψ_1 and ψ_2

Although we talk more about this in a separate section, we produced mathematical equations that were separated off from the text ("displayed") by placing them between the commands \[and \], or between \begin{equation} and \end{equation}, or between \begin{eqnarray} and \end{eqnarray}.

22.4.2 Special Characters

The characters

    # $ % & ~ _ ^ \ { }

are called "special characters" because LATEX uses them for its own purposes. This means that you cannot use them unless you do something special. If you simply want the special character to be printed just as any other letter, include a \ in front of the character:

    $ \$

There are two exceptions to this rule. You cannot produce \ via \\, because LATEX uses \\ to indicate the end of a line. So produce it by typing $\backslash$:

    \ $\backslash$

The second exception is the tilde. Seeing that \~ means "place a tilde accent over the following letter," a ˜ is produced by \~{}, that is, having nothing there (empty braces) for the tilde to go over:

˜name   \~{}name

22.4.3 Paragraphs, Spaces, and Breaks

Look now at the two short paragraphs below the headings in `Sample.tex`. A new paragraph is indicated by one (or more) skipped lines. LATEX then automatically indents the paragraph as appropriate for its place in the document, for example, it does not indent at the beginning of a new section. To ensure that our first paragraph after the table is *not* indented, we placed a \noindent command there.

Ordinary text is entered with no special commands. In general you do not even have to worry about the spacing between words and lines, or where lines begin and end. LATEX treats any number of spaces as equivalent to a single space, and views the carriage return (← Enter) at the end of a line as though it were just another space. If you want to insist on an extra blank space being inserted at some point, then you insert a \ command, that is, a blank space preceded by a *backslash*. This means that you do not have to worry about spaces in your input, although you should give it some structure with spaces and new lines to make the content clear, as you would with any coding.

Though you should not have to do this for most of your work, sometimes you do need to insert a horizontal or vertical blank space in your document. You request that LATEX does that (a "request" because LATEX has its own ideas about spacing, and it gets the last word) with the \hspace{} and \vspace{} commands. You become more insistent by using the \hspace*{} and \vspace*{} forms. These commands take the length of the space as an argument in the braces. The length is specified with a number of dimensional units that include:

ex   em   pt   pc   in   cm   mm

Here, ex and em are the sizes of a typeset x and m, pt and pc are the typesetting measures of points and picas, and the others are obvious.

Here is a 4ex horizontal space.	`Here \hspace{4ex} is a 4ex horizontal space.`
Here is a 9mm horizontal space.	`Here \hspace{9mm} is a 9mm horizontal space.`
Negative space & overst̶r̶iking	`Negative space & overstriking\hspace{-3em}---`
A 3ex vertical space between here	`A 3ex vertical space between here \vspace{3ex}`
and this line.	`and this line.`

If you want to insist on a line ending someplace and a new paragraph beginning, then you insert a double *backslash* \\ to end the line. In addition, you add some extra blank space after the line by including an argument to \\. To illustrate, we place *[3ex] here,

and you see that it skips three ex's of space before printing this line.

Usually LATEX decides where to start a new page according to its own internal rules. As an example, it tries not to split up tables or place the last line of a paragraph on a new page. If you disagree with LATEX's decision and wish to force a page break, use:

\pagebreak	hint to LATEX if embedded, command if on separate line
\newpage, \clearpage	no attempt to fill page

Though you would never "double-space" a book or journal article, there are occasions when you want to double-space a draft, or to make a business letter fill the page. If you want to vary the interline spacing, you need to change the LATEX environmental variable \baselinestretch from its default value of 1. Generally you do this in the *preamble* with:

```
\renewcommand{\baselinestretch}{1.75}
```

where we have set the spacing to one and three-quarter lines. The command then holds for the entire document. (You may try to reset the spacing locally, but that may mess up the length of the page.)

22.4.4 Quotation Marks and Dashes

Despite most of us never worrying about such things, LATEX is fairly serious when it comes to quotation marks and dashes. This is a consequence of its being a typesetting program, and typesetters are very serious about such things. When writing in LATEX, we usually place a word in quotation by placing two left quotes on the left side and two right quotes on the right. As a case in point, the quotes in

"golfballs appear to 'drop out of the sky' near the end of their trajectories"

is produced from the input

```
''golfballs appear to 'drop out of the sky' near the end of their
trajectories''
```

Scrutinize how the left double quote " is entered as *two* left single quotes in succes-

sion, ' and ', and the right double quote is entered as *two* right single quotes, ' and
'. As a general rule, one should not use the (undirected) 'double quote' character
" on the keyboard. (Some text editors, like emacs, automatically substitute either
" or " when you enter " if they know you are entering a LATEX document.)

LATEX and typesetters deal with dashes of three lengths:

intra-word dash or hyphen, as in intra-word	`intra-word dash or hyphen, as in intra-word`
double dash indicates range, as in 3–8	`double dash indicates range, as in 3--8`
triple or punctuation dash—popular in news	`triple or punctuation dash---popular in news`

22.5 FONTS FOR TEXT

The basic theory behind LATEX is that the user should worry about content and
let the program worry about presentation. So it follows that you should tell
LATEX whether you want some material to be *emphasized*, or **emboldened**, or
presented as mathematics, but you should not have to worry about the name or
size of the actual font being used. To give an instance, you *emphasize* text, and
LATEX usually reacts by placing that text in italic font. However, LATEX uses a different italic font for text than it does for mathematics; for example, *this* $(math)$
is different from *this (text)*.

By default, LATEX uses the *Computer Modern* fonts, which give a characteristic look to LATEX documents. If you really want some material to have a certain
presentation that differs from LATEX's standard, then you may have to change some
things "by hand" or develop some macros. However, those occasions should be
rare and should be done only at the last minute before final presentation. The
words you wish to have in a specific format are usually given as the arguments, for
example:

Emphasized text	`\emph{Emphasized text}`
Bold text	`\textbf{Bold text}`
Teletype (monospaced) text	`\texttt{Teletype (monospaced)`
SMALL CAPITAL LETTERS	`\textsc{small capital letters}`
$f = md^2x/dt^2$ (math)	`$f = m d^2 x/dt^2$` (math)

Explicit fonts are obtained with commands of the sort:

Roman font	`\textrm{Roman font}`
Italic font	`\textit{Italic font}`
Sans serif font	`\textsf{\small Sans serif font}`
Slanted, but not italics	`\textsl{Slanted, but not italics}`

If you are working with someone else's document, you may run into some old style
commands for font changes. Though not strictly LATEX 2e, these still work:

Emphasized	`{\em Emphasized}`
Bold	`{\bf Bold}`
`Teletype`	`{\tt Teletype}`

22.5.1 Type Sizes

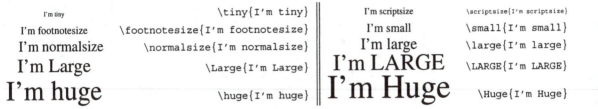

I'm tiny	`\tiny{I'm tiny}`	I'm scriptsize	`\scriptsize{I'm scriptsize}`
I'm footnotesize	`\footnotesize{I'm footnotesize}`	I'm small	`\small{I'm small}`
I'm normalsize	`\normalsize{I'm normalsize}`	I'm large	`\large{I'm large}`
I'm Large	`\Large{I'm Large}`	I'm LARGE	`\LARGE{I'm LARGE}`
I'm huge	`\huge{I'm huge}`	I'm Huge	`\Huge{I'm Huge}`

22.5.2 Fancy Text Accents

English appears to be an underachiever when it comes to accents. However, if you wish to include some foreign text in your documents, then you may well need some of the accents LATEX provides:

`\'{o}`	ó	`\'{o}`	ò	`\^{o}`	ô	`\"{o}`	ö	`\~{o}`	õ	`\={o}`	ō
`\.{o}`	ȯ	`\u{o}`	ŏ	`\v{o}`	ǒ	`\H{o}`	ő	`\t{oo}`	o͡o	`\c{o}`	ǫ
`\d{o}`	ọ	`\b{o}`	o̲	`\'{i}`	í	`\'{j}`	ȷ́				

If you want to accent mathematics, then different commands are needed yet, and we will get to that.

22.5.3 Math Symbols in Text

Placing mathematics in text, such as $\int f(x)dx$, is done by placing the mathematics between dollar signs, for example, `$\int f(x) dx$`. Other symbols are created in math mode with the commands:

#	`\#`	$	`\$`	%	`\%`	&	`\&`
\	`$\backslash$`	\	`\verb'\'`	ˆ	`\verb'^'`	^	`\char94`
ˆ	`\^{}`	~	`\char126`	{	`\{`	}	`\}`
_	`\_`	œ, Œ	`\oe, \OE`	æ, Æ	`\ae, \AE`	ra, rA	`\aa, \AA`
ω, Ω	`\o, \O`	ł, Ł	`\l, \L`	ß	`\ss`	¿	`?'`
¡	`!'`	†	`\dag`	‡	`\ddag`	§	`\S`
P	`\P`	©	`\copyright`	£	`\pounds`		

22.6 ENVIRONMENTS

A LaTeX *Environment* usually begins with \begin{name} and ends with \end{name}. Indeed, since a LaTeX document begins and ends as \begin{document} ... \end{document}, the entire source file is in a *document* environment. Other environments include:

array	math arrays	center	centered text or tables
description	definition list	document	the full LaTeX document
enumerate	numbered and lettered list	eqnarray	aligned equations
figure	floating figure	itemize	bullet list
list	custom list	minipage	page within a page
picture	basic diagram drawn by LaTeX	quotation	long quotation
quote	short quotation	tabbing	define and use tabs
table	floating and referenced table	tabular	in-place table
verbatim	set as entered in \texttt	\verb|text|	in-line verbatim

22.7 LISTS

LaTeX supports three types of lists:

enumerate: for numbered lists;

itemize: for bullet lists;

description: for definition lists like this;

list: custom lists.

```
\LaTeX supports three types of lists:
\begin{description}
\item [enumerate] for numbered lists,
\item [itemize ] for bullet lists,
\item [description ] for definition lists like this.
\item [list ] Custom lists
\end{description}
\end{enumerate}
```

The numbers or bullets are provided automatically by LaTeX, so all the user has to do is separate items by an \item command:

1. This is a numbered list, but you need not enter numbers.
2. This second item contains math $\sin^2 x + \cos^2 x = 1$.

```
\begin{enumerate}
\item This is a numbered list, but no numbers are entered.
\item This second item contains math $\sin^2 x+\cos^2 x =1$.
\end{enumerate}
```

Sublists are created just by starting another list within an existing list. LATEX generates yet different symbols for sublists:

1. First item in list
   a. First item in sublist
   b. Second item in sublist
2. Second item in list

```
\begin{enumerate}
\item First item in list
    \begin{enumerate}
    \item First item in sublist
    \item Second item in sublist
    \end{enumerate}
\item Second item in list
\end{enumerate}
```

22.7.1 Text Tables

Tables are produced in the LATEX text mode by entering the **tabular** environment. It is entered via \begin{tabular}{...}, and exited via \end{tabular}. The table is placed in the text at the location in which it is entered. If you want a table that is numbered, that has a caption, and that can be referenced, then you insert your \tabular commands between a set of \table commands. We describe that later.

Here is a table from one of our Java chapters:

Description	Data Types	Size	Examples
single character	char	2 B	a, e, I, $, 6
integer	byte, short, int, long	1, 2, 4, 8 B	12, -30, -128, 127
floating point	float, double	4, 8 B	9.34F, 7.2867
logical	boolean $(\leq, \geq)$	1 bit	true or false

It is the result of:

```
\begin{tabular}{|l||c|c|r|}
\hline\hline \textbf{Description} & \textbf{Data Types} &
\textbf{Size} & \textbf{Examples} \\*[2ex] \hline
single character & \tell{char} & 2B & {a, e, I, \$, 6} \\
integer & \tell{byte, short, int, long} & {1, 2, 4, 8 B} & 12, -30, -128, 127\\
floating point & \tell{float, double} & {4, 8 B} & {9.34F, 7.2867}\\
logical & \tell{boolean} ($\leq,\geq$) & 1 bit&true or false\\
\hline
\end{tabular}
```

The argument in braces after the \begin{tabular} command specifies the format for the columns in the table. The l indicates that the first column is left-justified.

The two c's indicates that the next two columns are centered, and the last r indicates that the fourth column is right-justified. The vertical bars | are optional and instruct LATEX to place vertical bars in the columns indicated. The fact that we have bars before the first column and after the last means that we want bars on the outsides of the table.

Peer at how we have two \hline commands before we enter the data, a single \hline command after we enter the column headings, and a single \hline command after we have entered all the data. These commands cause the horizontal lines in the table to be drawn. They too are optional and must be placed *after* a row separator \\ or before the rows begin.

Data are entered into the table one row at a time. Each row ends with a double backslash \\, and the columns are separated by an ampersand character &. Mathematical symbols or equations are placed in the table by switching to math mode, which we did with ≤ and ≥.

You do not have to specify the number of rows in your tables; LATEX will know when you are done from the \end{tabular} command. In the present example we end the last row with a \\. Normally that is not necessary, but we include it because we have a \hline command to follow. If you need some more vertical space between two rows, include a space option such as *[2ex] to end a row. We did that after the heading.

22.7.2 Floating Tables

In published books and journals, tables and figures often "float" on the page. This means that they are placed where they fit in best, which is often not at the place where they are first mentioned. Clearly, this becomes more important as your table or figure gets larger and harder to fit in someplace. Table 22.1 is an example of a floating table. It is produced with the commands:

```
\begin{table}\caption{A sample floating table with a number and a caption.}
\begin{tabular}{|c|ccc|c|}
\hline\hline
Binary $abc$ & $=  a\times 2^2$ & $+ b\times2^1$ & $+c \times 2^0$ & = Decimal \\
\hline
000 & 0 & 0 & 0 & 0\\
001 & 0 & 0 & 1 & 1\\
010 & 0 & 1 & 0 & 2\\
111 & 1 & 1 & 1 & 7\\ \hline
\end{tabular}
\label{tab.binary2}
\end{table}
```

Table 22.1 A sample floating table with a number and a caption.

Binary abc	$= a \times 2^2$	$+b \times 2^1$	$+c \times 2^0$	$=$ Decimal
000	0	0	0	0
001	0	0	1	1
010	0	1	0	2
111	1	1	1	7

Inspect how the table is made by inserting the standard \begin{tabular} and \end{tabular} pair within a \begin{table} and \end{table} pair. In addition, there are \caption{} and \label{} commands within the table environment but outside of the tabular environment. The argument to \caption contains the caption that appears under the table. (If the caption command appears before the tabular command, the caption will be above the table.) The argument to \label is a tag that is used to reference the table with the \ref command (the numbering is done automatically):

Table 22.1 is referenced   Table~\ref{tab.binary2} is referenced

This same scheme of labeling and referencing is used with equations.

22.8 SECTIONS

and

22.8.1 Subsections

and

22.8.1.1 Subsubsections

LATEX permits you to have sections, subsections, and subsubsections in your documents. You give each a title, and LATEX gives each a sequential number, which changes automatically as other sections are inserted or removed, and a different sized heading. By way of example, the section, subsection, and subsubsection right above this paragraph were produced with the commands:

\section{Sections} and \subsection{Subsections} and \subsubsection{Subsubsections}

Placing an asterisk before the title of the section or subsection will suppress LaTeX's automatic numbering, as in `\section*{A Section without a Number}`.

22.8.2 Quotations and Footnotes

LaTeX contains two commands for setting off text from its surroundings. The **quote** environment is used for short quotations, while the **quotation** environment is appropriate for longer ones. They differ in indentation:

> This is a quote. Look at how this first paragraph is indented. The **quote** environment is used for short quotations.
>
> This is still the quote Observe how this second paragraph is indented. To repeat, a **quote** environment is for short quotations.

> This is a quotation. Observe how this first paragraph is indented. The **quotation** environment is appropriate for longer quotations.
> This is still the quotation. Check how this second paragraph is indented and spaced. A **quotation** environment is for longer quotations.

```
\begin{quote} ... \end{quote}

\begin{quotation} ... \end{quotation}.
```

Footnotes are created with the `\footnote{text}` command. You place the command where you want a reference to the footnote, and LaTeX automatically places a reference there and sets the note at the bottom of the page. For instance, we place a footnote here[2] with `\footnote{Sample note with its own period.}`. You should find it below and below a horizontal line.

---

[2] Sample note with its own period.

Chapter Twenty-Three

LaTeX for Mathematics

23.1 ENTERING MATHEMATICS: MATH MODE

Typesetting mathematics properly is a challenge for humans and their computer counterparts. In order for mathematical symbols to convey their meanings properly, their size and vertical and horizontal placements must adhere exactly to accepted mathematical notation. LaTeX does a beautiful job at mathematical typesetting, better than any other program, in our opinion, and is almost as good as a human typesetter.

To input an equation or mathematical symbol you enter *math mode*, and then leave math mode when you want to enter text again. The equations or symbols may be embedded in text or displayed (set off) between lines of text. In-text mathematics, such as $R = \sqrt{N}$, is surrounded by dollar signs R = \sqrt{N}$, the first one indicating a switch from text to math mode, the second one indicating a switch back from math to text:

R varies as $R \propto \sqrt{N}$ for   `$R$ varies as $R \propto \sqrt{N}$ for`

In addition to dollar signs, you may also use \ (and \) to mark the beginning and the end of a mathematical formula or symbol embedded in text:

R varies as $R \propto \sqrt{N}$ `\(R\) varies as \(R \propto \sqrt{N}\)`

Though probably just a matter of taste, we find it easier to read and edit a LaTeX source file when there are dollar signs in the text; to us, the \(and \) look too much like part of the equation.

Mathematics that is *displayed* (separated from the text) looks like:

$$\frac{-\hbar^2}{2m}\frac{d^2\psi(x)}{dx^2} + V(x)\psi(x) = E\psi(x). \tag{23.1}$$

Check that this equation has a number on the extreme right (automatically assigned by LaTeX) and a period for punctuation (put there because we prefer equations with punctuation). This equation was obtained with the LaTeX input:

```
\begin{equation}
   {-\hbar^2 \over 2m} {d^2 \psi (x)\over dx^2} + V(x)\psi(x) = E \psi(x).
\end{equation}
```

The \begin{equation} and \end{equation} commands define the environment for numbered mathematical equations. If you do *not* want the equation to be numbered, that is, so it appears as:

$$\frac{-\hbar^2}{2m}\frac{d^2\psi(x)}{dx^2} + V(x)\psi(x) = E\psi(x),$$

then use \[and \] to begin and end the displayed equation environment:

```
\[
   {-\hbar^2 \over 2m} {d^2 \psi (x)\over dx^2} + V(x)\psi(x) = E \psi(x).
\]
```

23.2 MATHEMATICAL SYMBOLS AND GREEK

Most characters have their standard meaning in math mode. However, letters used as symbols appear in a special mode of italic, and function names and subscripts appear in Roman. The special characters, already discussed in §22.4.2, are entered in math mode as:

\# $ \$ %   \%   &   \&   _   _   {   \{   }   \}   \   \backslash

The spacings between math symbols will be different than the spacings in text mode and are designed to make the mathematics clearer. As always, LaTeX ignores extra spaces or carriage returns in the your source file, unless you force the issue. This means that you may insert extra spaces in your source file for clarity, or distribute your equations over several lines. LaTeX will put it all together and make it look nice. If you insist on inserting spaces (not worth the trouble unless you are publishing the document). For example, if you enter xyyou get xy, otherwise:

$x\ y$	x\ y	normal space	$x\ y$	x\:y	medium space	$x\,y$	x\,y	thin space
$x\;y$	x\;y	thick space	xy	x\!y	back space	$x\ \ y$	x\ \ y	double space

23.2.1 Greek Letters

Greek letters are produced in math mode by preceding the full name of the letter by a backslash \. For example, $C = 2\pi r$ is input as $C = 2 \pi r$. The lowercase Greek letters are obtained as:

α	\alpha	β	\beta	γ	\gamma	δ	\delta	ϵ	\epsilon
ε	\varepsilon	ζ	\zeta	η	\eta	θ	\theta	ϑ	\vartheta
ι	\iota	κ	\kappa	λ	\lambda	μ	\mu	ν	\nu
ξ	\xi	o	o (text o)	π	\pi	ρ	\rho	ϱ	\varrho
σ	\sigma	ς	\varsigma	τ	\tau	υ	\upsilon	ϕ	\phi
φ	\varphi	χ	\chi	ψ	\psi	ω	\omega		

For those that are different from their Roman counterparts, uppercase Greek letters are obtained by capitalizing the first character of their names:

Γ	\Gamma	Δ	\Delta	Θ	\Theta	Λ	\Lambda	Ξ	\Xi	Π	\Pi
R	R (text R)	Σ	\Sigma	Υ	\Upsilon	Φ	\Phi	Ψ	\Psi	Ω	\Omega

23.2.2 Relations

$\leq$	\leq	$\le$	\le	$\geq$	\geq	$\ge$	\ge	$\equiv$	\equiv
$\prec$	\prec	$\succ$	\succ	$\sim$	\sim	$\preceq$	\preceq	$\succeq$	\succeq
$\simeq$	\simeq	$\ll$	\ll	$\gg$	\gg	$\asymp$	\asymp	$\subset$	\subset
$\supset$	\supset	$\approx$	\approx	$\subseteq$	\subseteq	$\supseteq$	\supseteq	$\cong$	\cong
$\sqsubseteq$	\sqsubseteq	$\sqsupseteq$	\sqsupseteq	$\bowtie$	\bowtie	$\in$	\in	$\ni$	\ni
$\ni$	\owns	$\propto$	\propto	$\vdash$	\vdash	$\dashv$	\dashv	$\models$	\models
$\smile$	\smile	$\mid$	\mid	$\vert$	\vert	$\doteq$	\doteq	$\frown$	\frown
$\parallel$	\parallel	$\Vert$	\Vert	$\perp$	\perp	$\colon$	\colon	$\wedge$	\wedge
$\wedge$	\land	$\vee$	\vee	$\vee$	\lor	$\cdots$	\cdots	$\ldots$	ldots

23.2.3 Negative Relations

Most negative relations are formed by including a \not command in front of the normal relation:

$\not\leq$ \not\leq $\not\equiv$ \not\equiv

This is just \not placed in front of \leq and \equiv. In addition, the symbol $\neq$ may be formed in a number of ways:

$\neq$ \neq   \ne   \not\equal

23.2.4 Binary (and Other) Operators

±	\pm	∩	\cap	∨	\vee	∓	\mp	∪	\cup
∧	\wedge	\	\setminus	⊎	\uplus	⊕	\oplus	·	\cdot
⊓	\sqcap	⊖	\sqcap	×	\times	⊔	\sqcup	⊗	\otimes
*	\ast	◁	\triangleleft	⊘	\oslash	⋆	\star	▷	\triangler
⊙	\odot	◇	\diamond	≀	\wr	†	\dagger	○	\circ
○	\bigcirc	‡	\ddagger	•	\bullet	△	\bigtriangleup	Ⅱ	\amalg
÷	\div	▽	\bigtriangledown						

23.2.5 Arrows

←	\leftarrow	→	\rightarrow	⟵	\longleftarrow
⟶	\longrightarrow	⇐	\Leftarrow	⇒	\Rightarrow
⟸	\Longleftarrow	⟹	\Longrightarrow	↔	\leftrightarrow
⇔	\Leftrightarrow	↙	\swarrow	⟺	\Longleftrightarrow
↩	\hookleftarrow	↪	\hookrightarrow	↼	\leftharpoonup
⇀	\rightharpoonup	↽	\leftharpoondown	↓	\downarrow
↑	\uparrow	⇁	\rightharpoondown	⇑	\Uparrow
⇓	\Downarrow	↕	\updownarrow	⇕	\Updownarrow
↗	\nearrow	↖	\nwarrow	↘	\searrow
⟷	\longleftrightarrow	↦	\mapsto	⟼	\longmapsto

23.2.6 Math Parentheses

[	\lbrack	]	\rbrack	⌊	\lfloor	⌋	\rfloor	⌈	\lceil	⌉	\rceil
{	\lbrace	}	\rbrace	⟨	\langle	⟩	\rangle	{	\{ (alt)	}	\} (alt)

23.2.7 Miscellaneous Math Symbols

ℵ	\aleph	′	\prime	∀	\forall	ℏ	\hbar	∅	\empt
∃	\exists	ı	\imath	∇	\nabla	¬	\neg	ȷ	\jmat
√	\surd	⊥	\bot	ℓ	\ell	⊤	\top	♮	\natu
℘	\wp	♭	\flat	♯	\sharp	∠	\angle	‖	|
△	\triangle	Im	\Im	Re	\Re		\backslash	∂	\part
	\clubsuit	♡	\heartsuit	♠	\spadesuit	◇	\diamondsuit	∞	\inft

23.2.8 "Big" Operators

$\sum$	\sum	$\bigcap$	\bigcap		\bigodot	$\prod$	\prod	$\bigcup$	\bigcup
$\bigotimes$	\bigotimes	$\coprod$	\coprod		\bigsqcup	$\bigoplus$	\bigoplus	$\int$	\int
$\bigvee$	\bigvee		\biguplus	$\oint$	\oint	$\bigwedge$	\bigwedge		

23.3 MATH ACCENTS

$\underline{e}$	\underline{e}	$\overline{e}$	\overline{e}	$\hat{e}$	\hat{e}	$\check{e}$	\check{e}	$\tilde{e}$	\tilde{e}	$\acute{e}$	\acute{e}
$\grave{e}$	\grave{e}	$\dot{e}$	\dot{e}	$\ddot{e}$	\ddot{e}	$\breve{e}$	\breve{e}	$\bar{e}$	\bar{e}	$\vec{e}$	\vec{e}

23.4 SUPERSCRIPTS AND SUBSCRIPTS

A subscript is created by adding an underscore _ to a symbol and following that with the subscript, as in `I_x`. A superscript is created by adding a caret ^ to a symbol and following that with the superscript, as in `x^2`. And by doing both, a symbol may contain both a superscript and subscript:

$$I_x = m_1 x_1^2 + m_2 x_2^2$$

is obtained with either order of super- and subscripts:

`I_x = m_1 x_1^2 +  m_2 x_2^2,` or `I_x = m_1 x^2_1 + m_2 x^2_2.`

Inasmuch as the sub- and superscripts here are above each other, the two ways of inputting are equivalent. If the sub- or superscript contains more than one character, then the characters must be placed together within braces:

$$I_{11} = m_a x_{a,1}^2 + m_b x_{b,1}^2$$

is obtained by with either order of super- and subscripts:

`I_{11} = m_a x_{a,1}^2 + m_b x_{b,1}^2` or `I_{11} = m_a x^2_{a,1} + m_b x^2_{b,1}.`

23.5 CALCULUS AND SUMS

$\frac{dx}{dt}$	`{dx\over dt}`	$\frac{d^2x}{dt^2}$	`{d^2 x\over dt^2}`
$\frac{\partial u}{\partial t}$	`{\partial u\over \partial t}`	$\lim_{e\to0}$	`\lim_{e \to 0}`
$\frac{\partial^2\psi}{\partial x^2}$	`{\partial^2\psi\over \partial x^2}`	$\sum_{i=1}^{N} x^i/i!$	`\sum_{i=1}^N x^i/i!`
$\int_a^b f(x)\,dx$	`\int_a^b f(x)\,dx`	$\int\int f(z)\,dx\,dy$	`\int\int f(z) \,dx\,dy`

23.6 CHANGING MATH FONTS

We have seen that LaTeX sets mathematics in an italic font that is different from the italics of text mode. You obtain Roman and bold fonts within math mode with the commands \mathrm and \mathbf:

$$\mathbf{S} = \mathbf{E} \times \mathbf{B}$$ `\mathbf{S}  = \mathbf{E} \times \mathbf{B}`

If you start running out of letters, why not try the uppercase calligraphic letters in math mode: `\,\cal{A}`:

$$\mathcal{ABCDEFGHIJKLMNOPQRSTUVWXYZ}.$$

Sometimes you need to include text in an equation. You do that by making a box with `\mbox{text}` and placing the text in the box:

$$x = 3, \text{ for } y > 12$$ `x = 3, \mbox{ for } y > 12`

In view of the fact that LaTeX removes single blank spaces in math mode but not in text mode, the two single spaces we placed within the box above will remain. Alternatively, we could have inserted spaces with \ as `x = 3,\ \mbox{for}\ y > 12}`.

23.7 MATH FUNCTIONS

The basic mathematical functions are obtained by entering a backlash \ before the name. To cite an instance, $x^3 \sin y^2$ is obtained from `x^3 \sin y^2`. Look at how you need to leave a space after the function name as a separator, unless another backslash follows. Available functions include:

\arccos	\arcsin	\arctan	\arg	\cos	\cosh	\cot	\coth
\csc	\deg	\det	\dim	\exp	\gcd	\hom	\inf
\ker	\lg	\lim	\liminf	\limsup	\ln	\log	\max
\min	\Pr	\sec	\sin	\sinh	\sup	\tan	\tanh

Other mathematical function names are obtained by switching to Roman math font, and then writing the function name; for example, $\mathrm{cosec}(A)$ as `$\mathrm{cosec}(A)$`.

23.8 FRACTIONS

To make a fraction with num over denom, use the `\frac{num}{denom}` command:

$$v = \frac{dx}{dt}$$ `v = \frac{dx}{dt}`

Even though this LATEX command works fine, we prefer the simpler \over TEX command:

$$v = \frac{dx}{dt}$$ `v = {dx \over dt}`

23.9 ROOTS

The square root symbol $\sqrt{N}$ is obtained with the `\sqrt{N}` command. LATEX automatically adjusts the height and lengths of root symbols to fit into the equation and to span the argument:

$$\sqrt{x} = \frac{a \pm \sqrt{b^2 - 4ac}}{z}$$ `\sqrt{x} = {a \pm \sqrt{b^2-4ac} \over z}`

Higher roots are obtained by including an optional order parameter in square brackets to `\sqrt[n]{}`:

$$\sqrt[3]{x} = \frac{a + \sqrt[5]{b^2 - 4ac}}{z}$$ `\sqrt[3]{x} = {a + \sqrt[5]{b^2-4ac} \over z}`

23.10 BRACKETS (DELIMITERS)

Except for braces, which are used for commands, most normal-sized brackets or delimiters are entered into mathematics as typed:

((   ))   [[   ]]   { \{   } \} | | ‖   \|

As an instance: $\{a\} = (b) * [c] + |d| \times \|e\|$ `\{a\} =  (b)*[c] + |d| \times \|e\|`

Just as it does for roots, LATEX scales the size of these delimiters to match the size of the rest of the equation. However, since an equation may have a number of nested brackets, LATEX needs some help in deciding just which brackets you want to match. Thus, you give it help by tacking on the commands `\left` and `\right` to the delimiters that you wish to match up:

$$\left[\left| \frac{1}{\sqrt{z}} \right| = \left\{ a + \aleph \right\} \right]$$

`\left[ \left|{1\over\sqrt{z}} \right|= \left\{ a + \aleph \right\} \right].`

In order for LATEX to do all the work for you in sizing and placing these limiters, it demands that all the `\right`s be balanced by an equal number of `\left`s. LATEX does not demand that the types match up, just the number of rights and lefts. So, for example, `\left(` may be paired off with `\right]`. Although this all makes sense, it introduces a problem if you try to create something like

$$\int_a^b \frac{d^2 f}{dx^2} dx = \frac{df}{dx}\bigg|_a^b,$$

where there is no delimiter to match the left |. For this purpose, LaTeX contains the *null delimiters* `\left.` and `\right.` that count as delimiters but do not show up when typeset. As an instance, the above formula was obtained with:

```
$\int_a^b {df^2\over dx^2} dx = \left. {df\over dx} \right|_a^b$
```

23.11 MULTILINE EQUATIONS

Having LaTeX arrange multiline equations is essentially the same as working with the *tabular* environment for text. You place each equation on a separate line (row), and then align the equal signs in each equation by placing them in the same column. To cite an instance, `Sample.tex` on the CD creates

$$\frac{-\hbar^2}{2m_1} \frac{d^2\psi_1(x)}{dx^2} + V(x)\psi_1(x) + U(x)\psi_2(x) = E\psi_1(x) \tag{23.2}$$

$$\frac{-\hbar^2}{2m_2} \frac{d^2\psi_2(x)}{dx^2} + V(x)\psi_2(x) + U(x)\psi_1(x) = E\psi_2(x) \tag{23.3}$$

```
\begin{eqnarray}
 {-\hbar^2 \over 2m_1} {d^2 \psi_1 (x) \over dx^2} + V(x)\psi_1(x) +
           U(x)\psi_2(x)      &=& E \psi_1(x) \\
 {-\hbar^2 \over 2m_2} {d^2 \psi_2 (x) \over dx^2} + V(x)\psi_2(x) +
           U(x)\psi_1(x)      &=& E \psi_2(x)
\end{eqnarray}
```

Observe here that we display these equations with the *equation-array* environment `eqnarray` rather than the *equation* environment that we used for single-line equations. We begin with `\begin{eqnarray}` and end with `\end{eqnarry}`. These commands produce numbered equations. If unnumbered, multiline equations are desired, they are produced with the `\begin{eqnarray*}` and `\end{eqnarry*}` forms. The equations are entered into an `eqnarray` environment in the same way as they would be with `{equation}`, except that the equal signs are enclosed by ampersands `&=&`, and each line of the equation ends with a double backslash `\\`. As also occurs in the tabular environment, this produces a column with all the equal signs aligned, and permits there to be as many lines with equations as you enter.

Because `eqnarray` is just a tabular environment, it is possible to align symbols other than the equal sign, or to use this environment to split a very long equation onto two lines, with the continuation being indented:

$$-\frac{d^2\psi_1(x)}{dx^2} - \frac{d^2\psi_2(x)}{dx^2} + V(x)\psi_1(x) + V(x)\psi_2(x)$$

$$+ U(x)\psi_2(x) + U(x)\psi_1(x)$$
$$= \quad E\psi_1(x) + E\psi_2(x)$$

```
\begin{eqnarray*}
 - {d^2 \psi_1 (x)\over dx^2}   -   {d^2 \psi_2 (x)\over dx^2}
                        &+&  V(x)\psi_1(x)  + V(x)\psi_2(x) \\
                        &+&  U(x)\psi_2(x)  + U(x)\psi_1(x) \\
= && E \psi_1(x) +E \psi_2(x)
\end{eqnarray*}
```

23.12 MATRICES AND MATH ARRAYS

The **array** environment is used to produce matrices and mathematical arrays:

$$\begin{pmatrix} x & x^2 & y \\ \sqrt{y} & x^y & z \\ z^a & z^{-1} & i \end{pmatrix} \Rightarrow \begin{bmatrix} \alpha - \mu & \beta & \Gamma \\ \delta & \beta^3 & \alpha + \gamma \\ -x & y & \lambda \end{bmatrix}$$

```
\left( \begin{array}{ccc}
       x & x^2 & y \\
       \sqrt{y} & x^y & z \\
       z^a & z^{-1} & i \end{array} \right)          \Rightarrow
       \left[ \begin{array}{ccc}
              \alpha - \mu & \beta & \Gamma \\
              \delta & \beta^3 & \alpha + \gamma \\
              -x & y & \lambda
              \end{array} \right]
```

This is essentially identical to how tables are constructed for text. All that is new is the use of large right and left delimiters to produce a matrix symbol that fits the array. The alignment characters {ccc} are the same as with tabular.

Another approach to matrices, which we personally find easier and more compact than the LATEX standard, is the TEX command \pmatrix:

$$\begin{pmatrix} \frac{mb^2}{12} & 0 & 0 \\ 0 & \frac{ma^2}{12} & 0 \\ 0 & 0 & m\frac{a^2+b^2}{12} \end{pmatrix} = \begin{pmatrix} 1 & 0 & 0 \\ 0 & 4 & 0 \\ 0 & 0 & 5 \end{pmatrix}$$

```
\pmatrix{{mb^2\over 12} & 0 & 0 \cr
         0 & {ma^2\over 12} & 0 \cr
         0 & 0 & m{a^2+b^2\over 12}}
 = \pmatrix{1 & 0 & 0 \cr
            0 & 4 & 0 \cr
            0 & 0 & 5}
```

We see that pmatrix takes care of its own delimiters and uses the carriage return command \cr to end the rows.

The array environment is also used to produce an equation containing cases:

$$\theta(x) = \left\{ \begin{array}{ll} 1, & \text{if } x \geq 0, \\ 0, & \text{if } x < 0. \end{array} \right.$$

```
\theta(x) = \left\{ \begin{array}{ll}
            1 & \mbox{if $x \geq 0$};\\
            0 & \mbox{if $x < 0$}.\end{array} \right.
```

Here too, our preference is the TEX command \cases, which we find simpler:

$$\theta(x) = \left\{ \begin{array}{ll} 1, & \text{if } x \geq 0, \\ 0, & \text{if } x < 0. \end{array} \right.$$

```
\theta(x) = \cases{1, & if $x \geq 0$, \cr
            0, & if $x < 0$.    \cr}
```

23.13 INCLUDING GRAPHICS

Most drawing and graphing programs have a number of options to determine the file format in which to save graphics. Because LATEX is used to produce publication quality typesetting, if you include graphics, then they too should be publication quality. PostScript (.ps) and Encapsulated PostScript (.eps) figures are of publication quality, so it should not be a surprise that there are nice packages to include these formats in LATEX documents.

We will discuss how to include .eps figures, with the same commands used for .ps figures. Given a choice, use encapsulated figures, since it may be easier to adjust their size to fit the document. If your figure is of a different type, you should be able to open it in a drawing program and save it as an .eps figure. In addition, we recommend that you embed the fonts used in your figure with the figure; this does make for a larger file, but also avoids the possibility of some inappropriate local font being substituted when the document is printed (especially likely if you scale the figure).

We recommend the *graphics* package for including figures, although we have also had success with the *psfig* package, especially for placing figures at desired points on the page. If a package is not part of your LATEX installation, it may be added. Before you use a package, you must include it in your document's preamble (the part before the \begin{document} command):

```
\usepackage[dvips]{graphicx, color}
```

On the CD is the sample graphics file Latex_Compile.eps used to create Figure 22.1. It is redrawn on this page as Figure 23.1 with the commands

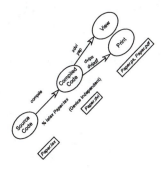

Figure 23.1 A scaled-down and rotated Figure 9.1.

```
\begin{figure}
\begin{center}
\includegraphics[angle=45, scale=0.35]{Latex_Compile.eps}
\caption{A scaled-down and rotated Figure~\ref{javacompile.eps}.
\label{sample.fig}}
\end{center}
\end{figure}
```

The `figure` environment is standard LATEX. It is also used to draw pictures with LATEX, or to leave room for and label figures to be pasted in later (use `\vspace` to make the room). The `\includegraphics` command is placed within the figure environment. To ensure that the figure is centered on the page, we place the figure in a `center` environment. The `angle=45, scale=0.25` specification in square brackets is optional and leads to a figure that is slanted and scaled to 25% of its original size.[1] The name of the figure `Latex_Compile.eps` is given in curly braces, with a path indication if it is not in current directory. Scrutinize how after the name of the figure we issue the `\caption` command containing the caption as its argument. Within the caption's argument (still within the curly braces) we have placed the label command `\label{sample.fig}`. We then refer to this figure as `\ref{sample.fig}`, as we do in the sample `\includegraphics` command above, and let LATEX take care of its actual number.

As an example of `\psfig`, examine Figure 15.1 (p. 310) with its multiple parts:

```
\begin{figure}
\psfig{file=FIGS/planet.eps, height=1.85in} \hspace{6ex}
\psfig{file=FIGS/PlanetApplet.eps, width=1.5in}
\caption{\emph{Left: } The gravitational ....)} \label{planet.eps}
\end{figure}
```

---

[1]We are able to scale and rotate with no loss in quality because PostScript figures are not bit maps, but instead contain a text description of the figure and the fonts.

23.14 EXERCISE: PUTTING IT ALL TOGETHER

1. Enter `Sample.tex` as given in §22.3. Use a text editor and save the file as `Sample.tex`. We recommend *WinEdt* and *MikTex* for Windows, and *gnu xemacs* for Unix/Linux.

2. Compile the file by pressing the LaTeX button or by issuing a command from a shell:

```
> latex Sample.tex                         Compile latex source Sample.tex
```

If there are no errors in your file, you should get a fairly verbose response with statements of the sort

```
This is TeX, Version 3.14159 (MiKTeX 2 UP 1) 2 NOV 2003 10:44 1478
**Sample.tex (Sample.tex LaTeX2e <2000/06/01> Babel <v3.6Z> ...
C:\Program Files\MiKTeX\tex\latex\base\article.cls Document Class:
article No file Sample.aux. LaTeX Warning: Reference 'eq.1' on
page 1 undefined on input line 37. LaTeX Warning: Reference 'eq.2'
on page 1 undefined on input line 37.
 [1] (sample.aux)
Output written on sample.dvi (1 page, 2676 bytes).
```

3. The warnings that there is `No file Sample.aux` and that `Reference 'eq.1'` (`'eq.2'`) `undefined` are to be expected on first compilation. The `Sample.aux` file contains the information LaTeX needs to cross-reference the source `Sample.tex`. Yet LaTeX does not write it until the end of compilation, and, consequently, it does not yet know that you have defined references `eq.1` and `eq.2`.

4. Compile the source file again. This time the compiler should find a `Sample.aux` file to use for cross-references and not warn you about undefined references.

5. The last part of LaTeX's message tells you that the files `sample.aux` and `sample.dvi` were written, and that the typeset document is one page long. If you have changed some labels or references, then LaTeX may request that you compile the source file again in order to incorporate the updated `.aux` file.

6. If there were no errors, your working directory should now contain the files

`Sample.tex`	source file
`sample.aux`	auxiliary working file with reference numbers and such
`sample.log`	log of LaTeX messages; similar to messages flashed on screen
`sample.dvi`	device-independent, viewable version of typeset document

7. If you are lucky enough to get a `sample.dvi` file, then look at it to admire your work. On Unix you do this with:

```
> xdvi sample.dvi                                      Preview .dvi file
```

On Windows use *Yap* (yet another previewer) or the DVI button.

8. If you get complaints that LATEX was not happy with the way a line fits on the page, just ignore them unless you are really going to publish the paper. If there are real errors, correct them one at a time and proceed. If you cannot figure out where the error is, try forcing LATEX to skip it by continually entering Enter. Alternatively, you isolate the location of an error by moving the %\end{document} up in your document until LATEX compiles with no errors. Then move it down gradually, recompiling at each stage until the error is uncovered.

9. To see how LATEX responds to errors, make these mistakes:

Correct	Change to incorrect
\item	\iten
$N=6$	$N=6

The first error should illicit the response

```
! Undefined control sequence.
l.19      \iten
                Use this sequence to simulate a random walk and
! LaTeX Error: Something's wrong--perhaps a missing \item.
```

This error message indicates with a carriage return where LATEX notices something is wrong, in this case, that it has never heard of \iten. Below that, LATEX indicates that it thinks you meant to write \item. In the second case where a $ is left off, LATEX responds with

```
! LaTeX Error: Bad math environment delimiter. 1.17 \[
      3, 7, 3, 1, 8, 2 \]
```

We see that LATEX knows something is wrong in the math environment (we left off the second $, but it does not know it until the *next* math environment begins with a \[on line 17. Consequently, you need to look at line 17 in the source file, and work back from there to see where there is a missing math delimiter.

10. Once you have produced a complete .dvi file, you convert it into the PostScript file sample.ps for printing with the dvips command:

```
> dvips -o sample.ps sample.dvi                    Convert .dvi file to .ps file
> dvips -o sample.ps sample                    Also converts .dvi file to .ps file
```

Here the -o option places the output into the file whose name follows. If you leave off the -o option, then the .ps file might well be sent directly to some printer. In WinEdt, the dvips command is issued by pushing the *dvi* ↪ *ps* button. You should get an output statement showing you all the page numbers that have been converted, and indicating that the output is placed in the file `sample.ps`. There is also the *pslatex* version of LaTeX that uses PostScript fonts in place of LaTeX's standard *Computer Modern* fonts. This does produce a smaller `.ps` file in the end.

11. If you want a `.pdf` file, you may issue the `pdfLATEX` command in the first place, or use the `dvipdf` command to convert your `.div` file. However, if the `.eps` figures in your file do not get placed in the `.pdf` file properly, we recommend the use of Adobe *Distiller* to convert the entire `.ps` file to a `.pdf` one.

12. If your document does not contain any embedded PostScript figures, then you may be able to print it successfully from the `.dvi` previewer. Otherwise, we have found it best to create a `.ps file` of your document and to print that.

13. Now print your `sample.ps` file. You do that from a *GhostScript* viewer, such as *GSview*, or with Unix printer commands:

```
>  lpr -Pps497 sample.ps                              Print to printer ps497
>  lp -d  ps497 sample.ps                          Print to device (printer) ps497
```

14. Now let us go back and add some more features to `Sample.tex`:

a. Include the sample PostScript figure `Latex_Compile.eps` from the disk or Web into your document.

b. Include Table 22.1 into your document (the commands are all given in the text). First keep the table in one place by using just the `tabular` environment, and then let it float by placing the `tabular` environment within a `table` environment.

c. Include a line in your document that uses the `\ref` command to refer to the floating table by its label.

d. Create a title page by placing your personalized versions of these commands into the preamble:

```
\title{My Title}
\author{My Name \and My Friend\\ Our Institution}
\date{Someday}
\thanks{To those who have supported this noble effort with cash.}
```

After placing these commands in the preamble, you need to create the title in the body of the document with:

```
\maketitle
```

Appendix A

Glossary

absolute value Value of a quantity expressed as a positive number, *e.g.*, $|f(x)|$.

accuracy The degree of exactness provided by a description or a theory. *Accuracy* usually refers to an absolute quality, while *precision* usually refers to the number of digits used to represent a number.

address The numerical designation of a location in memory. An identifier, such as a label, that points to an address in memory or a data source.

algorithm A set of rules for solving a problem in a finite number of steps. Usually independent of the software or hardware.

allocate To assign a resource for use, often memory.

alphanumeric The combination of alphabetic letters, numerical digits, and special characters, such as %, $, and /.

analog The mapping of a continuous physical observable to numbers. As an instance, a car's speed to its speedometer.

animation A process in which motion is simulated by presenting a series of slightly different pictures (frames) in succession.

append To add on, especially to the end of an object or word.

application A self-contained executable program containing tasks to be performed by a computer, usually for a practical purpose.

architecture The overall design of a computer in terms of its major components: memory, processor, I/O, and communication.

archive To copy programs and data to an auxiliary medium or file system for long-term and compact storage.

argument A parameter passed from one program part to another, or to a command.

arithmetic unit Part of the central processing unit that performs arithmetic.

array (matrix) A group of numbers stored together in rows and columns that may be referenced by one or more subscripts. Each number in an array is an array element.

assignment statement Command that sets a value to a variable or symbol.

B Abbreviation for byte (8 bits).

b Abbreviation for bit or baud (1 bit/sec).

background (1) A technique of having a programming run at low priority ("in background") while a higher-priority program runs "in foreground." (2) The part of video display not containing windows.

base The radix of a number system. (10 is the radix of the decimal system.)

basic machine language Instructions telling the hardware to do basic operations such as store or add binary numbers.

batch The running of programs without user interaction; often in background.

baud 1 bit per second.

binary Related to the number system with base 2.

BIOS Basic Input/Output System.

bit Contraction of "binary digit"; the digits 0 or 1 used in binary representation.

Boolean algebra A branch of symbolic logic dealing with logical relations as opposed to numerical values.

boot To "bootstrap"; to start a computer by loading the operating system.

branch To pick a path within a program based on the value of variables.

bug A mistake in a computer program or operating system; a malfunction.

bus A communication channel (bunch of wires) used for transmitting information quickly among computer parts.

byte Eight bits of storage. Java uses two bytes to store a single character in extended unicode.

byte code Compiled code that is read by all computer systems, but still needs to be interpreted (or recompiled) on each system. Contained in class file.

cache Small, very fast part of memory used as temporary storage between the very fast CPU registers and main memory.

calling sequence The data and setup needed to call a method or a subprogram.

central processing unit (CPU) The part of a computer that accepts and acts on instructions; where calculations are done and communications controlled.

checkpoint A statement within a program that stops normal execution and provides some output to assist in debugging.

checksum The summation of digits or bits used to check the integrity of data.

child Object created by presently existing parent object.

class A group of objects or methods having a common characteristic. Collection of data types and associated methods. An instance of an object. Byte code version of a Java program.

clock Electronics that generate the periodic signal to begin execution.

code A program or the writing of a program.

column The vertical line of numbers in an array.

column-major order The method used by Fortran to store matrices in which the leftmost subscript varies most rapidly and attains its maximum value before the subscript to the right is incremented. (Java uses row-major order.)

command A computer instruction. A control signal.

command key A keyboard key, or combination of keys, that performs a predefined function.

compilation Translation of a program written in a high-level language into (more) basic machine language.

compiler A program that translates source code from a high-level computer language to machine language or object code.

concatenate To join together two or more strings, head to tail.

concurrent processing Same as parallel processing; simultaneous execution of several related instructions.

conditional statement Statement to be executed only under certain conditions.

control character A character that modifies or controls the running of a program (e.g., *control +c*).

control statement A statement within a program that transfers control to another section of the program.

copy To transfer data *without* removing the original.

CPU See central processing unit.

crash   The abnormal termination of a program or a piece of hardware due to some malfunction.

cycle time (clock speed)   Time it takes CPU to execute simplest instruction.

data   Information stored in numerical form; plural of datum.

data type   Definitions that permits proper interpretation of character string.

debug   To detect, locate, and remove mistakes in a program or hardware.

default   The assumption made when no specific directive is given.

delete   To remove and leave no record.

digital   Representation of quantities in discrete form; contrast analog.

dimension of array   Number of subscripts needed to access single array element.

directory   A collection of files given their own name.

disc, disk   A circular magnetic medium used for storage.

discrete   Related to distinct elements.

double precision   Use of two memory words to store a number.

download   To transfer data *from* a remote computer *to* a local computer.

driver   A set of instructions needed to transmit data to/from external device.

dump   Data resulting from listing all information in memory.

dynamic RAM   Computer memory that must be refreshed at frequent intervals.

E   A symbol for exponent. To illustrate, $1.97E2 = 1.97 \times 10^2$.

element   An item of data within an array; a component of a language.

enable   To make a computer part operative.

ethernet   A high-speed local area network (LAN) composed of specific cable technology and communication protocols.

executable program   A set of instructions that can be loaded into the computer's memory and executed.

executable statement   A statement that causes some computational action, such as assigning a value to a variable.

fetch   To locate and retrieve information from storage.

floating point   Representation of numbers as mantissa times base raised to a power. Scientific notation.

FLOP   Floating Point Operation.

foreground   Running high-priority programs before low.

Fortran   An acronym for **for**mula **tran**slation.

fragmentation   File storage in many small, dispersed pieces.

G   Abbreviation for giga; one billion in USA; 10^9.

garbage   Meaningless numbers, usually the result of error or improper definition. Obsolete data in memory waiting to be removed ("collected").

giga   Prefix indicating one billion, 10^9, of something (USA).

GUI   Graphical user interface; a window environment.

hard disk   A circular, spinning, storage device using magnetic memory.

hardware   Physical components of a computer system.

hashing   A transformation that converts keystrokes to data values.

heuristic   A trial-and-error approach to problem solving.

hexadecimal   Base 16; {0,1,2,3,4,5,6,7,8,9,A,B,C,D,E,F}.

hidden line surface   Part of a graphics object normally hidden from view.

high-level language   Programming language similar to normal language.

host computer   A central computer providing services to terminals.

icon   Small on-screen symbol that activates an application.

increment   The amount added to a variable, especially an array index.

index   The symbol used to locate a variable in an array, the subscript. A reference table kept in memory.

infinite loop   The endless repeating of a set of instructions.

input   Introduction of data from an external device into main storage.

instructions   Orders to the hardware to do basic things such as fetch and add.

instruction stack   Group of instructions currently in use.

interpolation   Finding values between known values.

interpreter   A language translator that converts each line of source code into machine code and immediately executes each line.

interrupt   A command that stops execution of a program when some abnormal condition is encountered.

iterate   To repeat a series of steps automatically.

jump   A departure from the linear processing of code; branch, transfer.

just-in-time compiler   A procedure that takes a Java class file that would ordinarily be interpreted and recompiles it into a more efficient machine code.

K   Abbreviation for KILO, one thousand, 10^3.

kernel   The central part of a large program or operating system that does not get significantly modified when run on different computers.

kill   To delete or stop a process.

language   Rules, representations, and conventions used to convey information.

library (lib)   A collection of programs or methods usually on a related topic.

linking   The connecting of separate pieces of code to form an executable program.

literal   A symbol that defines itself, such as the letter A.

load   To read information into the computer's memory.

load module   A program that is loaded into memory and run immediately.

log in (on)   To sign onto the computer, to begin a session.

loop   A set of instructions executed repeatedly as long as some condition is met.

low-level language   Machine-related programming not easy for humans to read.

machine language   The set of instructions understood by the computer hardware.

machine precision   The maximum positive number that, when added to the number stored as 1, does not change it.

macro   A single, higher-level statement resulting in several lower-level ones.

main method   Part of application program where execution begins; may call other methods but cannot be called by them.

main storage   The fast, electronic memory; physical memory.

mantissa   The significant digits in a floating-point number; e.g., 1.2 in 1.2E3.

mega, M   A prefix denoting a million, or $1,048,576 = 2^{20}$.

metalanguage   A language used to define other languages.

method   A subroutine used to calculate a function or manipulate data.

modular programming   The technique of writing program with many, reusable, and independent parts.

modulo (mod)   Function that yields only remainder after division of numbers.

multiprocessors   Computers with more than one processor.

multitasking   The system by which several jobs reside in a computer's memory simultaneously; may run in parallel or sequentially.

nesting   Embedding a group of statements within another group.

object   A software component with properties like physical objects. A combination of data (variables, properties) and methods (behaviors) to interact with the data; and abstract data type containing multiple parts.

object-oriented programming   A modular programming style focused on classes of data objects and associated methods to interact with the objects.

object program (code)   A program in basic machine language produced by compiling a high-level language.

octal   Base 8; easy to convert to or from binary.

operating system (OS)   The program that controls the computer and runs applications, processes I/O, and shells.

optimization   The modification of a program to make it run more quickly.

overflow   A number that is larger than the largest number a computer can store accurately.

package   A collection of related programs or classes.

page   A segment of disk memory that gets read into central memory in one block.

parallel (concurrent) processing   Simultaneous or independent processing in different CPUs.

parallelization   Rewriting an existing program to run on a parallel computer.

partition   The section of memory assigned to a program during its execution.

physical memory   The fast, electronic memory of a computer; main memory; contrast to *virtual memory*.

physical record   The physical unit of data for input or output that may contain a number of logical records.

pipeline (segmented) arithmetic units   Assembly-line approach to central processing in which CPU simultaneously gathers, stores, and processed data.

pixel   A picture element, a dot on the screen. See also voxel.

portable document format, pdf A document format developed by Adobe that is of high quality and still readable within a Web browser.

PostScript, ps A standard language developed by Adobe for sending text and graphics to printers.

precision The degree of exactness with which a quantity is presented. High-precision numbers are not necessarily *accurate*.

program A set of instructions that a computer interprets and executes.

protocol A set of rules or conventions.

pseudocode A mixture of normal language and coding that provides a symbolic guide to a program.

queue An ordered group of items waiting to be acted upon in turn.

radix The base number in a number system that gets raised to powers.

RAM Random access (central) memory that is reached directly.

random access Reading or writing memory independent of storage order.

record A collection of data items treated as a unit.

recurrence (recursion) The use of a loop to produce new values of a variable computed in previous iterations.

registers Very high-speed memory used by the central processing unit.

reserved words Words that cannot be used in an application program.

RISC Reduced Instruction Set Computer; a CPU design that increases arithmetic speed by decreasing the number of instructions the CPU must follow.

row-major order The method used by Java to store matrices in which the right-most subscript varies most rapidly and attains its maximum value before the subscript to the left is incremented.

run To execute a program.

scalar A data value or number, for example, π.

serial/scalar processing Calculations in which numbers are processed in sequence. Contrast to vector and parallel processing.

shell The command line interpreter; the part of the operating system in which the user enters commands.

simulation The modeling of a real system by a computer program. The use of one system to represent or model another one.

single precision The use of one computer word to store a variable.

software Programs or instructions.

source code Program in high-level language needing compilation to run.

stochastic A process in which there is an element of chance.

string A connected sequence of characters treated as a single object.

structure The organization or arrangement of a program or a computer.

subprogram The part of a program invoked by another program unit, a *method*.

supercomputer The class of fastest and most computers available.

syntax The rules governing the structure of a language.

telnet Protocols for computer–computer communications.

tera, T 10^{12}, or $2^{30} = 1,073,741,824$.

top-down programming Designing a program from the most general view of the problem, down to the specific subroutines.

unary An operation that uses only one operand; monadic.

underflow A result that is smaller than the smallest number that a computer stores properly.

unit A device having a special function.

upload To transfer data *from* a local *to* a remote computer; opposite of download.

utility programs Programs to enhance other programs or do chores.

vector A group of N numbers in memory arranged in one-dimensional order.

vector processing Calculations in which an entire vector of numbers is processed with one operation.

virtual memory Memory on the slow, hard disk and not in fast RAM.

visualization The production of two- and three-dimensional pictures or graphs of the numerical results of computations.

volume A physical unit of a storage medium, such as a disk.

word A unit of main storage, usually 1, 2, 4, 6, or 8 bytes.

word length The amount of memory used to store a computer word.

Appendix B

Maple Quick Reference, Debugging Help

From Unix Prompt

```
% xmaple                                          # Start X Windows Maple in background
% maple                                           # Start text Maple in background
```

Select Modes

```
 T, ``text'' input                               # Useful for notes or reports
> Maple input                                     # To enter mathematics
Σ Calculation                                     # Insert and edit math into text
```

Execute Commands

```
> restart;                                        # De-assign all variables
> 3 + 7; then Enter                     # Enter and Return may be different keys
```

Basic Operations and Representations

```
>  (4/2)*3 - 7^8 + 7**8;                          # This should be 6
> 2485 / 3479;                                    # Reduces to 5/7
> 2485.  / 3479;                    # Decimal point implies float; limited precision
> Digits := 40;                                   # Save floats with 40 digits
> evalf( 2485/3479, 20);               # Evaluate rational number as 20-digit float
> 1.0*10^(-6);                        # Floating-point number in scientific notation
> Float( 1, -6 );                                 # Alternative form of above
> 1E-6;                                   # Alternative form of above, not e
> 1.*E-6;                                         # Variable E -6
> log(1.*E-6);                                    # Test exponential
> 1.E-6;                              # Syntax error without the* or with the.
> exp(1.);        exp(1);             # Two versions of e, base of natural logs
```

```
> log( exp(1) );                                                    # Test of log
> sqrt(10!);                                          # Maple even simplifies for you
> Pi;                                                          # Name for 3.1415...
> ln(x);          log10(x);          cos(Pi);          cos(x);      # Math functions
> (2+3*I)/(5-4*I);                                            # Complex numbers
> convert( %, polar );                              # Polar form of complex number
> polar(2+3*I); map(evalc,polar(Z));                # Polar form of complex number
> op(1,Polar);          op(2,Polar);          # Extract first, second operand from Polar
> String := "whatever I put here";                          # String within quotes
> ?command;                                                     # Help on *command*
```

Sums and Products

```
> sum( (-1)^i* x^(2*i)/(2*i)!, i = 0..2 );          # First 3 terms in cosine series
> sum( (-1)^i * x^(2*i)/(2*i)!, i = 0..infinity );                  # All terms
> Sum( (-1)^i * x^(2*i)/(2*i)!, i = 0..infinity );                  # Inert sum
> value(%);     expand(%);     factor(%);     expand(%);     simplify(%);   # Manipulate!
> allvalues(%);     eval(%);     collect(%);     normal(%);              # Manipulate!
> Product( (i^2+3*i-11)/(i+3), i = 0..10 );                 # Form product of symbols
> sum( i,i = 1 ..  n );                                     # Should be $n(n+1)/2$
> convert( sin(x), exp );                        # Express as exponents (many variants)
> seq(2*n-1, n = 1..4);                                       # Create sequence
> list1 := [4,4,8,6]; list2 := [seq(2*n-1, n = 1..4)];              # Create lists
> NiceSet := 0,2,4,6;                                           # Create set
```

Statements, Expressions, and Functions

```
> 1+4;          exp(x)-1;                        # Expressions (evaluated or stored)
> y := 3* z^2 + 1;                            # Assignment statement, has side effects
> eval( y, z = 2 );                                    # Evaluate $y$ for $z = 2$
> f :=(x) -> x * sin(x);                      # Define function $f(x)$ equal to $x \sin x$
> R :=(x,y,z) -> sqrt( x*x + y*y + z*z );              # Define function of 3 variables
> g := unapply( 3*z^2 + 1, z );          g(2);   # Convert expression into function, evaluate
> x := 'x';                                                     # De-assign x
```

Solving Single Equations

```
> solve( a*x^2 + b*x +c = 0, x );                             Find $x$ that solves
> y := a* x^2 + b*x + c = 0;                          # Symbol y represents equation
> solve( y, x );                                            # Solve equation y
> eval( y, x = a/2 );                                        # Verify answer
> roots( x^2-1 );                          # Real roots and multiplicity of polynomials
```

```
> roots( x^2 + 1, I );                                    # Find complex roots
> ans := solve( a* x^2 + b*x +c = 0, x);                  # ans equals sequence
> ans[2];                                        # Second answer or element in sequence
> fsolve( x*sin(x) - 1, x );                          # Floating point solve for x
> fsolve( x*sin(x) - 1, x = 0..6 );            # Floating point solve for 0 < x < 6
```

Simultaneous Equations

```
> eqn1 := a +3*b +4*c = 4;   eqn2 := 5*a +6*b +7*c = 2;          # 2 equations
> solve( eqn1, eqn2, a, b );                # Solve for a, b in terms of c
> x := Linsolve(A,b) mod 5;                 # Solve matrix equation [A]x = b
```

Plotting Along

```
> with(plots);       with(plottools);              # Load the plotting package
> plot( tan(x), x = -7...3 );                                   # Basic plot
> plot(tan(x), x = -7..7, y = -5..5, labels=['x','tan(x)'], title='tan');
> plot({cos(x), sin(x), x^2}, x = -Pi..Pi );       # Multiple functions in 1 plot
> plot( max(0, cos(x)), x = -2*Pi..2*Pi );                 # Eliminate y < 0
> plot([sin(x), cos(x), x = 0..2*Pi], scaling = constrained);  # Parametric plot
> implicitplot(x^2+y^2 = 1, y = exp(x),x=-2..2, y=-2..2); # Implicit 2 variable eqtn
> plot3d( x*(x^2-3*y^2), x = -1..1, y = -1..1,title = 'saddle' );  # 3-D plot
> polarplot( [ r, theta, theta = 0..2*Pi ] );                  # Polar plot
> contourplot(V(x,y), x = -4..4, y = -4..4);                 # Contour plot
> fieldplot( [Ex(x,y), Ey(x,y)], x = -3.5..3.5,           # Vector field plot
        y = -3.5..3.5, color = Ex(x,y), arrows = THICK );
> fieldplot3d( [Ex(x,y,z), Ey(x,y,z), Ez(x,y,z)],
>   x = -3.5..3.5, y = -3.5..3.5, z = -3.5..3.5, arrows = THICK);
> animate( cos(t*x) *sin(t*x), x = 0..Pi, t = 1..20 );       # 2-D animation
> animate3d(cos(t*x) * sin(t*y), x=0..Pi, y=0..Pi, t=1..2 );   # 3-D animate
> complexplot3d( [x^2 - y^2, 2*x*y], x =-2..2, y =-2..2);    # Separate Re and Im
> complexplot3d( z^2, z = -2-2*I..2+2*I, axes = framed );     # Complex function
```

Plotting Numerical Data

```
> with(statplots);       with(stats);        # Need statistics packages (not math!)
> Xdata :  = [1, 2, 3, 6, 10];                       # A list of all x values
> Ydata := [1, 4, 9, 36, 100];                # A list of corresponding y values
> scatterplot( Xdata, Ydata, color = RED);        # Can have several plots
> pointplot(List, connect = true);          # Plot points in a list or set
> display( plot1, plot2 );                  # Display two plots in one figure
```

Differentiation

```
> diff( f(x), x );                                              # df(x)/dx
> diff( f(x), x$2 );                              # Second derivative ($ not ^)
> diff( (sin(x))^y, x );                                   # Partial derivative
> diff( (sin(x))^y, x, y );              # Second partial derivative wrt x and y
> Diff( f(x), x );                                             # Inert derivative
> D(f)(x);                                        # Function = derivative of f(x)
> Diff( f(x,y,z), x, z );                      # Differentiate multivariate function
> g := (x) -> D(f)(x);               # Define function as derivative of function
> h := (x, y, z) -> sin(x*y*z);                 # Define multivariate function
> g := D [1] (h);                          # Differentiate h wrt its first argument
> limit( (1+x/n)^n, n = infinity );                                   # Limit
> D (cos);                                       # New function = derivative of cos
> g := (x) -> D(f)(x);                               # New function = derivative
```

Integration

```
> int ( x/sqrt(1+x), x );                                     # Indefinite integral
> diff ( %, x );                                # Check answer by differentiation
> int ( x/sqrt(1+x), x = 0..1 );                             # Definite integration
> g := unapply ( int( f(x), x ),x );                  # Integrate to produce a function
> g := (y) -> int( f(x,y), x = a..b );           # Function of y after integrate out x
```

Differential Equations

```
> with( DEtools ):                             # Load differential-equation tools
> diff_eq := D( D(x) ) (t) = -w*w*x;             # ODE of simple harmonic motion
> diff_eq := ( D@@2 ) (x) (t) = -w*w *x;               # Alternate form of above
> DEplot([diff(theta(t),t) -omega = 0, diff(omega(t), t) + sin(theta) = 0],
  [t, theta, omega], 0..12, [0,0,1.0], scene = [t, omega] );      # Solve and plot
> diff_eq1 := D ( D(y) ) (x) + 5*D(y)(x) + 6*y(x) = 0;                 # PDE
> init_con := y(0)=0, D(y)(0)=1;                            # Initial conditions
> dsolve( {diff_eq1, init_con},{y(x)} );                       # Solve equation
> sys := (D@@2)(y)(x) = z(x), (D@@2)(z)(x) = y(x);           # System of ODEs
> dsolve( {sys}, {y(x), z(x)});          # Maple generates initial condition parameters
```

Linear Algebra

```
> with(LinearAlgebra):      with (linalg):                  # Load, list packages
> N := matrix(2, 2, [2, x, 1, y^3]);             # Assign 2 × 2 matrix with symbols
> A := matrix(3, 3, (i,j)-> i*j);               # Matrix with function as elements
```

```
> ID := IdentityMatrix(3);                    # Identity matrix
> v := vector([1, 2, 3]);                      # Enter column vector with list
> ucol := matrix(3, 1, [1, 2, 3]);            # Explicit column vector
> urow := matrix(1, 3, [1, 2, 3]);            # Explicit row vector, NB no commas!
> print (A);                                   # View matrix
> evalm( A &* B );                             # Matrix multiply of two square matrices
> evalm( A^2 );                                # Square of matrix
> evalm( 1/B );                                # inverse of nonsingular matrix
> det( A );                                    # Determinant of matrix
> inverse( A );                                # Inverse, another way
> P := multiply(A, B);                         # Matrix multiplication, another way
> eigenvals( B );                              # Eigenvalues of matrix B
> eigenvects( B );                             # Eigenvectors of 3 × 3 matrix
> x := linsolve (A, b);                        # Solve $Ax = b$ for $x$
```

LinearAlgebra vs. linalg Commands

N := Matrix(2,2, [[2,x],[1, y^3]])	N := matrix(2,2, [[2,x],[1, y^3]])
A := Matrix(3,3, (i,j)-> i*j)	A := matrix(3,3, (i,j)-> i*j)
B := Array(1..2, 1..2, [[2,2,3],[2,1,6]])	B := array(1..3, 1..3,[[2,2,3],[2,1,6]])
type(A, Matrix)	type(A,matrix)
Vec := Vector([1/M[1, 2], M[1, 1], B[3, 3]])	
evalm(A &* B)	evalm(A &* B)
A . B	ID := IdentityMatrix(4)
Multiply(A,B)	multiply(A, B)
Map(f, {a,b,c})	map(f, {a,b,c})
ID := matrix(3, 3, [[1, 0, 0], [0, 1, 0], [0, 0, 1]])	
Determinant(A)	det(A)
Binv := 1/B	Binv := evalm(1/B)
B . Binv	evalm (B &* Binv)
Transpose(A)	transpose(A)
Ainv := MatrixInverse(A)	inverse(A)
vec := Vector([x, y*x^2,y])	vec := vector([x, y*x^2,y])
DotProduct(vec,vec2)	dotprod(vec,vec2)
CrossProduct(vec,vec2)	crossprod(vec,vec2)
Curl(vec,[x,x,x])	curl(vec, [x,x,x])
linalg[diverge](vec, [x,y,z])	diverge(vec, [x,x,x])
linalg[grad](x^3,[x,y,x])	grad(x^3,[x,y,x])
Eigenvectors(A)	eigenvectors(A)
Eigenvalues(A)	eigenvalues(A)
X := LinearSolve (A,	X := linsolve (A,

Generating Java, Matlab, Fortran, and C Code

```
> with (codegen):
> CodeGeneration (Java);                    # Code generation; also for Fortran, C, Matlab
```

Statistics and Fitting

```
> with ( stats );                                              # Load the package
> with ( fit );                                          # Load the fitting package
> X := [2,4,6,8];                                    # Define independent variable
> Y := [0,20,28,44];                                   # Define dependent variable
> leastsquare [ [x,y], y = a*x^2 + b*x + c, a, b, c ] ( [X,Y] ); # Fit quadratic
> with ( describe );                                 # Load the package for means
> mean_X := mean ( X );                                                  # Mean
> median ( X );
> variance ( X );
> dev := standarddeviation ( X );
> with(statplots);                            # Load the statistical plotting package
> scatterplot( X, Y, color = black);                           # Make scatterplot
```

Maple Procedures

```
Chebyshev := proc( n )
local p, k;
p[0] := 1;
p[1] := x;
if n <= 1 then
RETURN ( eval(p) )
fi;
for k from 2 to n do
p[k] := expand( 2*x*p[k-1] - p[k-2] )
od;
RETURN ( eval(p) )
end;
> a := Chebyshev(5); a[3];                                       # Call procedure
```

Maple Debugging

Built in debuggers: `tracelast, mint, trace, printlevel`

1. Check example in help file for proper use of options.

2. `restart`: try if something that was just working no longer does.

3. Maple confused: delete command or line and start again; there may be hidden control characters.

4. Check against backup copy (see Edit/Preferences for automatic backups).

5. Check if used = when wanted := (or vice versa).

6. `"; unexpected"`: possibly unbalanced parentheses.

7. `empty plot`: numerical values for parameters may not be assigned.

8. ... instead of [...], or vice versa.

9. `wrong number (or type) of parameter`, invalid arguments a symbolic variable may be numeric, or vice versa.

10. No response from Maple: Maple gave up. Try numerical evaluation, if that works then the problem is not you. May need to assign variable type to assist Maple.

11. No action: forgotten ";" to end line.

Maple's Standard Library Functions

about	abs	add	addcoords	additionally
addproperty	addressof	AFactor	AFactors	AIrreduc
AiryAi	AiryAiZeros	AiryBi	AiryBiZeros	algebraic
algsubs	alias	allvalues	anames	andmap
AngerJ	antihermitian	antisymm	apply	applyop
applyrule	arccos	arccosh	arccot	arccoth
arccsc	arccsch	arcsec	arcsech	arcsin
arcsinh	arctan	arctanh	argument	Array
array	ArrayDims	ArrayElems	ArrayIndFns	ArrayOptions
assemble	assign	assigned	asspar	assume
assuming	asympt	attributes	band	Berlekamp
bernoulli	bernstein	BesselI	BesselJ	BesselJZeros
BesselK	BesselY	BesselYZeros	Beta	BivariatePolynomial
branches	cat	ceil	changecoords	charfcn
CheckArgs	Chi	chrem	Ci	close
coeff	coeffs	coeftayl	collect	combine
comparray	compiletable	COMPILE_OPTIONS	compoly	CompSeq
conjugate	constant_indfcn	Content	content	convergs
convert	coords	copy	CopySign	cos
cosh	cot	coth	coulditbe	csc
csch	csgn	currentdir	curry	CustomWrapper
CylinderD	CylinderU	CylinderV	dawson	Default0
DefaultOverflow	DefaultUnderflow	define	define_external	degree
denom	depends	DESol	Det	diagonal
Diff	diff	diffop	Digits	dinterp
Dirac	disassemble	discont	discrim	dismantle
DistDeg	Divide	divide	dsolve	efficiency
Eigenvals	eliminate	ellipsoid	EllipticCE	EllipticCK
EllipticCPi	EllipticE	EllipticF	EllipticK	EllipticModulus
EllipticNome	EllipticPi	elliptic_int	entries	erf
erfc	erfi	euler	eulermac	Eval
eval	evala	evalapply	evalb	evalc
evalf	evalfint	evalhf	evalindets	evalm
evaln	evalr	evalrC	events	Excel
exists	Expand(inert)	Expand	expand	expandoff
expandon	exports	ExternalCalling	extract	extrema
Factor	factor	Factors	factors	fclose
fdiscont	feof	fflush	FFT	filepos
fixdiv	float	floor	fnormal	fold
fopen	forall	forget	fprintf	frac
freeze	frem	fremove	FresnelC	Fresnelf
Fresnelg	FresnelS	FromInert	frontend	fscanf

Maple's Standard Library Functions (cont)

fsolve	galois	GAMMA	GaussAGM	Gausselim
Gaussjord	gc	Gcd	gcd	Gcdex
gcdex	genpoly	getenv	GetResultDataType	GetResultShape
GF	Greek	HankelH1	HankelH2	harmonic
has	hasassumptions	hasfun	hasoption	hastype
heap	Heaviside	Hermite	HermiteH	hermitian
Hessenberg	hfarray	history	icontent	identity
IEEEdiffs	ifactor	ifactors	iFFT	igcd
igcdex	ilcm	ilog10	ilog2	ilog[b]
Im	implicitdiff	ImportMatrix	ImportVector	in
indets	index	indexed	indices	inifcn
ininame	initialcondition	initialize	insert	int
intat	interface	Interp	interp	Inverse
invfunc	invztrans	iostatus	iperfpow	iquo
iratrecon	irem	iroot	Irreduc	irreduc
is	iscont	isdifferentiable	isdir	IsMatrixShape
isolate	isolve	ispoly	isprime	isqrfree
isqrt	issqr	ithprime	JacobiAM	JacobiCD
JacobiCN	JacobiCS	JacobiDC	JacobiDN	JacobiDS
JacobiNC	JacobiND	JacobiNS	JacobiSC	JacobiSD
JacobiSN	JacobiTheta1	JacobiTheta2	JacobiTheta3	JacobiTheta4
JacobiZeta	KelvinBei	KelvinBer	KelvinHei	KelvinHer
KelvinKei	KelvinKer	KummerM	KummerU	
LambertW	last_name_eval	latex	latex_filter	lattice
lcm	Lcm	lcoeff	leadterm	LegendreP
LegendreQ	length	LerchPhi	lexorder	lhs
Li	Limit	limit	Linsolve	listdir
ln	lnGAMMA	log	log10	LommelS1
LommelS2	lprint	map	map2	Maple_floats
maptype	match	MatlabMatrix	Matrix	matrix
MatrixOptions	max	maximize	maxnorm	maxorder
member	membertype	min	minimize	mkdir
ModifiedMeijerG	modp	modp1	modp2	modpol
mods	Modular	module	MOLS	mserver
msolve	mtaylor	mul	NextAfter	Nextpoly
Nextprime	nextprime	nops	norm	Normal(inert)
Normal	normal	nprintf	Nullspace	numboccur
numer	NumericClass	NumericEvent	NumericEventHandler	NumericException
numerics	NumericStatus	numeric_type	odetest	op
open	order	OrderedNE	ormap	parse
patmatch	pclose	PDEplot_options	pdesolve	pdetest
pdsolve	pi	piecewise	plot	plot3d

plotsetup	pochhammer	pointto	poisson	polar
polylog	polynom	polytools	Power	Powmod
powmod	Prem	prem	Preprocessor	Prevpoly
Prevprime	prevprime	Primitive	Primpart	primpart
print	printf	ProbSplit	procbody	ProcessOptions
procmake	Product	product	proot	property
protect	Psi	psqrt	queue	Quo
quo	radfield	radnormal	radsimp	rand
randomize	Randpoly	randpoly	Randprime	range
ratinterp	rationalize	Ratrecon	ratrecon	Re
readbytes	readdata	readlib	readline	readstat
realroot	Record	Reduce	references	Regular_Expressions
release	Rem	rem	remove	repository
requires	residue	RESol	Resultant	resultant
rhs	RiemannTheta	rmdir	root	rootbound
RootOf	Roots	roots	round	Rounding
rsolve	rtable	rtable_algebra	rtable_dims	rtable_elems
rtable_indfns	rtable_options	rtable_printf	rtable_scanf	SampleRTable
savelib	scalar	Scale10	Scale2	scan
scanf	Searchtext	searchtext	sec	sech
select	selectfun	selectremove	seq	series
setattribute	SFloatExponent	SFloatMantissa	shake	SharedLibrary
Shi	showprofile	showtime	Si	sign
signum	sigpipe	Simplify	simplify	sin
singular	sinh	sinterp	smartplot3d	Smith
solve	solvefor	sort	sparse	spec_eval_rules
spline	spreadsheet	SPrem	sprem	sprintf
Sqrfree	sqrfree	sqrt	sscanf	Ssi
ssystem	storage	string	StruveH	StruveL
sturm	sturmseq	subs	subsindets	subsop
substring	subtype	Sum	sum	surd
Svd	symmdiff	symmetric	syntax	system
table	tan	tanh	taylor	testeq
testfloat	TEXT	thaw	thiele	time
timelimit	ToInert	TopologicalSort	traperror	triangular
trigsubs	trunc	type	typematch	unames
unapply	unassign	undefined	unit	Unordered
unprotect	UseHardwareFloats	userinfo	value	Vector
vector	verify	WeberE	WeierstrassP	WeierstrassPPrime
WeierstrassSigma	WeierstrassZeta	whattype	WhittakerM	WhittakerW
with	worksheet	WRAPPER	writebytes	writedata
writeline	writestat	writeto	zero	Zeta
zip	ztrans			

Maple Packages

algcurves	algebraic curves	codegen	translate Maple
CodeGeneration	translate Maple	combinat	combinatorial functions
combstruct	combinatorial structures	context	context sensitive menus
CurveFitting	functions for curve fitting	DEtools	differential equations tool
diffalg	differential algebra	difforms	differential forms
Domains	create computation domains	finance	financial mathematics
GaussInt	gaussian integers	genfunc	rational generating functic
geom3d	Euclidean 3-D geometry	geometry	Euclidean geometry
Groebner	Groebner basis calculations	group	permutation and finite gro
inttrans	integral transforms	LargeExpressions	computation sequences
LibraryTools	library manipulation utilities	liesymm	Lie symmetries
linalg	array-based linear algebra	LinearAlgebra	rtable-based linear algebra
LinearFunctionalSystems	linear functional equations	LinearOperators	linear functional equations
ListTools	manipulating lists	LREtools	linear recurrence relations
Maplets	graphical user interfaces	MathML	import and export MathMl
Matlab	MATLAB Link	MatrixPolynomialAlgebra	polynomial matrices
networks	graph networks	numapprox	numerical approximation
numtheory	number theory	Ore_algebra	algebras of linear operator
OrthogonalSeries	orthogonal poly series	orthopoly	orthogonal polynomials
padic	p-adic numbers	PDEtools	PDE tools
plots	graphics	plottools	basic graphical objects
PolynomialTools	polynomial tools	powseries	formal power series
process	(Unix)-multi-processing	RandomTools	random objects
RationalNormalForms	rational normal forms	RealDomain	real number context
Rif	nonlinear ODEs and PDEs	ScientificConstants	scientific constants
simplex	linear optimization	Slode	ODE series solution
SNAP	symbolic-numeric algorithms	Sockets	network communication
SoftwareMetrics	code complexity	SolveTools	solution tools
Spread	spreadsheets	stats	statistics
StringTools	string manipulations	Student	undergraduate math
student	student calculus	Student[Calculus1]	calculus education
SumTools	closed form sums	sumtools	indefinite/definite sums
tensor	tensors, Gen Relativity	TypeTools	extending type tools
Units	unit conversions	VariationalCalculus	Calculus of Variations
VectorCalculus	vector calculus	Worksheet	worksheet tools
XMLTools	XML tools		

Appendix C

Java Quick Reference and Installing Software

C.1 JAVA ELEMENTS

Compilation and Interpretation of Application

```
> javac Hello.java
> java Hello
```

Compile Hello.java
Run Hellow.class

Application Program Structure

`public class Hello`	Class definition, in file Hello.java
`{`	Beginning brace; must have mate
`  public int a = 2;`	Class variable a
`  public static void main(String[] args)`	main method
`  {`	Opening brace for main
`    double b = 3., c;`	Variables local to main
`    int three;`	Integer variable
`    final double HBARC = 197.32;`	Unchangeable constant
`    three = add(1,a);`	Call to method
`    c = Math.sin(b);`	Call to math xlibe
`    System.out.println("sin(b)= "+ c);`	Print to screen
`  }`	Closing brace for main
`// -end main, begin add-`	Comment
`  public static int add(int x, int y)`	Silly method to add to int's
`  {return x + y;}`	Returns value of "add"
`}`	Ending brace for class
`/* Comment field (multiple lines OK) */`	Comment in field
`// One line comment`	One line comment
`/** Documentation comment **/`	Documenting comment
`public static double f(double x)`	Method (function) $f(x)$
`{return x*x ;}`	Multiple lines within brace OK too

Data (Variable) Types

Description	Type	Size/Format
Integer	`byte, short, int, long`	1B (8b), 2B, 4B, 8B
Floating Point	`float, double`	Single, Double precision (8B)
Single Character	`char`	16-bit (2B)
Logical	`boolean`	1 bit, true or false

Sample Data Representations

Representation	Meaning	Representation	Meaning
`i = 10 L; i = 10 l;`	long integer	`i = 3.1e+8, 3.1E+08`	Scientific
`i = 10.;`	decimal (double)	`i = OxA;`	Hexidecimal
`i = 10.0 F;, 10.0 f;`	float (single)	`i = O17;`	Octal

Naming Convention

variable, variableName; ClassName, Classname; CONSTANT.

Reserved Words

abstract	double	int	static	do	instanceof
boolean	else	interface	super	short	while
break	extends	long	switch	default	import
byte	final	native	synchronized	return	volatile
case	finally	new	this	continue	implements
catch	float	null	throw	public	void
char	for	package	throws	const *	if
class	goto *	private	transient	protected	try

Arrays

`int [] i;`	Declare integer array
`double [] x = new double[10];`	Declare & create (allocate memory) array
`double [][] y = new double [8][9];`	Declare & create 2D array
`arrayname [i][j] = i*j;`	Assign value to array element
`int a[3] = {1, 2, 3};`	Assign values to array elements
`int size = arrayname.length;`	Extract length of array (any array)

Arithmetic Operators

Operator	Example	Description
+	x + y	Add x to y (also concatenates strings)
-	x - y	Subtract y from x
*	x * y	Multiply x by y
/	x / y	Divide x by y
%	x % y	Remainder from x/y; the modular op

Unary Operators

Operator	Example	Description
+	+x	Promotes x to int if it is a byte, short, or char
-	-x	Arithmetically negates x
( )	x = (double) 1	Cast (converts data types)

Shortcuts

Operator	Example	Description
++	x++	Use x, then set x = x + 1
++	++x	Set x = x + 1, use x
--	x--	Use x, then set x = x - 1
--	--x	Set x = x - 1, then use x

Relational Operators

Operator	Example	Return true if
>	x > y	x is greater than y
>=	x >= y	x is greater than or equal to y
<	x < y	x is less than y
<=	x <= y	x is less than or equal to y
==	x == y	x and y are same *object*
!=	x != y	x and y are not equal

Logical Operators

Operator	Example	Name: Return true if
&&	x && y	**Logical and:** x and y both true, conditionally evaluates y
||	x || y	**Logical or:** either x or y true, conditionally evaluates y
!	!x	**Not:** x is false
&	x & y	**And:** x and y both true, always evaluates x and y
|	x | y	**Or:** either x or y true, always evaluates x and y

Bitwise Operators

Operator	Example	Operation
>>	x >> y	Shift bits of x right by distance y
<<	x << y	Shift bits of x left by distance y
>>>	x >>> y	Shift bits of x right by distance y (unsigned)
&	x & y	Bitwise and
|	x | y	Bitwise or
^	x ^ y	Bitwise xor
~	~y	Bitwise complement

Compound Assignment Operators

Operator	Example	Equivalent to
+=	x += y	x = x + y
-=	x -= y	x = x - y
*=	x *= y	x = x * y
/=	x /= y	x = x / y
%=	x %= y	x = x % y
&=	x &= y	x = x & y
|=	x |= y	x = x | y
^=	x ^= y	x = x^y
<<=	x <<= y	x = x << y
>>=	x >>= y	x = x >> y

Order of Precedence

1. unary then binary ops	2. left to right	3. assignment ops	4. RHS then LHS
5. x++	6. ++x	7. cast	8. *
9. +	10. >>>	11. ==	12. =

Mathematical Function Library [Use: Math.sin(b)]

E	PI	sin	cos	tan	asin	acos	atan	atan2(y,x)	exp
log	pow(x,3.)	sqrt	random	abs	max	min	ceil	floor	rint

Flow Control

```while (x <= 0.) {y = y * y; 'x = x + 2.;}```	Evaluate as long as true; Second line to be evaluated, etc.
` if ( (x < 3) && (y == 12) ) z = y * x;`	Evaluate once if true
```if (x <= 0.) { y = y * y; } else y = 2 * y;```	Can have one or more lines in {} Only one `else` permitted (catchall)
```if (score >= 90) { grade = 'A'; } else if (score >= 80) { grade = 'B'; } else if (score >= 70) { grade = 'C'; }```	The "if" condition Any number of `else if`'s OK Inaccessible if earlier `else` satisfied
```switch (month) { case 1: s = "Jan"; break ... case 12: s = "Dec"; break;}```	Fall through if no break Can have many cases
```for (i = 0; i < 100; i++) { <statements> }```	(initial value; repeat for; increment) Multiline code block
```do { <statements> } while (<boolean>) <labelname>: x = x*y; ... break <labelname>; if (i==99) continue;```	Goes through at least once Break send control back here Use `continue` within loops for new iterati Unlabelled continue, jump to loop end Break out of loop if no label

Input and Output, Screen and Keyboard

`System.out.println ( "count = " + j );`	Screen output
```import java.io.*; main(String[] argv) throws IOException, FileNotFoundException```	Include input/output package Main method to handle exceptions; the exception
```BufferedReader b=new Buffered Reader (new InputStreamReader(System.in));```	Read via 3 filters; "
`String s = b.readLine();`	Line read stored as string
`r = Double.valueOf(s).doubleValue();`	Convert string to double

Input and Output, Files

```import java.io.*; main(String[] argv) throws IOException, FileNotFoundException```	Need for all but screen & keyboard `main` with exception throwing
```BufferedReader b = new BufferedReader (new InputStreamReader (new FileInputStream("radius.dat")));```	Open file with JDK 1.1; " "
`String s = b.readLine();`	Read 1 line, save as string
```double x = Double.parseDouble(s); int i = Integer.parseInt(s);```	Convert string to double Convert string to integer
```PrintWriter q = new PrintWriter (new FileOutputStream("area.dat", true);```	Open output file with JDK 1.1; appends file
```PrintWriter q = new PrintWriter (new FileOutputStream("area.dat", false);```	Open output file with JDK 1.1; overwrites file
`q.println("radius = " + radius);`	Output word `radius` and its value
`q.close();`	Closes file

Compiling Options	javac [*options*]⟨source files ⟩
-g	Generate all debugging info
-g:none	Generate no debugging info
-g:lines,vars,source	Generate only some debugging info
-O	Optimize; may hinder debugging or enlarge class files
-nowarn	Generate no warnings
<u>**-verbose**</u>	Output messages about what the compiler is doing
-deprecation	Output source locations where deprecated APIs are used
-classpath ⟨path⟩	Specify where to find user class files
-sourcepath ⟨path⟩	Specify where to find input source files
-bootclasspath ⟨path⟩	Override location of bootstrap class files
-extdirs ⟨dirs⟩	Override location of installed extensions
-d ⟨directory⟩	Specify where to place generated class files
-encoding ⟨encoding⟩	Specify character encoding used by source files
-target ⟨release⟩	Generate class files for specific VM version
<u>**-cp -classpath ⟨ directories and zip/jar files⟩**</u>	
-cp -classpath dir	Use files in directory dir
	set search path for application classes and resources
-D⟨name⟩=⟨value⟩	set a system property
-verbose[:class|gc|jni]	enable verbose output
-showversion	print version of Java being used
-?	print help message
-help	print help message
-X	print help on non-standard options

Execution

```
> java [-options] class [args...]           To execute a class
> java -jar [-options] jarfile [args...]     To execute a jar file
```

C.2 TRANSFERRING FILES FROM THE CD

The Maple and Java worksheets and programs given on the CD do not need any special installation. You just need to pick a directory/folder on your computer where you want them stored, and copy the appropriate folder from the disk into that directory. Of course you will need to insert the CD into the CD drive, and open that drive to see the contents of the CD. (On Windows computers you get to that drive by clicking on the My Computer icon.)

C.3 USING OUR MAPLE WORKSHEETS

You open one of our Maple worksheets by starting Maple on your computer and then opening the worksheet from within Maple. Of course you must have Maple installed on your computer for this to work, and that is done with the installer that comes on the Maple CD.

We have written the Maple worksheets with Maple Versions 6–9.5. We have not tried to specialize the worksheets to just the latest version, so most every command should work with any recent version of Maple. You may get a complaint from Maple when you first load the worksheet that it was created with a more recent version (that the Maple people would not mind you running out and purchasing), but that should cause no problems. You may find that the response shown in the text does not quite match that given by your version of Maple. In any case, learning how to cope with ever-advancing software and hardware is part of the learning experience we wish to present.

C.4 USING OUR JAVA PROGRAMS

The Java programs on the CD are almost all source (.java) files and therefore need to be compiled before they will execute. There are a number of ways in which you may work with and execute our Java programs. The least painful is probably to use a complete programming workbench like *Code Warrior* or the *Forte Suite*. With these you need only punch some buttons to compile, debug, and execute programs. We view these programming environments as powerful tools that will increase the productivity of professional programmers. However, we believe that the more basic approach is preferable for the purpose of this introductory book.

The basic approach to Java programming that we prefer is to use an editor to modify the Java source file, *save the file*, and then execute the resulting class file from the prompt (command line) of a shell. In this way the beginning programmer learns that there are just two basic types of files to deal with, and that they are universal for all operating systems. In contrast, the programming environments often produce an assortment of files containing formatting and other such information, with the user not sure just what is truly needed to write and run a program.

On Windows computers you may use a text editor such as *Notepad* to modify Java source file. You should not, in contrast, use a word processor such as *MS Word*, since it formats text by inserting control characters that are invisible to you but stop the Java compiler from getting its job done. We prefer using the *WinEdt* [WinEdt] editor on Windows, which also provides immediate access to a shell in the same directory as the source (it is also excellent for LaTeX).

On Unix systems we recommend the free *gnu emacs* (especially *xemacs*) editor [Gnu]. It is powerful and permits compilation and execution from within the editor. It is excellent too with LaTeX. In addition, the *jEdit* Java editor is an excellent and free Java editor that is written in Java. Thus, it runs identically on all operating systems and provides some very useful color coding of codes.

Once you have your .java file open in an editor, you need a shell or command line from which to issue the javac and java commands. On Unix this is easy if you first change to the appropriate directory and open your editor from there. It is equally easy on Windows computers if you open a shell from your editor. However, if you use the Start > Run > Open > Command route, then you will have to navigate the Window's file directory structure with the dir and cd commands.

C.5 INSTALLING PTPLOT (OR OTHER) PACKAGES

The first step in setting up PtPlot is to download its latest version and then uncompress it.[1] The plotting package we call PtPlot is part of a larger Java project called *Ptolemy* [PtPlot], all free for downloading.

After you have properly unzipped or untarred the PtPlot package, a directory such as ptplot5.2 should be created. The number 5.2 here is the version number of the PtPlot package that we are now using; there may be a newer version when you do your download. For our examples, we have renamed the directory in which PtPlot resides as simply ptplot, with no version number attached. On Unix, we assume that your ptplot directory is ^/java_packages/ptplot, where the ^ indicates your home directory. On Windows, we assume that your ptplot directory is C:\ptplot.[2] Advanced users may prefer to keep the version number in the directory name, or use a different organizational system. However, if this is the first time that you have installed a Java package, we recommend that you use the same directory names as we have.

Now that we have placed the PtPlot package in its own directory, we need to tell Java where to find it. As a matter of convention, the Java compiler javac and interpreter java assume that the value of a variable named CLASSPATH contains the information on where packages such as PtPlot are stored. This type of variable that controls the environment in which programs run is called an *environment variable*. On account of the programs in the packages having already been compiled into class files, the variable that directs Java to the classes is called the 1"1 CLASSPATH. To get PtPlot to work under Java you need to modify the CLASSPATH variable to include the location where PtPlot is stored:

---

[1]If you have never done this before, you may want to do it with a friend who has. In Windows, you use *WinZip* [WinZip] to unzip files. In Unix, you try double-clicking on an icon of the file, or decompress it from within a shell with gunzip and tar -xvf.

[2]If you use the Windows automatic installer, you should install to C:\ptplot, rather than C:\ptolemy\ptplot5.2, if you want to follow our examples verbatim.

Windows 95: Open the `autoexec.bat` file (usually `C:\autoexec.bat`) in a text editor such as *Notepad*. At the end of the file, add the line

```
SET CLASSPATH=%CLASSPATH%;C:\ptplot
```

Save the `autoexec.bat` file and restart your computer.

Windows 98/ME: Click Start and then Run under that. Key in the command name `msconfig`, and press Enter. The System Configuration Utility should appear. Select the tab named Autoexec.bat and look for a line that says SET CLASSPATH. If you cannot find that line, click New, and enter SET CLASSPATH = C:\ptplot. If the SET CLASSPATH line already exists, select it, choose Edit, add a semicolon *;* to the end of the line, and then add C:\ptplot after the semicolon. The semicolon is a separator that tells Java that it should look in more than one location for class files. Make sure that the checkbox by the CLASSPATH line is checked, and click OK. Answer Yes when Windows asks you whether you want to restart the computer.

Windows NT/2000/XP Open the Control Panel (Start, Settings, Control Panel in NT/2000, or Start, Control Panel in XP). Open the System icon (you may need to switch to the Classic View in Windows XP). Under the System Properties window, select the Advanced tab, and choose Environment Variables. Two lists should be shown. One contains environment variables just for you, and one contains environment variables for all users on the system. In your personal environment variable list, look for CLASSPATH. If you cannot find the CLASSPATH variable, click *New*, enter CLASSPATH for the variable name, and C:\ptplot for the value. If the CLASSPATH variable already exists, select it, choose *Edit*, add a semicolon *;* to the end of the current value, and then add C:\ptplot after the semicolon. The semicolon is a separator that tells Java that it should look in more than one location for class files. Click *OK* until you get back to the Control Panel, and then restart your machine.

Solaris: We assume that you do not have system authority for your computer, and so will install PtPlot in your home directory. We suggest that you make a subdirectory called `java_packages` in your home directory and install PtPlot there:

```
> cd                              Change to my home directory
> mkdir java_packages             Create subdirectory in present directory
> mkdir java_packages/ptplot      Create subdirectory in java_packages
```

If the ˜ is used to represent your home directory, this assumes that you will be installing the PtPlot package in ˜/java_packages/ptplot/

Your CLASSPATH variable that needs updating is contained in the initiation (init) file `.cshrc` in your home directory. Because this file name begins with a . it is usually hidden from view. Beware; it is easy to mess up your `.cshrc` file and end up in a quagmire in which you cannot enter commands. For this reason we suggest that you first create a backup copy of your `.cshrc` file, in case anything goes wrong:

```
> cp .cshrc .cshrc_bk
```
Make a backup, just in case

Next, open the .cshrc file in a text editor. Because this file may contain some very long lines that must be kept intact, if your text editor has an "automatic word wrap" feature, make sure it is turned off. Next look for a line that starts with setenv CLASSPATH. If you cannot find that line, add setenv CLASSPATH ~/java_packages/ptplot on its own line at the end of your .cshrc file. If the setenv CLASSPATH line already exists, add a colon : to the end of the existing line, and then add ~/java_packages/ptplot after the colon. The colon is a separator that tells Java that it should look in more than one location for class files. Save your .cshrc file, then close and reopen all shells that you have open (or log off and then back on).

Once you have the CLASSPATH variable set, you should make sure that it is working. To check, go to a command prompt in a shell and enter

```
> echo %CLASSPATH%
> echo $CLASSPATH
```
Windows check
Unix check

The complete value for the CLASSPATH variable should be printed to the screen, for example:

```
/home/jan/java/classes:/home/jan:/home/jan/mpiJava:/usr/local/mpiJava/
lib/classes:/home/jan/java_packages:/home/jab/java_packages/ptplot:
```

If your changes do not take, carefully follow the directions again, then ask for help.

At this point, you are ready to try out PtPlot. Get the file EasyPtPlot.java containing a sample plot program from the disk or the Web and enter

```
> javac EasyPtPlot.java
> java EasyPtPlot
```
Compile sample plot program
Run sample plot program

If the PtPlot package was installed correctly, you should get a nice graph on your screen. If this does not work, ask for help.

C.6 INSTALLING JAVA DEVELOPER'S KIT

Sun Microsystem's Java Web site [SunJ] contains the latest, and free, version of JDK, the Java Developer's Kit (presently j2sdk1.4.1). Though most operating systems have all that is needed to *run* Java programs, you need the developer's kit to compile Java programs from a source file. The actual JDK tools occupy about 7 MB, with its (optional) documentation occupying more than ten times this space (the documentation is in HTML). This means that you may want only the tools if space is an issue.

On Windows computers, JDK is usually placed in `C:\jdk1.2\bin`, while on Unix it is in `/usr/local/jdk1.2`. Once installed, you need to update the PATH and the CLASSPATH environment variables so that the shell knows where to find the Java compiler and classes you make. This is essentially the same procedure we used to include the PtPlot classes in the CLASSPATH. Under Windows you need to go to the System control panel and then select the Environment tab. You then need to add `;C:\jdk1.2\bin` (or whatever file JDK was installed into) to the PATH variable. Likewise, the CLASSPATH need to be added, for example,

```
> set CLASSPATH=C:\...
```

Finally, you need to reboot for the changes to take effect.

Bibliography

MAPLE AND MATHEMATICA

[Corl 02] CORLESS, R. M. (2002), *Essential Maple 7, An Introduction for Scientific Programmers,* Springer, New York.

[Gass 98] GASS, R. (1998), *Mathematica for Scientists and Engineers,* Prentice-Hall, Upper Saddle River, NJ.

[Hass 03] HASSANI, H. (2003), *Mathematical Methods Using Mathematica,* Springer, New York.

[Heck 03] HECK, A. (2003), *Introduction to Maple, Third Ed.,* Springer, New York.

[Meissner 95] MEISSNER, L. P. (1995), *Maple, Fortran 90,* PWS Publishers, Boston.

[N&W 96] NICOLAIDES, R., AND N. WALKINGTON (1996), *Maple, A Comprehensive Introduction,* Cambridge University Press, Cambridge.

[R&M 01] ROMANO, A., AND A. MARASCO (1996), *Mathematica Navigator, Second Ed.,* Elsevier/Academic Press, New York.

[Rusk 04] RUSKEEPAA, H. (2001), *Scientific Computing with Mathematica,* (ODEs) Birkhäuser, Boston.

[Wolf 99] WOLFRAM, S. (1999), *The Mathematica Book,* Wolfram Media, Champaign, and Cambridge University Press, Cambridge.

[Zimm 02] ZIMMERMAN, R. L., AND F. I. OLNESS, (2002), *Mathematica for Physicists,* Addison-Wesley, San Francisco.

JAVA AND FORTRAN

[Bron 03] BRONSON, G. J. (2003), *Java for Engineers and Scientists,* Thompson, Brooks/Cole, Toronto.

[Chap 04] CHAPMAN, S. J. (2004), *Java for Engineers and Scientists*, Second
           Ed., Pearson, Prentice Hall, Upper Saddle River, NJ.

[ChapF 04] CHAPMAN, S. J. (2004), *Fortran 90/95 for Engineers and Scientists*,
            Second Ed., McGraw-Hill, New York.

[Dav 99] DAVIES, R. (1999), *Introductory Java for Scientists and Engineers*,
          Addison-Wesley, Harlow, UK.

[Eck 02] ECK, D. (2002), *Introduction to Programming Using Java, Version 4.0*,
          (a free textbook), http://math.hws.edu/javanotes.

[Flan 97] FLANAGA, D. (1997), *Java in a Nutshell, Desktop Quick Reference*,
           Second Ed., O'Reilly, Sebastopol, CA.

[F90_CSEP] THE COMPUTATIONAL SCIENCE EDUCATION PROJECT, *Fortran
            90 and Computational Science*, http://csep1.phy.ornl.gov/pl/pl.html.

[F90_UL] MARSHALL, A. C. *The University of Liverpool Fortran 90 Course
          Notes*, http://www.liv.ac.uk/HPC/F90page.html.

[Smit 91] SMITH, D. N. (1991), *Concepts of Object-Oriented Programming*,
           McGraw-Hill, New York.

COMPUTATIONAL SCIENCES

[CP 05] LANDAU, R. H., AND M. J. PÁEZ (1997), *Computational Physics,
         Problem Solving with Computers*, Wiley, New York;
         LANDAU, R. H., M. J. PÁEZ, AND C. C. BORDEIANU (2005), *Computa-
         tional Physics, Problem Solving with Computers*, Second Ed., Wiley, New
         York.

[G&T 96] GOULD, H., AND J. TOBOCHNIK (1996), *An Introduction to Com-
          puter Simulation Methods*, Second Ed., Addison-Wesley, Reading, PA.

[Gar 00] GARCIA, A. L. (2000), *Numerical Methods for Physics*, Prentice Hall,
          Upper Saddle River, NJ.

[Knuth 86] KNUTH, D. E. (1986), *The TeXbook*, Addison-Wesley, Reading, PA.

[L&F 93] LANDAU, R. H., AND P. J. FINK (1993), *A Scientist's and Engineer's
          Guide to Workstations and Supercomputers*, Wiley, New York.

[Lap 85] LAMPORT, L., (1986), *LaTeX: A Document Preparation System*, Second
          Ed. Addison-Wesley, Reading, PA.

[LAP 95] ANDERSON, E., Z. BAI, C. BISCHOF, J. DEMMEL, J. DONGARRA,
          J. DU CROZ, A. GREENBAUM, S. HAMMARLING, A. MCKENNEY, S. OS-
          TROUCHOV, AND D. SORENSEN (1995), *Lapack Users' Guide*, Second Ed.,
          SIAM, Philadelphia; http://netlib.org.

[Press 94] PRESS, W. H., B. P. FLANNERY, S. A. TEUKOLSKY, AND W. T. VETTERLING (1994), *Numerical Recipes*, Cambridge University Press, Cambridge, UK.

[UCES] UNDERGRADUATE COMPUTATIONAL ENGINEERING AND SCIENCE, http://www.krellinst.org/UCES/.

[Wilk 95] WILKINS, D. R., *Getting Started with LaTeX*, Second Ed., http://www.maths.tcd.ie/~dwilkins/LaTeXPrimer/, (1995).

[Zach 96] ZACHARY, J. L. (1993), *Introduction to Scientific Programming, Computational Problem Solving using Maple and C*, Springer-Telos, Santa Clara, CA.

MATHEMATICS

[A&S 64] ABRAMOWITZ, M., AND I. A. STEGUN (1964), *Handbook of Mathematical Functions,* U.S. Govt. Printing Office, Washington.

[B&R 92] BEVINGTON, P. R., AND D. K. ROBINSON (1992), *Data Reduction and Error Analysis for the Physical Sciences*, McGraw-Hill, New York.

[Fral 76] FRALEIGH, J. B. (1976), *A First Course in Abstract Algebra*, Second Ed., Addison-Wesley, Reading, PA.

[Krey 88] KREYSZIG, E. (1988), *Advanced Engineering Mathematics*, Sixth Ed., Wiley, New York.

SCIENCE

[D&A 00] DEGAUDENZI, M. E., AND C. M. ARIZMENDI, *Wavelet-Based Fractal Analysis of Electrical Power Demand*, Fractals, **8,** no. 3 (2000) 239–245.

[Feig 79] FEIGENBAUM, M. J. (1979), *J. Stat. Physics* **21**, 669.

[Fein 76] G. FEINBERG, Phys. Rev. **159** (1976) 1089–1105.

[Feyn 63] FEYNMAN, R. P., R. B. LEIGHTON, AND M. SANDS, (1963), *The Feynman Lectures on Physics* §9.7.

[M&T 88] MARION, J. B., AND S. T. THORNTON (1988), *Classical Dynamics of Particles and Systems*, Third Ed., Harcourt Brace Jovanovich, Orlando, FL.

[R & M 93] REITZ, J. R., F. J. MILFORD, AND CHRISTY, R. W. (1993), *Foundations of Electromagnetic Theory,* Fourth Ed., Addison-Wesley, Reading, PA.

[Rash 90] RASBAND, S. N. (1990), *Chaotic Dynamics of Nonlinear Systems*, Wiley, New York.

[Ser 00] SERWAY, R. A., AND R. J. BEICHNER (2000), *Physics for Scientists and Engineers,* Fifth Edition, Saunders, Orlando, FL.

[Smith 65] SMITH, J. H. (1965), *Introduction to Special Relativity*, Benjamin, New York.

[USN&WR] *US News & World Report*, 1/28/99.

WEB RESOURCES

Web pages change so often that we expect some of these URLs to fail. If so, we suggest searching on the name.

[Black] *The Java-Linux Porting Project*, http://www.blackdown.org/.

[CPlets] *Interactive Computational Physics Applets,* http://www.physics.orst.edu/~rubin/nacphy/CPapplets/, http://www.physics.orst.edu/~rubin/TALKS/CPtalk/DEMO/samples.html.

[Dislin] H. Michels, MPI fuer Sonnensystemforschung, *Dislin Scientific Plotting Software*, http://www.mps.mpg.de/dislin/.

[DX] *Open DX, Data Explorer* (formerly IBM's DataExplorer), http://www.opendx.org/.

[Energy] *Edison Electrical Institute, Climatron Research Technical Reports*, http://www.climatron.com; *California Independent System Operator*, http://www.caiso.com; *Platte River Power Authority*, http://www.prpa.org.

[Game] *Gamelan Repository of Java Code*, http://www.gamelan.com/.

[Gnu] *The GNU Project, Emacs*, http://www.gnu.org/.

[Gnuplot] A command-line interactive datafile and function plotting utility, http://www.gnuplot.info/.

[Grace] A WYSIWYG 2D plotting tool (descendant of ACE/gr, Xmgr), http://plasma-gate.weizmann.ac.il/Grace/.

[Jama] HICKLIN, J., C. MOLER, P. WEBB, R. F. BOISVERT, B. MILLER, R. POZO, AND K. REMINGTON, *JAMA: Java Matrix Library*, http://math.nist.gov/javanumerics/jama/.

[Jampack] *Java Matrix Package,* http://www.mathematik.hu-berlin.de/~lamour/software/JAVA/Jampack/Doc/00_Manual.html.

[jEdit] *jEdit*, http://www.jedit.org.

[JF] *NPAC JavaForce*, http://www.npac.syr.edu/projects/javaforce/.

[Jgran] *Java Grande Forum*, http://www.javagrande.org/.

[JHPC] *Java for High Performance Computing*, http://www.jhpc.org/.

[JNL] VISUAL NUMERICS, *Java Numerical Library*, http://www.vni.com/products/imsl/jmsl.html.

[Jopt] *Java Optimization*, http://www-2.cs.cmu.edu/⌐jch/java/optimization.html.

[JsimS] *Physics Simulation with Java*, http://www.particle.kth.se/⌐fmi/kurs/PhysicsSimulation/.

[Jtut] *Sun's Java Tutorial*, http://java.sun.com/docs/books/tutorial.

[MapWeb2] *Indiana Maple WWW Tutorial*, http://www.indiana.edu/⌐statmath/math/maple.

[MMM] *Mathematica, Maple, Matlab, IDL, Translations*, http://amath.colorado.edu/computing/mmm/.

[Net] *Netlib*, http://www.netlib.org/.

[NIST] *Java Numerics at National Inst of Sci and Tech*, http://math.nist.gov/javanumerics/.

[OSS] *Open Source Software*, http://www.opensource.org/.

[Printf] BENGTSSON, H., *Java Printf Package*, http://www.braju.com/.

[PtPlot] Ptolemy plotting project, http://ptolemy.eecs.berkeley.edu/java/ptplot/.

[SunJ] *Sun Microsystems Java Home Page*, http://java.sun.com/.

[UnixWeb] LANDAU, R. H., P. J. FINK, AND M. JOHNSON, *Unix Survival Guide*, http://www.physics.orst.edu/⌐rubin/nacphy/UNIX/.

[Visad] *VisAD, Java Component Library for Interactive and Collaborative Visualization and Analysis of Numerical Data*, http://www.ssec.wisc.edu/⌐billh/visad.html.

[WinEdt] SIMONIC, A., *WinEdt*, http://www.winedt.com/.

[WinZip] *WinZip Extractor and Compactor*, http://www.winzip.com/.

Index